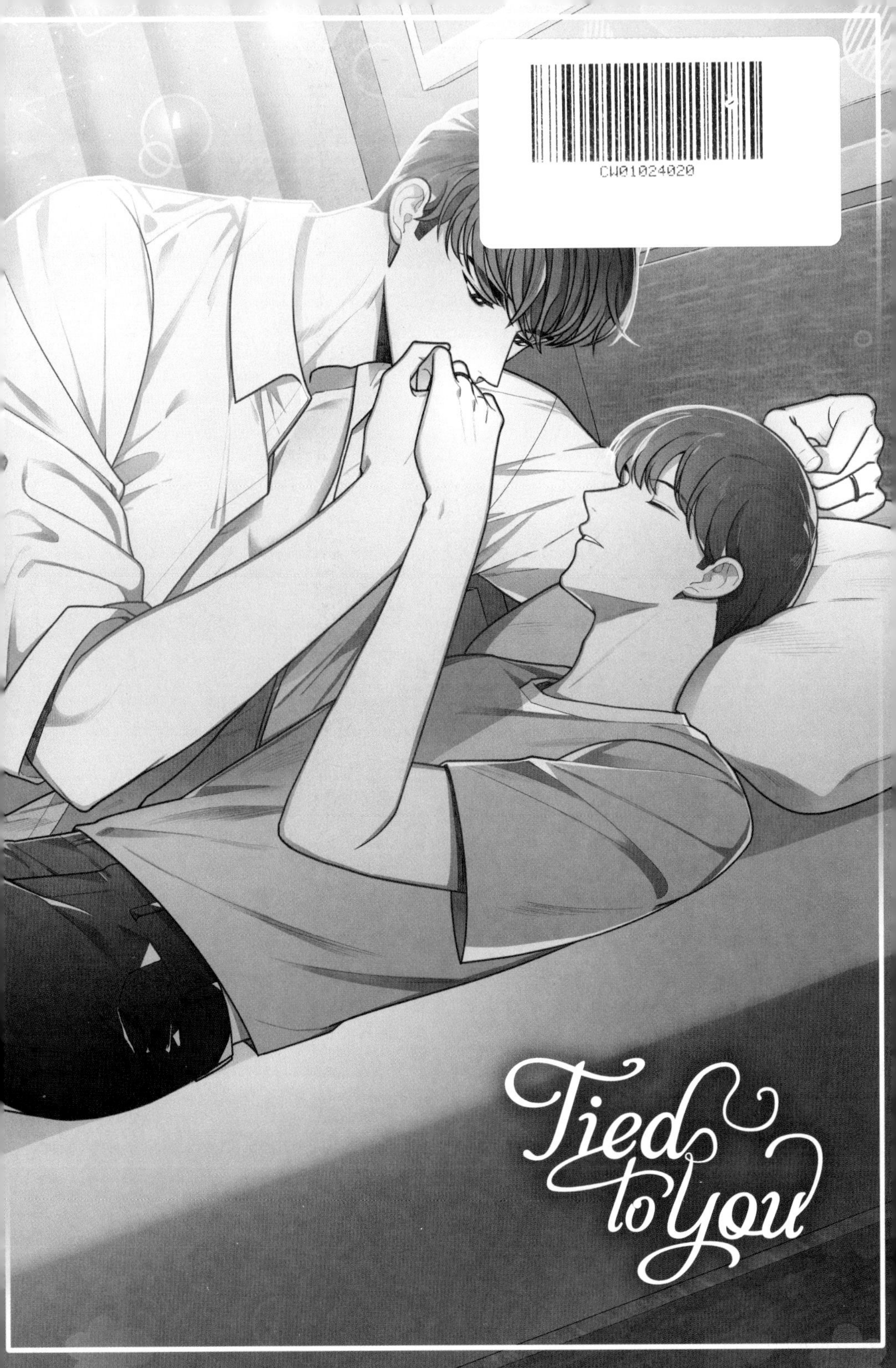
Tied
to You

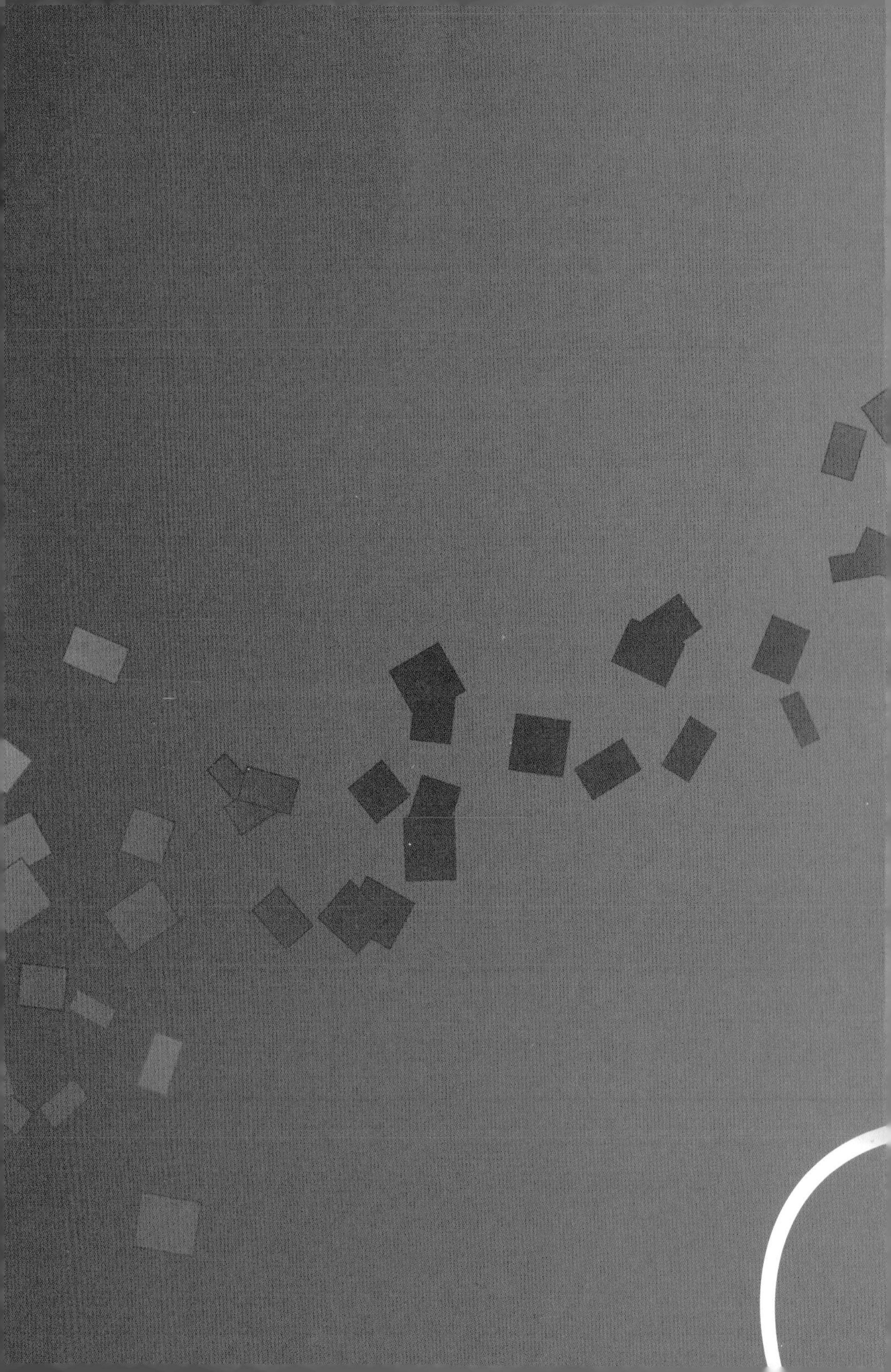

Table of Contents

Chapter 1

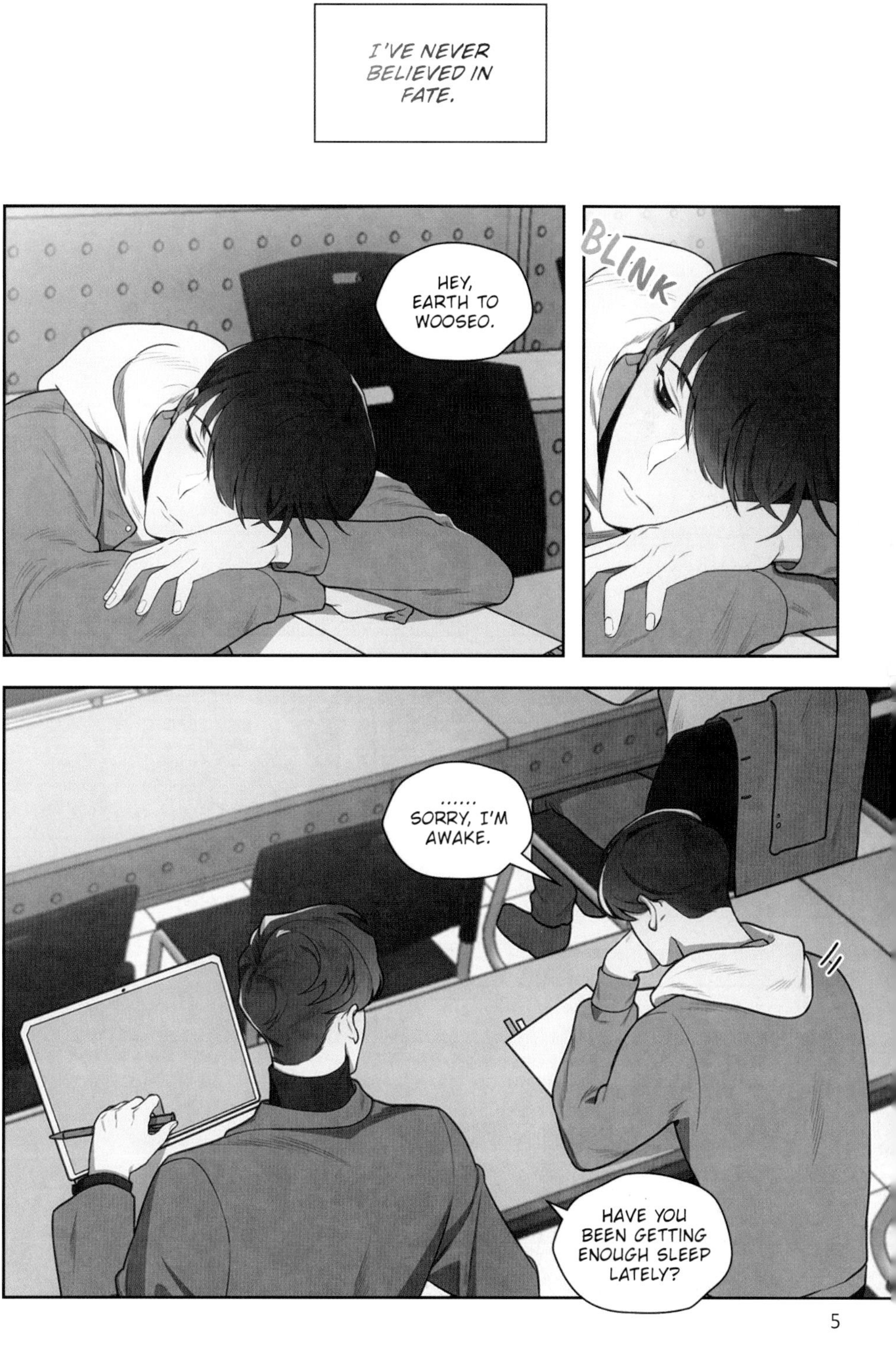
I'VE NEVER BELIEVED IN FATE.
HEY, EARTH TO WOOSEO.
BLINK
......
SORRY, I'M AWAKE.
HAVE YOU BEEN GETTING ENOUGH SLEEP LATELY?

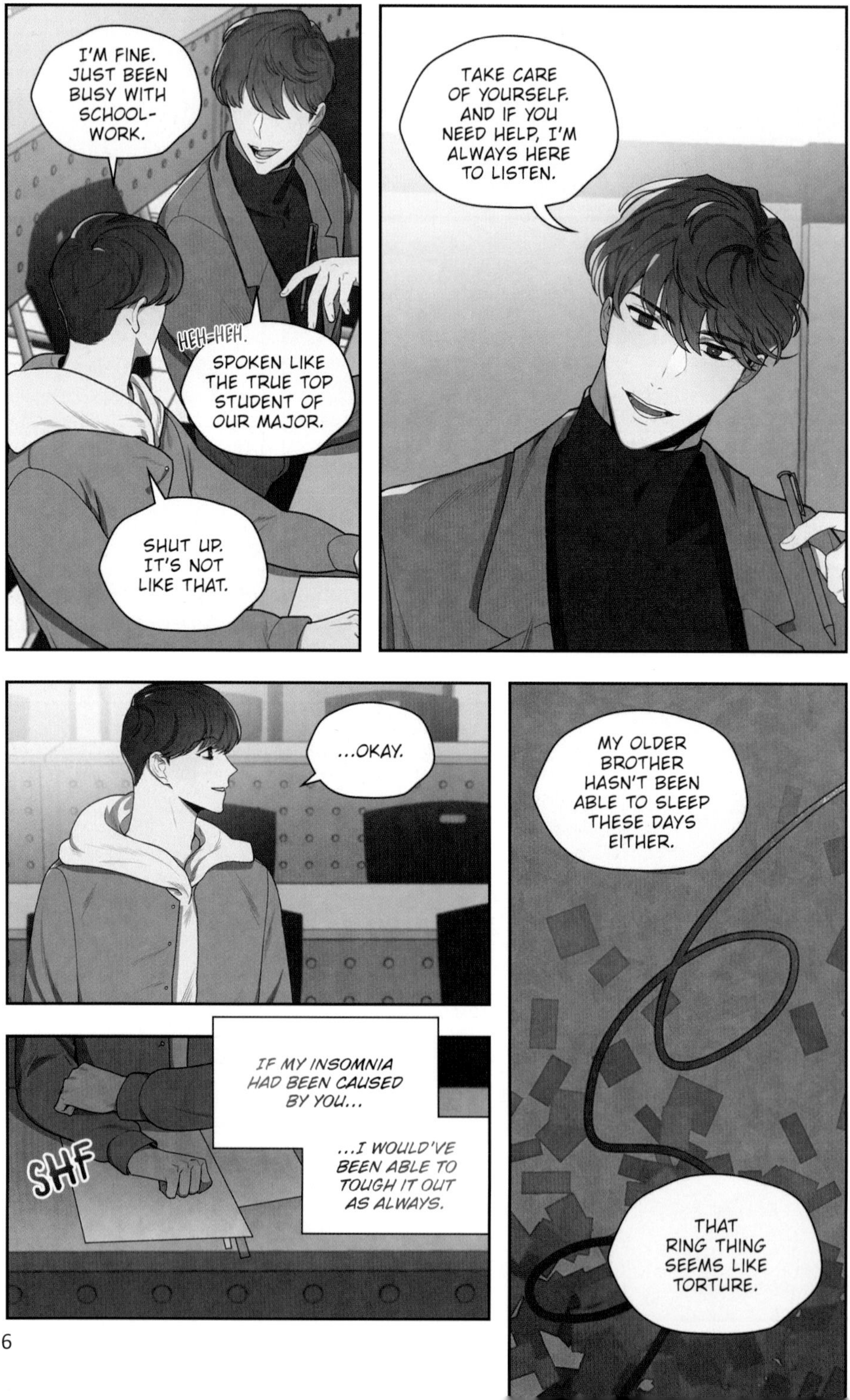
I'M FINE. JUST BEEN BUSY WITH SCHOOL-WORK.
HEH-HEH.
SPOKEN LIKE THE TRUE TOP STUDENT OF OUR MAJOR.
SHUT UP. IT'S NOT LIKE THAT.
TAKE CARE OF YOURSELF. AND IF YOU NEED HELP, I'M ALWAYS HERE TO LISTEN.
...OKAY.
IF MY INSOMNIA HAD BEEN CAUSED BY YOU...
SHF
...I WOULD'VE BEEN ABLE TO TOUGH IT OUT AS ALWAYS.
MY OLDER BROTHER HASN'T BEEN ABLE TO SLEEP THESE DAYS EITHER.
THAT RING THING SEEMS LIKE TORTURE.

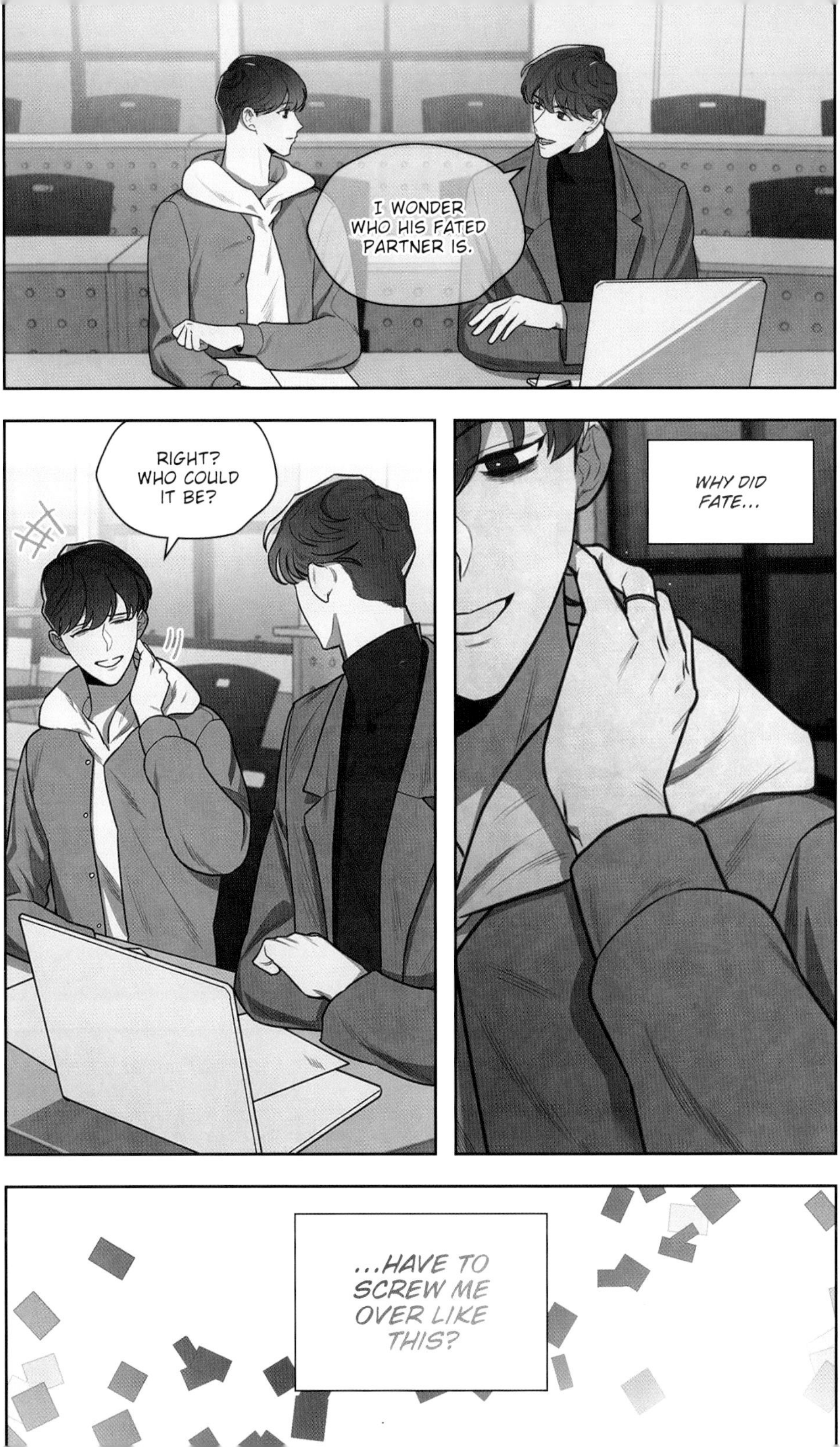
I WONDER WHO HIS FATED PARTNER IS.
RIGHT? WHO COULD IT BE?
WHY DID FATE...
...HAVE TO SCREW ME OVER LIKE THIS?

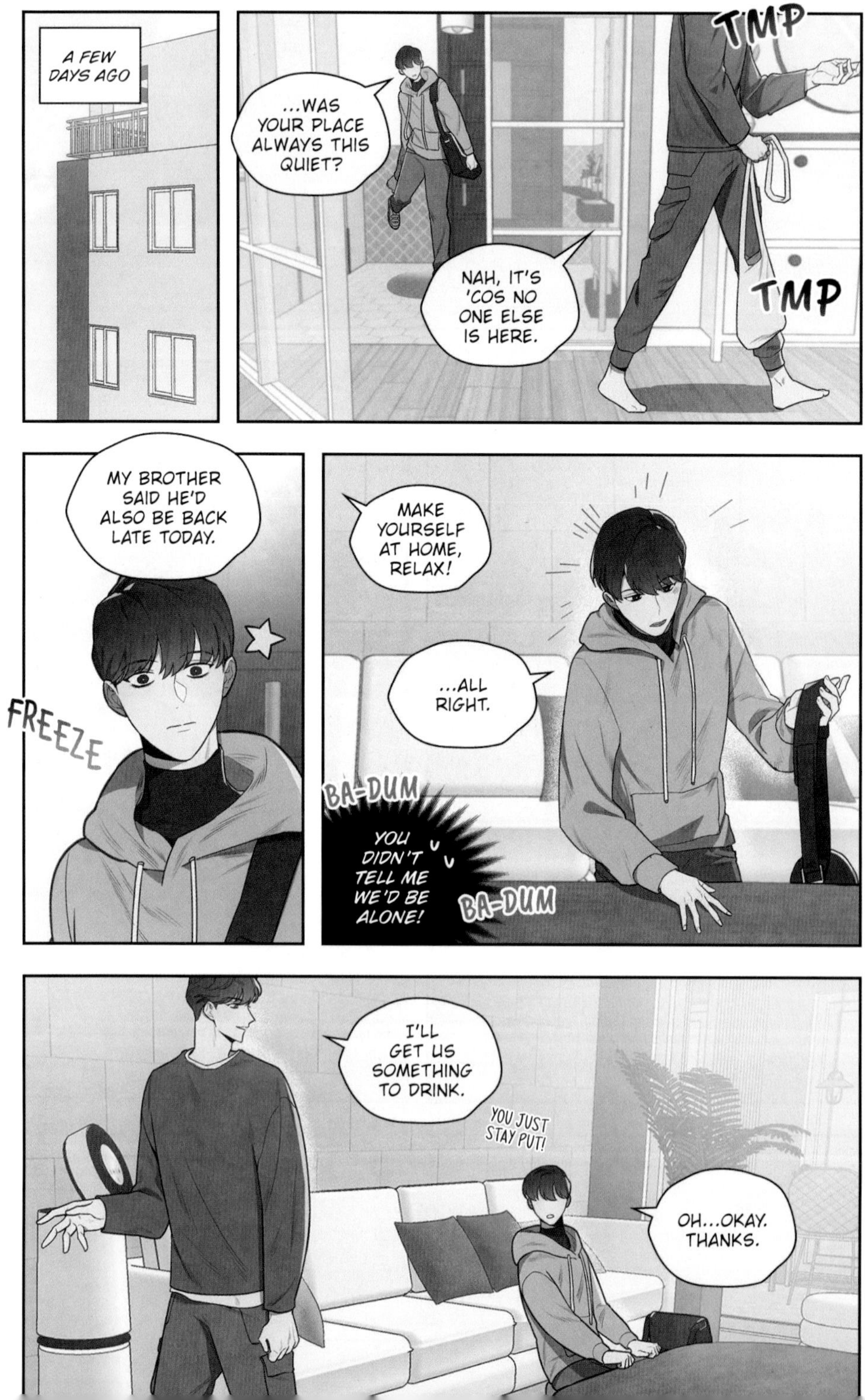
A FEW DAYS AGO
TMP
...WAS YOUR PLACE ALWAYS THIS QUIET?
NAH, IT'S 'COS NO ONE ELSE IS HERE.
TMP
MY BROTHER SAID HE'D ALSO BE BACK LATE TODAY.
FREEZE
MAKE YOURSELF AT HOME, RELAX!
...ALL RIGHT.
BA-DUM
YOU DIDN'T TELL ME WE'D BE ALONE!
BA-DUM
I'LL GET US SOMETHING TO DRINK.
YOU JUST STAY PUT!
OH...OKAY. THANKS.

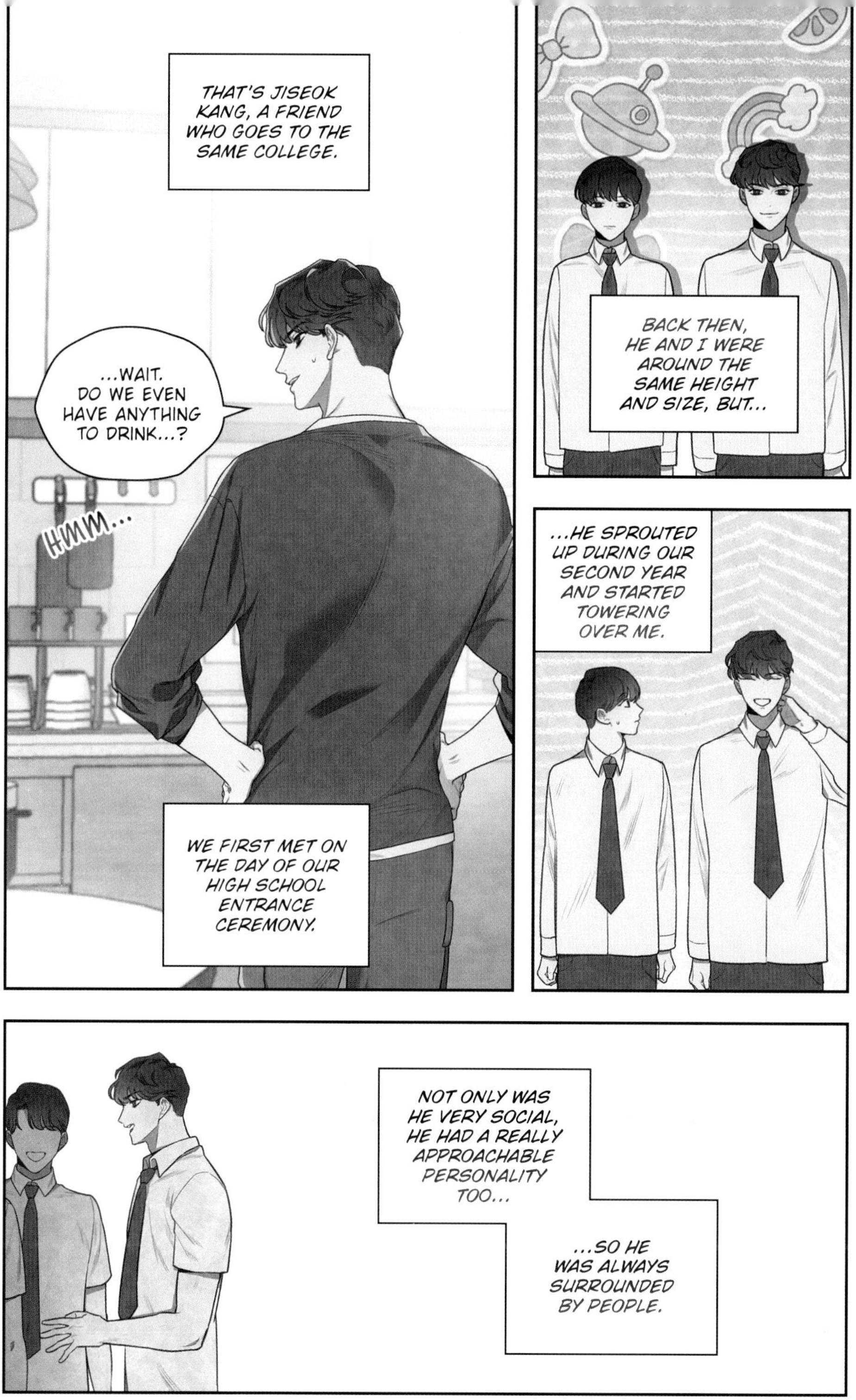

THAT'S JISEOK KANG, A FRIEND WHO GOES TO THE SAME COLLEGE.
...WAIT. DO WE EVEN HAVE ANYTHING TO DRINK...?
HMM...
WE FIRST MET ON THE DAY OF OUR HIGH SCHOOL ENTRANCE CEREMONY.
BACK THEN, HE AND I WERE AROUND THE SAME HEIGHT AND SIZE, BUT...
...HE SPROUTED UP DURING OUR SECOND YEAR AND STARTED TOWERING OVER ME.
NOT ONLY WAS HE VERY SOCIAL, HE HAD A REALLY APPROACHABLE PERSONALITY TOO...
...SO HE WAS ALWAYS SURROUNDED BY PEOPLE.

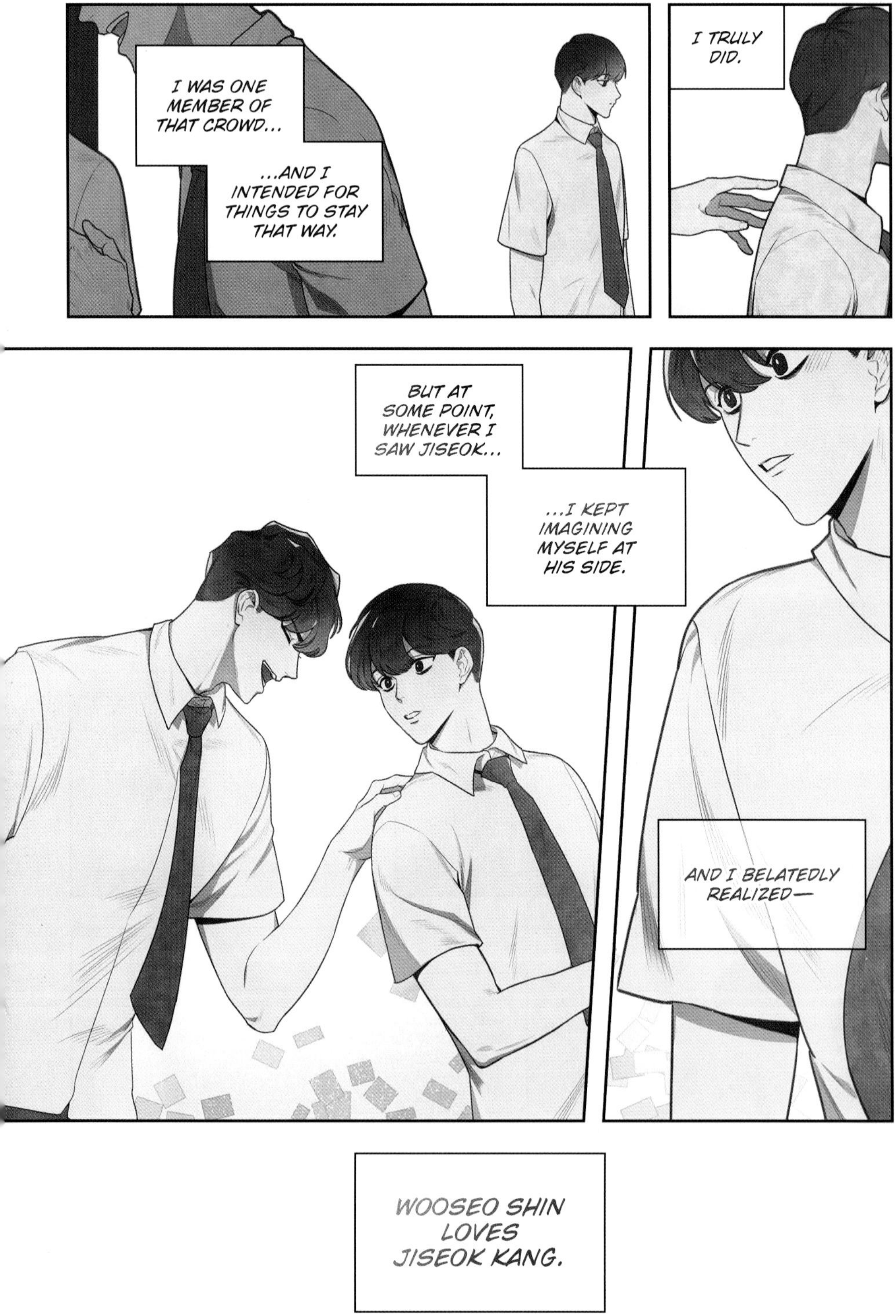
I WAS ONE MEMBER OF THAT CROWD...
...AND I INTENDED FOR THINGS TO STAY THAT WAY.
I TRULY DID.
BUT AT SOME POINT, WHENEVER I SAW JISEOK...
...I KEPT IMAGINING MYSELF AT HIS SIDE.
AND I BELATEDLY REALIZED—
WOOSEO SHIN LOVES JISEOK KANG.

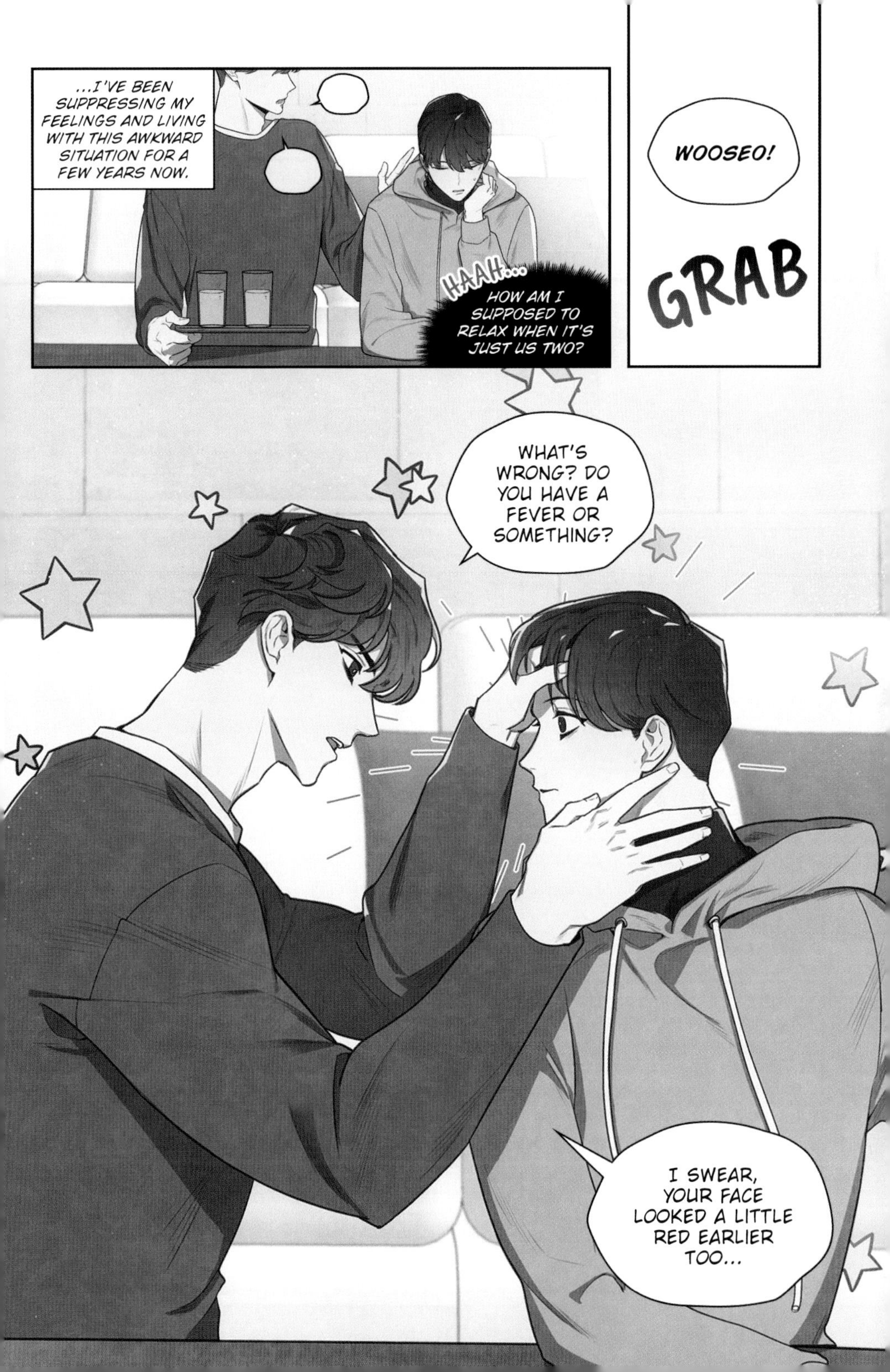
...I'VE BEEN SUPPRESSING MY FEELINGS AND LIVING WITH THIS AWKWARD SITUATION FOR A FEW YEARS NOW.
HAAH...
HOW AM I SUPPOSED TO RELAX WHEN IT'S JUST US TWO?
WOOSEO!
GRAB
WHAT'S WRONG? DO YOU HAVE A FEVER OR SOMETHING?
I SWEAR, YOUR FACE LOOKED A LITTLE RED EARLIER TOO...

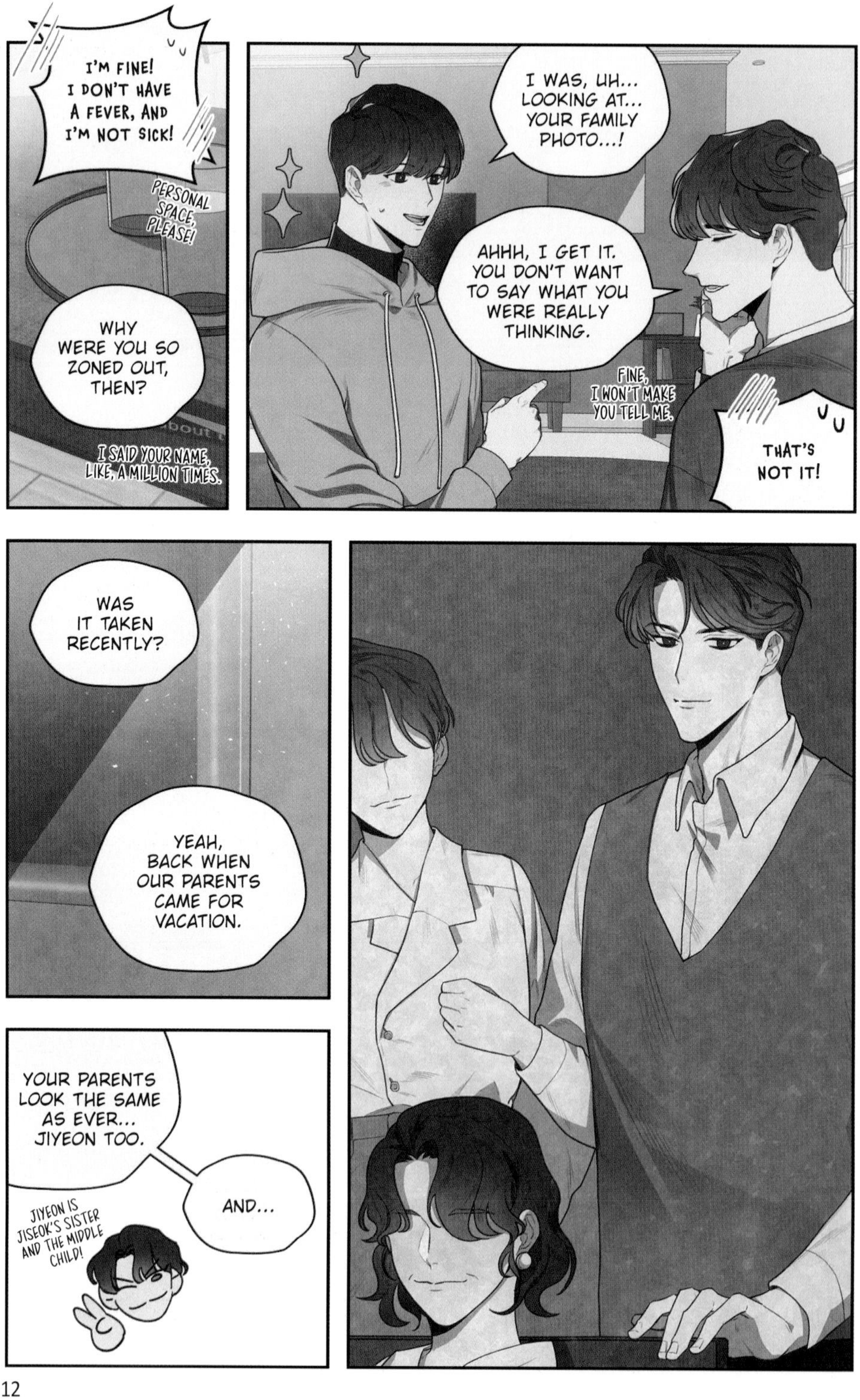

I'M FINE! I DON'T HAVE A FEVER, AND I'M NOT SICK!
PERSONAL SPACE, PLEASE!
WHY WERE YOU SO ZONED OUT, THEN?
I SAID YOUR NAME, LIKE, A MILLION TIMES.
I WAS, UH... LOOKING AT... YOUR FAMILY PHOTO...!
AHHH, I GET IT. YOU DON'T WANT TO SAY WHAT YOU WERE REALLY THINKING.
FINE, I WON'T MAKE YOU TELL ME.
THAT'S NOT IT!
WAS IT TAKEN RECENTLY?
YEAH, BACK WHEN OUR PARENTS CAME FOR VACATION.
YOUR PARENTS LOOK THE SAME AS EVER... JIYEON TOO.
AND...
JIYEON IS JISEOK'S SISTER AND THE MIDDLE CHILD!

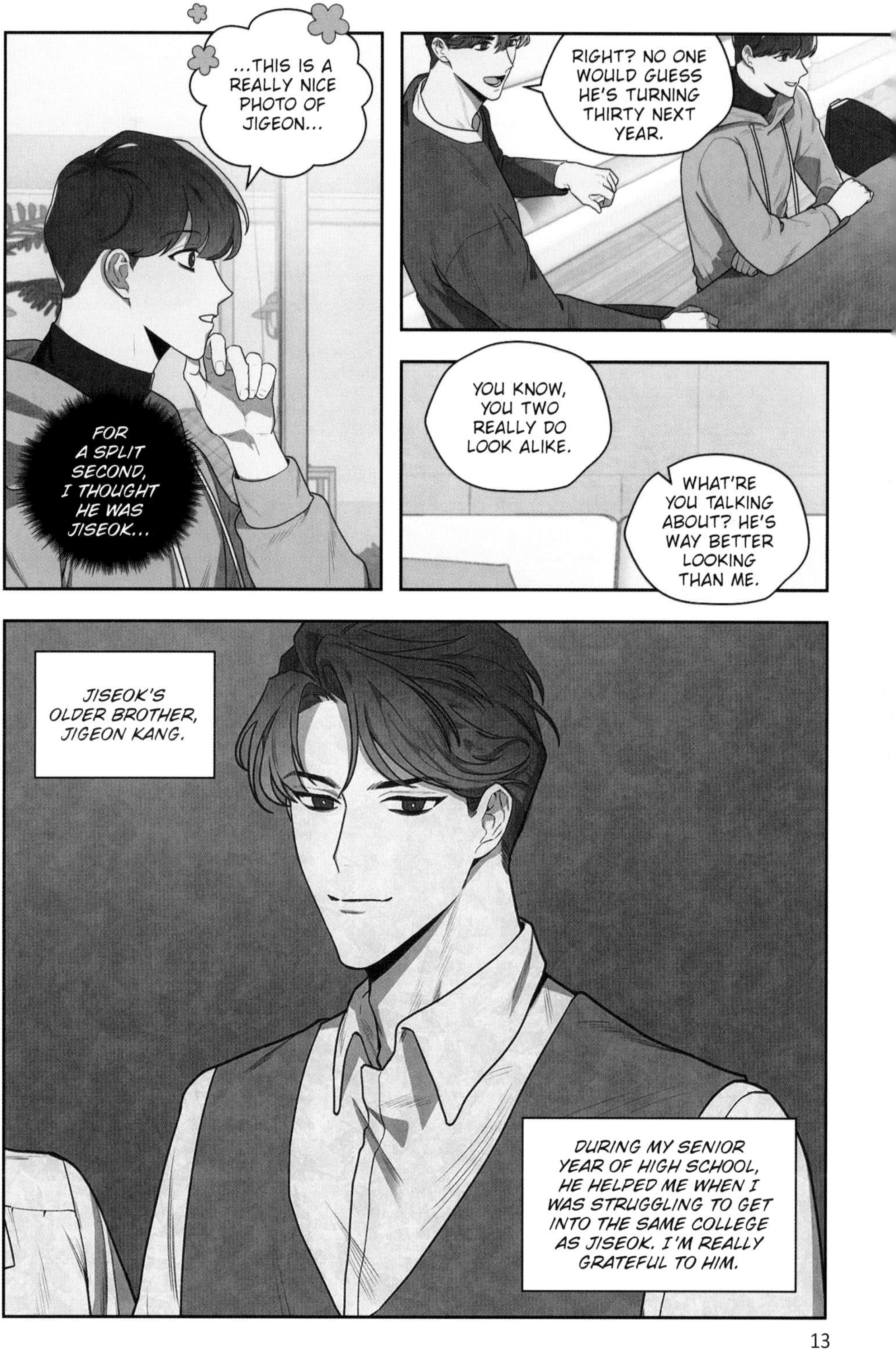

...THIS IS A REALLY NICE PHOTO OF JIGEON...
FOR A SPLIT SECOND, I THOUGHT HE WAS JISEOK...
RIGHT? NO ONE WOULD GUESS HE'S TURNING THIRTY NEXT YEAR.
YOU KNOW, YOU TWO REALLY DO LOOK ALIKE.
WHAT'RE YOU TALKING ABOUT? HE'S WAY BETTER LOOKING THAN ME.
JISEOK'S OLDER BROTHER, JIGEON KANG.
DURING MY SENIOR YEAR OF HIGH SCHOOL, HE HELPED ME WHEN I WAS STRUGGLING TO GET INTO THE SAME COLLEGE AS JISEOK. I'M REALLY GRATEFUL TO HIM.

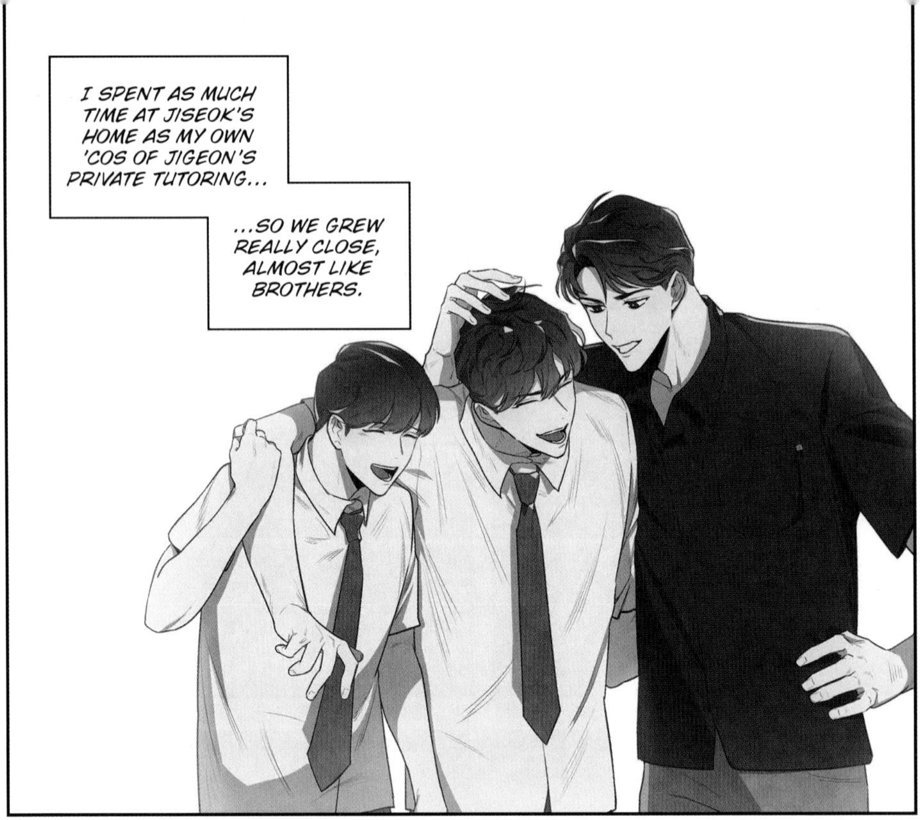
I SPENT AS MUCH TIME AT JISEOK'S HOME AS MY OWN 'COS OF JIGEON'S PRIVATE TUTORING...
...SO WE GREW REALLY CLOSE, ALMOST LIKE BROTHERS.

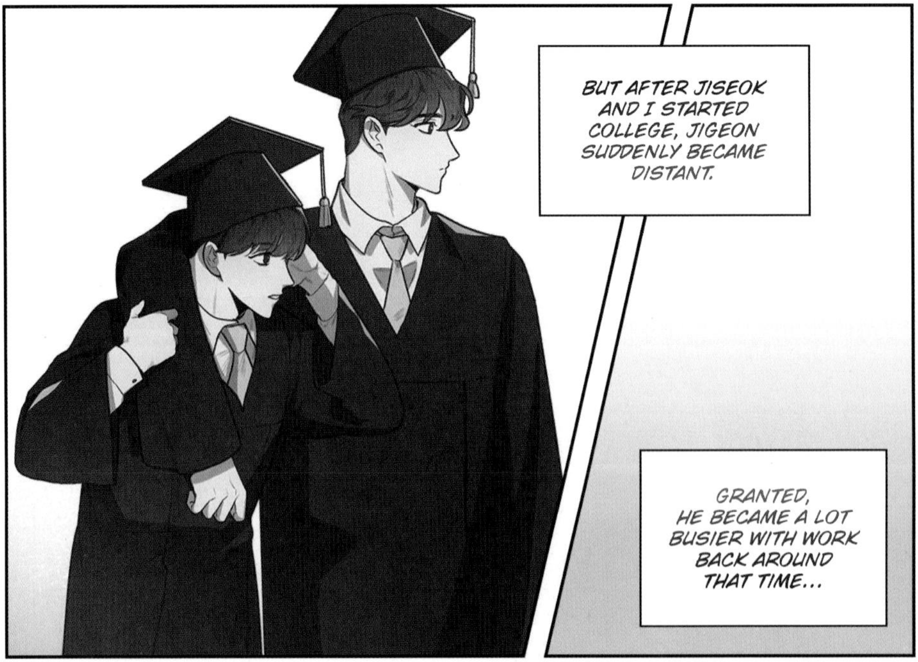
BUT AFTER JISEOK AND I STARTED COLLEGE, JIGEON SUDDENLY BECAME DISTANT.
GRANTED, HE BECAME A LOT BUSIER WITH WORK BACK AROUND THAT TIME...

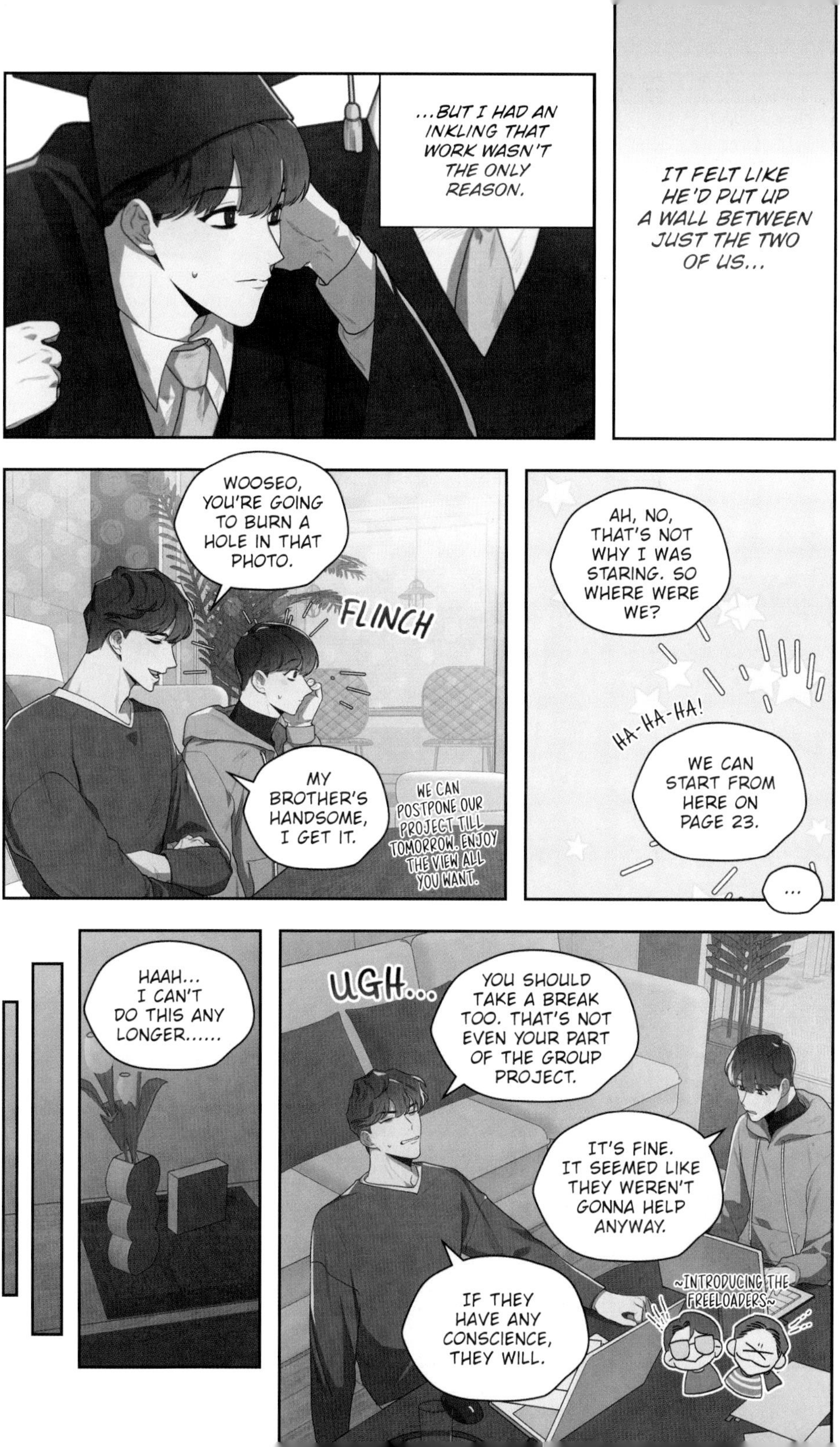
...BUT I HAD AN INKLING THAT WORK WASN'T THE ONLY REASON.
IT FELT LIKE HE'D PUT UP A WALL BETWEEN JUST THE TWO OF US...
WOOSEO, YOU'RE GOING TO BURN A HOLE IN THAT PHOTO.
FLINCH
MY BROTHER'S HANDSOME, I GET IT.
WE CAN POSTPONE OUR PROJECT TILL TOMORROW. ENJOY THE VIEW ALL YOU WANT.
AH, NO, THAT'S NOT WHY I WAS STARING. SO WHERE WERE WE?
HA-HA-HA!
WE CAN START FROM HERE ON PAGE 23.
...
HAAH... I CAN'T DO THIS ANY LONGER......
UGH...
YOU SHOULD TAKE A BREAK TOO. THAT'S NOT EVEN YOUR PART OF THE GROUP PROJECT.
IT'S FINE. IT SEEMED LIKE THEY WEREN'T GONNA HELP ANYWAY.
IF THEY HAVE ANY CONSCIENCE, THEY WILL.
~INTRODUCING THE FREELOADERS~

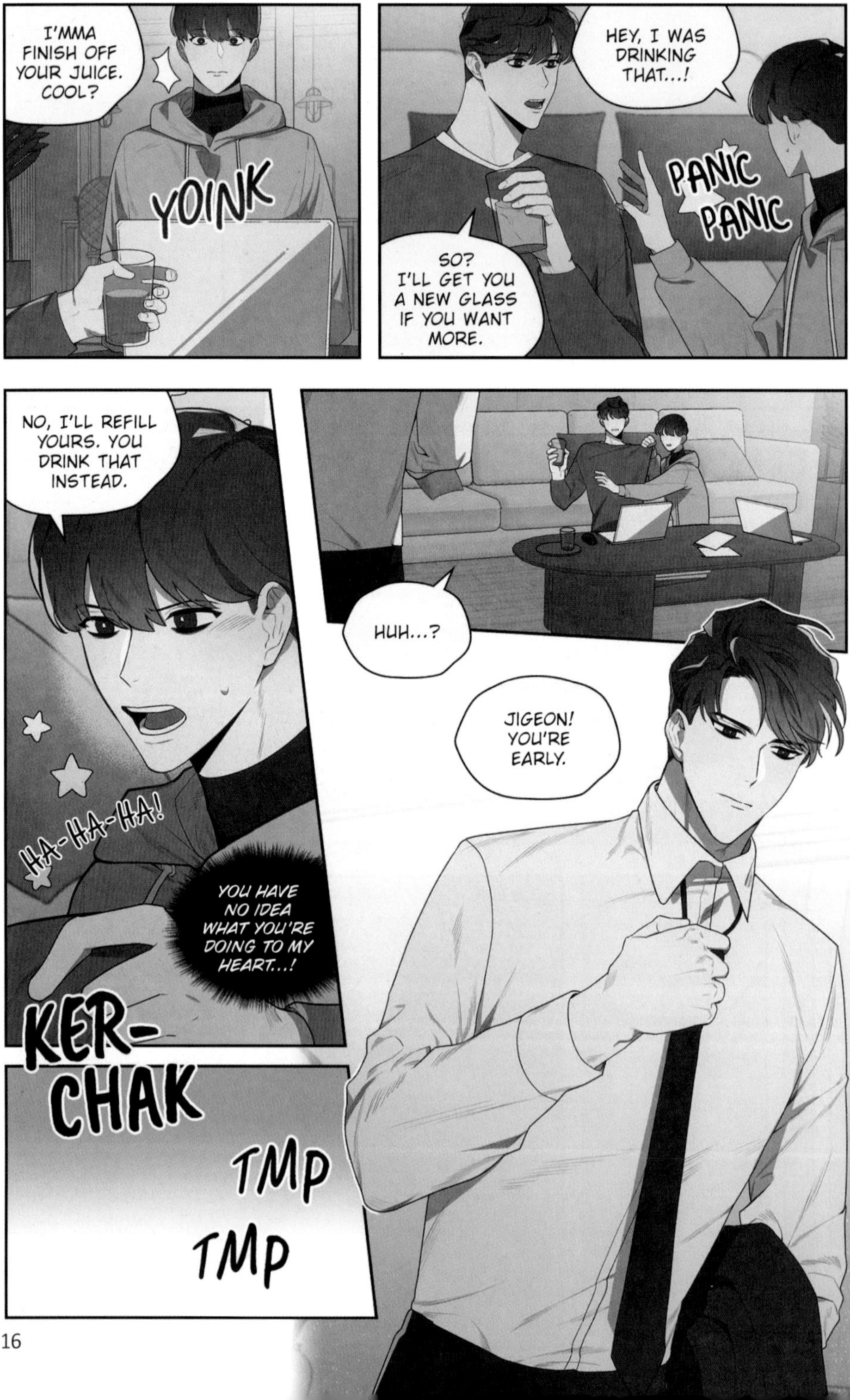
I'MMA FINISH OFF YOUR JUICE. COOL?
YOINK
HEY, I WAS DRINKING THAT...!
PANIC PANIC
SO? I'LL GET YOU A NEW GLASS IF YOU WANT MORE.
NO, I'LL REFILL YOURS. YOU DRINK THAT INSTEAD.
HA-HA-HA!
YOU HAVE NO IDEA WHAT YOU'RE DOING TO MY HEART...!
HUH...?
KER-CHAK
TMP
TMP
JIGEON! YOU'RE EARLY.

I THOUGHT YOU SAID YOU'D BE HOME LATE 'COS OF A SEMINAR OR WHATEVER.

I NEEDED TO SWING BY AND GRAB SOMETHING. MIND YOUR OWN BUSINESS.

YES, SIR. SORRY, SIR.

SHRUG

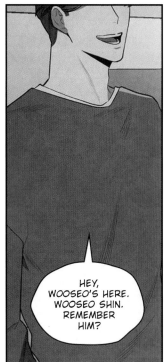

HEY, WOOSEO'S HERE. WOOSEO SHIN. REMEMBER HIM?

WAVER

GOOD EVENING...

GLANCE

FLINCH

I MEAN, YOU HAVE TO REMEMBER— HE'S THE ONLY ONE I EVER TALK ABOUT.

...HE'S GLARING DAGGERS AT ME.

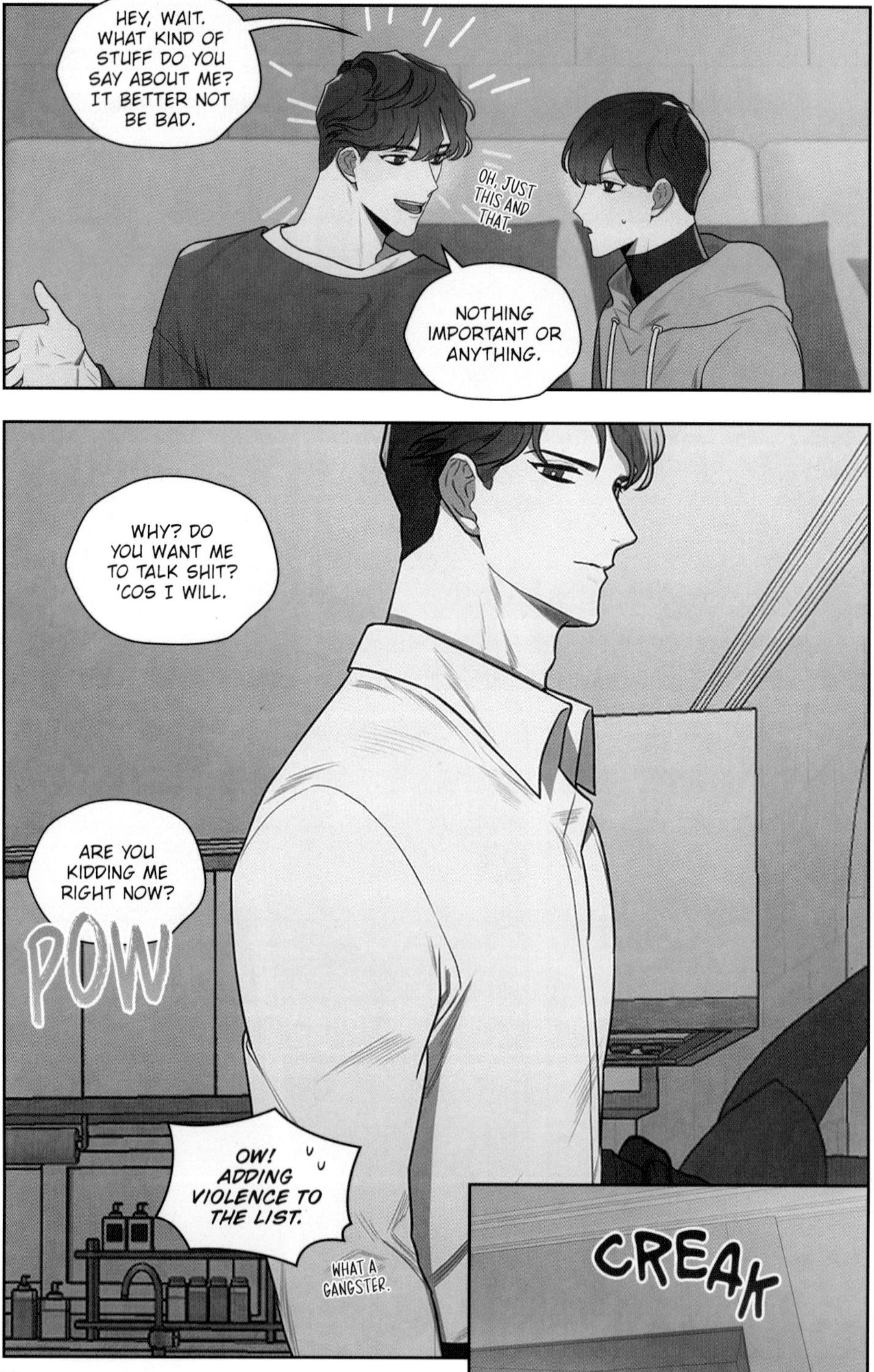
HEY, WAIT. WHAT KIND OF STUFF DO YOU SAY ABOUT ME? IT BETTER NOT BE BAD.
OH, JUST THIS AND THAT.
NOTHING IMPORTANT OR ANYTHING.
WHY? DO YOU WANT ME TO TALK SHIT? 'COS I WILL.
ARE YOU KIDDING ME RIGHT NOW?
POW
OW! ADDING VIOLENCE TO THE LIST.
WHAT A GANGSTER.
CREAK

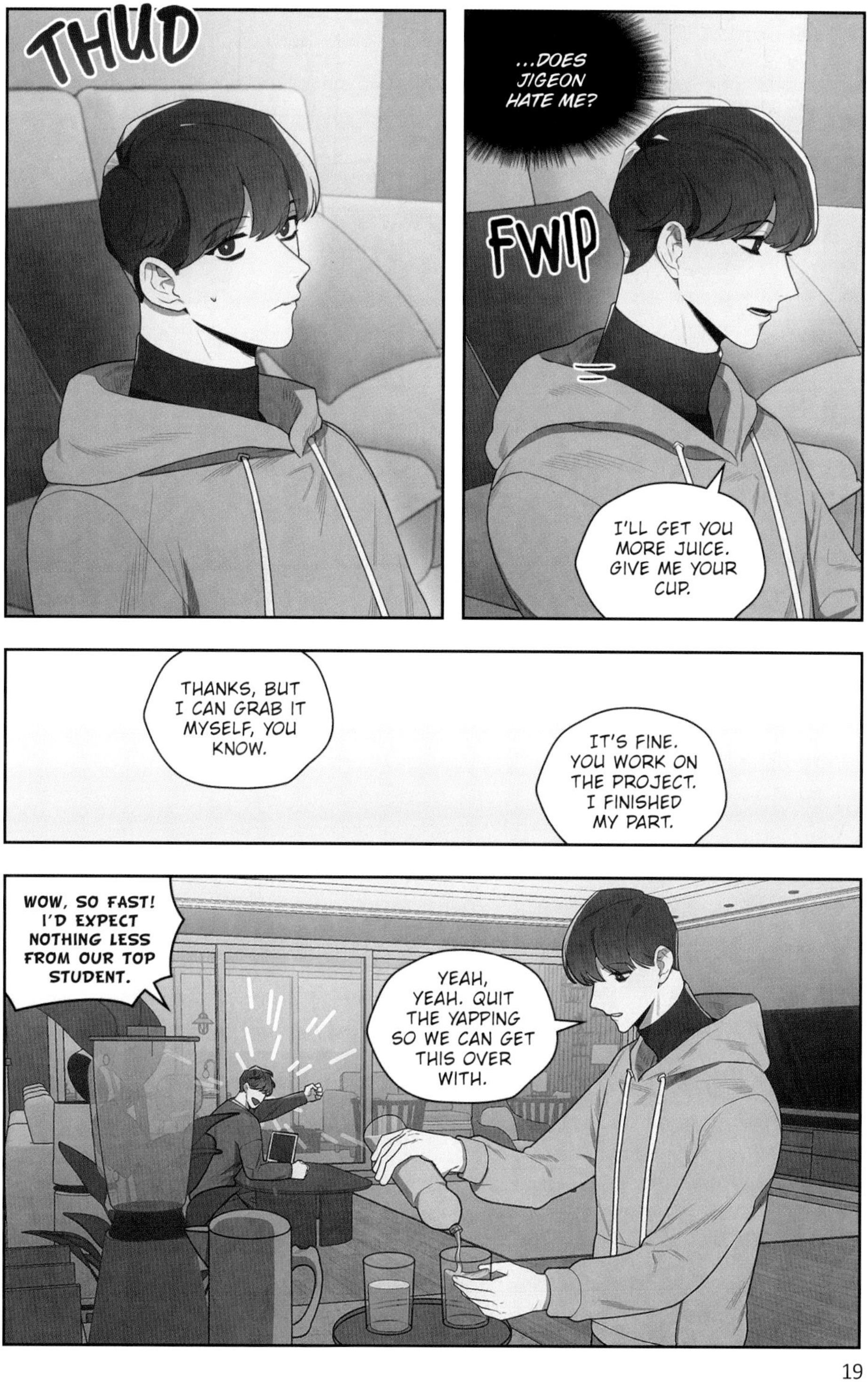
THUD
...DOES JIGEON HATE ME?
FWIP
I'LL GET YOU MORE JUICE. GIVE ME YOUR CUP.
THANKS, BUT I CAN GRAB IT MYSELF, YOU KNOW.
IT'S FINE. YOU WORK ON THE PROJECT. I FINISHED MY PART.
WOW, SO FAST! I'D EXPECT NOTHING LESS FROM OUR TOP STUDENT.
YEAH, YEAH. QUIT THE YAPPING SO WE CAN GET THIS OVER WITH.

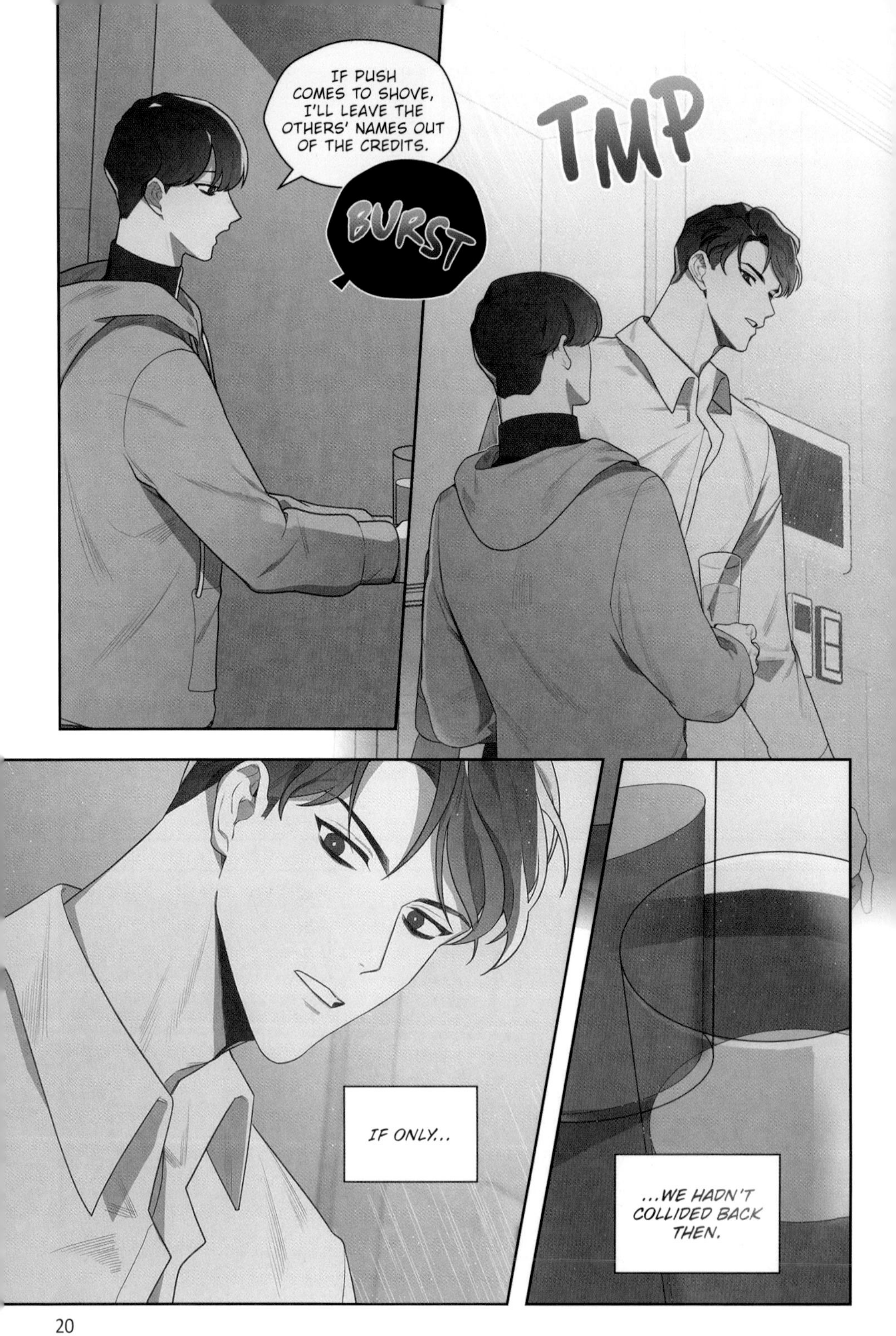
IF PUSH COMES TO SHOVE, I'LL LEAVE THE OTHERS' NAMES OUT OF THE CREDITS.
BURST
TMP
IF ONLY...
...WE HADN'T COLLIDED BACK THEN.

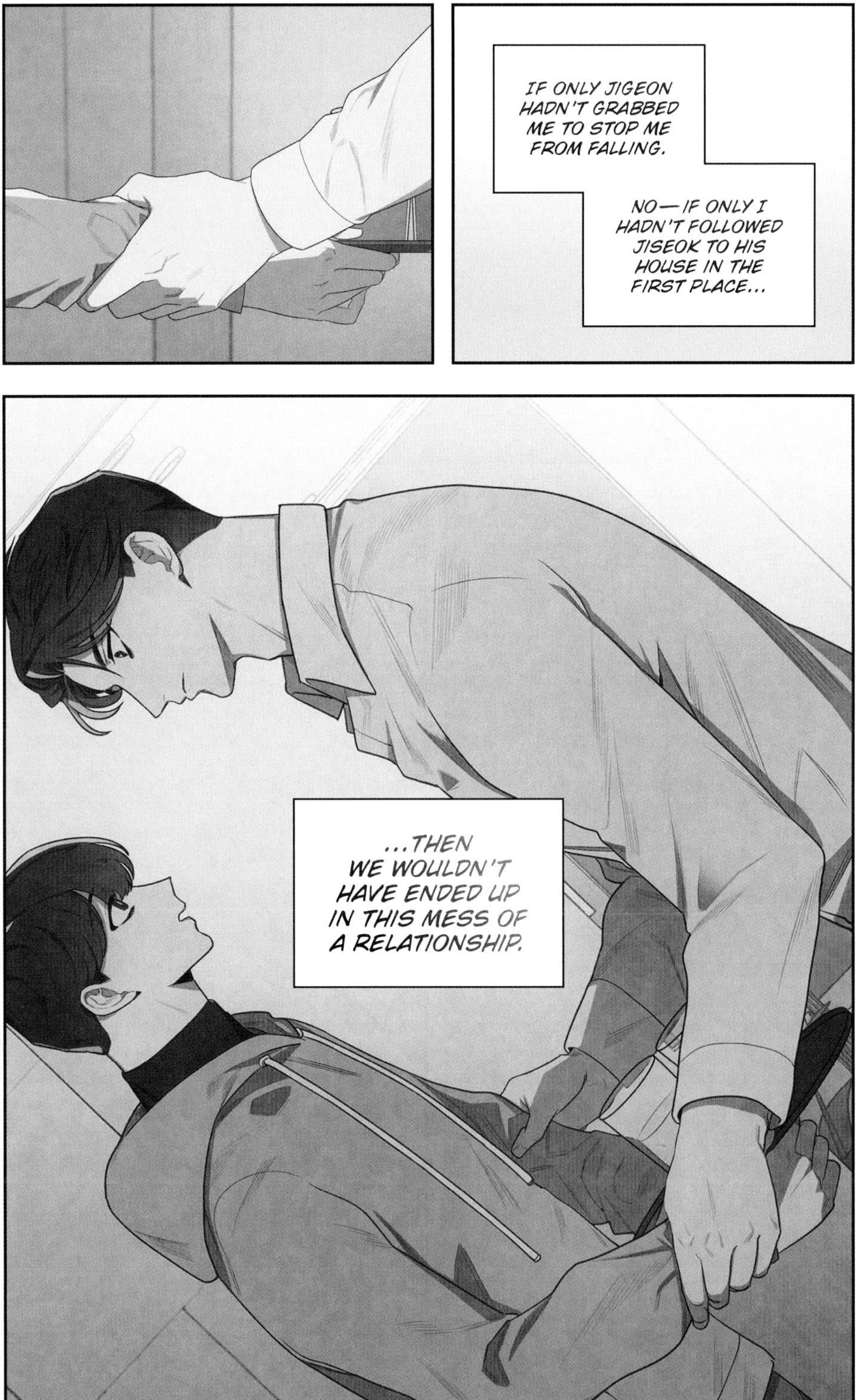
IF ONLY JIGEON HADN'T GRABBED ME TO STOP ME FROM FALLING.
NO— IF ONLY I HADN'T FOLLOWED JISEOK TO HIS HOUSE IN THE FIRST PLACE...
...THEN WE WOULDN'T HAVE ENDED UP IN THIS MESS OF A RELATIONSHIP.

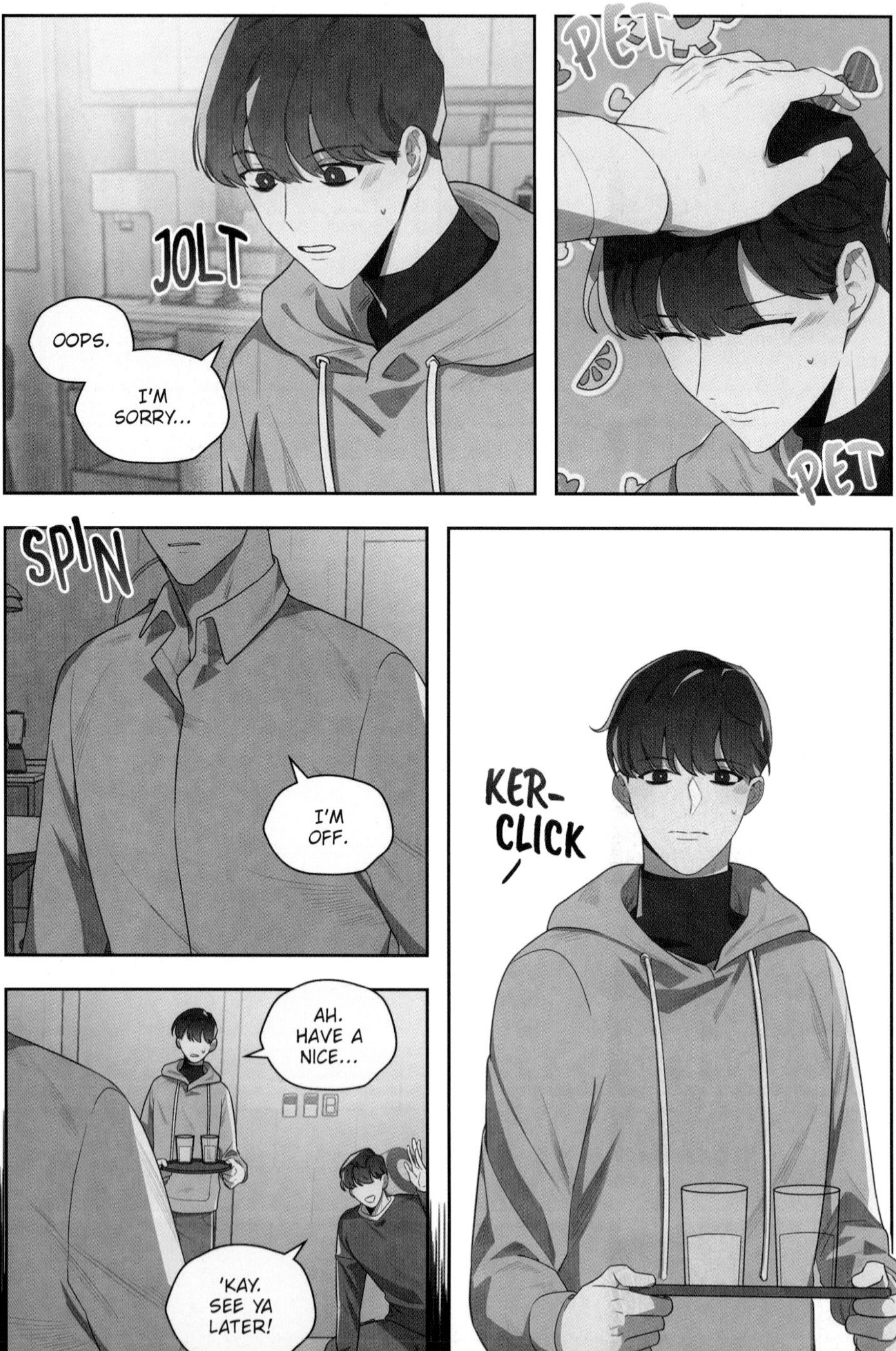
JOLT
OOPS.
I'M SORRY...
PET
PET
SPIN
I'M OFF.
KER-CLICK
AH. HAVE A NICE...
'KAY. SEE YA LATER!

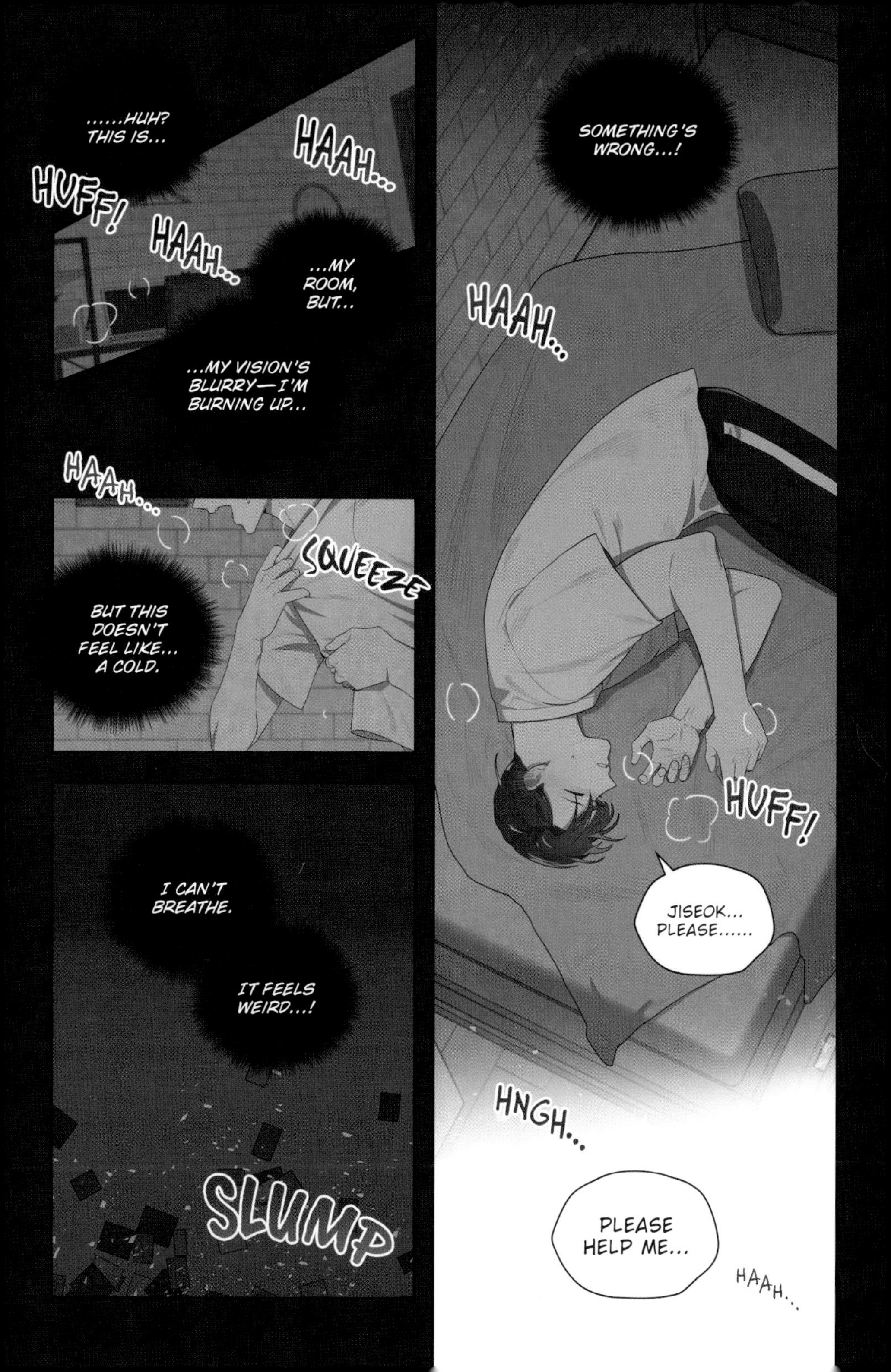
......HUH? THIS IS...
HAAAH...
HUFF!
HAAAH...
...MY ROOM, BUT...
...MY VISION'S BLURRY—I'M BURNING UP...
HAAAH...
SQUEEZE
BUT THIS DOESN'T FEEL LIKE... A COLD.
I CAN'T BREATHE.
IT FEELS WEIRD...!
SLUMP
SOMETHING'S WRONG...!
HAAAH...
HUFF!
JISEOK... PLEASE......
HNGH...
PLEASE HELP ME...
HAAAH...

Chapter 2

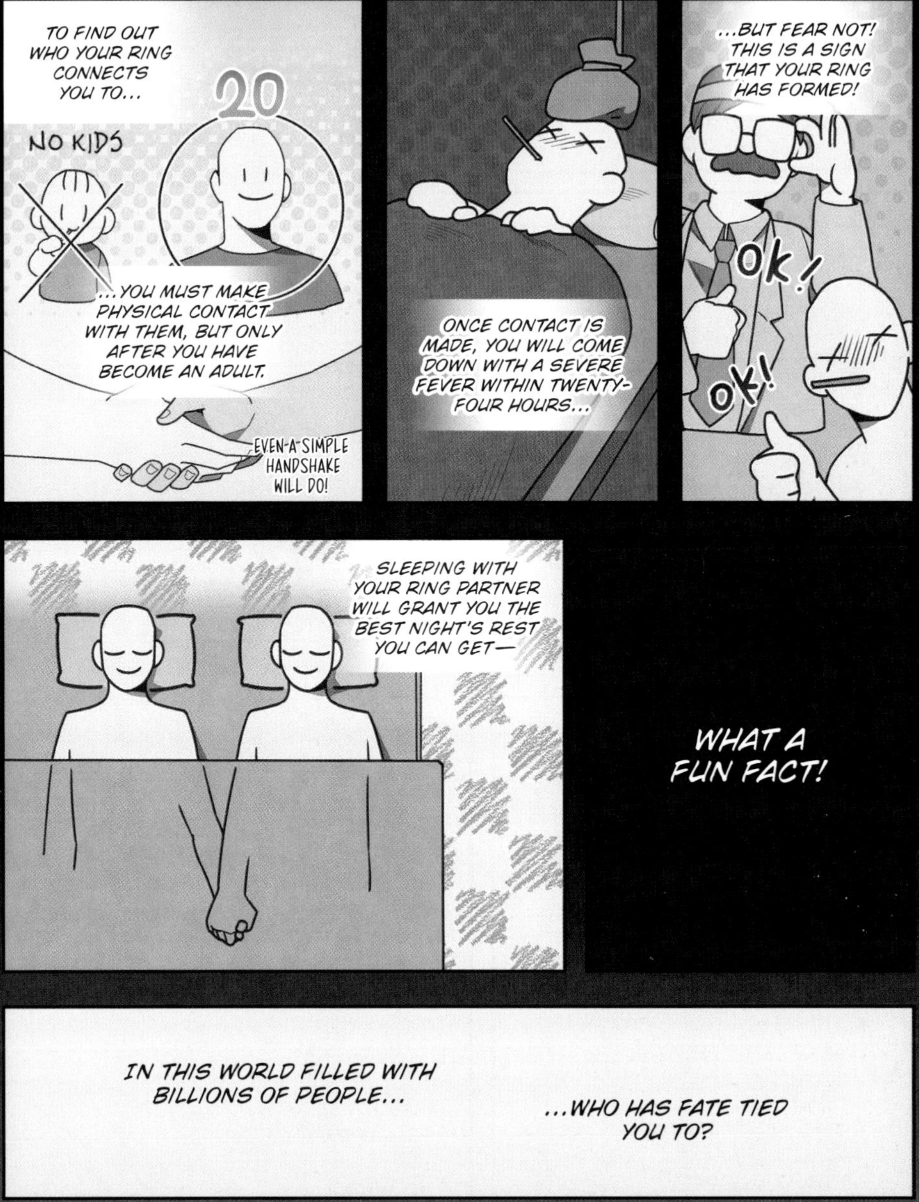
TO FIND OUT WHO YOUR RING CONNECTS YOU TO...
20
NO KIDS
...YOU MUST MAKE PHYSICAL CONTACT WITH THEM, BUT ONLY AFTER YOU HAVE BECOME AN ADULT.
EVEN A SIMPLE HANDSHAKE WILL DO!
ONCE CONTACT IS MADE, YOU WILL COME DOWN WITH A SEVERE FEVER WITHIN TWENTY-FOUR HOURS...
...BUT FEAR NOT! THIS IS A SIGN THAT YOUR RING HAS FORMED!
OK!
OK!
SLEEPING WITH YOUR RING PARTNER WILL GRANT YOU THE BEST NIGHT'S REST YOU CAN GET—
WHAT A FUN FACT!
IN THIS WORLD FILLED WITH BILLIONS OF PEOPLE...
...WHO HAS FATE TIED YOU TO?

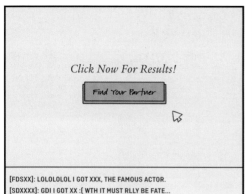

Click Now For Results!

Find Your Partner

[FDSXX]: LOLOLOLOL I GOT XXX, THE FAMOUS ACTOR.
[SDXXXX]: GDI I GOT XX :(WTH IT MUST RLLY BE FATE...
[HGXX]: OMG NOOO WHY'D I GET A POLITICIAN ASDFGHJKL

CLACK

THROB

A FEW DAYS AGO, I WASN'T EVEN SURE IF RINGS ACTUALLY EXISTED.

AND NOW HERE I AM, ACTUALLY LOOKING THIS CRAP UP.

IF YOU HAPPEN TO MAKE DIRECT CONTACT WITH YOUR PARTNER AFTER TURNING TWENTY...

...THE RING APPEARS, AS IF IT WERE DESTINY.

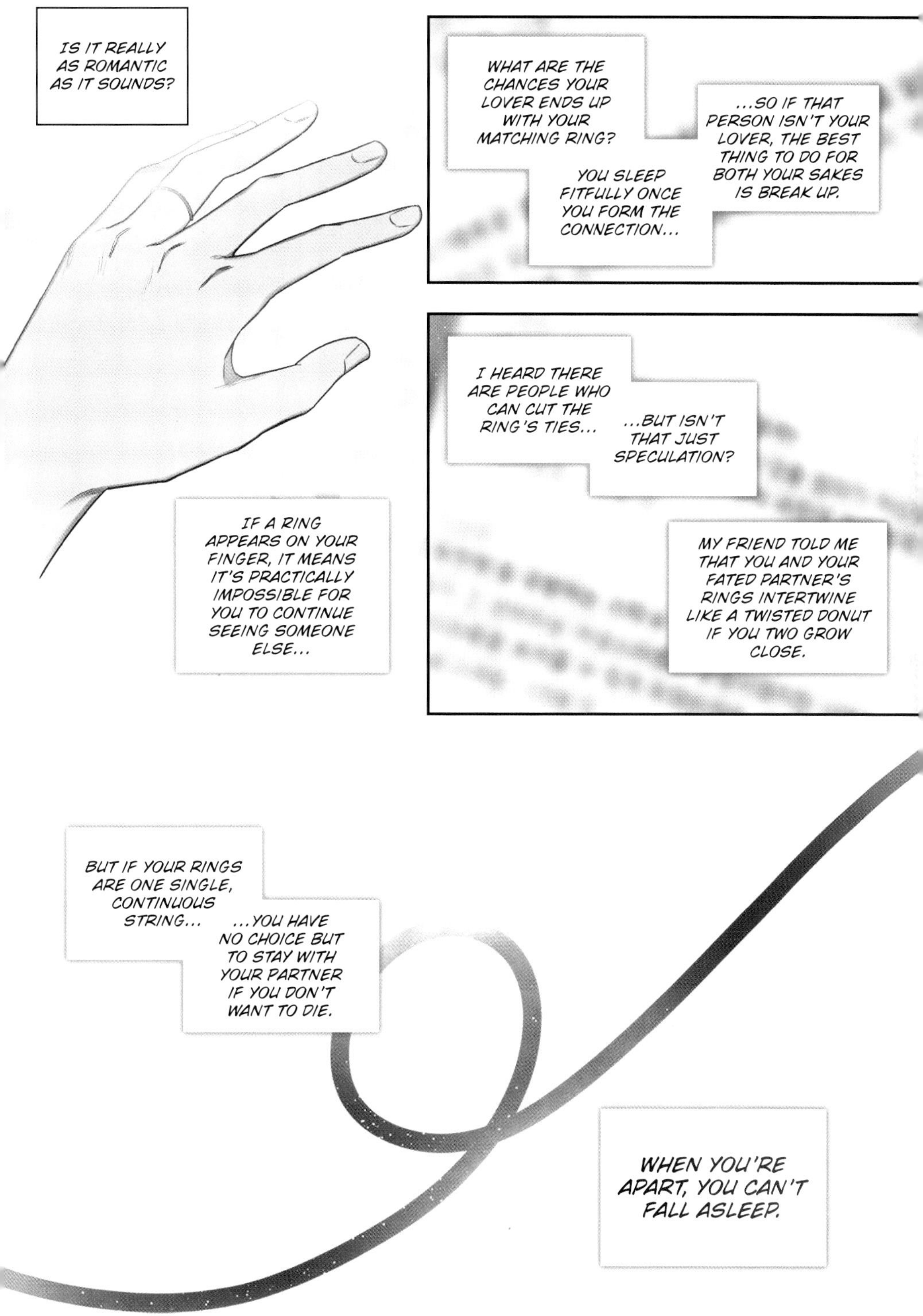
IS IT REALLY AS ROMANTIC AS IT SOUNDS?
WHAT ARE THE CHANCES YOUR LOVER ENDS UP WITH YOUR MATCHING RING?
YOU SLEEP FITFULLY ONCE YOU FORM THE CONNECTION...
...SO IF THAT PERSON ISN'T YOUR LOVER, THE BEST THING TO DO FOR BOTH YOUR SAKES IS BREAK UP.
IF A RING APPEARS ON YOUR FINGER, IT MEANS IT'S PRACTICALLY IMPOSSIBLE FOR YOU TO CONTINUE SEEING SOMEONE ELSE...
I HEARD THERE ARE PEOPLE WHO CAN CUT THE RING'S TIES...
...BUT ISN'T THAT JUST SPECULATION?
MY FRIEND TOLD ME THAT YOU AND YOUR FATED PARTNER'S RINGS INTERTWINE LIKE A TWISTED DONUT IF YOU TWO GROW CLOSE.
BUT IF YOUR RINGS ARE ONE SINGLE, CONTINUOUS STRING...
...YOU HAVE NO CHOICE BUT TO STAY WITH YOUR PARTNER IF YOU DON'T WANT TO DIE.
WHEN YOU'RE APART, YOU CAN'T FALL ASLEEP.

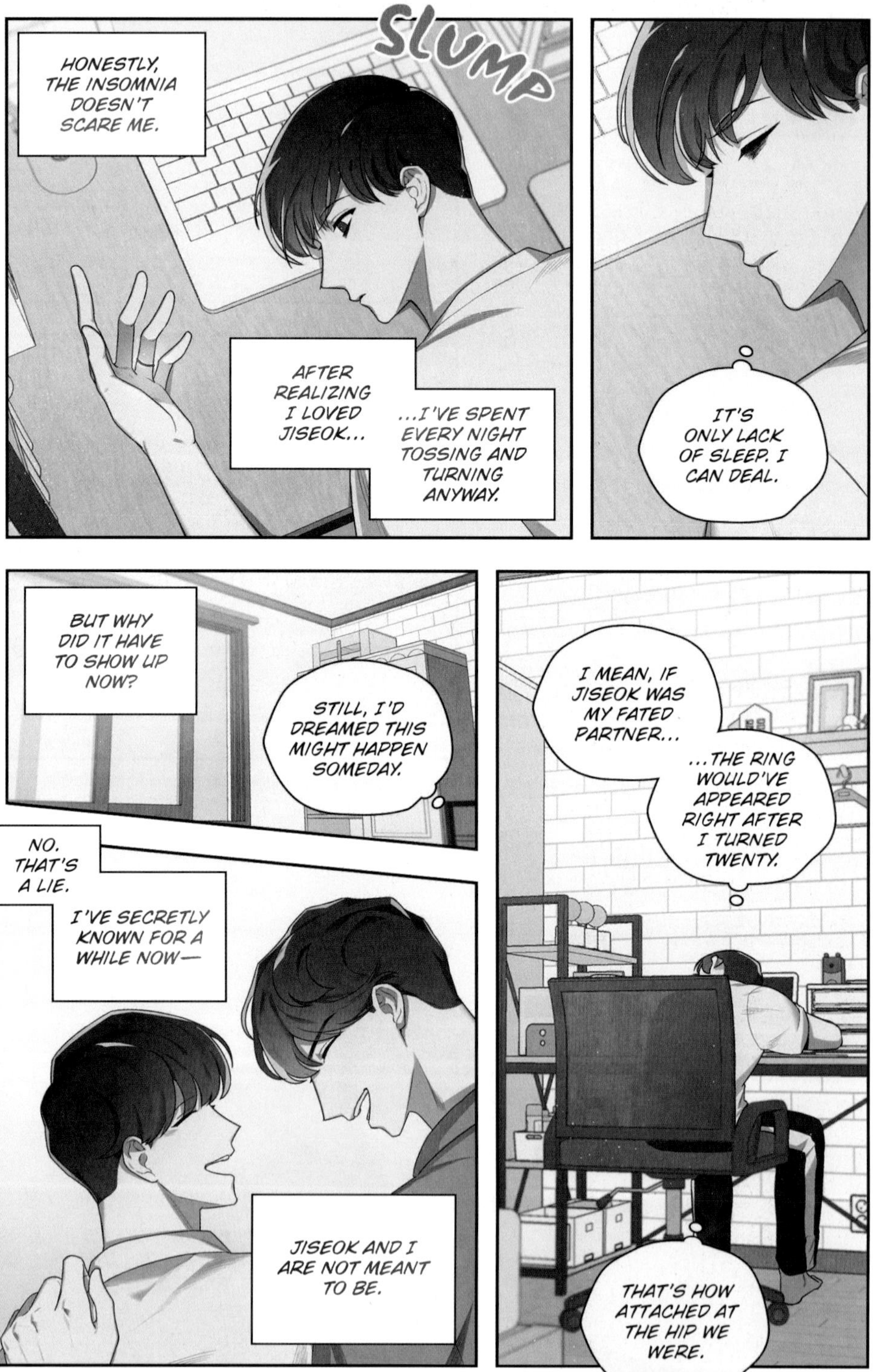
SLUMP
HONESTLY, THE INSOMNIA DOESN'T SCARE ME.
AFTER REALIZING I LOVED JISEOK...
...I'VE SPENT EVERY NIGHT TOSSING AND TURNING ANYWAY.
IT'S ONLY LACK OF SLEEP. I CAN DEAL.
BUT WHY DID IT HAVE TO SHOW UP NOW?
STILL, I'D DREAMED THIS MIGHT HAPPEN SOMEDAY.
I MEAN, IF JISEOK WAS MY FATED PARTNER...
...THE RING WOULD'VE APPEARED RIGHT AFTER I TURNED TWENTY.
THAT'S HOW ATTACHED AT THE HIP WE WERE.
NO. THAT'S A LIE.
I'VE SECRETLY KNOWN FOR A WHILE NOW—
JISEOK AND I ARE NOT MEANT TO BE.

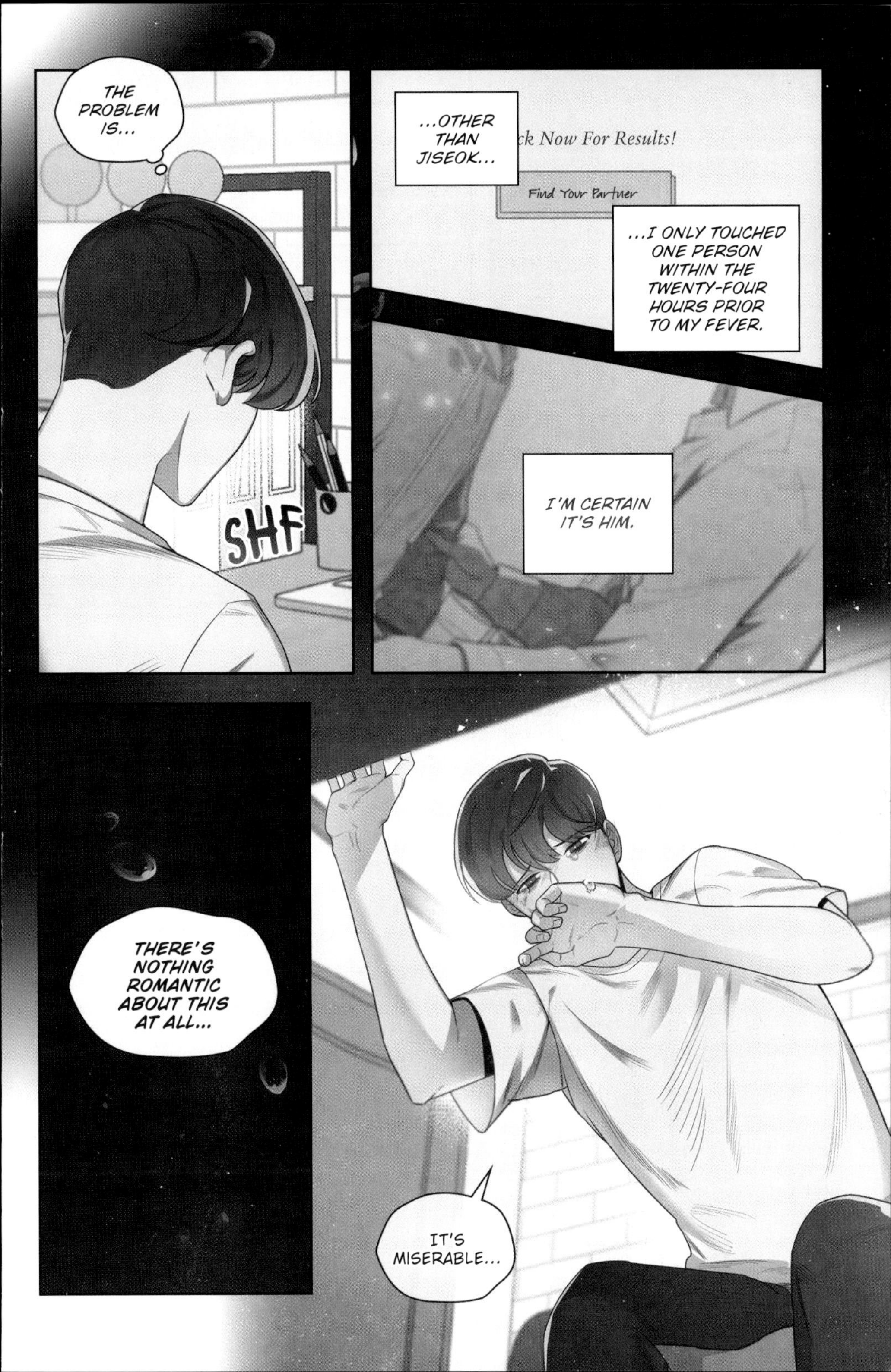
THE PROBLEM IS...
...OTHER THAN JISEOK...
ck Now For Results!
Find Your Partner
...I ONLY TOUCHED ONE PERSON WITHIN THE TWENTY-FOUR HOURS PRIOR TO MY FEVER.
SHF
I'M CERTAIN IT'S HIM.
THERE'S NOTHING ROMANTIC ABOUT THIS AT ALL...
IT'S MISERABLE...

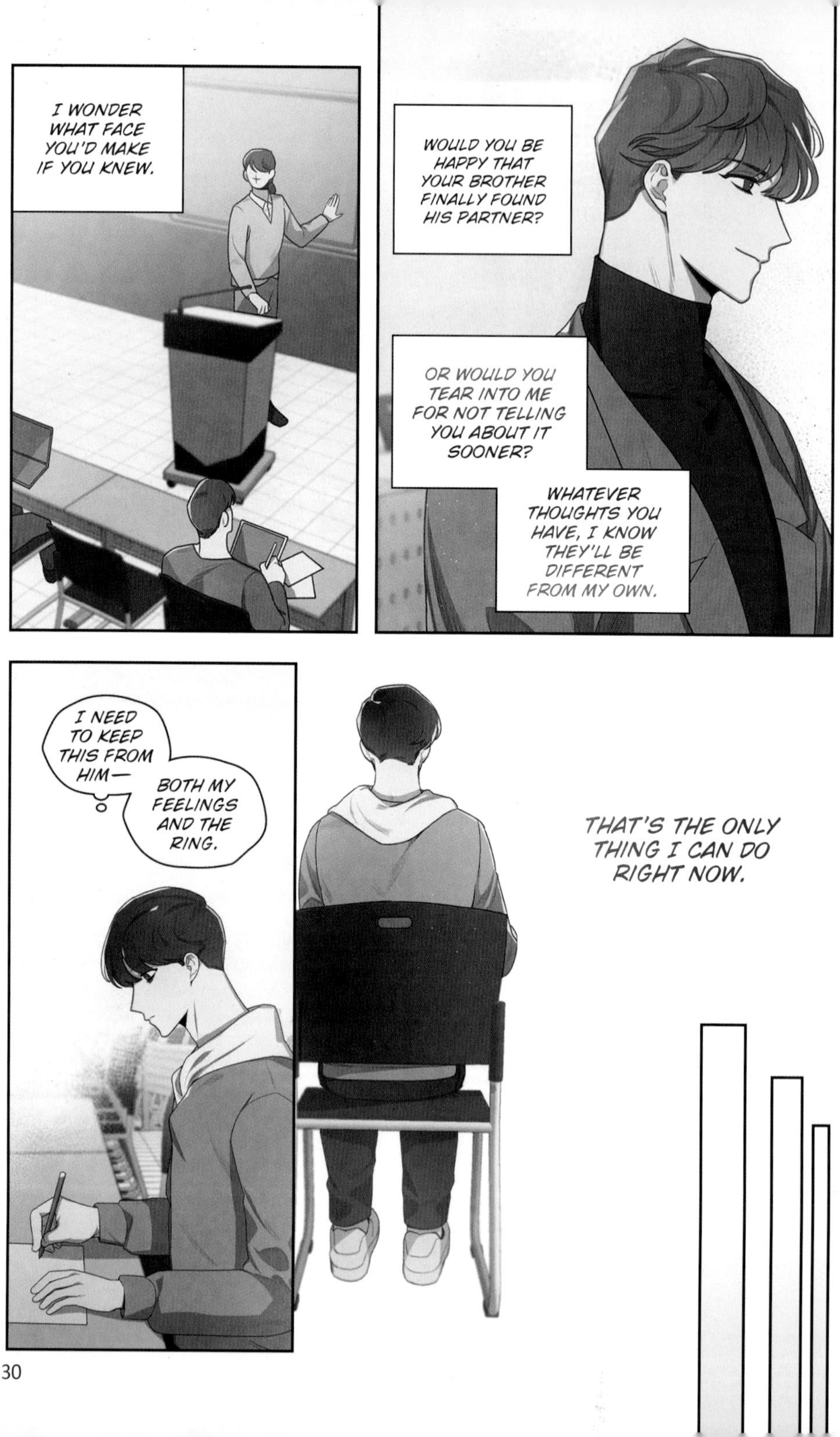

I WONDER WHAT FACE YOU'D MAKE IF YOU KNEW.
WOULD YOU BE HAPPY THAT YOUR BROTHER FINALLY FOUND HIS PARTNER?
OR WOULD YOU TEAR INTO ME FOR NOT TELLING YOU ABOUT IT SOONER?
WHATEVER THOUGHTS YOU HAVE, I KNOW THEY'LL BE DIFFERENT FROM MY OWN.
I NEED TO KEEP THIS FROM HIM—
BOTH MY FEELINGS AND THE RING.
THAT'S THE ONLY THING I CAN DO RIGHT NOW.

...AT LEAST, THAT WAS THE PLAN.

...COME IN...

HEY...YOU DIDN'T HAVE TO BRING ME ANYTHING, Y'KNOW...

I'LL HELP YOU ONCE IF YOU NEED TO SIT UP. UNTIL THEN, SHUT UP AND LIE DOWN.

PUSH

ACK!

YOU DIDN'T EAT LUNCH, RIGHT?

YEAH... I DIDN'T HAVE THE STRENGTH TO GO TO THE KITCHEN...

TEE-HEE.

I KNEW IT.

BURLY GUYS LIKE YOU GET PRETTY DARN SICK EVERY SO OFTEN.

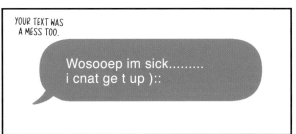

YOUR TEXT WAS A MESS TOO.

Wosooep im sick.........
i cnat ge t up)::

I THOUGHT I WAS GONNA DIE. I THINK I'LL BE OKAY NOW THAT YOU'RE HERE, THOUGH.

IT'S THE PORRIDGE'S DOING, NOT MINE.

AWW, DON'T SAY THAT.

31

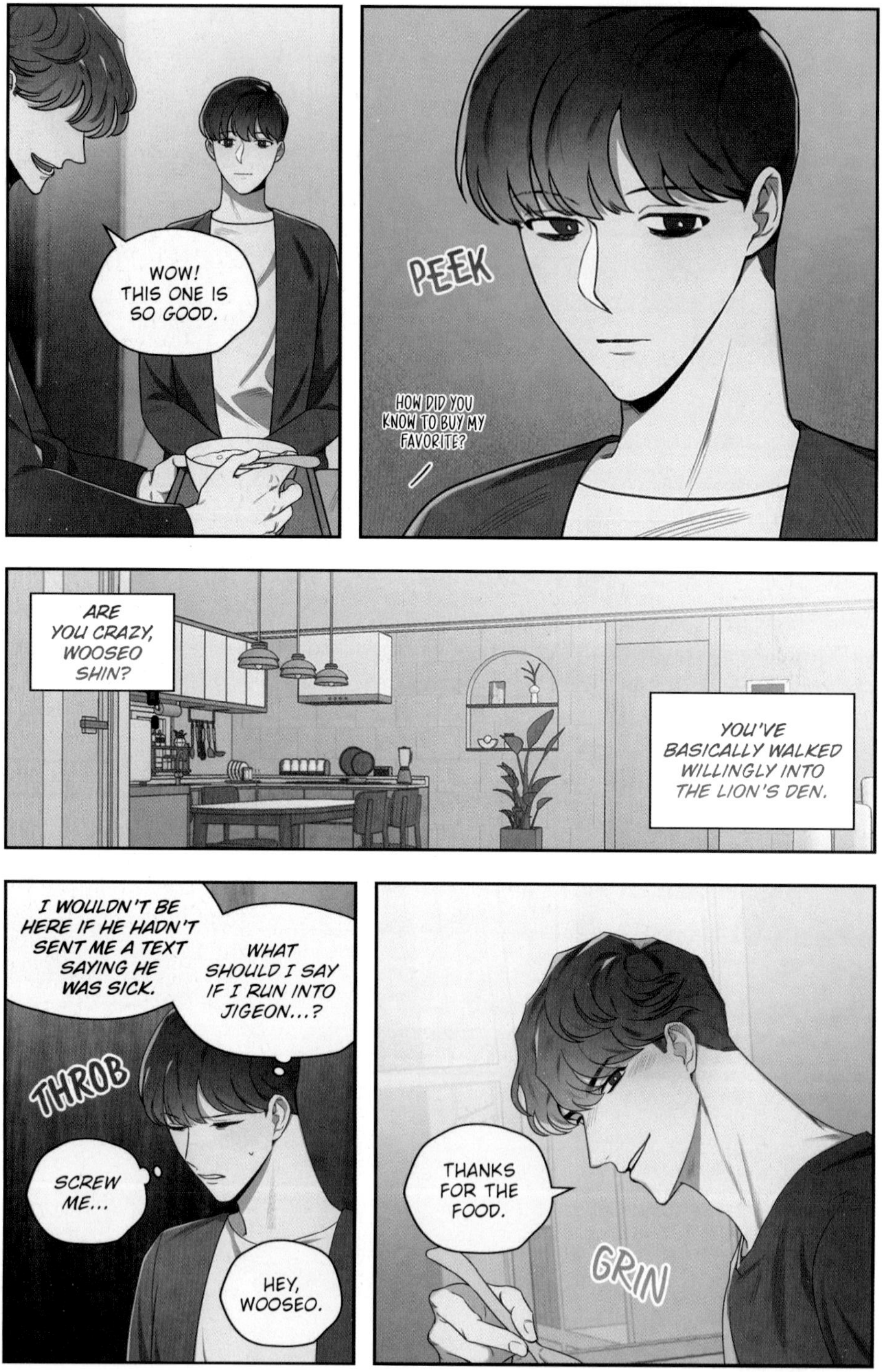
WOW! THIS ONE IS SO GOOD.
PEEK
HOW DID YOU KNOW TO BUY MY FAVORITE?
ARE YOU CRAZY, WOOSEO SHIN?
YOU'VE BASICALLY WALKED WILLINGLY INTO THE LION'S DEN.
I WOULDN'T BE HERE IF HE HADN'T SENT ME A TEXT SAYING HE WAS SICK.
WHAT SHOULD I SAY IF I RUN INTO JIGEON...?
THROB
SCREW ME...
HEY, WOOSEO.
THANKS FOR THE FOOD.
GRIN

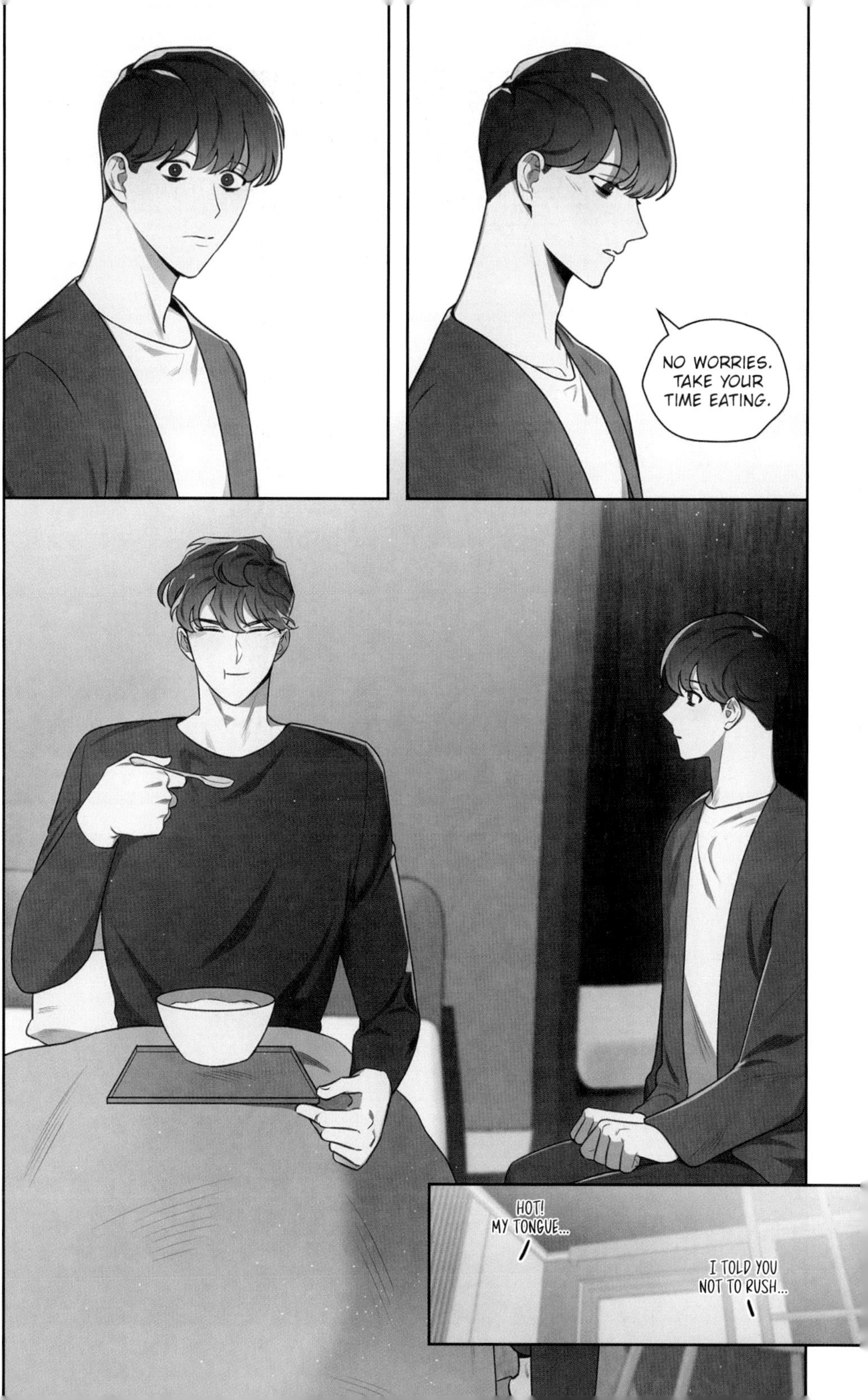

NO WORRIES. TAKE YOUR TIME EATING.
HOT! MY TONGUE...
I TOLD YOU NOT TO RUSH...

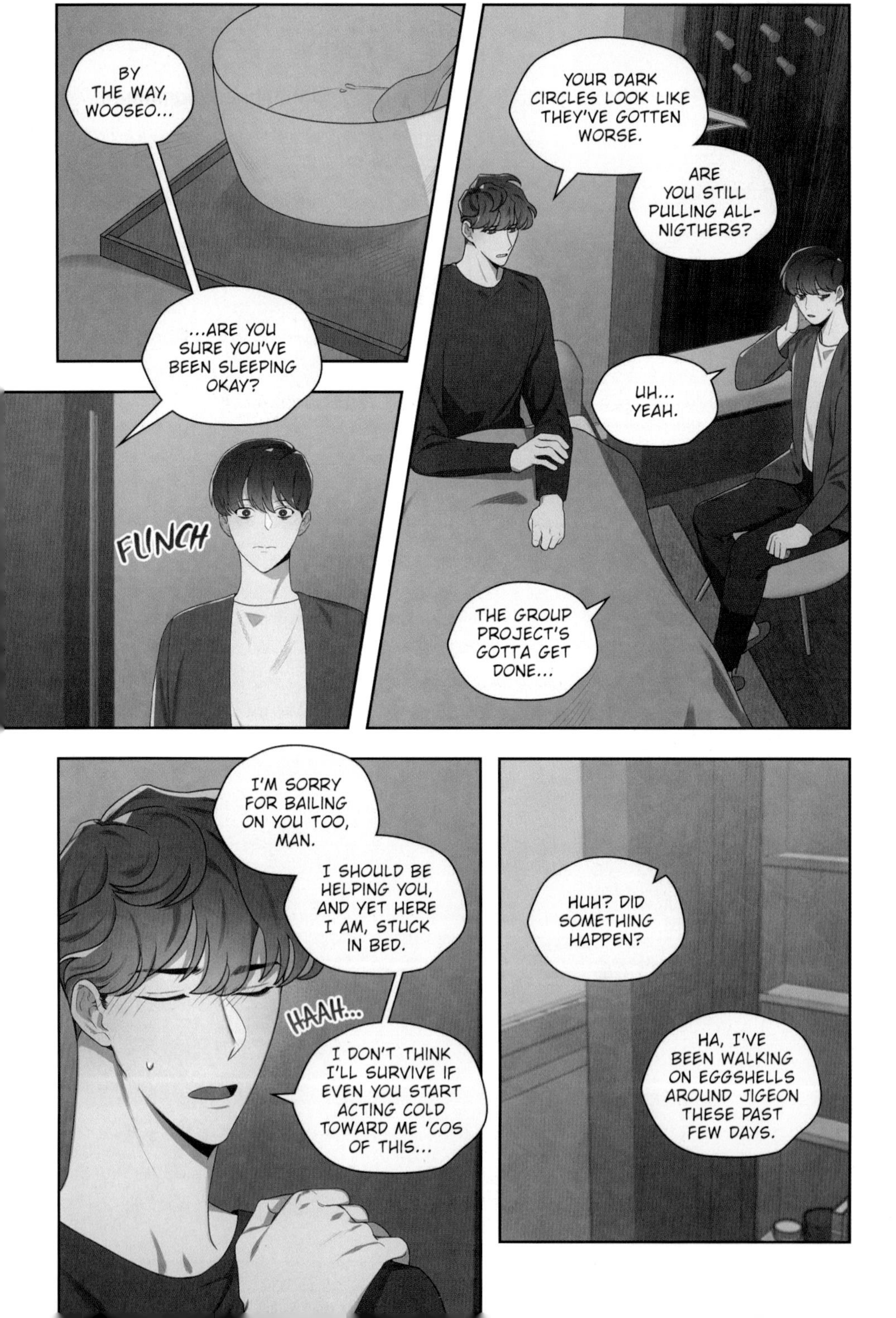

BY THE WAY, WOOSEO...
YOUR DARK CIRCLES LOOK LIKE THEY'VE GOTTEN WORSE.
ARE YOU STILL PULLING ALL-NIGTHERS?
...ARE YOU SURE YOU'VE BEEN SLEEPING OKAY?
FLINCH
UH... YEAH.
THE GROUP PROJECT'S GOTTA GET DONE...
I'M SORRY FOR BAILING ON YOU TOO, MAN.
I SHOULD BE HELPING YOU, AND YET HERE I AM, STUCK IN BED.
HAAH...
I DON'T THINK I'LL SURVIVE IF EVEN YOU START ACTING COLD TOWARD ME 'COS OF THIS...
HUH? DID SOMETHING HAPPEN?
HA, I'VE BEEN WALKING ON EGGSHELLS AROUND JIGEON THESE PAST FEW DAYS.

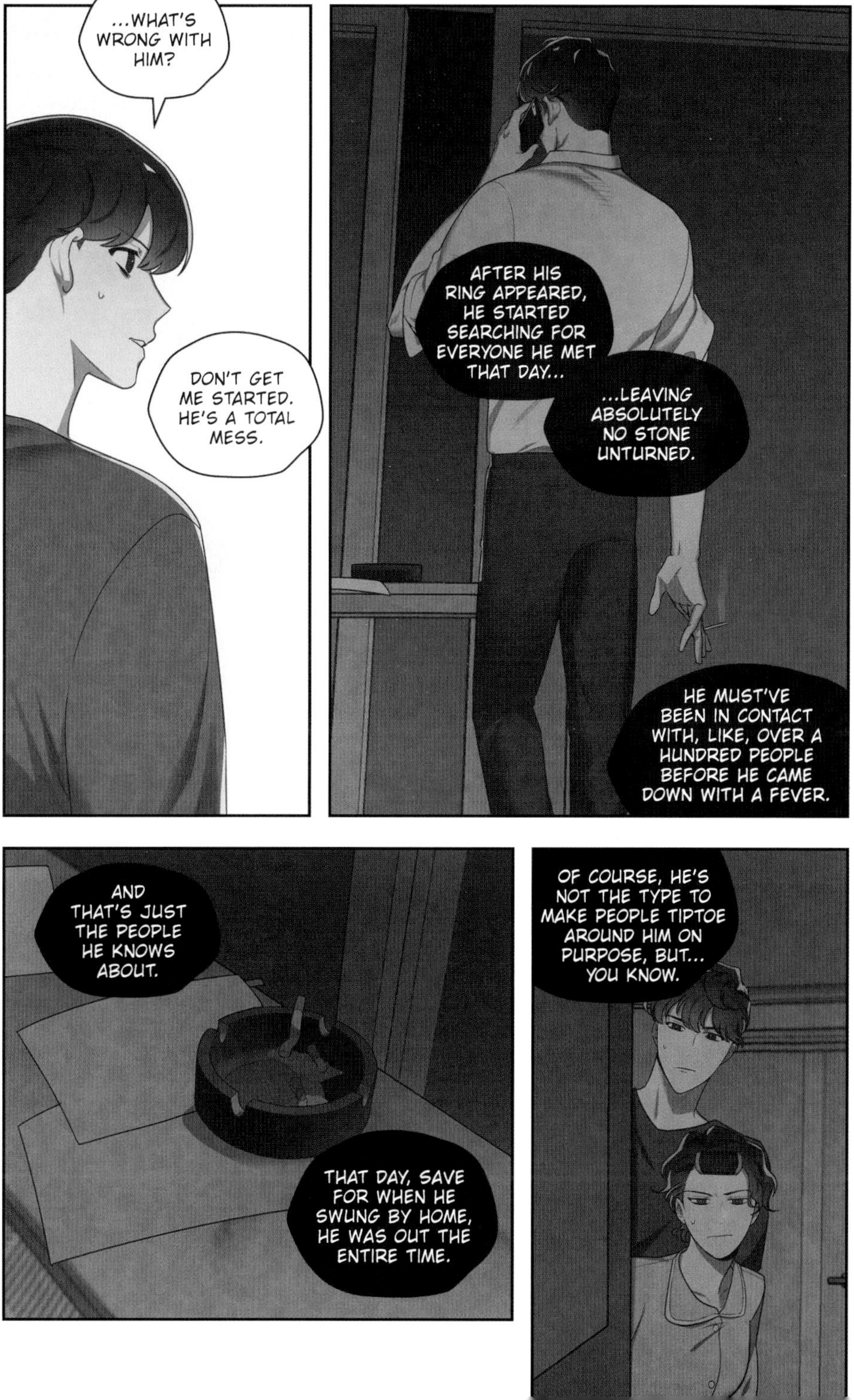
...WHAT'S WRONG WITH HIM?
DON'T GET ME STARTED. HE'S A TOTAL MESS.
AFTER HIS RING APPEARED, HE STARTED SEARCHING FOR EVERYONE HE MET THAT DAY...
...LEAVING ABSOLUTELY NO STONE UNTURNED.
HE MUST'VE BEEN IN CONTACT WITH, LIKE, OVER A HUNDRED PEOPLE BEFORE HE CAME DOWN WITH A FEVER.
AND THAT'S JUST THE PEOPLE HE KNOWS ABOUT.
THAT DAY, SAVE FOR WHEN HE SWUNG BY HOME, HE WAS OUT THE ENTIRE TIME.
OF COURSE, HE'S NOT THE TYPE TO MAKE PEOPLE TIPTOE AROUND HIM ON PURPOSE, BUT... YOU KNOW.

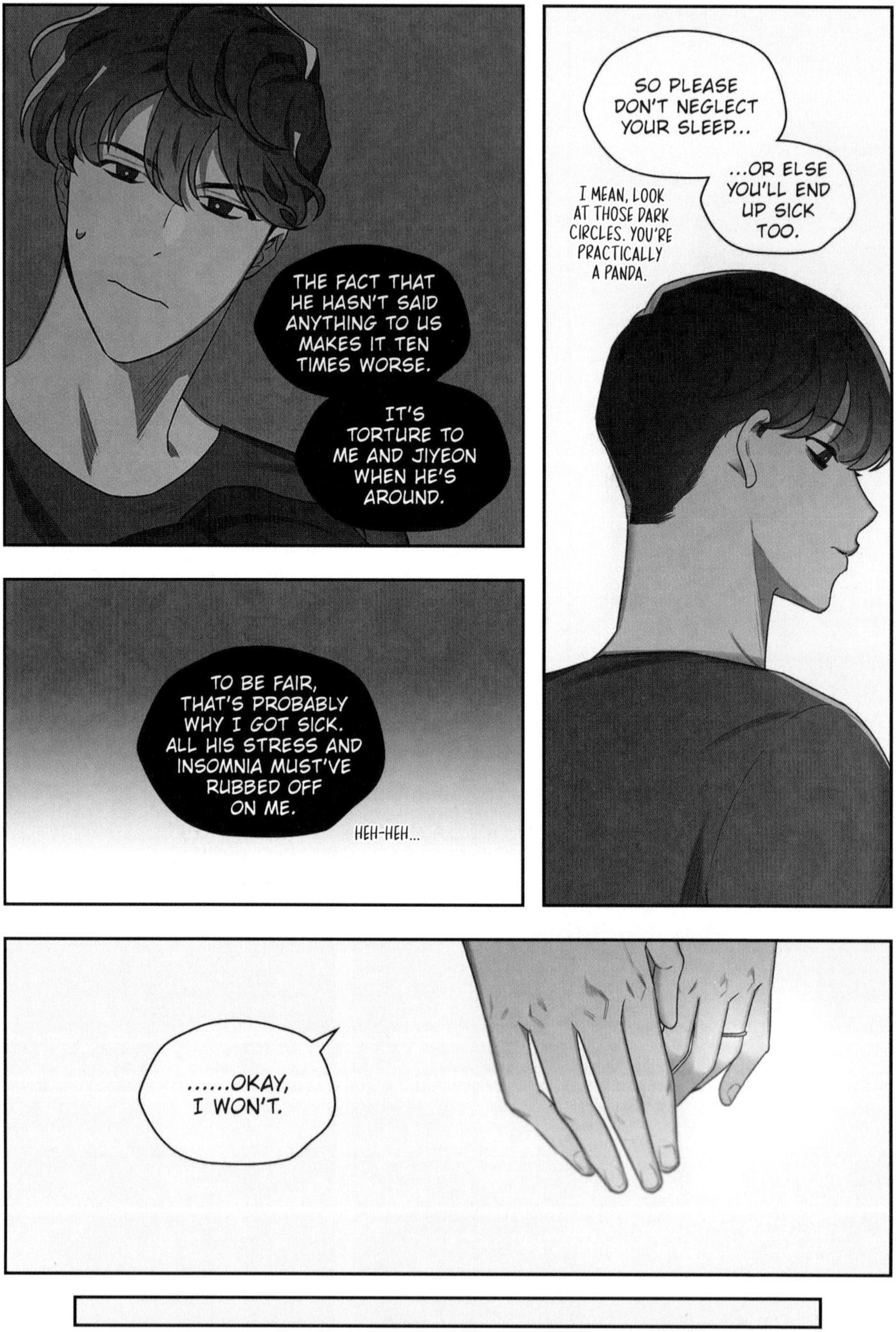

THE FACT THAT HE HASN'T SAID ANYTHING TO US MAKES IT TEN TIMES WORSE.
IT'S TORTURE TO ME AND JIYEON WHEN HE'S AROUND.
TO BE FAIR, THAT'S PROBABLY WHY I GOT SICK. ALL HIS STRESS AND INSOMNIA MUST'VE RUBBED OFF ON ME.
HEH-HEH...
SO PLEASE DON'T NEGLECT YOUR SLEEP...
...OR ELSE YOU'LL END UP SICK TOO.
I MEAN, LOOK AT THOSE DARK CIRCLES. YOU'RE PRACTICALLY A PANDA.
......OKAY, I WON'T.

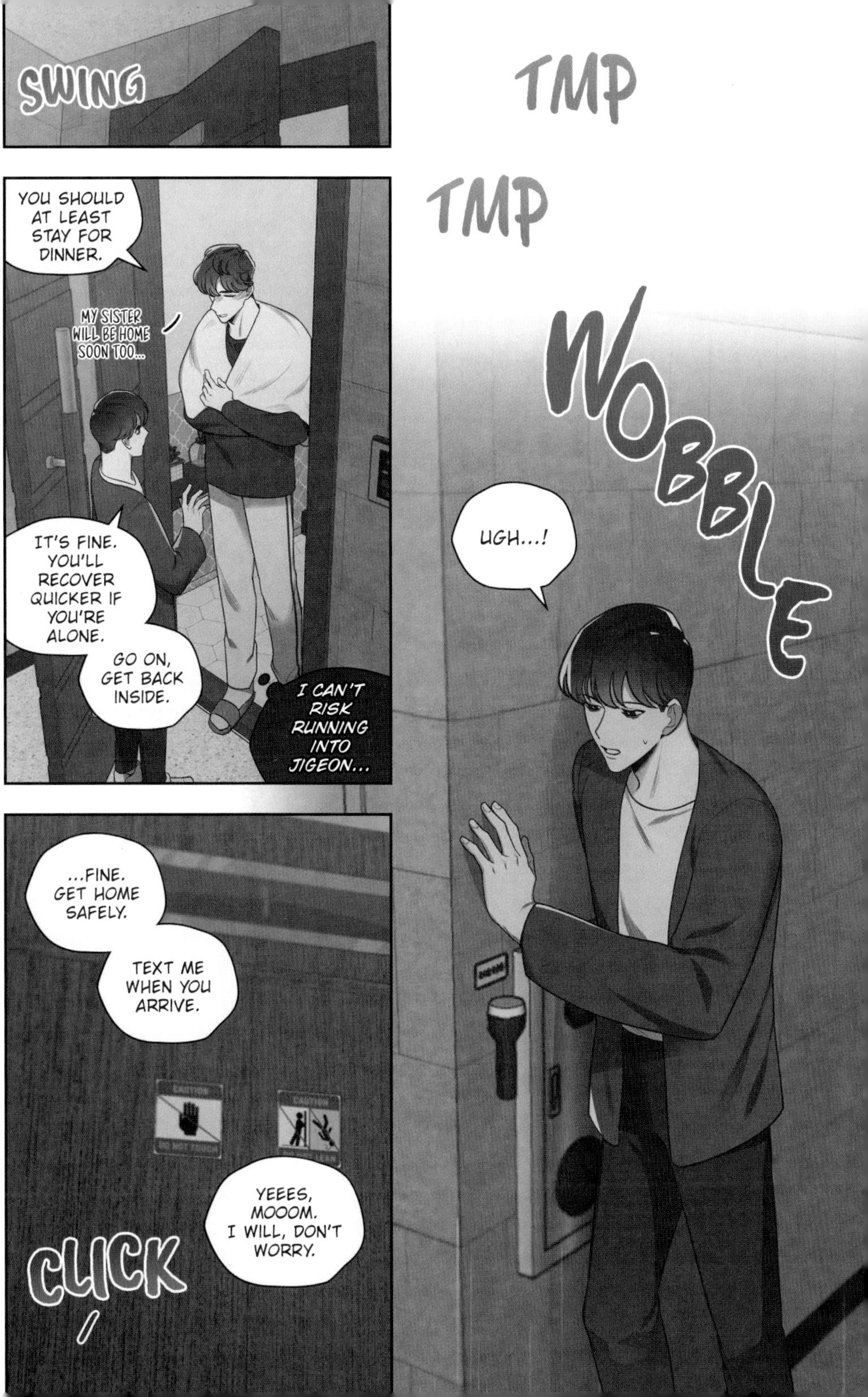
SWING
TMP
TMP
YOU SHOULD AT LEAST STAY FOR DINNER.
MY SISTER WILL BE HOME SOON TOO...
IT'S FINE. YOU'LL RECOVER QUICKER IF YOU'RE ALONE.
GO ON, GET BACK INSIDE.
I CAN'T RISK RUNNING INTO JIGEON...
...FINE. GET HOME SAFELY.
TEXT ME WHEN YOU ARRIVE.
YEEES, MOOOM. I WILL, DON'T WORRY.
CLICK
WOBBLE
UGH...!

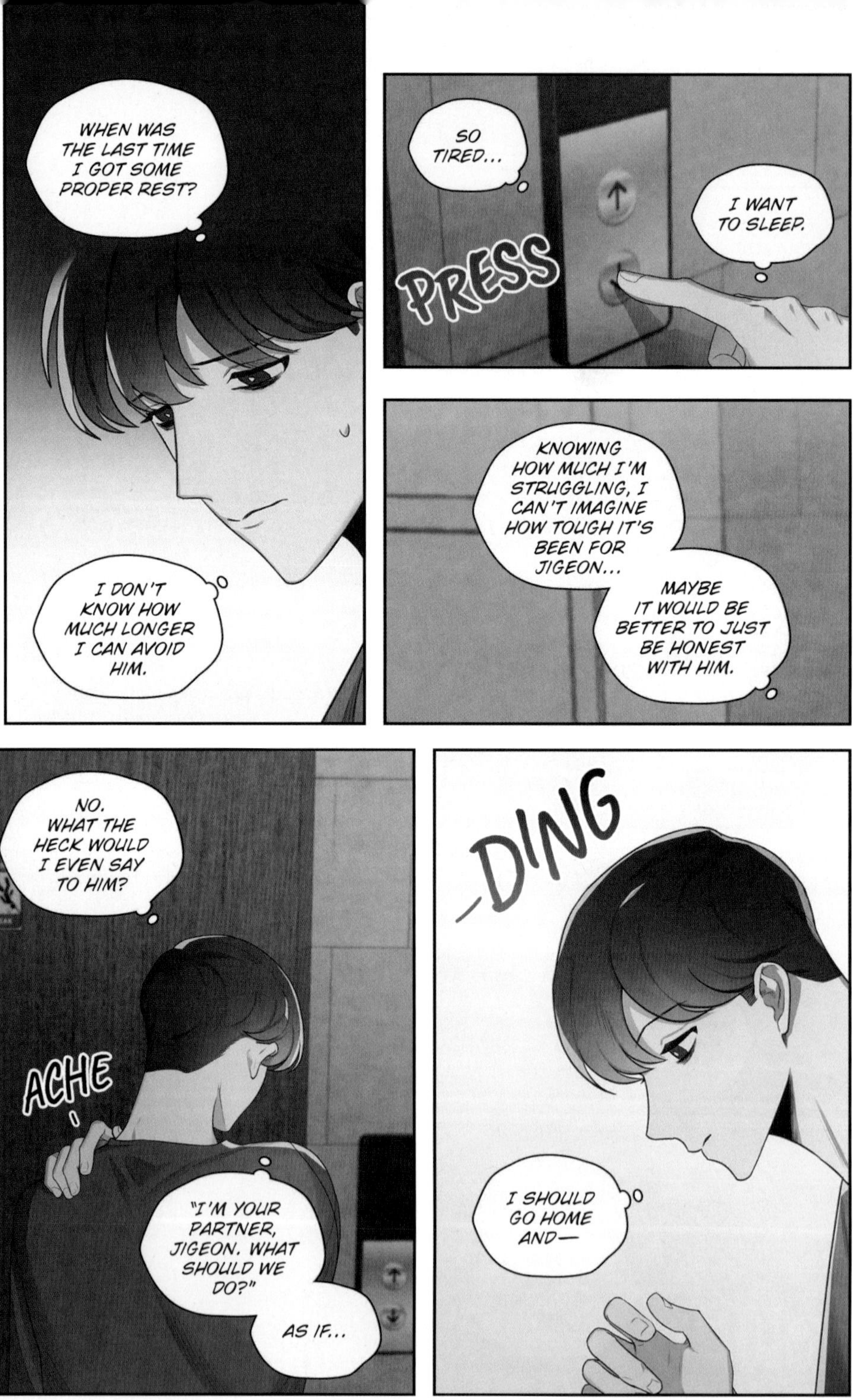
WHEN WAS THE LAST TIME I GOT SOME PROPER REST?
I DON'T KNOW HOW MUCH LONGER I CAN AVOID HIM.
SO TIRED...
PRESS
I WANT TO SLEEP.
KNOWING HOW MUCH I'M STRUGGLING, I CAN'T IMAGINE HOW TOUGH IT'S BEEN FOR JIGEON...
MAYBE IT WOULD BE BETTER TO JUST BE HONEST WITH HIM.
NO. WHAT THE HECK WOULD I EVEN SAY TO HIM?
ACHE
"I'M YOUR PARTNER, JIGEON. WHAT SHOULD WE DO?"
AS IF...
DING
I SHOULD GO HOME AND—

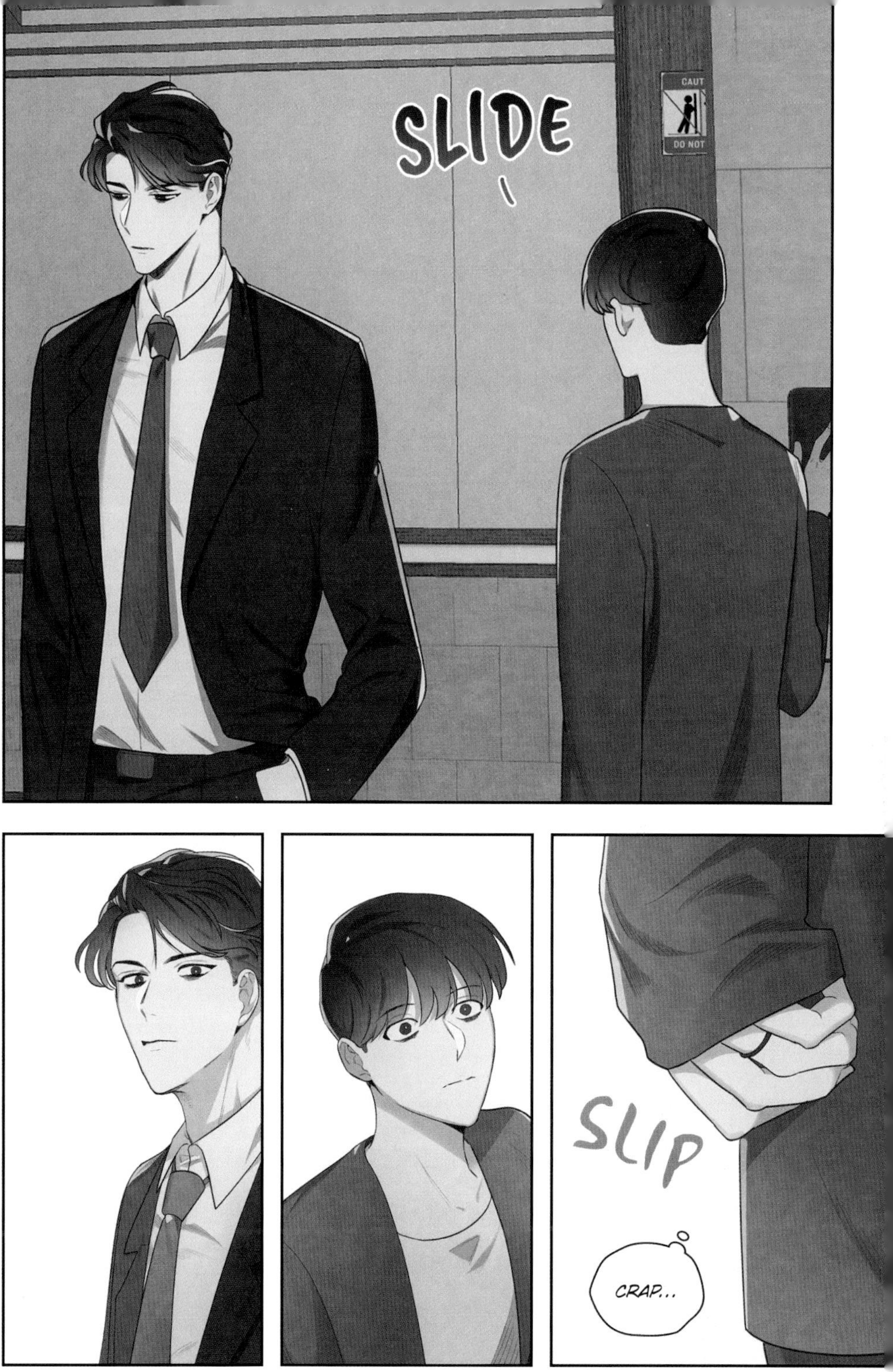
SLIDE
DO NOT
SLIP
CRAP...

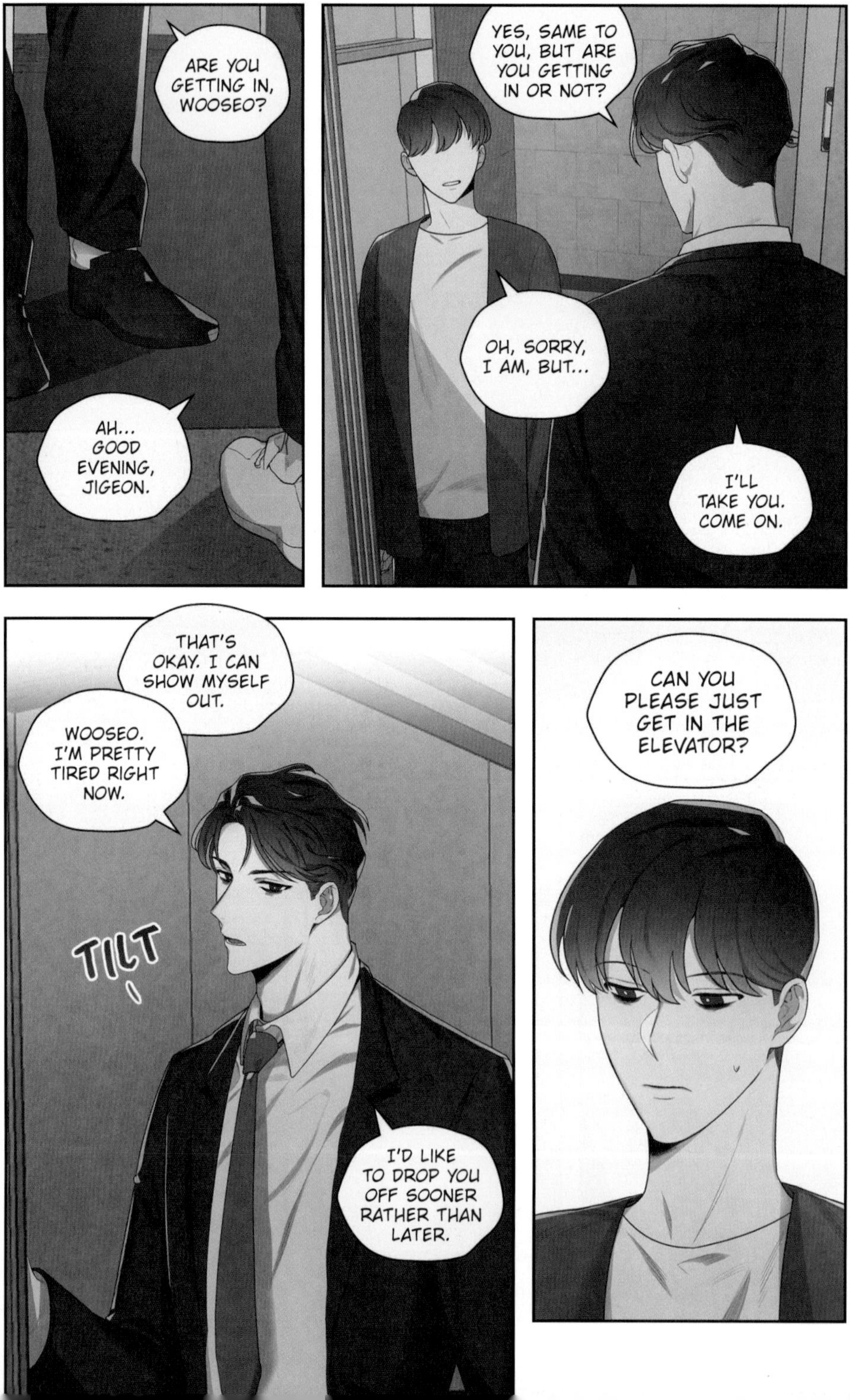
ARE YOU GETTING IN, WOOSEO?
AH... GOOD EVENING, JIGEON.
YES, SAME TO YOU, BUT ARE YOU GETTING IN OR NOT?
OH, SORRY, I AM, BUT...
I'LL TAKE YOU. COME ON.
THAT'S OKAY. I CAN SHOW MYSELF OUT.
WOOSEO. I'M PRETTY TIRED RIGHT NOW.
TILT
I'D LIKE TO DROP YOU OFF SOONER RATHER THAN LATER.
CAN YOU PLEASE JUST GET IN THE ELEVATOR?

Tied to You

Chapter 3

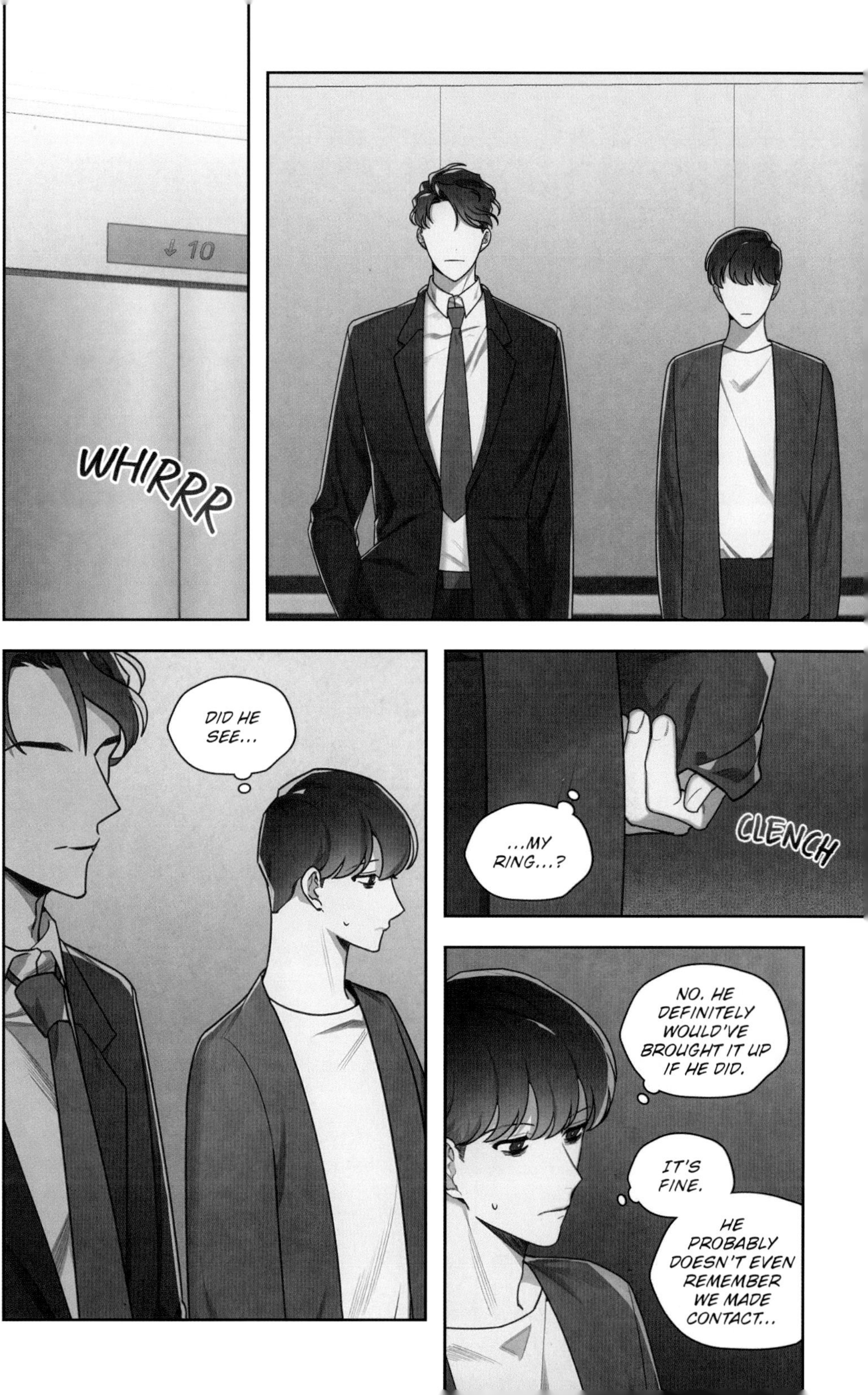
↓10
WHIRRR
DID HE SEE...
...MY RING...?
CLENCH
NO. HE DEFINITELY WOULD'VE BROUGHT IT UP IF HE DID.
IT'S FINE.
HE PROBABLY DOESN'T EVEN REMEMBER WE MADE CONTACT...

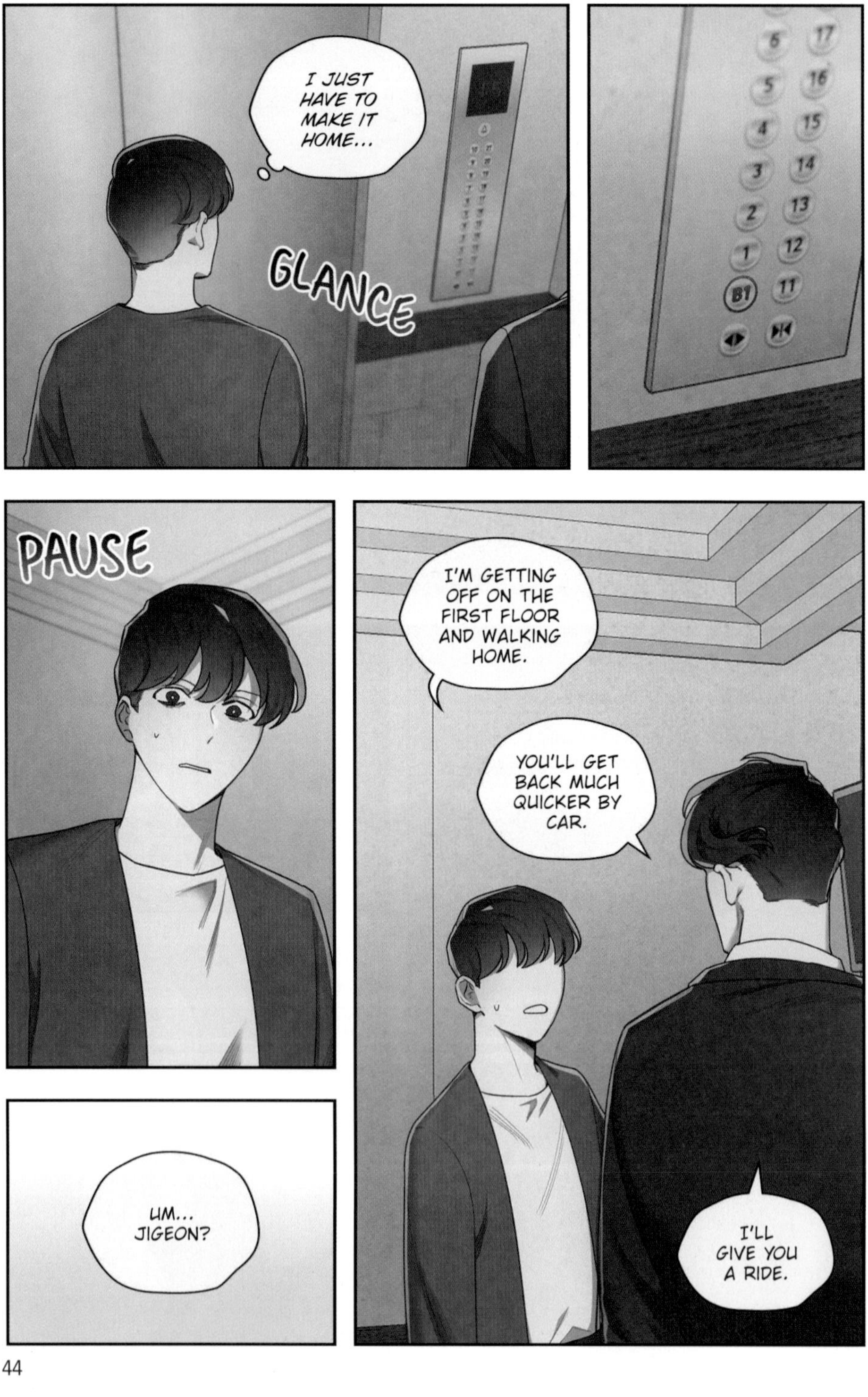
I JUST HAVE TO MAKE IT HOME...
GLANCE
PAUSE
I'M GETTING OFF ON THE FIRST FLOOR AND WALKING HOME.
YOU'LL GET BACK MUCH QUICKER BY CAR.
UM... JIGEON?
I'LL GIVE YOU A RIDE.

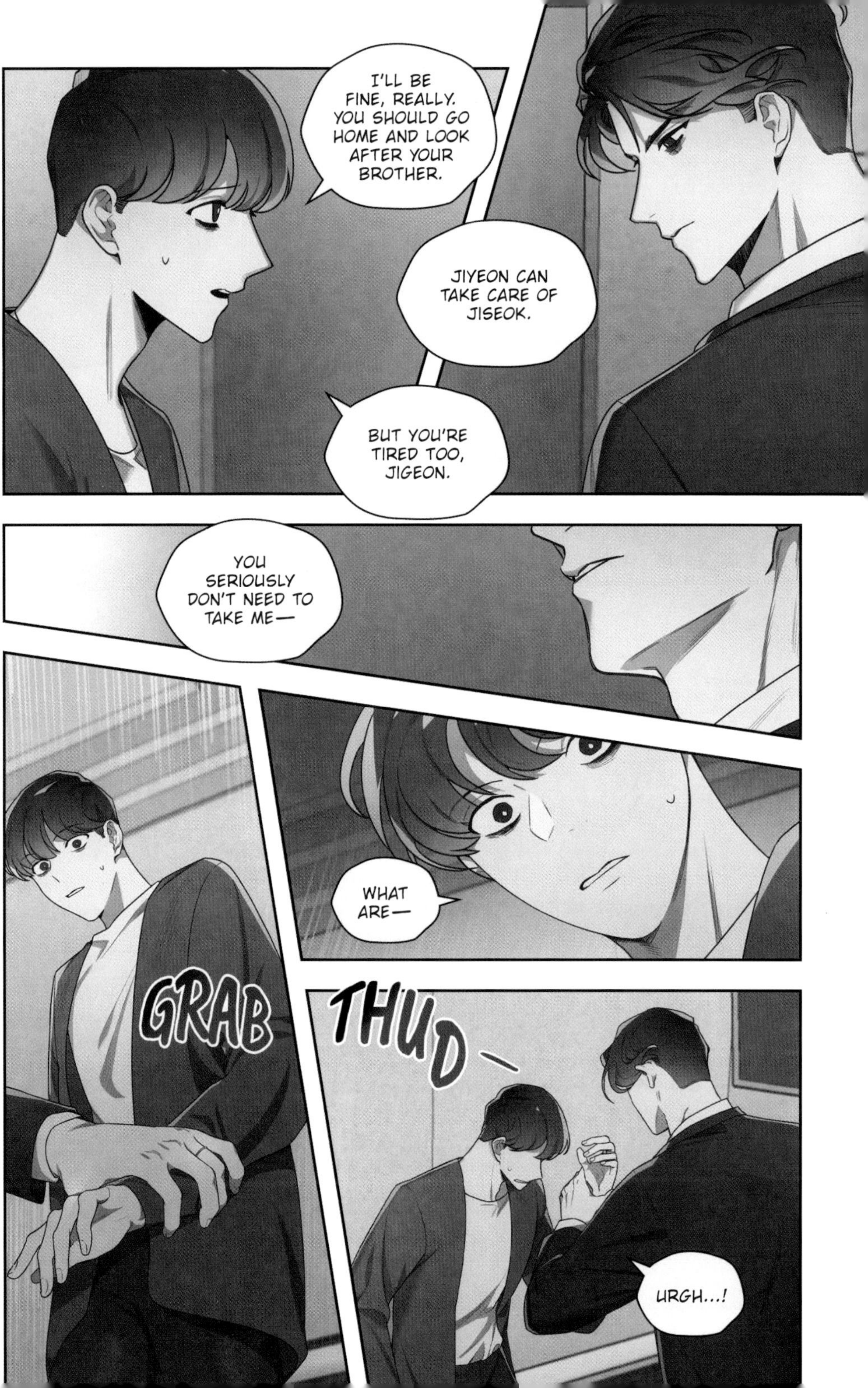
I'LL BE FINE, REALLY. YOU SHOULD GO HOME AND LOOK AFTER YOUR BROTHER.
JIYEON CAN TAKE CARE OF JISEOK.
BUT YOU'RE TIRED TOO, JIGEON.
YOU SERIOUSLY DON'T NEED TO TAKE ME—
WHAT ARE—
GRAB
THUD—
URGH...!

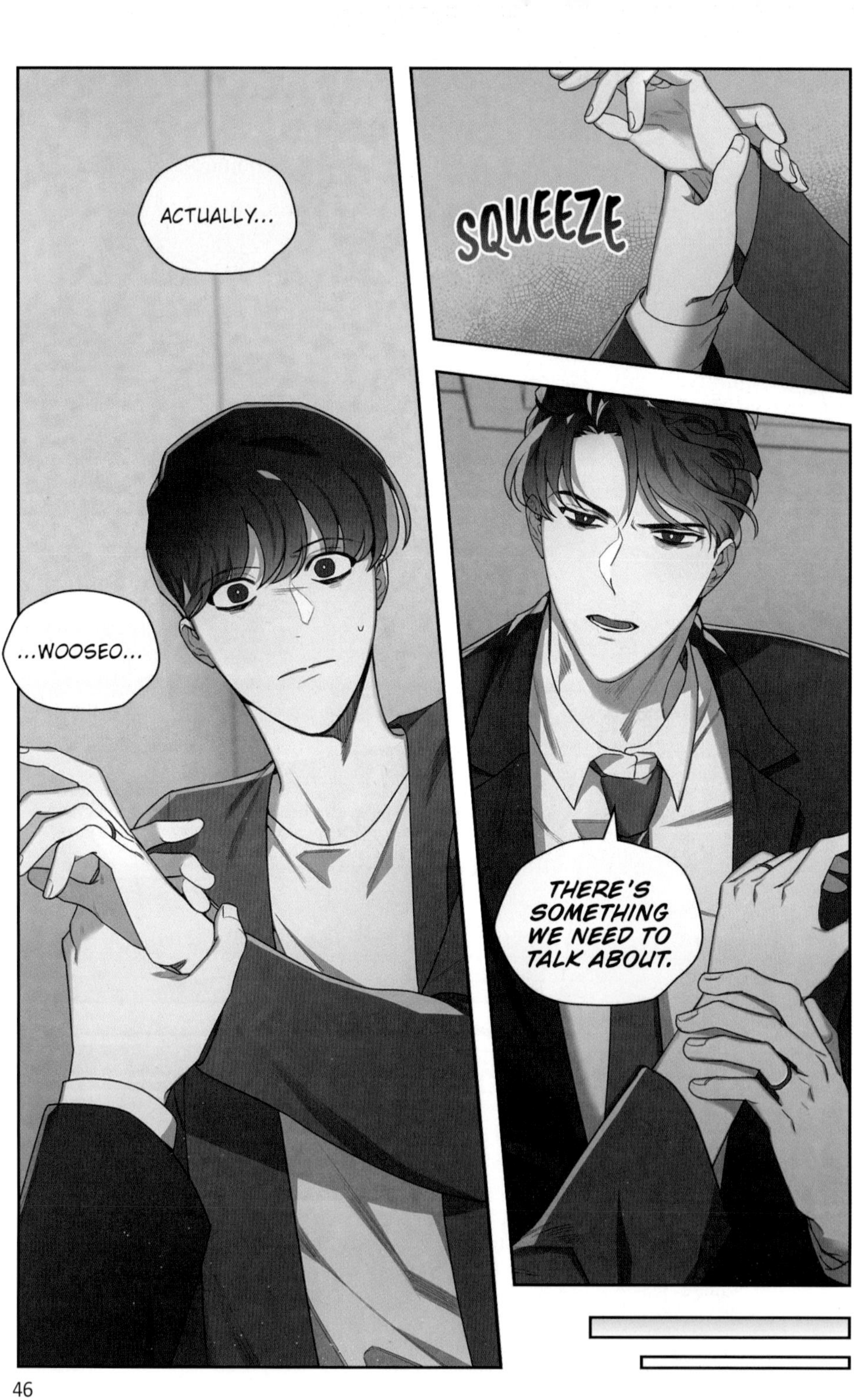

ACTUALLY...
SQUEEZE
...WOOSEO...
THERE'S SOMETHING WE NEED TO TALK ABOUT.

JIGEON! WAI—

HEY, JIGEON.

STRIDE

WAIT A SECOND... JIGEON!

STRIDE

THUMP

URK...!

WHAT DO I DO? HE SEEMS FURIOUS.

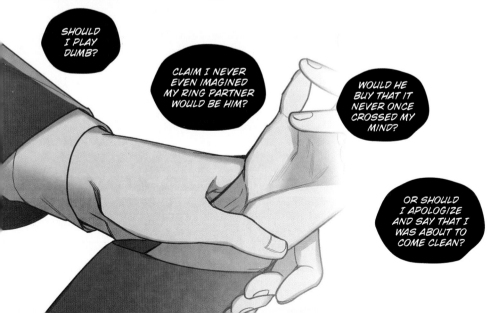

SHOULD I PLAY DUMB?

CLAIM I NEVER EVEN IMAGINED MY RING PARTNER WOULD BE HIM?

WOULD HE BUY THAT IT NEVER ONCE CROSSED MY MIND?

OR SHOULD I APOLOGIZE AND SAY THAT I WAS ABOUT TO COME CLEAN?

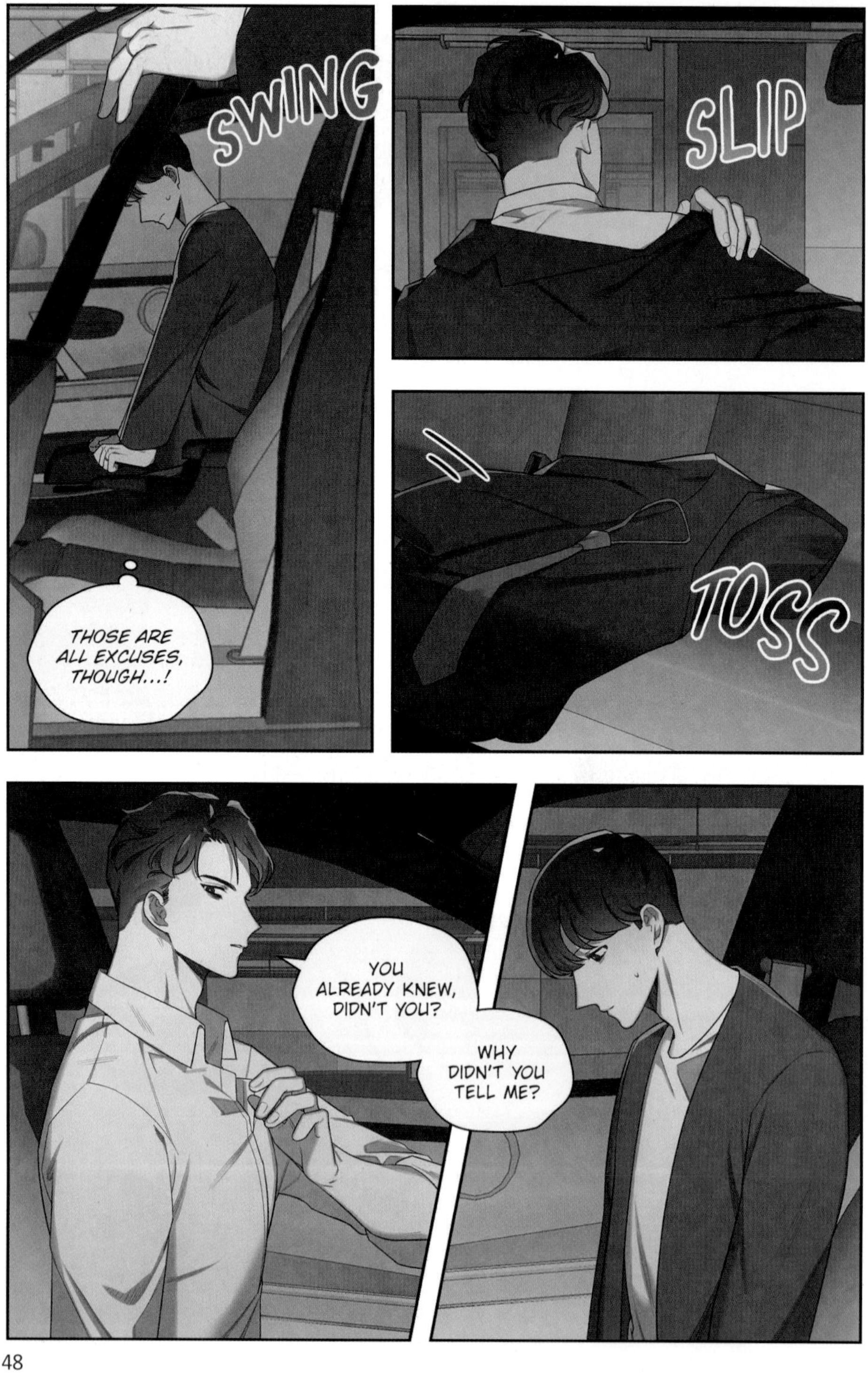
SWING
THOSE ARE ALL EXCUSES, THOUGH...!
SLIP
TOSS
YOU ALREADY KNEW, DIDN'T YOU?
WHY DIDN'T YOU TELL ME?

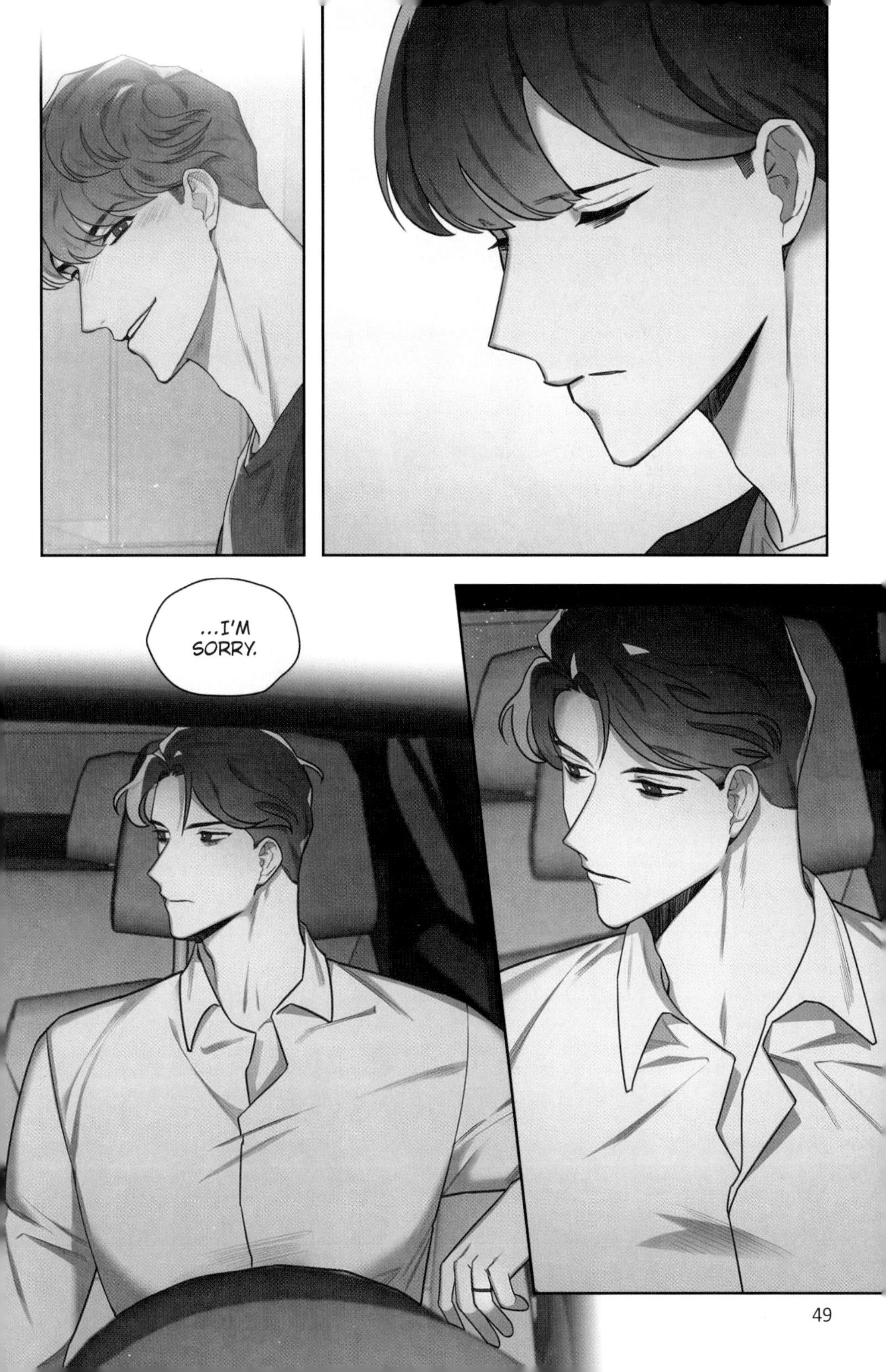
...I'M SORRY.

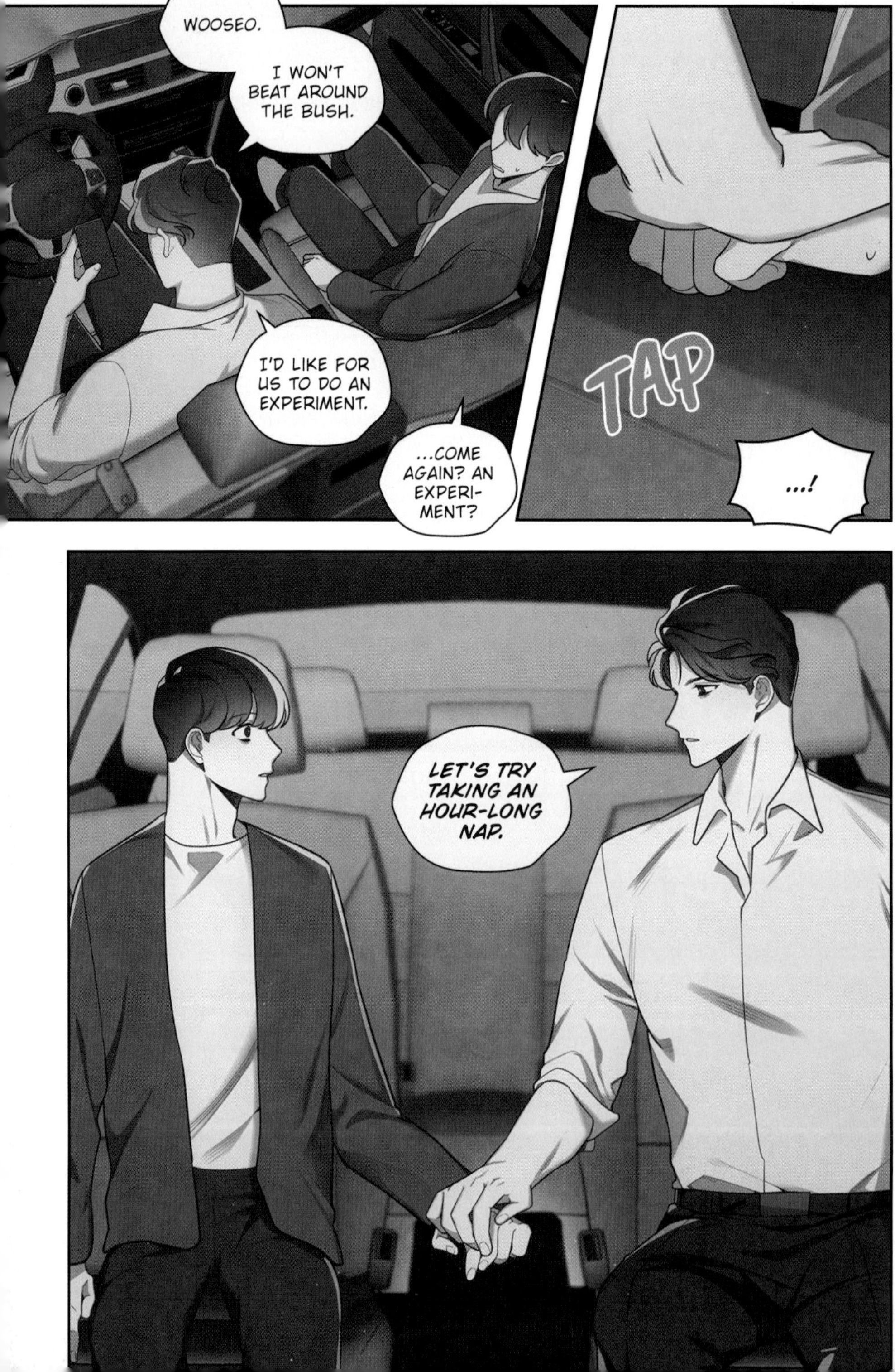
WOOSEO.
I WON'T BEAT AROUND THE BUSH.
I'D LIKE FOR US TO DO AN EXPERIMENT.
...COME AGAIN? AN EXPERI-MENT?
TAP
...!
LET'S TRY TAKING AN HOUR-LONG NAP.

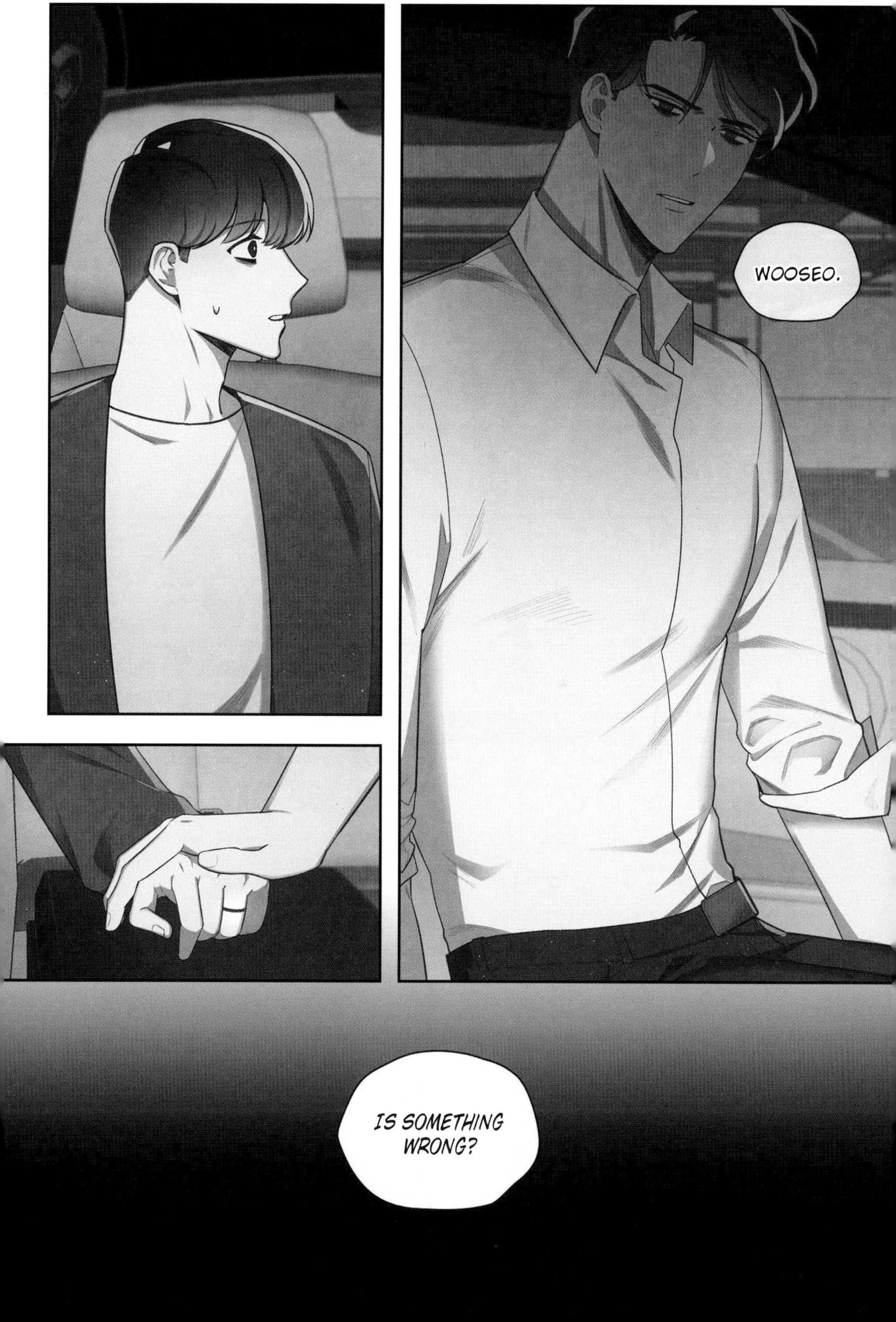
WOOSEO.
IS SOMETHING WRONG?

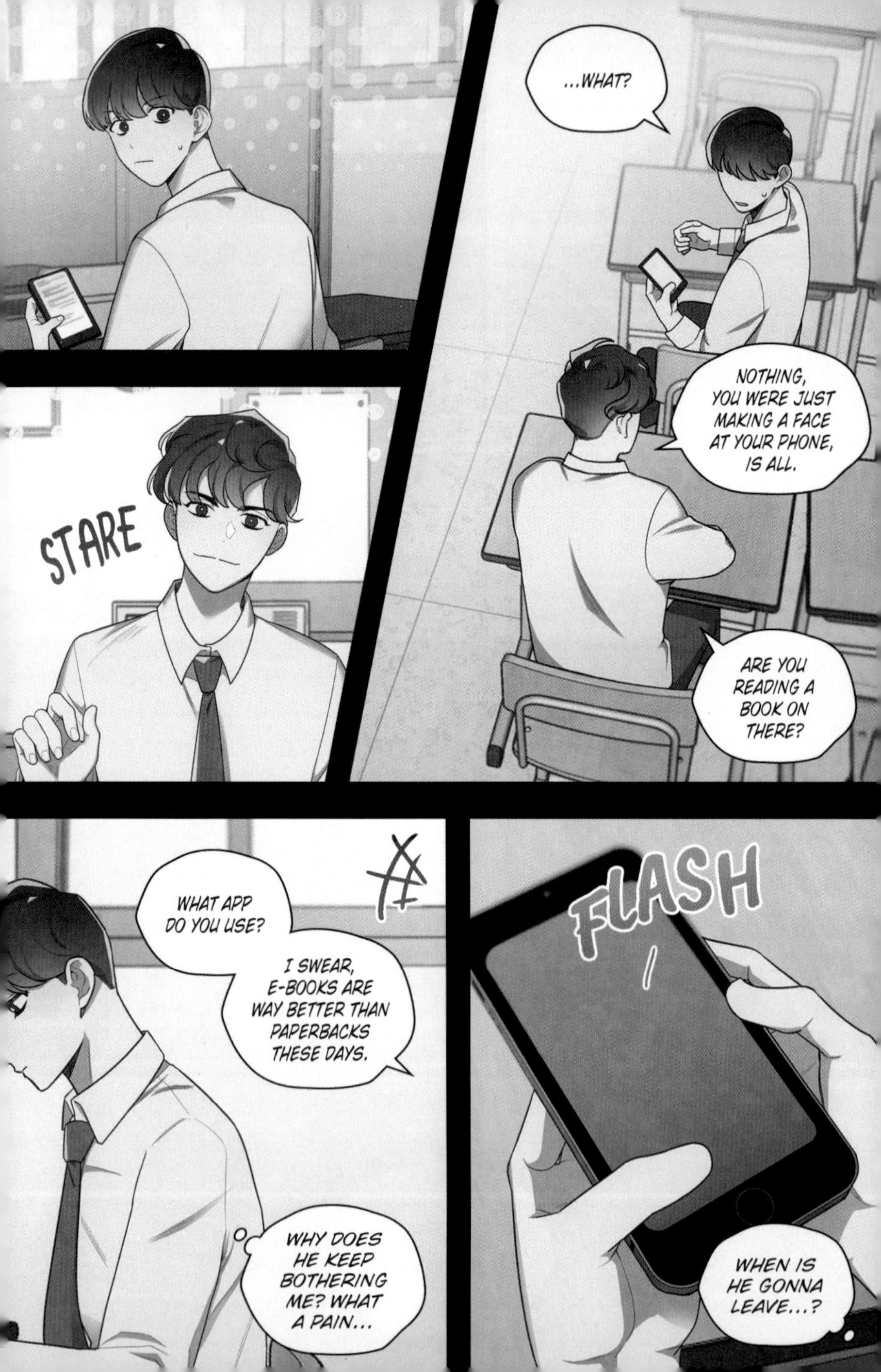
...WHAT?
STARE
NOTHING, YOU WERE JUST MAKING A FACE AT YOUR PHONE, IS ALL.
ARE YOU READING A BOOK ON THERE?
WHAT APP DO YOU USE?
I SWEAR, E-BOOKS ARE WAY BETTER THAN PAPERBACKS THESE DAYS.
WHY DOES HE KEEP BOTHERING ME? WHAT A PAIN...
FLASH
WHEN IS HE GONNA LEAVE...?

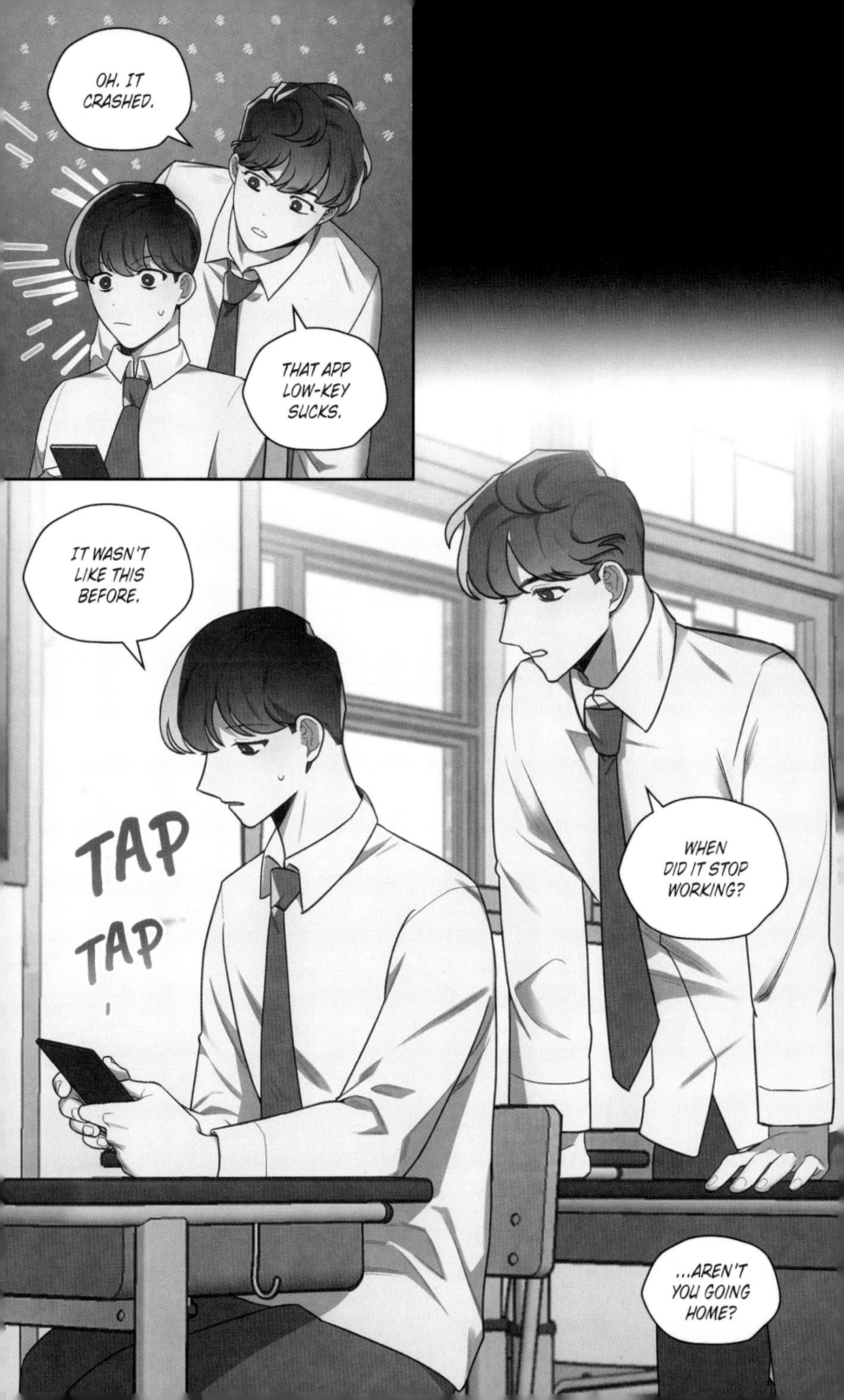
OH. IT CRASHED.
THAT APP LOW-KEY SUCKS.
IT WASN'T LIKE THIS BEFORE.
WHEN DID IT STOP WORKING?
TAP
TAP
...AREN'T YOU GOING HOME?

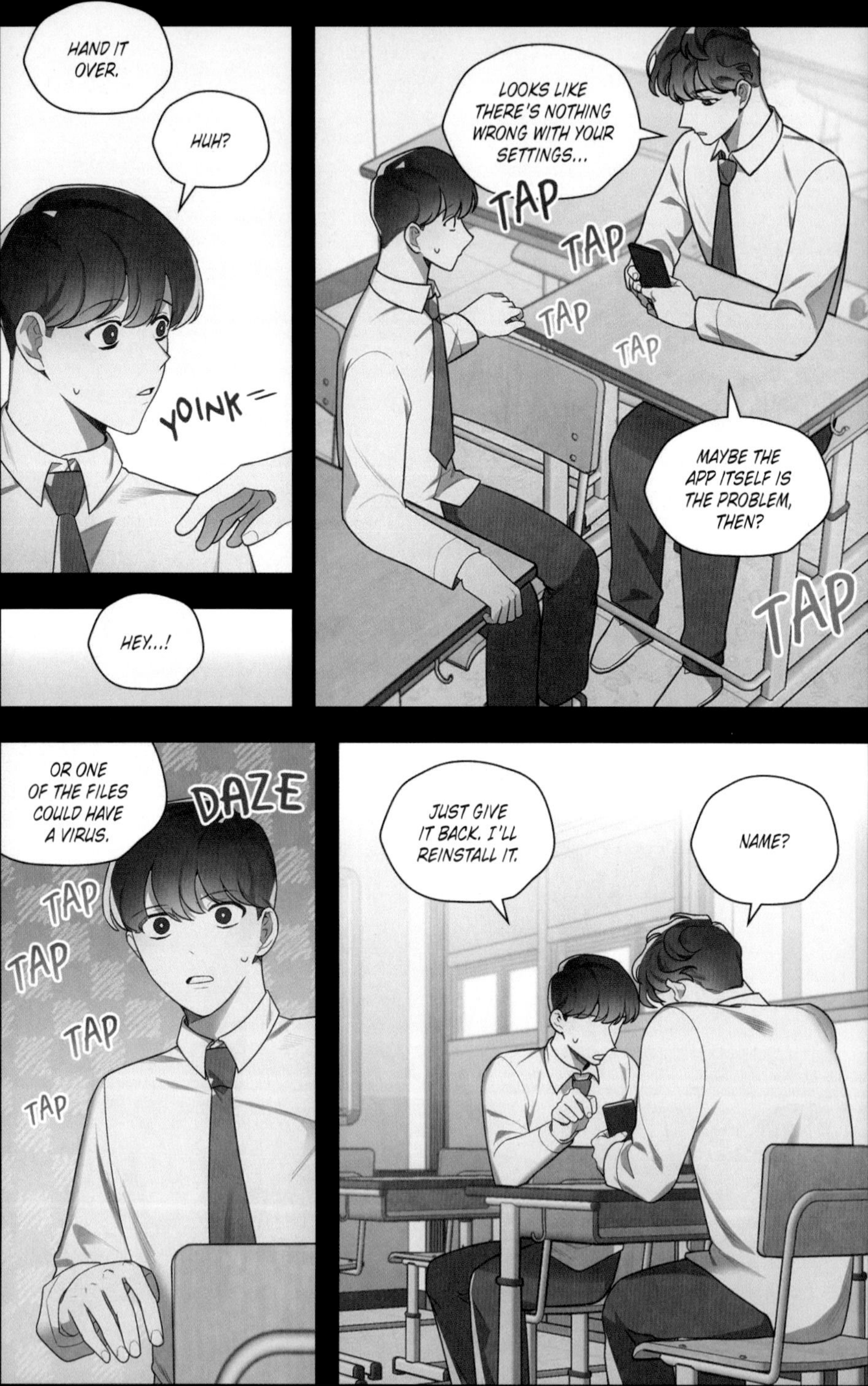
HAND IT OVER.
HUH?
YOINK
HEY...!
LOOKS LIKE THERE'S NOTHING WRONG WITH YOUR SETTINGS...
TAP
TAP
TAP
TAP
MAYBE THE APP ITSELF IS THE PROBLEM, THEN?
TAP
OR ONE OF THE FILES COULD HAVE A VIRUS.
DAZE
TAP
TAP
TAP
TAP
JUST GIVE IT BACK. I'LL REINSTALL IT.
NAME?

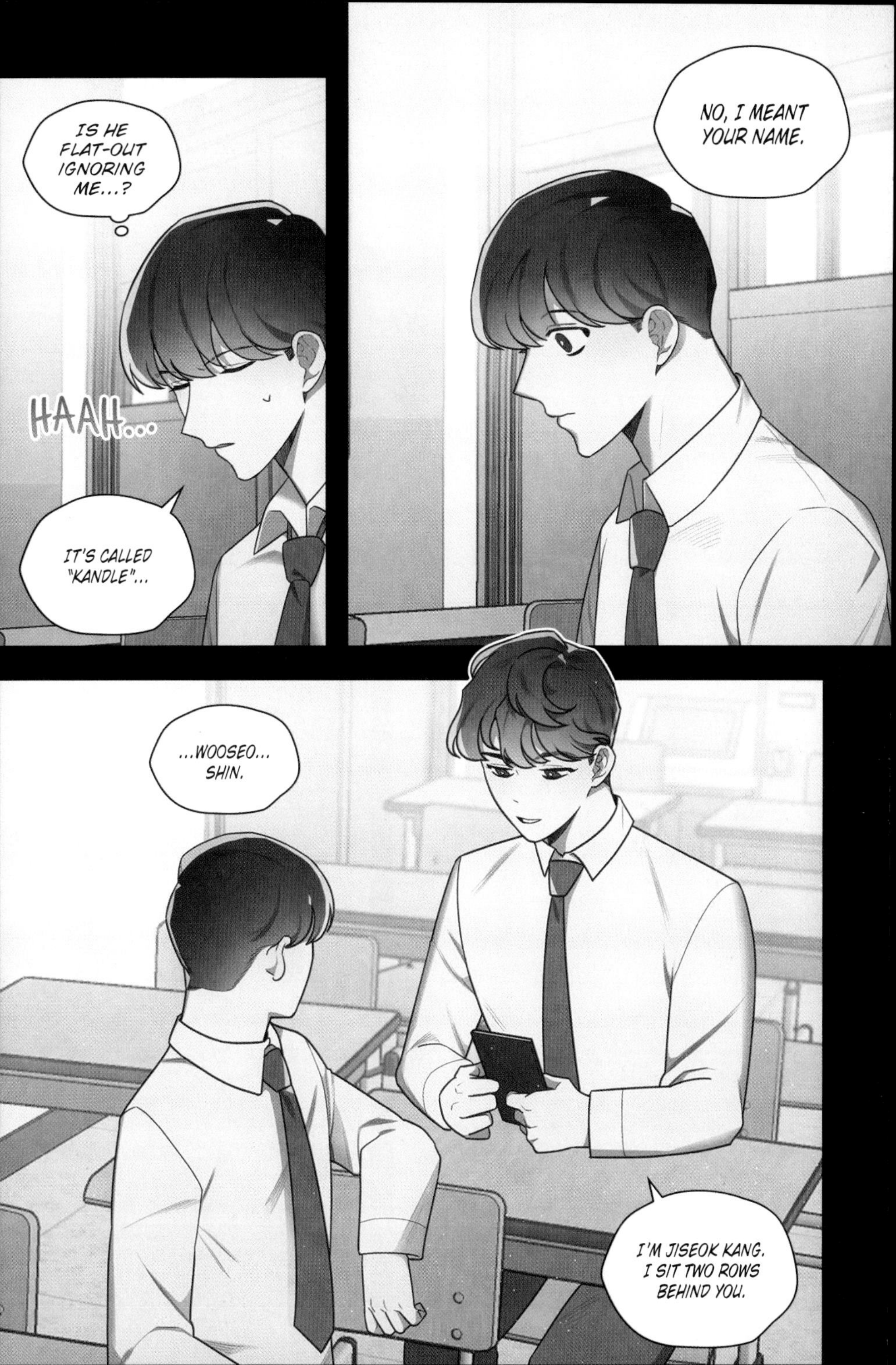
IS HE FLAT-OUT IGNORING ME...?
HAAH...
IT'S CALLED "KANDLE"...
NO, I MEANT YOUR NAME.
...WOOSEO... SHIN.
I'M JISEOK KANG. I SIT TWO ROWS BEHIND YOU.

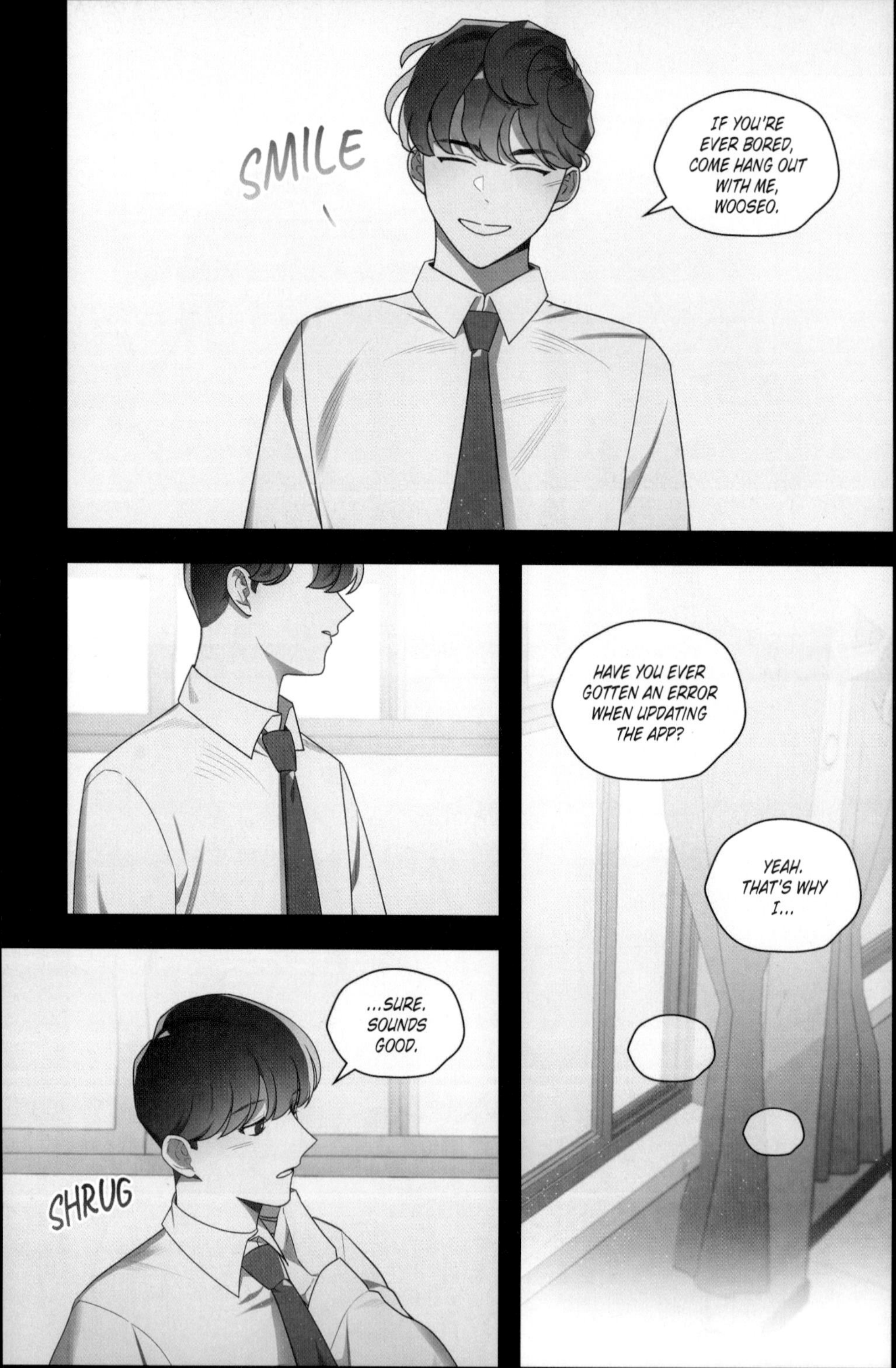
SMILE
IF YOU'RE EVER BORED, COME HANG OUT WITH ME, WOOSEO.
HAVE YOU EVER GOTTEN AN ERROR WHEN UPDATING THE APP?
YEAH. THAT'S WHY I...
...SURE. SOUNDS GOOD.
SHRUG

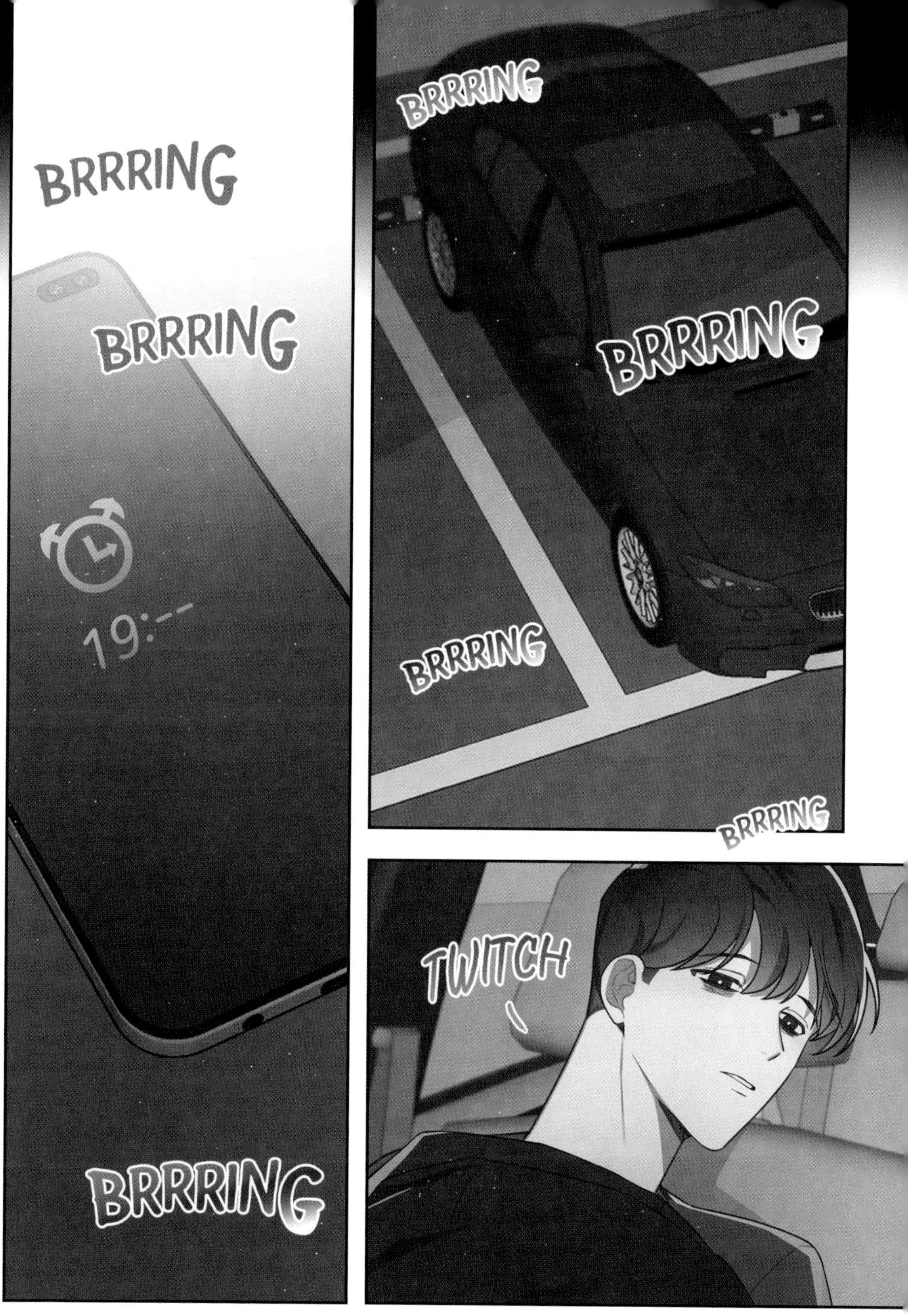
BRRRING
BRRRING
19:--
BRRRING
BRRRING
BRRRING
BRRRING
BRRRING
TWITCH

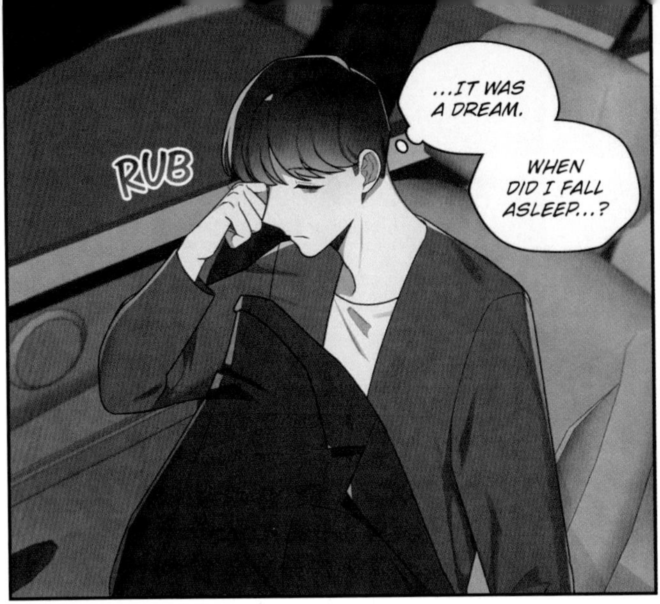
RUB
...IT WAS A DREAM.
WHEN DID I FALL ASLEEP...?

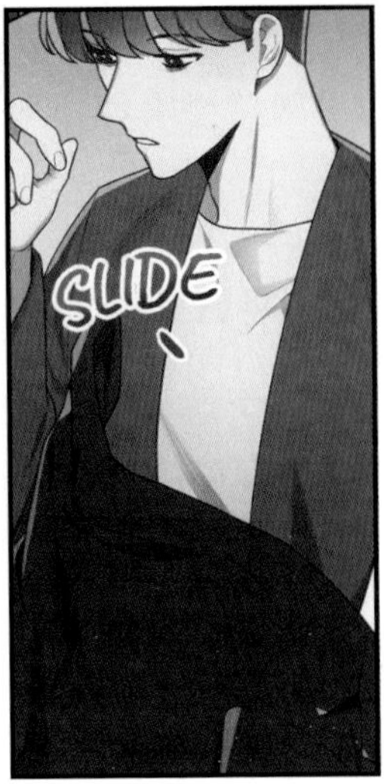
SLIDE

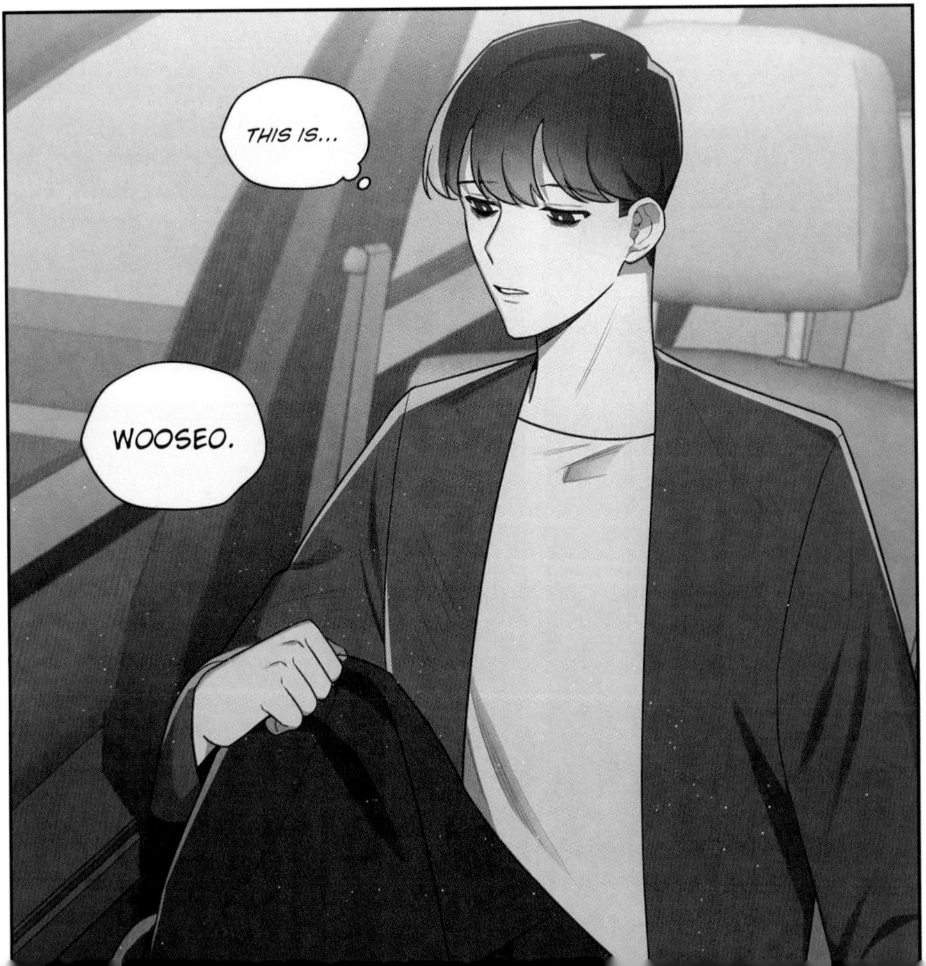
THIS IS...
WOOSEO.

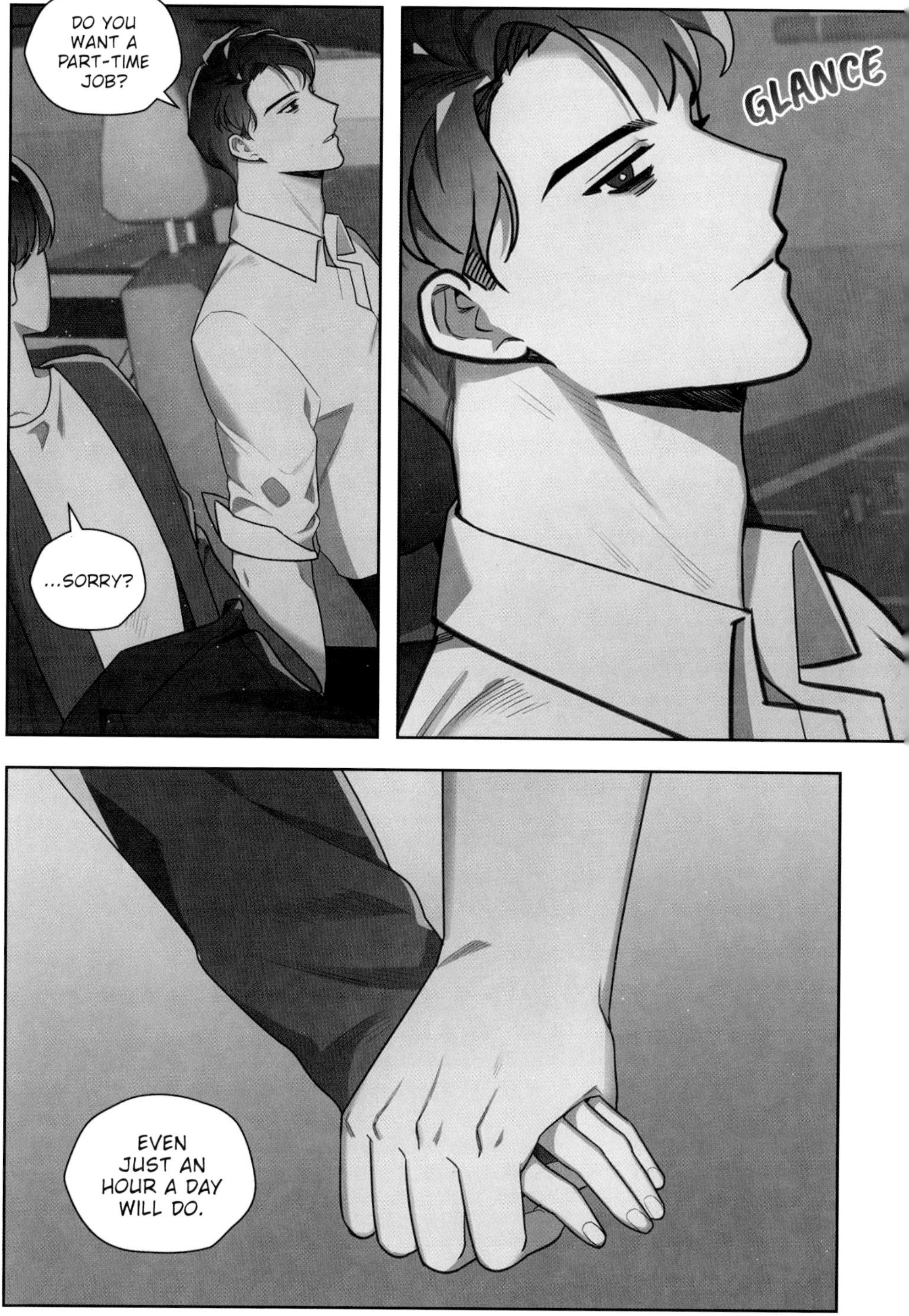
DO YOU WANT A PART-TIME JOB?
...SORRY?
GLANCE
EVEN JUST AN HOUR A DAY WILL DO.

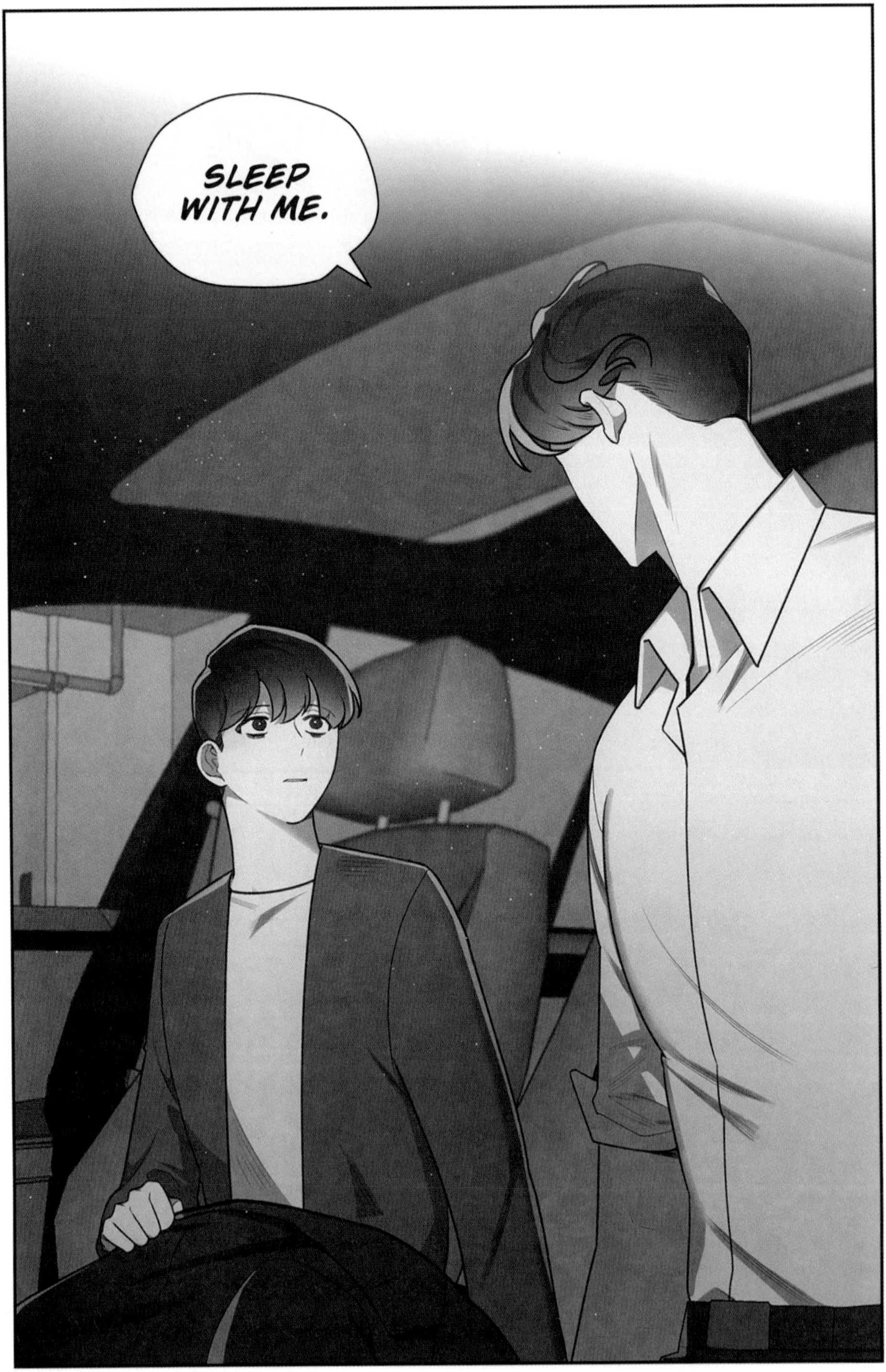
SLEEP WITH ME.

Tied to you

Chapter 4

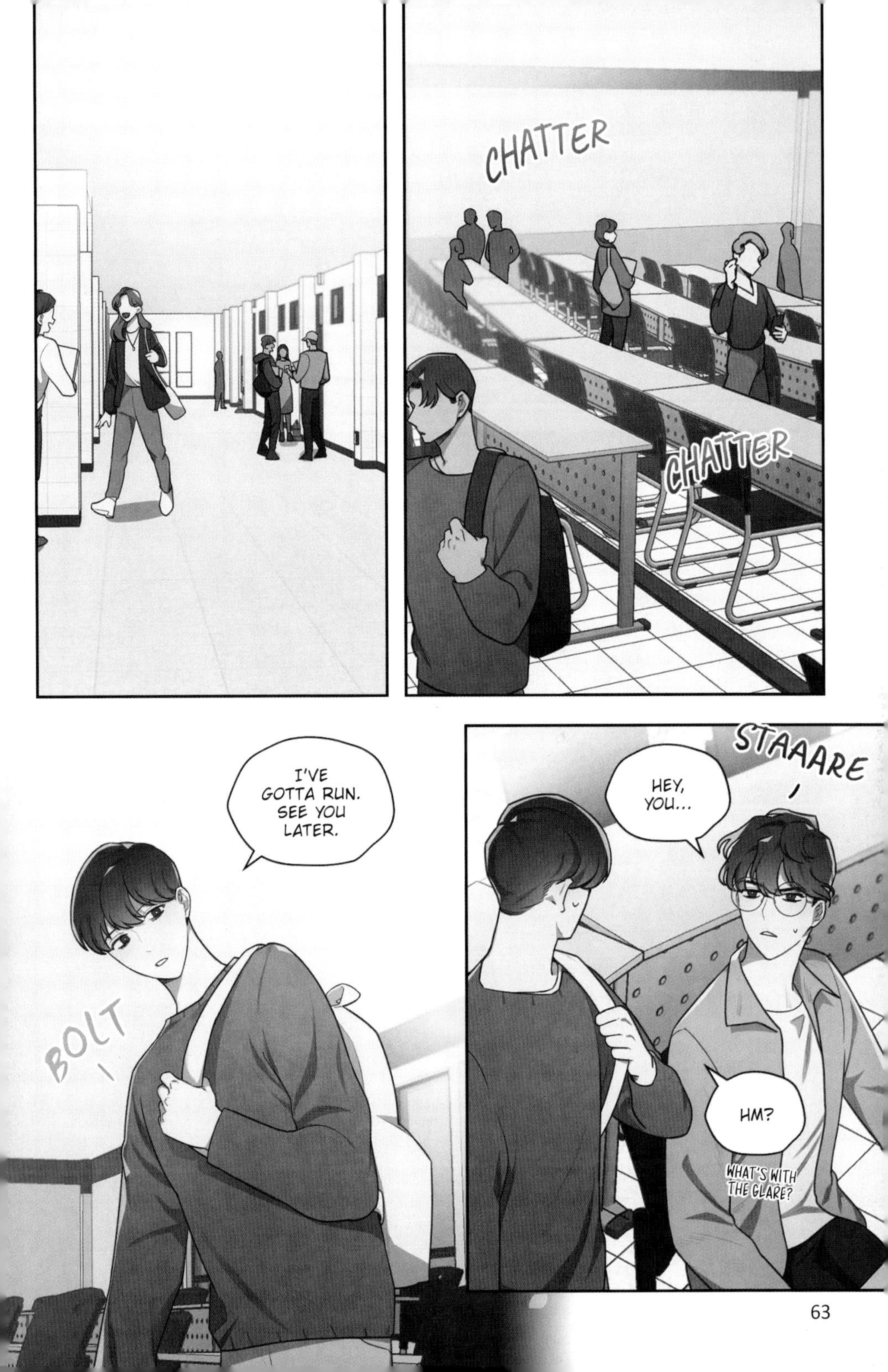
CHATTER
CHATTER
I'VE GOTTA RUN. SEE YOU LATER.
BOLT
HEY, YOU...
STAAARE
HM?
WHAT'S WITH THE GLARE?

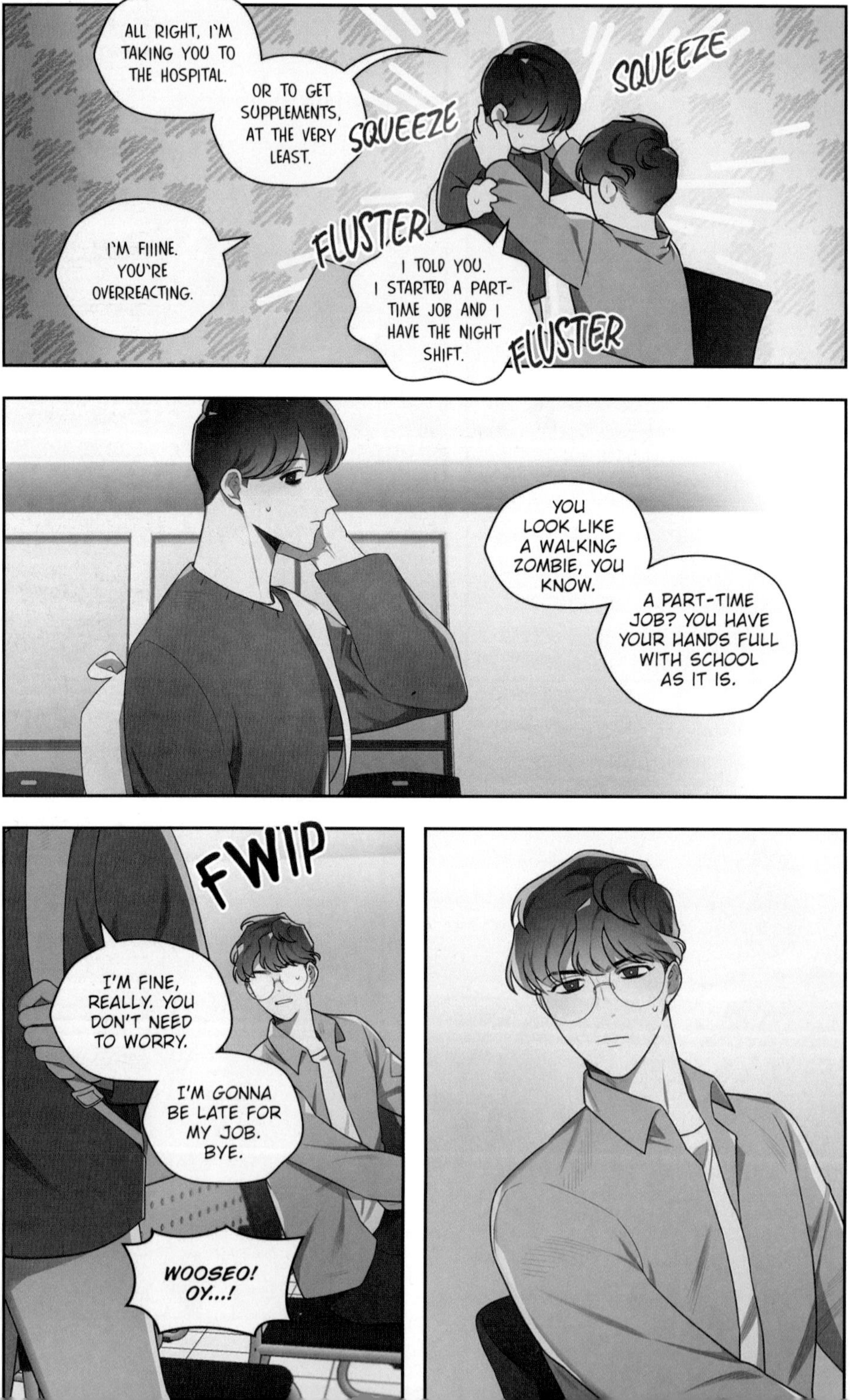
ALL RIGHT, I'M TAKING YOU TO THE HOSPITAL.
OR TO GET SUPPLEMENTS, AT THE VERY LEAST.
SQUEEZE
SQUEEZE
I'M FIIINE. YOU'RE OVERREACTING.
FLUSTER
I TOLD YOU. I STARTED A PART-TIME JOB AND I HAVE THE NIGHT SHIFT.
FLUSTER
YOU LOOK LIKE A WALKING ZOMBIE, YOU KNOW.
A PART-TIME JOB? YOU HAVE YOUR HANDS FULL WITH SCHOOL AS IT IS.
FWIP
I'M FINE, REALLY. YOU DON'T NEED TO WORRY.
I'M GONNA BE LATE FOR MY JOB. BYE.
WOOSEO! OY...!

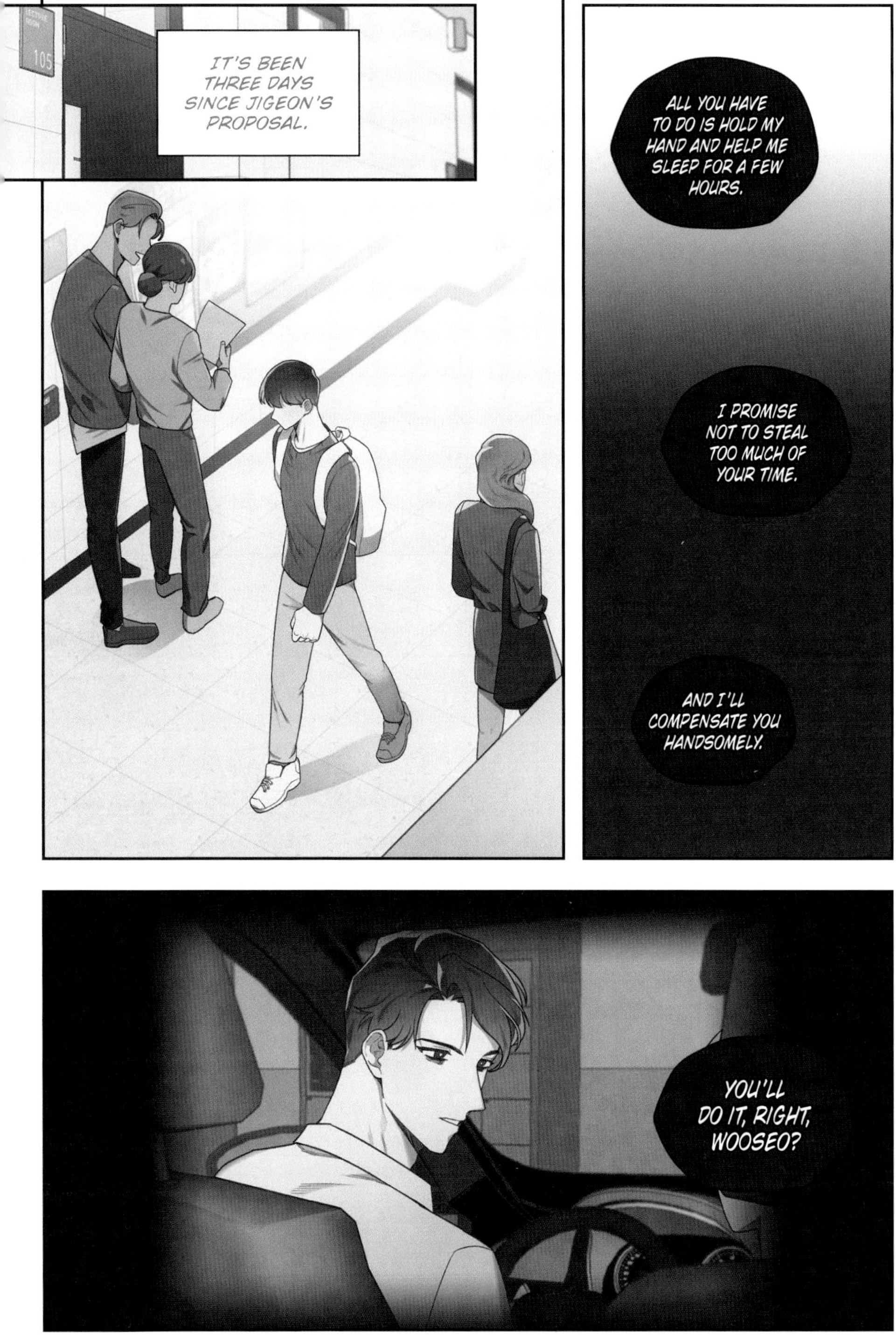
105
IT'S BEEN THREE DAYS SINCE JIGEON'S PROPOSAL.
ALL YOU HAVE TO DO IS HOLD MY HAND AND HELP ME SLEEP FOR A FEW HOURS.
I PROMISE NOT TO STEAL TOO MUCH OF YOUR TIME.
AND I'LL COMPENSATE YOU HANDSOMELY.
YOU'LL DO IT, RIGHT, WOOSEO?

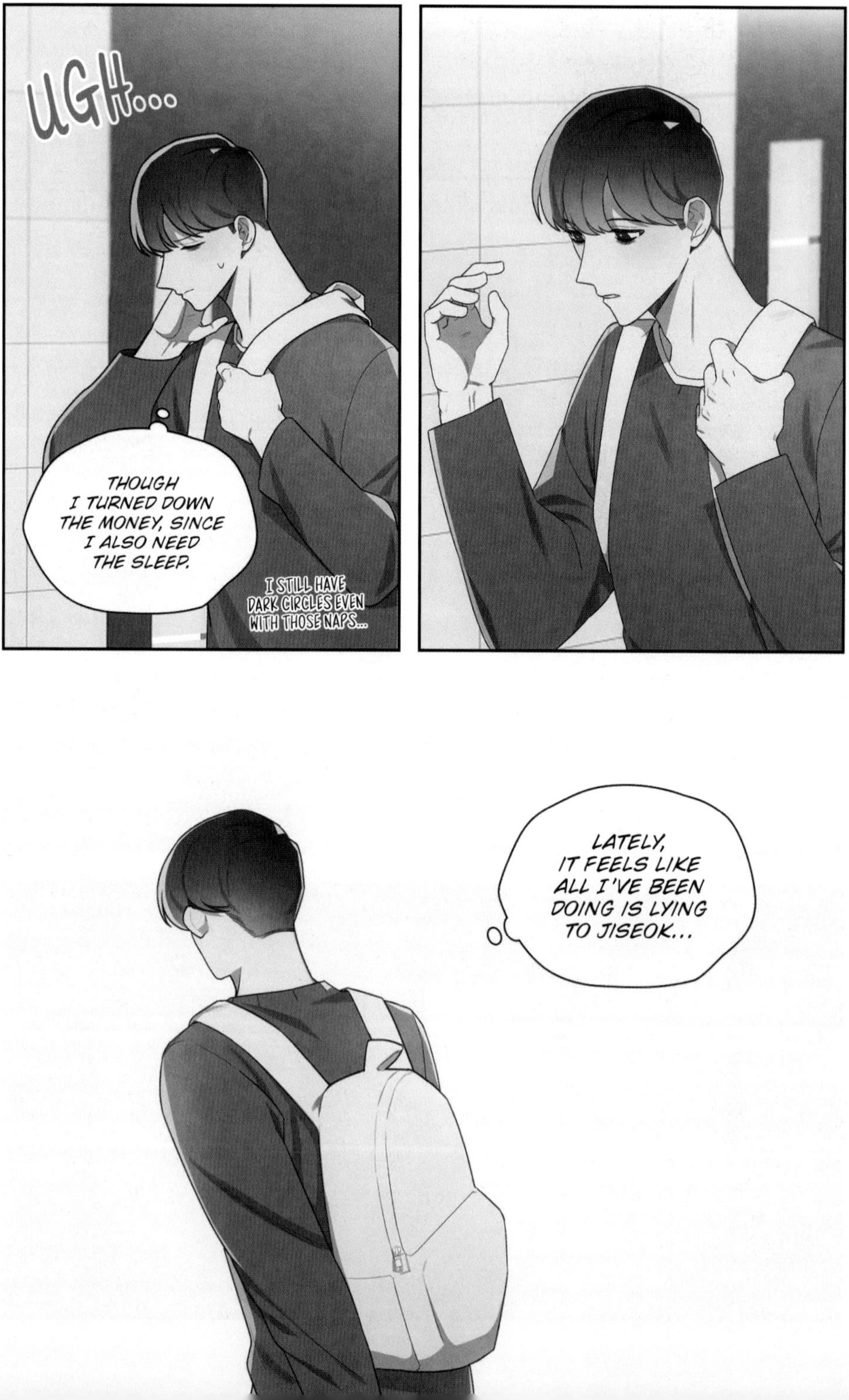
UGH...
THOUGH I TURNED DOWN THE MONEY, SINCE I ALSO NEED THE SLEEP.
I STILL HAVE DARK CIRCLES EVEN WITH THOSE NAPS...
LATELY, IT FEELS LIKE ALL I'VE BEEN DOING IS LYING TO JISEOK...

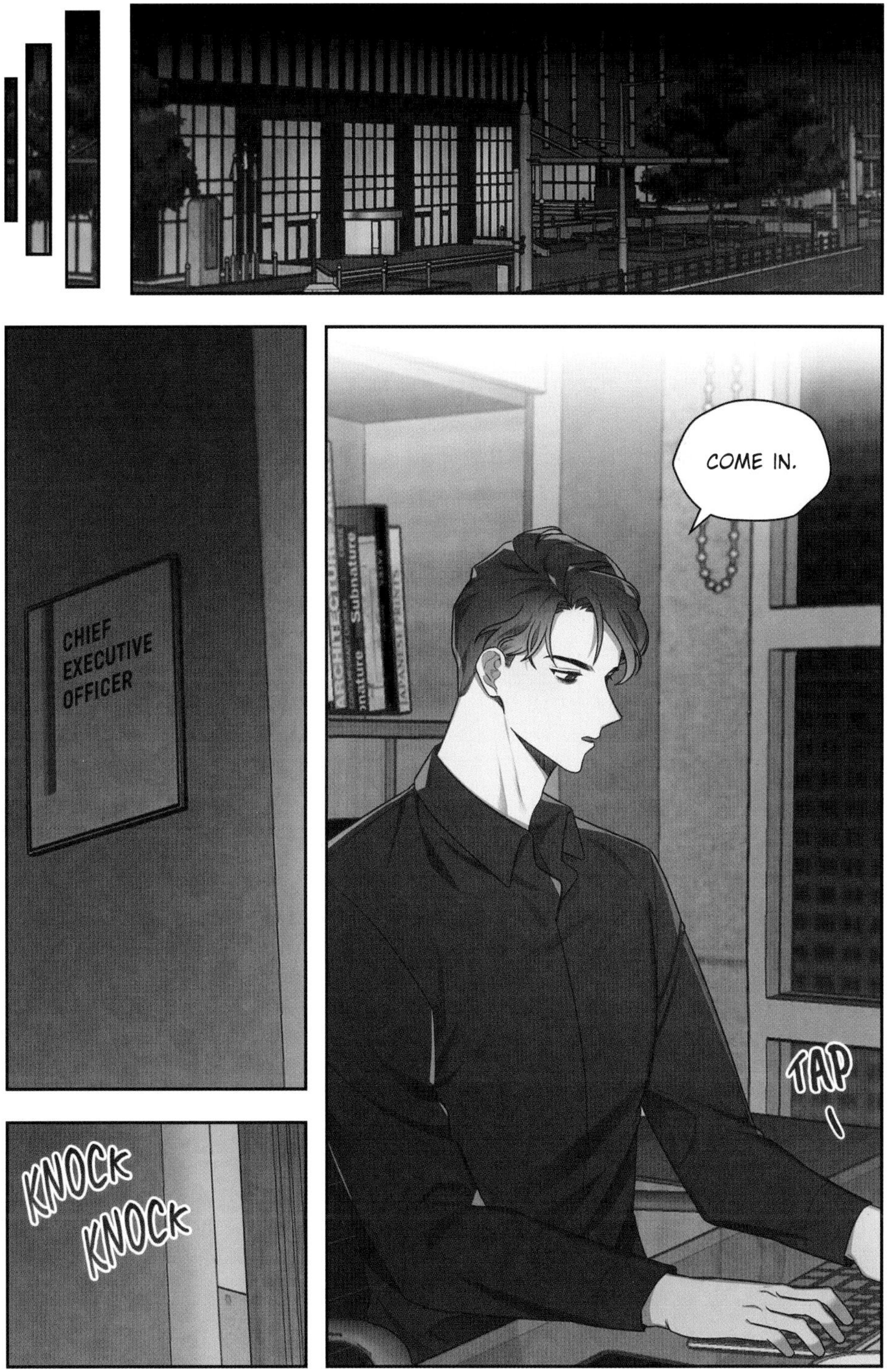
CHIEF EXECUTIVE OFFICER
KNOCK KNOCK
COME IN.
TAP

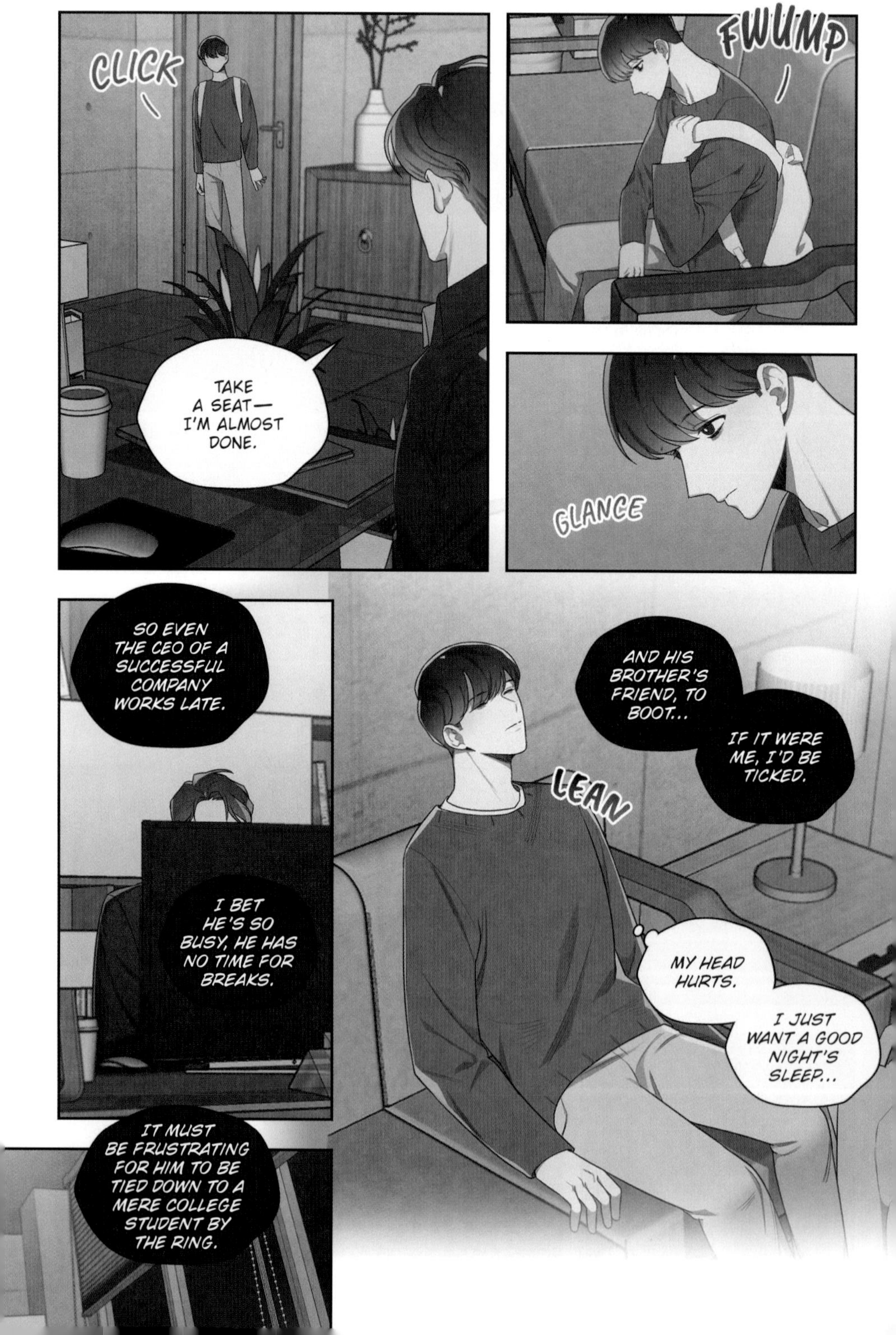
CLICK
TAKE A SEAT— I'M ALMOST DONE.
FWUMP
GLANCE
SO EVEN THE CEO OF A SUCCESSFUL COMPANY WORKS LATE.
AND HIS BROTHER'S FRIEND, TO BOOT...
IF IT WERE ME, I'D BE TICKED.
LEAN
I BET HE'S SO BUSY, HE HAS NO TIME FOR BREAKS.
MY HEAD HURTS.
I JUST WANT A GOOD NIGHT'S SLEEP...
IT MUST BE FRUSTRATING FOR HIM TO BE TIED DOWN TO A MERE COLLEGE STUDENT BY THE RING.

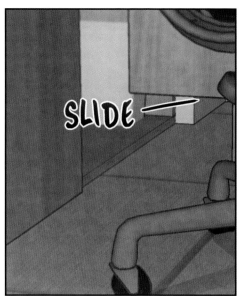

SLIDE

TMP

TMP

FWUMP

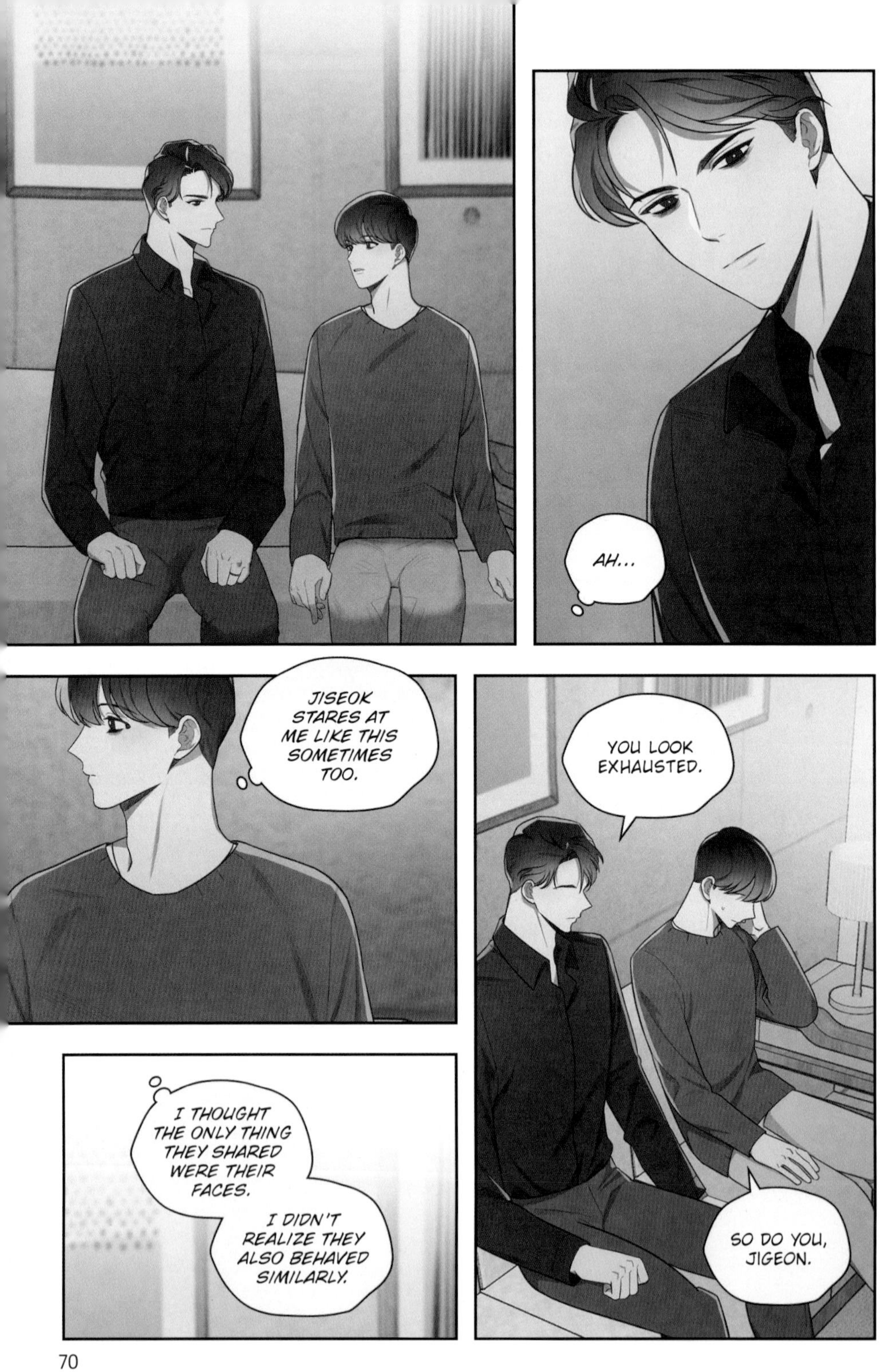
AH...
JISEOK STARES AT ME LIKE THIS SOMETIMES TOO.
I THOUGHT THE ONLY THING THEY SHARED WERE THEIR FACES.
I DIDN'T REALIZE THEY ALSO BEHAVED SIMILARLY.
YOU LOOK EXHAUSTED.
SO DO YOU, JIGEON.

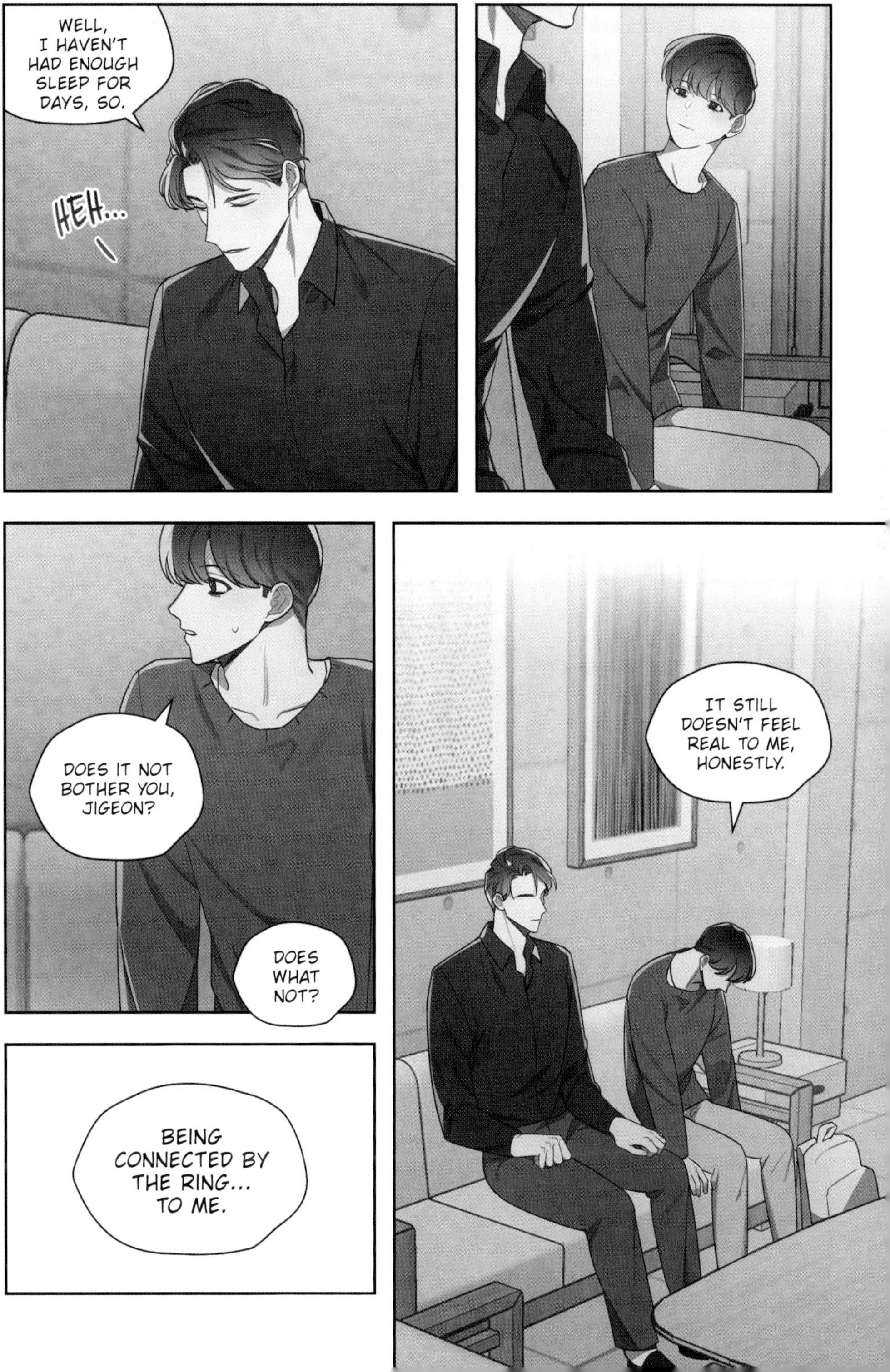
WELL, I HAVEN'T HAD ENOUGH SLEEP FOR DAYS, SO.
HEH...
DOES IT NOT BOTHER YOU, JIGEON?
DOES WHAT NOT?
IT STILL DOESN'T FEEL REAL TO ME, HONESTLY.
BEING CONNECTED BY THE RING... TO ME.

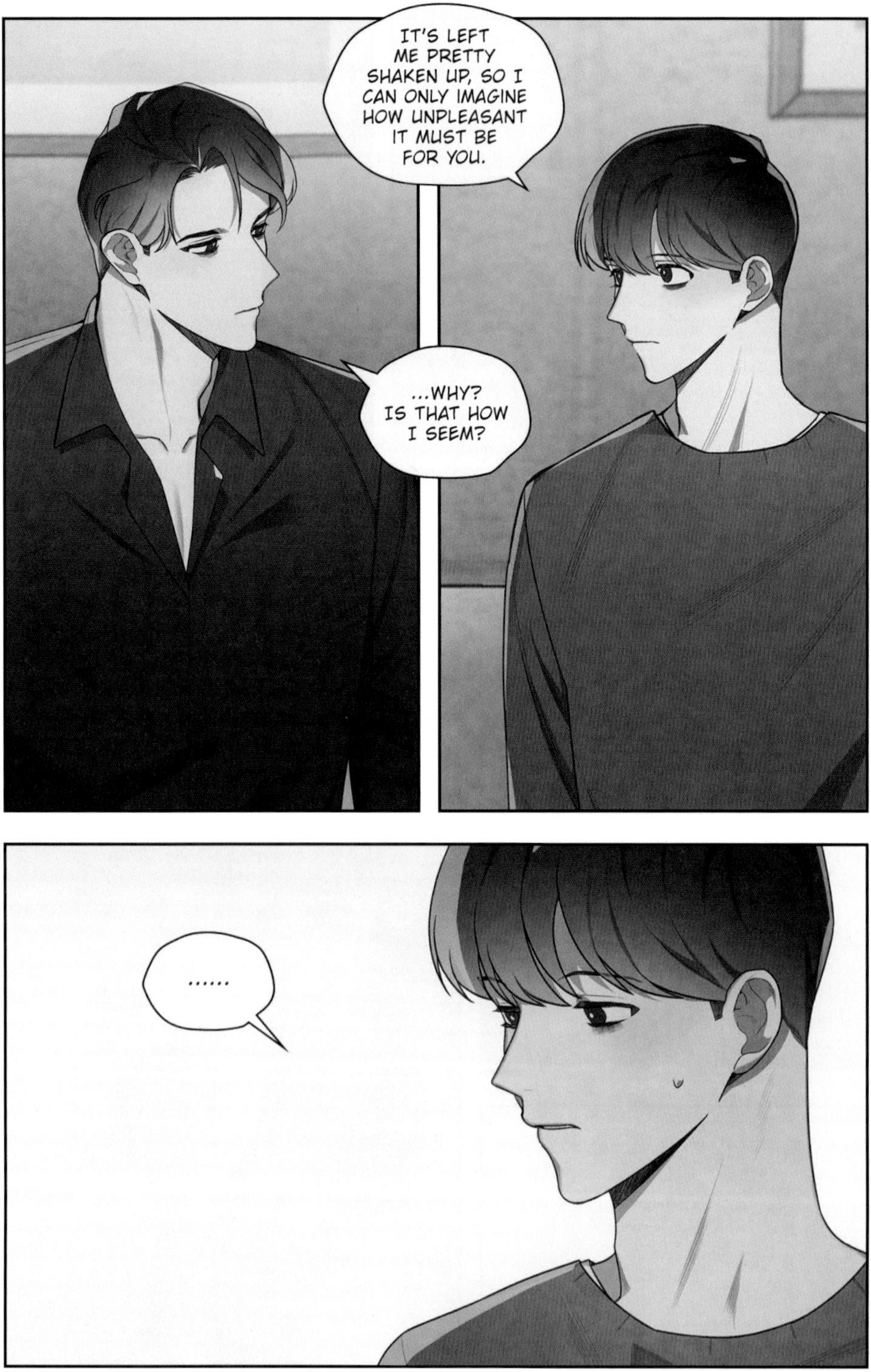
IT'S LEFT ME PRETTY SHAKEN UP, SO I CAN ONLY IMAGINE HOW UNPLEASANT IT MUST BE FOR YOU.
...WHY? IS THAT HOW I SEEM?
......

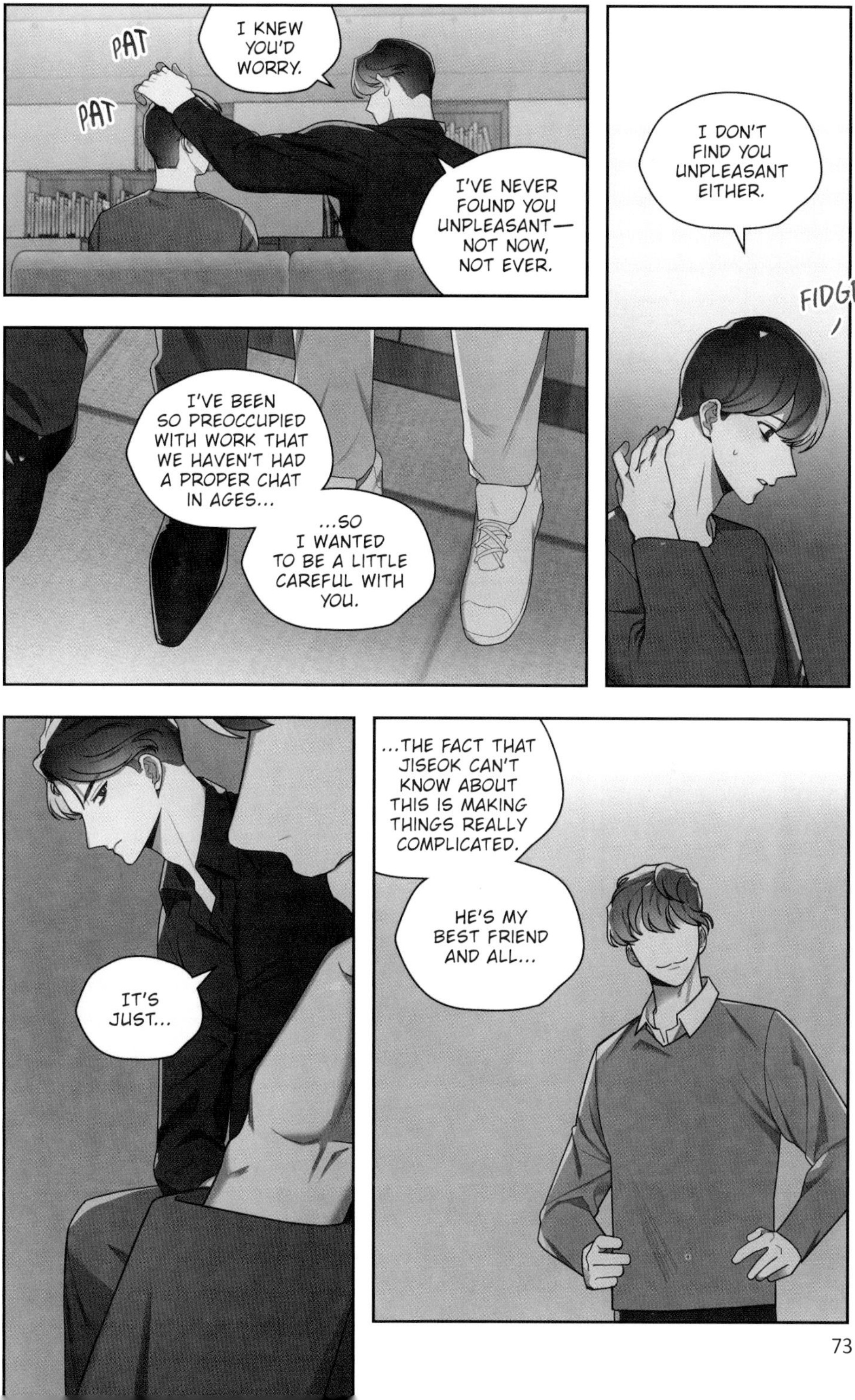
PAT
PAT
I KNEW YOU'D WORRY.
I'VE NEVER FOUND YOU UNPLEASANT— NOT NOW, NOT EVER.
I DON'T FIND YOU UNPLEASANT EITHER.
FIDGET
I'VE BEEN SO PREOCCUPIED WITH WORK THAT WE HAVEN'T HAD A PROPER CHAT IN AGES...
...SO I WANTED TO BE A LITTLE CAREFUL WITH YOU.
IT'S JUST...
...THE FACT THAT JISEOK CAN'T KNOW ABOUT THIS IS MAKING THINGS REALLY COMPLICATED.
HE'S MY BEST FRIEND AND ALL...

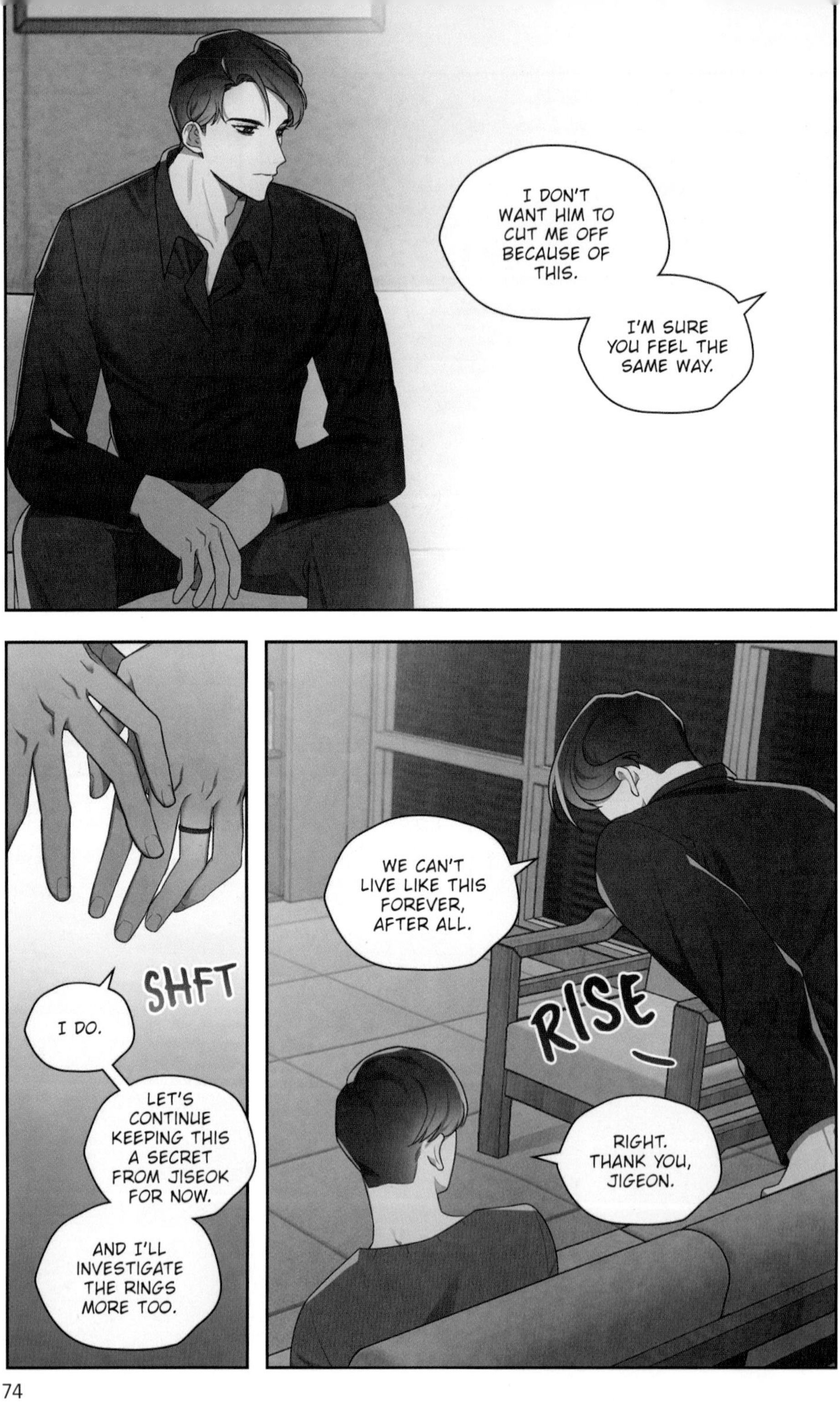

I DON'T WANT HIM TO CUT ME OFF BECAUSE OF THIS.
I'M SURE YOU FEEL THE SAME WAY.
SHFT
I DO.
LET'S CONTINUE KEEPING THIS A SECRET FROM JISEOK FOR NOW.
AND I'LL INVESTIGATE THE RINGS MORE TOO.
WE CAN'T LIVE LIKE THIS FOREVER, AFTER ALL.
RISE
RIGHT. THANK YOU, JIGEON.

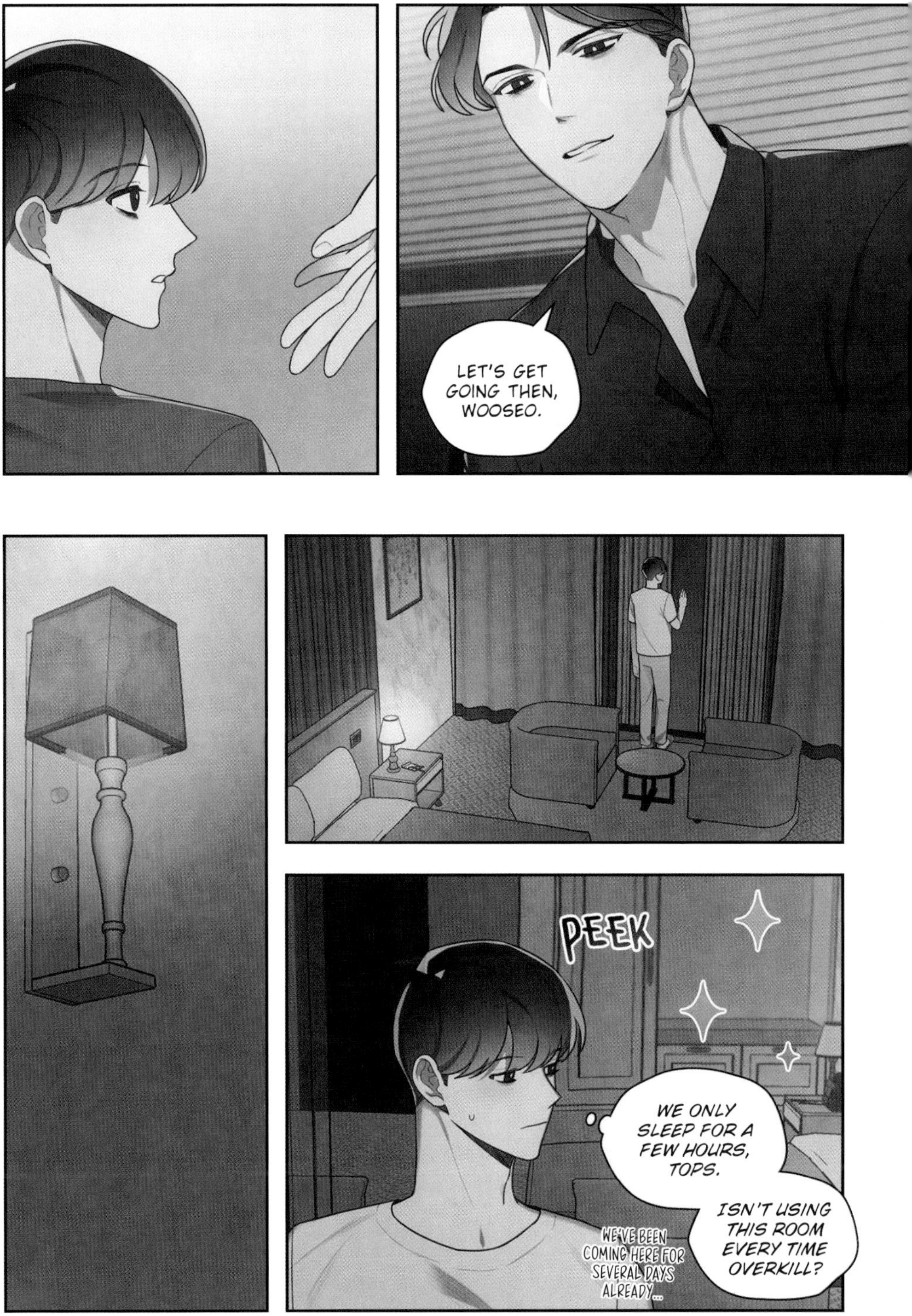
LET'S GET GOING THEN, WOOSEO.
PEEK
WE ONLY SLEEP FOR A FEW HOURS, TOPS.
ISN'T USING THIS ROOM EVERY TIME OVERKILL?
WE'VE BEEN COMING HERE FOR SEVERAL DAYS ALREADY...

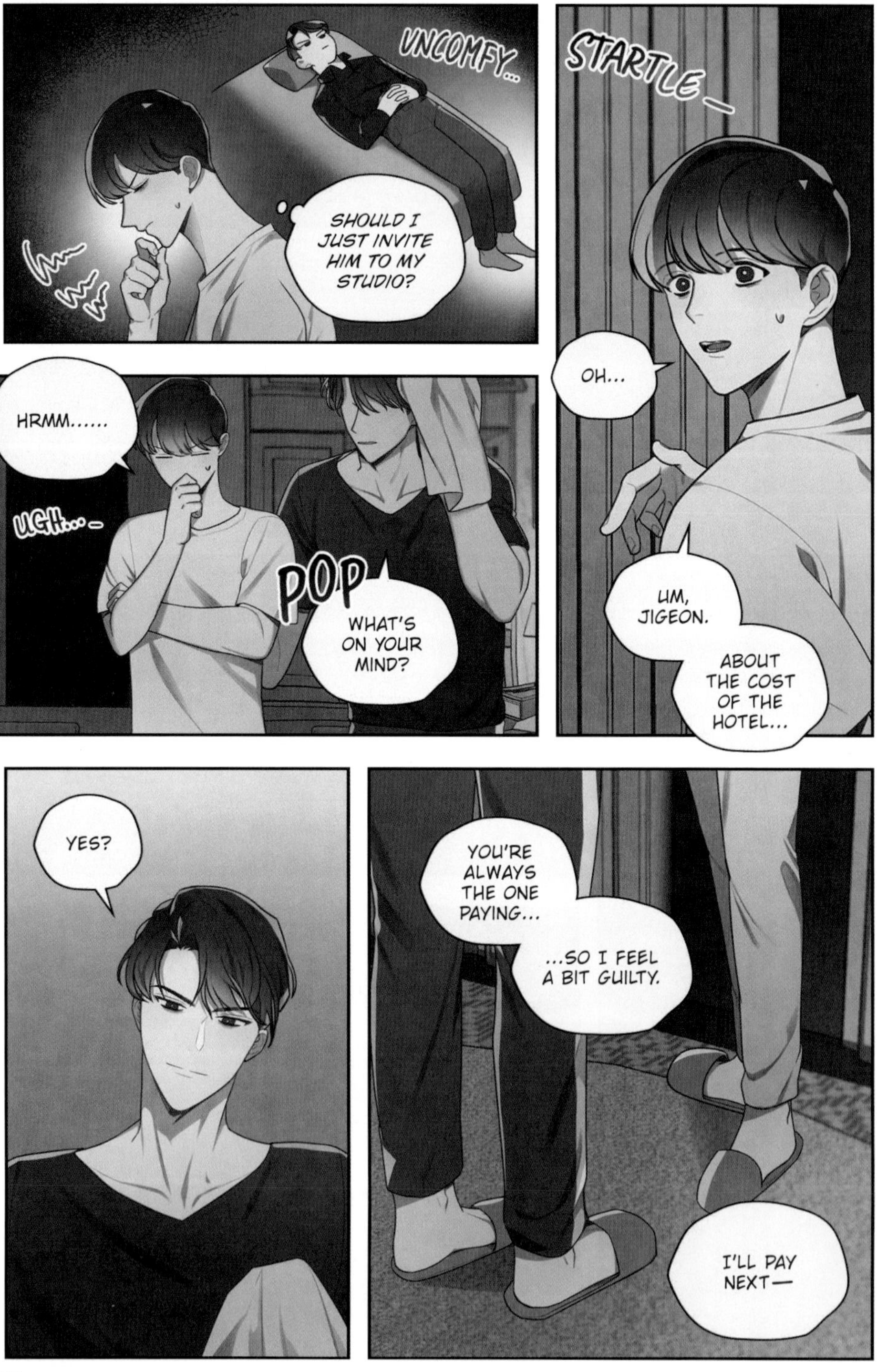
UNCOMFY...
SHOULD I JUST INVITE HIM TO MY STUDIO?
STARTLE—
OH...
HRMM......
UGH...—
POP
WHAT'S ON YOUR MIND?
UM, JIGEON.
ABOUT THE COST OF THE HOTEL...
YES?
YOU'RE ALWAYS THE ONE PAYING...
...SO I FEEL A BIT GUILTY.
I'LL PAY NEXT—

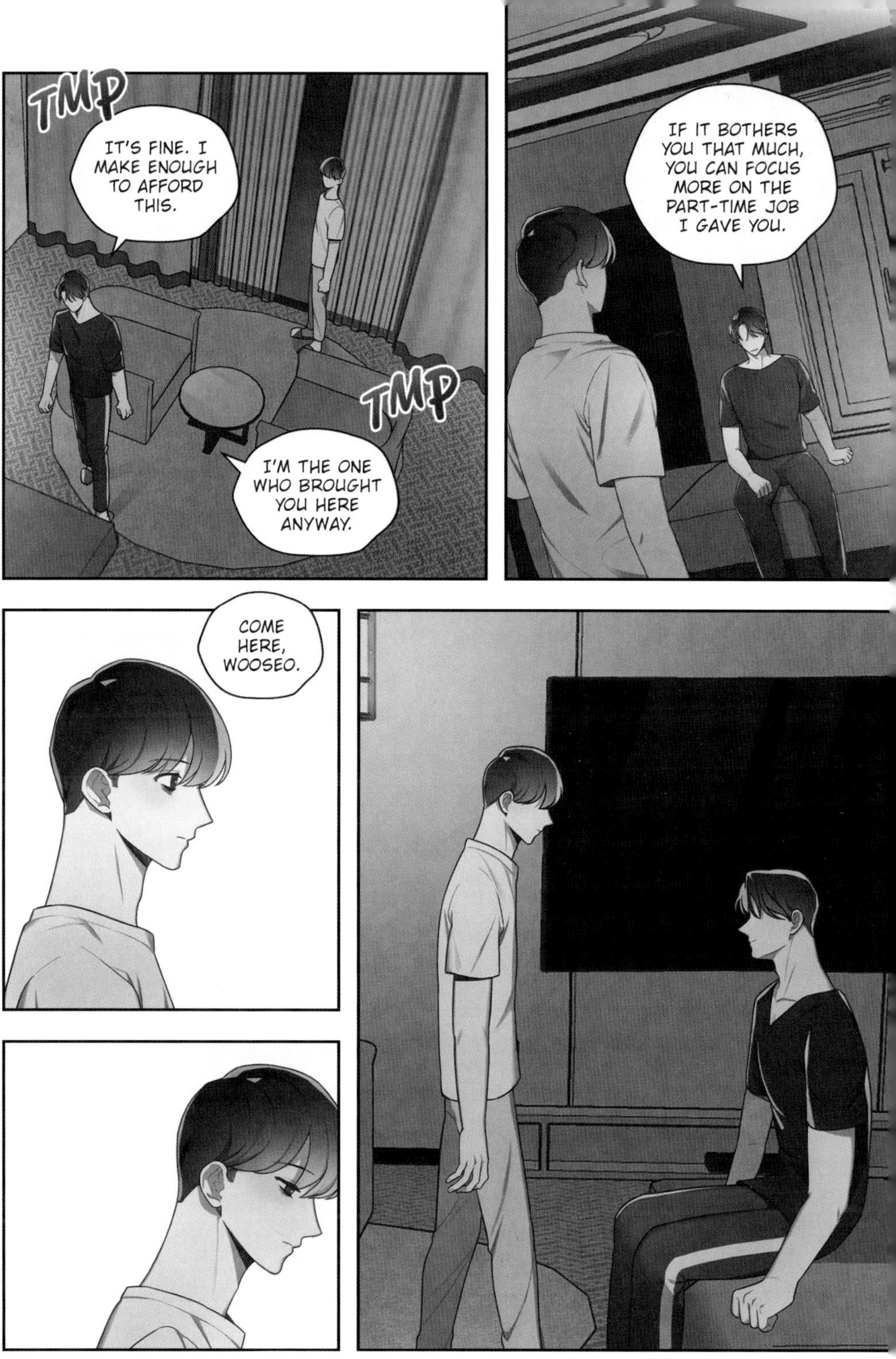
TMP
IT'S FINE. I MAKE ENOUGH TO AFFORD THIS.
TMP
I'M THE ONE WHO BROUGHT YOU HERE ANYWAY.
IF IT BOTHERS YOU THAT MUCH, YOU CAN FOCUS MORE ON THE PART-TIME JOB I GAVE YOU.
COME HERE, WOOSEO.

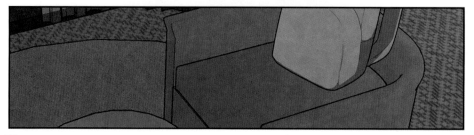

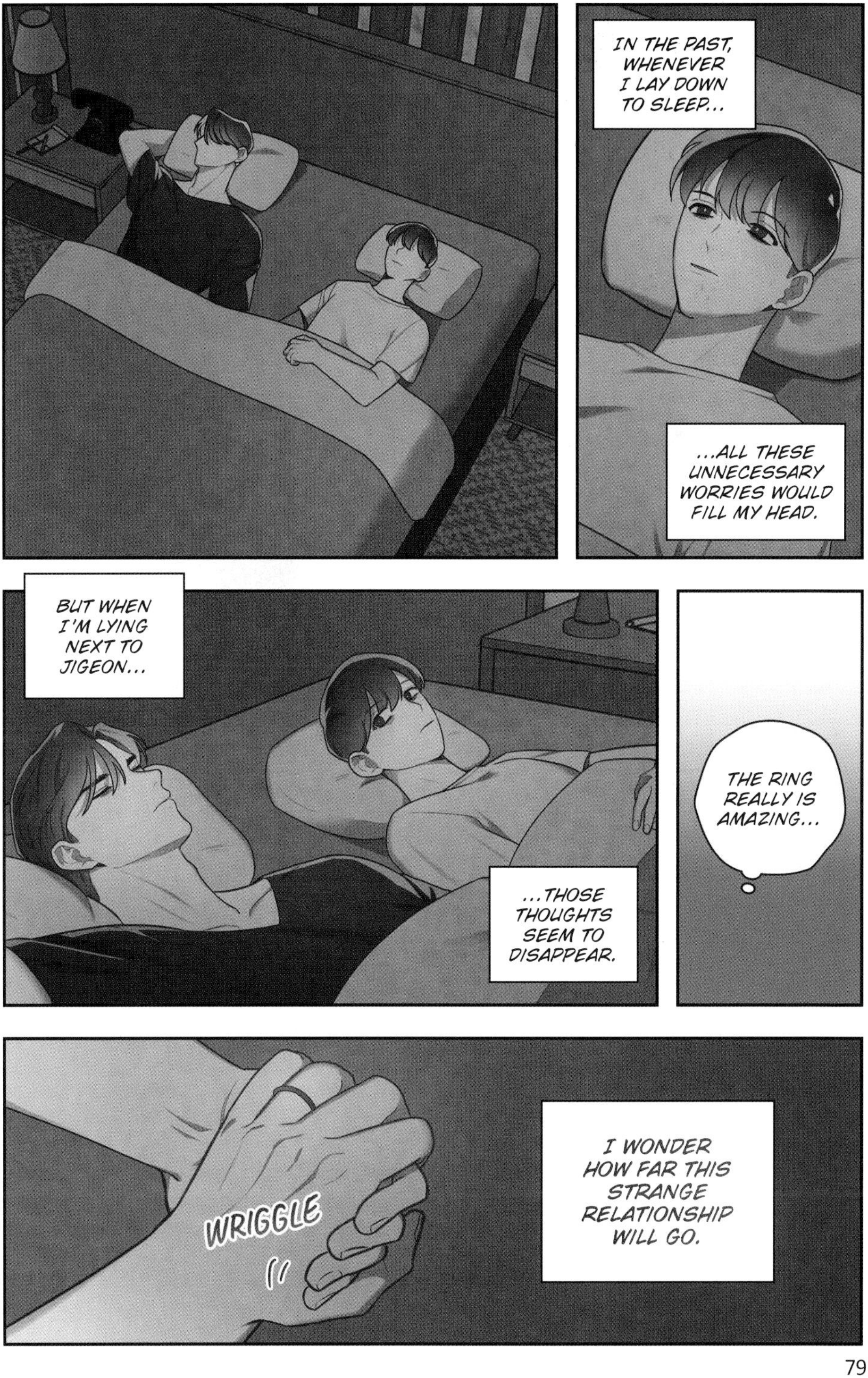
IN THE PAST, WHENEVER I LAY DOWN TO SLEEP...
...ALL THESE UNNECESSARY WORRIES WOULD FILL MY HEAD.
BUT WHEN I'M LYING NEXT TO JIGEON...
...THOSE THOUGHTS SEEM TO DISAPPEAR.
THE RING REALLY IS AMAZING...
WRIGGLE
I WONDER HOW FAR THIS STRANGE RELATIONSHIP WILL GO.

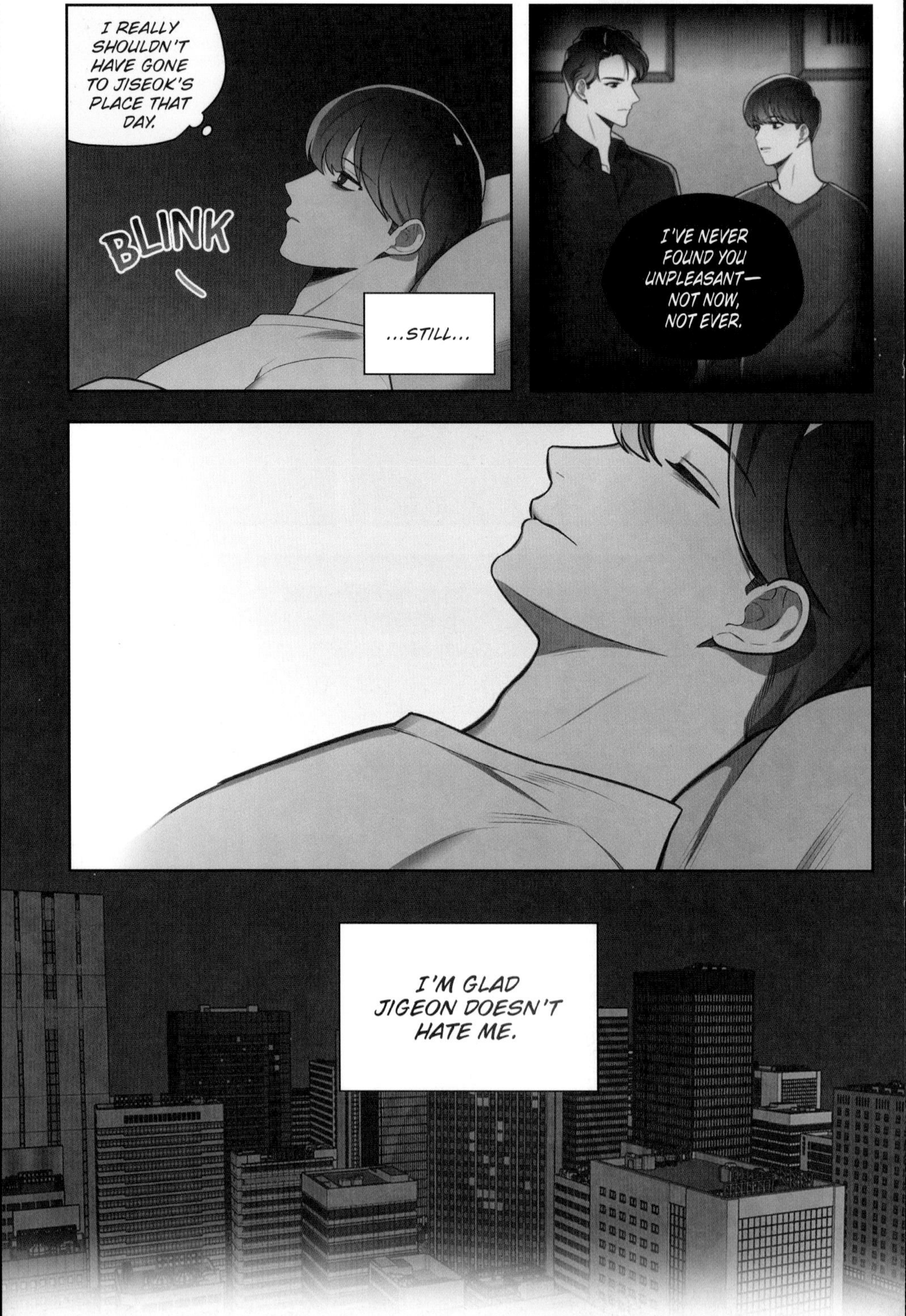
I REALLY SHOULDN'T HAVE GONE TO JISEOK'S PLACE THAT DAY.
BLINK
...STILL...
I'VE NEVER FOUND YOU UNPLEASANT—NOT NOW, NOT EVER.
I'M GLAD JIGEON DOESN'T HATE ME.

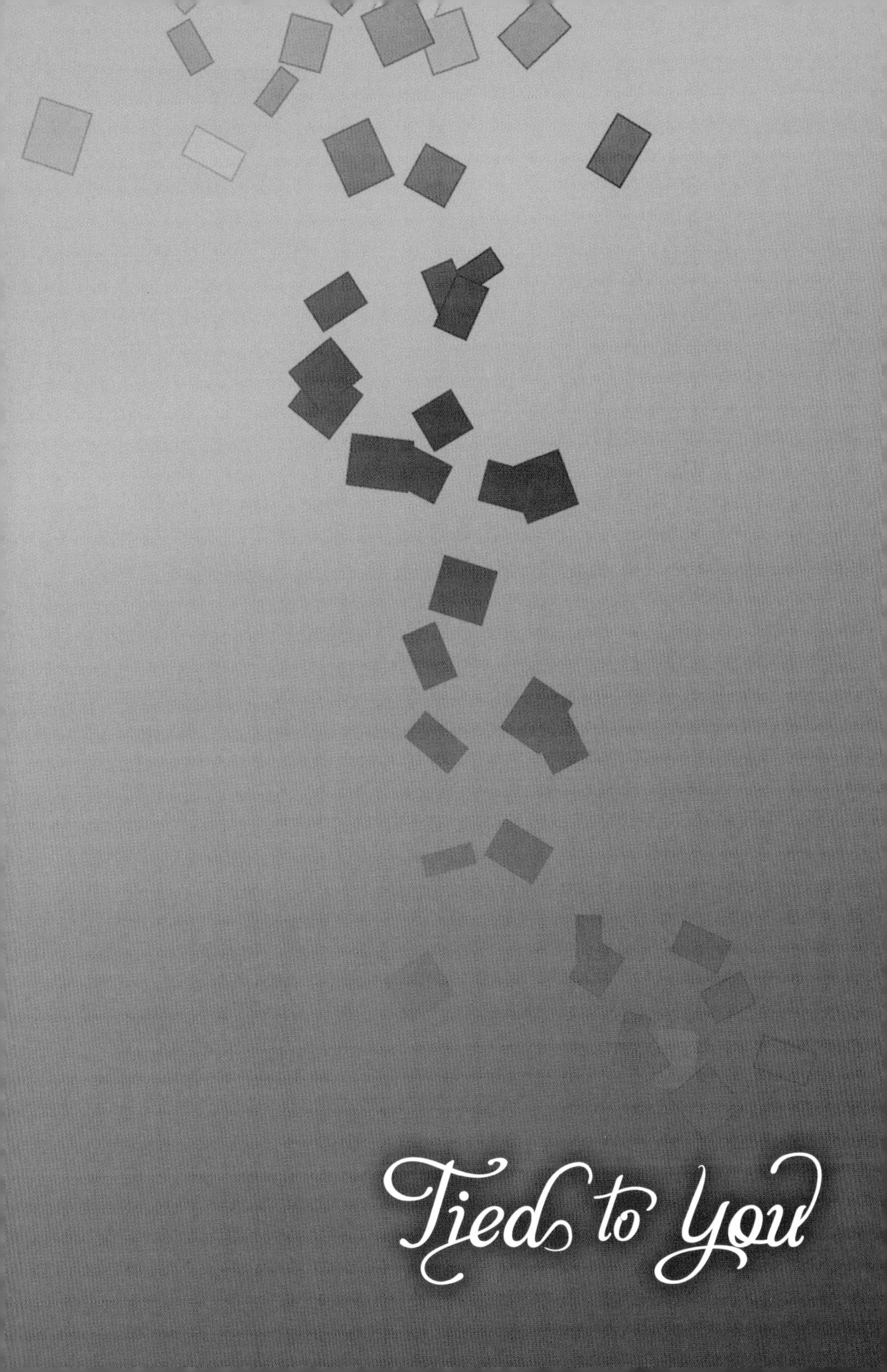

Tied to You

Chapter 5

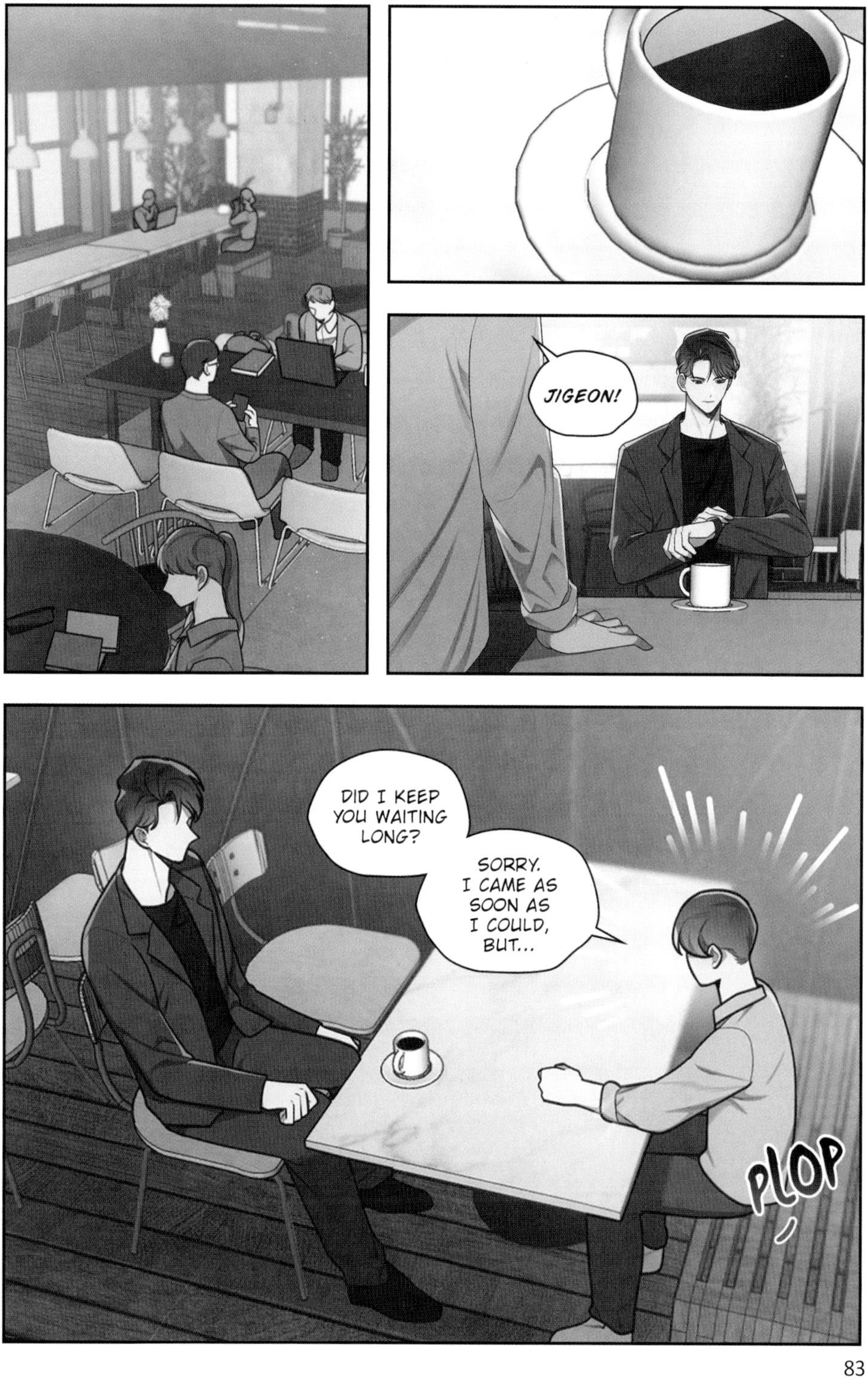
JIGEON!
DID I KEEP YOU WAITING LONG?
SORRY. I CAME AS SOON AS I COULD, BUT...
PLOP

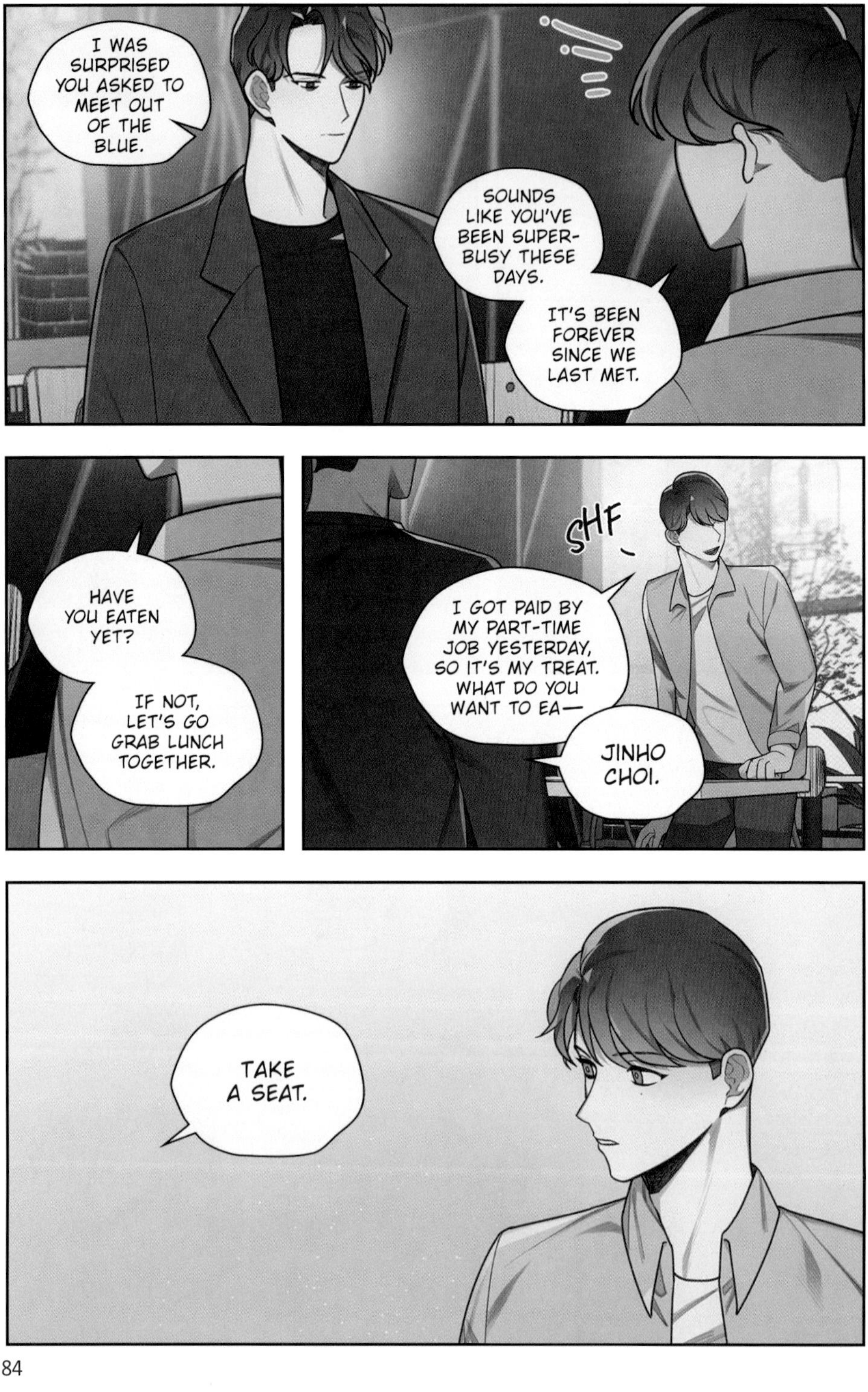
I WAS SURPRISED YOU ASKED TO MEET OUT OF THE BLUE.
SOUNDS LIKE YOU'VE BEEN SUPER-BUSY THESE DAYS.
IT'S BEEN FOREVER SINCE WE LAST MET.
HAVE YOU EATEN YET?
IF NOT, LET'S GO GRAB LUNCH TOGETHER.
SHF
I GOT PAID BY MY PART-TIME JOB YESTERDAY, SO IT'S MY TREAT. WHAT DO YOU WANT TO EA—
JINHO CHOI.
TAKE A SEAT.

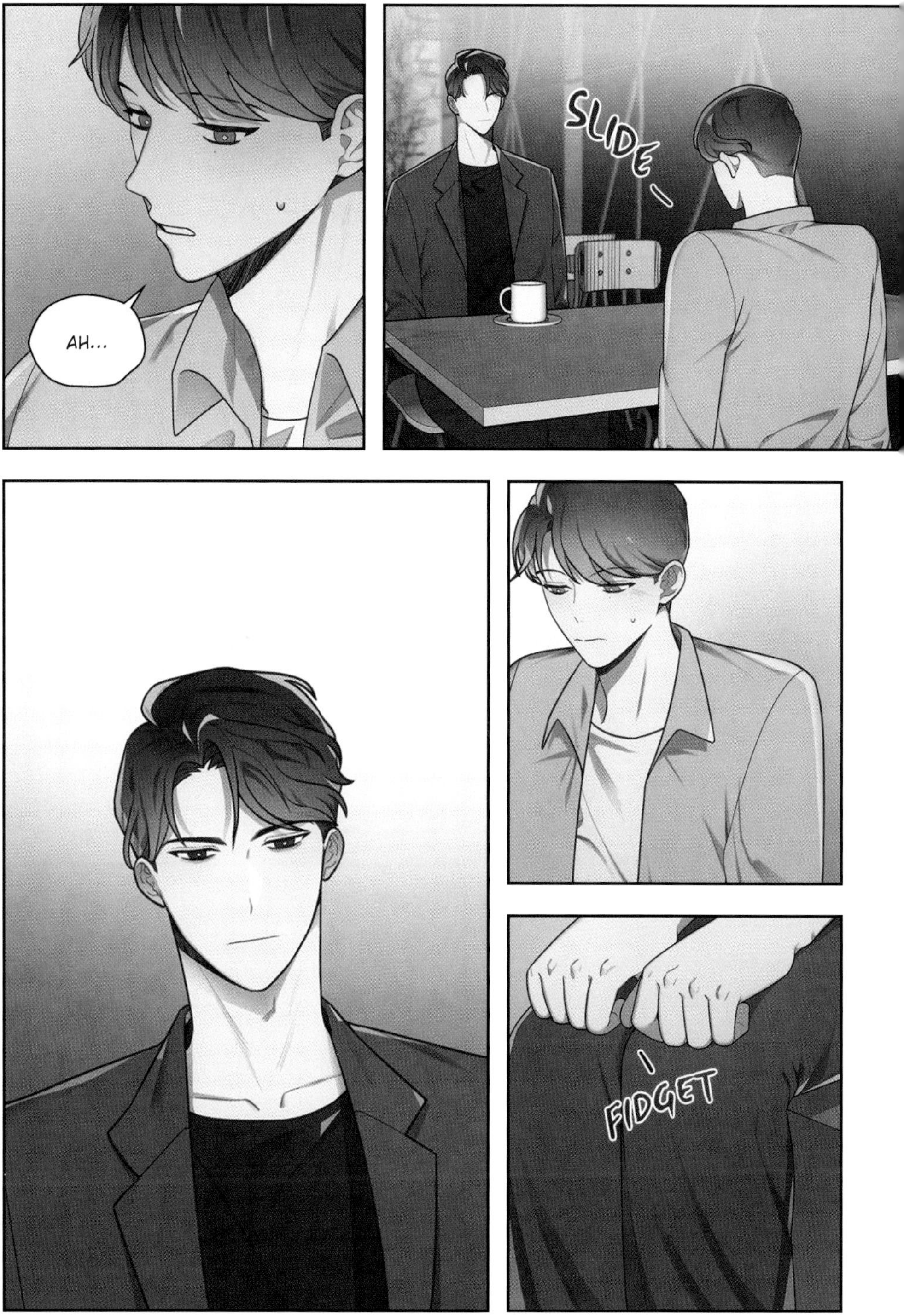
AH...
SLIDE
FIDGET

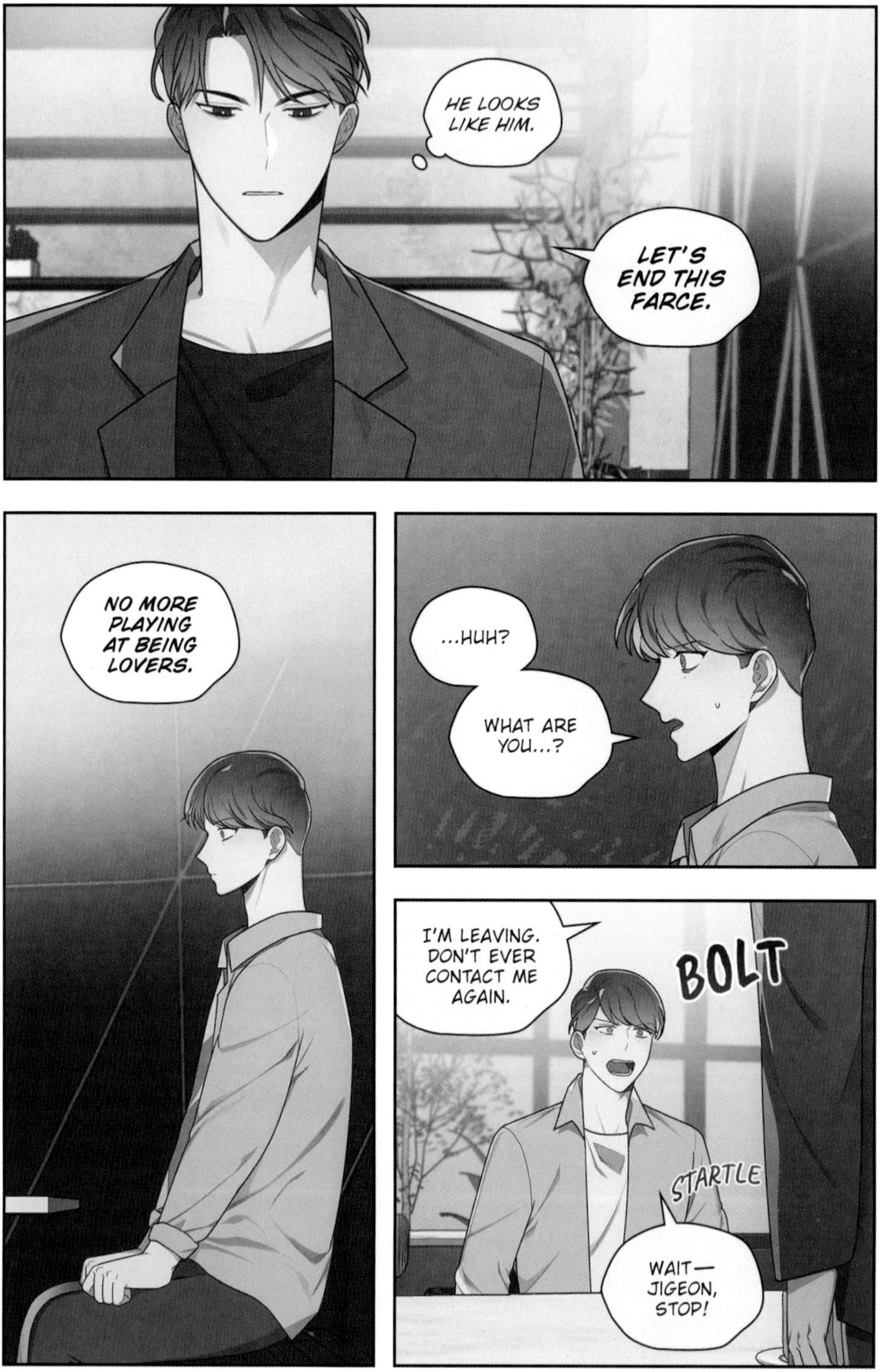
HE LOOKS LIKE HIM.
LET'S END THIS FARCE.
NO MORE PLAYING AT BEING LOVERS.
...HUH?
WHAT ARE YOU...?
I'M LEAVING. DON'T EVER CONTACT ME AGAIN.
BOLT
STARTLE
WAIT— JIGEON, STOP!

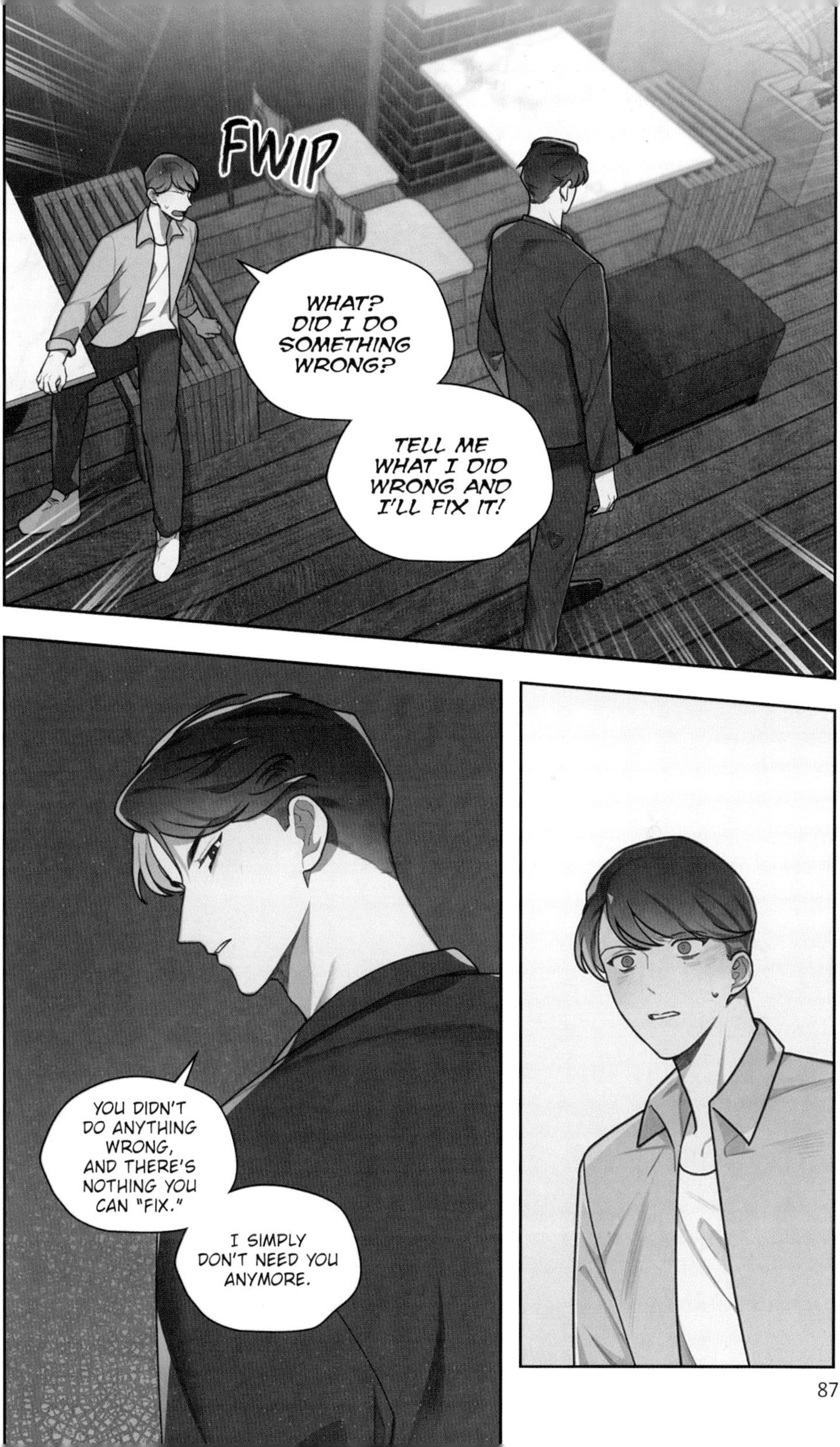
FWIP
WHAT? DID I DO SOMETHING WRONG?
TELL ME WHAT I DID WRONG AND I'LL FIX IT!
YOU DIDN'T DO ANYTHING WRONG, AND THERE'S NOTHING YOU CAN "FIX."
I SIMPLY DON'T NEED YOU ANYMORE.

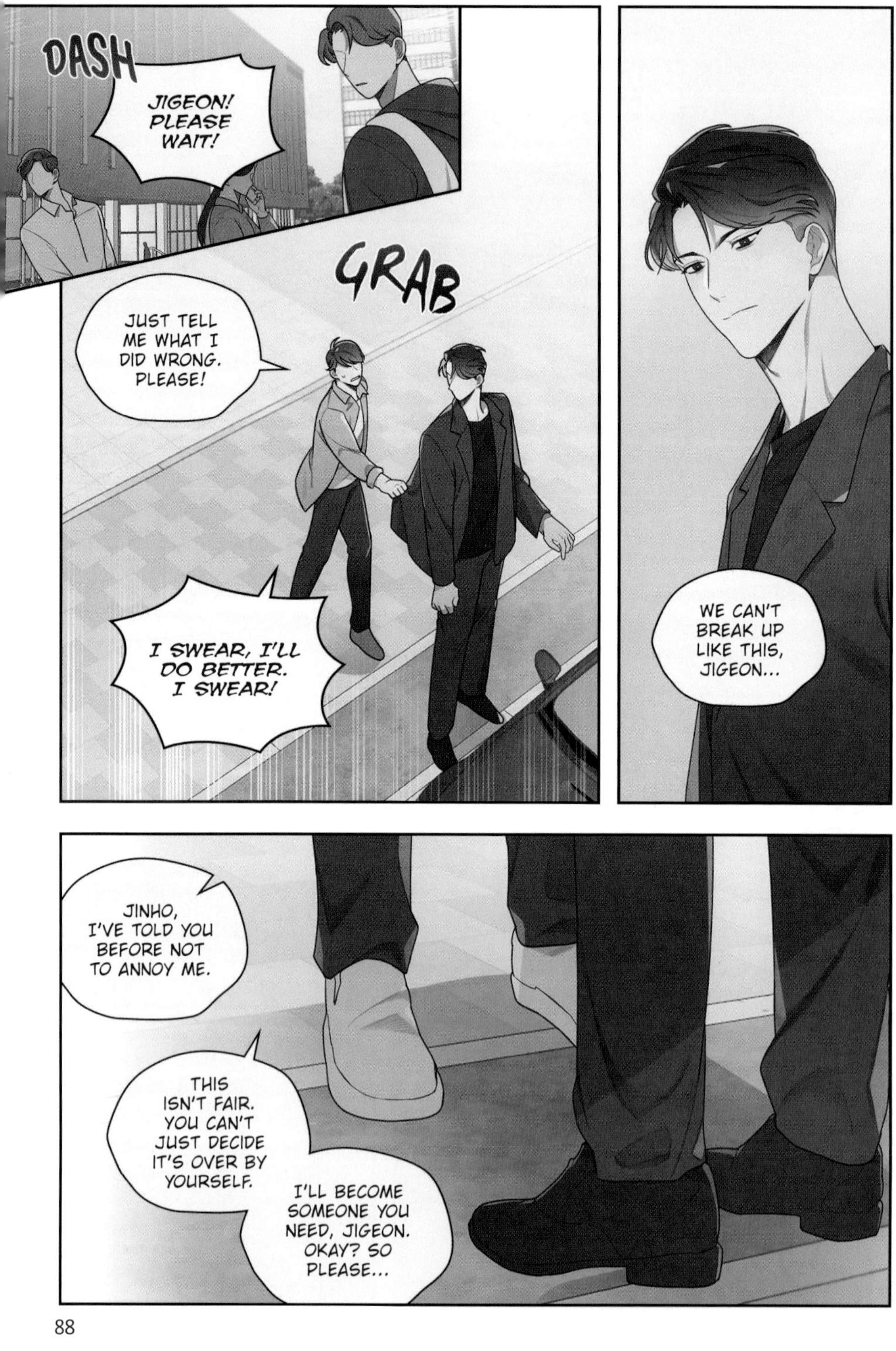
DASH
JIGEON! PLEASE WAIT!
GRAB
JUST TELL ME WHAT I DID WRONG. PLEASE!
I SWEAR, I'LL DO BETTER. I SWEAR!
WE CAN'T BREAK UP LIKE THIS, JIGEON...
JINHO, I'VE TOLD YOU BEFORE NOT TO ANNOY ME.
THIS ISN'T FAIR. YOU CAN'T JUST DECIDE IT'S OVER BY YOURSELF.
I'LL BECOME SOMEONE YOU NEED, JIGEON. OKAY? SO PLEASE...

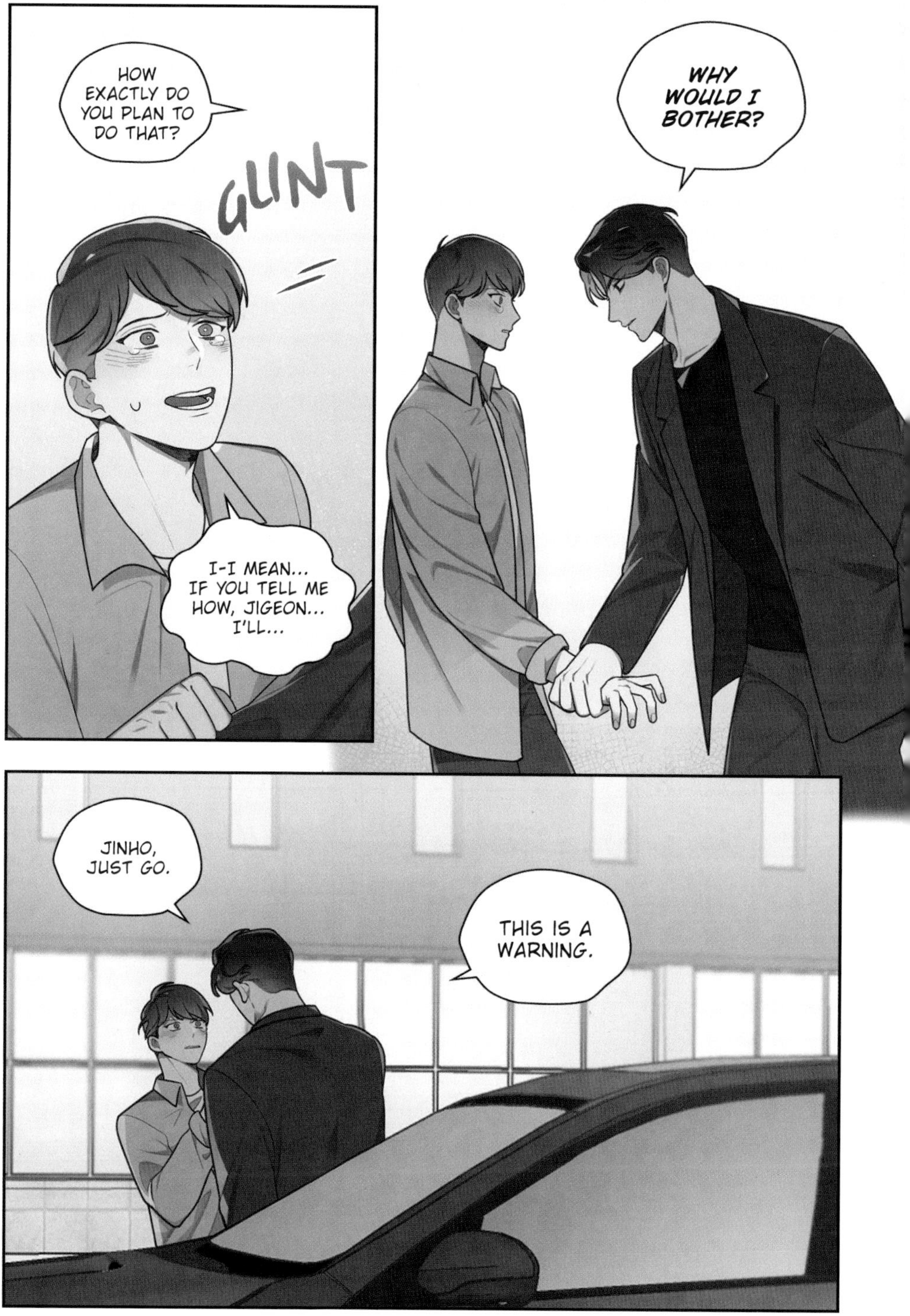
HOW EXACTLY DO YOU PLAN TO DO THAT?
GLINT
I-I MEAN... IF YOU TELL ME HOW, JIGEON... I'LL...
WHY WOULD I BOTHER?
JINHO, JUST GO.
THIS IS A WARNING.

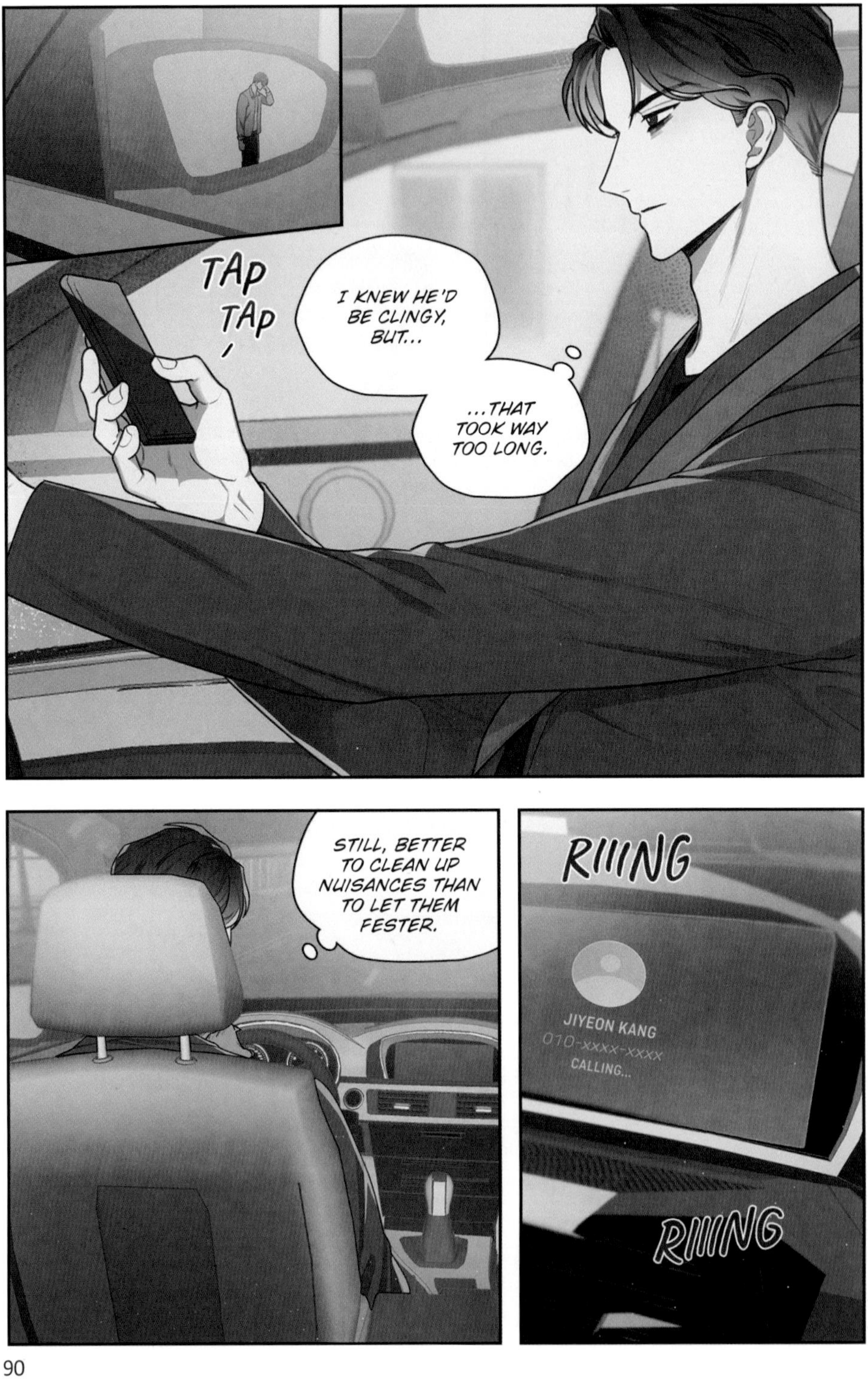
TAP TAP
I KNEW HE'D BE CLINGY, BUT...
...THAT TOOK WAY TOO LONG.
STILL, BETTER TO CLEAN UP NUISANCES THAN TO LET THEM FESTER.
RIIING
JIYEON KANG
010-XXXX-XXXX
CALLING...
RIIING

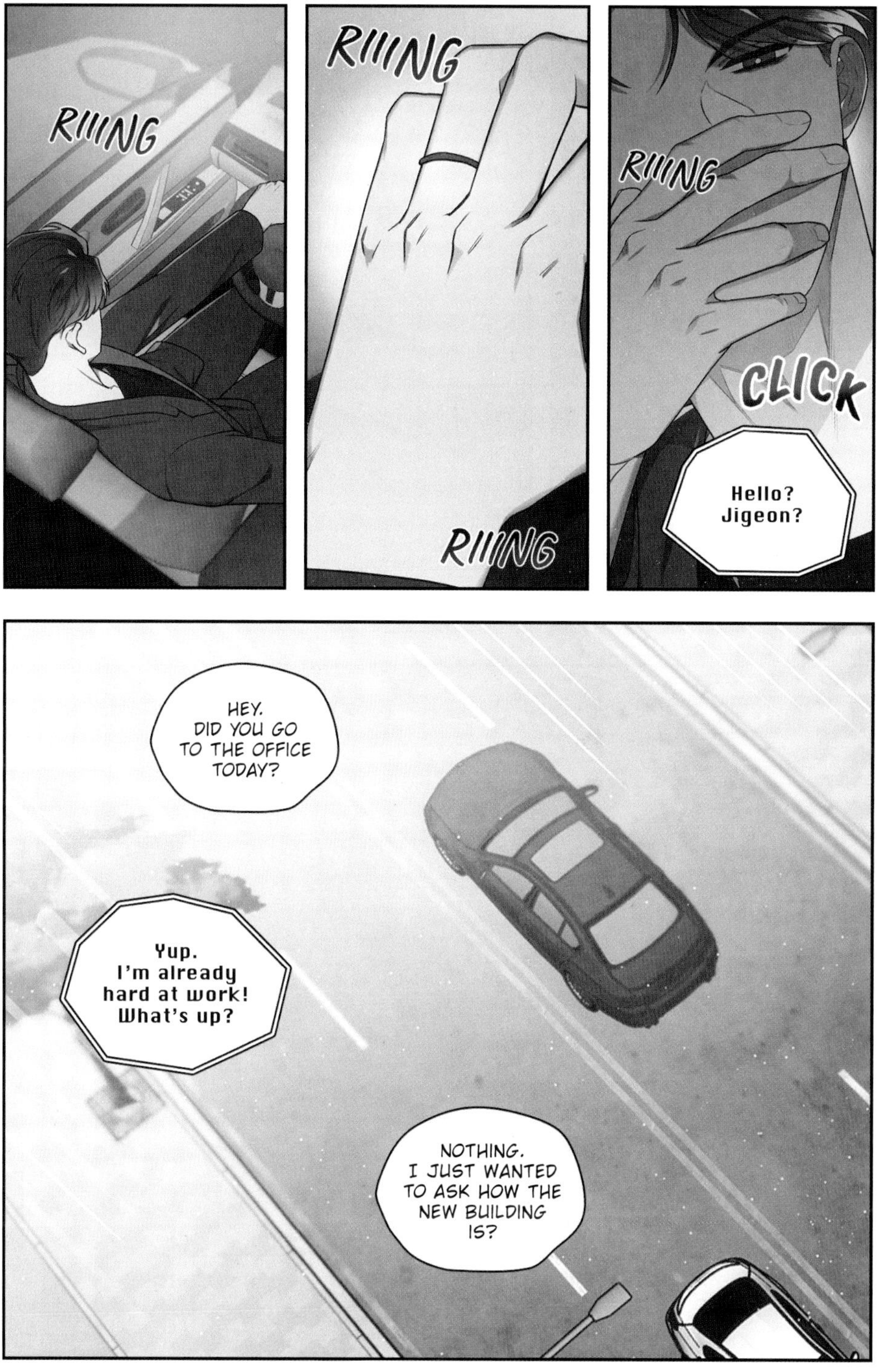
RIIING
RIIING
RIIING
RIIING
CLICK
Hello? Jigeon?
HEY. DID YOU GO TO THE OFFICE TODAY?
Yup. I'm already hard at work! What's up?
NOTHING. I JUST WANTED TO ASK HOW THE NEW BUILDING IS?

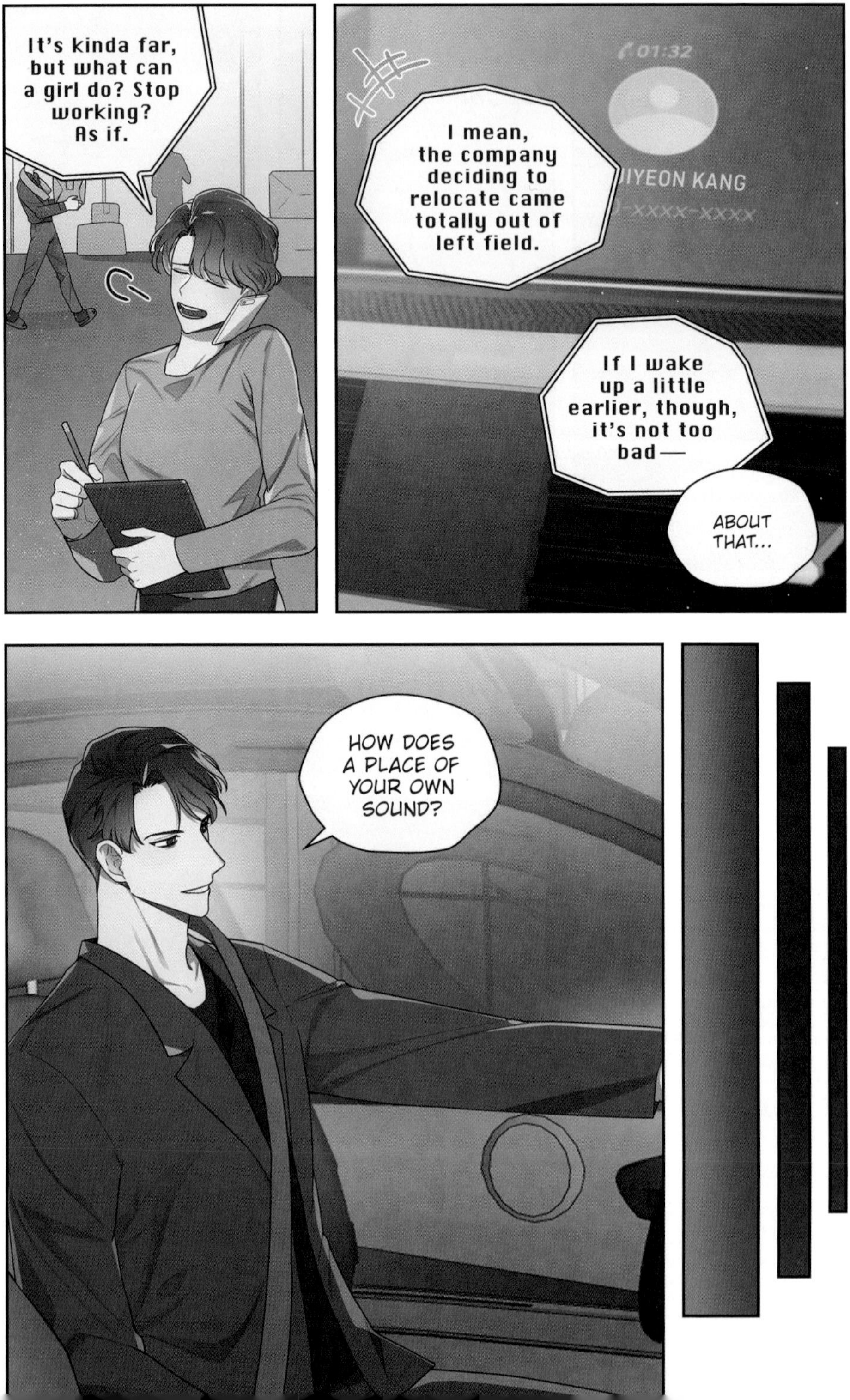

It's kinda far, but what can a girl do? Stop working? As if.
01:32
JIYEON KANG
I mean, the company deciding to relocate came totally out of left field.
If I wake up a little earlier, though, it's not too bad—
ABOUT THAT...
HOW DOES A PLACE OF YOUR OWN SOUND?

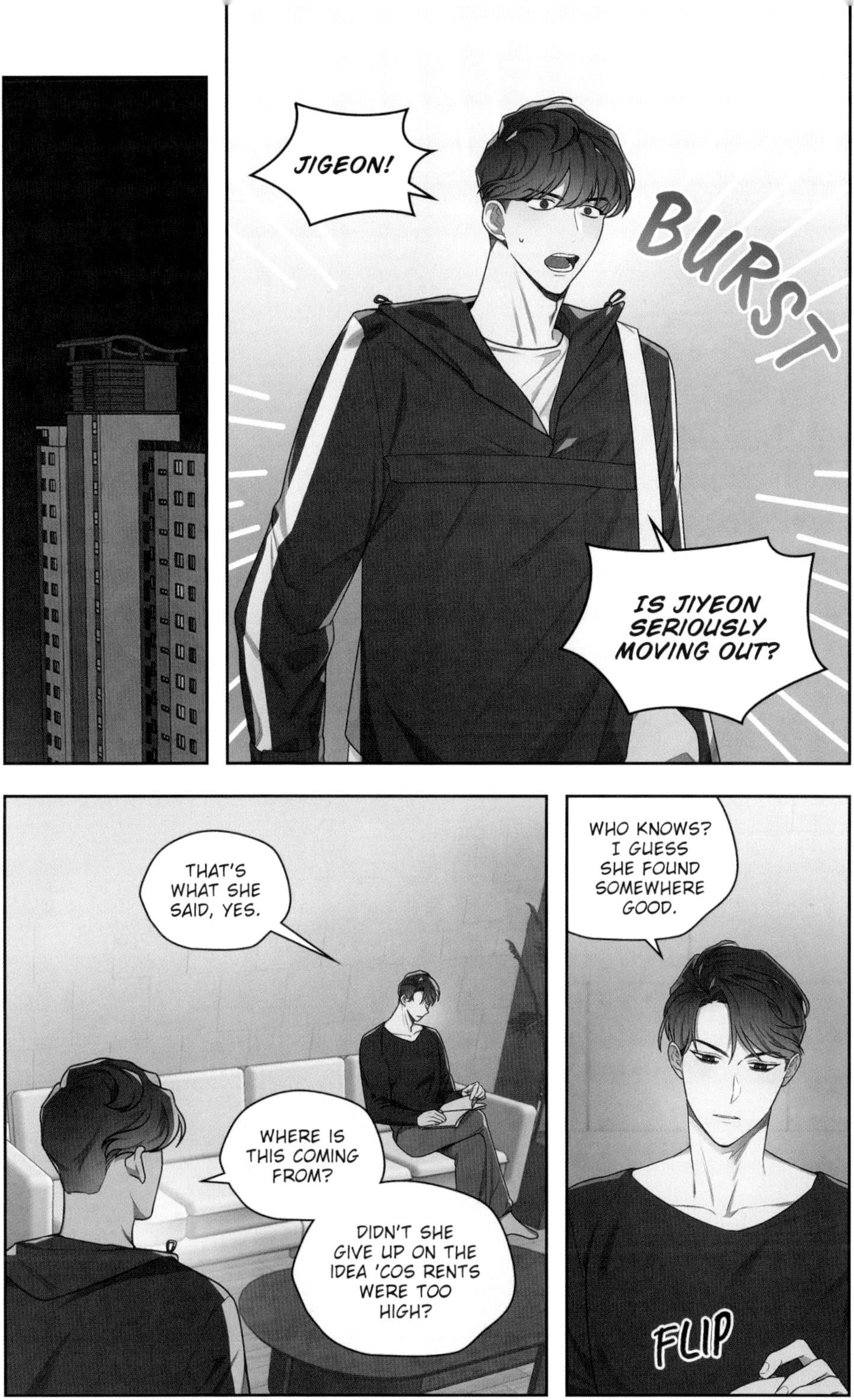
JIGEON!
BURST
IS JIYEON SERIOUSLY MOVING OUT?
THAT'S WHAT SHE SAID, YES.
WHERE IS THIS COMING FROM?
DIDN'T SHE GIVE UP ON THE IDEA 'COS RENTS WERE TOO HIGH?
WHO KNOWS? I GUESS SHE FOUND SOMEWHERE GOOD.
FLIP

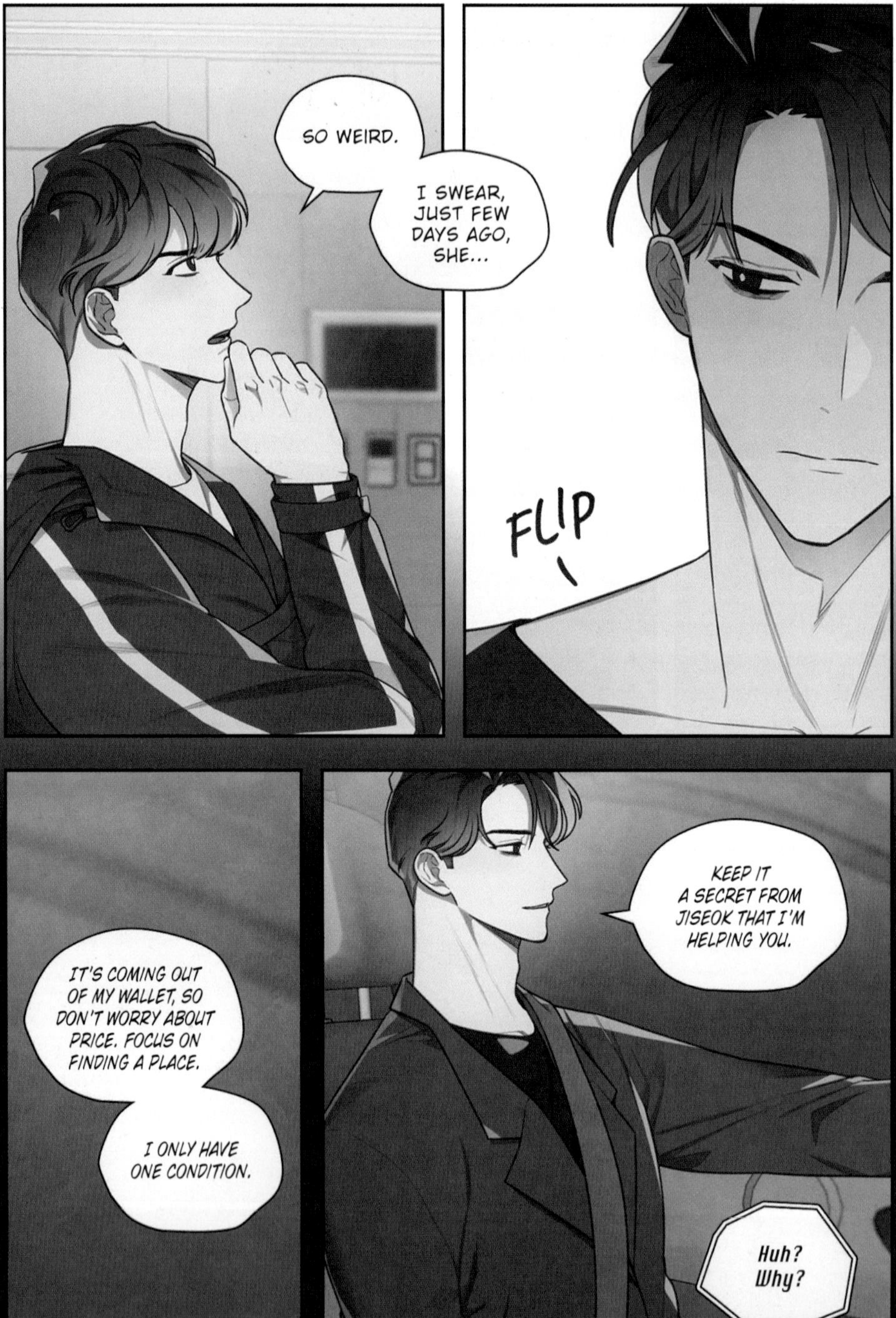
SO WEIRD.
I SWEAR, JUST FEW DAYS AGO, SHE...
FLIP
KEEP IT A SECRET FROM JISEOK THAT I'M HELPING YOU.
IT'S COMING OUT OF MY WALLET, SO DON'T WORRY ABOUT PRICE. FOCUS ON FINDING A PLACE.
I ONLY HAVE ONE CONDITION.
Huh? Why?

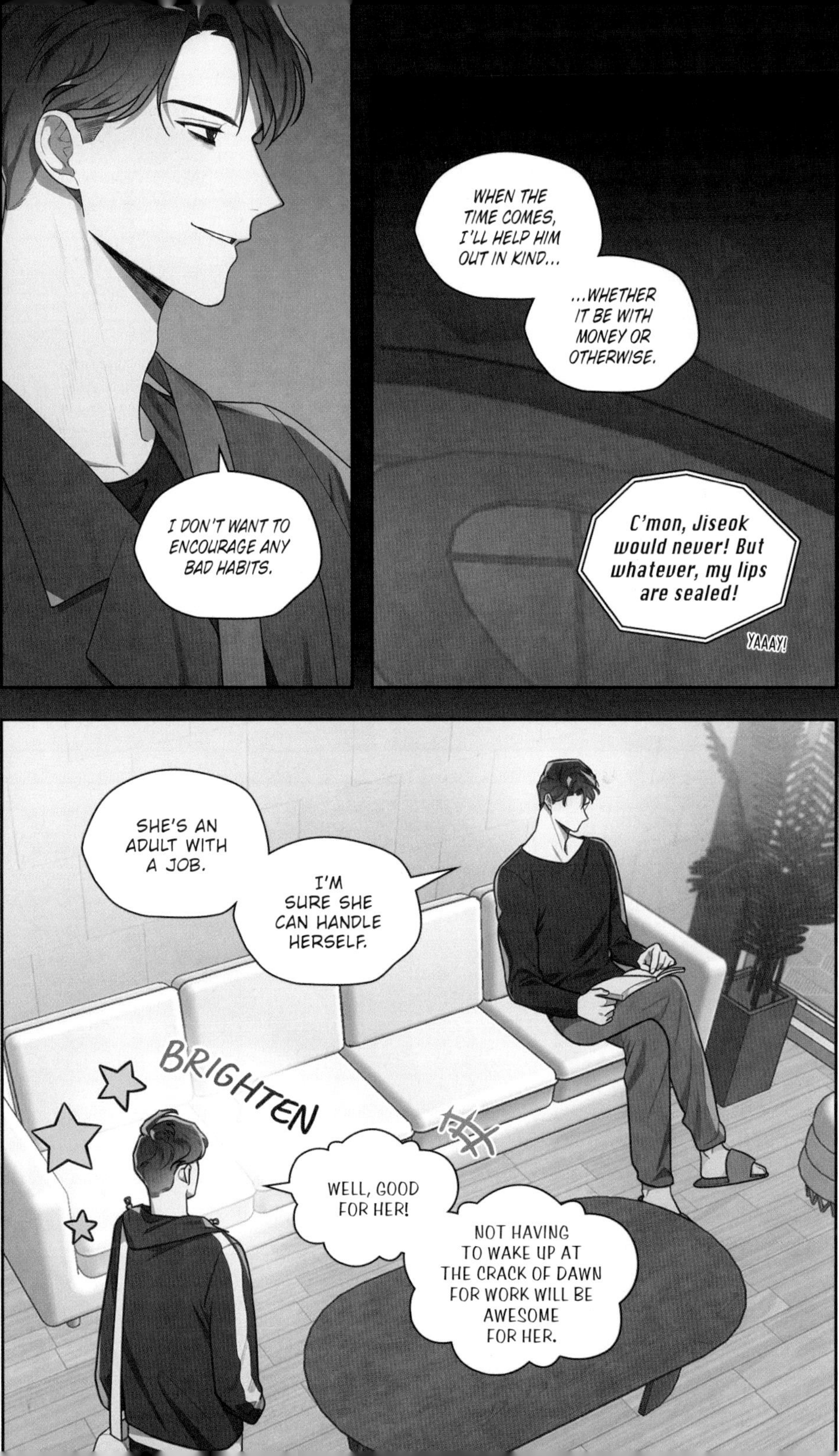
I DON'T WANT TO ENCOURAGE ANY BAD HABITS.
WHEN THE TIME COMES, I'LL HELP HIM OUT IN KIND...
...WHETHER IT BE WITH MONEY OR OTHERWISE.
C'mon, Jiseok would never! But whatever, my lips are sealed!
YAAAY!
SHE'S AN ADULT WITH A JOB.
I'M SURE SHE CAN HANDLE HERSELF.
BRIGHTEN
WELL, GOOD FOR HER!
NOT HAVING TO WAKE UP AT THE CRACK OF DAWN FOR WORK WILL BE AWESOME FOR HER.

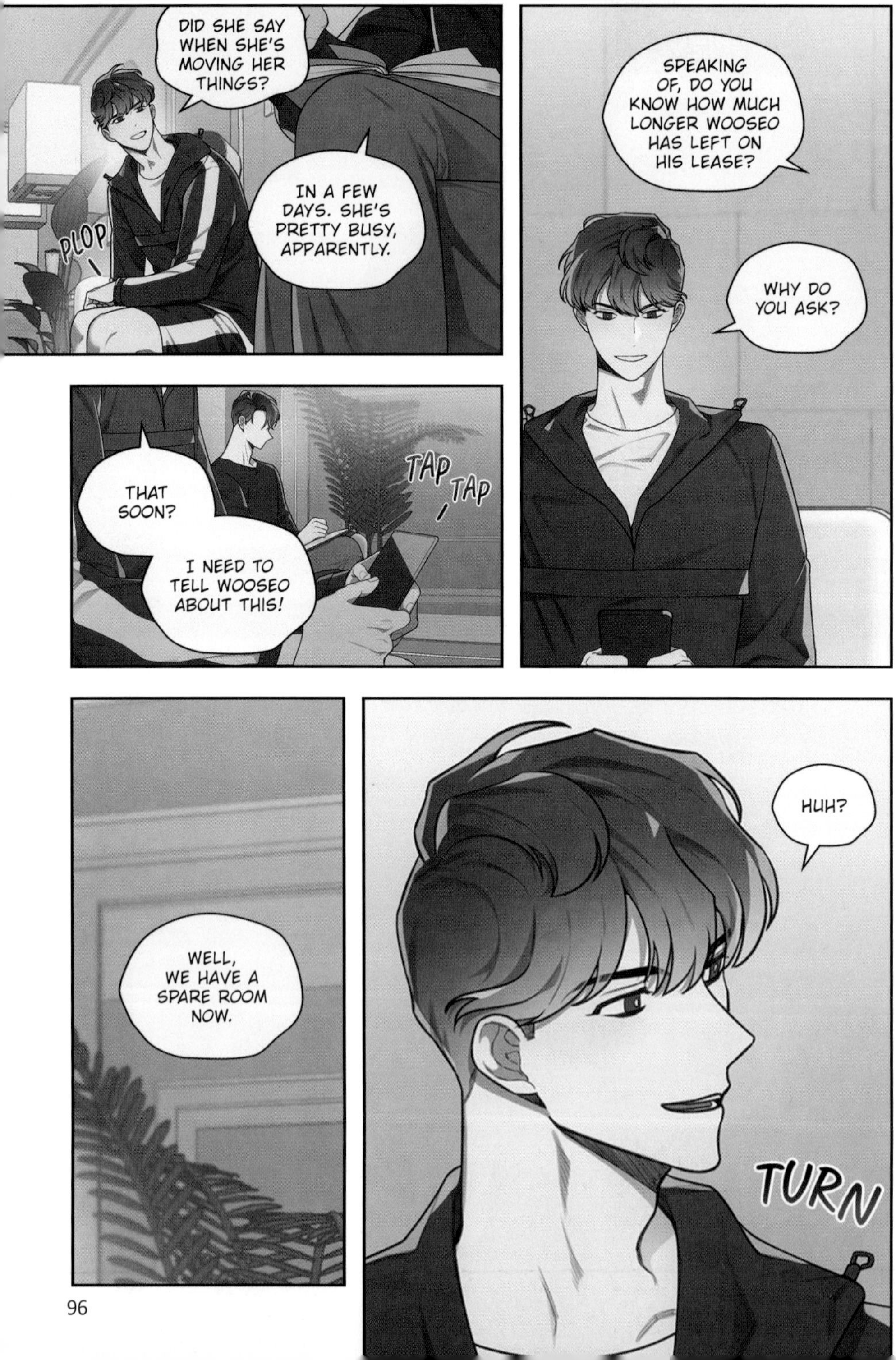
DID SHE SAY WHEN SHE'S MOVING HER THINGS?
IN A FEW DAYS. SHE'S PRETTY BUSY, APPARENTLY.
PLOP
THAT SOON?
I NEED TO TELL WOOSEO ABOUT THIS!
TAP
TAP
SPEAKING OF, DO YOU KNOW HOW MUCH LONGER WOOSEO HAS LEFT ON HIS LEASE?
WHY DO YOU ASK?
WELL, WE HAVE A SPARE ROOM NOW.
HUH?
TURN

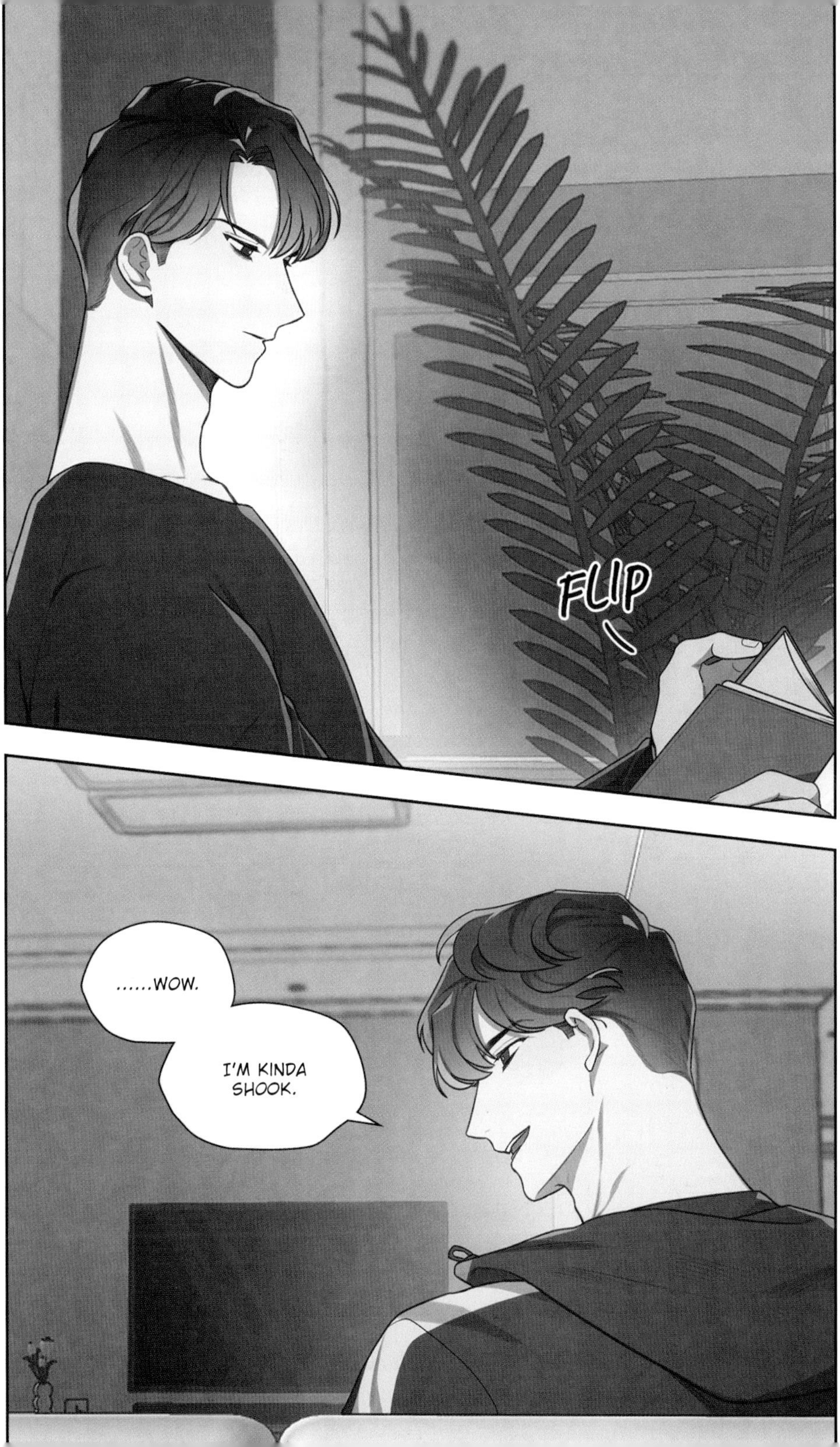
FLIP
......WOW.
I'M KINDA SHOOK.

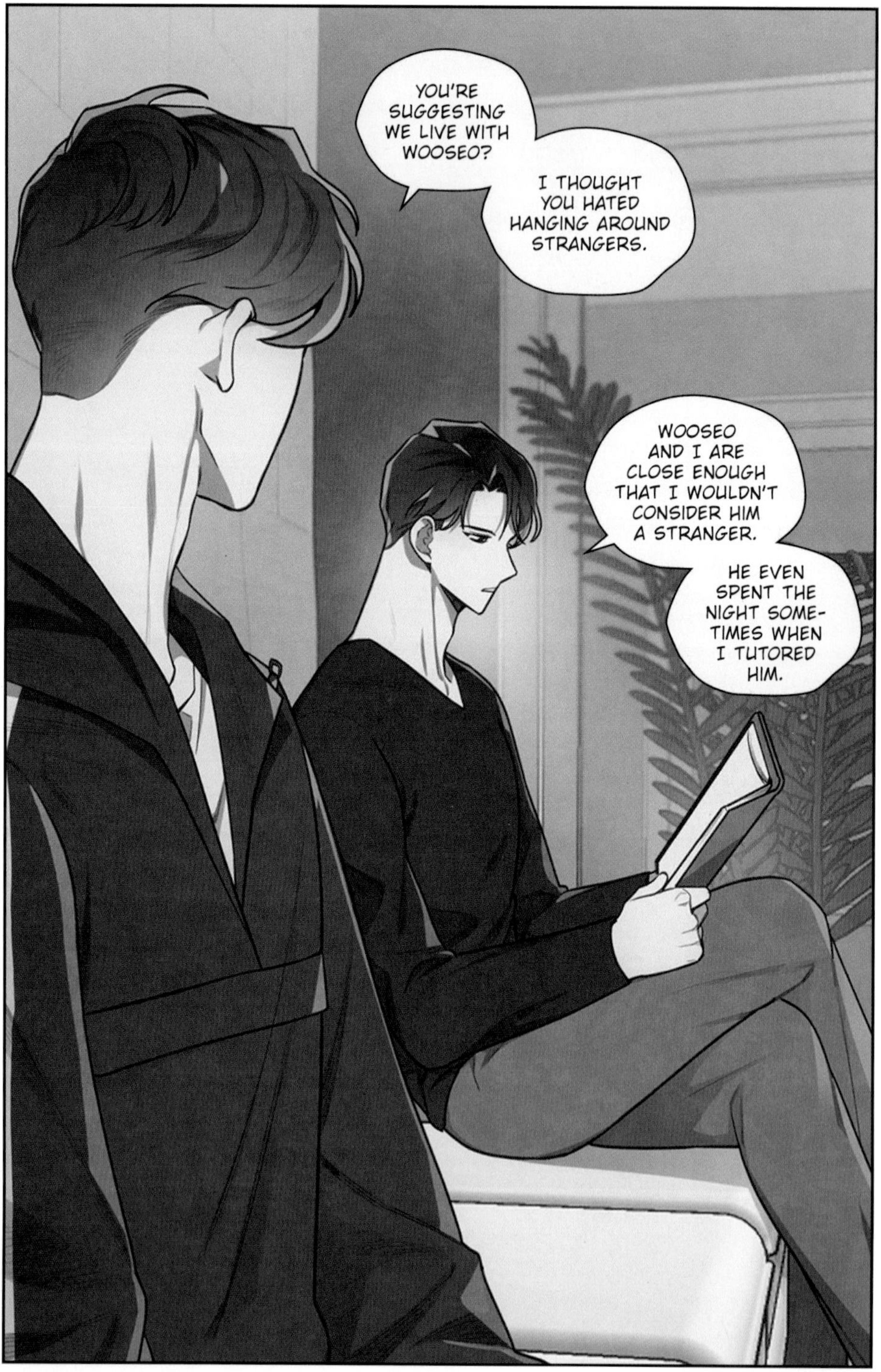
YOU'RE SUGGESTING WE LIVE WITH WOOSEO?
I THOUGHT YOU HATED HANGING AROUND STRANGERS.
WOOSEO AND I ARE CLOSE ENOUGH THAT I WOULDN'T CONSIDER HIM A STRANGER.
HE EVEN SPENT THE NIGHT SOME-TIMES WHEN I TUTORED HIM.

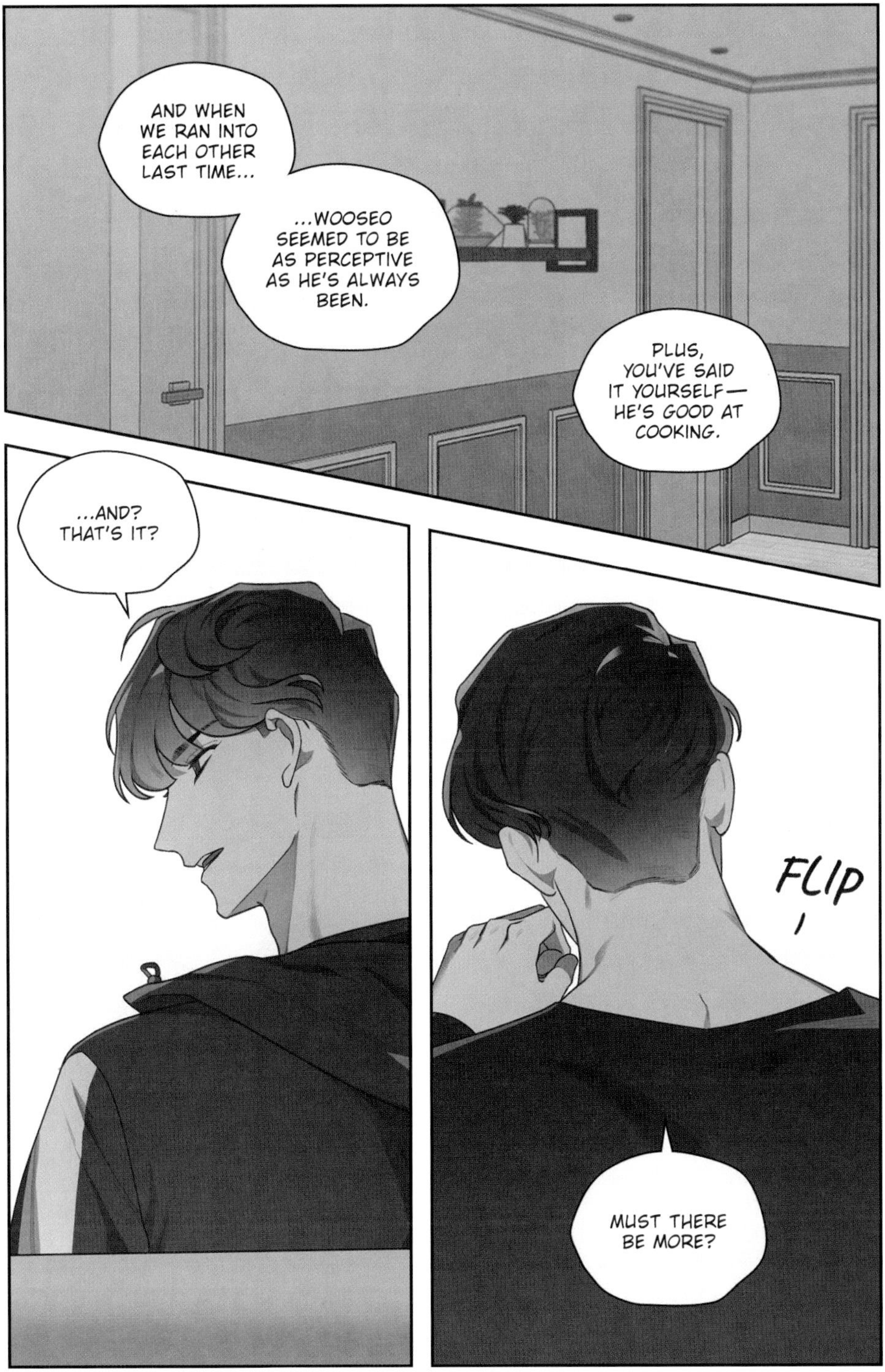
AND WHEN WE RAN INTO EACH OTHER LAST TIME...
...WOOSEO SEEMED TO BE AS PERCEPTIVE AS HE'S ALWAYS BEEN.
PLUS, YOU'VE SAID IT YOURSELF— HE'S GOOD AT COOKING.
...AND? THAT'S IT?
FLIP
MUST THERE BE MORE?

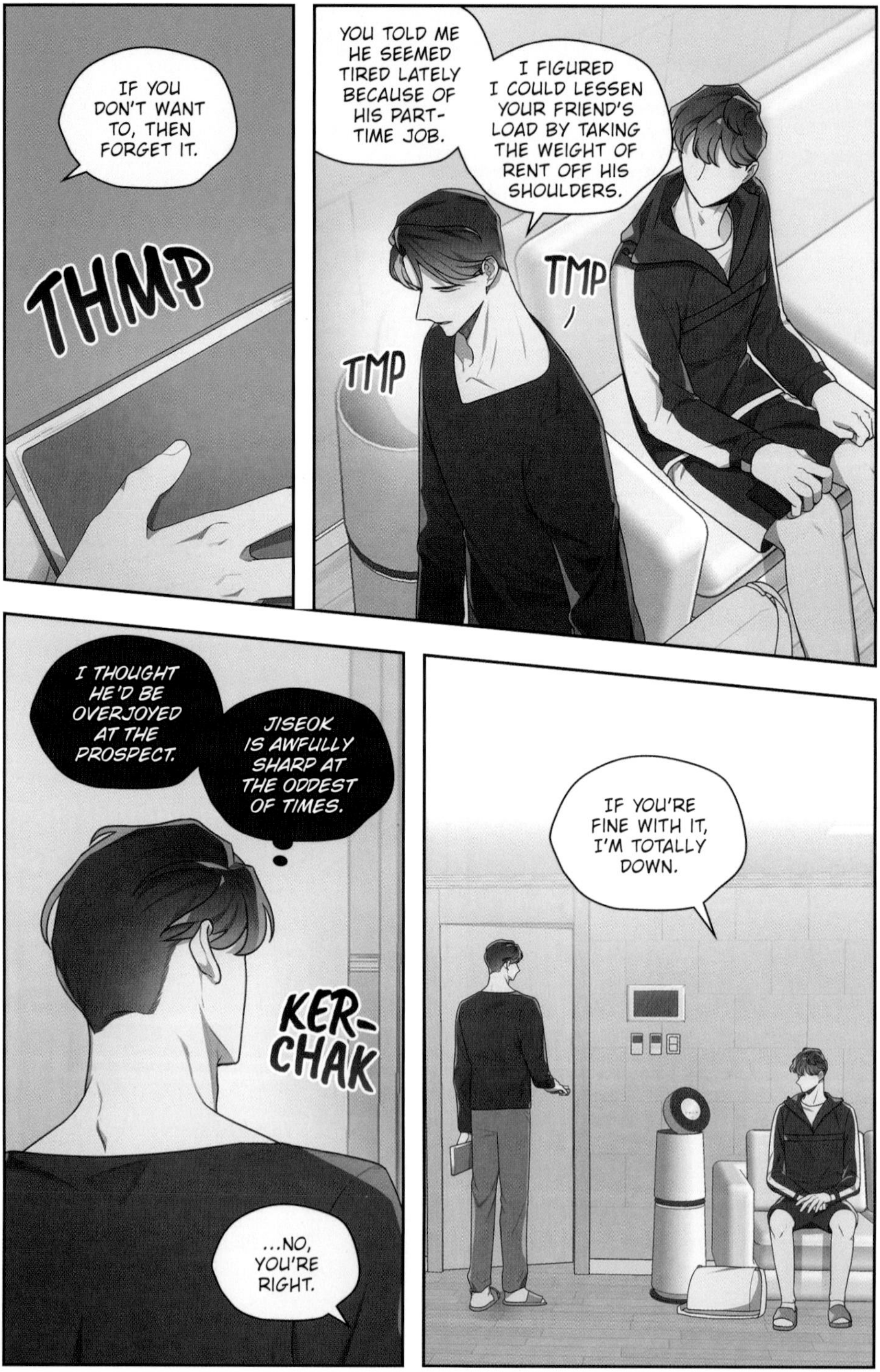
IF YOU DON'T WANT TO, THEN FORGET IT.
THMP
YOU TOLD ME HE SEEMED TIRED LATELY BECAUSE OF HIS PART-TIME JOB.
I FIGURED I COULD LESSEN YOUR FRIEND'S LOAD BY TAKING THE WEIGHT OF RENT OFF HIS SHOULDERS.
TMP
TMP
I THOUGHT HE'D BE OVERJOYED AT THE PROSPECT.
JISEOK IS AWFULLY SHARP AT THE ODDEST OF TIMES.
KER-CHAK
...NO, YOU'RE RIGHT.
IF YOU'RE FINE WITH IT, I'M TOTALLY DOWN.

BEAM

COOL.
I'LL LET HIM
KNOW.

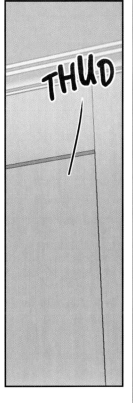

THUD

HMM...

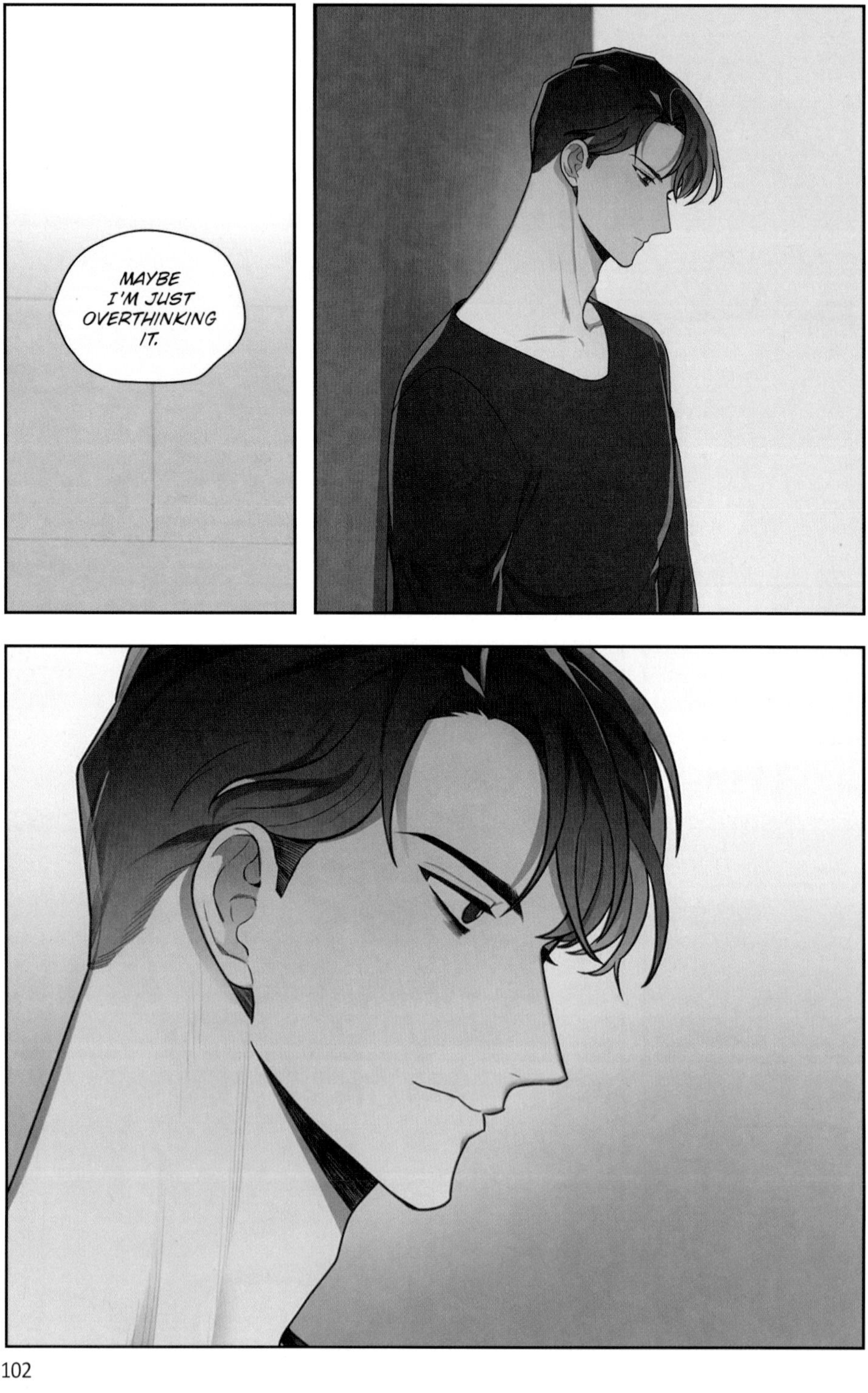
MAYBE I'M JUST OVERTHINKING IT.

Tied to You

Chapter 6

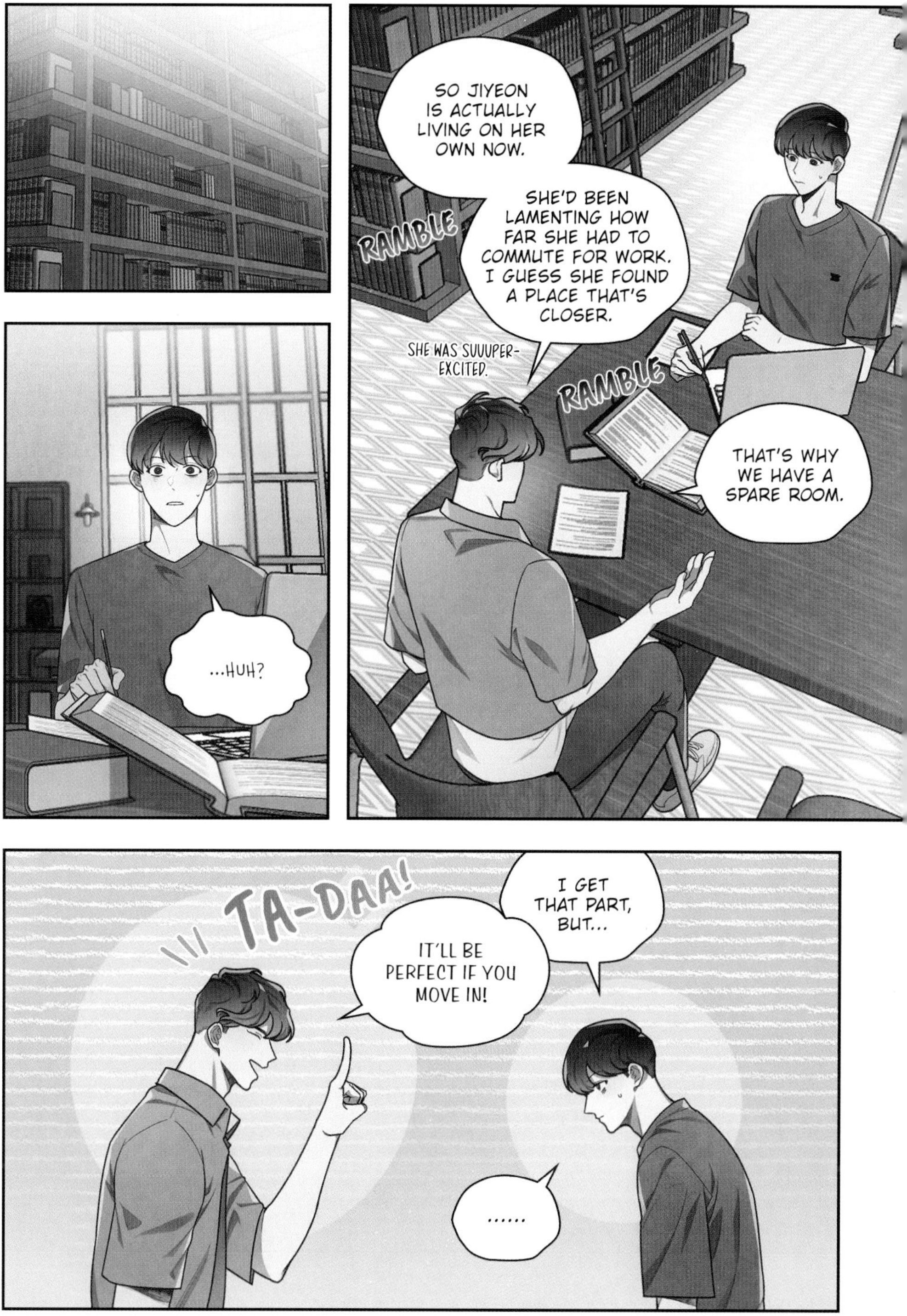
SO JIYEON IS ACTUALLY LIVING ON HER OWN NOW.
SHE'D BEEN LAMENTING HOW FAR SHE HAD TO COMMUTE FOR WORK. I GUESS SHE FOUND A PLACE THAT'S CLOSER.
RAMBLE
SHE WAS SUUUPER-EXCITED.
RAMBLE
THAT'S WHY WE HAVE A SPARE ROOM.
...HUH?
TA-DAA!
IT'LL BE PERFECT IF YOU MOVE IN!
I GET THAT PART, BUT...
......

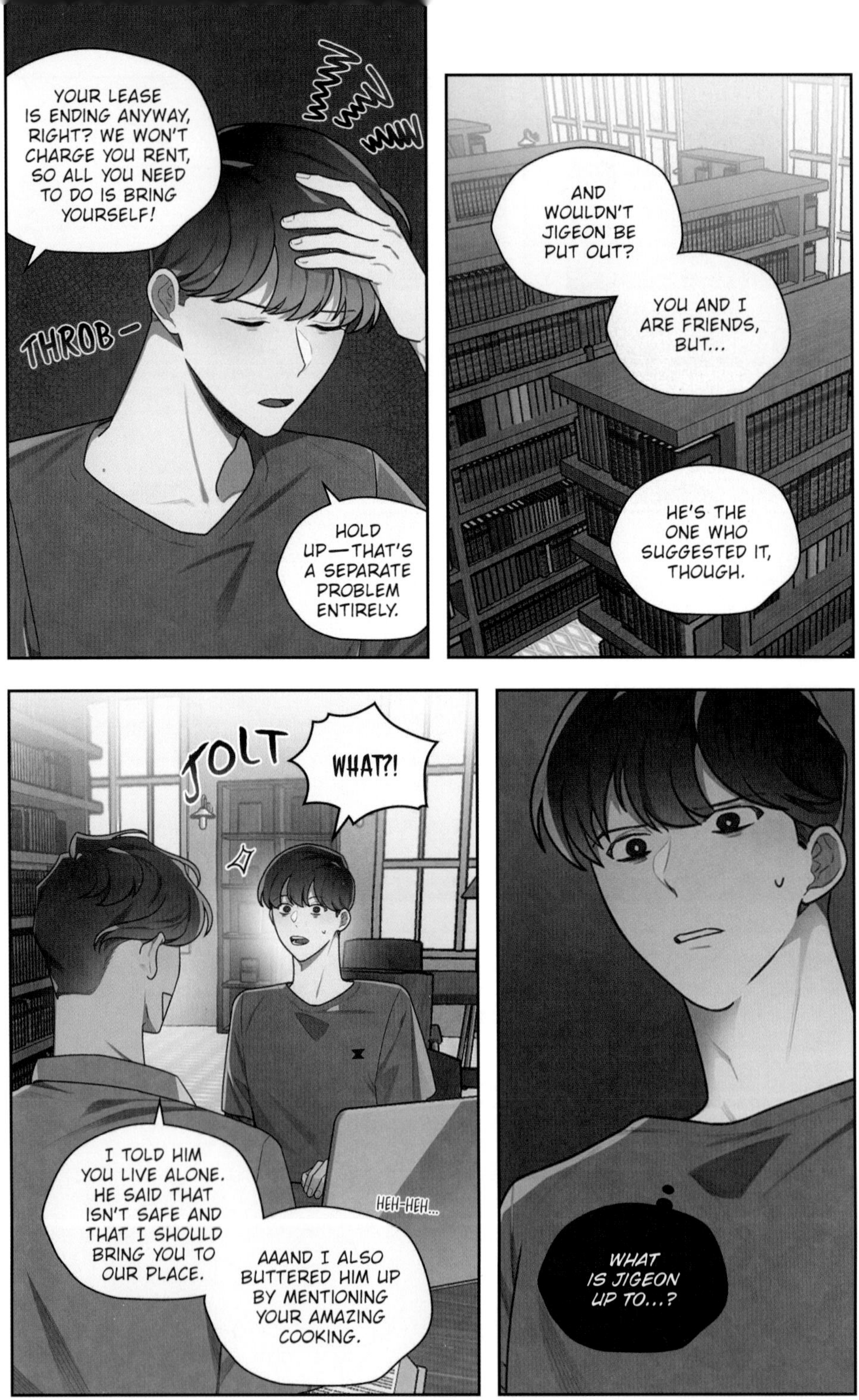
YOUR LEASE IS ENDING ANYWAY, RIGHT? WE WON'T CHARGE YOU RENT, SO ALL YOU NEED TO DO IS BRING YOURSELF!
WWW WW WWW
THROB
HOLD UP—THAT'S A SEPARATE PROBLEM ENTIRELY.
AND WOULDN'T JIGEON BE PUT OUT?
YOU AND I ARE FRIENDS, BUT...
HE'S THE ONE WHO SUGGESTED IT, THOUGH.
JOLT
WHAT?!
I TOLD HIM YOU LIVE ALONE. HE SAID THAT ISN'T SAFE AND THAT I SHOULD BRING YOU TO OUR PLACE.
HEH-HEH...
AAAND I ALSO BUTTERED HIM UP BY MENTIONING YOUR AMAZING COOKING.
WHAT IS JIGEON UP TO...?

SURE, IF WE'RE LIVING TOGETHER, WE DON'T HAVE TO GO TO A HOTEL ANYMORE...

...BUT THE ISSUE IS...

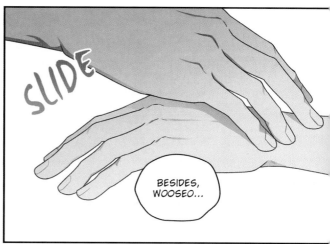

SLIDE

BESIDES, WOOSEO...

...I WORRY ABOUT YOU TOO. ESPECIALLY WITH YOU WORKING AT NIGHT NOW.

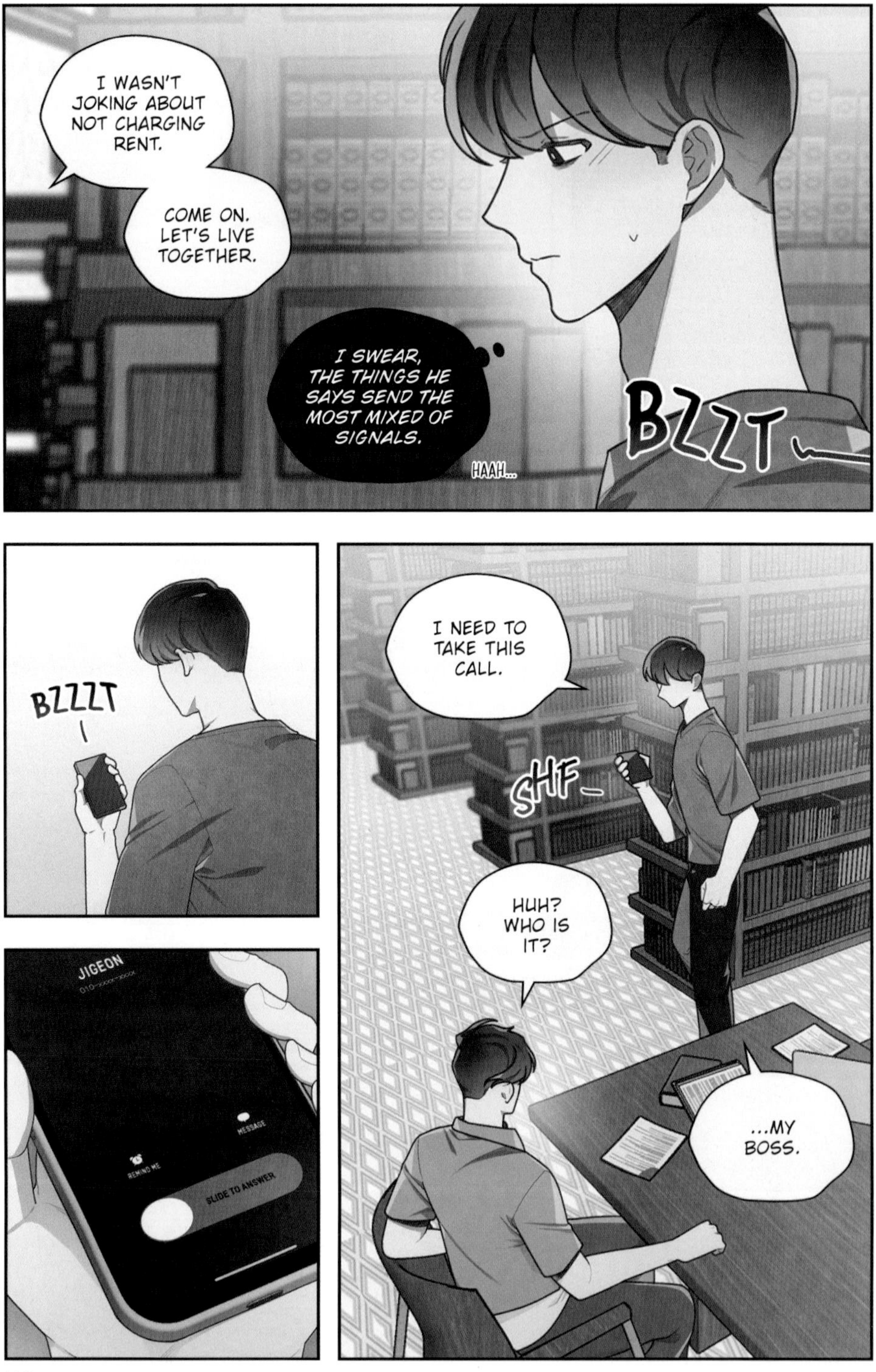
I WASN'T JOKING ABOUT NOT CHARGING RENT.
COME ON. LET'S LIVE TOGETHER.
I SWEAR, THE THINGS HE SAYS SEND THE MOST MIXED OF SIGNALS.
HAAH...
BZZT
BZZZT
JIGEON
MESSAGE
REMIND ME
SLIDE TO ANSWER
I NEED TO TAKE THIS CALL.
SHF
HUH? WHO IS IT?
...MY BOSS.

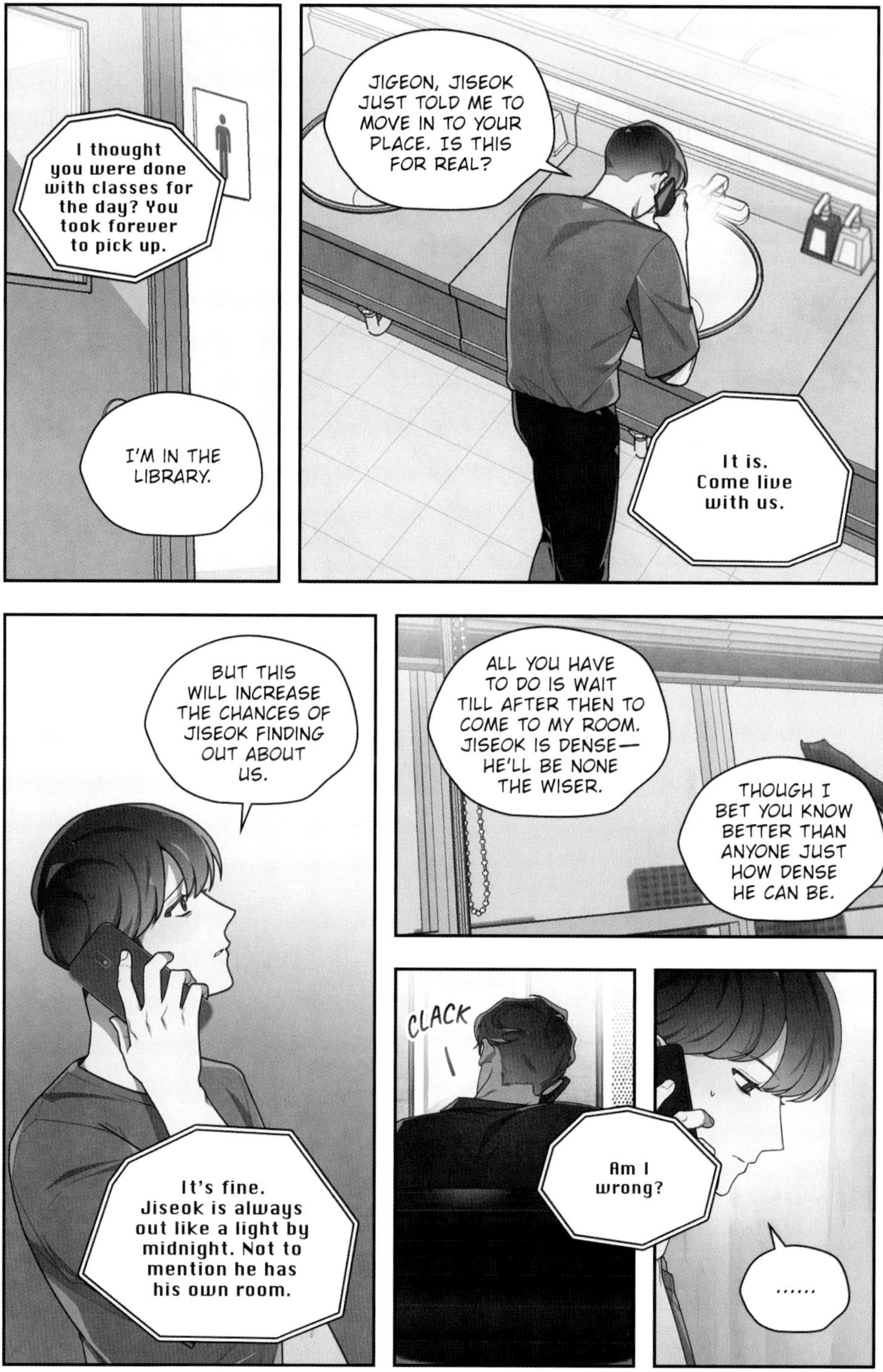
I thought you were done with classes for the day? You took forever to pick up.
I'M IN THE LIBRARY.
JIGEON, JISEOK JUST TOLD ME TO MOVE IN TO YOUR PLACE. IS THIS FOR REAL?
It is. Come live with us.
BUT THIS WILL INCREASE THE CHANCES OF JISEOK FINDING OUT ABOUT US.
It's fine. Jiseok is always out like a light by midnight. Not to mention he has his own room.
ALL YOU HAVE TO DO IS WAIT TILL AFTER THEN TO COME TO MY ROOM. JISEOK IS DENSE— HE'LL BE NONE THE WISER.
THOUGH I BET YOU KNOW BETTER THAN ANYONE JUST HOW DENSE HE CAN BE.
CLACK
Am I wrong?
……

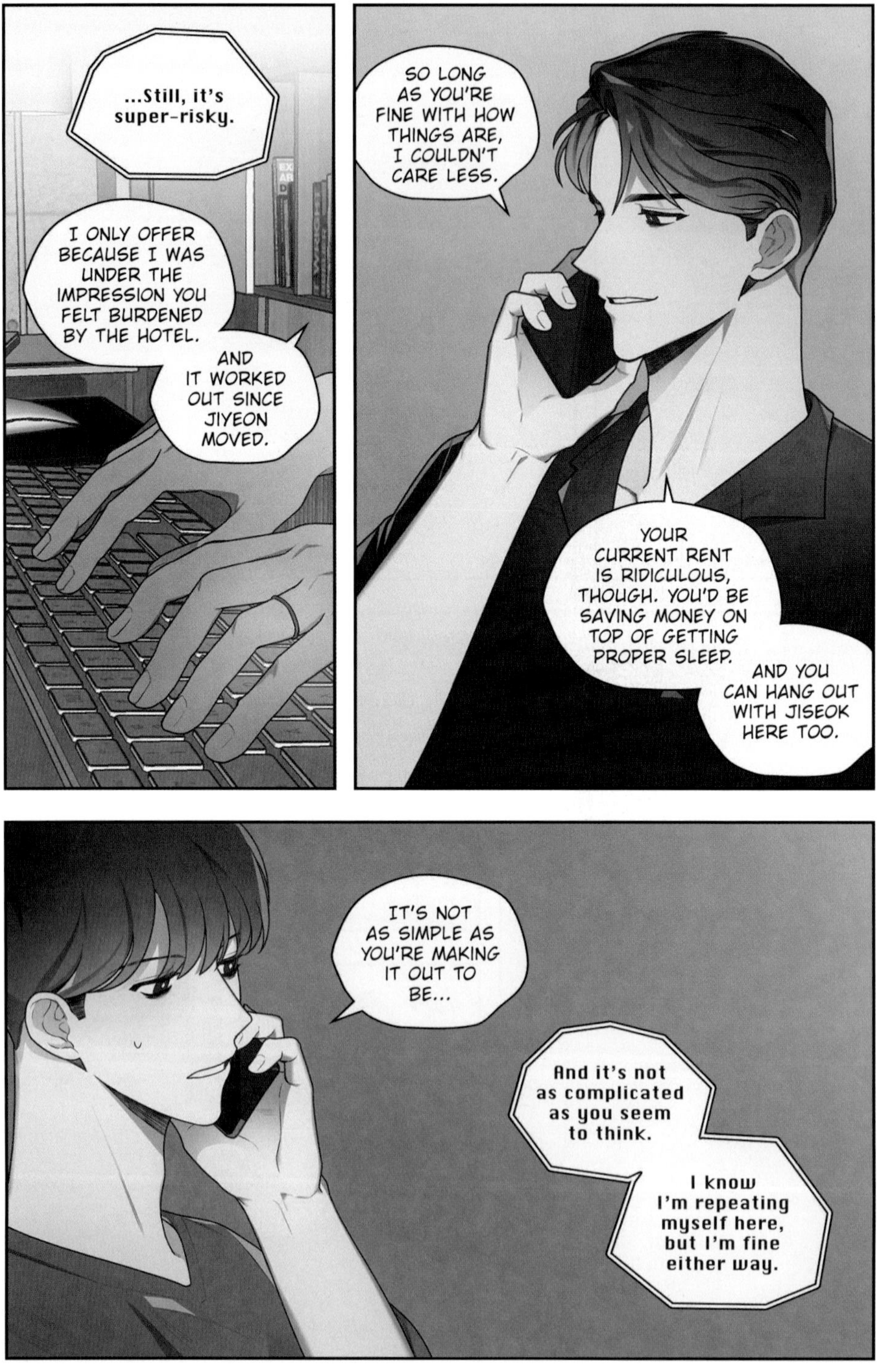
...Still, it's super-risky.
I ONLY OFFER BECAUSE I WAS UNDER THE IMPRESSION YOU FELT BURDENED BY THE HOTEL.
AND IT WORKED OUT SINCE JIYEON MOVED.
SO LONG AS YOU'RE FINE WITH HOW THINGS ARE, I COULDN'T CARE LESS.
YOUR CURRENT RENT IS RIDICULOUS, THOUGH. YOU'D BE SAVING MONEY ON TOP OF GETTING PROPER SLEEP.
AND YOU CAN HANG OUT WITH JISEOK HERE TOO.
IT'S NOT AS SIMPLE AS YOU'RE MAKING IT OUT TO BE...
And it's not as complicated as you seem to think.
I know I'm repeating myself here, but I'm fine either way.

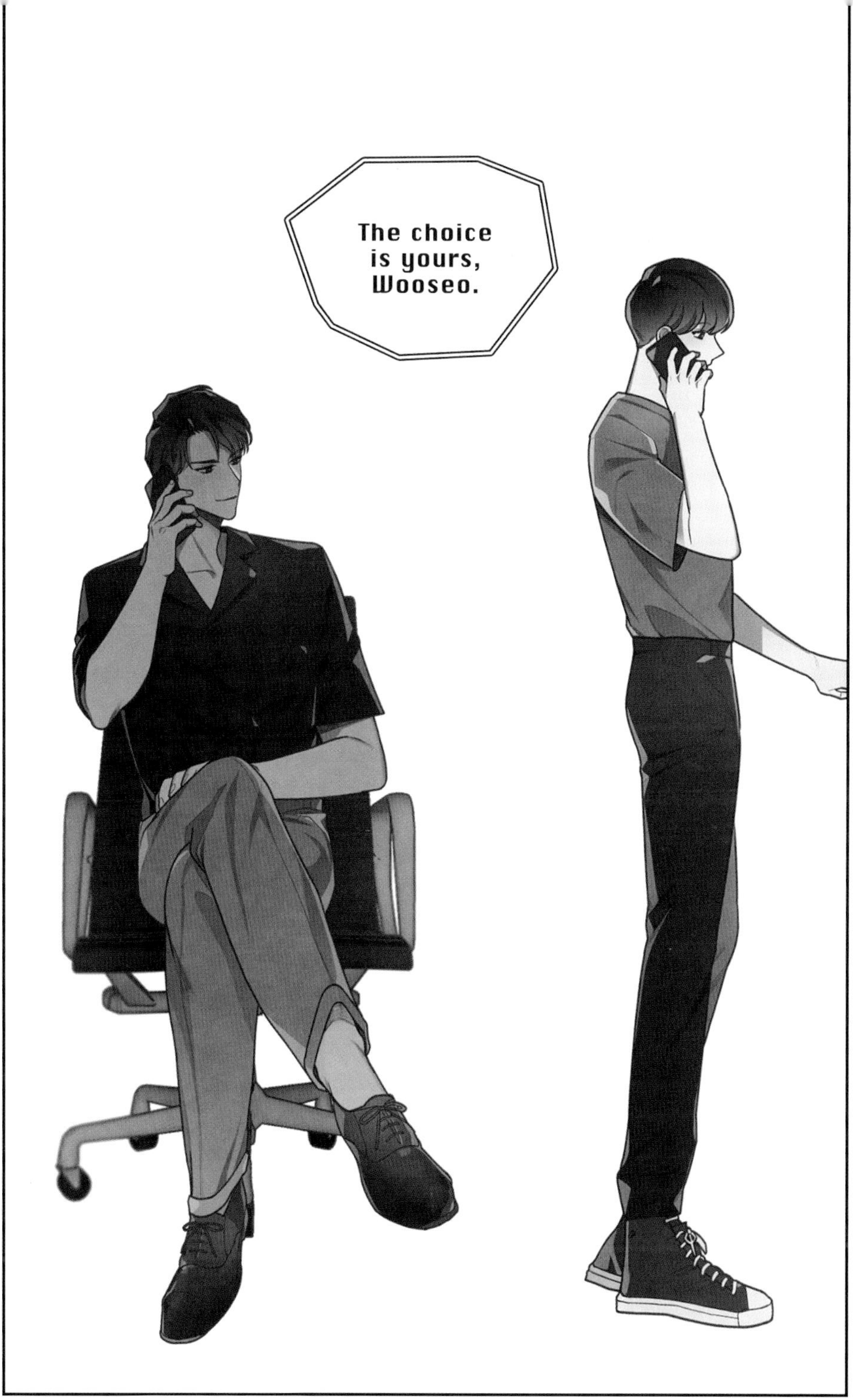
The choice is yours, Wooseo.

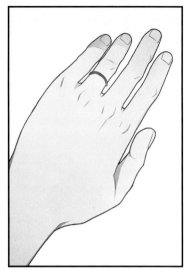

IN THE END, I DECIDED TO MOVE...

...BUT WAS THIS THE RIGHT CHOICE?

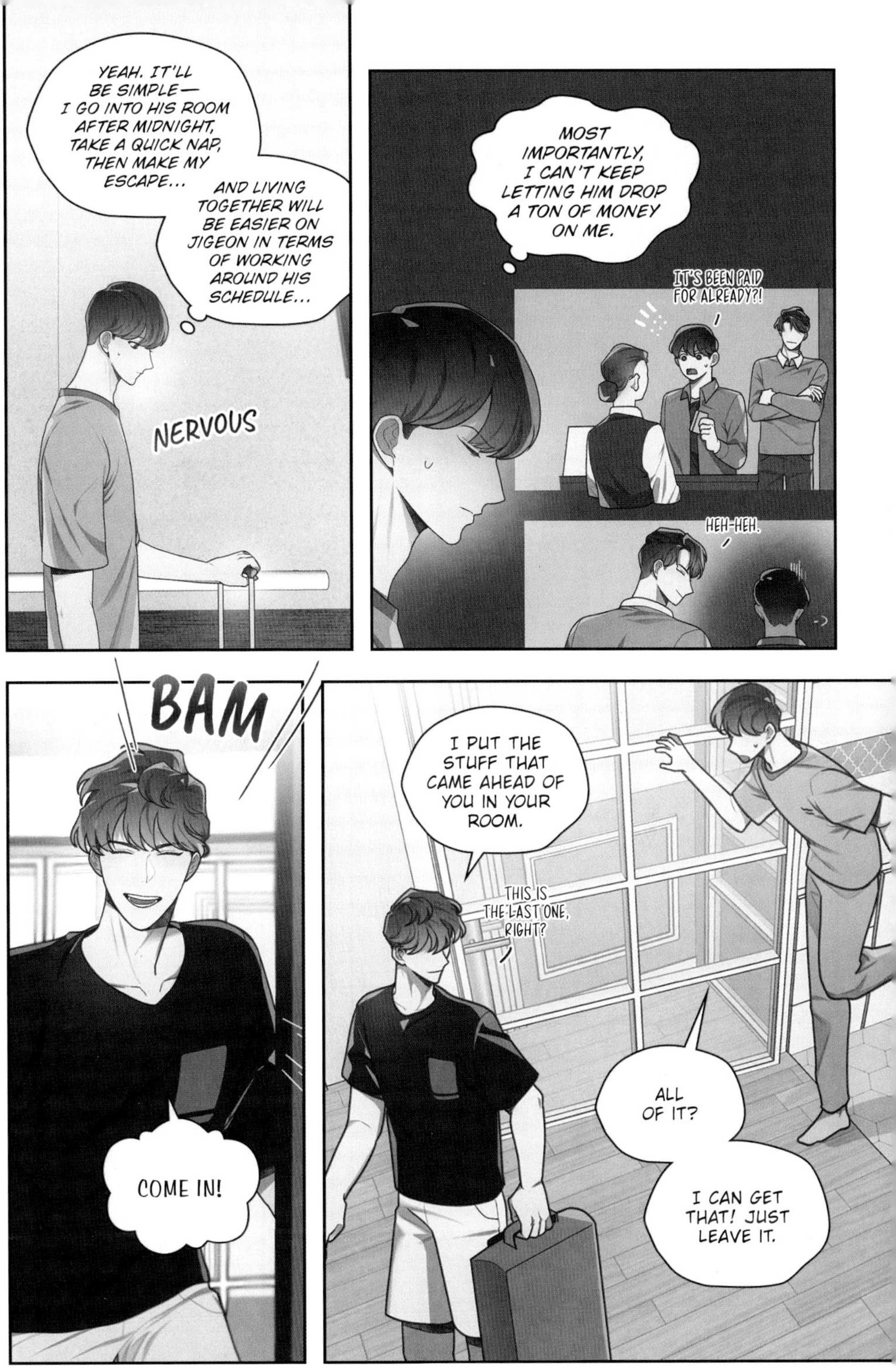
YEAH. IT'LL BE SIMPLE— I GO INTO HIS ROOM AFTER MIDNIGHT, TAKE A QUICK NAP, THEN MAKE MY ESCAPE...
AND LIVING TOGETHER WILL BE EASIER ON JIGEON IN TERMS OF WORKING AROUND HIS SCHEDULE...
NERVOUS
MOST IMPORTANTLY, I CAN'T KEEP LETTING HIM DROP A TON OF MONEY ON ME.
IT'S BEEN PAID FOR ALREADY?!
HEH-HEH.
BAM
COME IN!
I PUT THE STUFF THAT CAME AHEAD OF YOU IN YOUR ROOM.
THIS IS THE LAST ONE, RIGHT?
ALL OF IT?
I CAN GET THAT! JUST LEAVE IT.

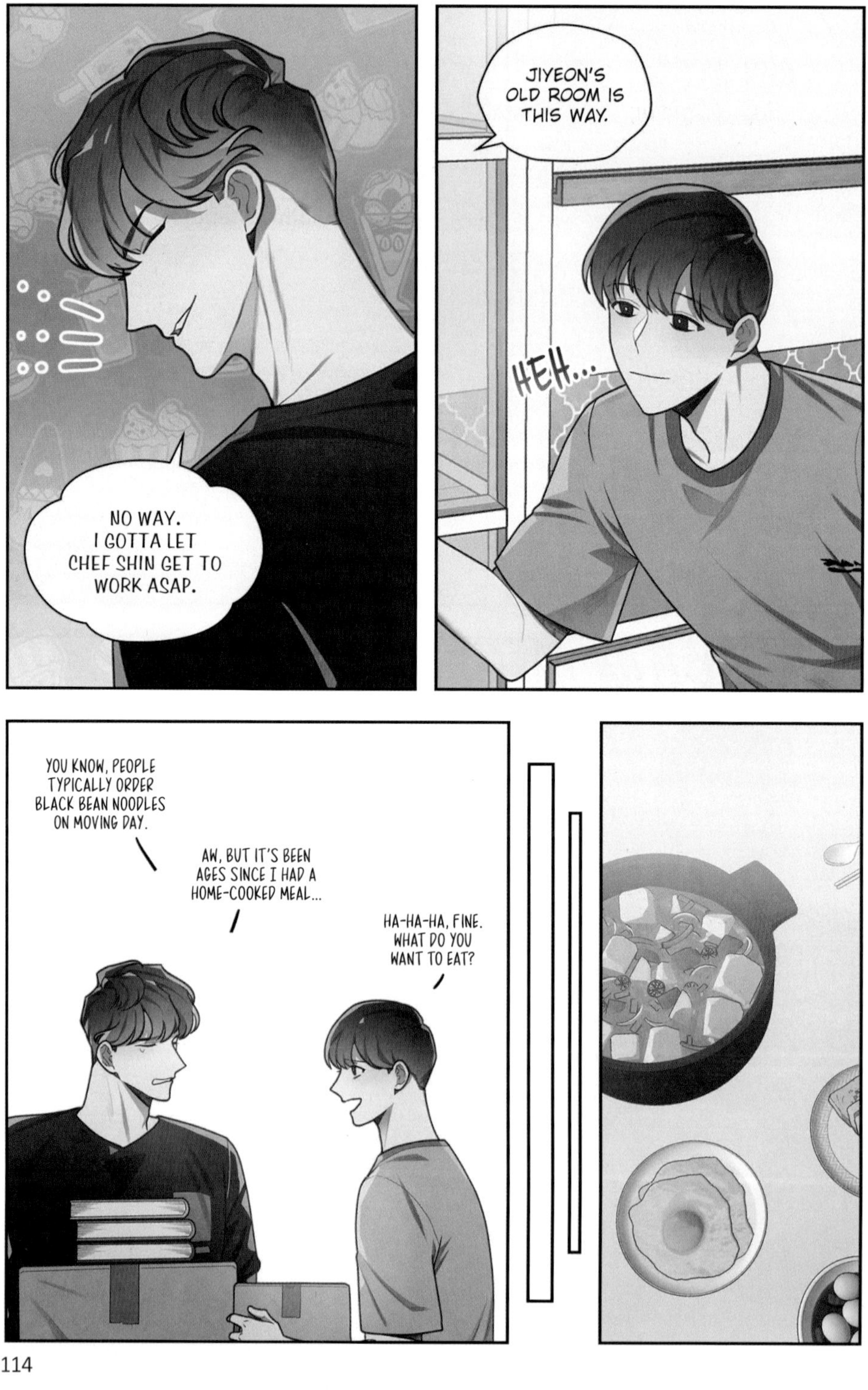
NO WAY. I GOTTA LET CHEF SHIN GET TO WORK ASAP.
JIYEON'S OLD ROOM IS THIS WAY.
HEH...
YOU KNOW, PEOPLE TYPICALLY ORDER BLACK BEAN NOODLES ON MOVING DAY.
AW, BUT IT'S BEEN AGES SINCE I HAD A HOME-COOKED MEAL...
HA-HA-HA, FINE. WHAT DO YOU WANT TO EAT?

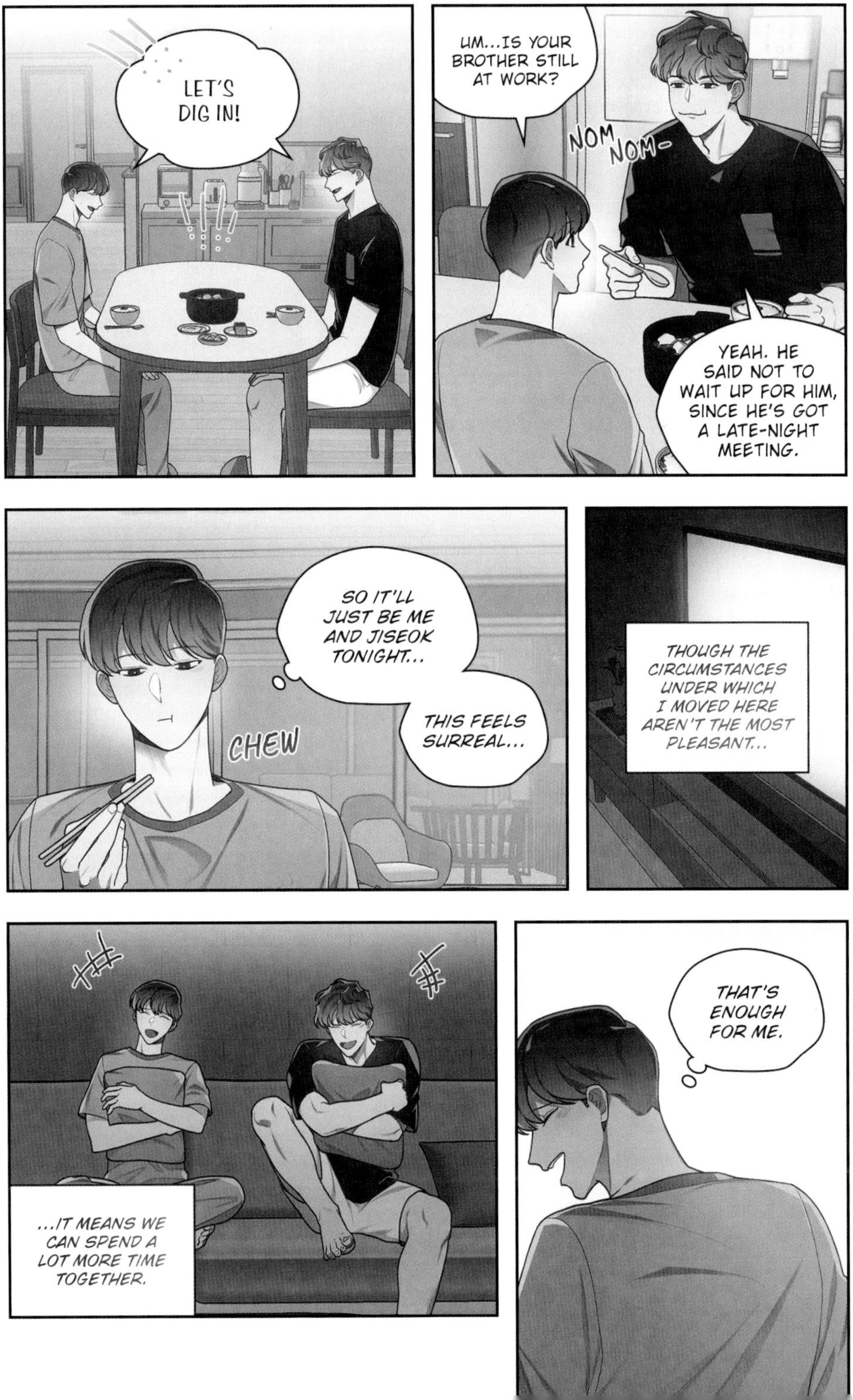
LET'S DIG IN!
UM...IS YOUR BROTHER STILL AT WORK?
NOM NOM-
YEAH. HE SAID NOT TO WAIT UP FOR HIM, SINCE HE'S GOT A LATE-NIGHT MEETING.
SO IT'LL JUST BE ME AND JISEOK TONIGHT...
THIS FEELS SURREAL...
CHEW
THOUGH THE CIRCUMSTANCES UNDER WHICH I MOVED HERE AREN'T THE MOST PLEASANT...
...IT MEANS WE CAN SPEND A LOT MORE TIME TOGETHER.
THAT'S ENOUGH FOR ME.

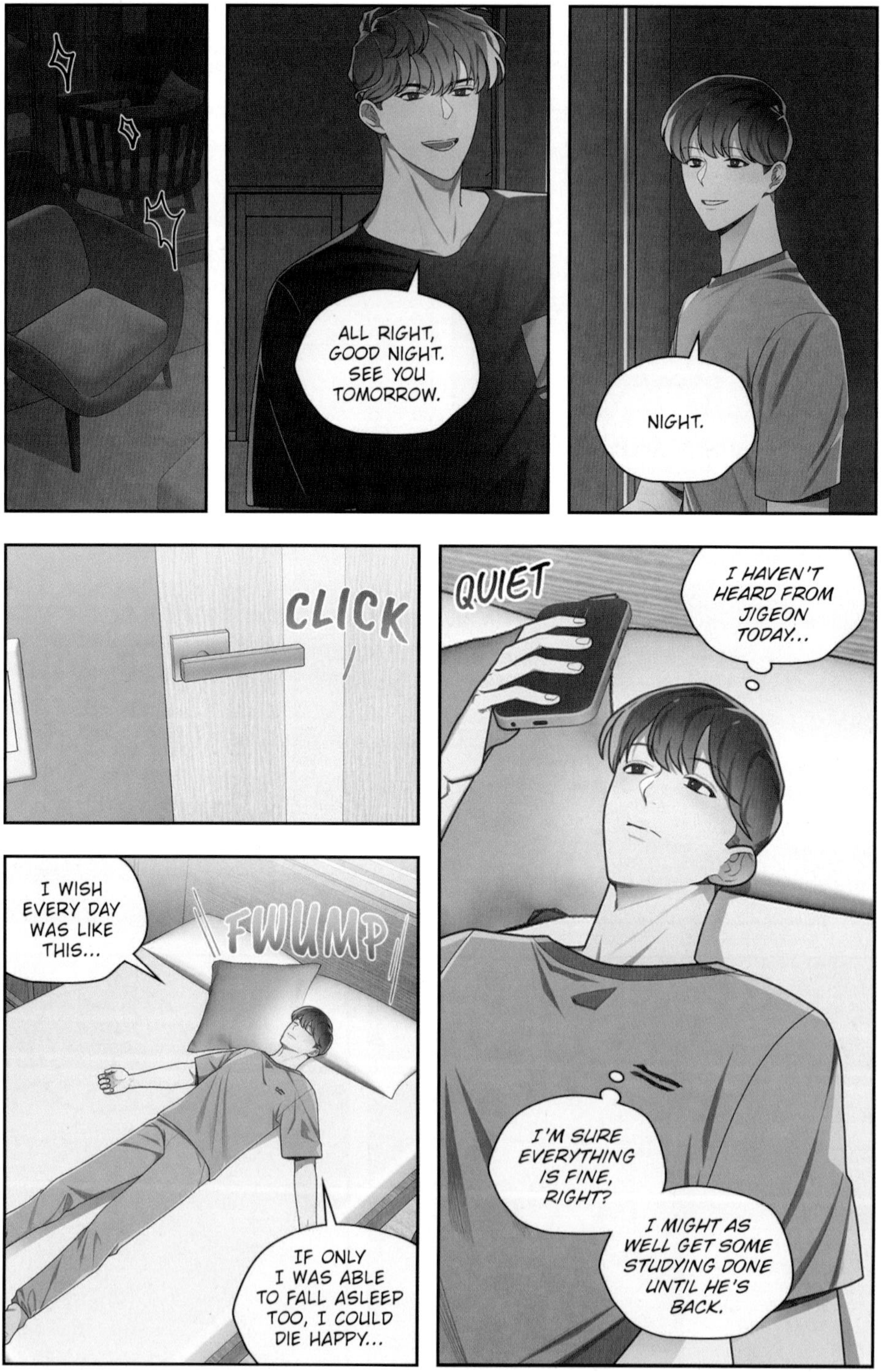
ALL RIGHT, GOOD NIGHT. SEE YOU TOMORROW.
NIGHT.
CLICK
QUIET
I HAVEN'T HEARD FROM JIGEON TODAY...
I'M SURE EVERYTHING IS FINE, RIGHT?
I MIGHT AS WELL GET SOME STUDYING DONE UNTIL HE'S BACK.
I WISH EVERY DAY WAS LIKE THIS...
FWUMP
IF ONLY I WAS ABLE TO FALL ASLEEP TOO, I COULD DIE HAPPY...

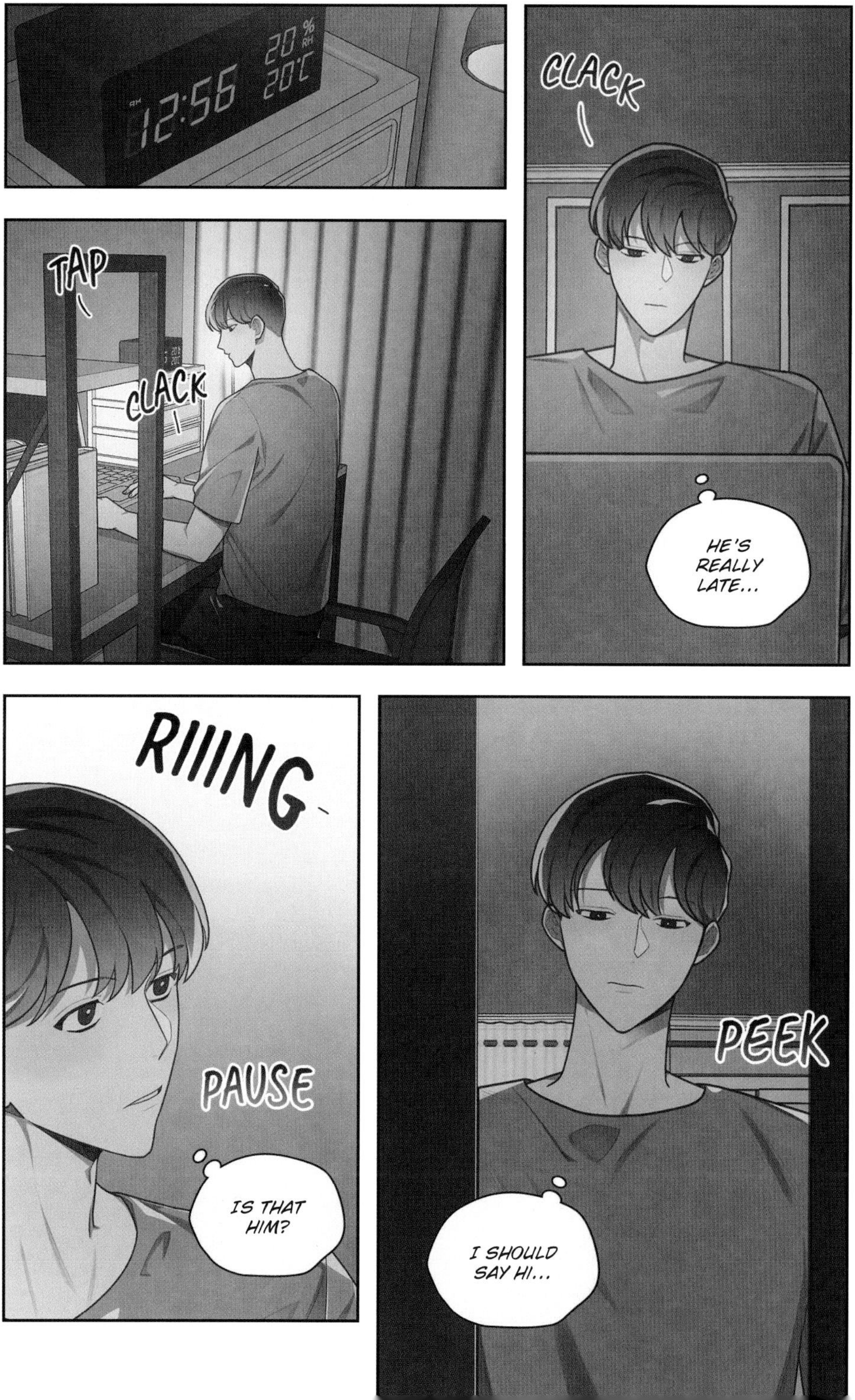
12:56
20 % RH
20°C
CLACK
TAP
CLACK
HE'S REALLY LATE...
RIIING
PAUSE
IS THAT HIM?
PEEK
I SHOULD SAY HI...

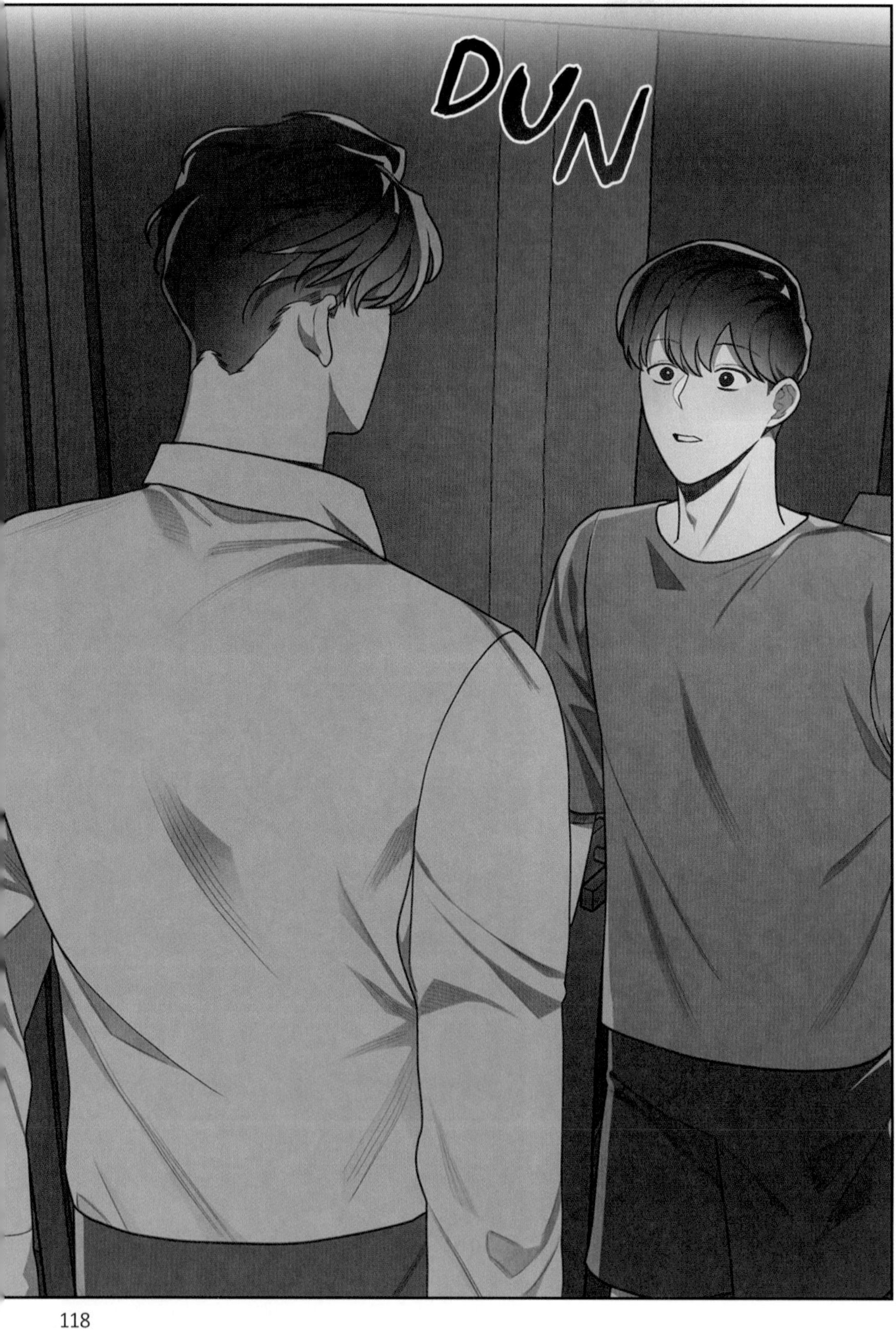
DUN

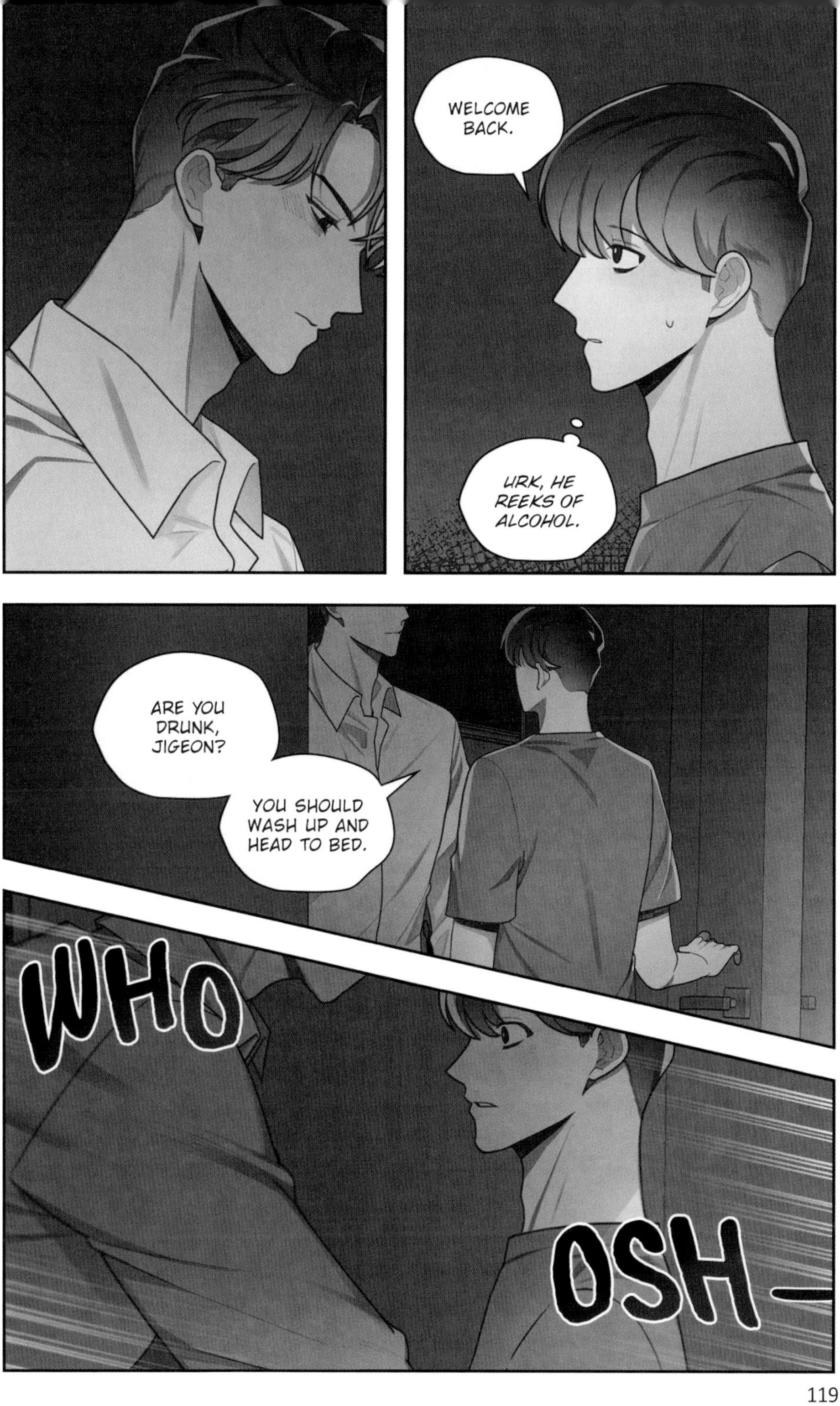
WELCOME BACK.
URK, HE REEKS OF ALCOHOL.
ARE YOU DRUNK, JIGEON?
YOU SHOULD WASH UP AND HEAD TO BED.
WHO
OSH-

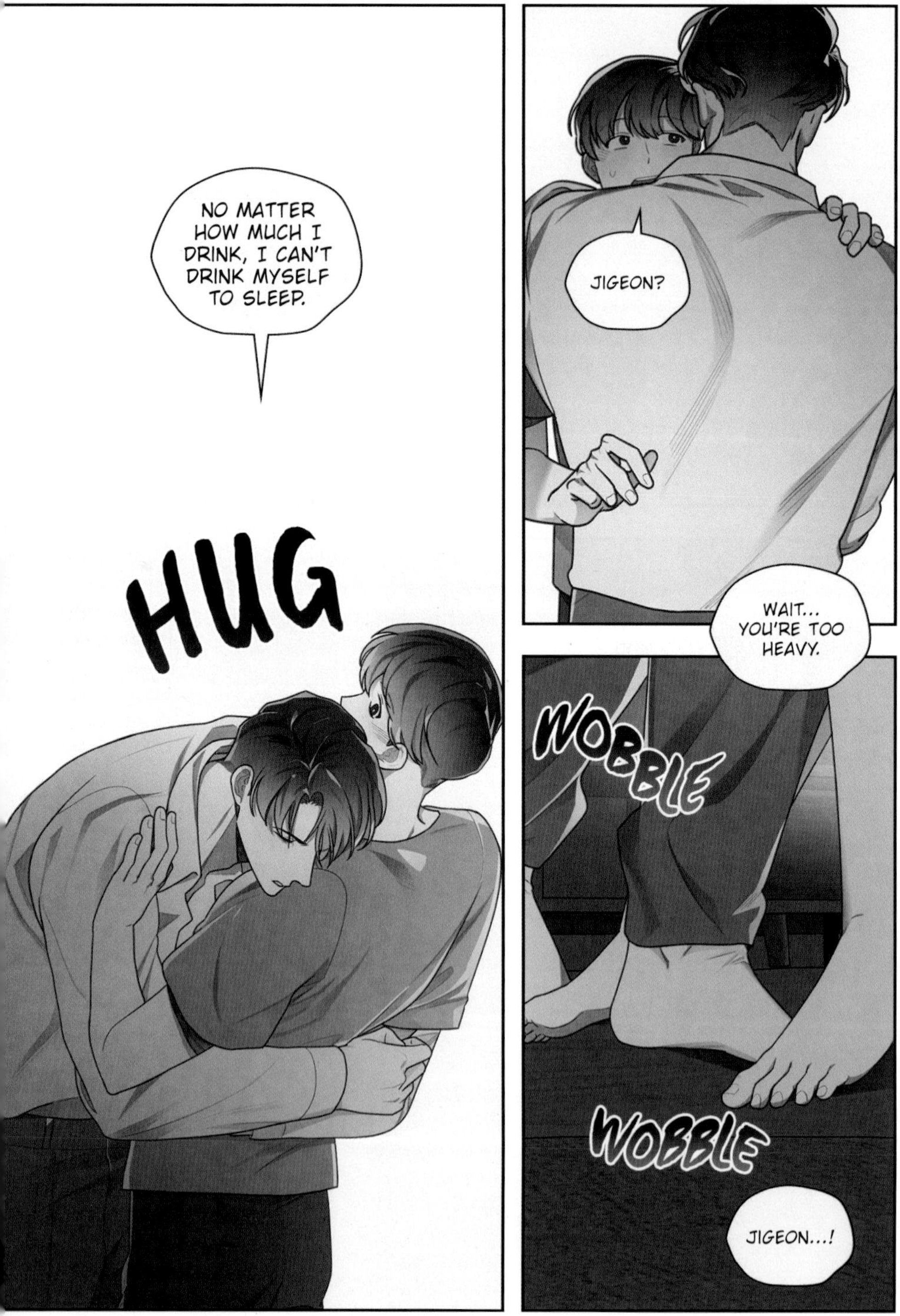
NO MATTER HOW MUCH I DRINK, I CAN'T DRINK MYSELF TO SLEEP.
HUG
JIGEON?
WAIT... YOU'RE TOO HEAVY.
WOBBLE
WOBBLE
JIGEON...!

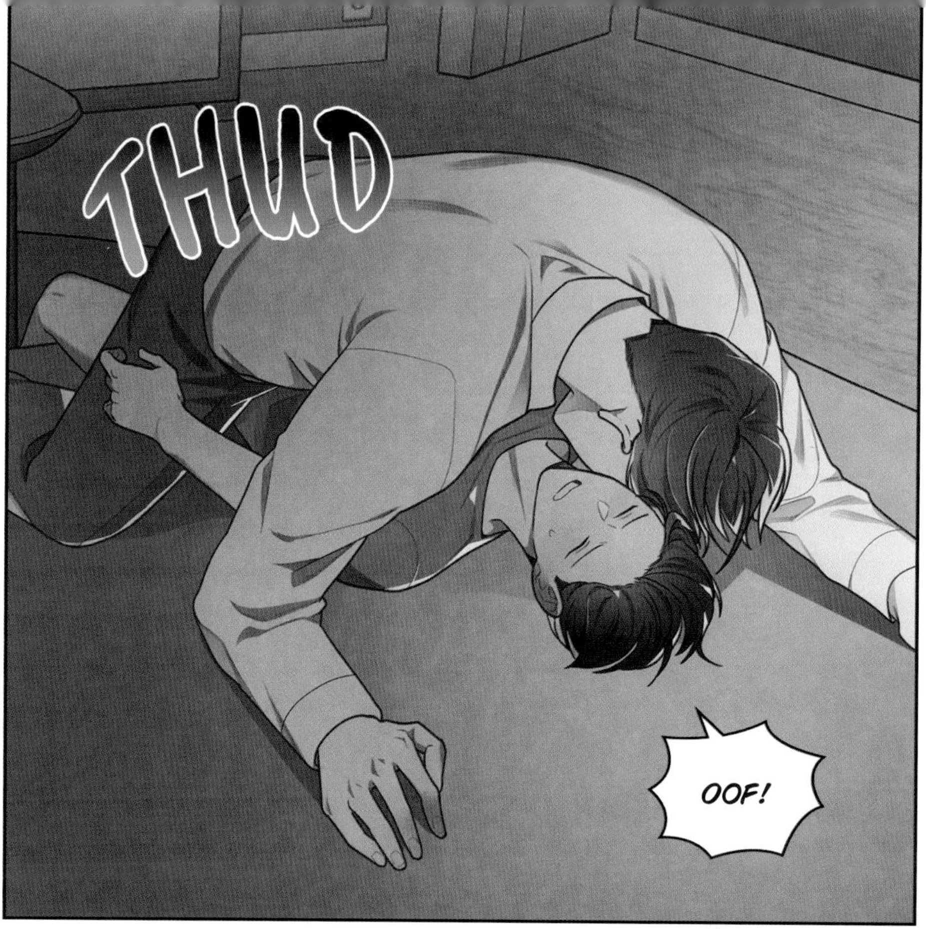
THUD
OOF!

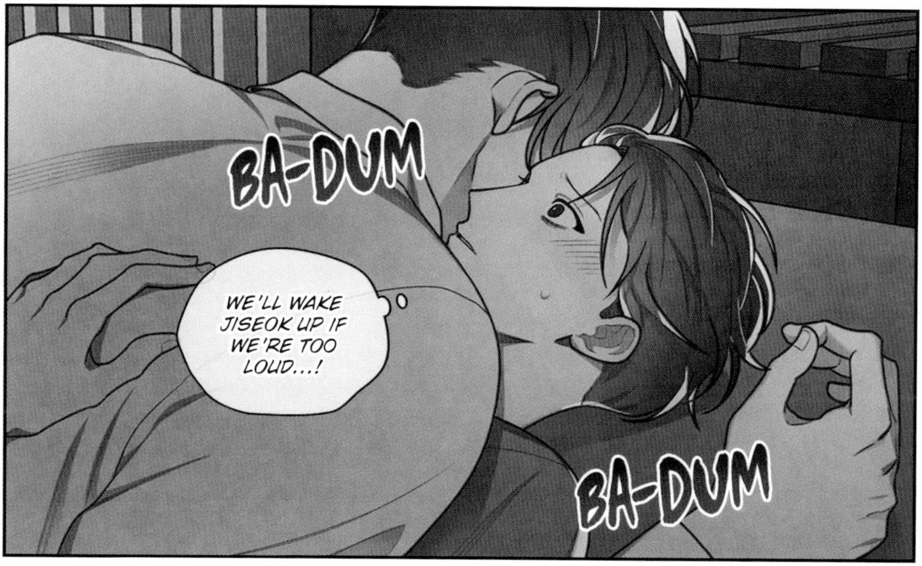
BA-DUM
WE'LL WAKE JISEOK UP IF WE'RE TOO LOUD...!
BA-DUM

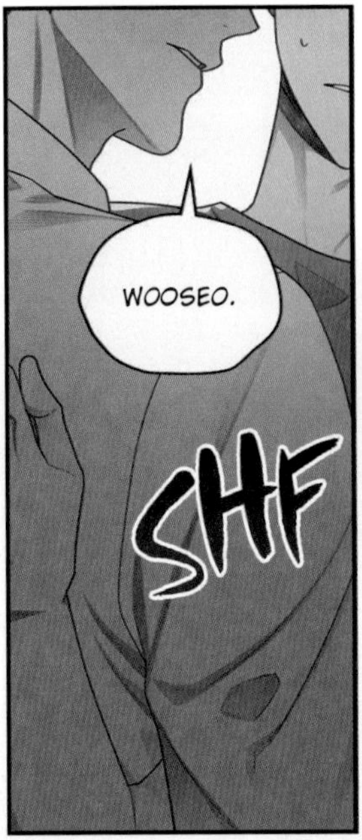
WOOSEO.
SHF
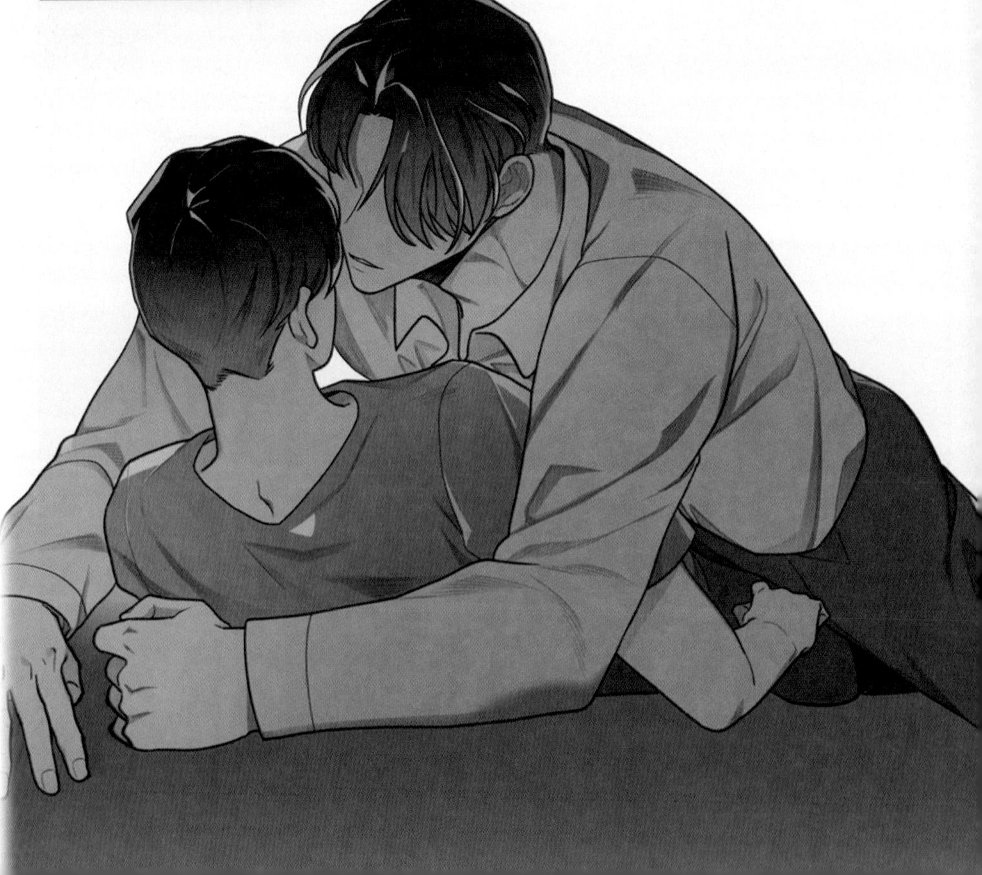
LET'S SLEEP TOGETHER.

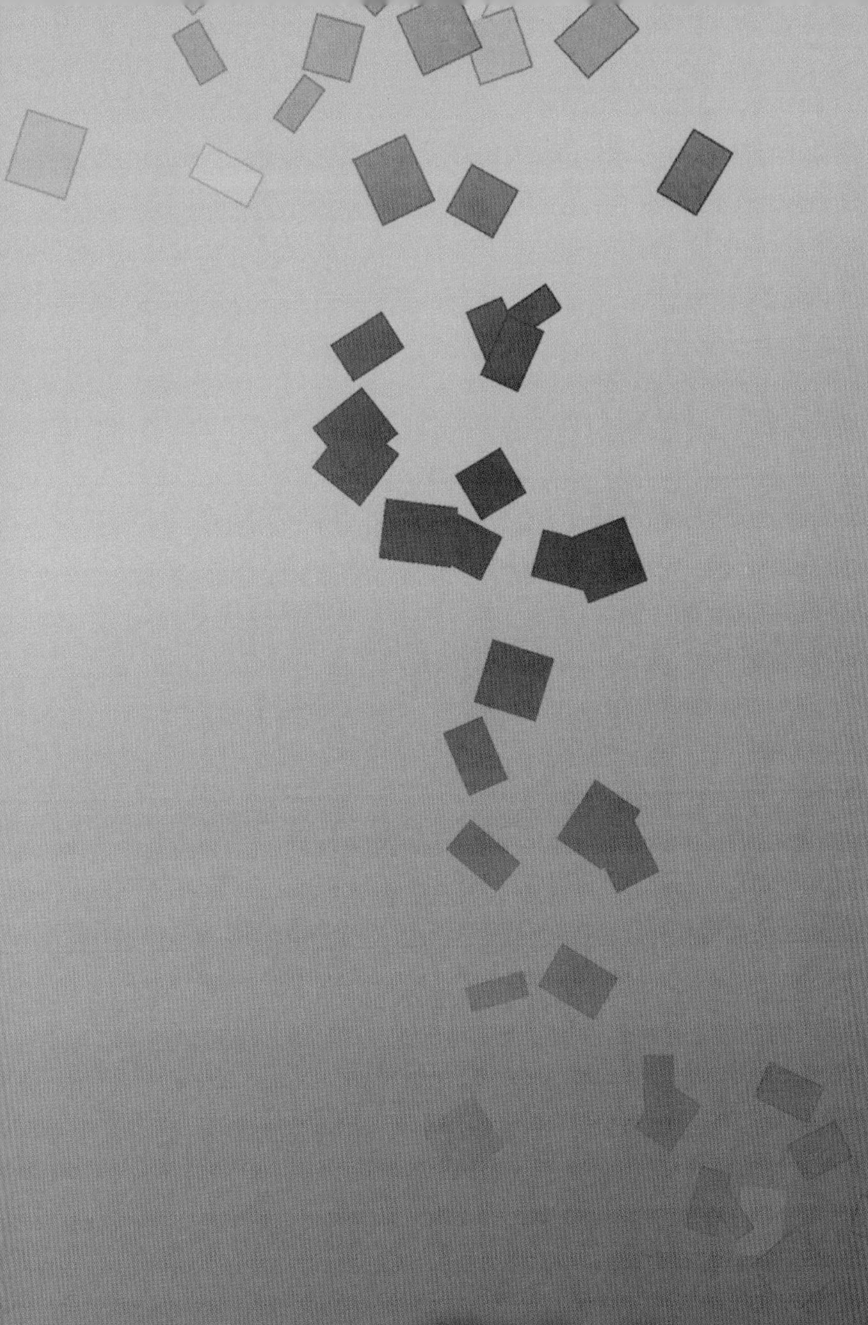

Tied to You

Chapter 7

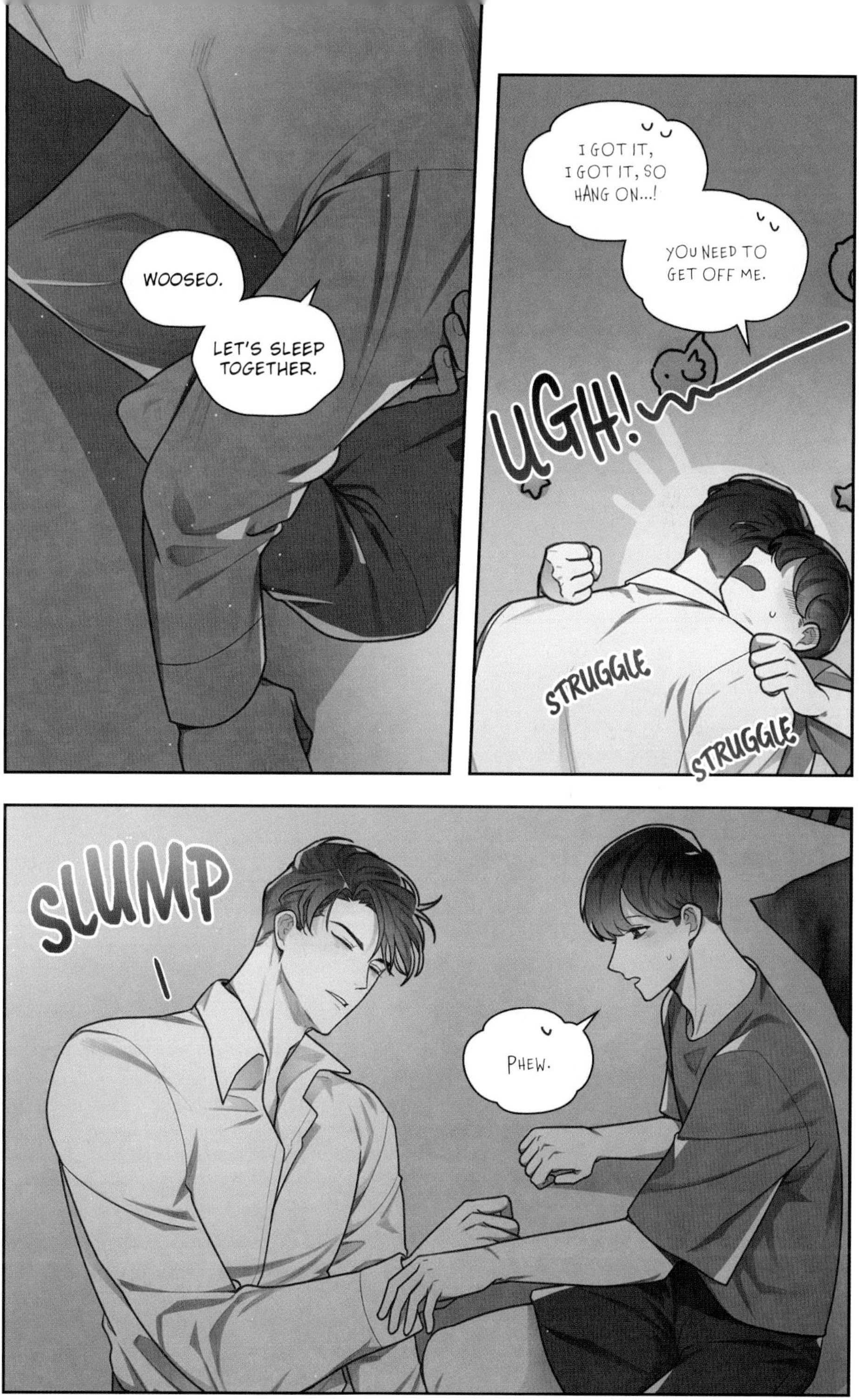
WOOSEO.
LET'S SLEEP TOGETHER.
I GOT IT, I GOT IT, SO HANG ON...!
YOU NEED TO GET OFF ME.
UGH!
STRUGGLE
STRUGGLE
SLUMP
PHEW.

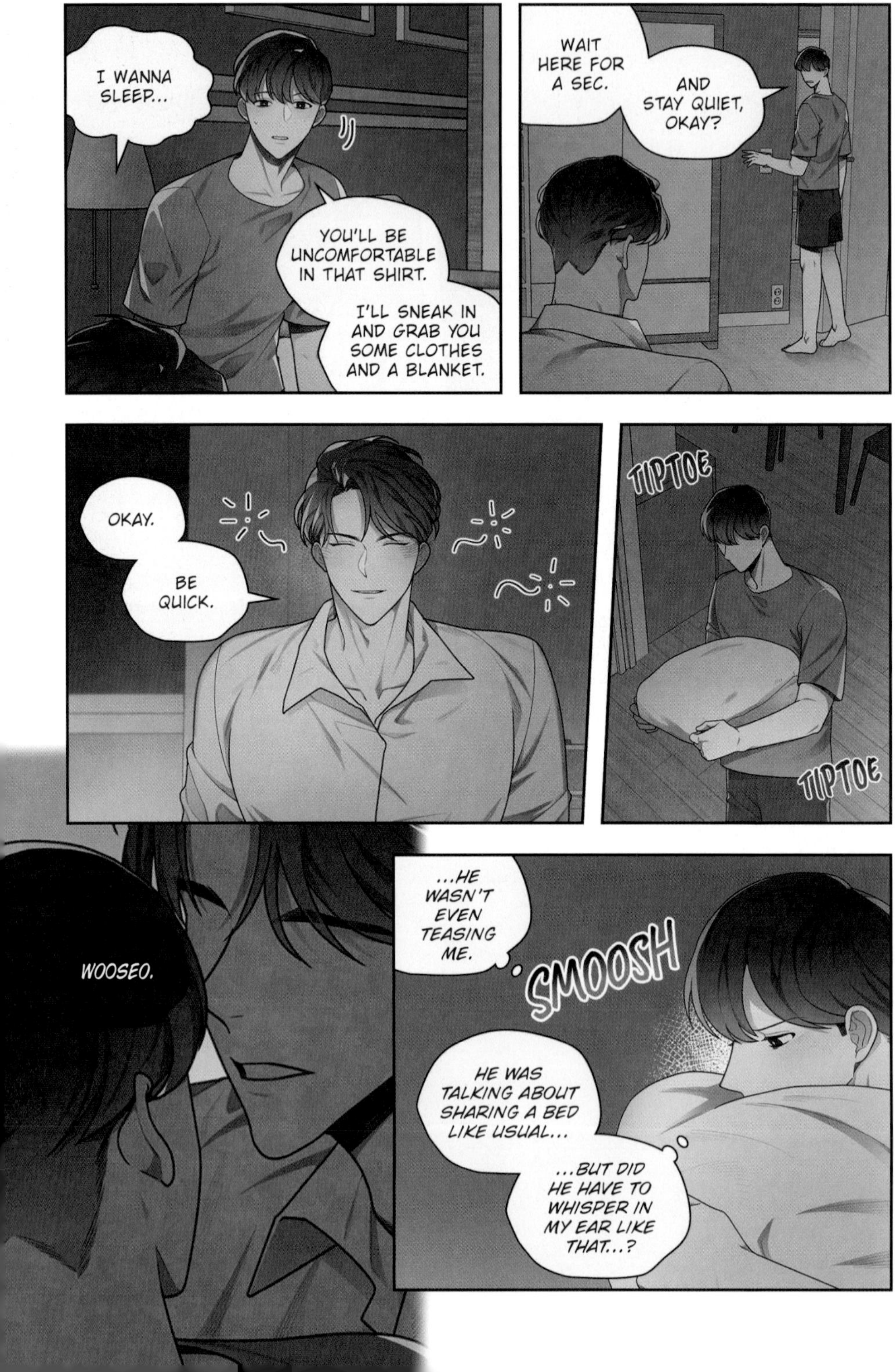
I WANNA SLEEP...
YOU'LL BE UNCOMFORTABLE IN THAT SHIRT.
I'LL SNEAK IN AND GRAB YOU SOME CLOTHES AND A BLANKET.
WAIT HERE FOR A SEC.
AND STAY QUIET, OKAY?
OKAY.
BE QUICK.
TIPTOE
TIPTOE
WOOSEO.
...HE WASN'T EVEN TEASING ME.
SMOOSH
HE WAS TALKING ABOUT SHARING A BED LIKE USUAL...
...BUT DID HE HAVE TO WHISPER IN MY EAR LIKE THAT...?

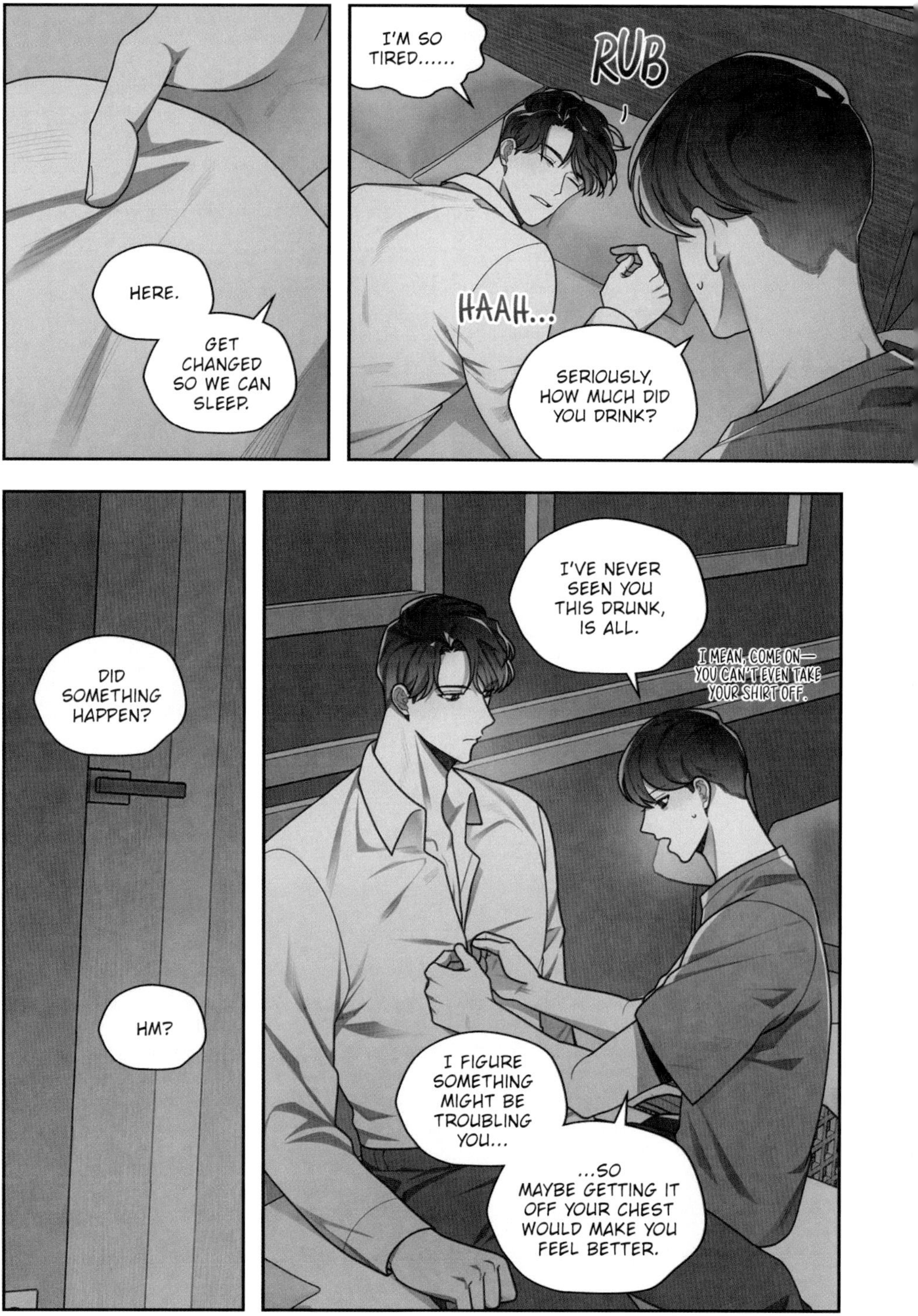
HERE.
GET CHANGED SO WE CAN SLEEP.
I'M SO TIRED......
RUB
HAAH...
SERIOUSLY, HOW MUCH DID YOU DRINK?
DID SOMETHING HAPPEN?
HM?
I'VE NEVER SEEN YOU THIS DRUNK, IS ALL.
I MEAN, COME ON— YOU CAN'T EVEN TAKE YOUR SHIRT OFF.
I FIGURE SOMETHING MIGHT BE TROUBLING YOU...
...SO MAYBE GETTING IT OFF YOUR CHEST WOULD MAKE YOU FEEL BETTER.

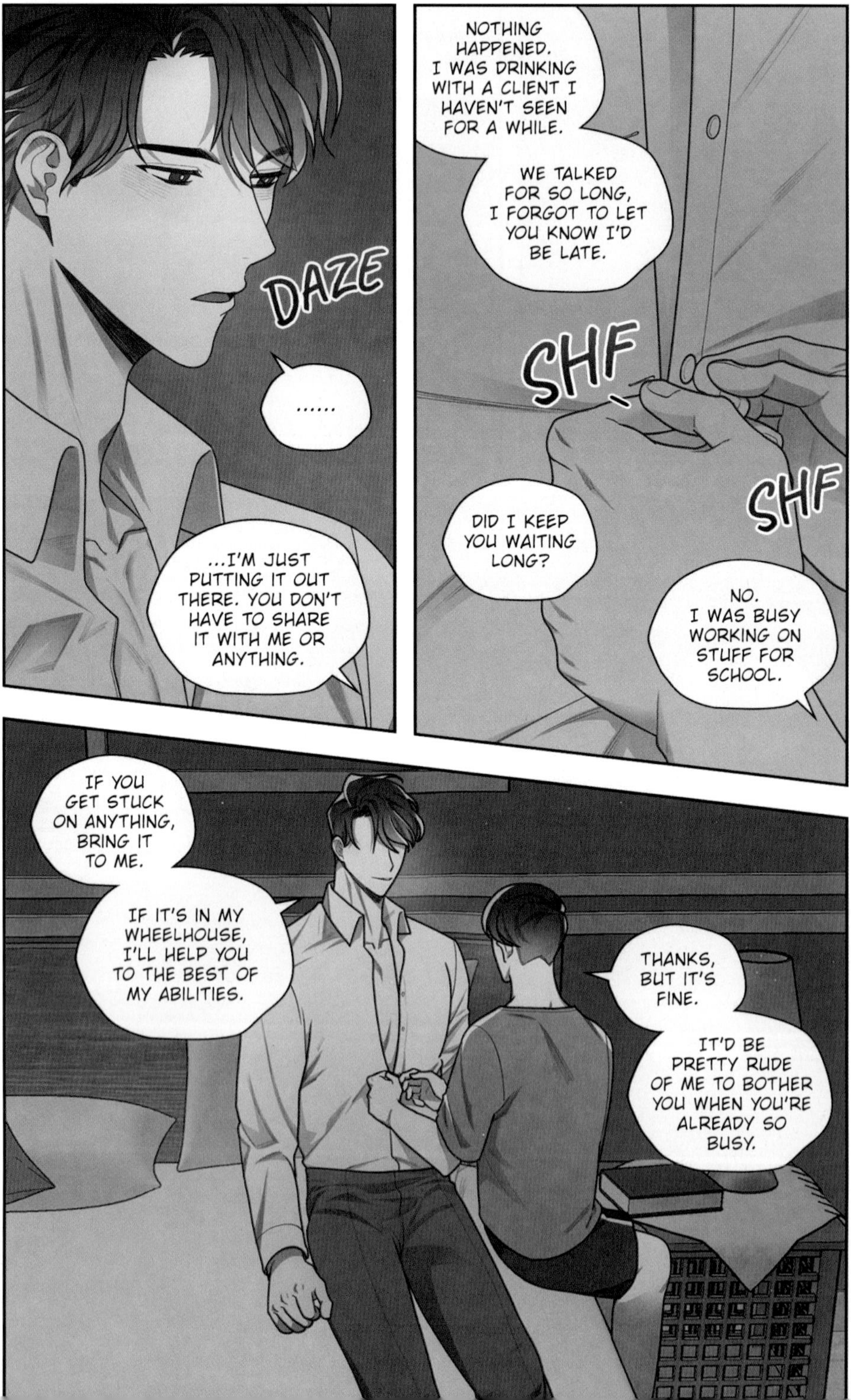
DAZE
......
...I'M JUST PUTTING IT OUT THERE. YOU DON'T HAVE TO SHARE IT WITH ME OR ANYTHING.
NOTHING HAPPENED. I WAS DRINKING WITH A CLIENT I HAVEN'T SEEN FOR A WHILE.
WE TALKED FOR SO LONG, I FORGOT TO LET YOU KNOW I'D BE LATE.
SHF
SHF
DID I KEEP YOU WAITING LONG?
NO. I WAS BUSY WORKING ON STUFF FOR SCHOOL.
IF YOU GET STUCK ON ANYTHING, BRING IT TO ME.
IF IT'S IN MY WHEELHOUSE, I'LL HELP YOU TO THE BEST OF MY ABILITIES.
THANKS, BUT IT'S FINE.
IT'D BE PRETTY RUDE OF ME TO BOTHER YOU WHEN YOU'RE ALREADY SO BUSY.

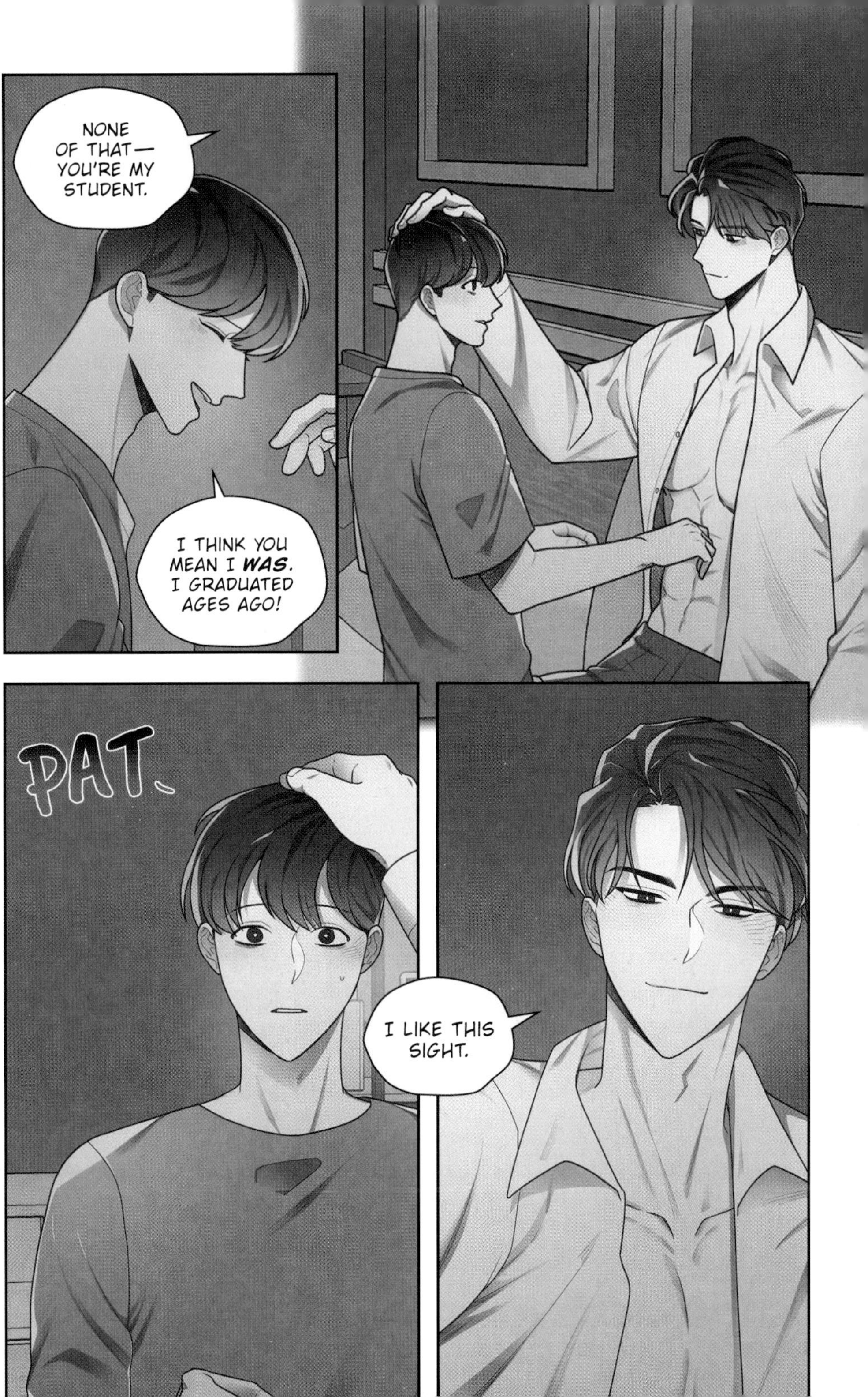
NONE OF THAT— YOU'RE MY STUDENT.
I THINK YOU MEAN I ***WAS***. I GRADUATED AGES AGO!
PAT.
I LIKE THIS SIGHT.

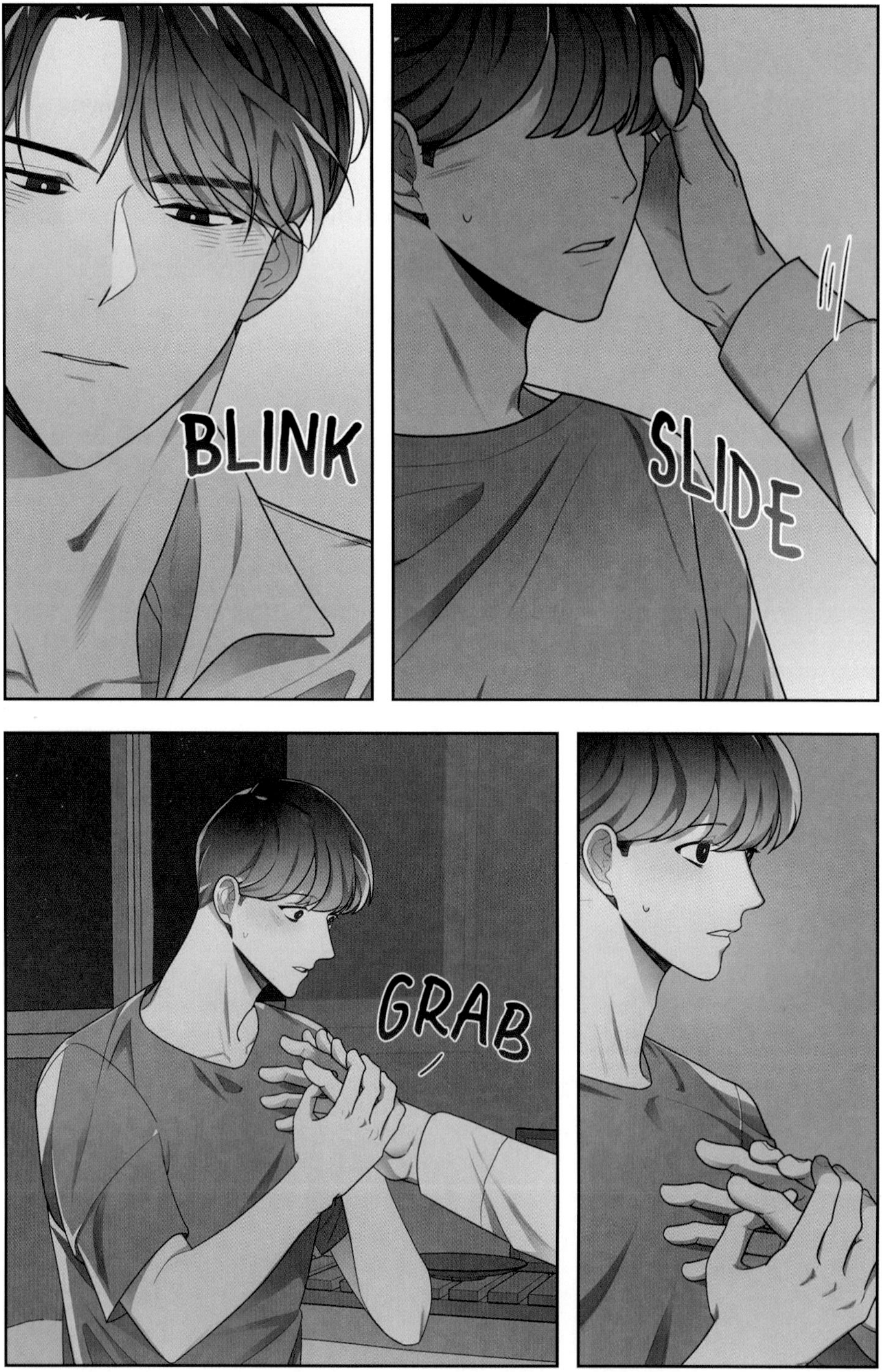
BLINK
SLIDE
GRAB

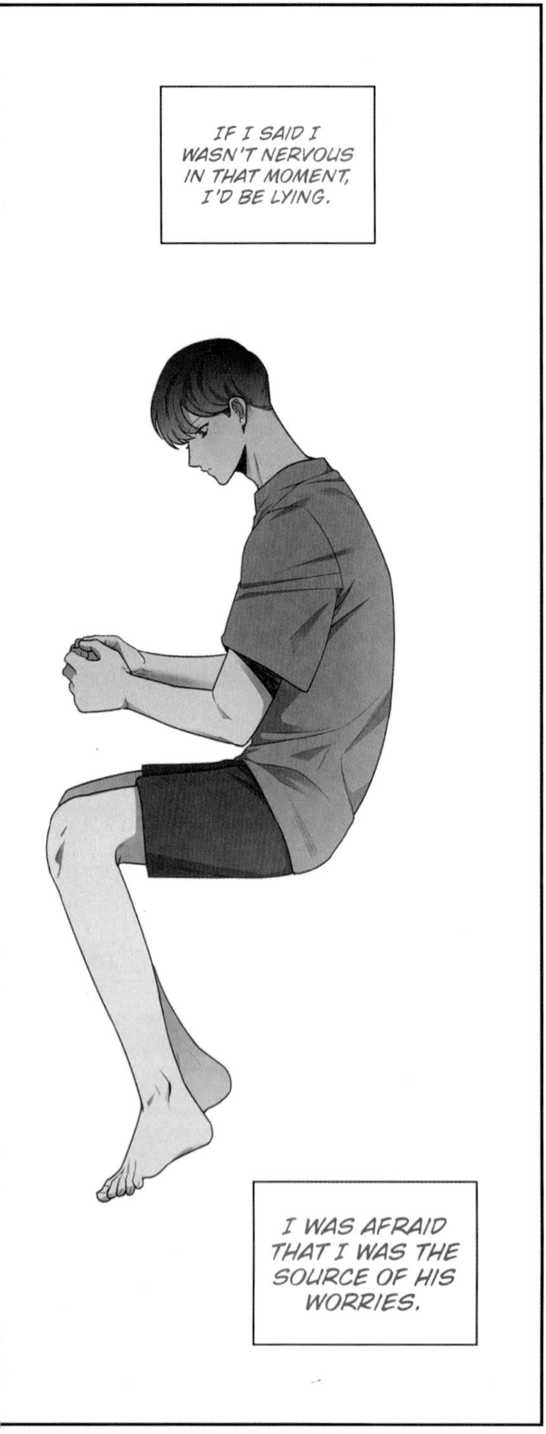
IF I SAID I WASN'T NERVOUS IN THAT MOMENT, I'D BE LYING.
I WAS AFRAID THAT I WAS THE SOURCE OF HIS WORRIES.
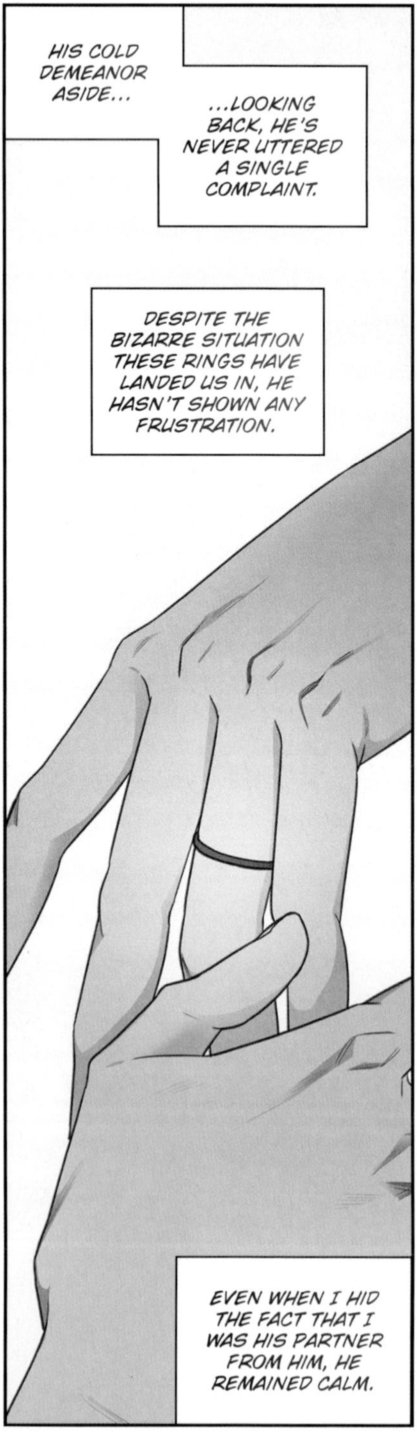
HIS COLD DEMEANOR ASIDE...
...LOOKING BACK, HE'S NEVER UTTERED A SINGLE COMPLAINT.
DESPITE THE BIZARRE SITUATION THESE RINGS HAVE LANDED US IN, HE HASN'T SHOWN ANY FRUSTRATION.
EVEN WHEN I HID THE FACT THAT I WAS HIS PARTNER FROM HIM, HE REMAINED CALM.

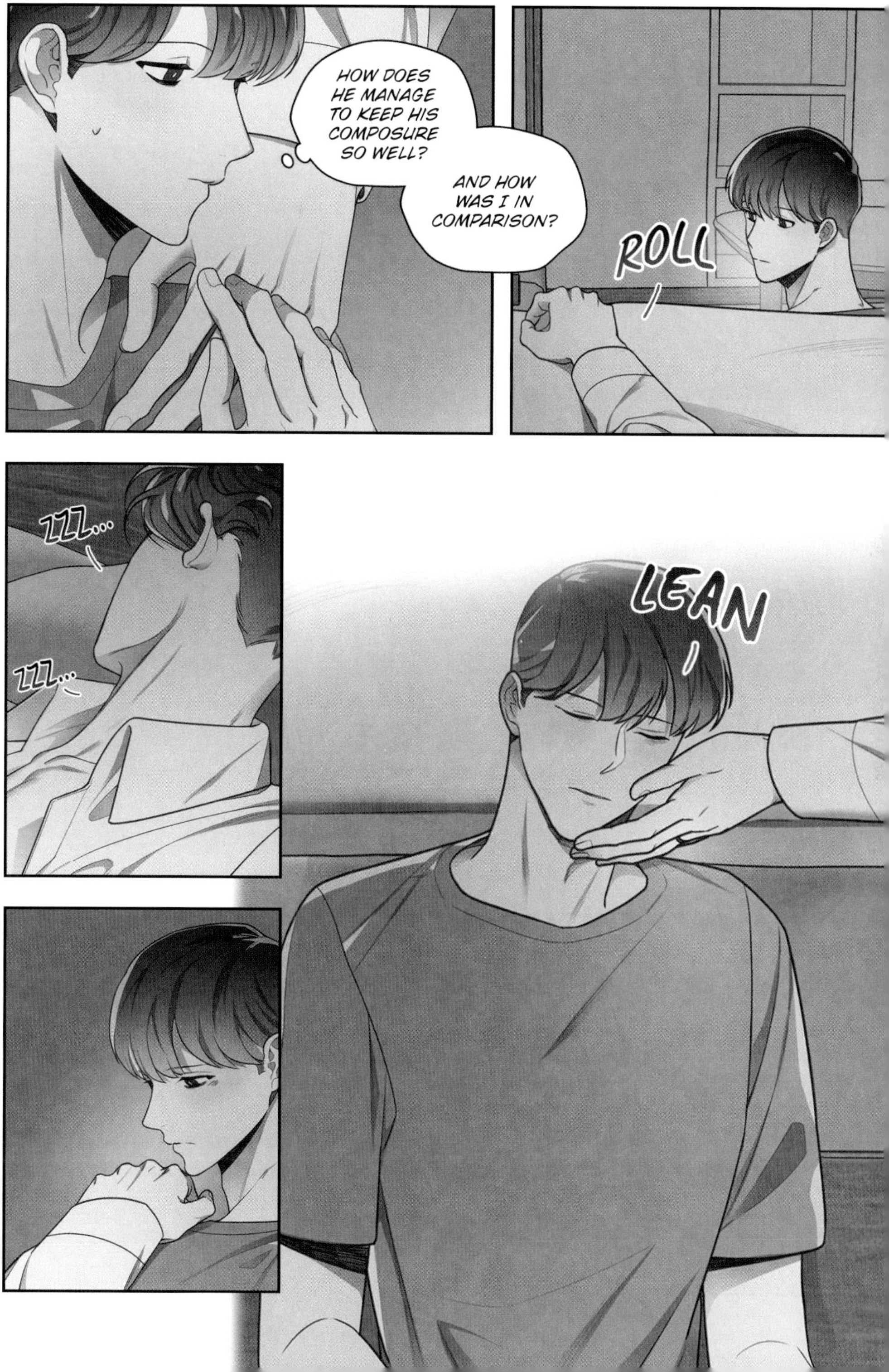
HOW DOES HE MANAGE TO KEEP HIS COMPOSURE SO WELL?
AND HOW WAS I IN COMPARISON?
ROLL
ZZZ...
ZZZ...
LEAN

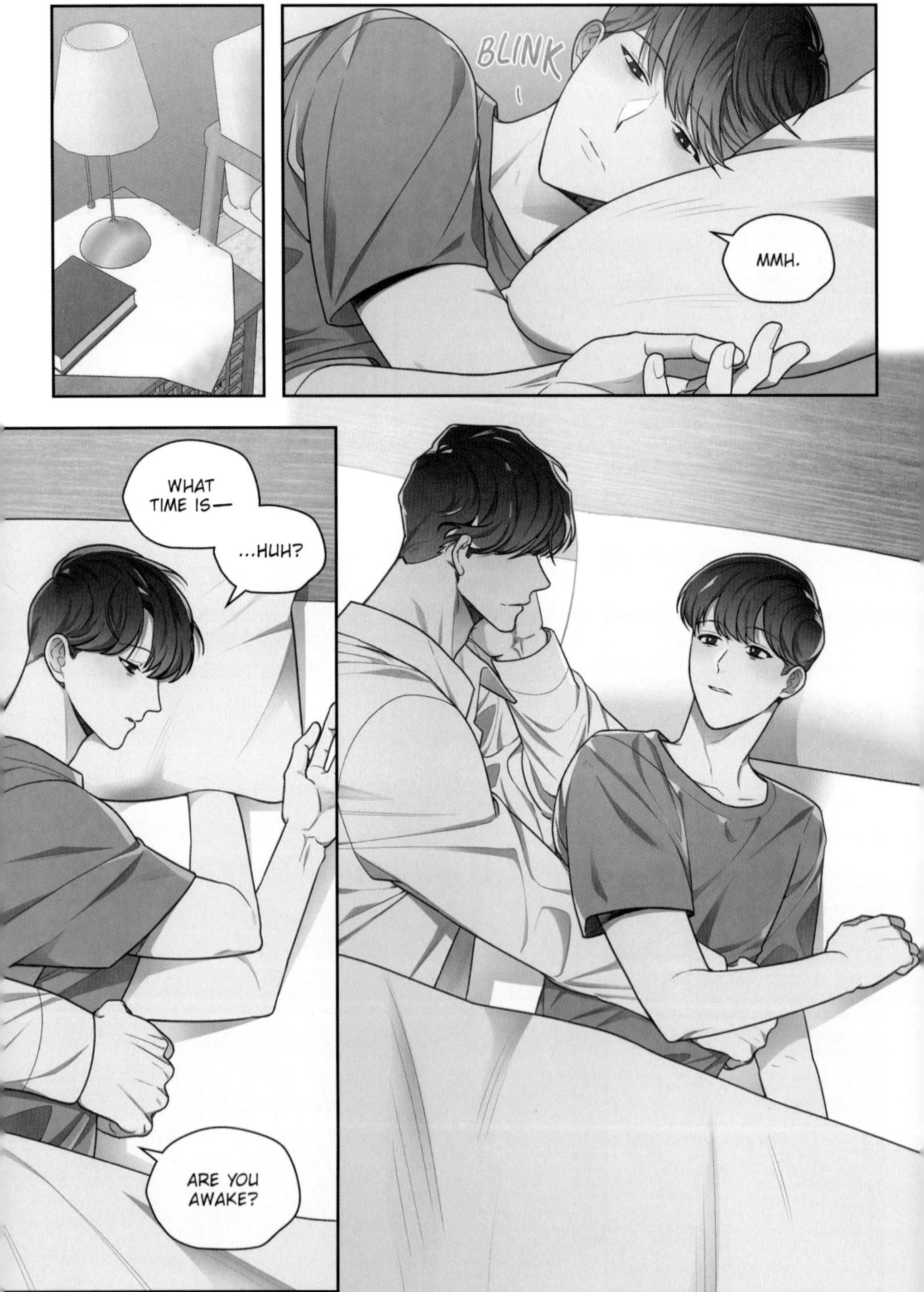
BLINK
MMH.
WHAT TIME IS—
...HUH?
ARE YOU AWAKE?

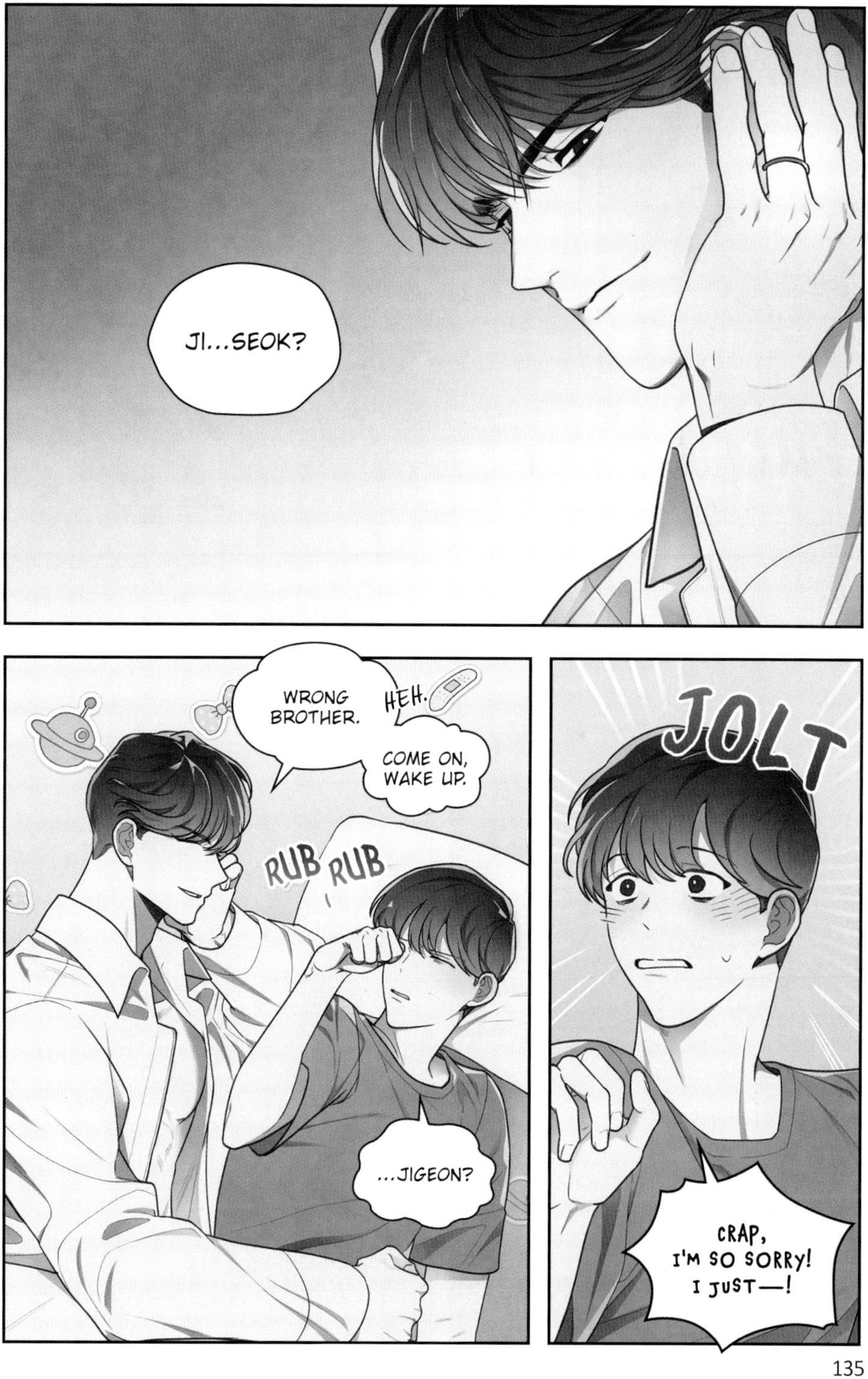
JI...SEOK?
WRONG BROTHER.
HEH.
COME ON, WAKE UP.
RUB RUB
...JIGEON?
JOLT
CRAP, I'M SO SORRY! I JUST—!

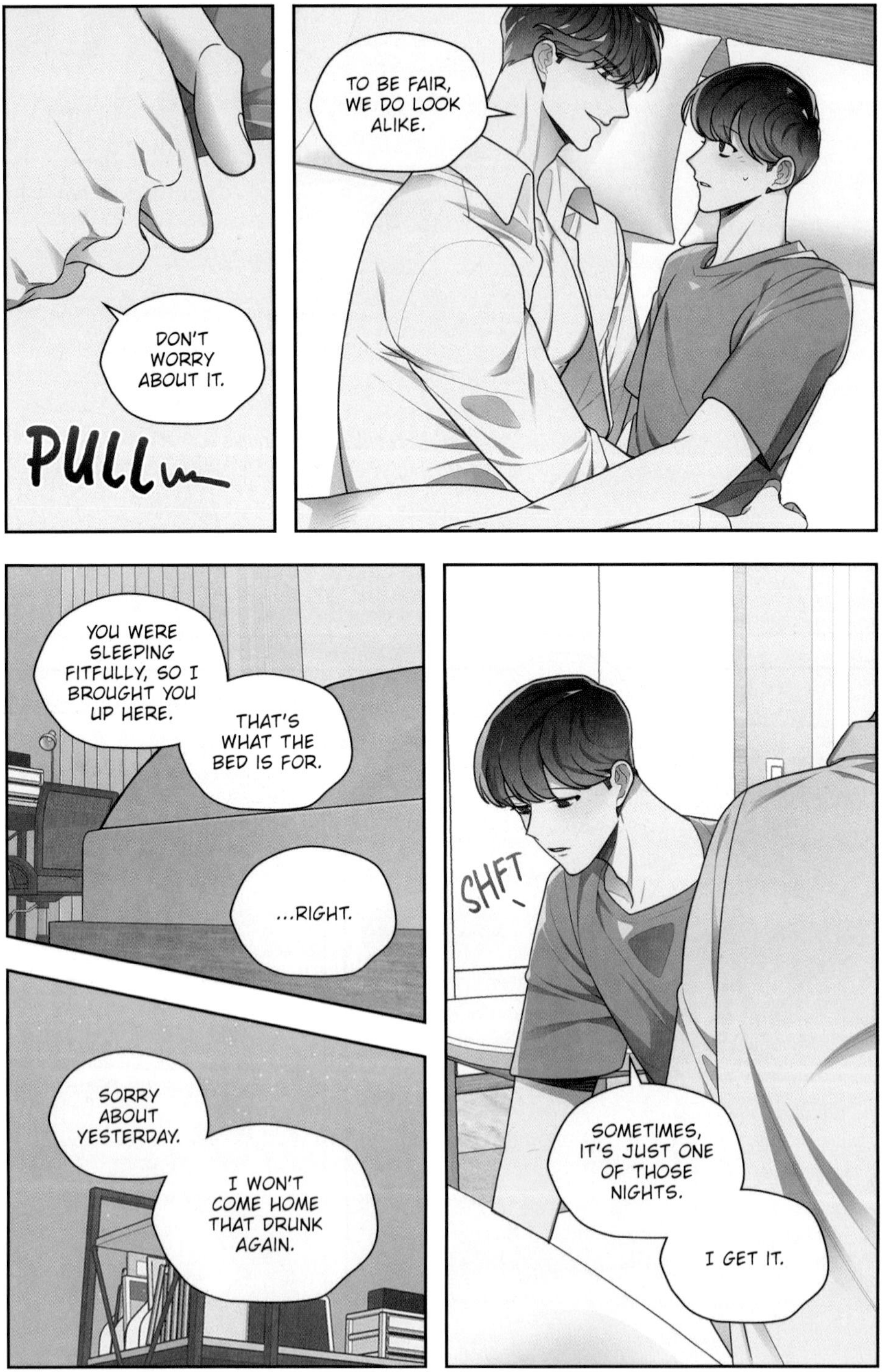
DON'T WORRY ABOUT IT.
PULL
TO BE FAIR, WE DO LOOK ALIKE.
YOU WERE SLEEPING FITFULLY, SO I BROUGHT YOU UP HERE.
THAT'S WHAT THE BED IS FOR.
...RIGHT.
SHFT
SORRY ABOUT YESTERDAY.
I WON'T COME HOME THAT DRUNK AGAIN.
SOMETIMES, IT'S JUST ONE OF THOSE NIGHTS.
I GET IT.

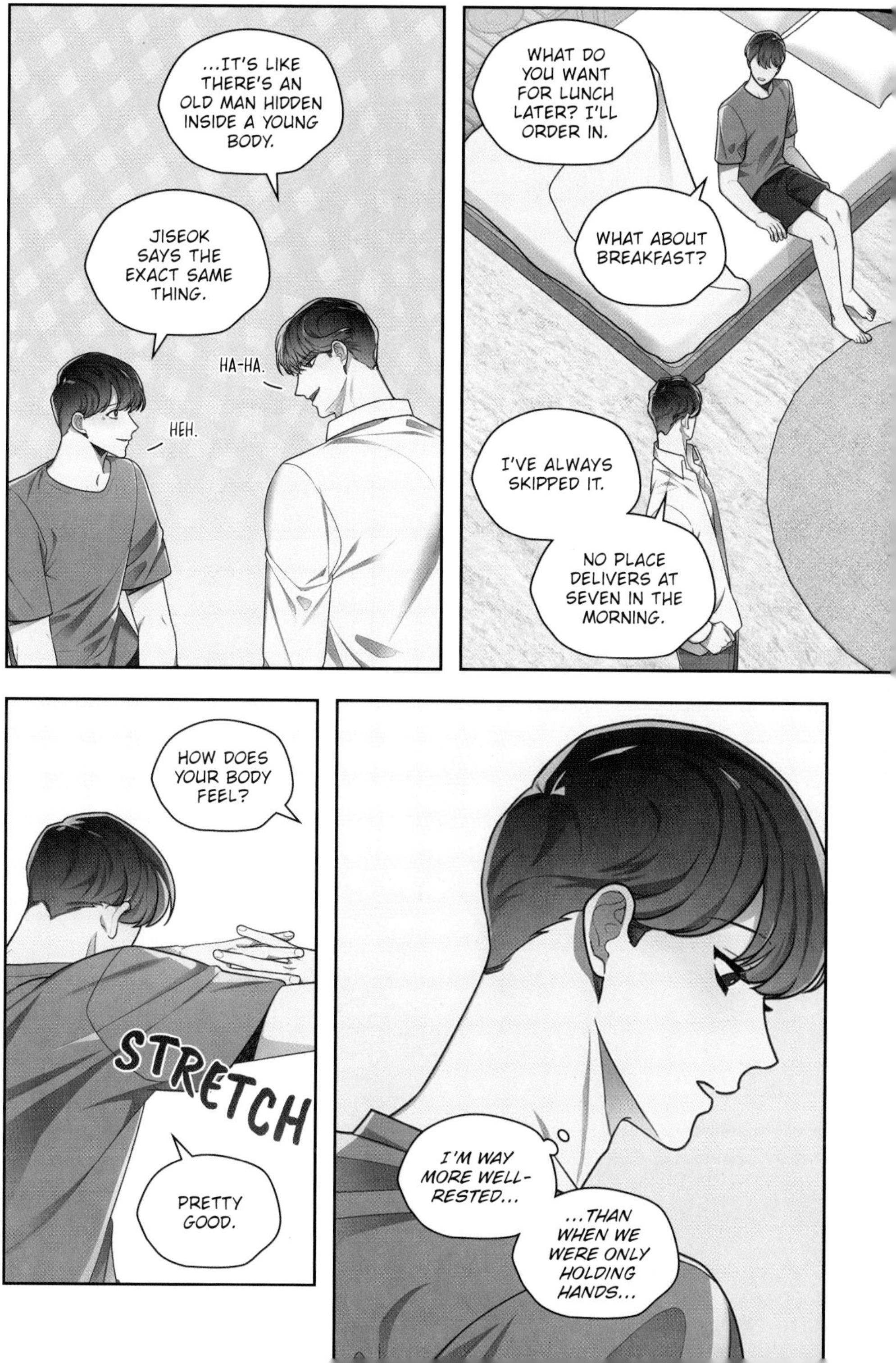
...IT'S LIKE THERE'S AN OLD MAN HIDDEN INSIDE A YOUNG BODY.
JISEOK SAYS THE EXACT SAME THING.
HA-HA.
HEH.
WHAT DO YOU WANT FOR LUNCH LATER? I'LL ORDER IN.
WHAT ABOUT BREAKFAST?
I'VE ALWAYS SKIPPED IT.
NO PLACE DELIVERS AT SEVEN IN THE MORNING.
HOW DOES YOUR BODY FEEL?
STRETCH
PRETTY GOOD.
I'M WAY MORE WELL-RESTED...
...THAN WHEN WE WERE ONLY HOLDING HANDS...

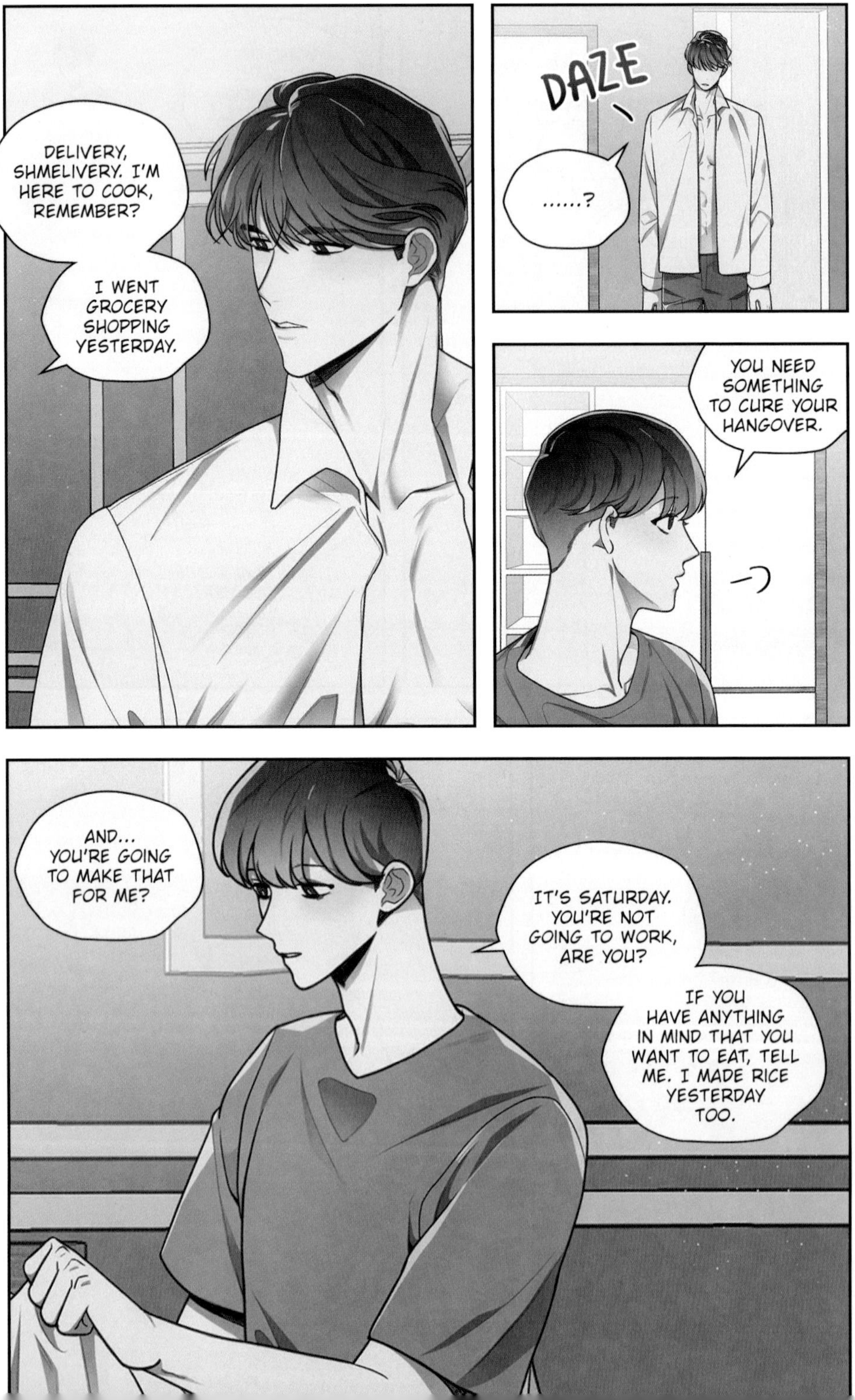
DELIVERY, SHMELIVERY. I'M HERE TO COOK, REMEMBER?
I WENT GROCERY SHOPPING YESTERDAY.
DAZE
......?
YOU NEED SOMETHING TO CURE YOUR HANGOVER.
AND... YOU'RE GOING TO MAKE THAT FOR ME?
IT'S SATURDAY. YOU'RE NOT GOING TO WORK, ARE YOU?
IF YOU HAVE ANYTHING IN MIND THAT YOU WANT TO EAT, TELL ME. I MADE RICE YESTERDAY TOO.

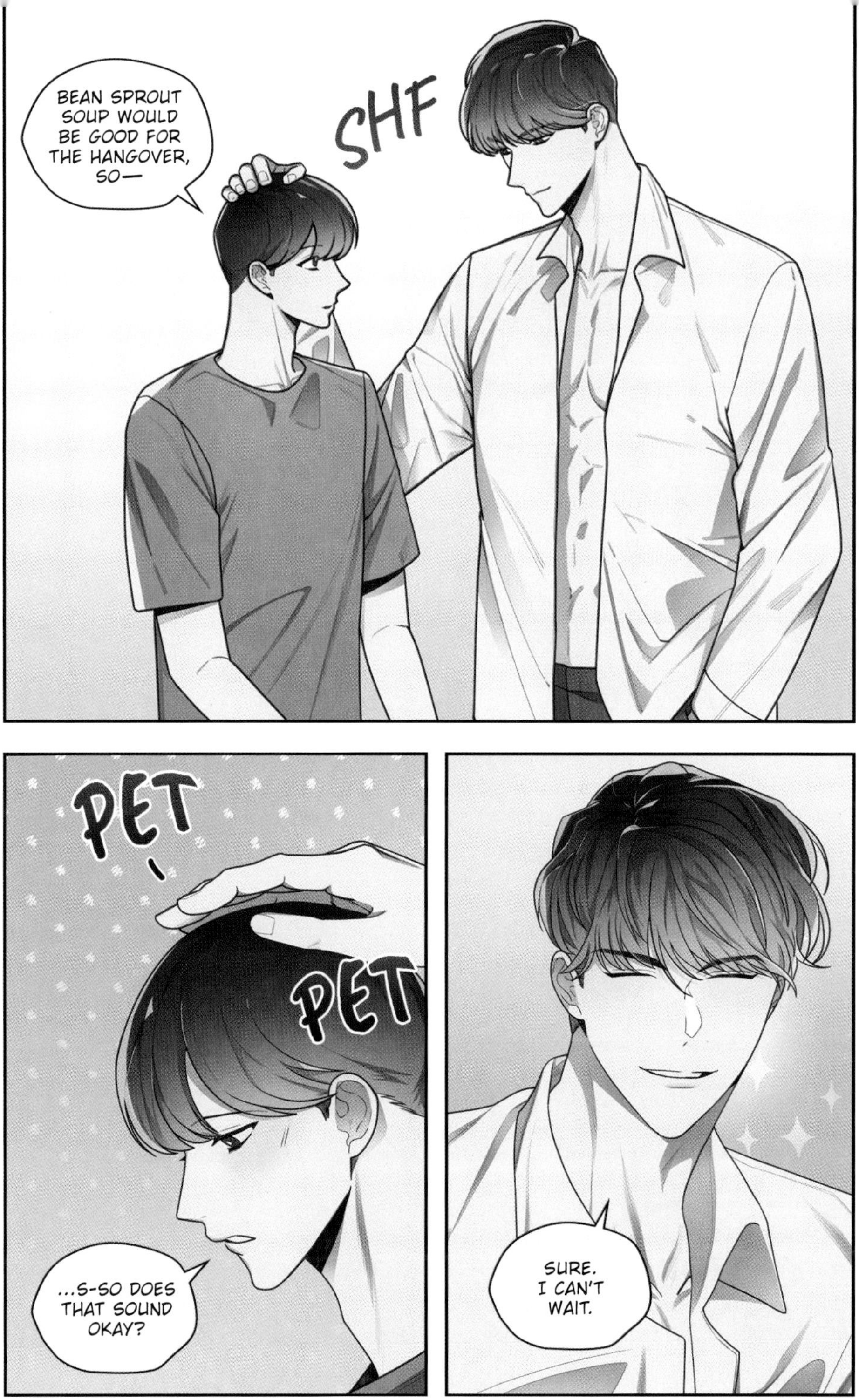
BEAN SPROUT SOUP WOULD BE GOOD FOR THE HANGOVER, SO—
SHF
PET
PET
...S-SO DOES THAT SOUND OKAY?
SURE. I CAN'T WAIT.

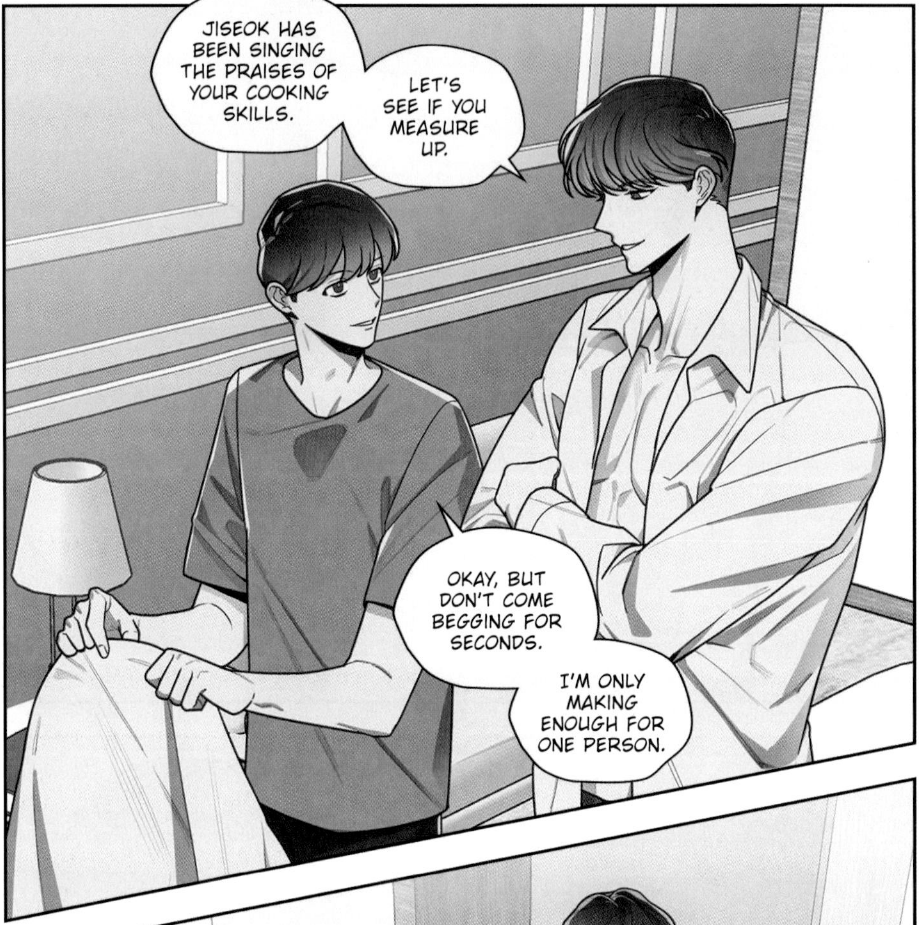
JISEOK HAS BEEN SINGING THE PRAISES OF YOUR COOKING SKILLS.
LET'S SEE IF YOU MEASURE UP.
OKAY, BUT DON'T COME BEGGING FOR SECONDS.
I'M ONLY MAKING ENOUGH FOR ONE PERSON.

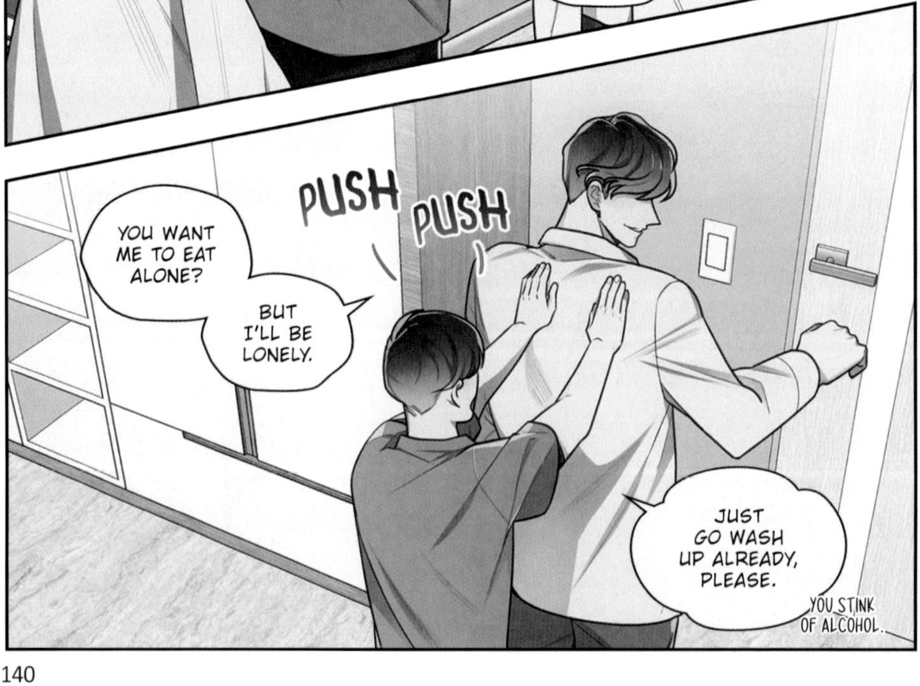
PUSH
PUSH
YOU WANT ME TO EAT ALONE?
BUT I'LL BE LONELY.
JUST GO WASH UP ALREADY, PLEASE.
YOU STINK OF ALCOHOL.

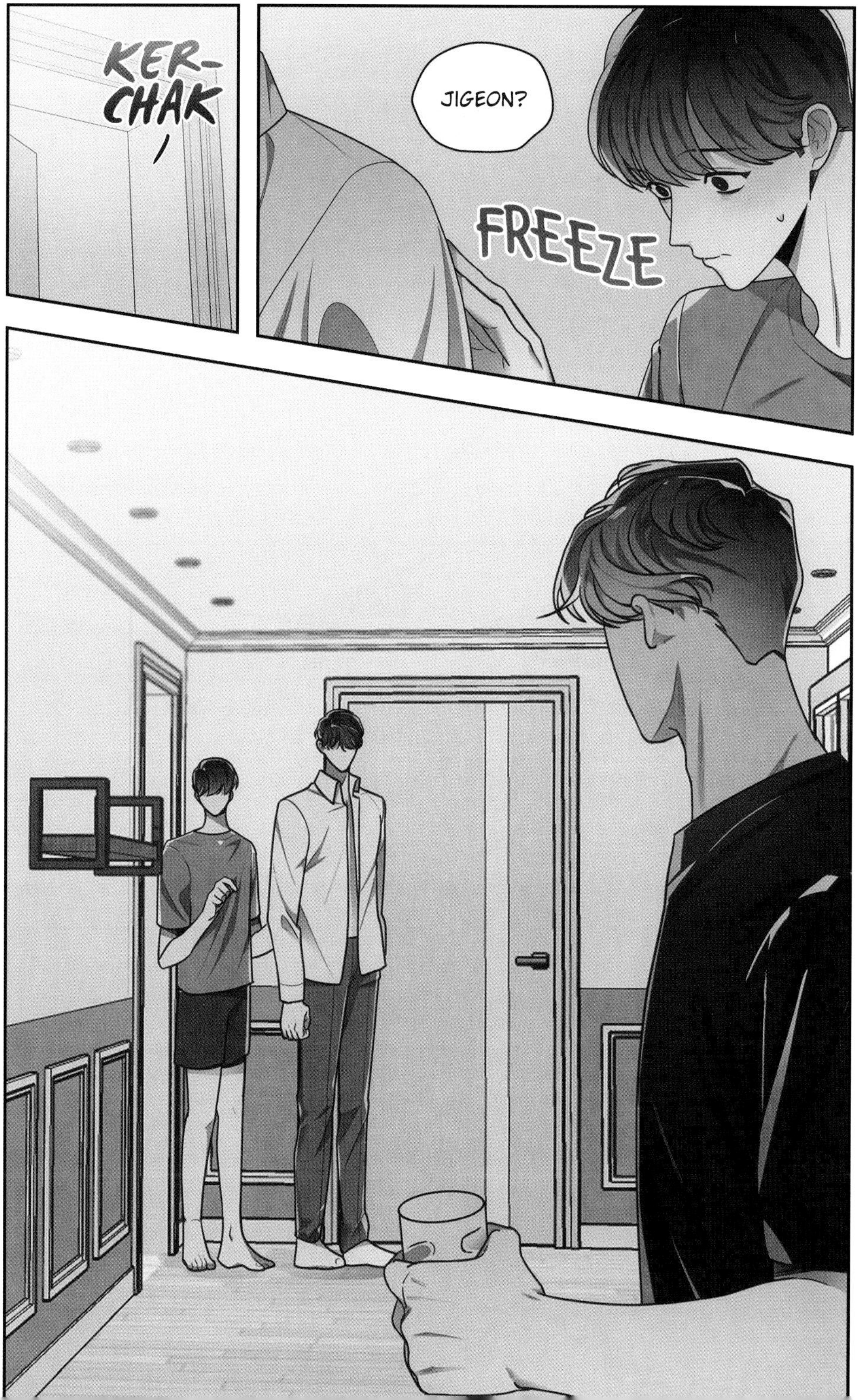
KER-CHAK
JIGEON?
FREEZE

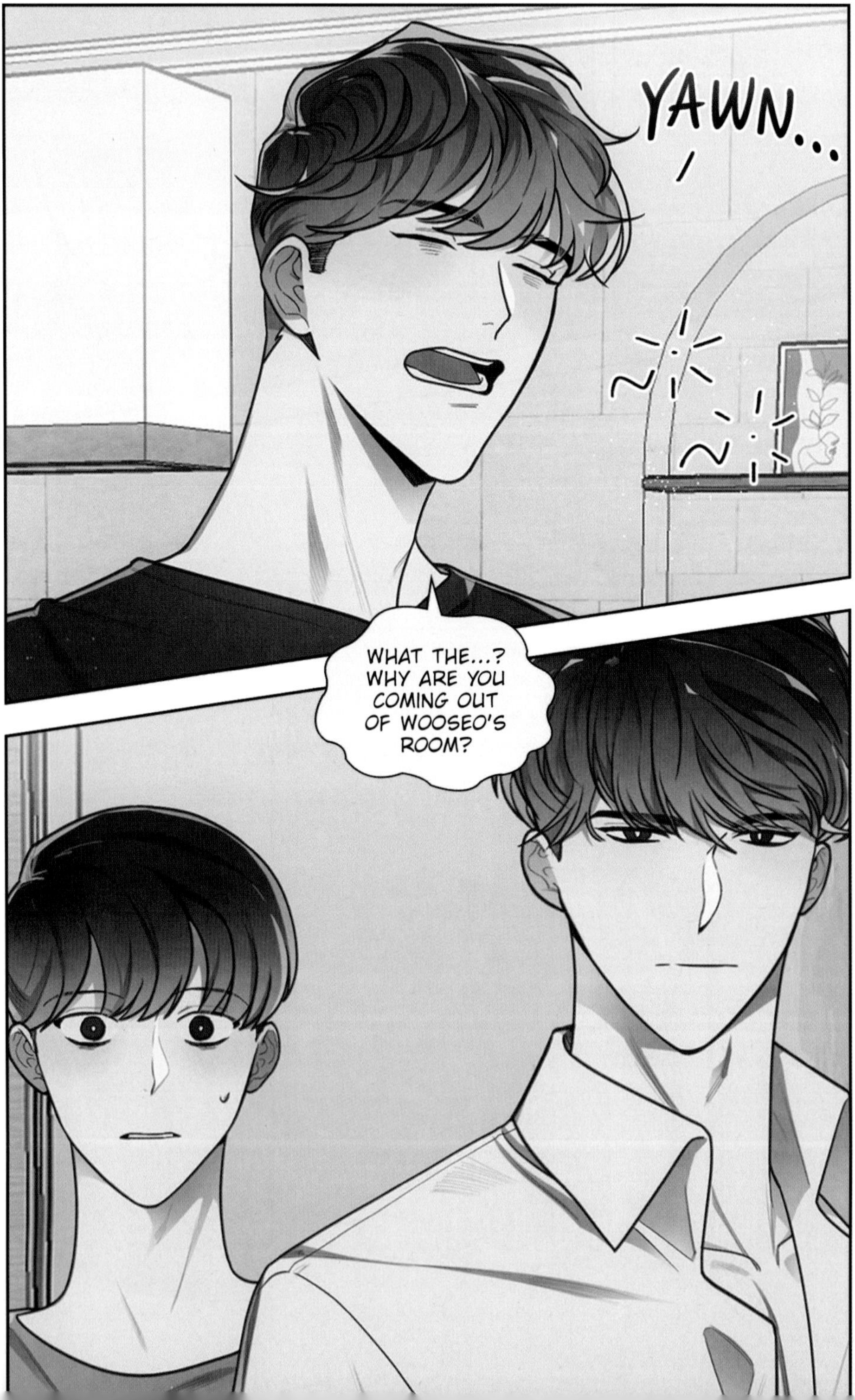
YAWN...
WHAT THE...? WHY ARE YOU COMING OUT OF WOOSEO'S ROOM?

Tied to you

Chapter 8

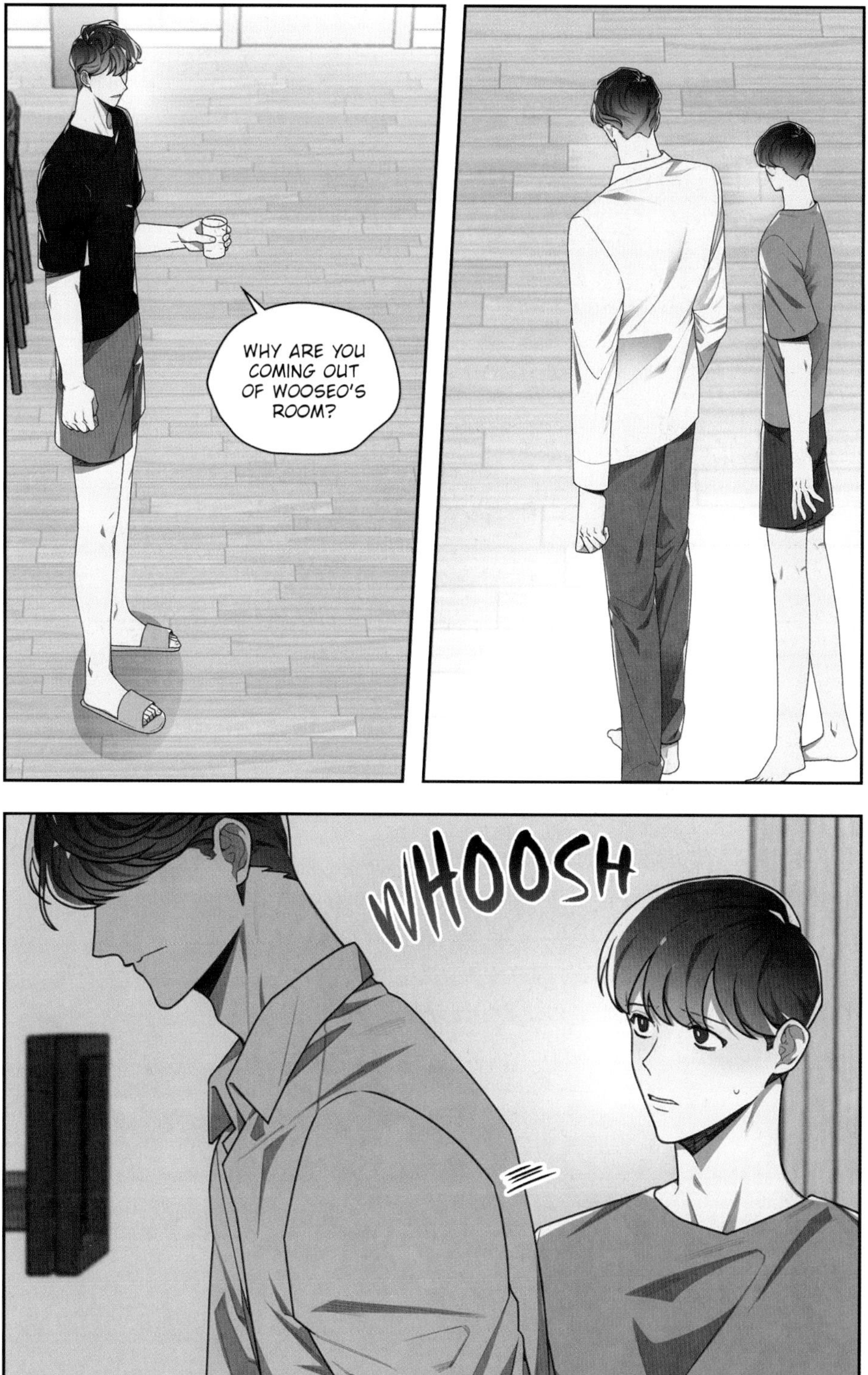
WHY ARE YOU COMING OUT OF WOOSEO'S ROOM?
WHOOSH

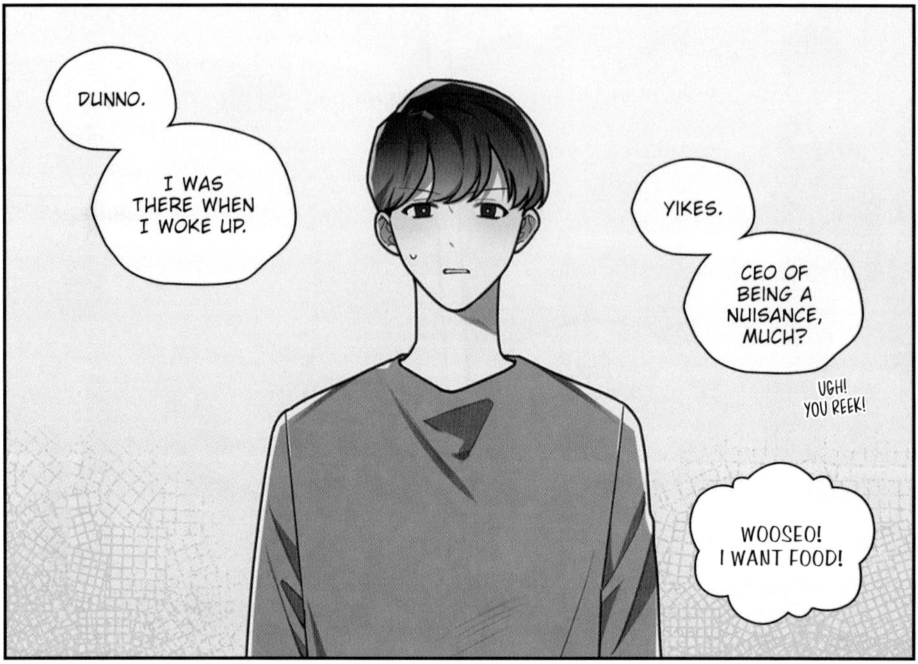
DUNNO.
I WAS THERE WHEN I WOKE UP.
YIKES.
CEO OF BEING A NUISANCE, MUCH?
UGH! YOU REEK!
WOOSEO! I WANT FOOD!

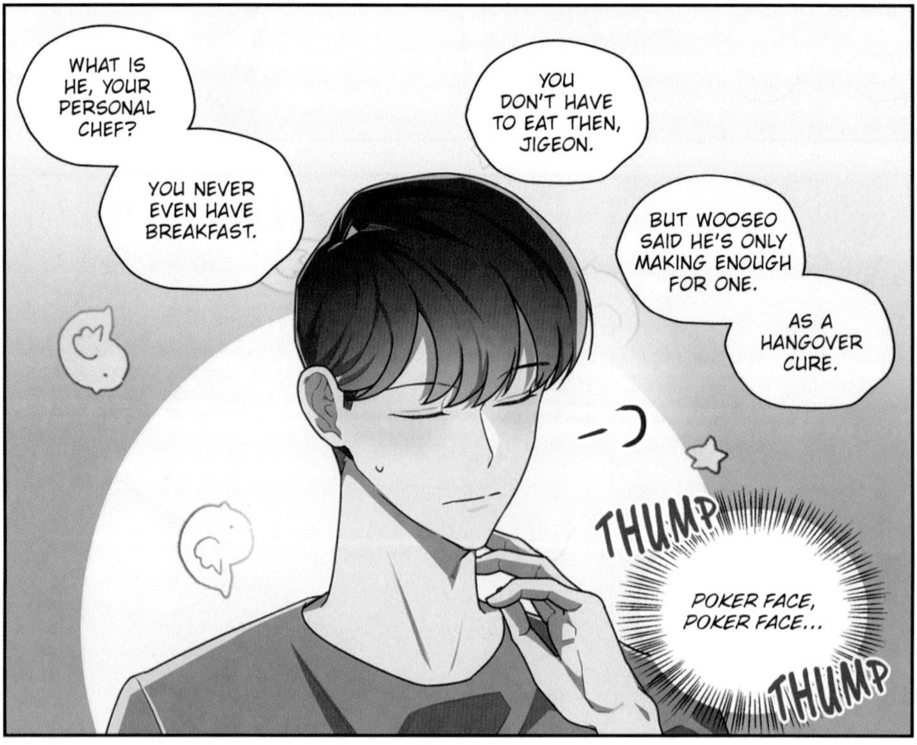
WHAT IS HE, YOUR PERSONAL CHEF?
YOU NEVER EVEN HAVE BREAKFAST.
YOU DON'T HAVE TO EAT THEN, JIGEON.
BUT WOOSEO SAID HE'S ONLY MAKING ENOUGH FOR ONE.
AS A HANGOVER CURE.
THUMP
POKER FACE, POKER FACE...
THUMP

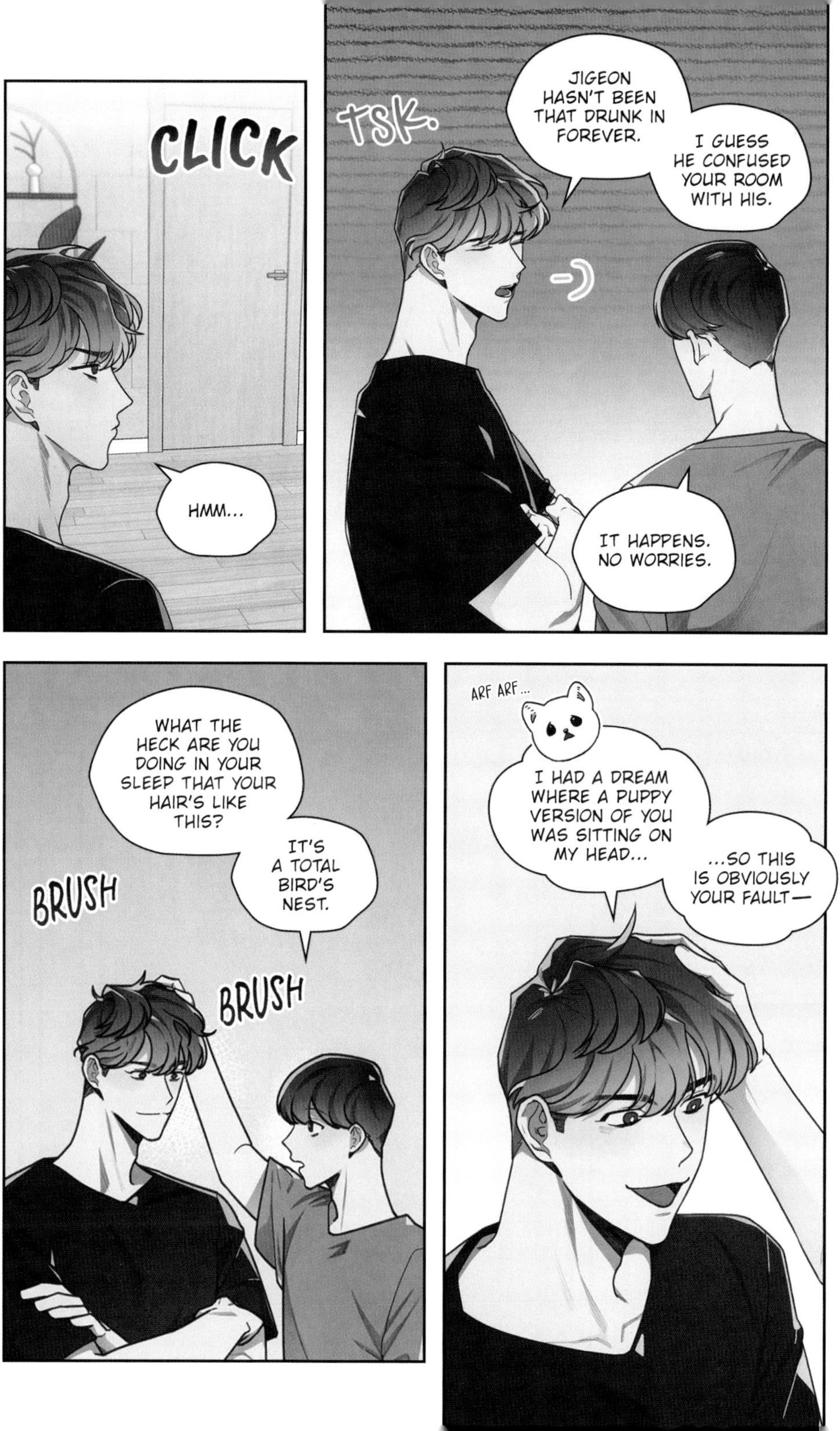
CLICK
HMM...
TSK.
JIGEON HASN'T BEEN THAT DRUNK IN FOREVER.
I GUESS HE CONFUSED YOUR ROOM WITH HIS.
IT HAPPENS. NO WORRIES.
WHAT THE HECK ARE YOU DOING IN YOUR SLEEP THAT YOUR HAIR'S LIKE THIS?
IT'S A TOTAL BIRD'S NEST.
BRUSH
BRUSH
ARF ARF...
I HAD A DREAM WHERE A PUPPY VERSION OF YOU WAS SITTING ON MY HEAD...
...SO THIS IS OBVIOUSLY YOUR FAULT—

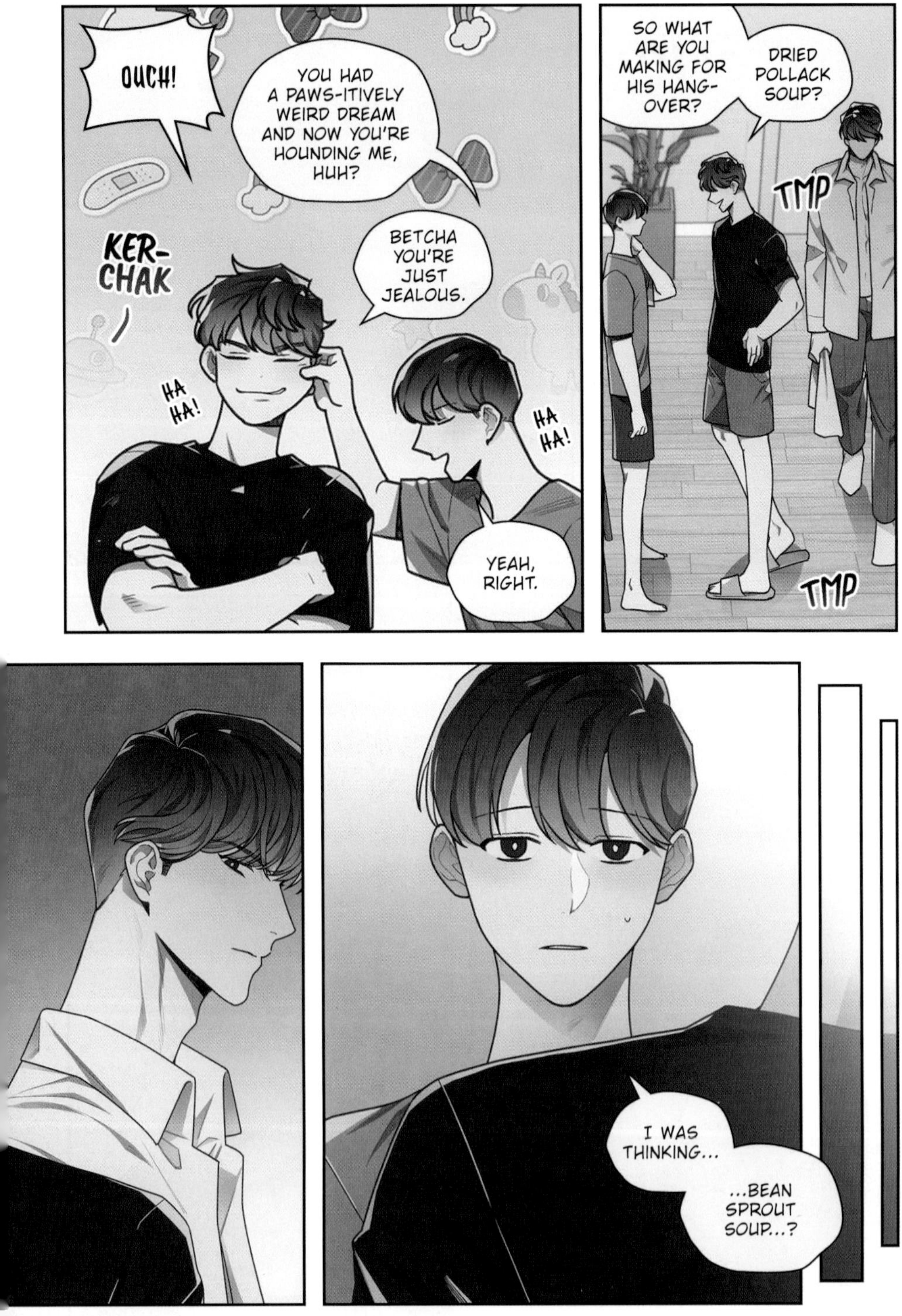
OUCH!
YOU HAD A PAWS-ITIVELY WEIRD DREAM AND NOW YOU'RE HOUNDING ME, HUH?
KER-CHAK
BETCHA YOU'RE JUST JEALOUS.
HA HA!
HA HA!
YEAH, RIGHT.
SO WHAT ARE YOU MAKING FOR HIS HANG-OVER?
DRIED POLLACK SOUP?
TMP
TMP
I WAS THINKING...
...BEAN SPROUT SOUP...?

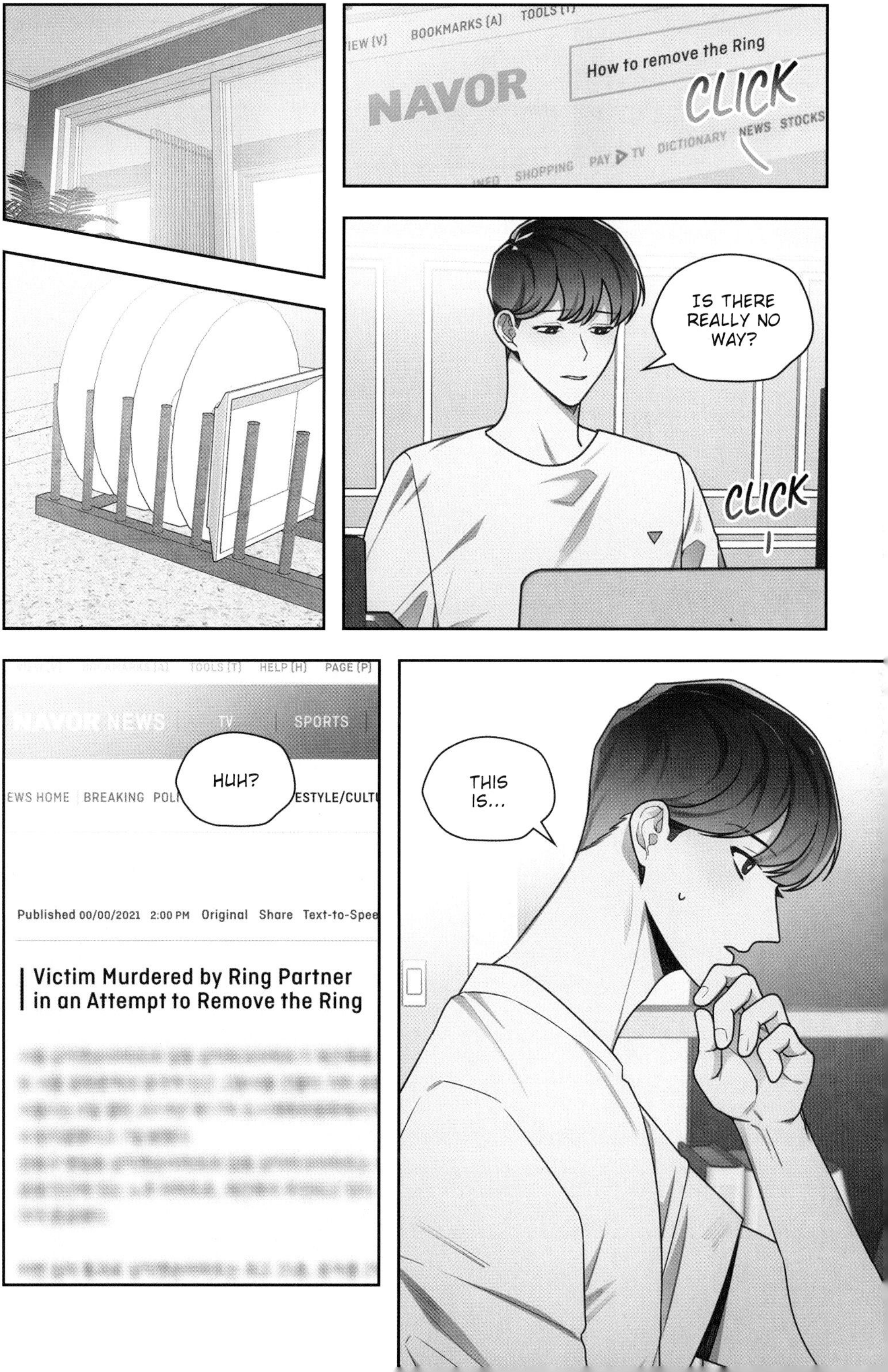

VIEW (V)
BOOKMARKS (A)
TOOLS (T)
NAVOR
How to remove the Ring
CLICK
SHOPPING
PAY
TV
DICTIONARY
NEWS
STOCKS
IS THERE REALLY NO WAY?
CLICK
TOOLS (T)
HELP (H)
PAGE (P)
NAVOR NEWS
TV
SPORTS
HUH?
EWS HOME
BREAKING
POLI
ESTYLE/CULTU
Published 00/00/2021 2:00 PM Original Share Text-to-Spee
Victim Murdered by Ring Partner in an Attempt to Remove the Ring
THIS IS...

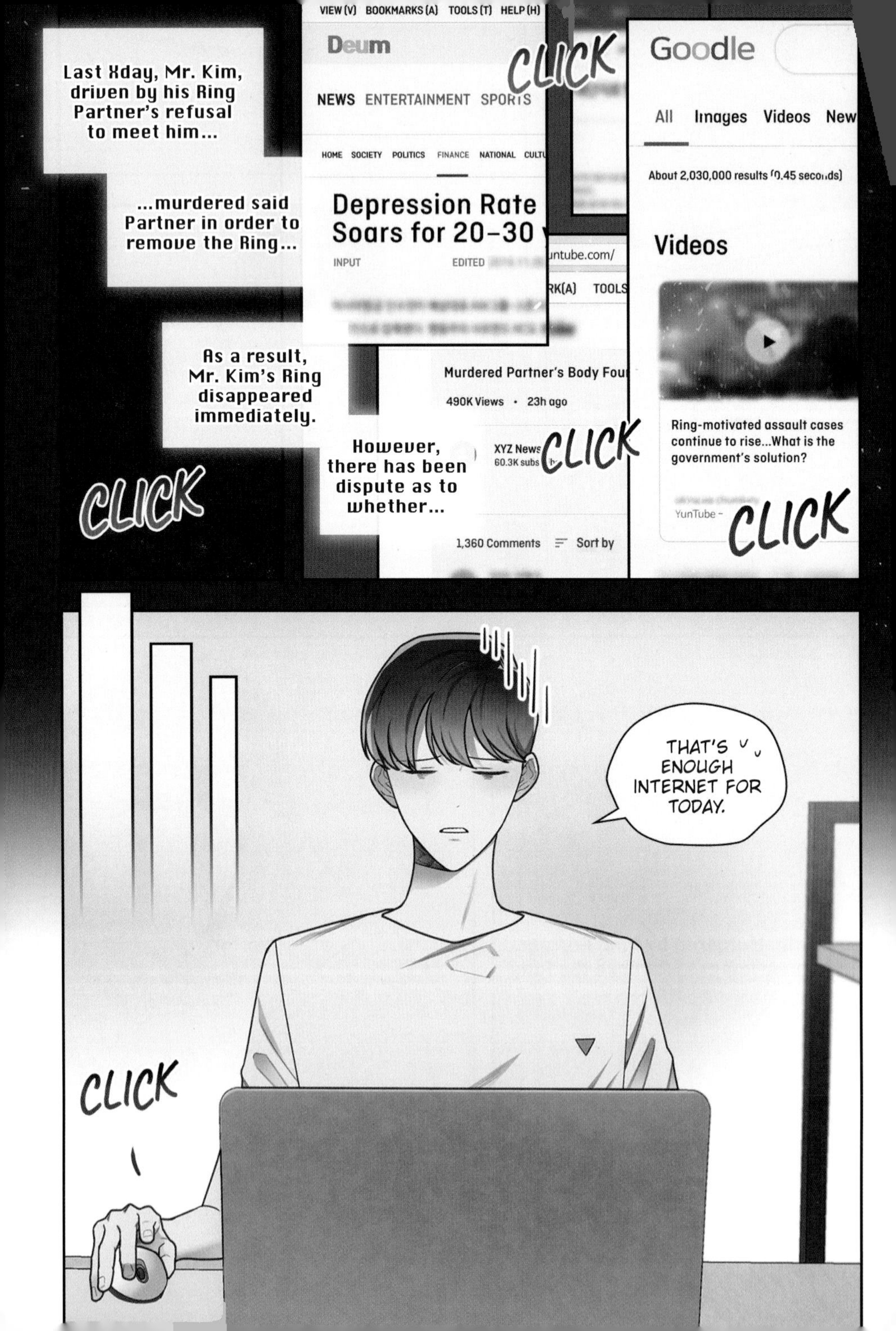

Last Xday, Mr. Kim, driven by his Ring Partner's refusal to meet him...
...murdered said Partner in order to remove the Ring...
As a result, Mr. Kim's Ring disappeared immediately.
CLICK
VIEW (V) BOOKMARKS (A) TOOLS (T) HELP (H)
Deum
NEWS ENTERTAINMENT SPORTS
HOME SOCIETY POLITICS FINANCE NATIONAL CULTU
Depression Rate Soars for 20-30
INPUT EDITED
CLICK
However, there has been dispute as to whether...
Murdered Partner's Body Fou
490K Views • 23h ago
XYZ News
60.3K subs
1,360 Comments Sort by
CLICK
Goodle
All Images Videos New
About 2,030,000 results (0.45 seconds)
Videos
Ring-motivated assault cases continue to rise...What is the government's solution?
YunTube -
CLICK
THAT'S ENOUGH INTERNET FOR TODAY.
CLICK

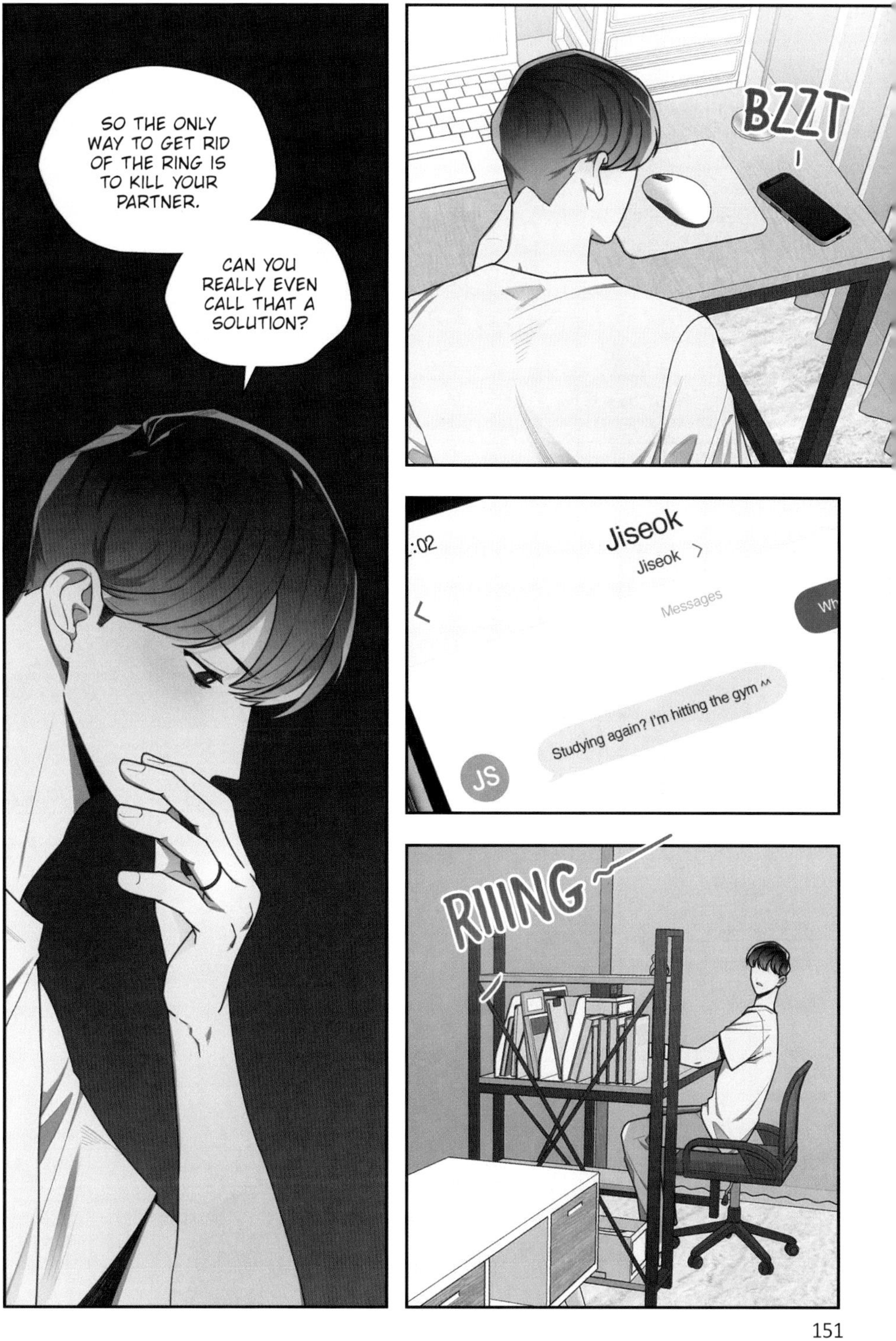
SO THE ONLY WAY TO GET RID OF THE RING IS TO KILL YOUR PARTNER.
CAN YOU REALLY EVEN CALL THAT A SOLUTION?
BZZT
Jiseok
Jiseok >
Messages
Studying again? I'm hitting the gym ^^
JS
RIIING ~

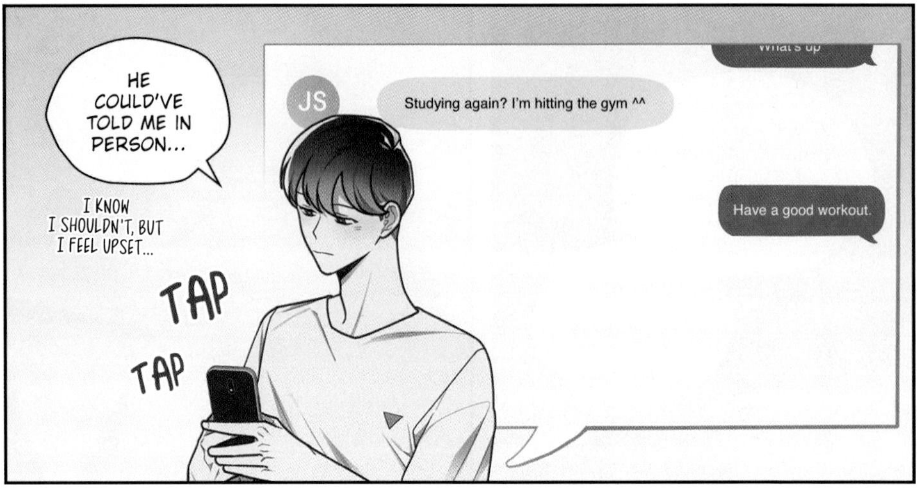
HE COULD'VE TOLD ME IN PERSON...
I KNOW I SHOULDN'T, BUT I FEEL UPSET...
TAP
TAP
JS
Studying again? I'm hitting the gym ^^
Have a good workout.

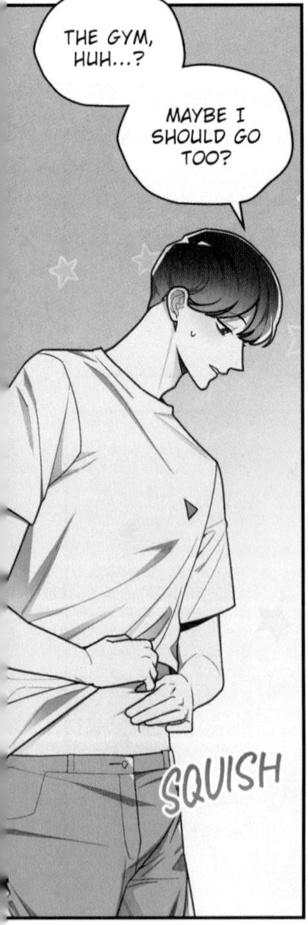
THE GYM, HUH...?
MAYBE I SHOULD GO TOO?
SQUISH

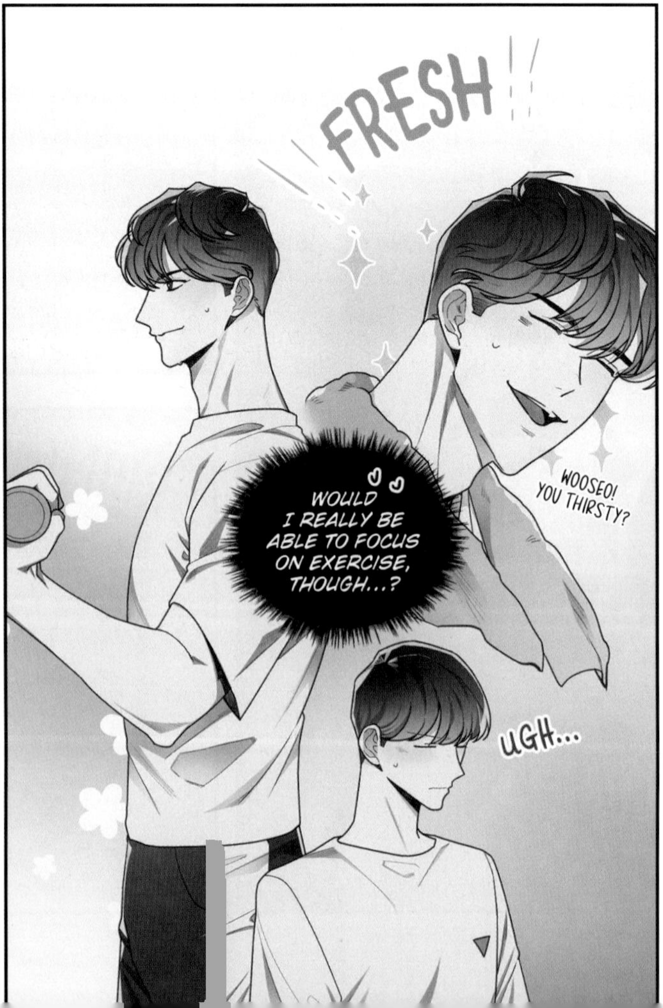
FRESH
WOULD I REALLY BE ABLE TO FOCUS ON EXERCISE, THOUGH...?
WOOSEO! YOU THIRSTY?
UGH...

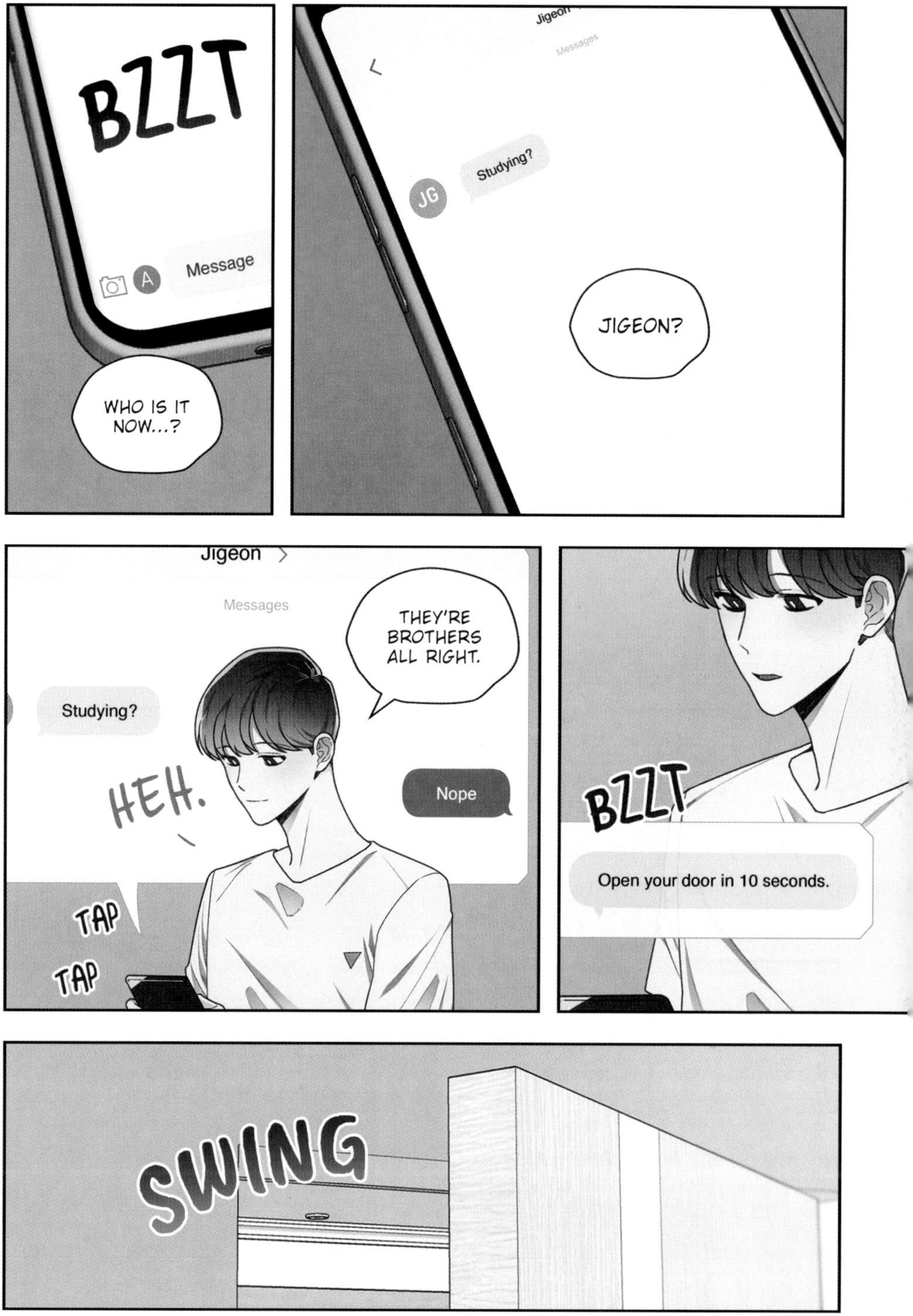
BZZT
A
Message
WHO IS IT NOW...?
Jigeon
Messages
Studying?
JG
JIGEON?
Jigeon
Messages
THEY'RE BROTHERS ALL RIGHT.
Studying?
Nope
HEH.
TAP
TAP
BZZT
Open your door in 10 seconds.
SWING

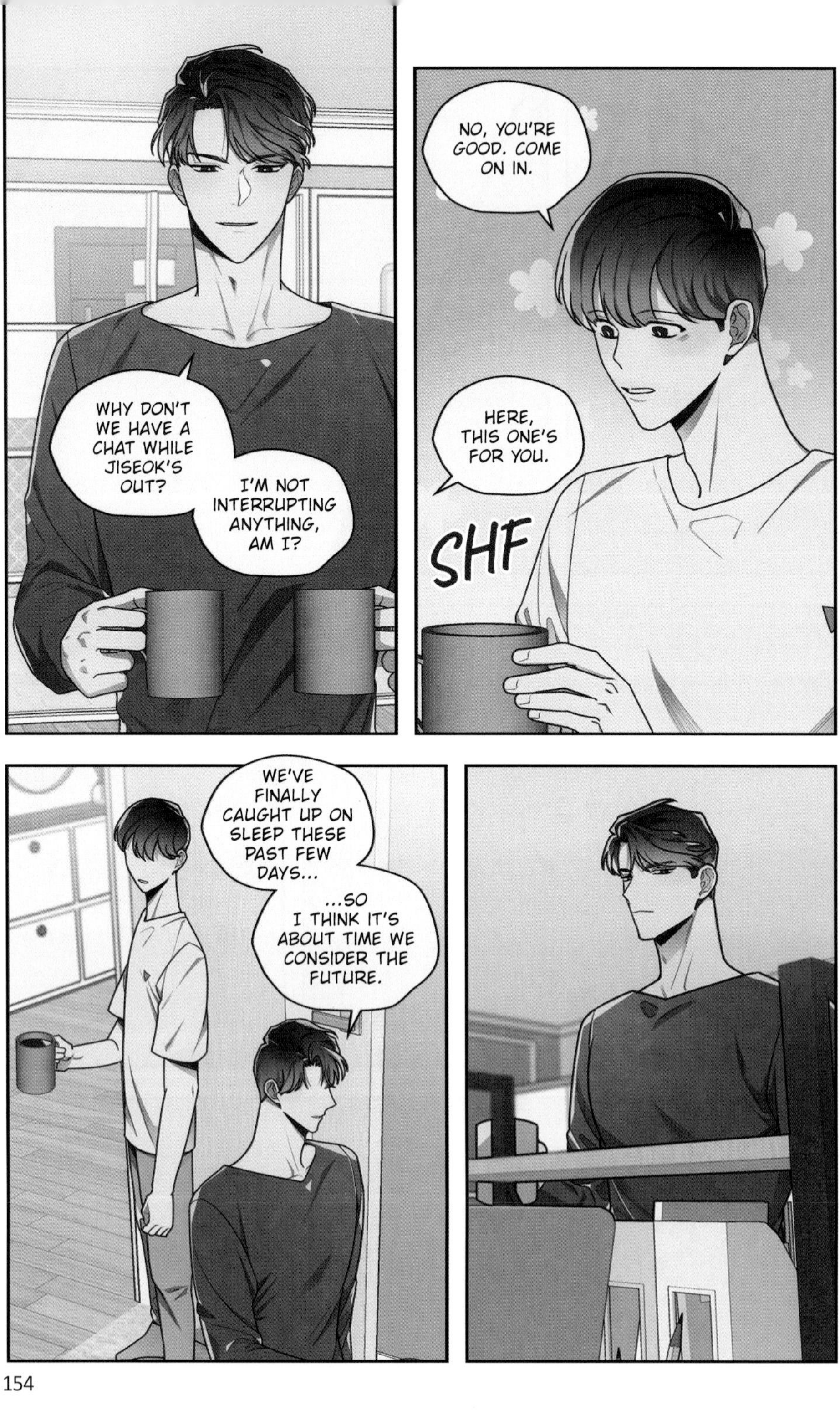
WHY DON'T WE HAVE A CHAT WHILE JISEOK'S OUT?
I'M NOT INTERRUPTING ANYTHING, AM I?
NO, YOU'RE GOOD. COME ON IN.
HERE, THIS ONE'S FOR YOU.
SHF
WE'VE FINALLY CAUGHT UP ON SLEEP THESE PAST FEW DAYS...
...SO I THINK IT'S ABOUT TIME WE CONSIDER THE FUTURE.

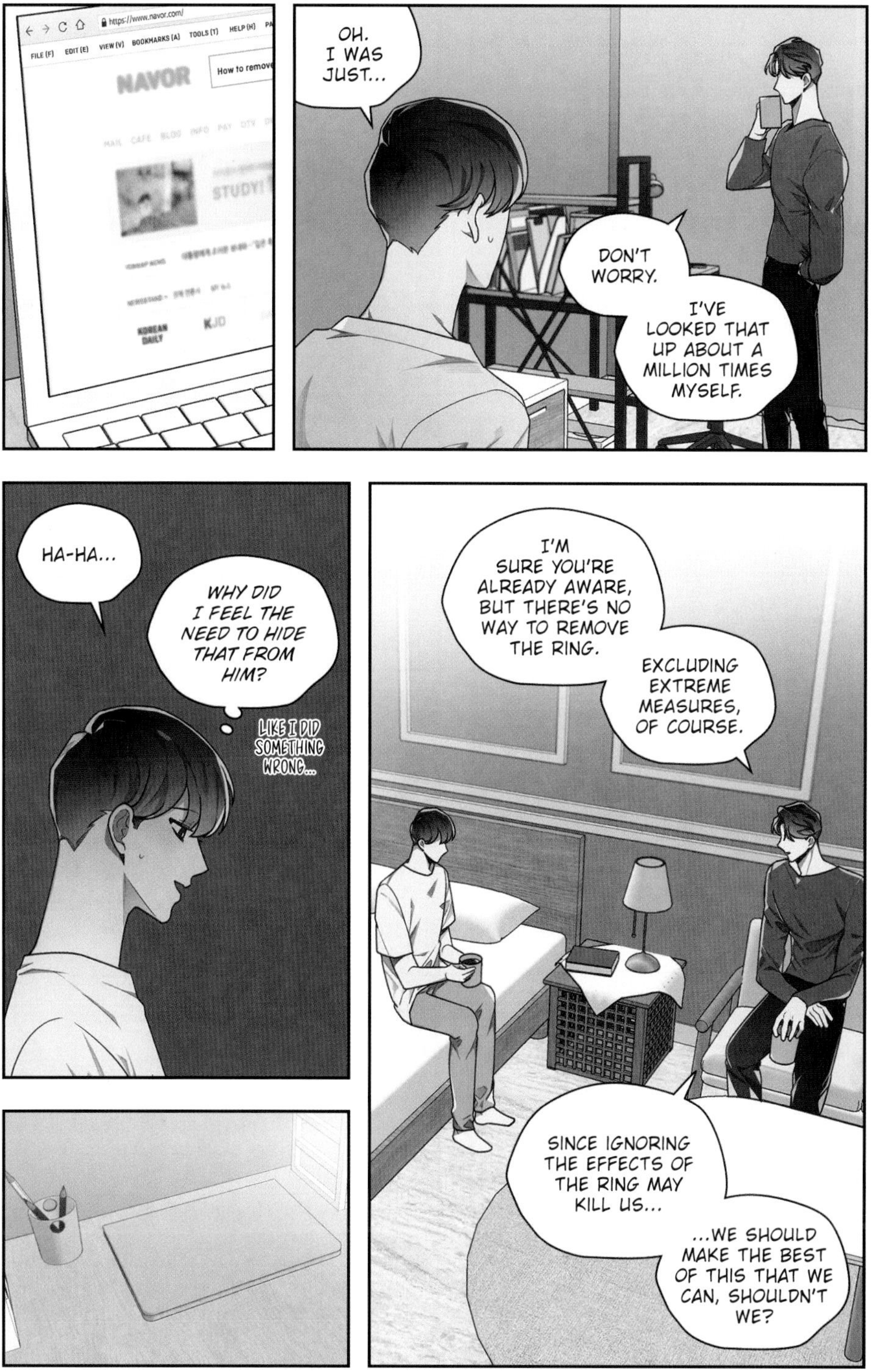
https://www.navor.com/
FILE (F) EDIT (E) VIEW (V) BOOKMARKS (A) TOOLS (T) HELP (H)
NAVOR
How to remove
OH. I WAS JUST...
DON'T WORRY.
I'VE LOOKED THAT UP ABOUT A MILLION TIMES MYSELF.
HA-HA...
WHY DID I FEEL THE NEED TO HIDE THAT FROM HIM?
LIKE I DID SOMETHING WRONG...
I'M SURE YOU'RE ALREADY AWARE, BUT THERE'S NO WAY TO REMOVE THE RING.
EXCLUDING EXTREME MEASURES, OF COURSE.
SINCE IGNORING THE EFFECTS OF THE RING MAY KILL US...
...WE SHOULD MAKE THE BEST OF THIS THAT WE CAN, SHOULDN'T WE?

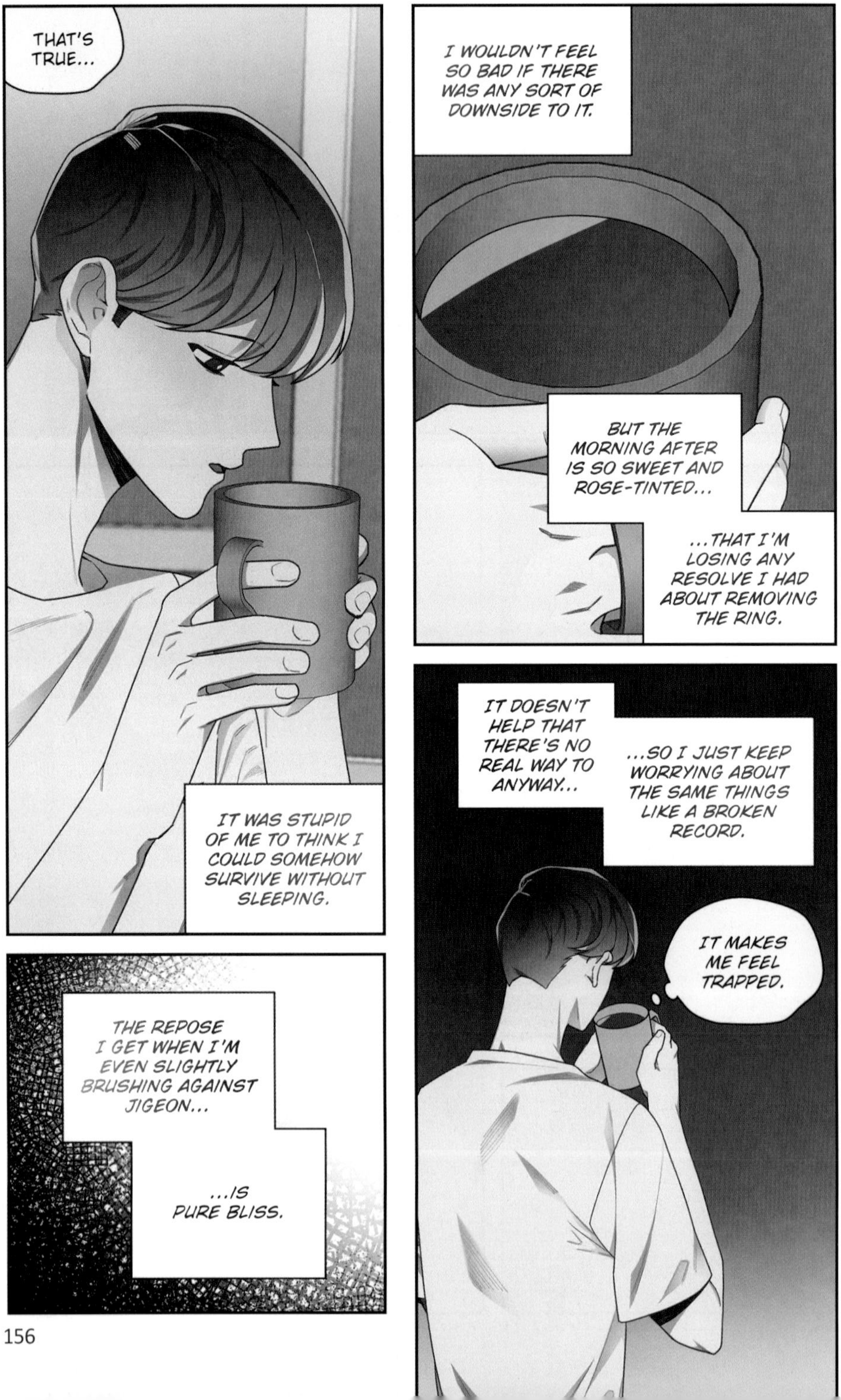
THAT'S TRUE...
IT WAS STUPID OF ME TO THINK I COULD SOMEHOW SURVIVE WITHOUT SLEEPING.
I WOULDN'T FEEL SO BAD IF THERE WAS ANY SORT OF DOWNSIDE TO IT.
BUT THE MORNING AFTER IS SO SWEET AND ROSE-TINTED...
...THAT I'M LOSING ANY RESOLVE I HAD ABOUT REMOVING THE RING.
THE REPOSE I GET WHEN I'M EVEN SLIGHTLY BRUSHING AGAINST JIGEON...
...IS PURE BLISS.
IT DOESN'T HELP THAT THERE'S NO REAL WAY TO ANYWAY...
...SO I JUST KEEP WORRYING ABOUT THE SAME THINGS LIKE A BROKEN RECORD.
IT MAKES ME FEEL TRAPPED.

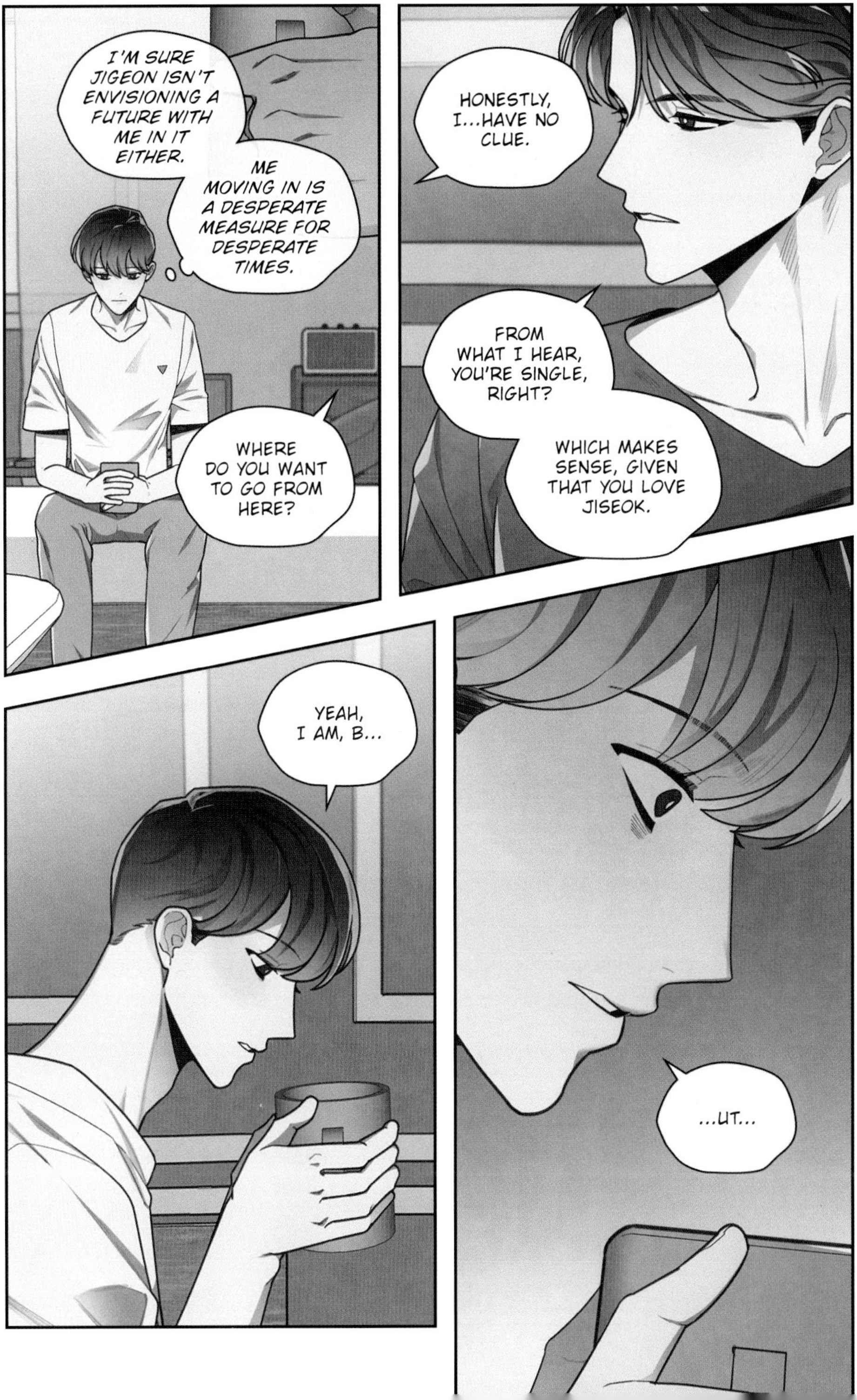
I'M SURE JIGEON ISN'T ENVISIONING A FUTURE WITH ME IN IT EITHER.
ME MOVING IN IS A DESPERATE MEASURE FOR DESPERATE TIMES.
HONESTLY, I...HAVE NO CLUE.
WHERE DO YOU WANT TO GO FROM HERE?
FROM WHAT I HEAR, YOU'RE SINGLE, RIGHT?
WHICH MAKES SENSE, GIVEN THAT YOU LOVE JISEOK.
YEAH, I AM, B...
...UT...

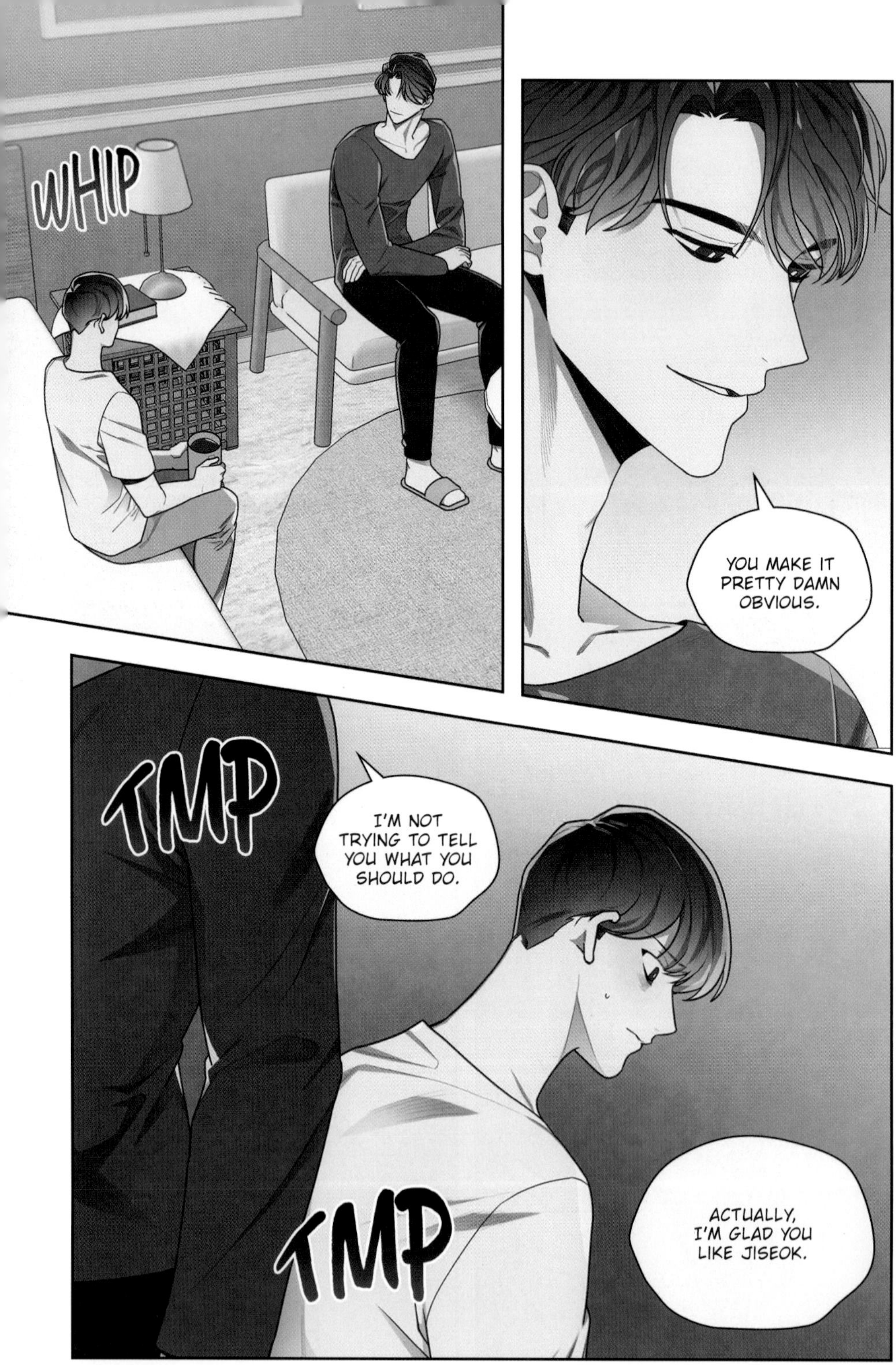
WHIP
YOU MAKE IT PRETTY DAMN OBVIOUS.
TMP
I'M NOT TRYING TO TELL YOU WHAT YOU SHOULD DO.
TMP
ACTUALLY, I'M GLAD YOU LIKE JISEOK.

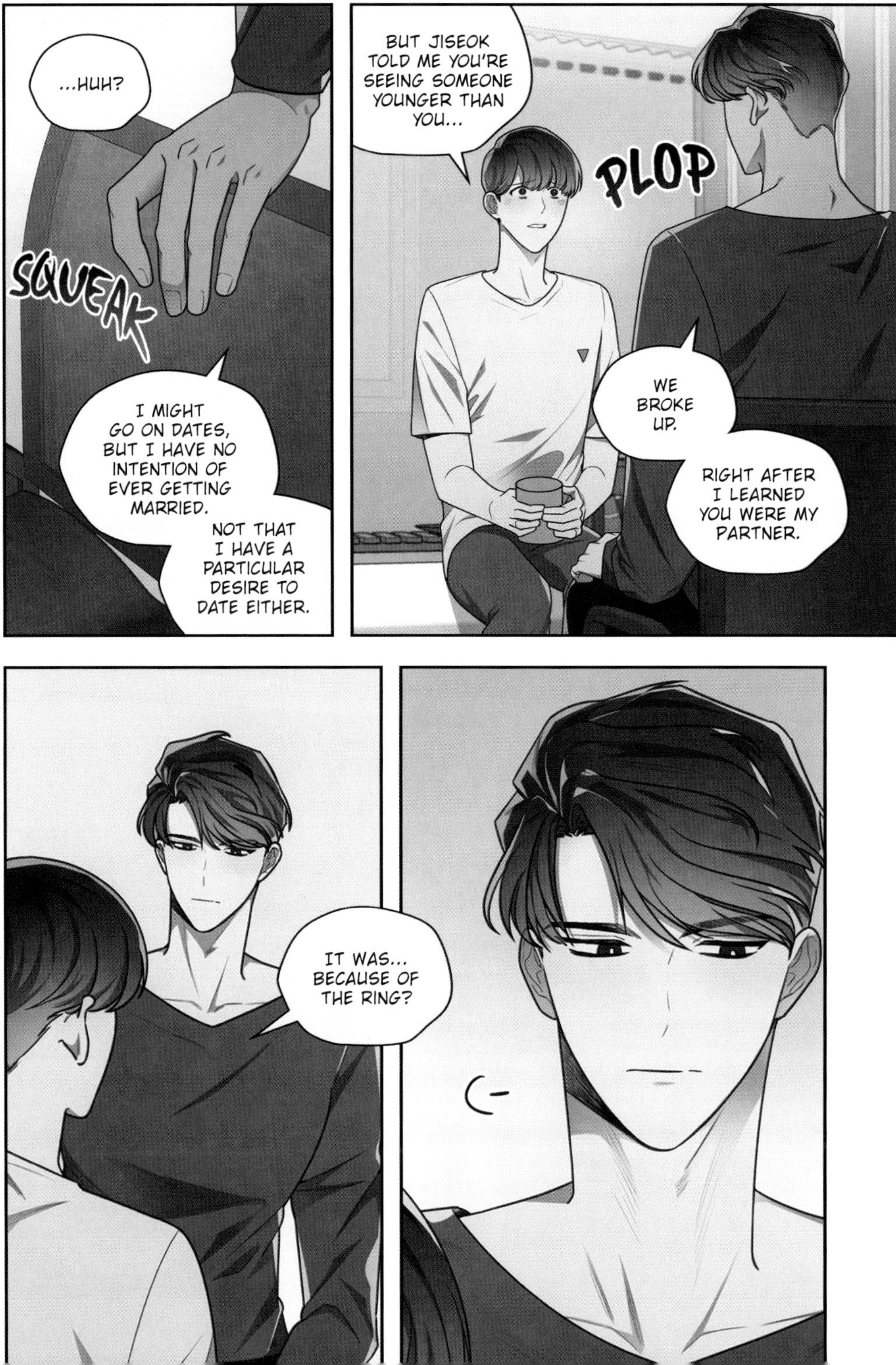
...HUH?
SQUEAK
I MIGHT GO ON DATES, BUT I HAVE NO INTENTION OF EVER GETTING MARRIED.
NOT THAT I HAVE A PARTICULAR DESIRE TO DATE EITHER.
BUT JISEOK TOLD ME YOU'RE SEEING SOMEONE YOUNGER THAN YOU...
PLOP
WE BROKE UP.
RIGHT AFTER I LEARNED YOU WERE MY PARTNER.
IT WAS... BECAUSE OF THE RING?

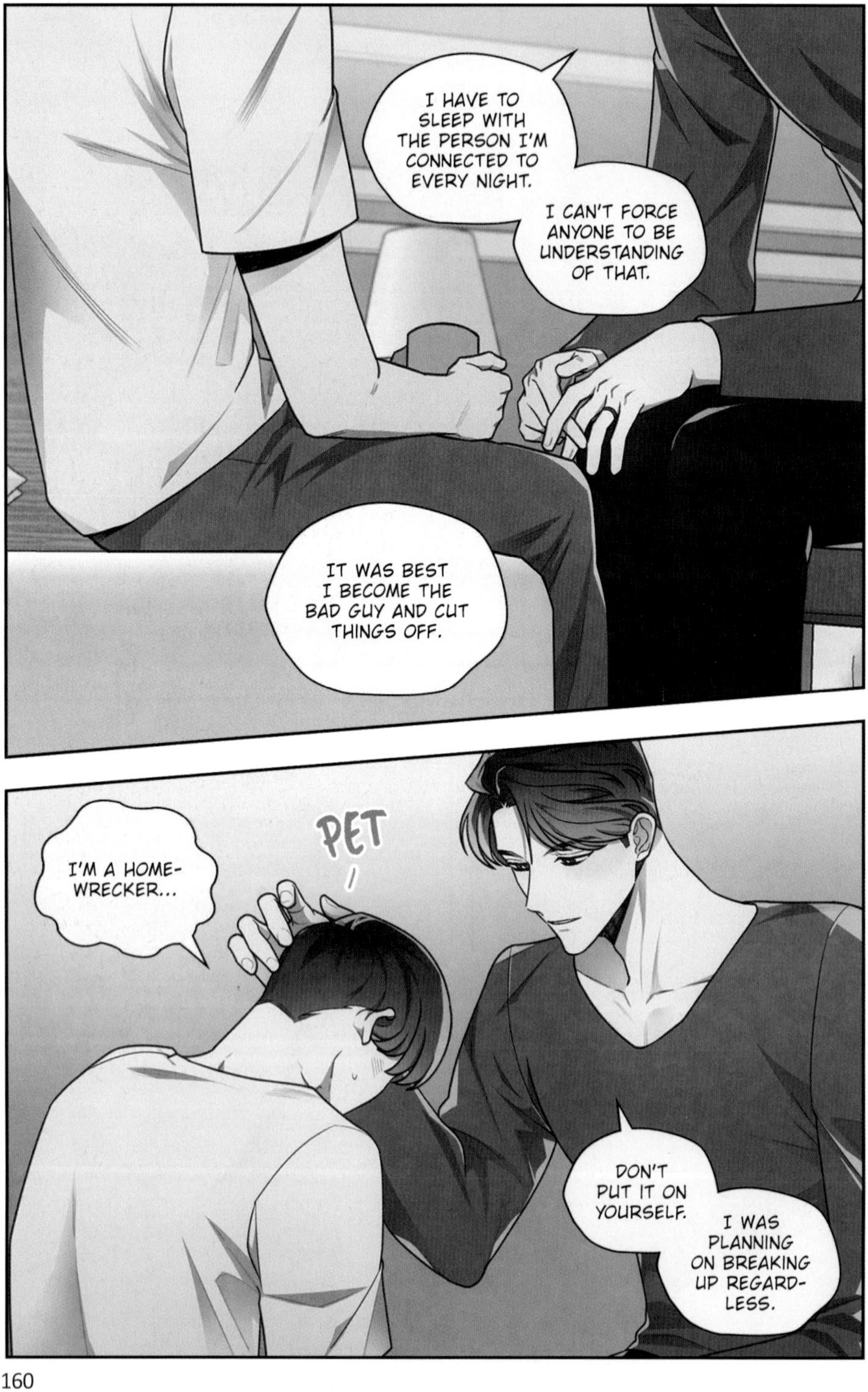
I HAVE TO SLEEP WITH THE PERSON I'M CONNECTED TO EVERY NIGHT.
I CAN'T FORCE ANYONE TO BE UNDERSTANDING OF THAT.
IT WAS BEST I BECOME THE BAD GUY AND CUT THINGS OFF.
I'M A HOME-WRECKER...
PET
DON'T PUT IT ON YOURSELF.
I WAS PLANNING ON BREAKING UP REGARD-LESS.

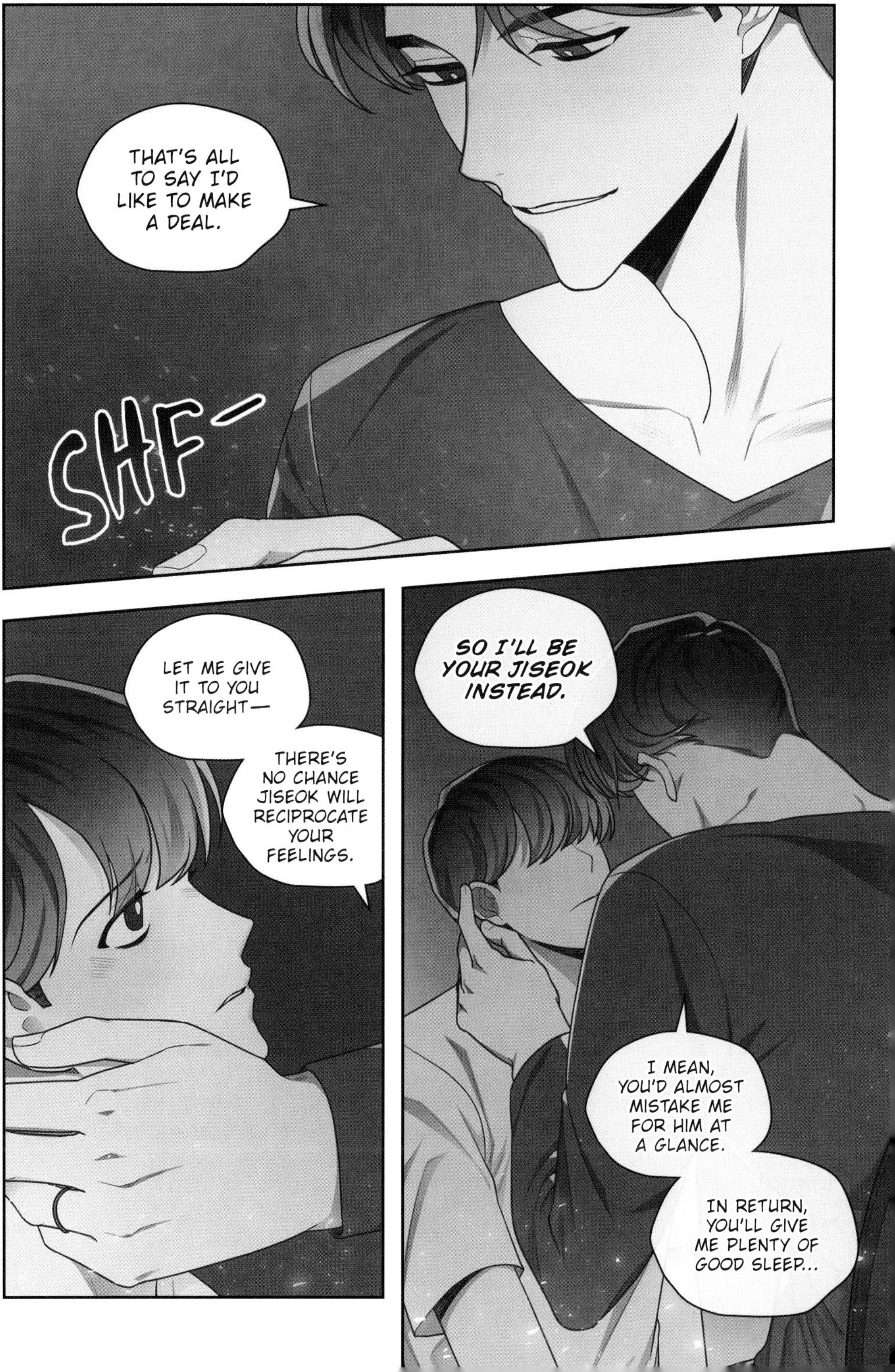
THAT'S ALL TO SAY I'D LIKE TO MAKE A DEAL.
SHF-
LET ME GIVE IT TO YOU STRAIGHT—
THERE'S NO CHANCE JISEOK WILL RECIPROCATE YOUR FEELINGS.
SO I'LL BE YOUR JISEOK INSTEAD.
I MEAN, YOU'D ALMOST MISTAKE ME FOR HIM AT A GLANCE.
IN RETURN, YOU'LL GIVE ME PLENTY OF GOOD SLEEP...

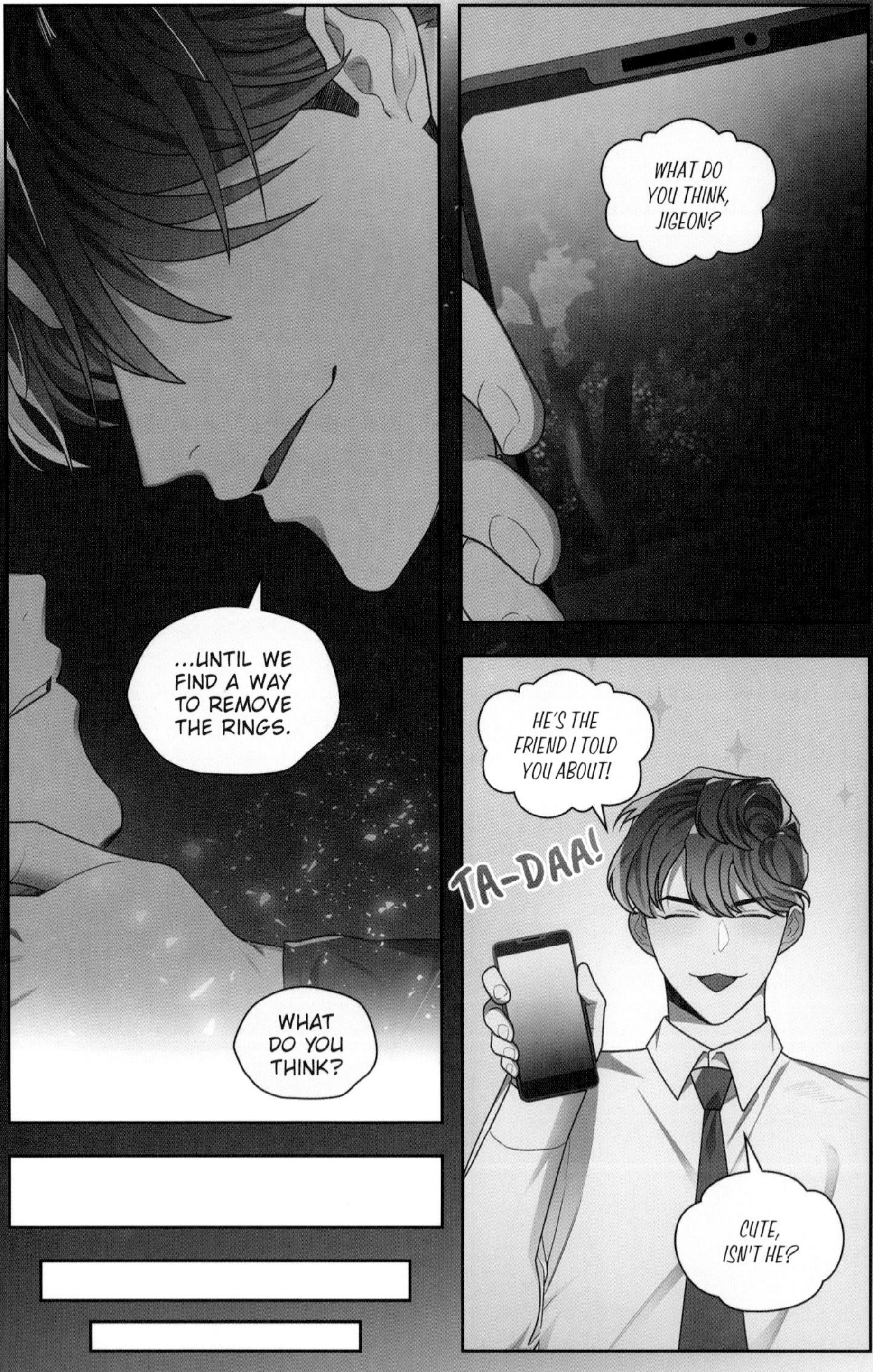
WHAT DO YOU THINK, JIGEON?
...UNTIL WE FIND A WAY TO REMOVE THE RINGS.
WHAT DO YOU THINK?
HE'S THE FRIEND I TOLD YOU ABOUT!
TA-DAA!
CUTE, ISN'T HE?

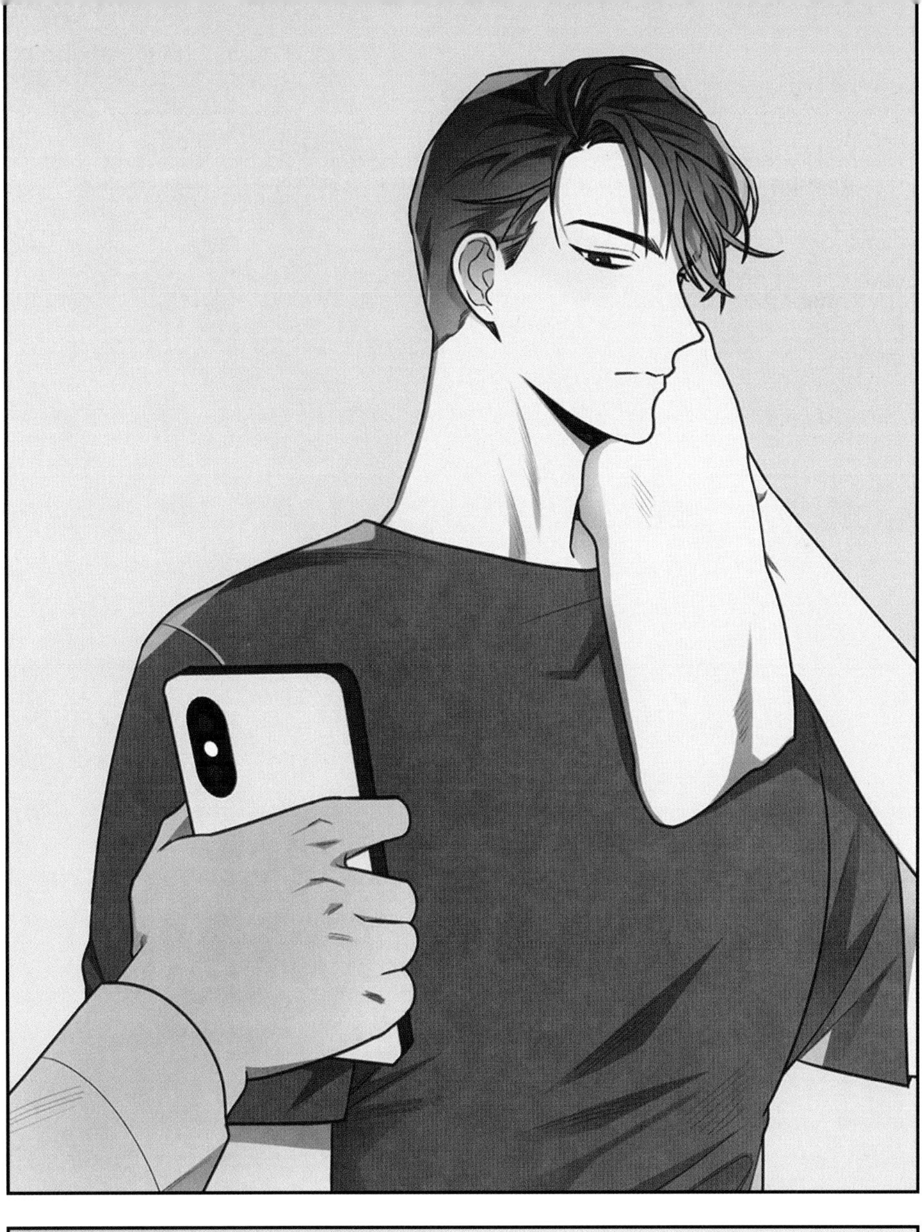

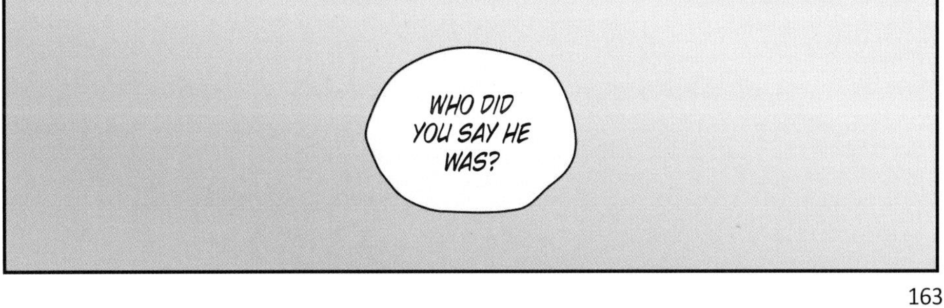
WHO DID YOU SAY HE WAS?

Chapter 9

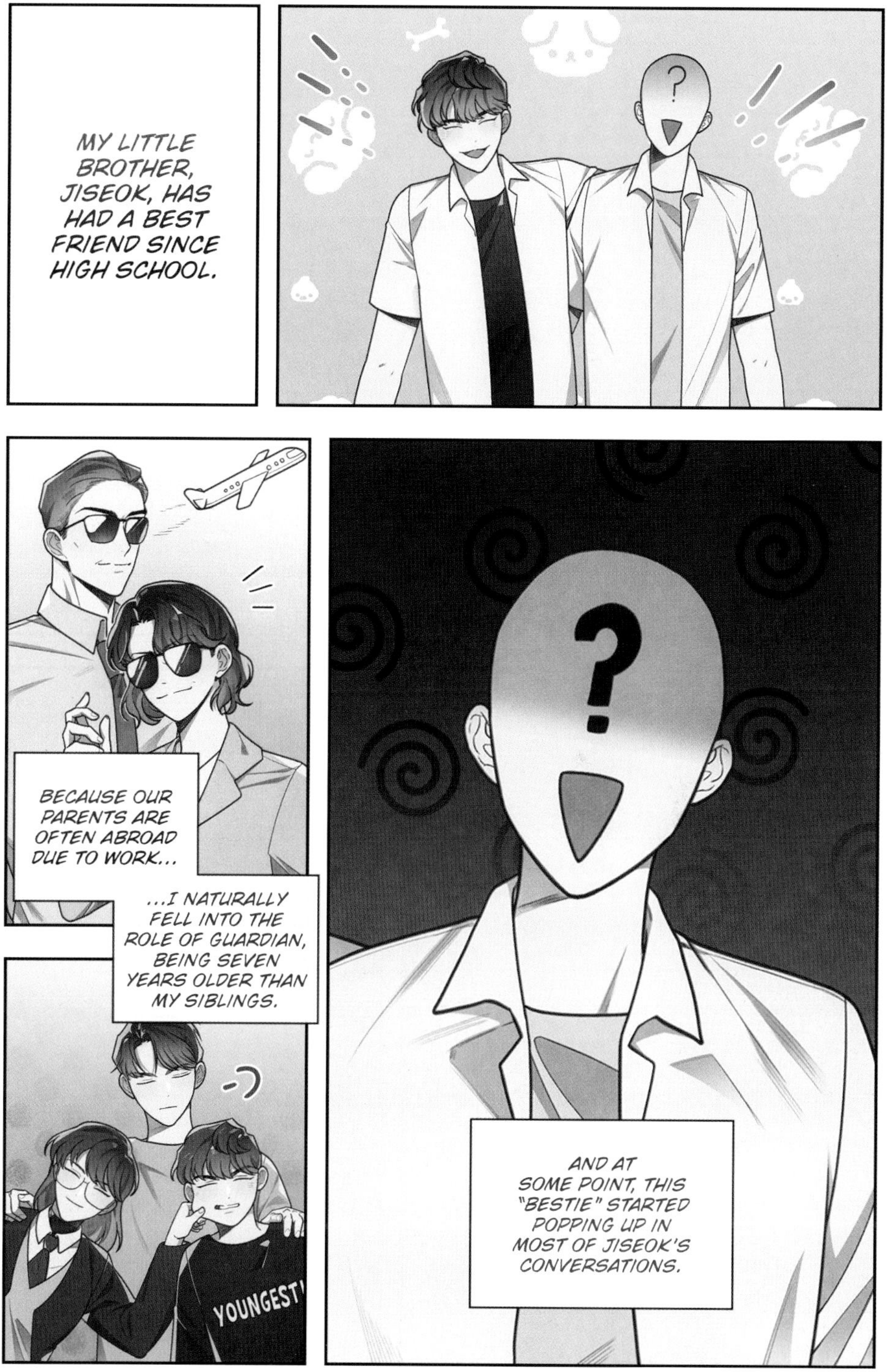
MY LITTLE BROTHER, JISEOK, HAS HAD A BEST FRIEND SINCE HIGH SCHOOL.
BECAUSE OUR PARENTS ARE OFTEN ABROAD DUE TO WORK...
...I NATURALLY FELL INTO THE ROLE OF GUARDIAN, BEING SEVEN YEARS OLDER THAN MY SIBLINGS.
YOUNGEST
AND AT SOME POINT, THIS "BESTIE" STARTED POPPING UP IN MOST OF JISEOK'S CONVERSATIONS.

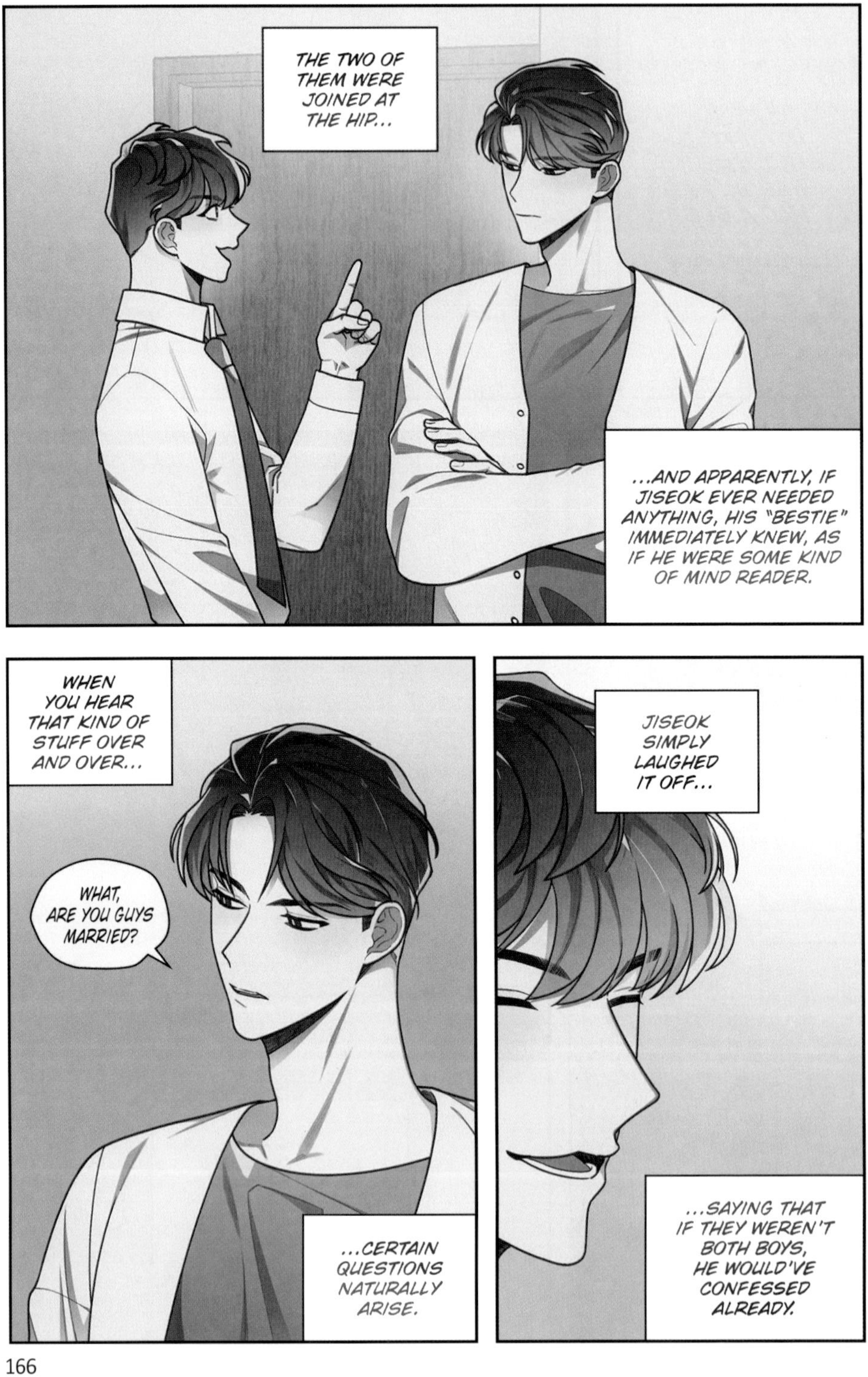
THE TWO OF THEM WERE JOINED AT THE HIP...
...AND APPARENTLY, IF JISEOK EVER NEEDED ANYTHING, HIS "BESTIE" IMMEDIATELY KNEW, AS IF HE WERE SOME KIND OF MIND READER.
WHEN YOU HEAR THAT KIND OF STUFF OVER AND OVER...
WHAT, ARE YOU GUYS MARRIED?
...CERTAIN QUESTIONS NATURALLY ARISE.
JISEOK SIMPLY LAUGHED IT OFF...
...SAYING THAT IF THEY WEREN'T BOTH BOYS, HE WOULD'VE CONFESSED ALREADY.

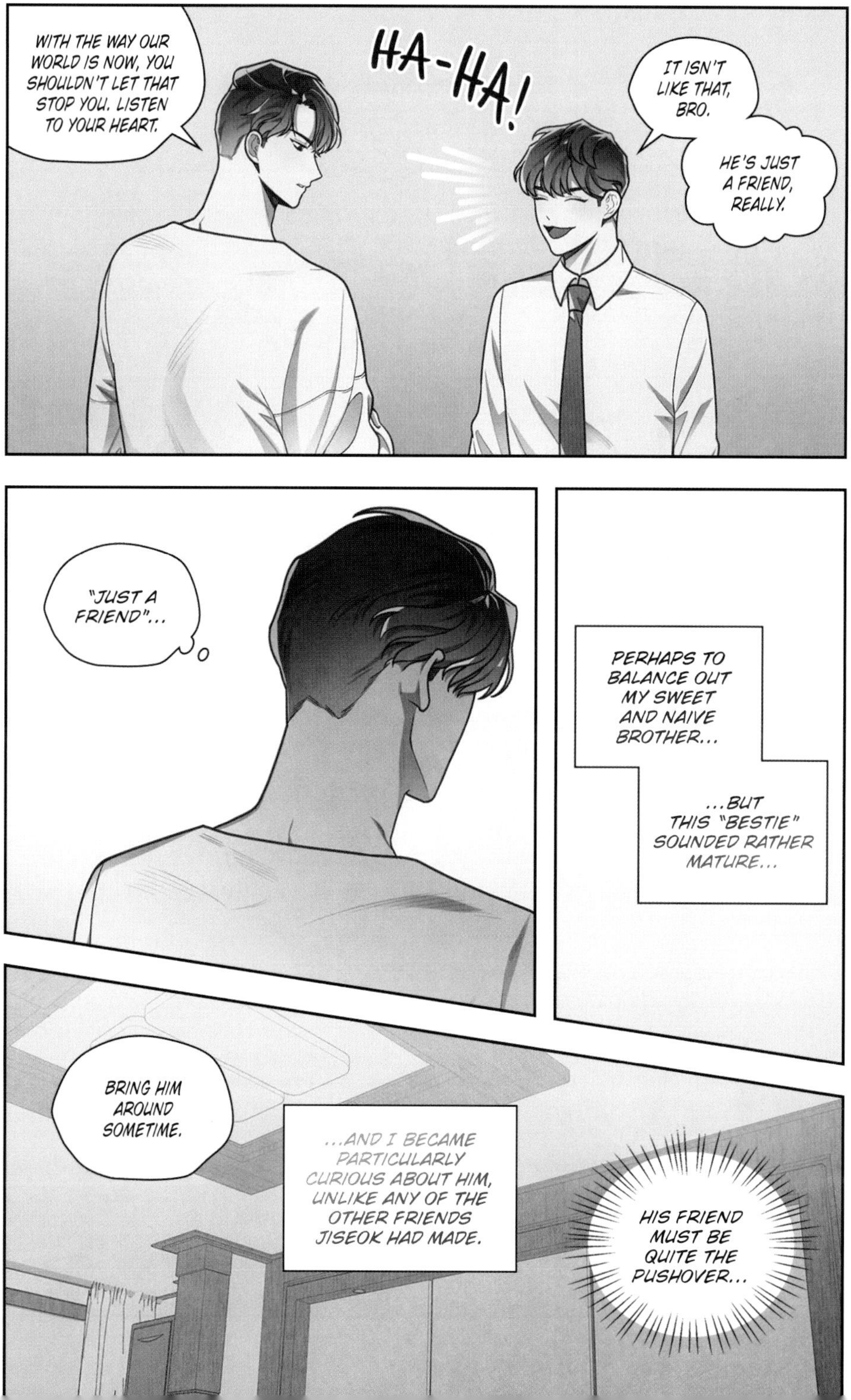
WITH THE WAY OUR WORLD IS NOW, YOU SHOULDN'T LET THAT STOP YOU. LISTEN TO YOUR HEART.
HA-HA!
IT ISN'T LIKE THAT, BRO.
HE'S JUST A FRIEND, REALLY.
"JUST A FRIEND"...
PERHAPS TO BALANCE OUT MY SWEET AND NAIVE BROTHER...
...BUT THIS "BESTIE" SOUNDED RATHER MATURE...
BRING HIM AROUND SOMETIME.
...AND I BECAME PARTICULARLY CURIOUS ABOUT HIM, UNLIKE ANY OF THE OTHER FRIENDS JISEOK HAD MADE.
HIS FRIEND MUST BE QUITE THE PUSHOVER...

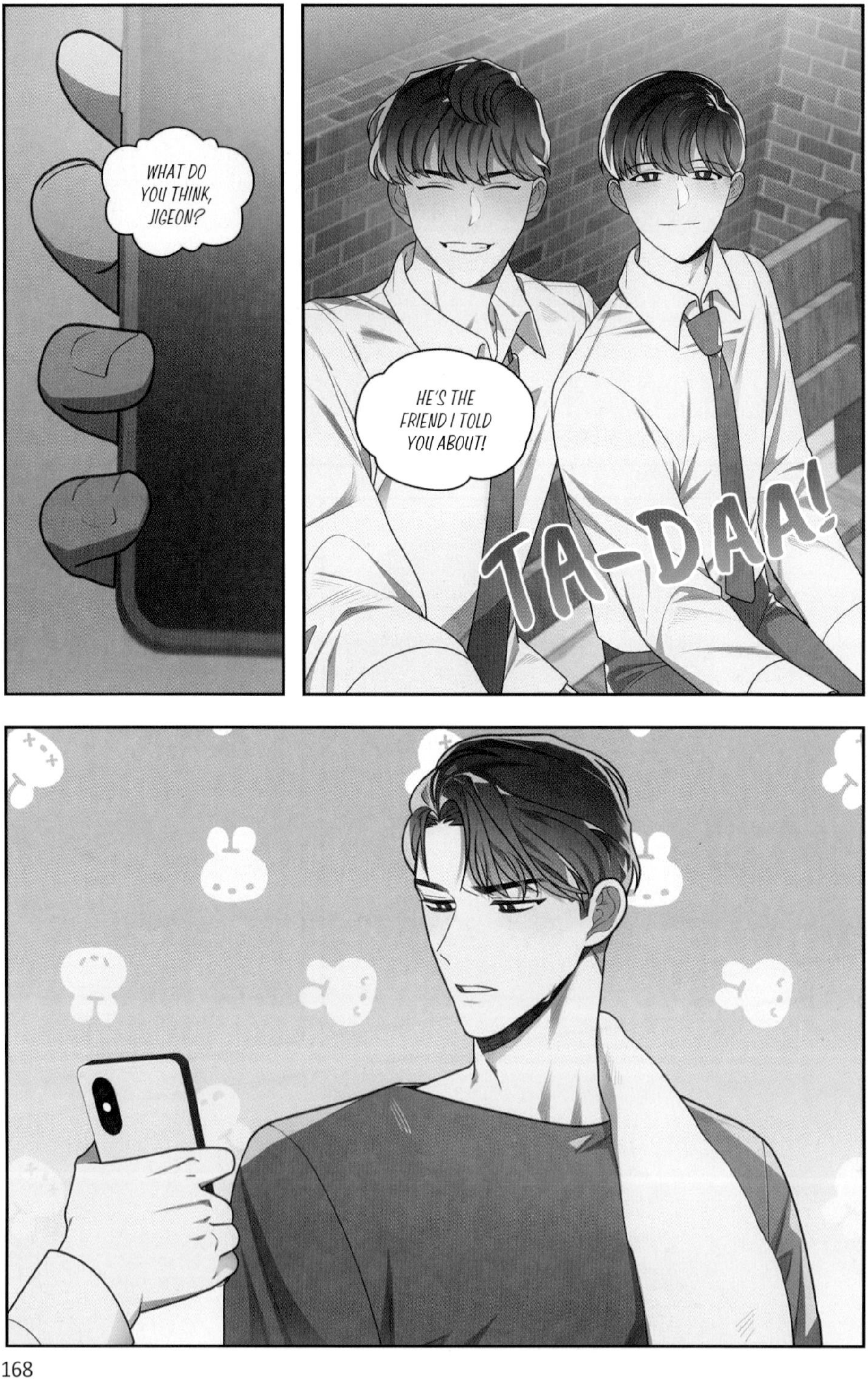
WHAT DO YOU THINK, JIGEON?
HE'S THE FRIEND I TOLD YOU ABOUT!
TA-DAA!

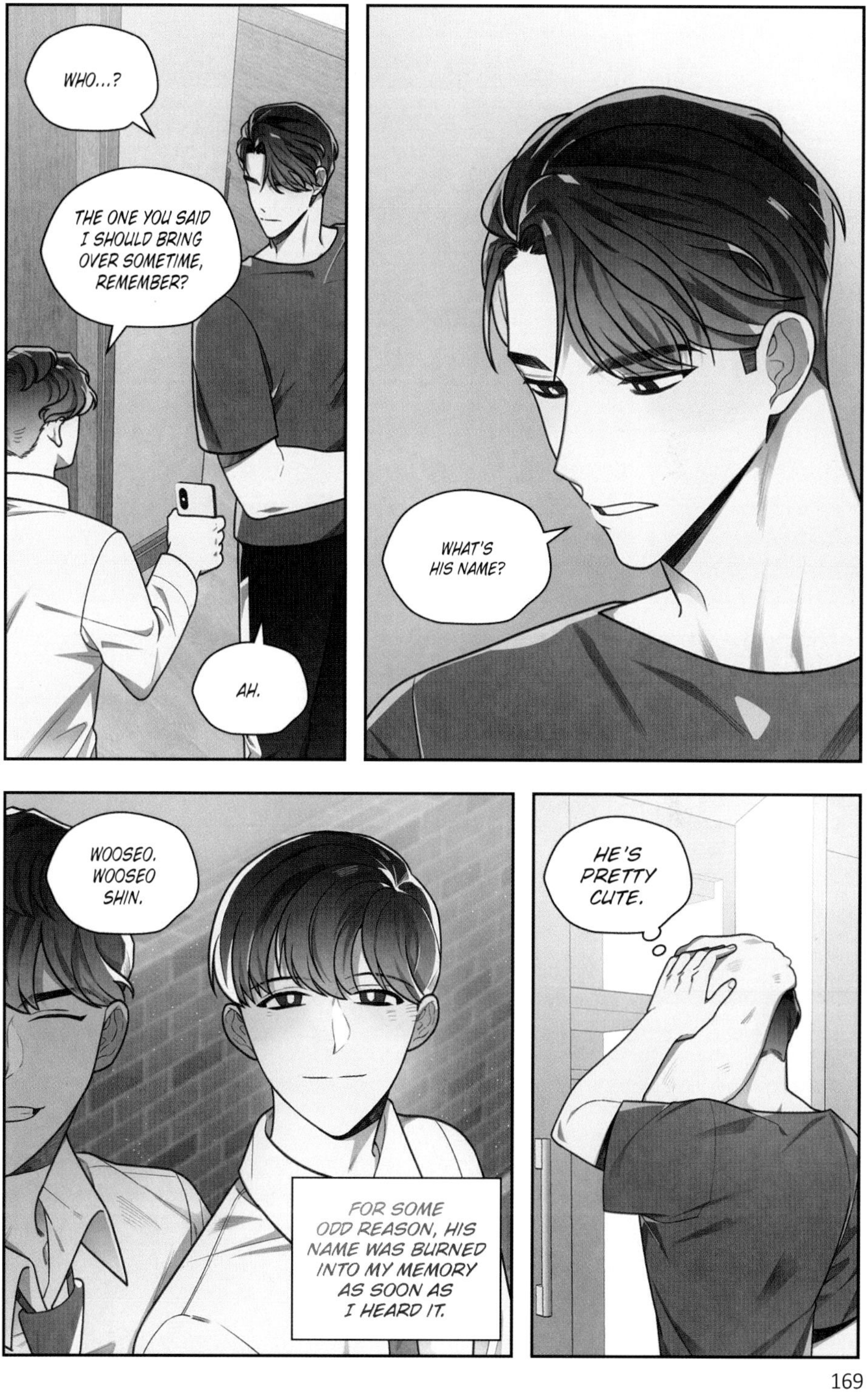
WHO...?
THE ONE YOU SAID I SHOULD BRING OVER SOMETIME, REMEMBER?
AH.
WHAT'S HIS NAME?
WOOSEO. WOOSEO SHIN.
FOR SOME ODD REASON, HIS NAME WAS BURNED INTO MY MEMORY AS SOON AS I HEARD IT.
HE'S PRETTY CUTE.

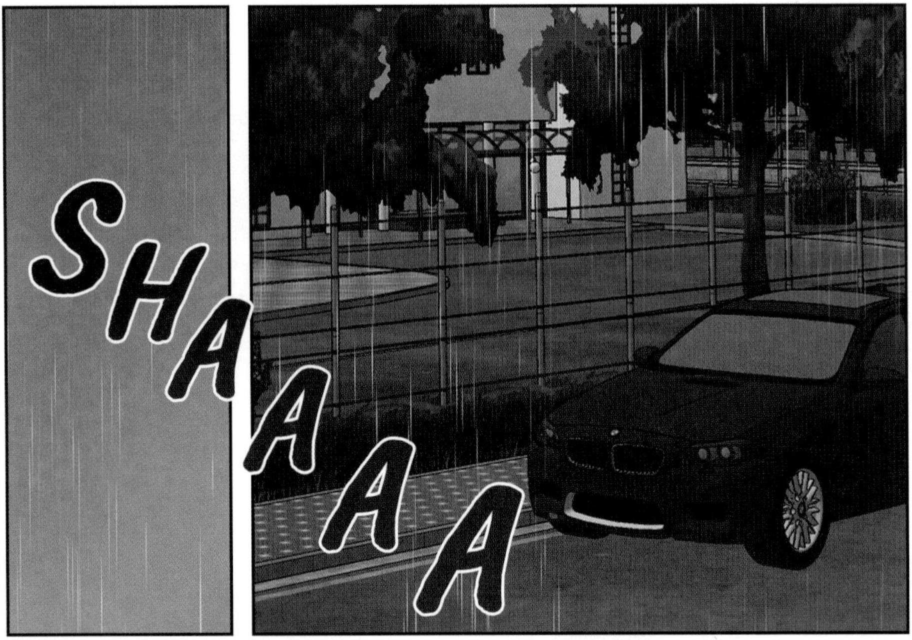
SHAAAAA

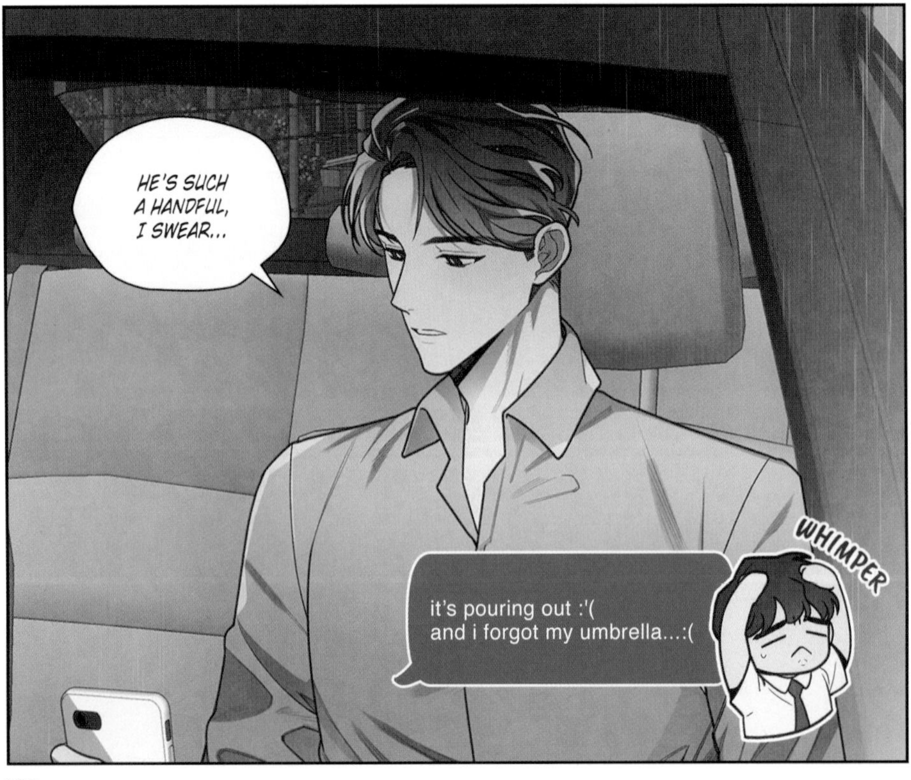
HE'S SUCH A HANDFUL, I SWEAR...
WHIMPER
it's pouring out :'(
and i forgot my umbrella...:(

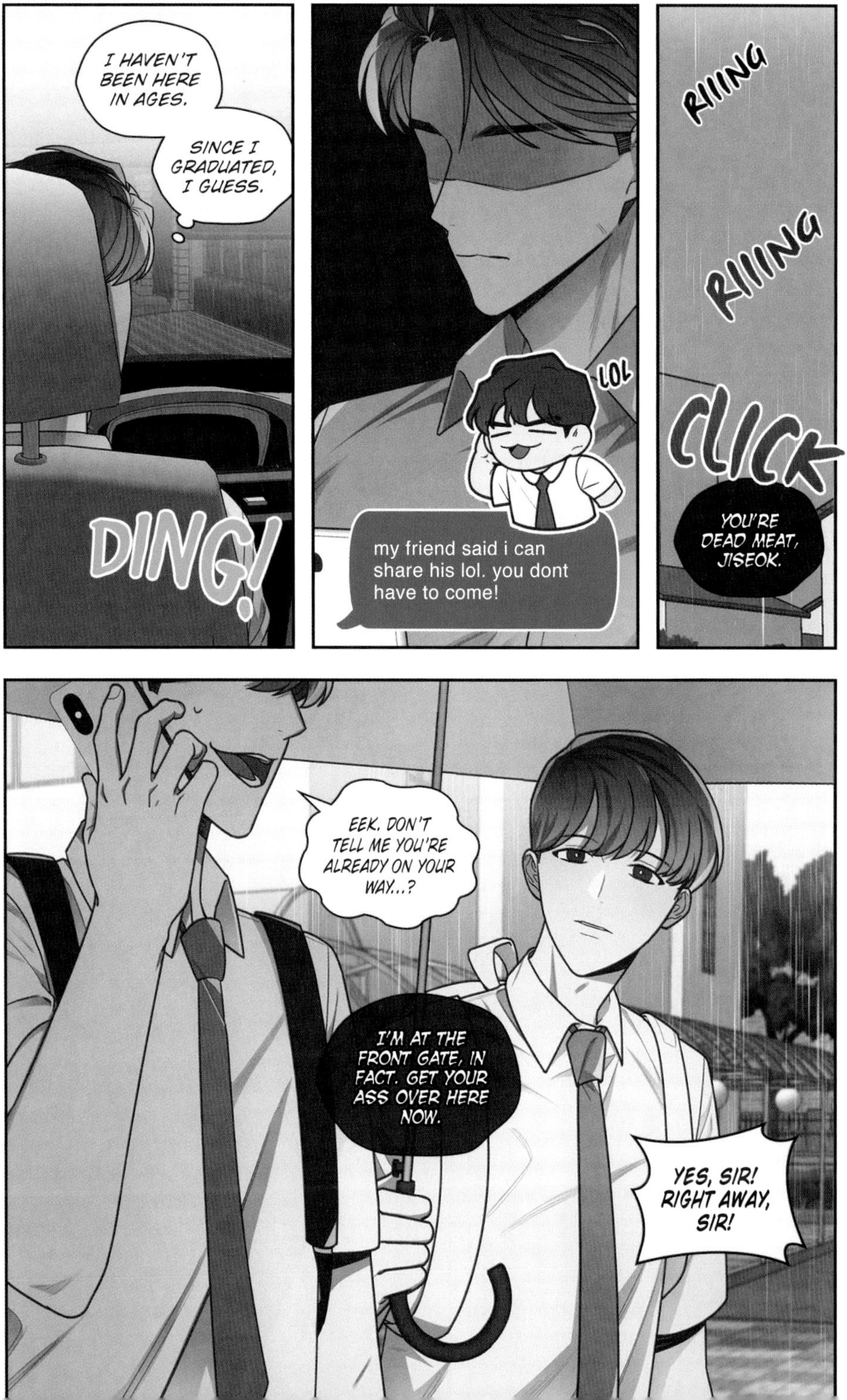
I HAVEN'T BEEN HERE IN AGES.
SINCE I GRADUATED, I GUESS.
DING!
LOL
my friend said i can share his lol. you dont have to come!
RIIING
RIIING
CLICK
YOU'RE DEAD MEAT, JISEOK.
EEK. DON'T TELL ME YOU'RE ALREADY ON YOUR WAY...?
I'M AT THE FRONT GATE, IN FACT. GET YOUR ASS OVER HERE NOW.
YES, SIR! RIGHT AWAY, SIR!

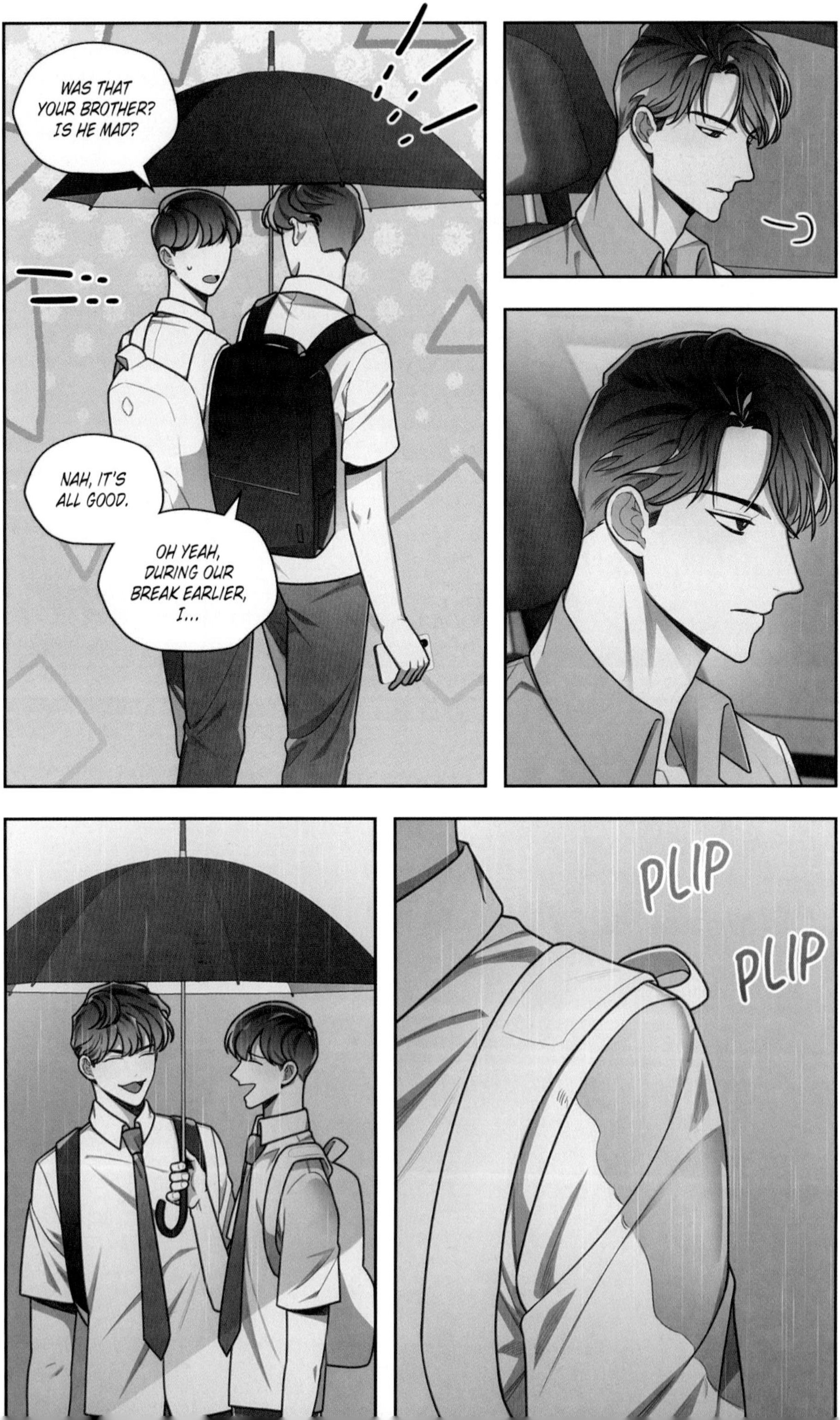
WAS THAT YOUR BROTHER? IS HE MAD?
NAH, IT'S ALL GOOD.
OH YEAH, DURING OUR BREAK EARLIER, I...
PLIP
PLIP

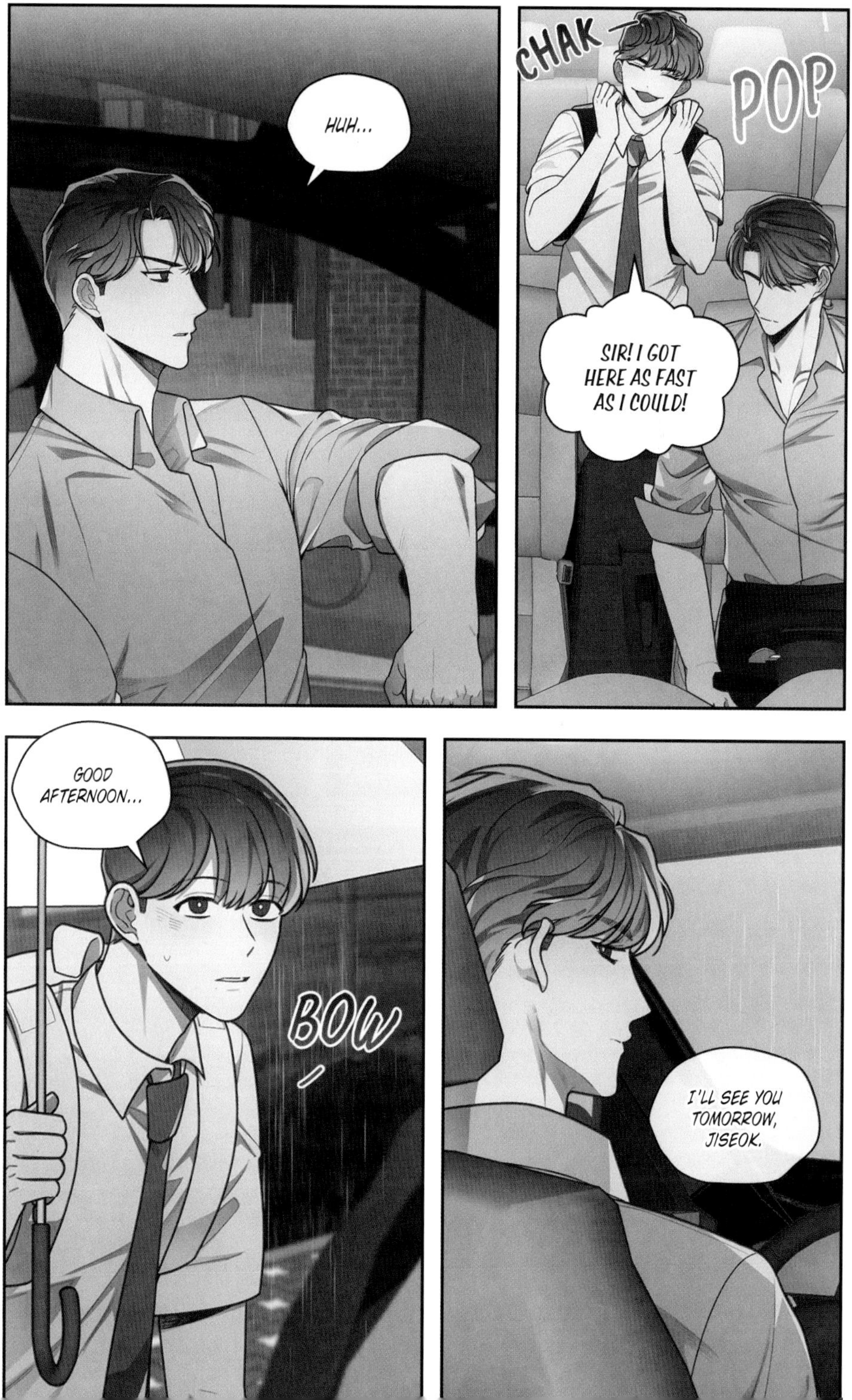
HUH...
CHAK
POP
SIR! I GOT HERE AS FAST AS I COULD!
GOOD AFTERNOON...
BOW
I'LL SEE YOU TOMORROW, JISEOK.

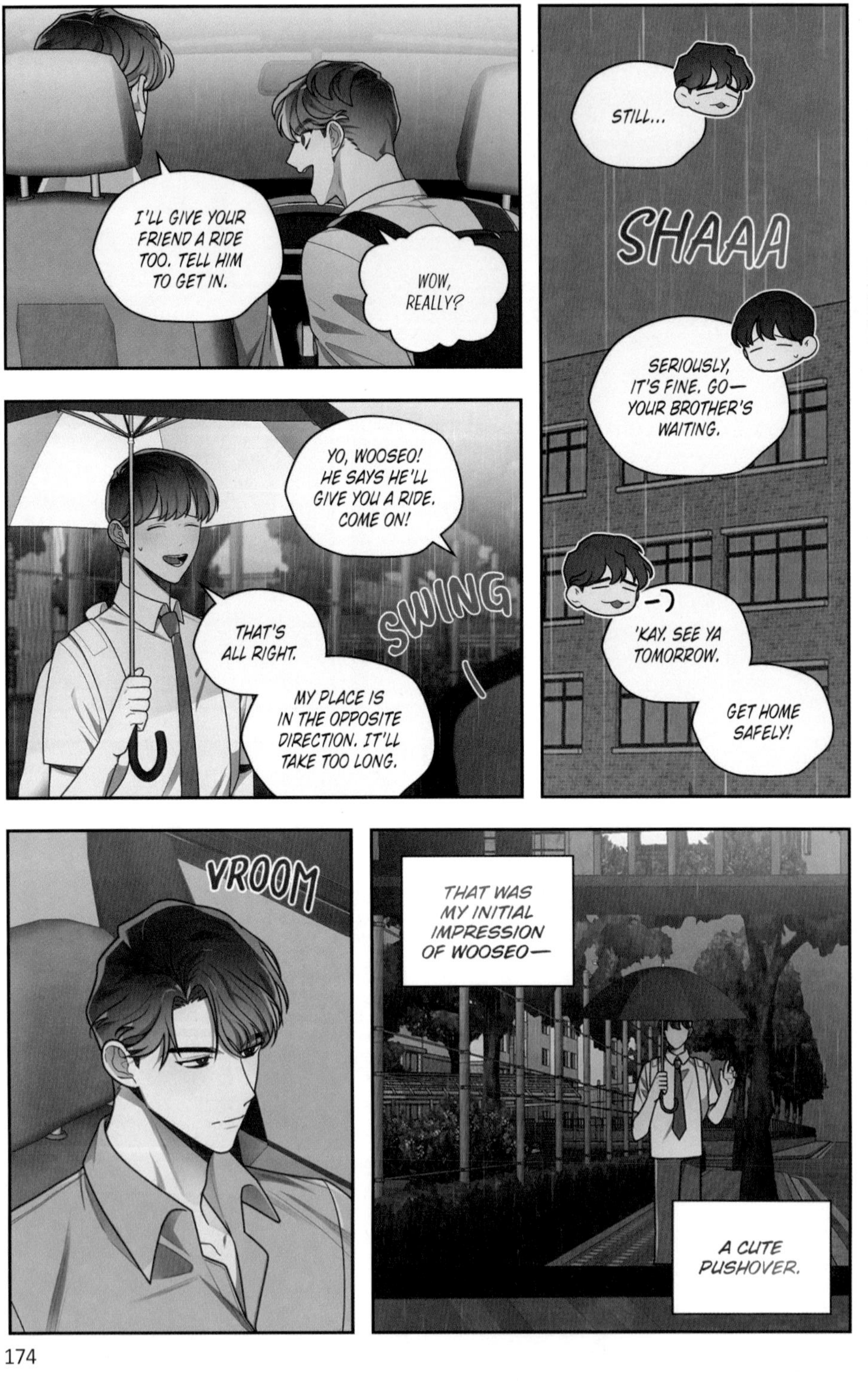

I'LL GIVE YOUR FRIEND A RIDE TOO. TELL HIM TO GET IN.
WOW, REALLY?
YO, WOOSEO! HE SAYS HE'LL GIVE YOU A RIDE. COME ON!
THAT'S ALL RIGHT.
MY PLACE IS IN THE OPPOSITE DIRECTION. IT'LL TAKE TOO LONG.
SWING
STILL...
SHAAA
SERIOUSLY, IT'S FINE. GO— YOUR BROTHER'S WAITING.
'KAY. SEE YA TOMORROW.
GET HOME SAFELY!
VROOM
THAT WAS MY INITIAL IMPRESSION OF WOOSEO—
A CUTE PUSHOVER.

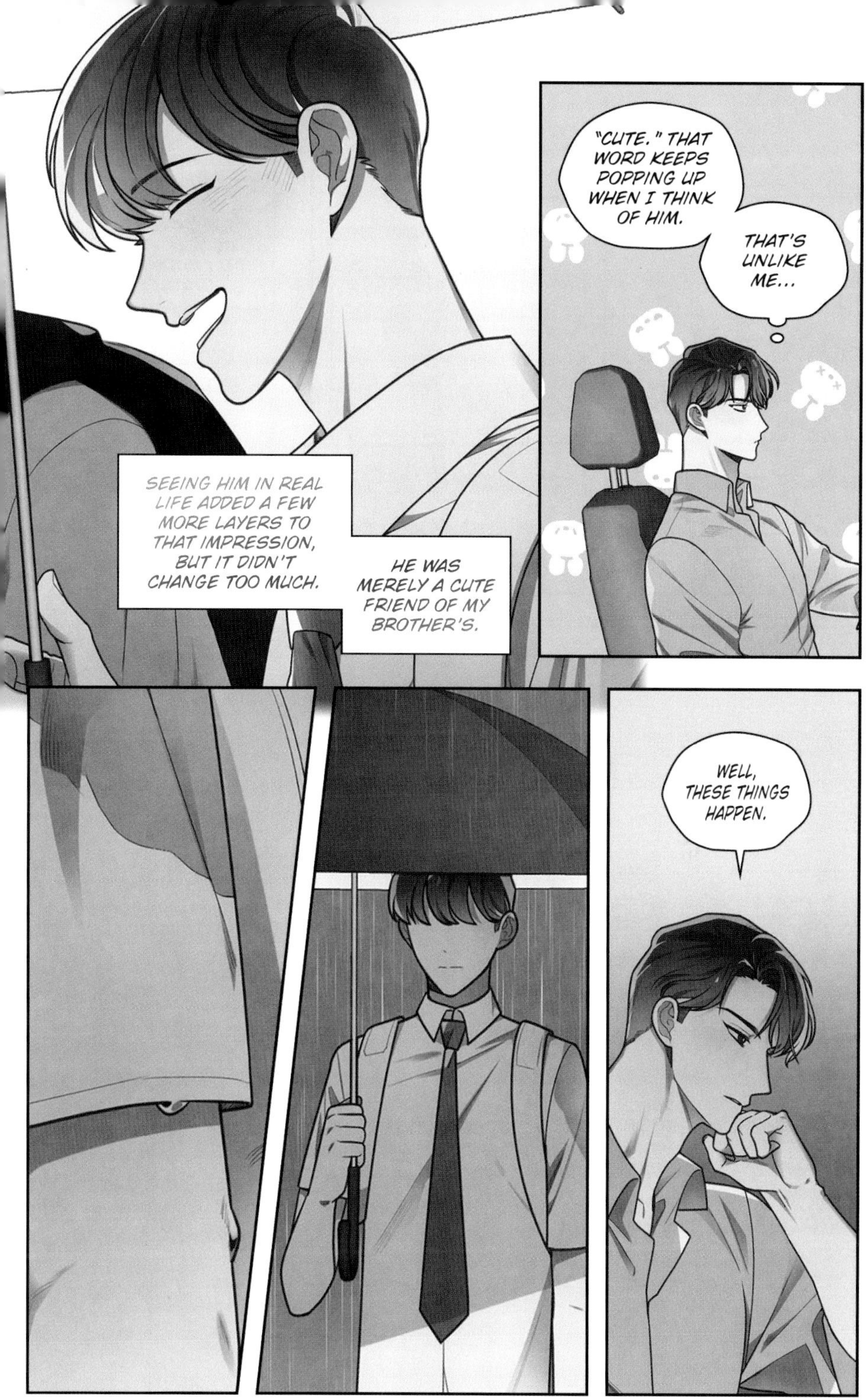
SEEING HIM IN REAL LIFE ADDED A FEW MORE LAYERS TO THAT IMPRESSION, BUT IT DIDN'T CHANGE TOO MUCH.
HE WAS MERELY A CUTE FRIEND OF MY BROTHER'S.
"CUTE." THAT WORD KEEPS POPPING UP WHEN I THINK OF HIM.
THAT'S UNLIKE ME...
WELL, THESE THINGS HAPPEN.

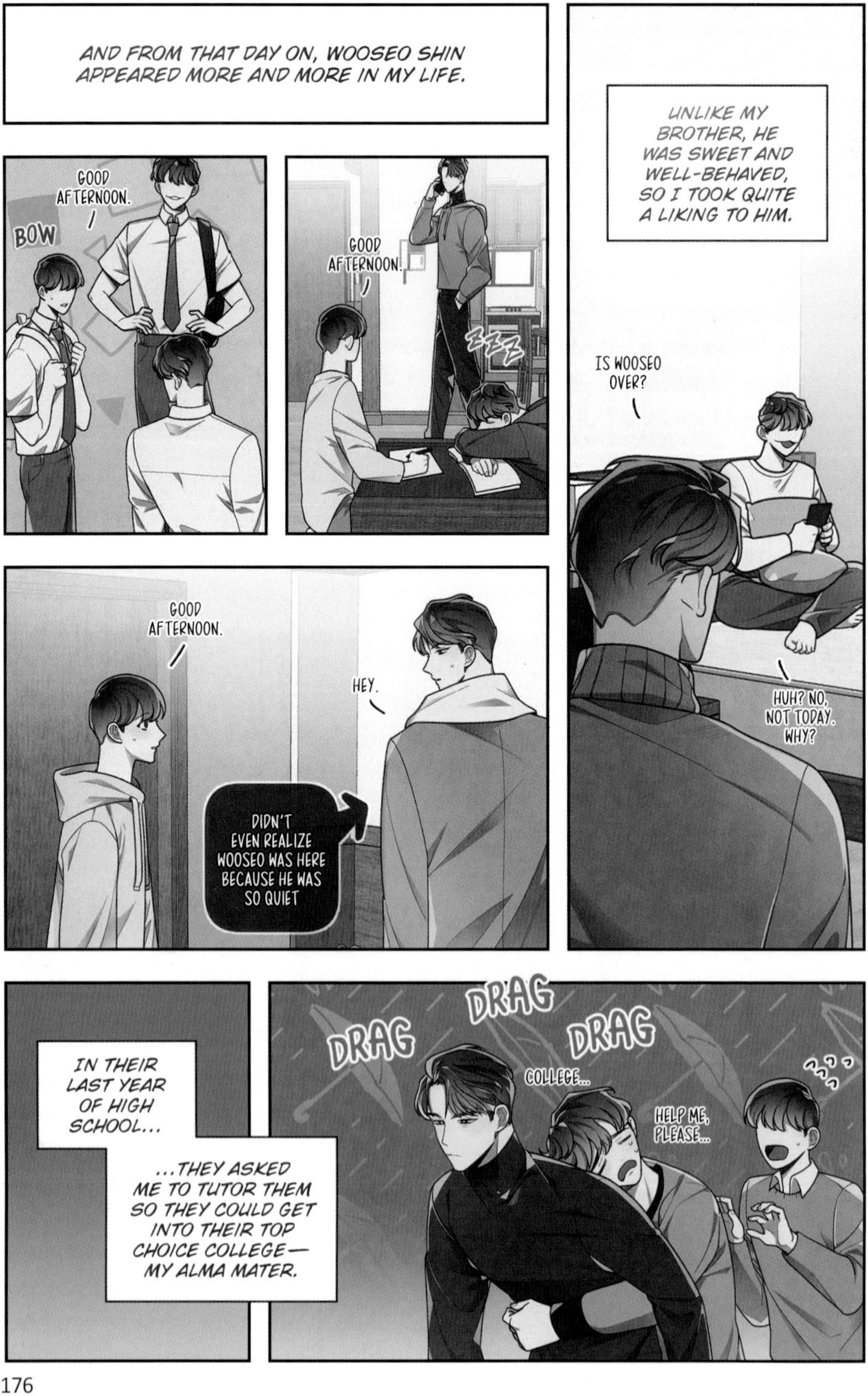
AND FROM THAT DAY ON, WOOSEO SHIN APPEARED MORE AND MORE IN MY LIFE.
GOOD AFTERNOON.
BOW
GOOD AFTERNOON.
ZZZ
UNLIKE MY BROTHER, HE WAS SWEET AND WELL-BEHAVED, SO I TOOK QUITE A LIKING TO HIM.
IS WOOSEO OVER?
HUH? NO, NOT TODAY. WHY?
GOOD AFTERNOON.
HEY.
DIDN'T EVEN REALIZE WOOSEO WAS HERE BECAUSE HE WAS SO QUIET
IN THEIR LAST YEAR OF HIGH SCHOOL...
...THEY ASKED ME TO TUTOR THEM SO THEY COULD GET INTO THEIR TOP CHOICE COLLEGE—MY ALMA MATER.
DRAG
DRAG
DRAG
COLLEGE...
HELP ME, PLEASE...

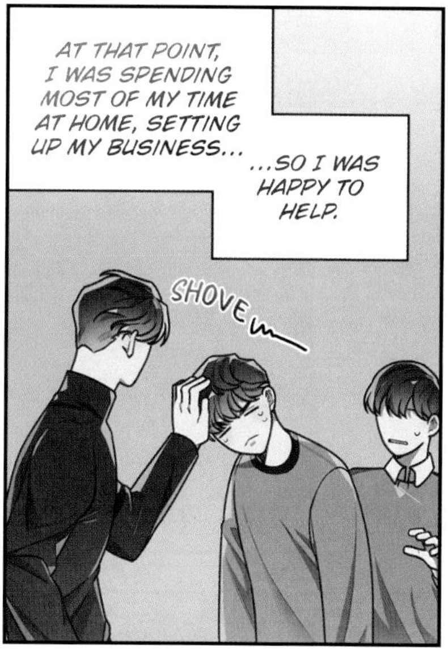
AT THAT POINT, I WAS SPENDING MOST OF MY TIME AT HOME, SETTING UP MY BUSINESS...
...SO I WAS HAPPY TO HELP.
SHOVE

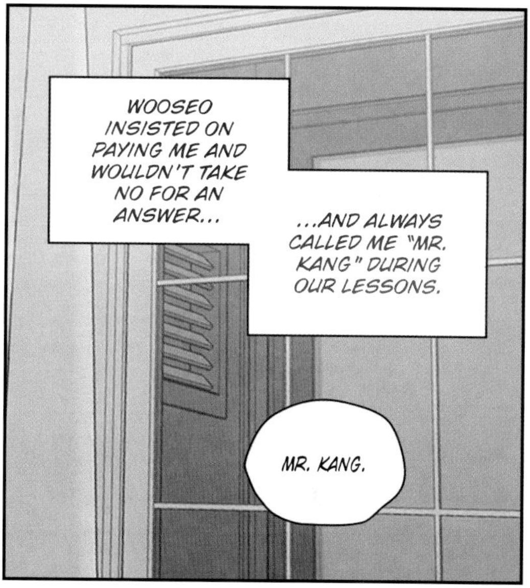
WOOSEO INSISTED ON PAYING ME AND WOULDN'T TAKE NO FOR AN ANSWER...
...AND ALWAYS CALLED ME "MR. KANG" DURING OUR LESSONS.
MR. KANG.

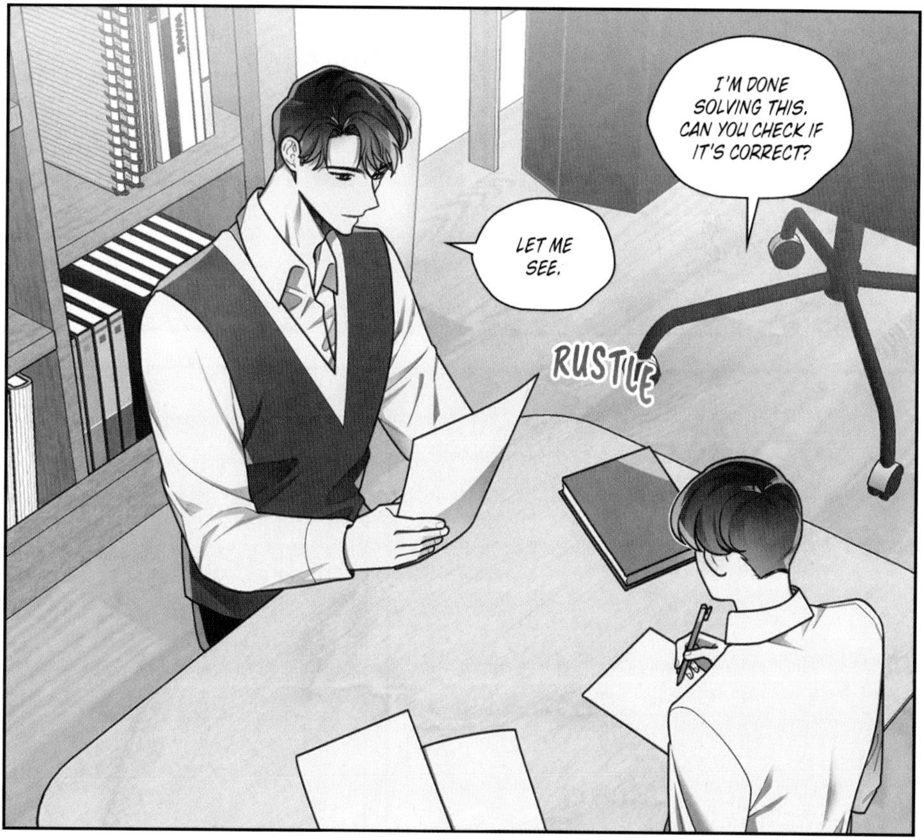
I'M DONE SOLVING THIS. CAN YOU CHECK IF IT'S CORRECT?
LET ME SEE.
RUSTLE

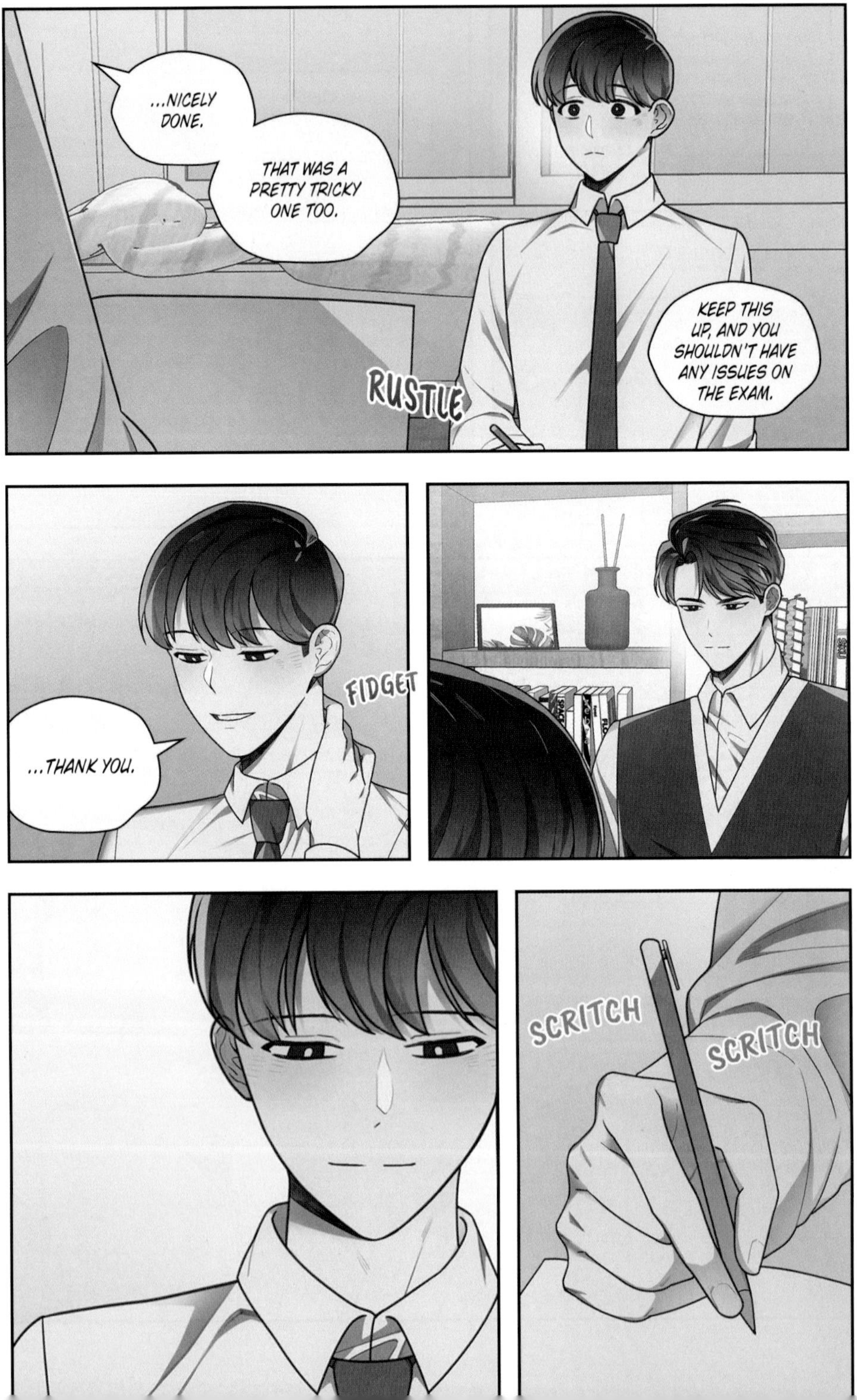
...NICELY DONE.
THAT WAS A PRETTY TRICKY ONE TOO.
RUSTLE
KEEP THIS UP, AND YOU SHOULDN'T HAVE ANY ISSUES ON THE EXAM.
FIDGET
...THANK YOU.
SCRITCH
SCRITCH

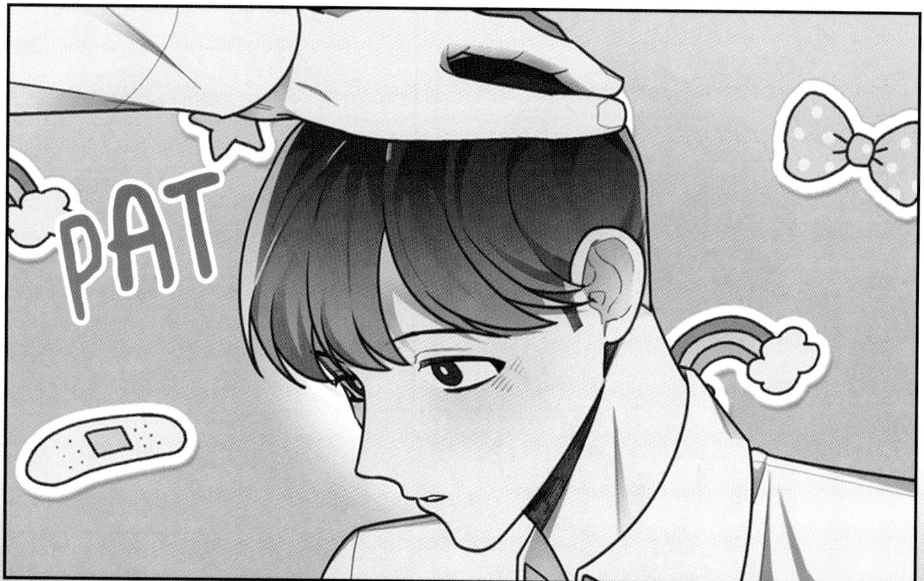
PAT

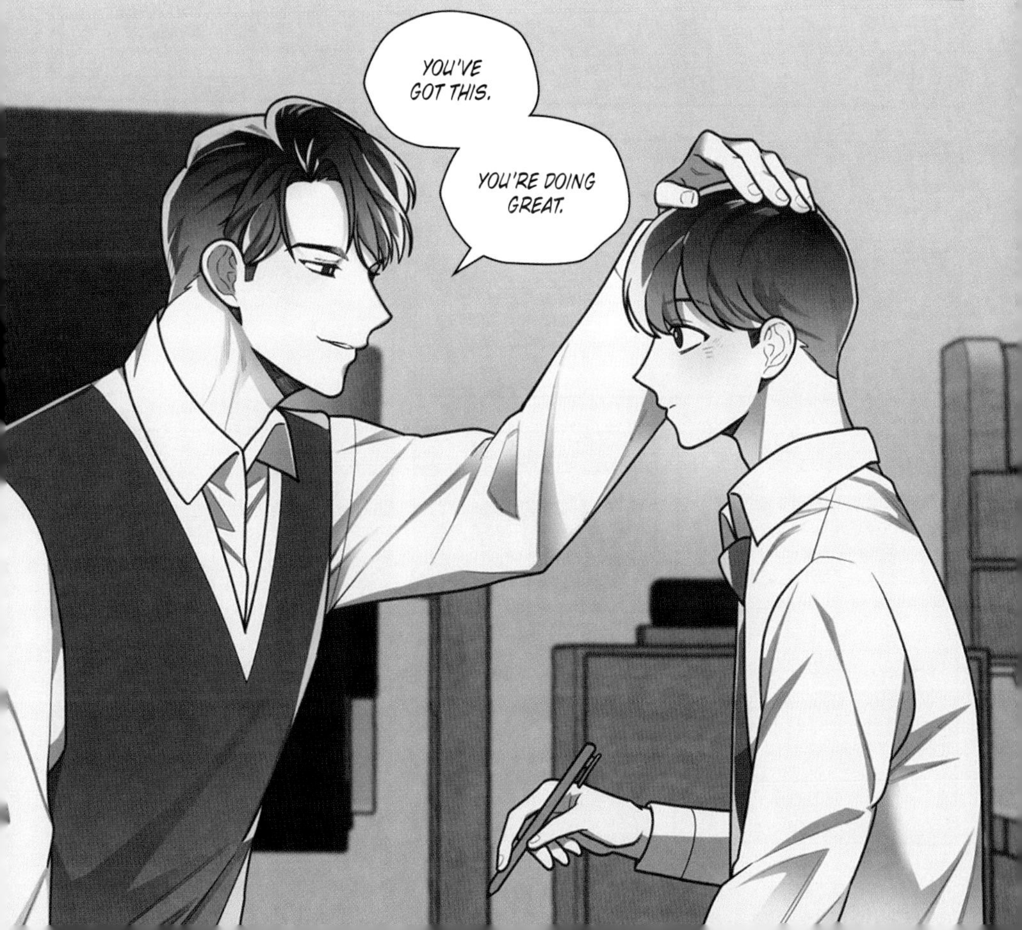
YOU'VE GOT THIS.
YOU'RE DOING GREAT.

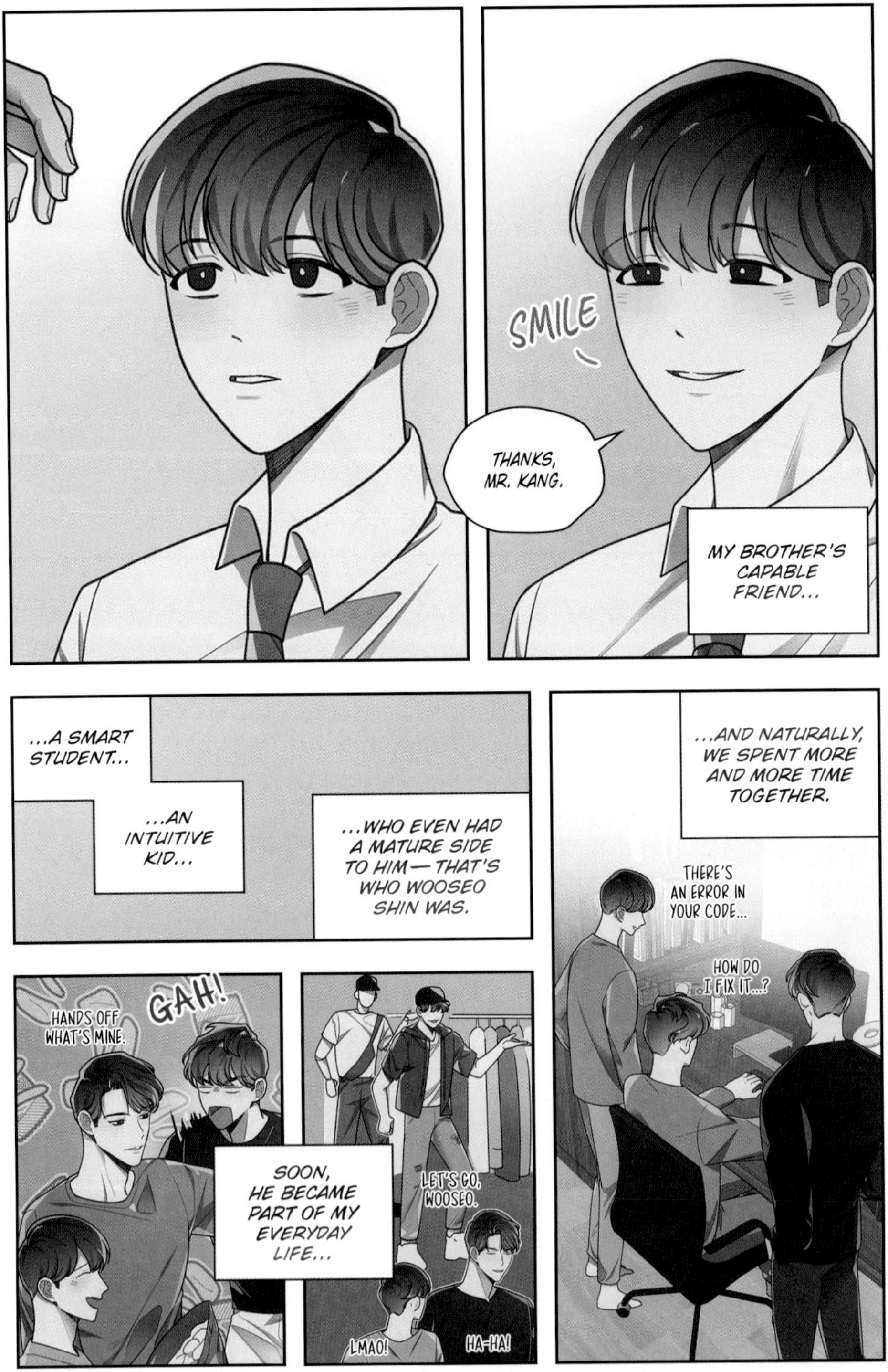
SMILE
THANKS, MR. KANG.
MY BROTHER'S CAPABLE FRIEND...
...A SMART STUDENT...
...AN INTUITIVE KID...
...WHO EVEN HAD A MATURE SIDE TO HIM—THAT'S WHO WOOSEO SHIN WAS.
...AND NATURALLY, WE SPENT MORE AND MORE TIME TOGETHER.
THERE'S AN ERROR IN YOUR CODE...
HOW DO I FIX IT...?
HANDS OFF WHAT'S MINE.
GAH!
SOON, HE BECAME PART OF MY EVERYDAY LIFE...
LET'S GO, WOOSEO.
LMAO!
HA-HA!

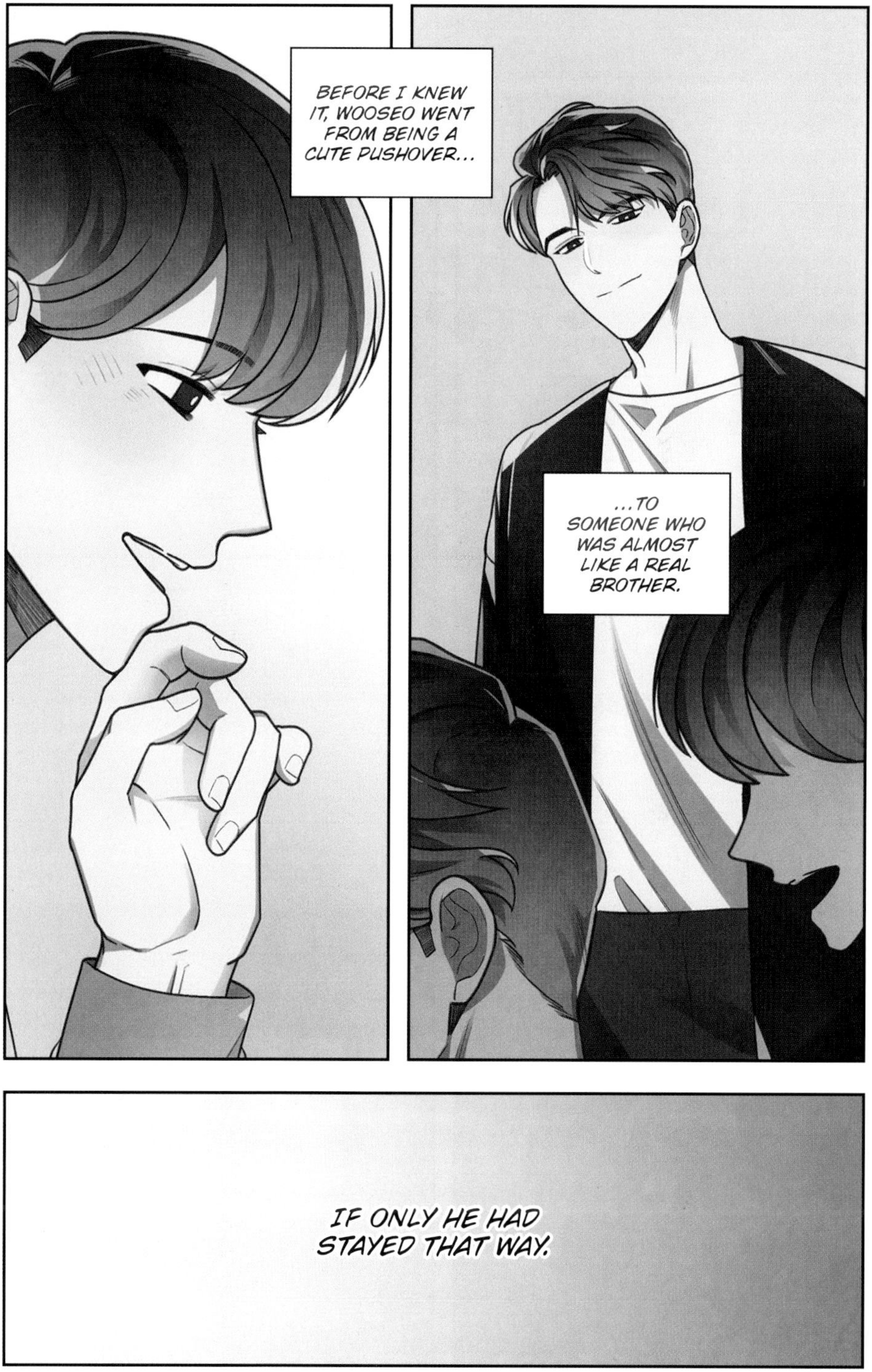
BEFORE I KNEW IT, WOOSEO WENT FROM BEING A CUTE PUSHOVER...
...TO SOMEONE WHO WAS ALMOST LIKE A REAL BROTHER.
IF ONLY HE HAD STAYED THAT WAY.

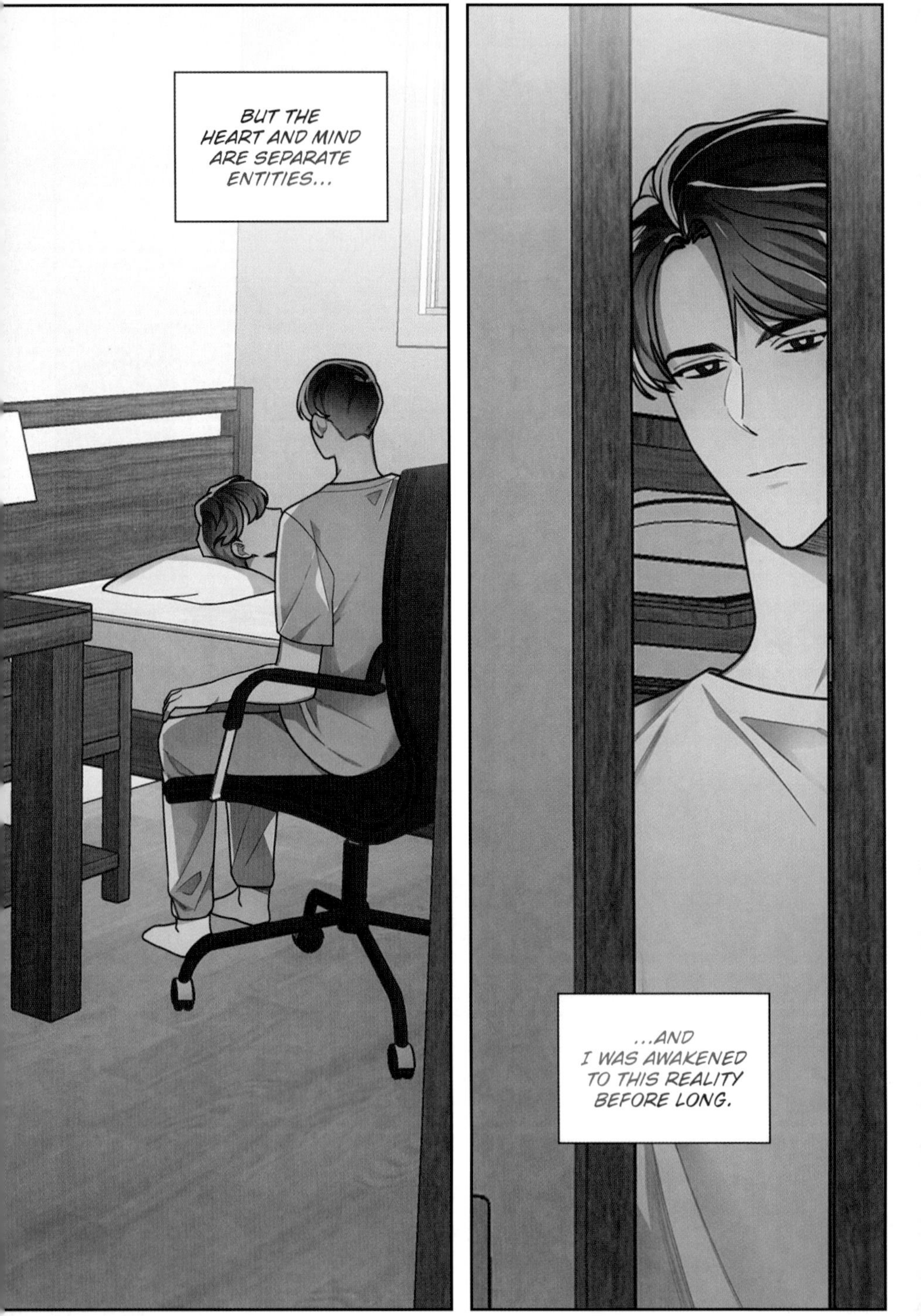
BUT THE HEART AND MIND ARE SEPARATE ENTITIES...
...AND I WAS AWAKENED TO THIS REALITY BEFORE LONG.

Tied to You

Chapter 10

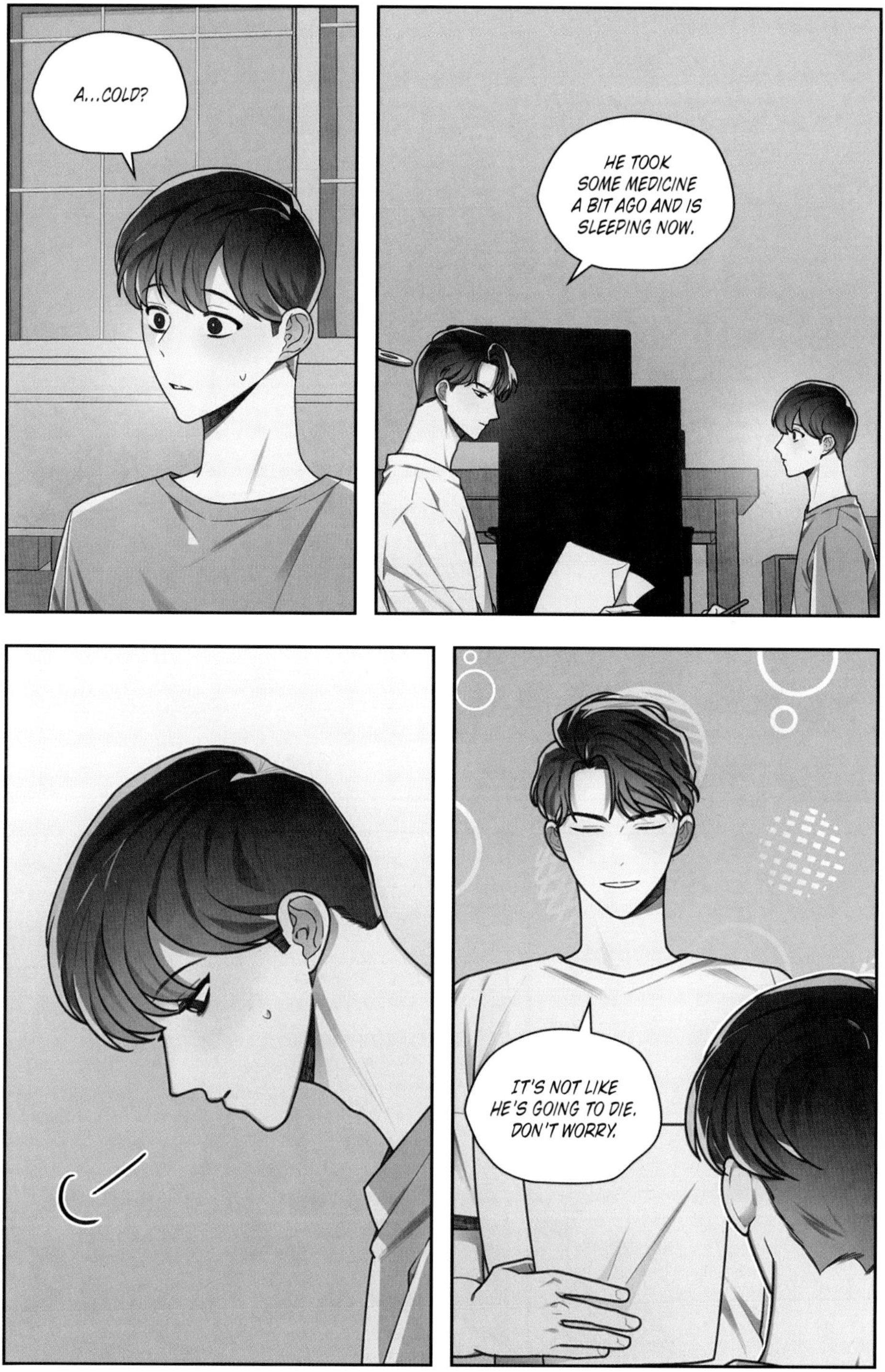
A...COLD?
HE TOOK SOME MEDICINE A BIT AGO AND IS SLEEPING NOW.
IT'S NOT LIKE HE'S GOING TO DIE. DON'T WORRY.

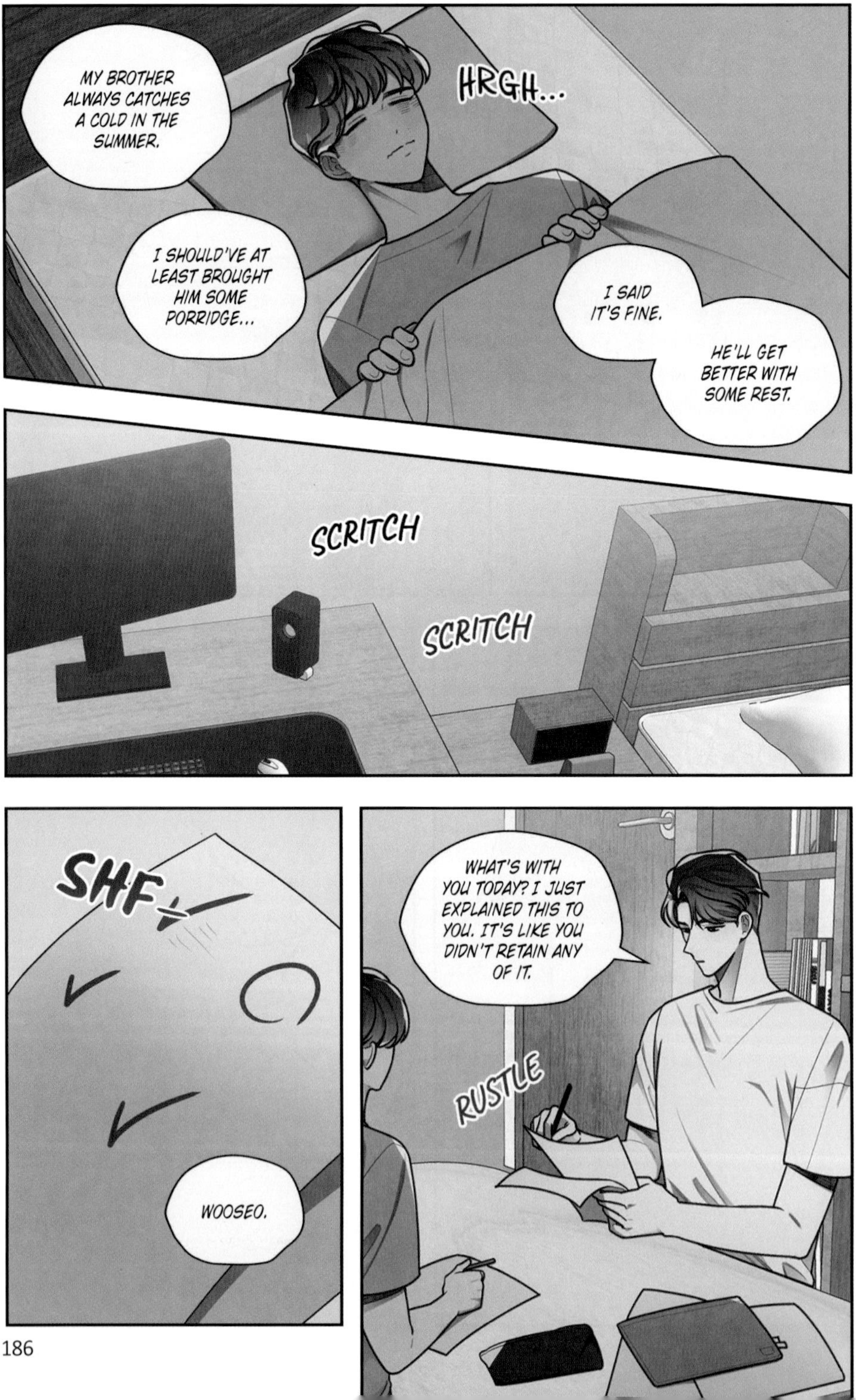

MY BROTHER ALWAYS CATCHES A COLD IN THE SUMMER.
HRGH...
I SHOULD'VE AT LEAST BROUGHT HIM SOME PORRIDGE...
I SAID IT'S FINE.
HE'LL GET BETTER WITH SOME REST.
SCRITCH
SCRITCH
SHF
WOOSEO.
WHAT'S WITH YOU TODAY? I JUST EXPLAINED THIS TO YOU. IT'S LIKE YOU DIDN'T RETAIN ANY OF IT.
RUSTLE

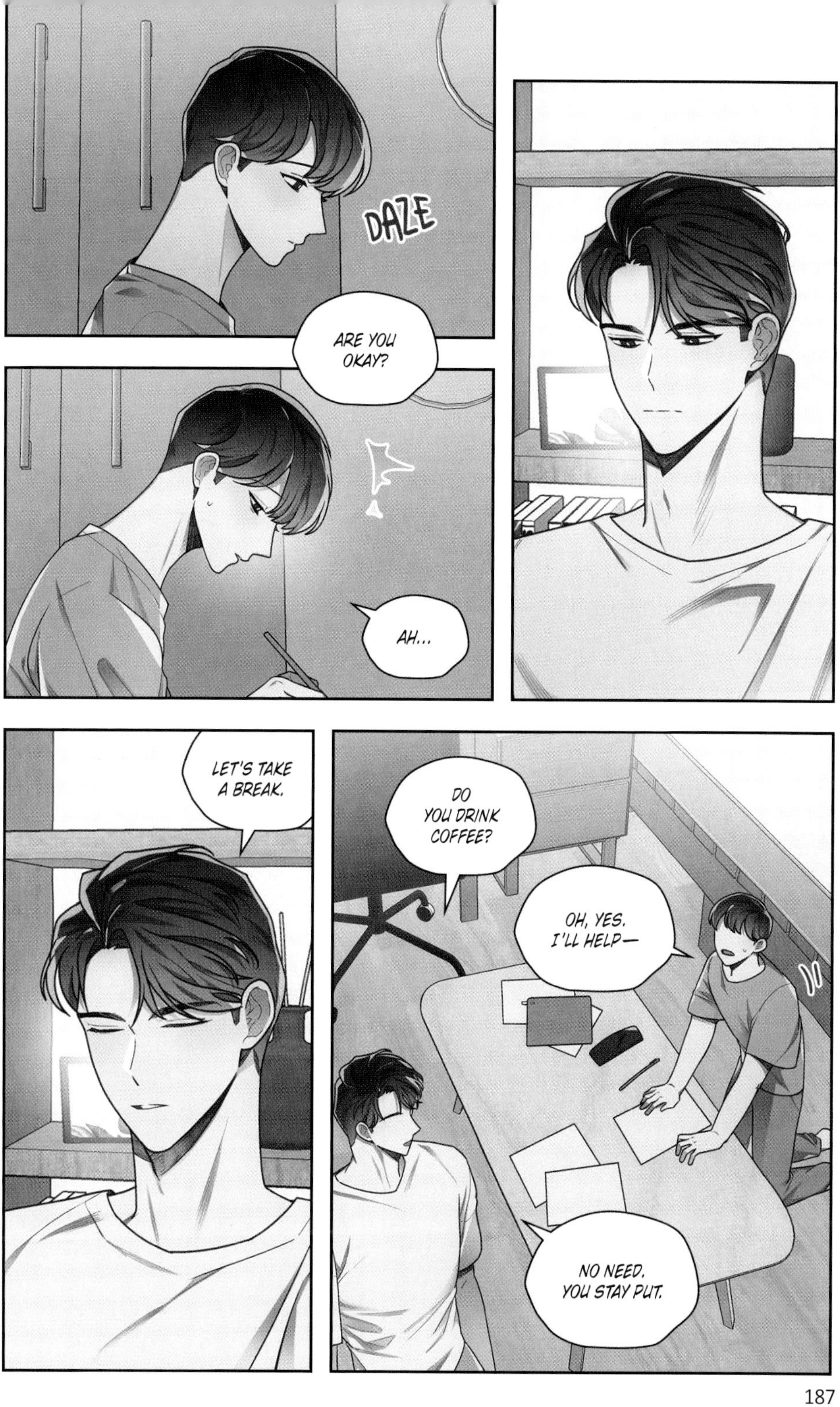
DAZE
ARE YOU OKAY?
AH...
LET'S TAKE A BREAK.
DO YOU DRINK COFFEE?
OH, YES. I'LL HELP—
NO NEED. YOU STAY PUT.

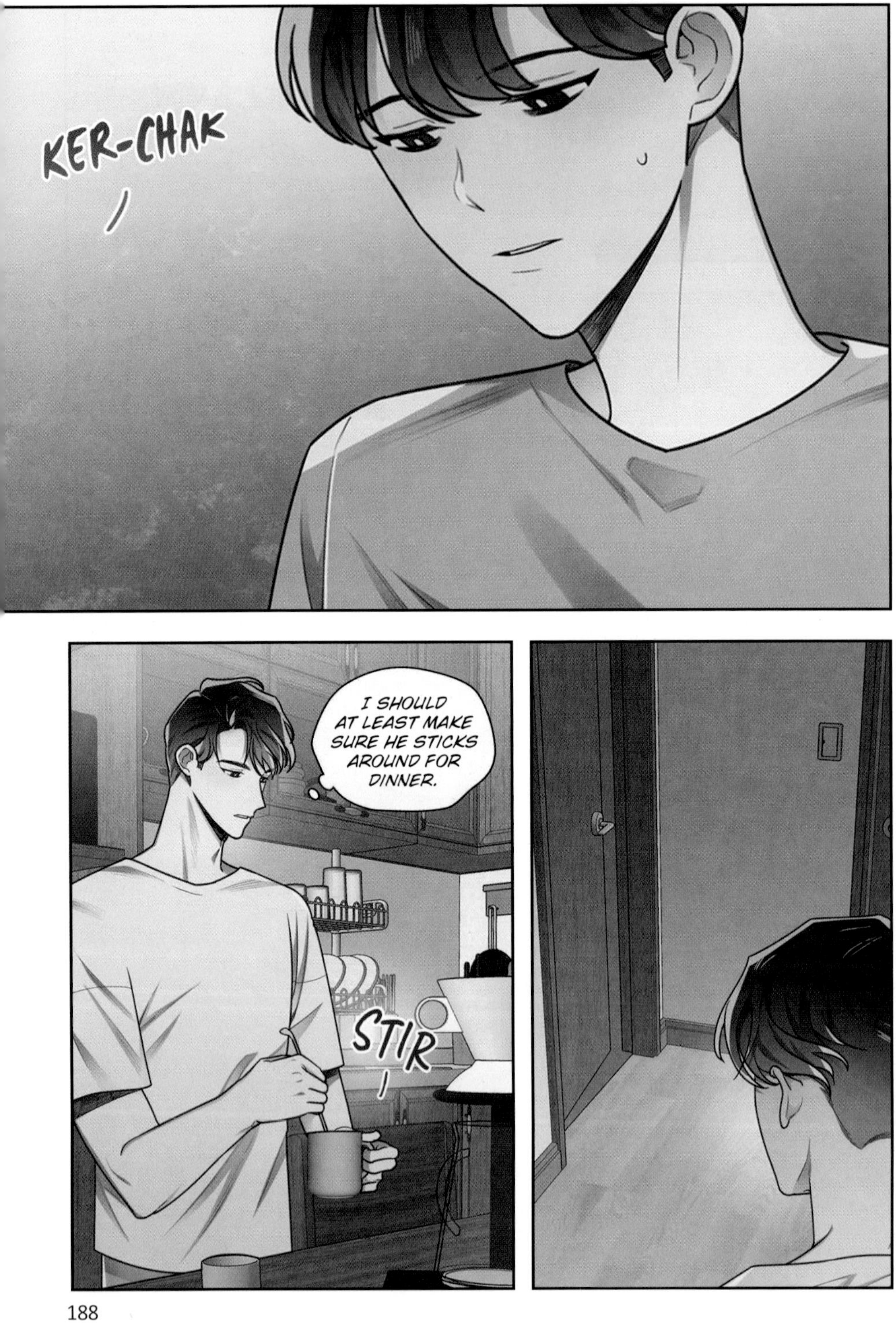
KER-CHAK
I SHOULD AT LEAST MAKE SURE HE STICKS AROUND FOR DINNER.
STIR

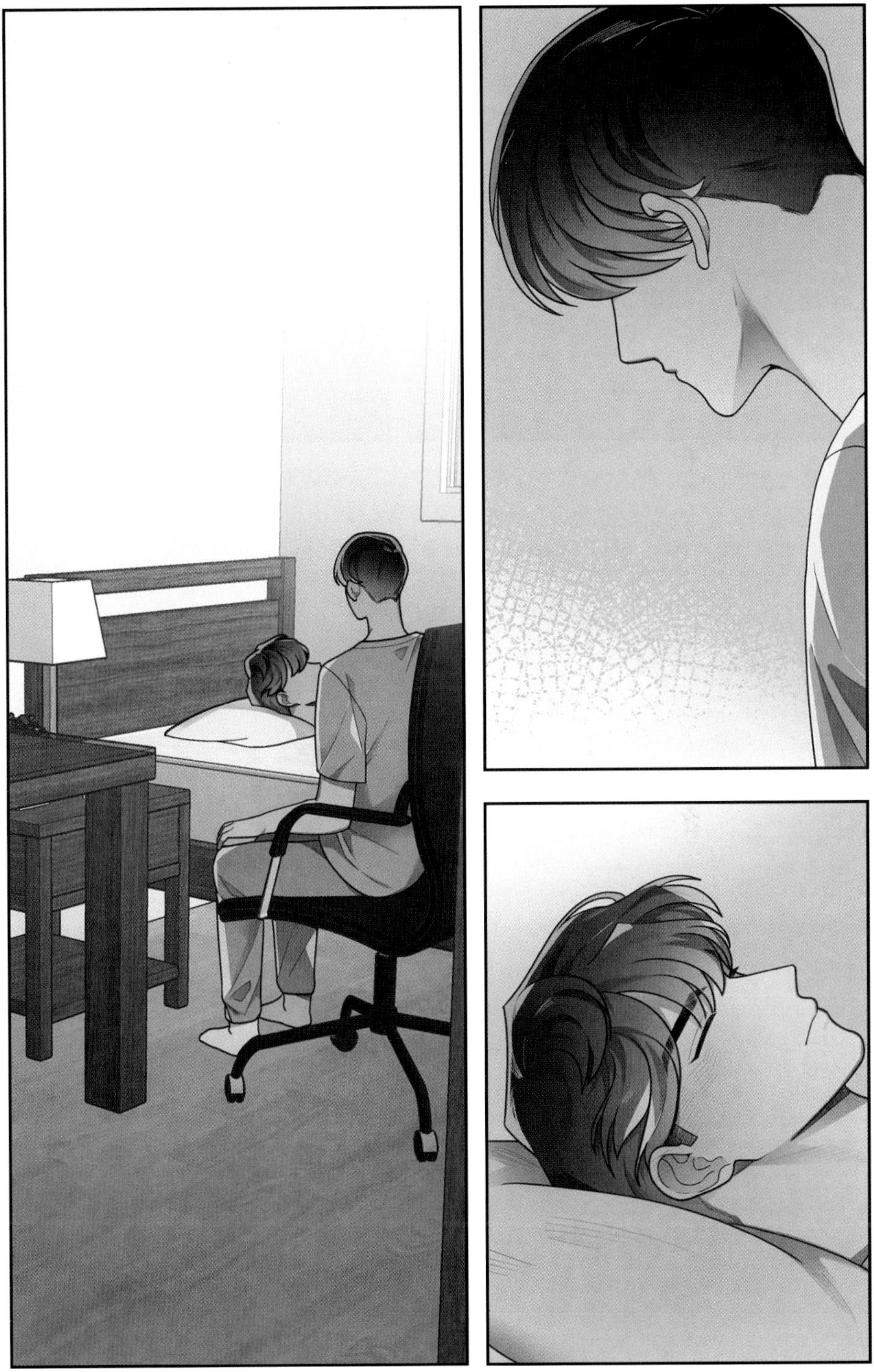

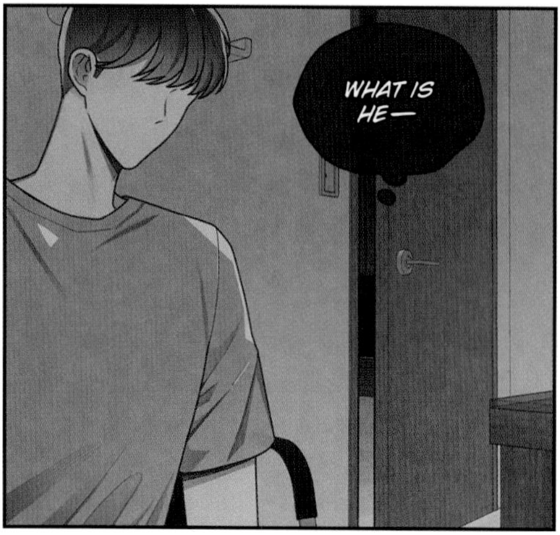
WHAT IS HE—

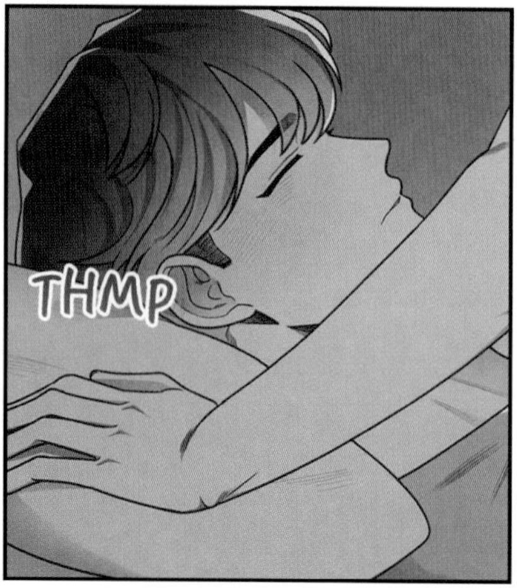
THMP

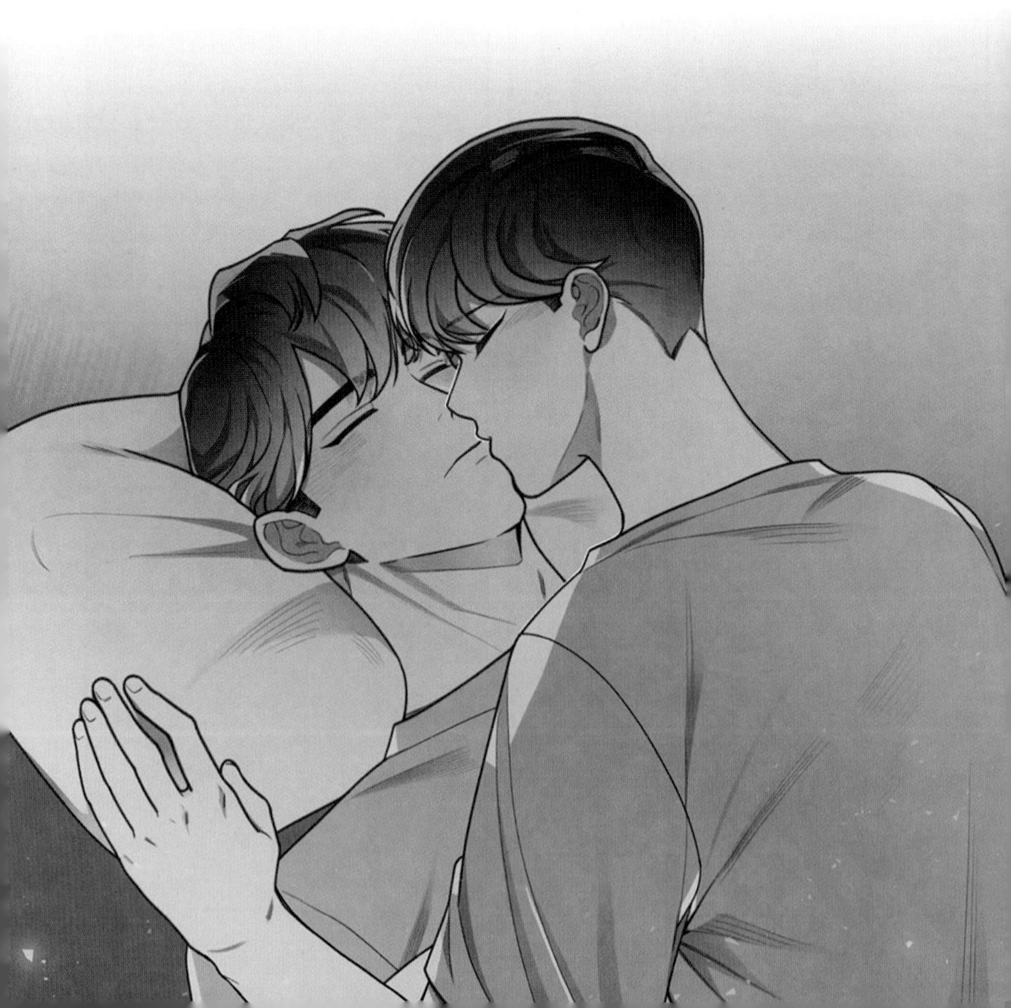

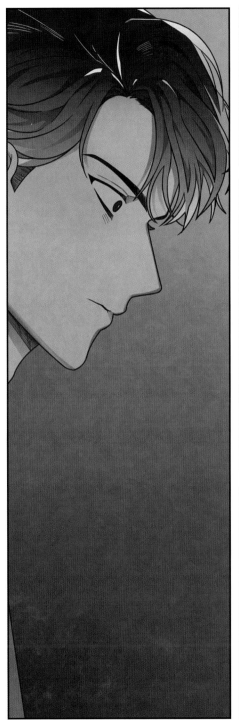

CLICK

FWUMP

SINCE WHEN...?

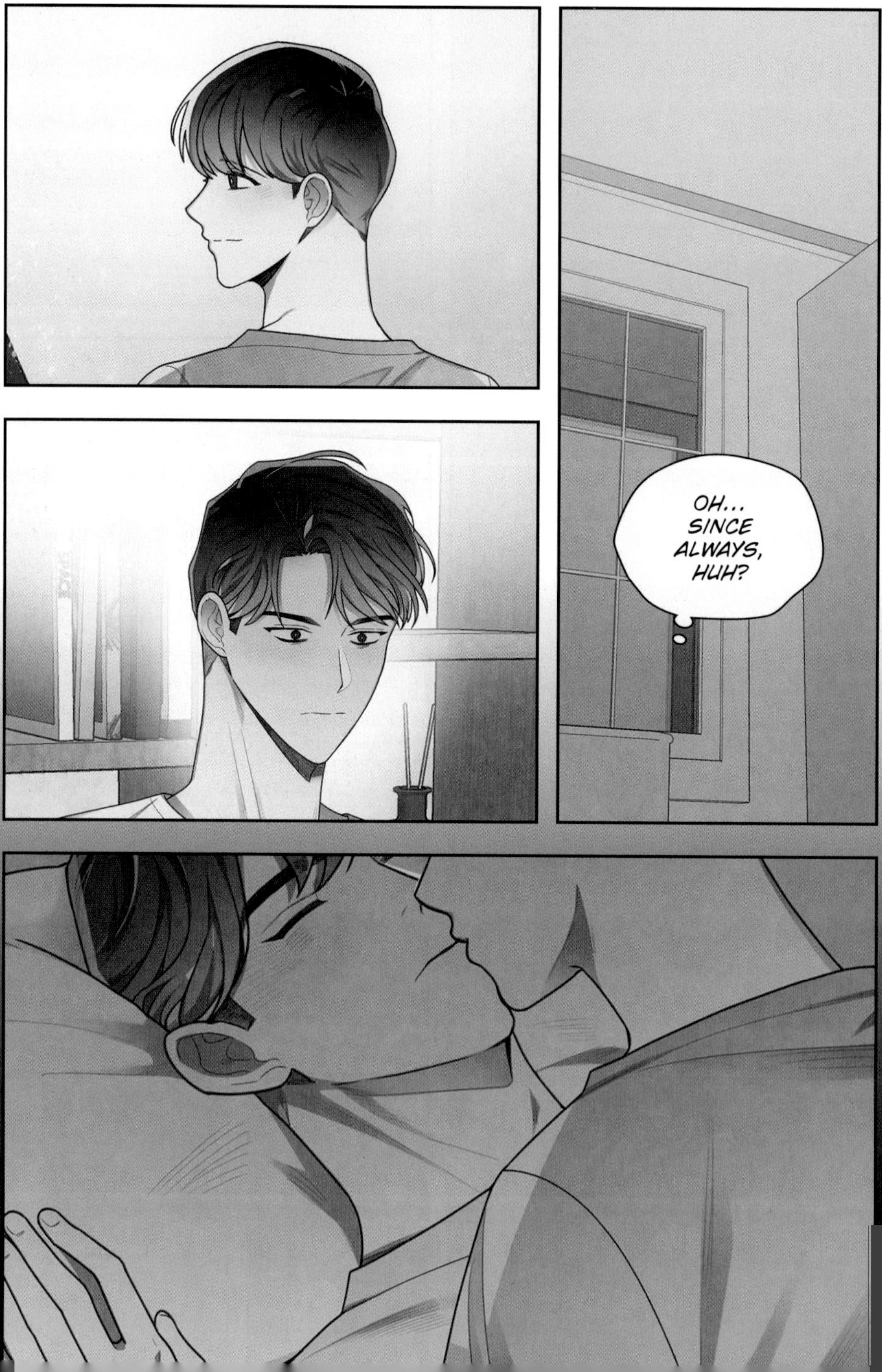
OH... SINCE ALWAYS, HUH?

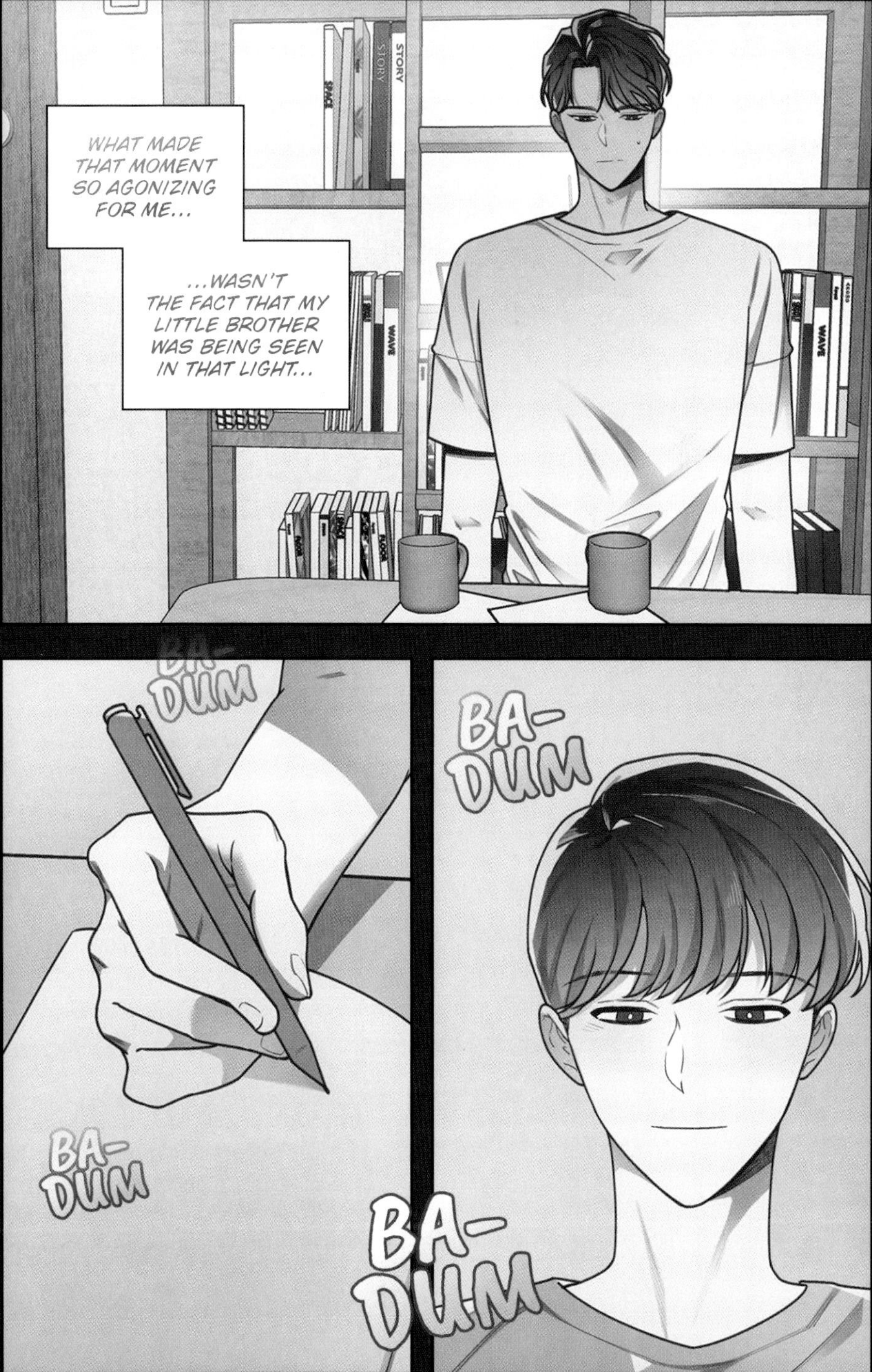
WHAT MADE THAT MOMENT SO AGONIZING FOR ME...
...WASN'T THE FACT THAT MY LITTLE BROTHER WAS BEING SEEN IN THAT LIGHT...
BA-DUM
BA-DUM
BA-DUM
BA-DUM

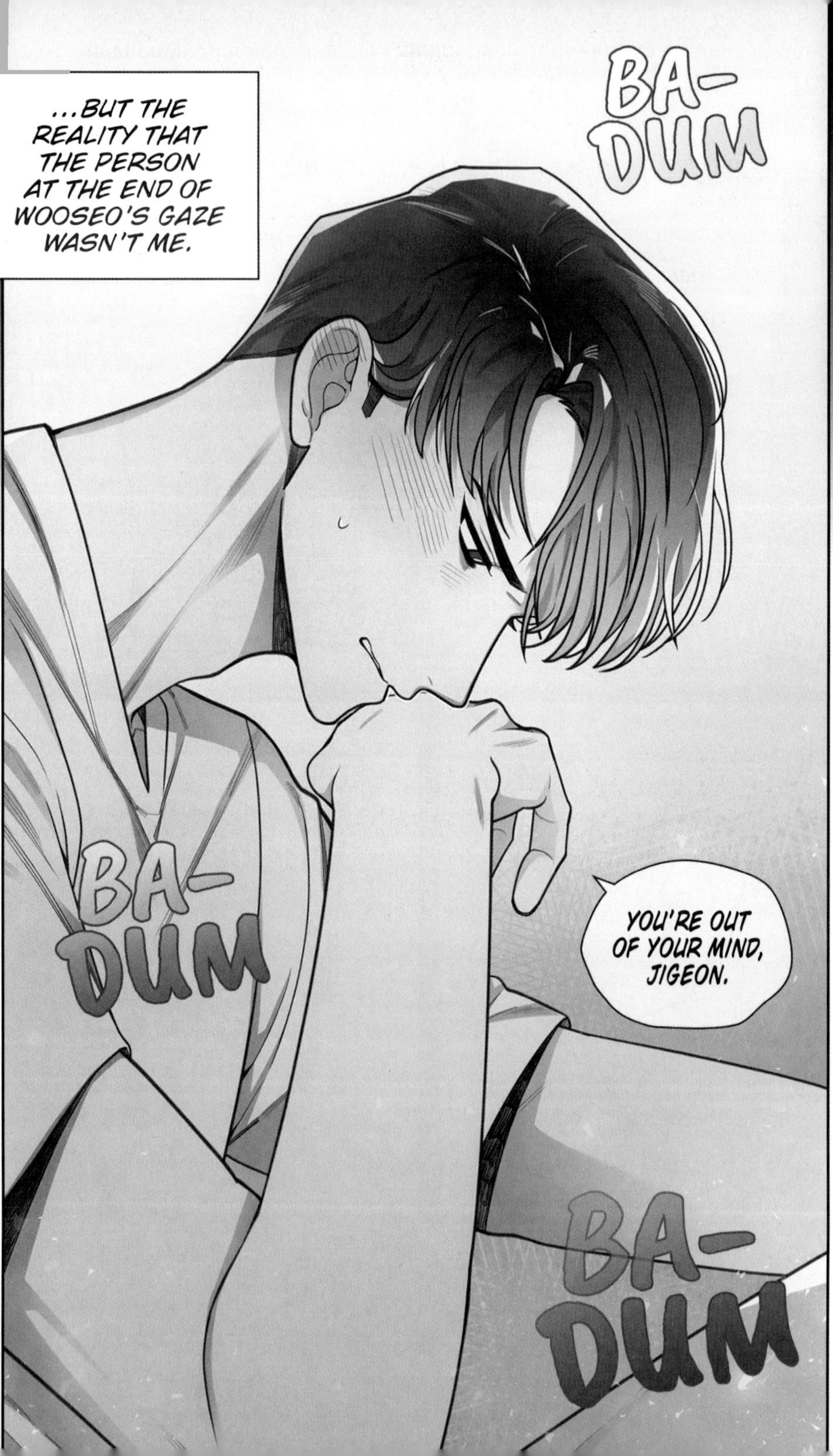
...BUT THE REALITY THAT THE PERSON AT THE END OF WOOSEO'S GAZE WASN'T ME.
BA-DUM
BA-DUM
YOU'RE OUT OF YOUR MIND, JIGEON.
BA-DUM

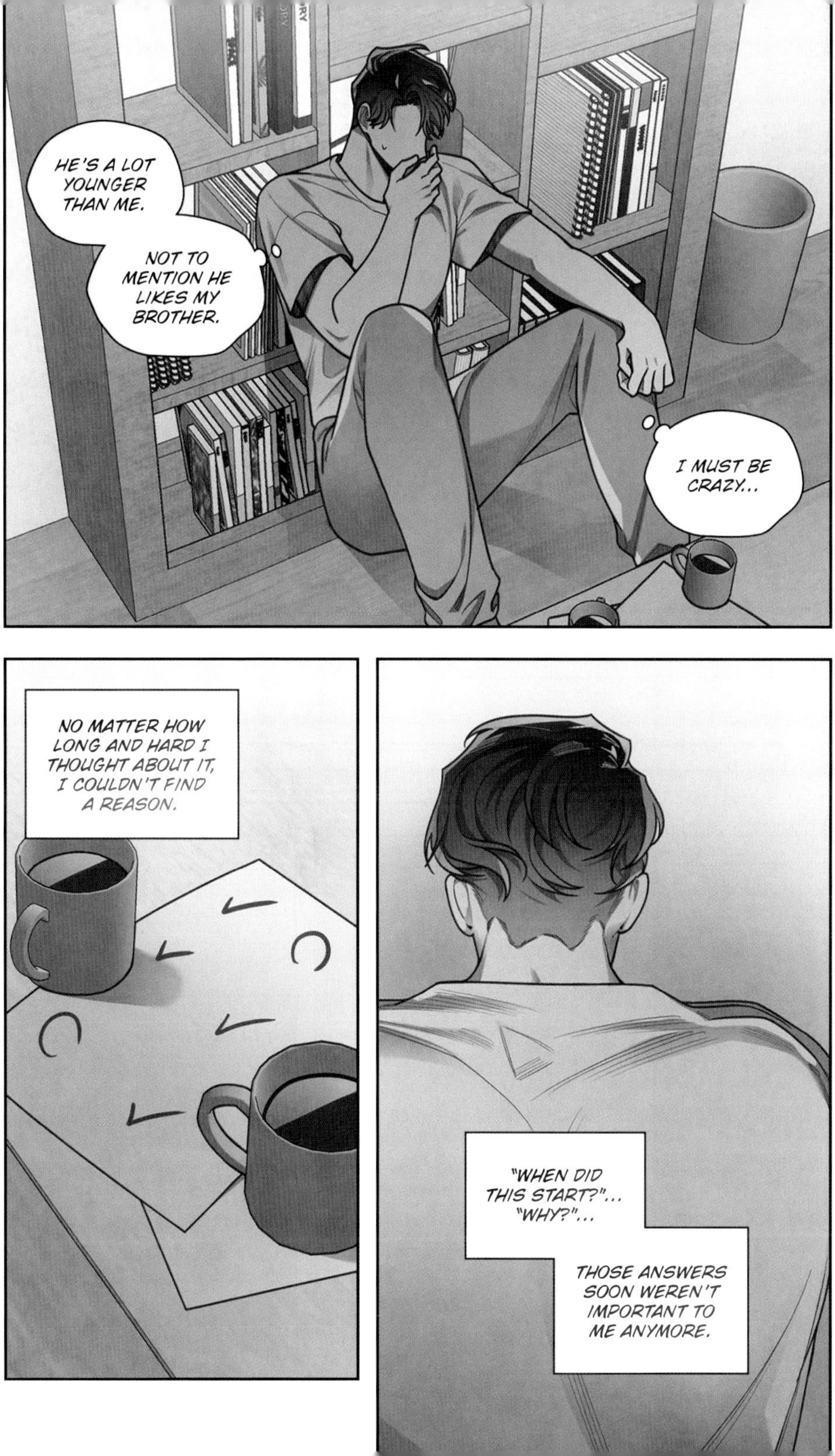
HE'S A LOT YOUNGER THAN ME.
NOT TO MENTION HE LIKES MY BROTHER.
I MUST BE CRAZY...
NO MATTER HOW LONG AND HARD I THOUGHT ABOUT IT, I COULDN'T FIND A REASON.
"WHEN DID THIS START?"... "WHY?"...
THOSE ANSWERS SOON WEREN'T IMPORTANT TO ME ANYMORE.

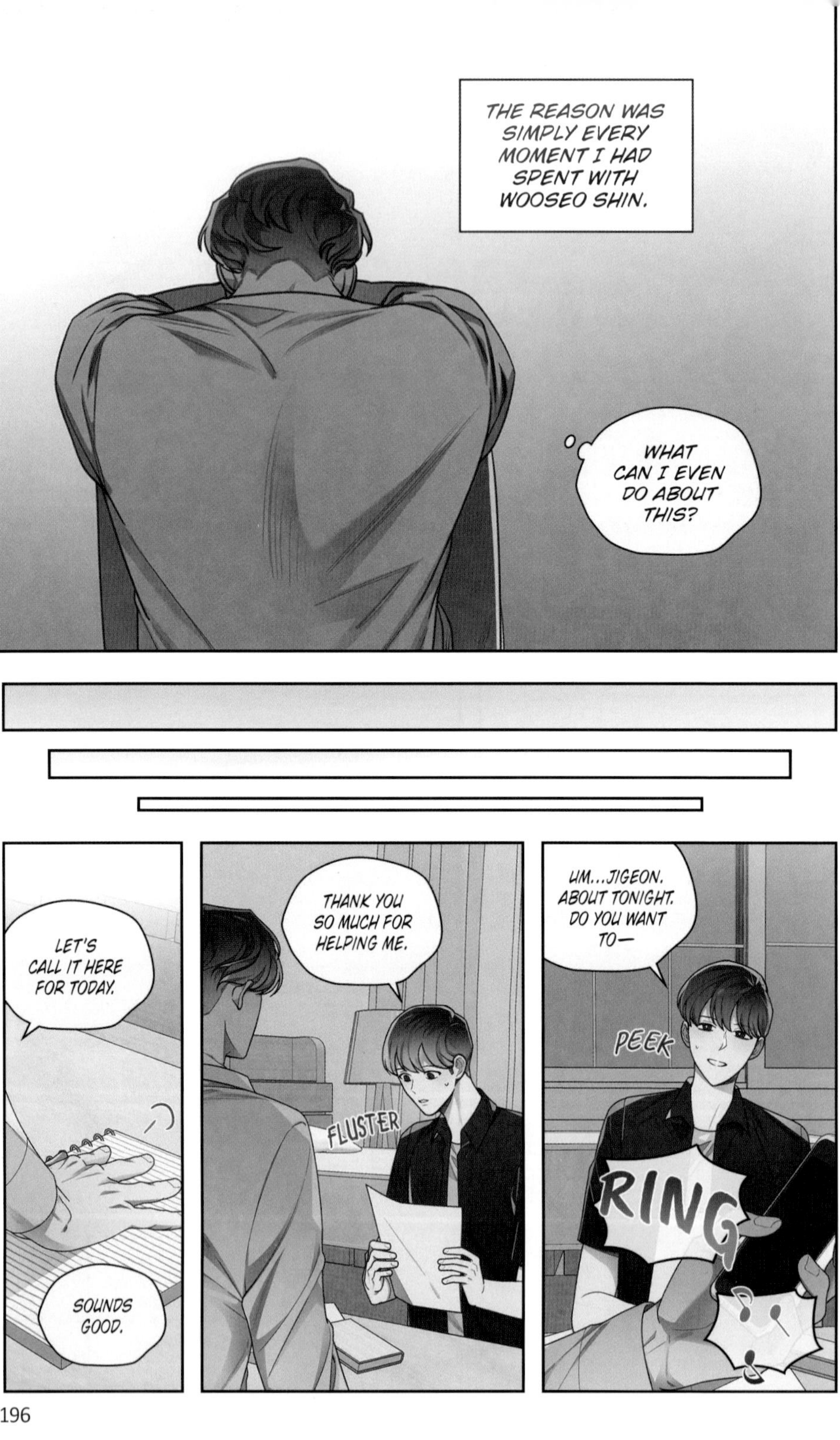
THE REASON WAS SIMPLY EVERY MOMENT I HAD SPENT WITH WOOSEO SHIN.
WHAT CAN I EVEN DO ABOUT THIS?
LET'S CALL IT HERE FOR TODAY.
SOUNDS GOOD.
THANK YOU SO MUCH FOR HELPING ME.
FLUSTER
UM...JIGEON. ABOUT TONIGHT. DO YOU WANT TO—
PEEK
RING

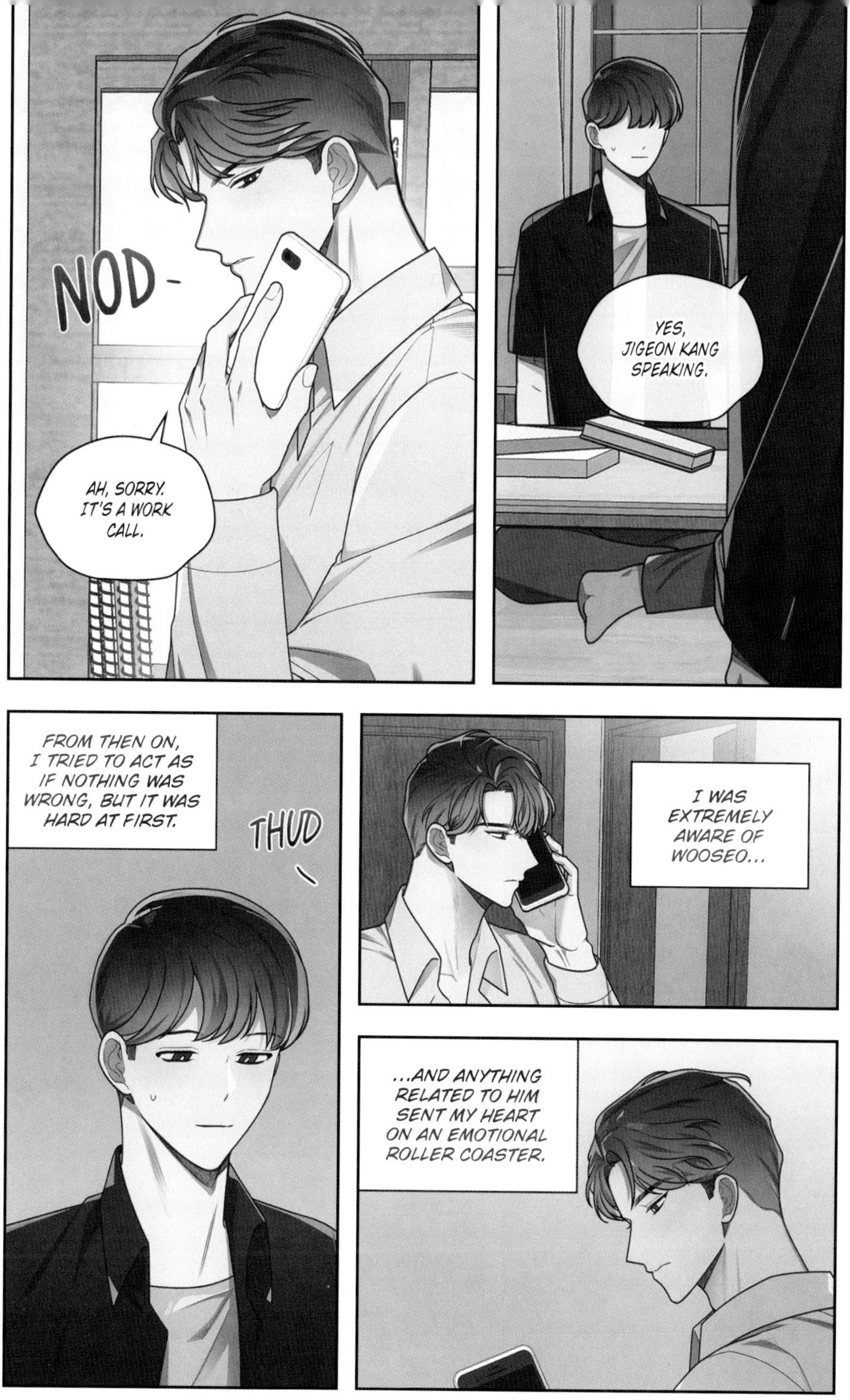
NOD
AH, SORRY. IT'S A WORK CALL.
YES, JIGEON KANG SPEAKING.
FROM THEN ON, I TRIED TO ACT AS IF NOTHING WAS WRONG, BUT IT WAS HARD AT FIRST.
THUD
I WAS EXTREMELY AWARE OF WOOSEO...
...AND ANYTHING RELATED TO HIM SENT MY HEART ON AN EMOTIONAL ROLLER COASTER.

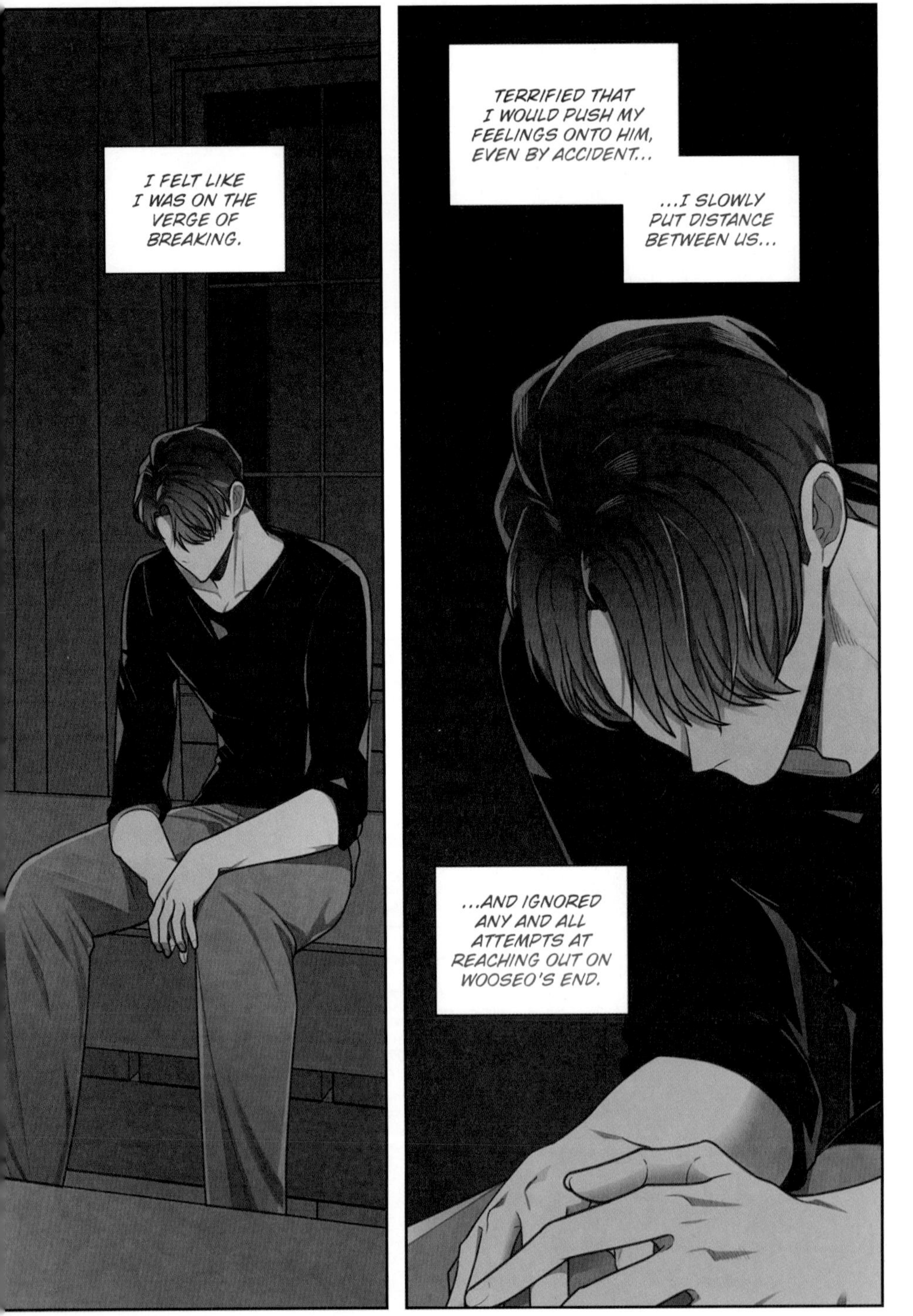
I FELT LIKE I WAS ON THE VERGE OF BREAKING.
TERRIFIED THAT I WOULD PUSH MY FEELINGS ONTO HIM, EVEN BY ACCIDENT...
...I SLOWLY PUT DISTANCE BETWEEN US...
...AND IGNORED ANY AND ALL ATTEMPTS AT REACHING OUT ON WOOSEO'S END.

BZZZT

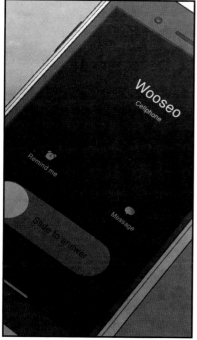

Wooseo
Cellphone

Remind me

Message

Slide to answer

I BELIEVED HIDING
MY FEELINGS WOULD
BE FOR THE BEST,
SINCE THEY'D NEVER
BE RECIPROCATED
ANYWAY.

I MAINTAINED THAT
DISTANCE FROM
HIM FOR THE FEW
YEARS AFTER
MY BROTHER
GRADUATED.

EVENTUALLY,
WOOSEO AND
I STOPPED
CONTACTING
EACH OTHER
COMPLETELY.

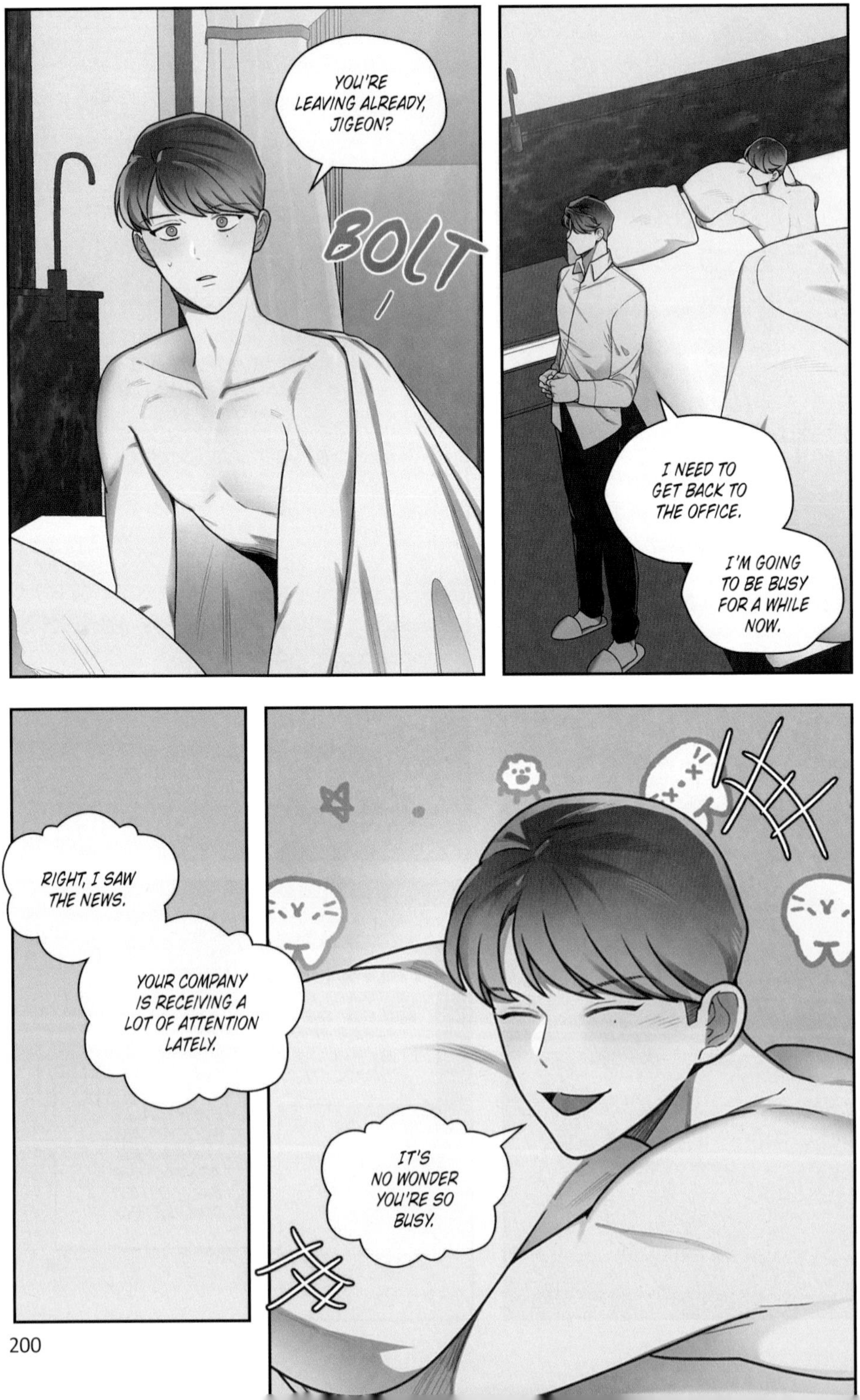
YOU'RE LEAVING ALREADY, JIGEON?
BOLT
I NEED TO GET BACK TO THE OFFICE.
I'M GOING TO BE BUSY FOR A WHILE NOW.
RIGHT, I SAW THE NEWS.
YOUR COMPANY IS RECEIVING A LOT OF ATTENTION LATELY.
IT'S NO WONDER YOU'RE SO BUSY.

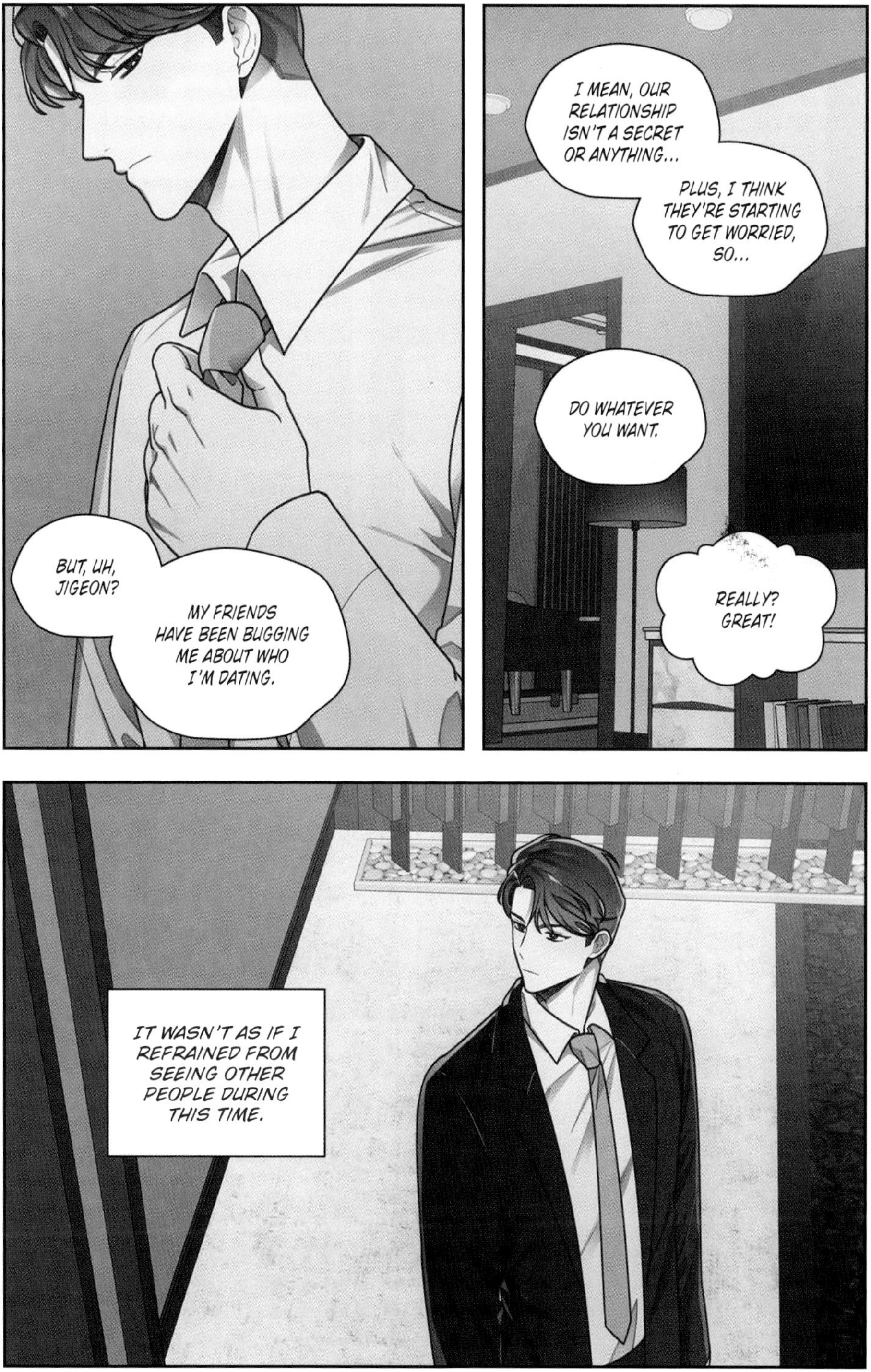
BUT, UH, JIGEON?
MY FRIENDS HAVE BEEN BUGGING ME ABOUT WHO I'M DATING.
I MEAN, OUR RELATIONSHIP ISN'T A SECRET OR ANYTHING...
PLUS, I THINK THEY'RE STARTING TO GET WORRIED, SO...
DO WHATEVER YOU WANT.
REALLY? GREAT!
IT WASN'T AS IF I REFRAINED FROM SEEING OTHER PEOPLE DURING THIS TIME.

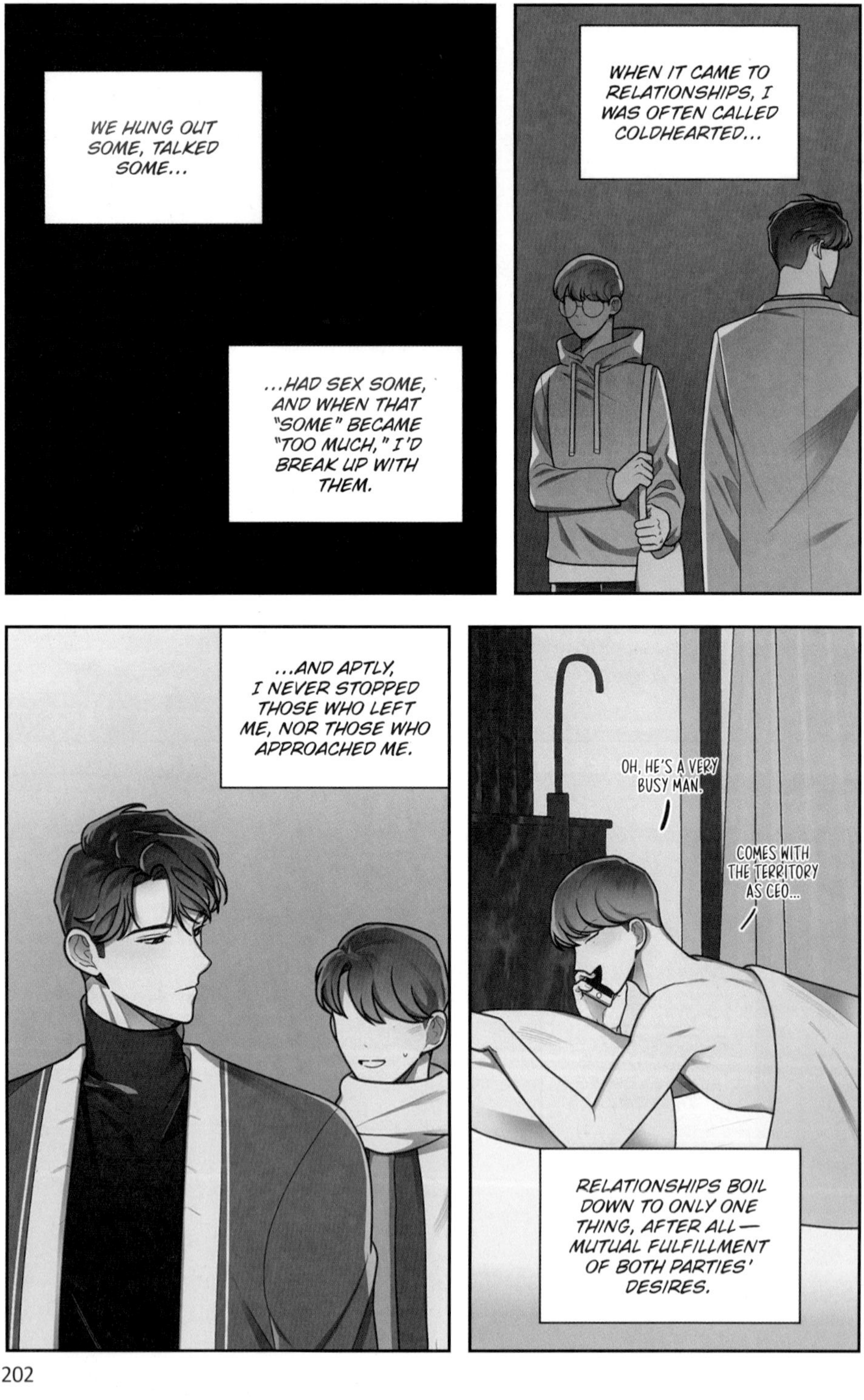
WE HUNG OUT SOME, TALKED SOME...
...HAD SEX SOME, AND WHEN THAT "SOME" BECAME "TOO MUCH," I'D BREAK UP WITH THEM.
WHEN IT CAME TO RELATIONSHIPS, I WAS OFTEN CALLED COLDHEARTED...
...AND APTLY, I NEVER STOPPED THOSE WHO LEFT ME, NOR THOSE WHO APPROACHED ME.
OH, HE'S A VERY BUSY MAN.
COMES WITH THE TERRITORY AS CEO...
RELATIONSHIPS BOIL DOWN TO ONLY ONE THING, AFTER ALL— MUTUAL FULFILLMENT OF BOTH PARTIES' DESIRES.

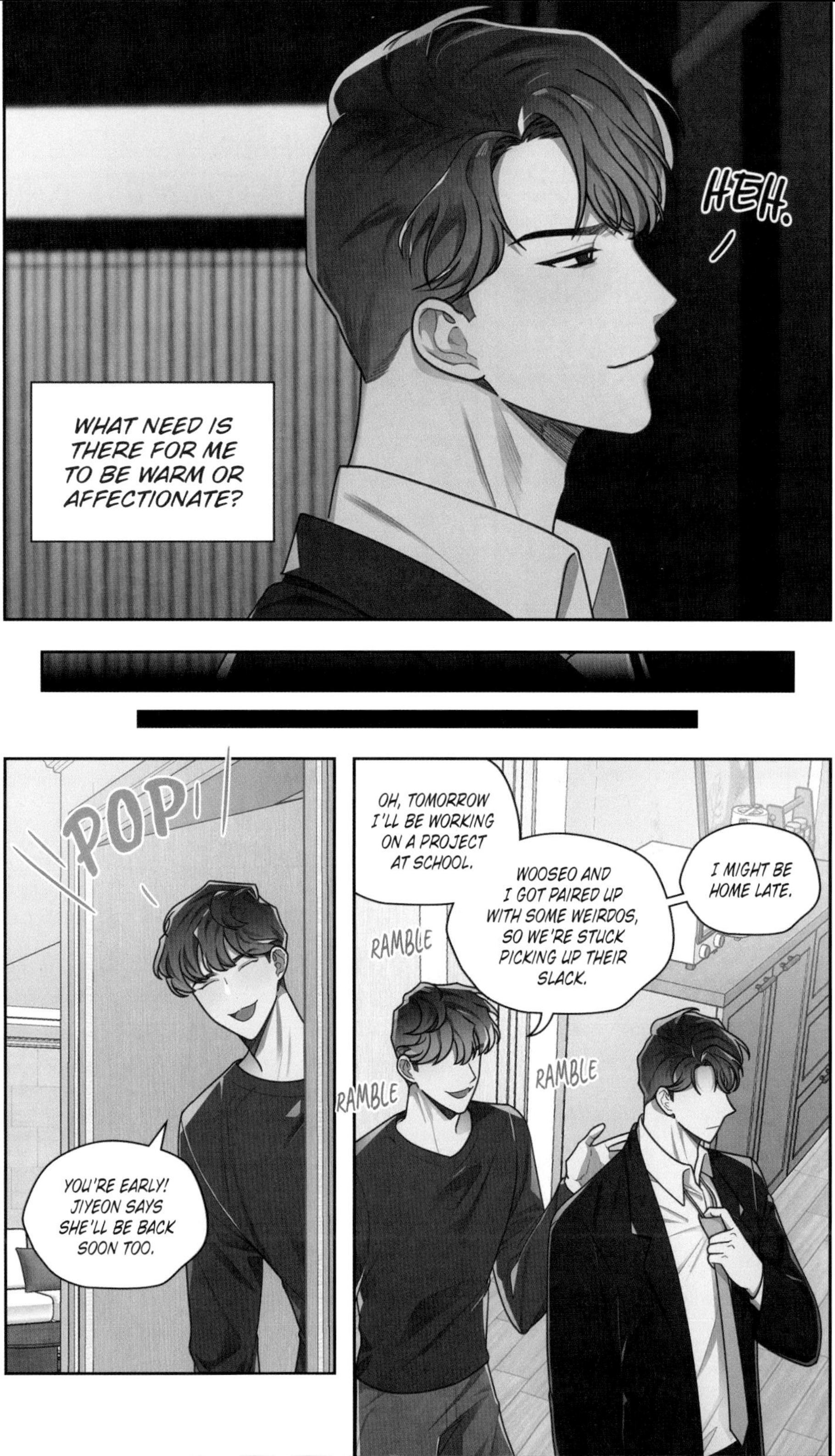
WHAT NEED IS THERE FOR ME TO BE WARM OR AFFECTIONATE?
HEH.
POP
YOU'RE EARLY! JIYEON SAYS SHE'LL BE BACK SOON TOO.
OH, TOMORROW I'LL BE WORKING ON A PROJECT AT SCHOOL.
WOOSEO AND I GOT PAIRED UP WITH SOME WEIRDOS, SO WE'RE STUCK PICKING UP THEIR SLACK.
I MIGHT BE HOME LATE.
RAMBLE
RAMBLE
RAMBLE

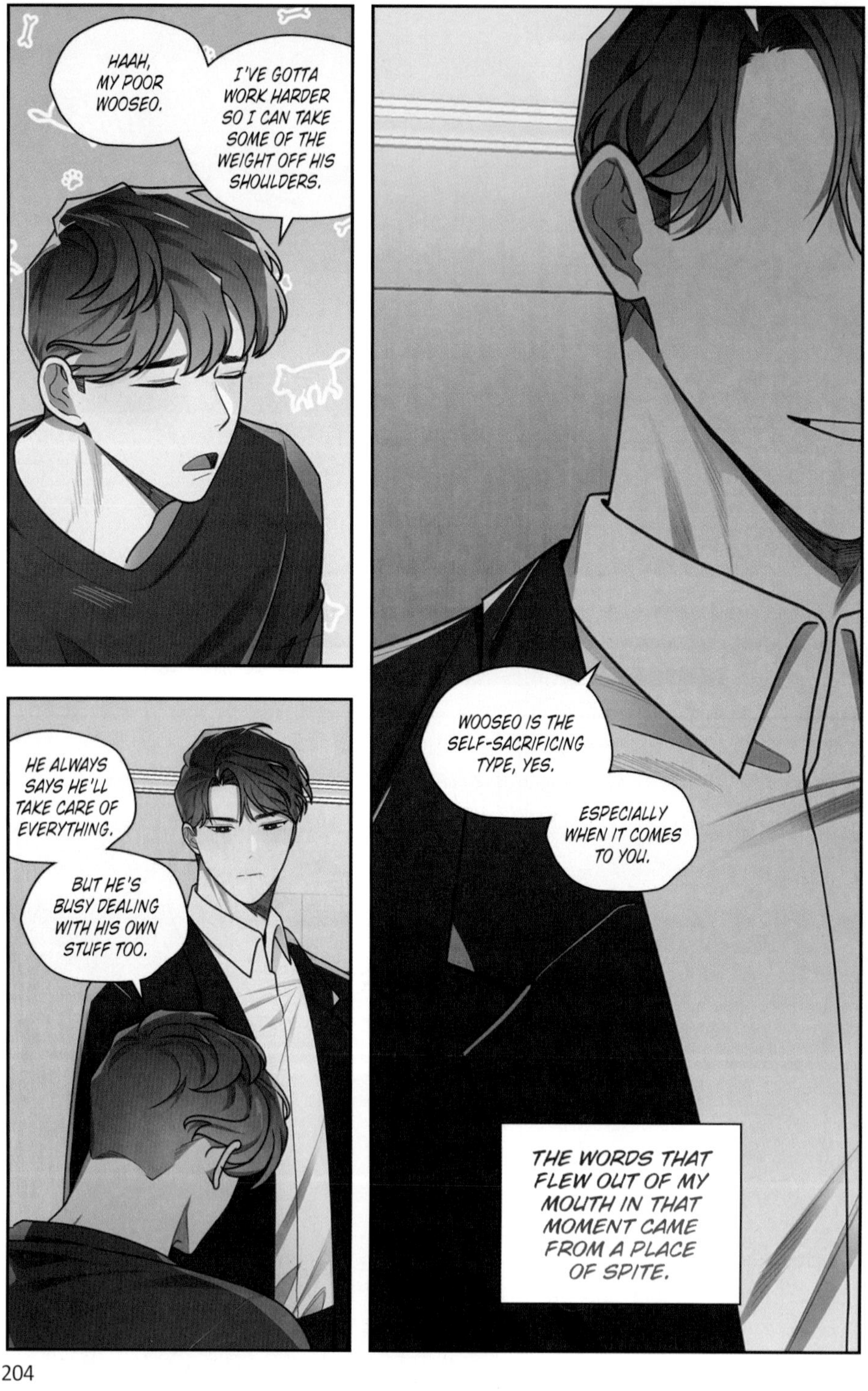
HAAH, MY POOR WOOSEO.
I'VE GOTTA WORK HARDER SO I CAN TAKE SOME OF THE WEIGHT OFF HIS SHOULDERS.
HE ALWAYS SAYS HE'LL TAKE CARE OF EVERYTHING.
BUT HE'S BUSY DEALING WITH HIS OWN STUFF TOO.
WOOSEO IS THE SELF-SACRIFICING TYPE, YES.
ESPECIALLY WHEN IT COMES TO YOU.
THE WORDS THAT FLEW OUT OF MY MOUTH IN THAT MOMENT CAME FROM A PLACE OF SPITE.

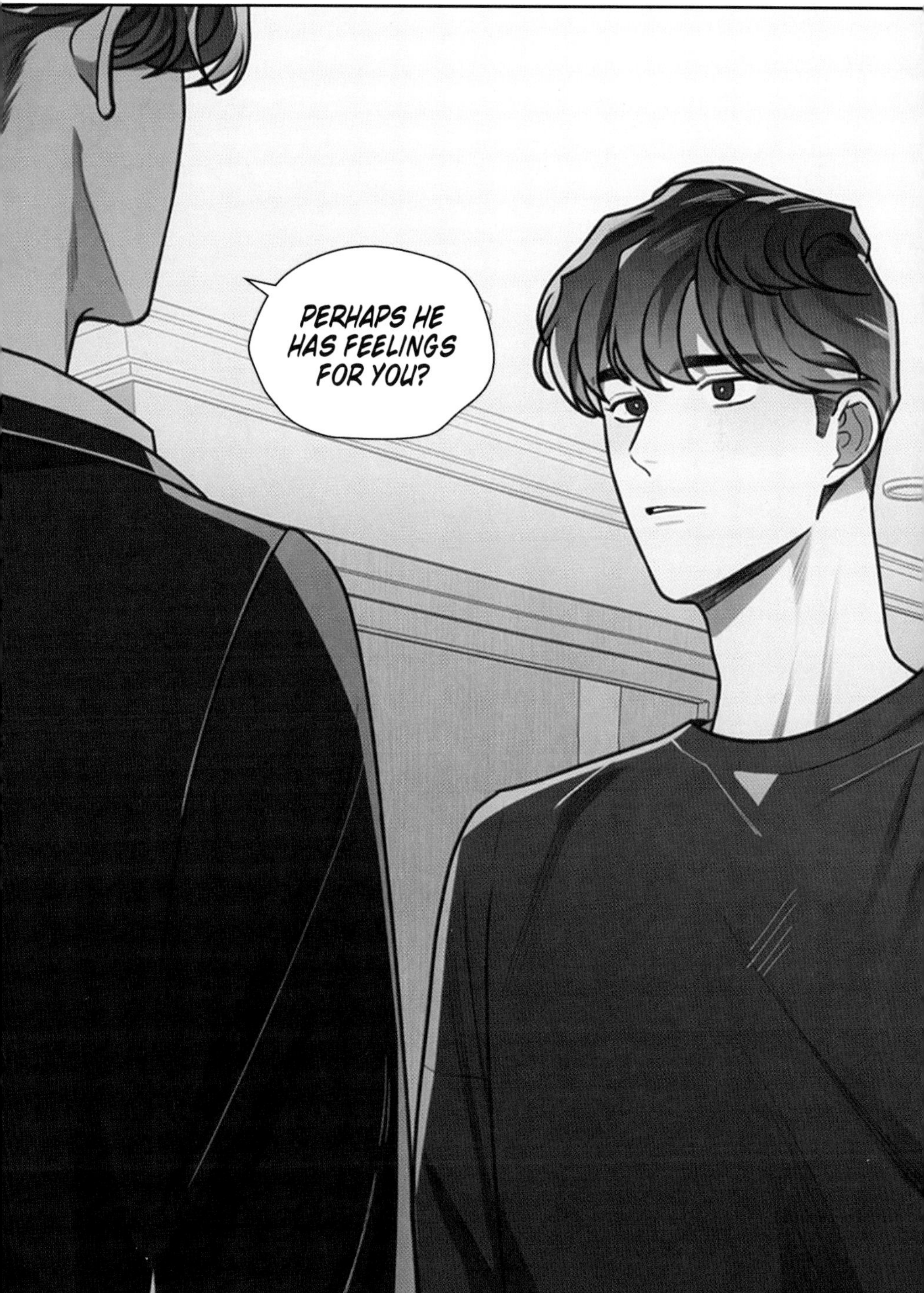
PERHAPS HE HAS FEELINGS FOR YOU?

Chapter 11

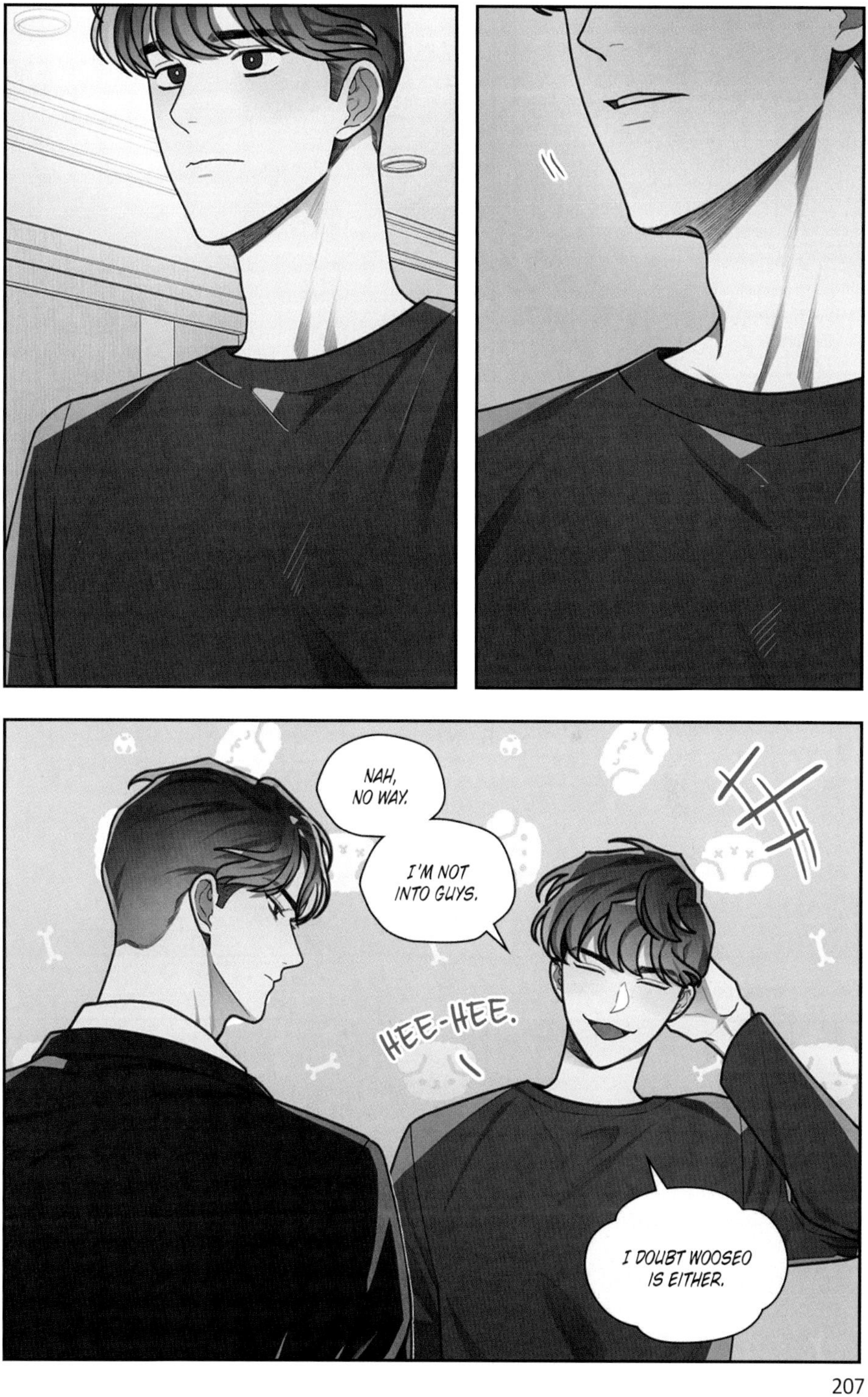
NAH, NO WAY.
I'M NOT INTO GUYS.
HEE-HEE.
I DOUBT WOOSEO IS EITHER.

JISEOK WAS 100% STRAIGHT...

...AND SO WOOSEO FAILED HIS MOST BASIC PREREQUISITE FOR ROMANTIC INTEREST.

IT'S REALLY QUITE SAD.

I'LL ALSO BE OUT LATE TOMORROW.

FIGURE OUT DINNER ON YOUR OWN AND EAT WITHOUT ME.

SURE THING!

WELL, IT NO LONGER CONCERNS ME.

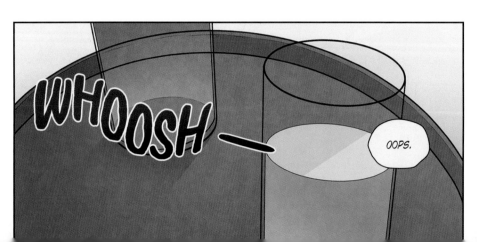

WHOOSH—

OOPS.

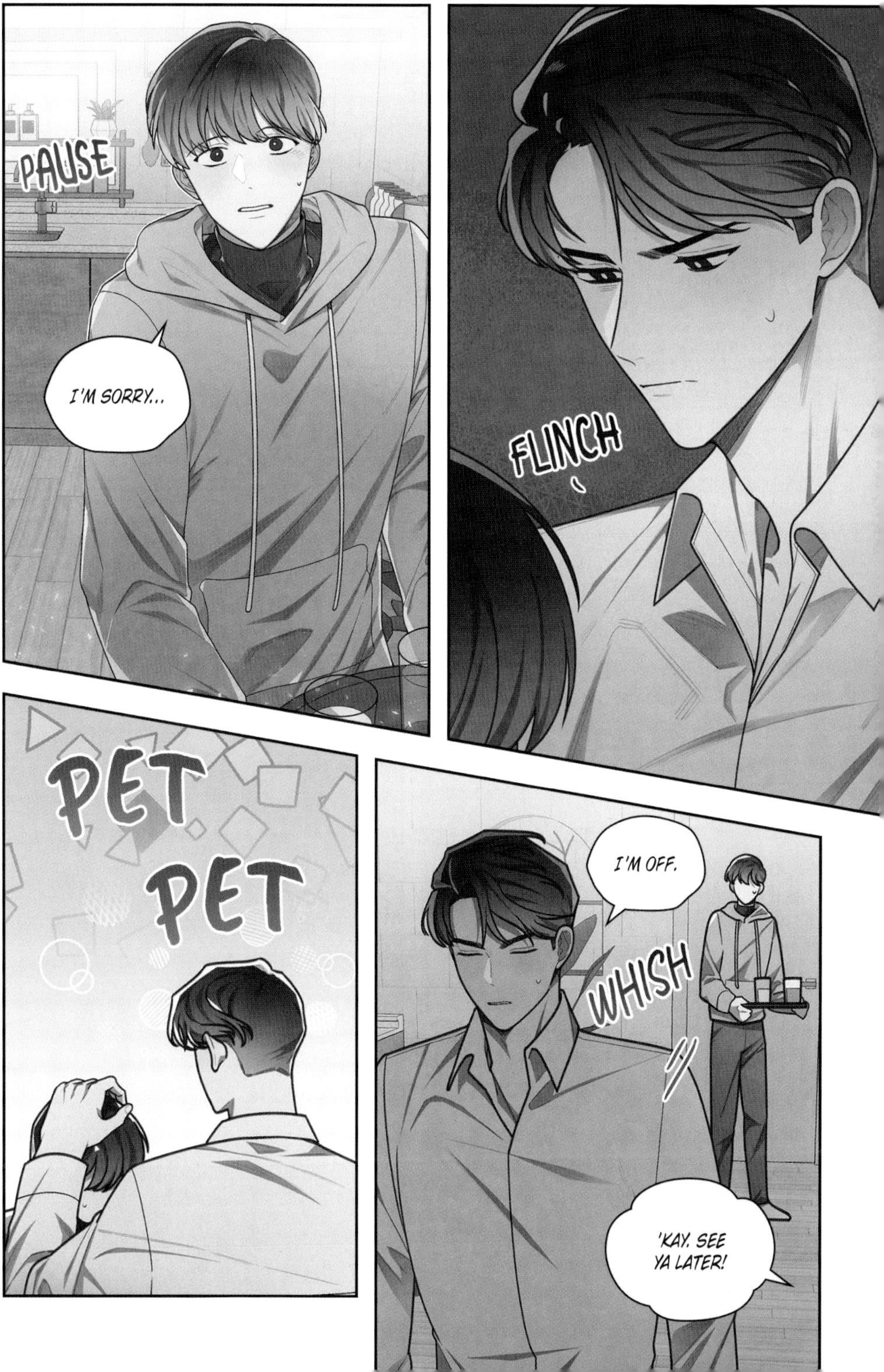
PAUSE
I'M SORRY...
FLINCH
PET
PET
I'M OFF.
WHISH
'KAY. SEE YA LATER!

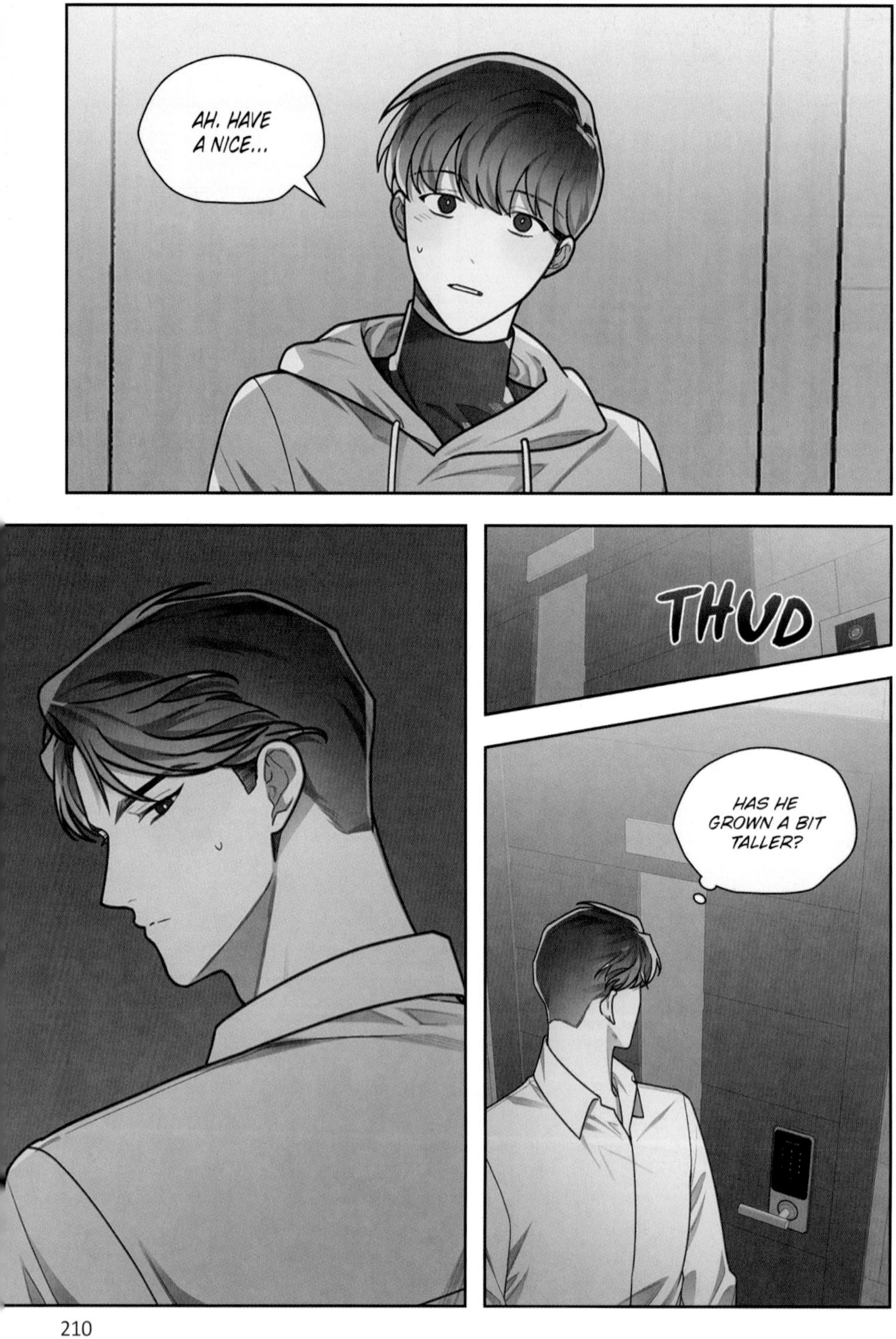
AH. HAVE
A NICE...
THUD
HAS HE
GROWN A BIT
TALLER?

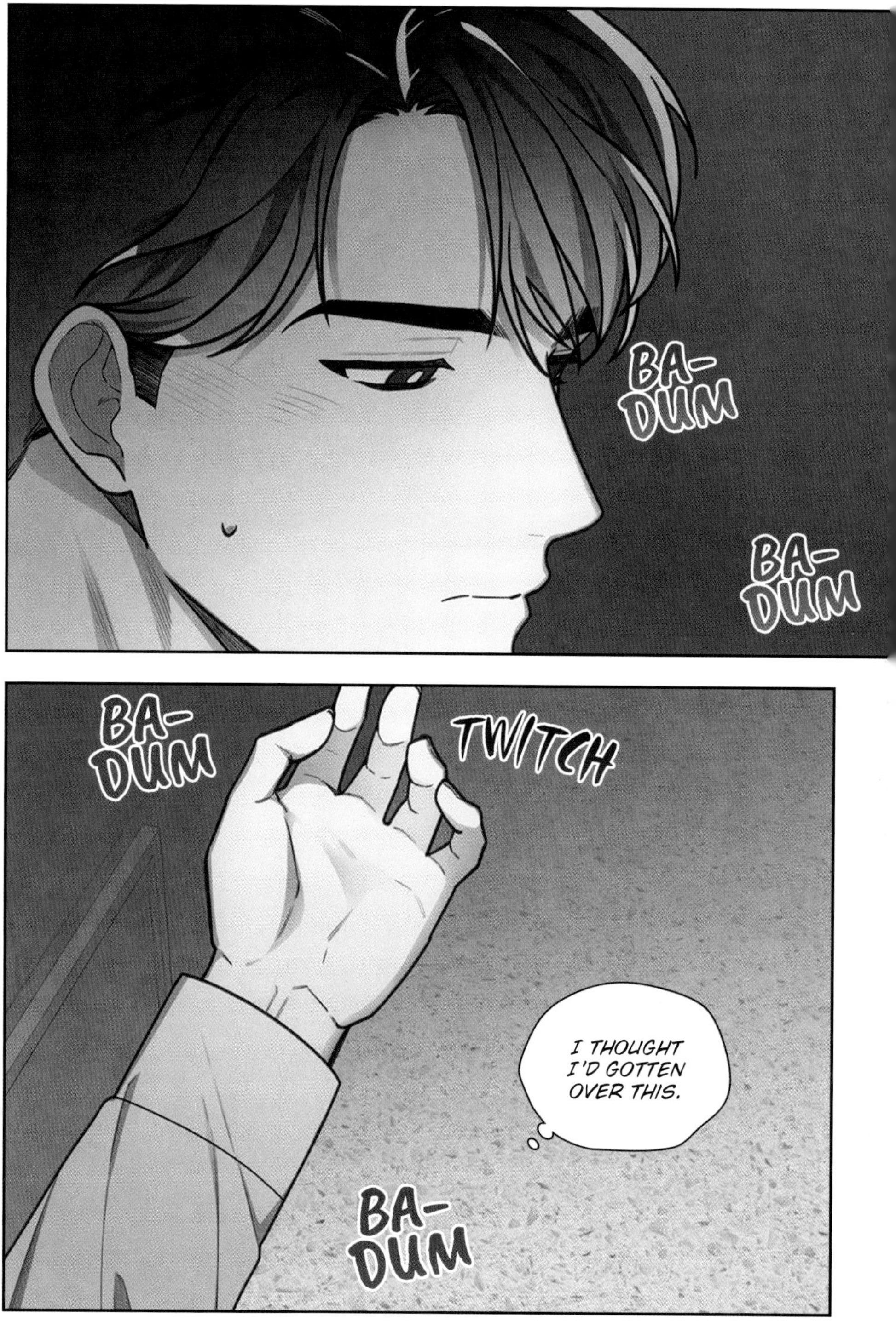
BA-
DUM
BA-
DUM
BA-
DUM
TWITCH
I THOUGHT I'D GOTTEN OVER THIS.
BA-
DUM

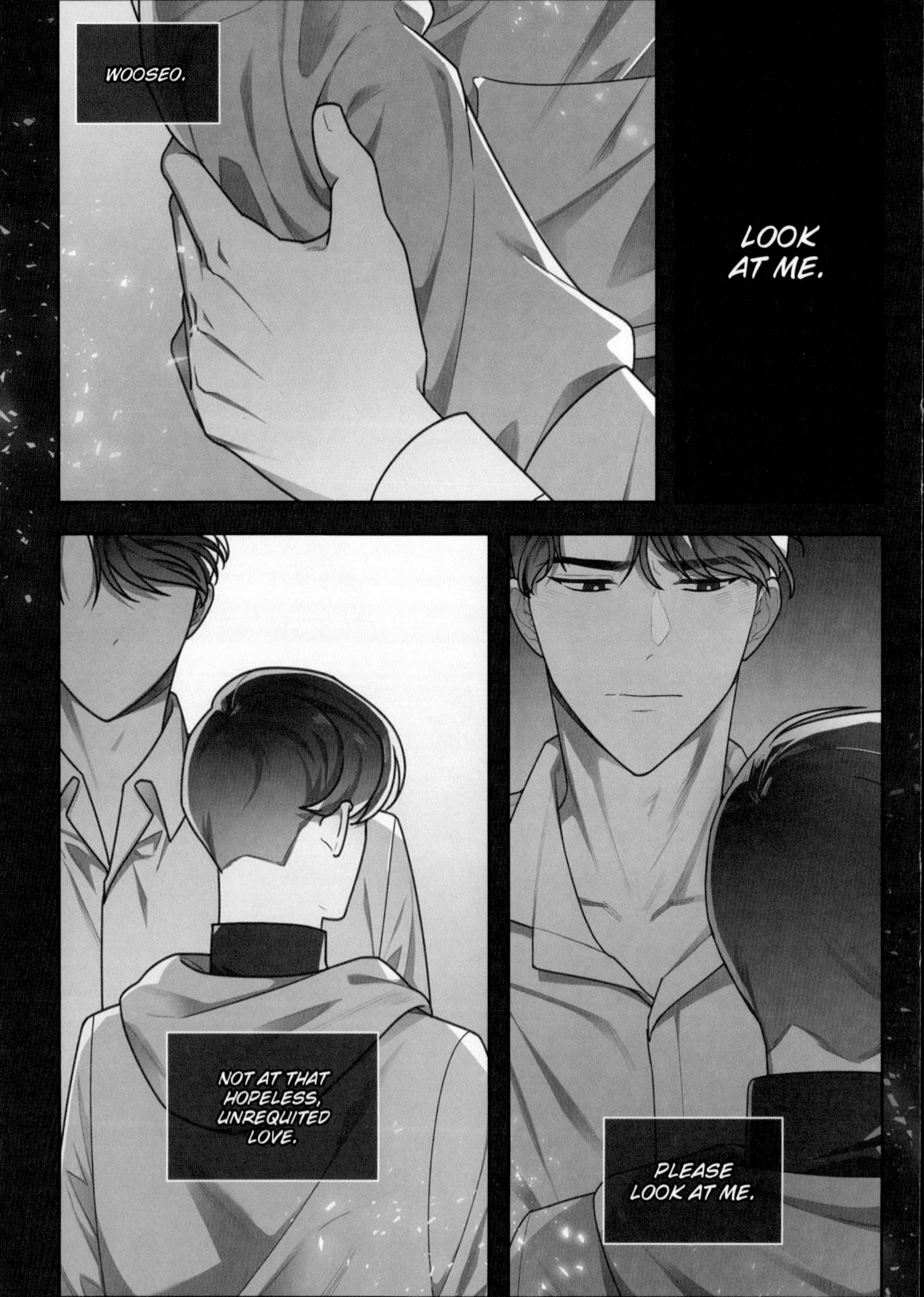
WOOSEO.
LOOK AT ME.
NOT AT THAT HOPELESS, UNREQUITED LOVE.
PLEASE LOOK AT ME.

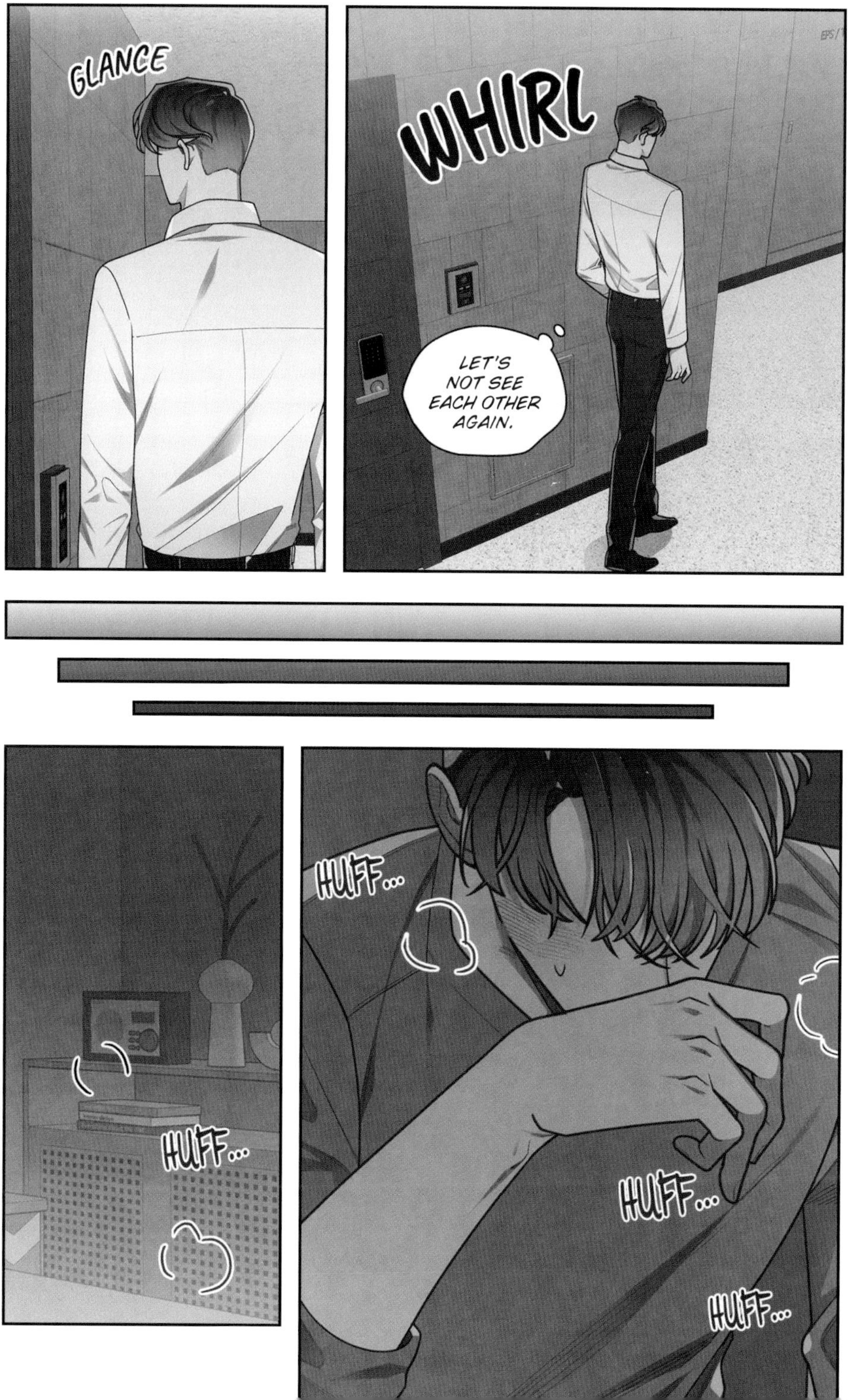
GLANCE
WHIRL
LET'S NOT SEE EACH OTHER AGAIN.
HUFF...
HUFF...
HUFF...
HUFF...

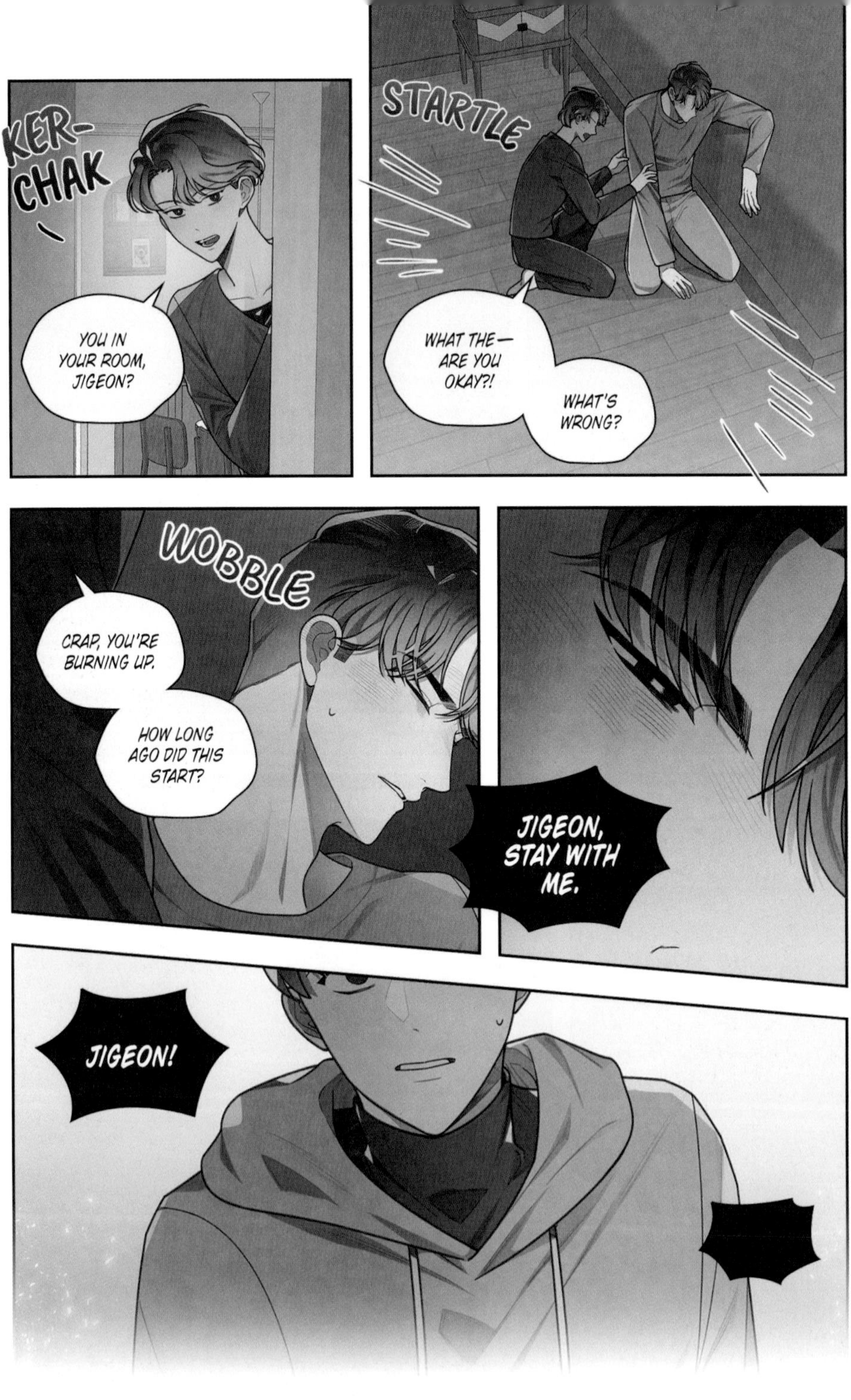
KER-CHAK
YOU IN YOUR ROOM, JIGEON?
STARTLE
WHAT THE— ARE YOU OKAY?!
WHAT'S WRONG?
WOBBLE
CRAP, YOU'RE BURNING UP.
HOW LONG AGO DID THIS START?
JIGEON, STAY WITH ME.
JIGEON!

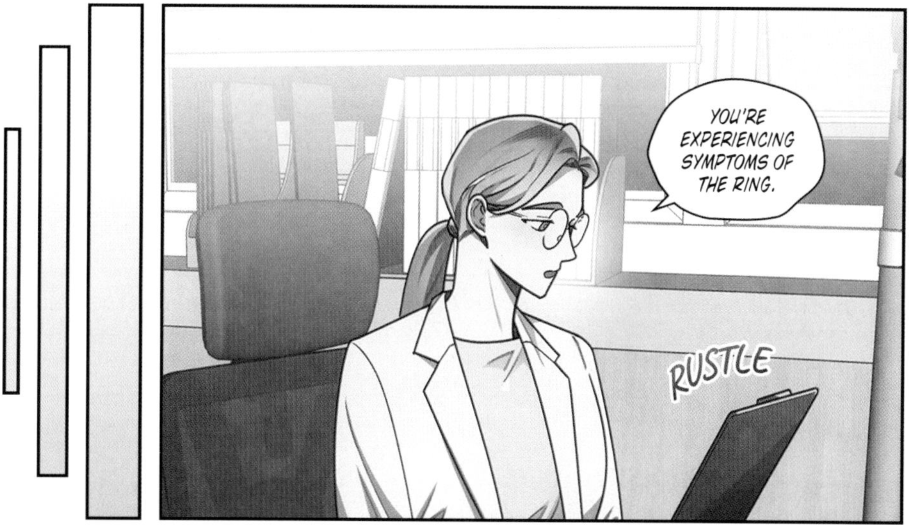
YOU'RE EXPERIENCING SYMPTOMS OF THE RING.
RUSTLE

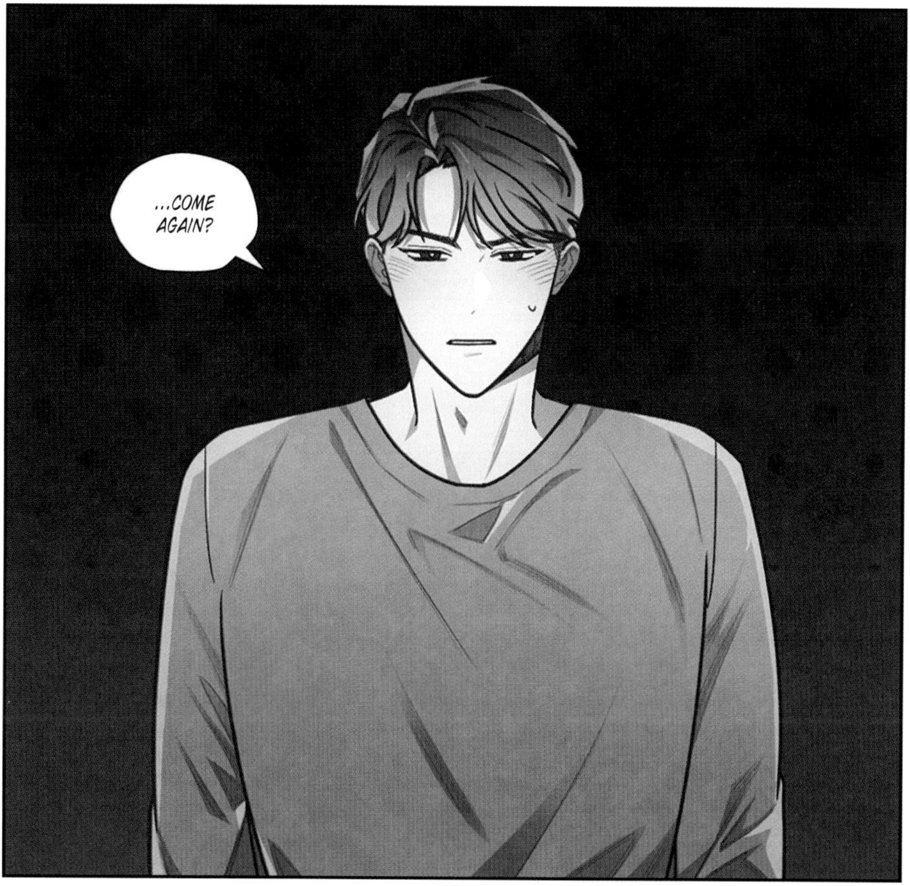
...COME AGAIN?

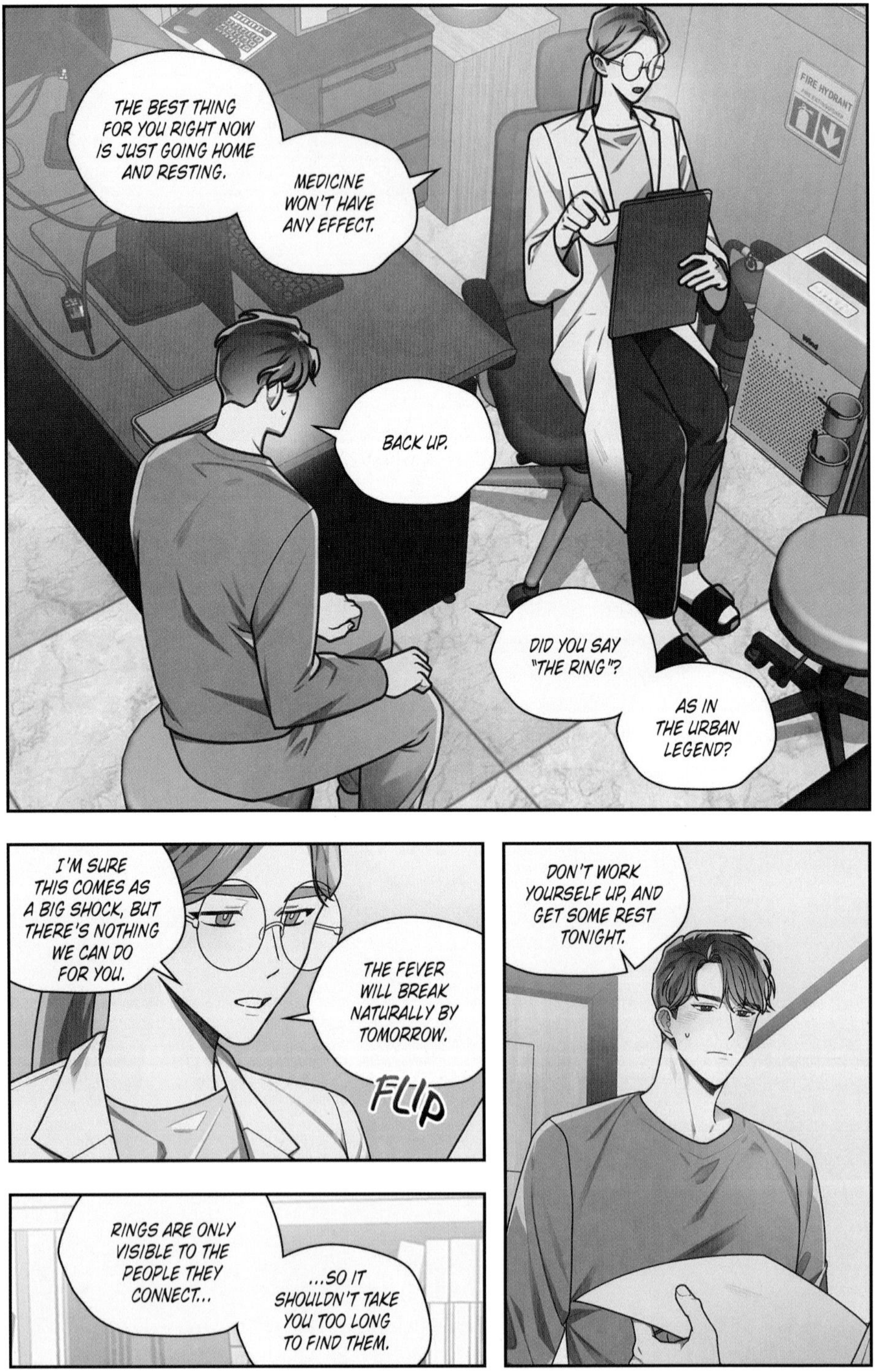
THE BEST THING FOR YOU RIGHT NOW IS JUST GOING HOME AND RESTING.
MEDICINE WON'T HAVE ANY EFFECT.
FIRE HYDRANT
BACK UP.
DID YOU SAY "THE RING"?
AS IN THE URBAN LEGEND?
I'M SURE THIS COMES AS A BIG SHOCK, BUT THERE'S NOTHING WE CAN DO FOR YOU.
THE FEVER WILL BREAK NATURALLY BY TOMORROW.
FLIP
DON'T WORK YOURSELF UP, AND GET SOME REST TONIGHT.
RINGS ARE ONLY VISIBLE TO THE PEOPLE THEY CONNECT...
...SO IT SHOULDN'T TAKE YOU TOO LONG TO FIND THEM.

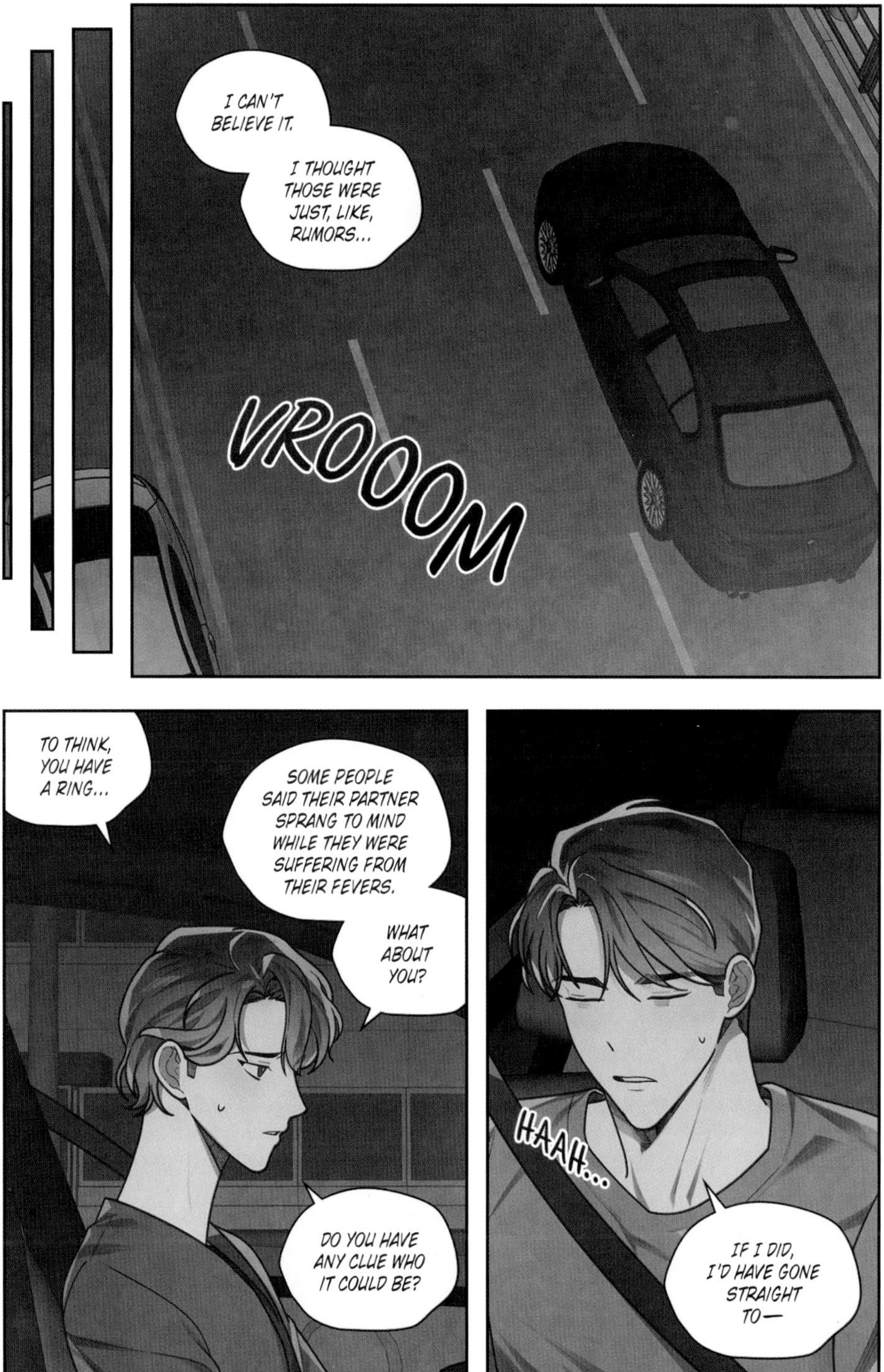
I CAN'T BELIEVE IT.
I THOUGHT THOSE WERE JUST, LIKE, RUMORS…
VROOOM
TO THINK, YOU HAVE A RING…
SOME PEOPLE SAID THEIR PARTNER SPRANG TO MIND WHILE THEY WERE SUFFERING FROM THEIR FEVERS.
WHAT ABOUT YOU?
DO YOU HAVE ANY CLUE WHO IT COULD BE?
HAAH…
IF I DID, I'D HAVE GONE STRAIGHT TO—

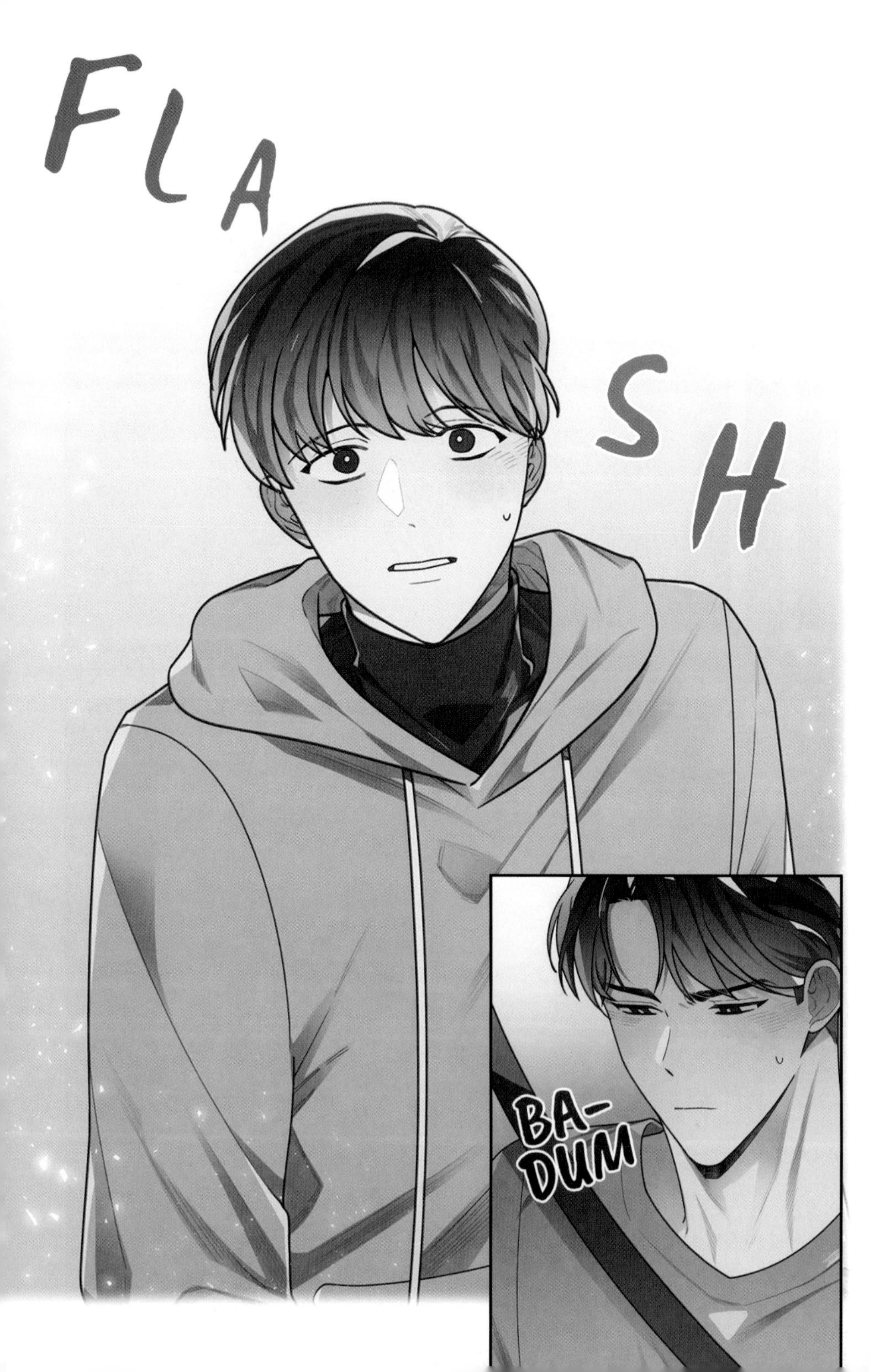
FLASH
BA-DUM

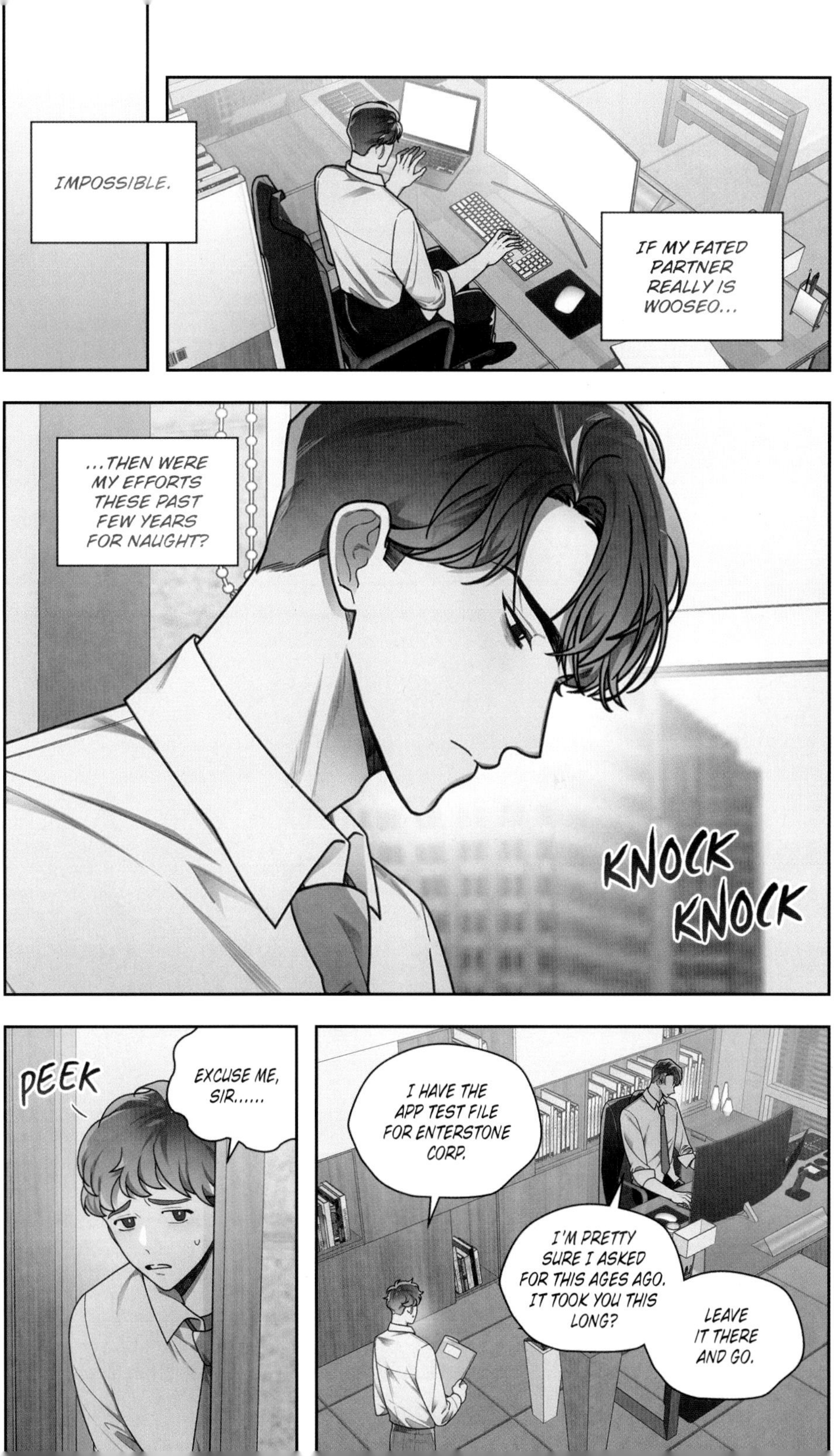
IMPOSSIBLE.
IF MY FATED PARTNER REALLY IS WOOSEO...
...THEN WERE MY EFFORTS THESE PAST FEW YEARS FOR NAUGHT?
KNOCK KNOCK
PEEK
EXCUSE ME, SIR......
I HAVE THE APP TEST FILE FOR ENTERSTONE CORP.
I'M PRETTY SURE I ASKED FOR THIS AGES AGO. IT TOOK YOU THIS LONG?
LEAVE IT THERE AND GO.

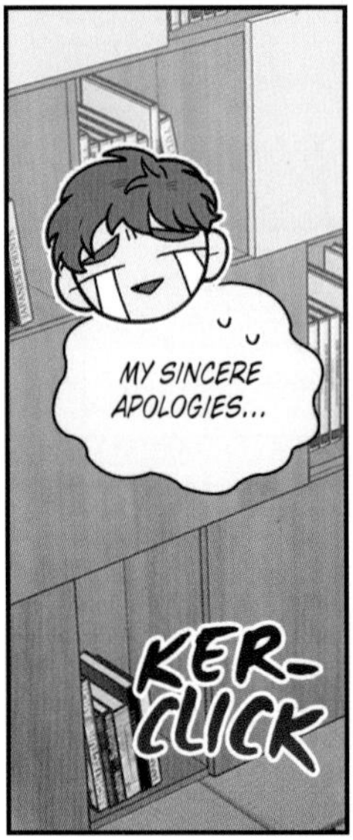
MY SINCERE APOLOGIES...
KER-CLICK

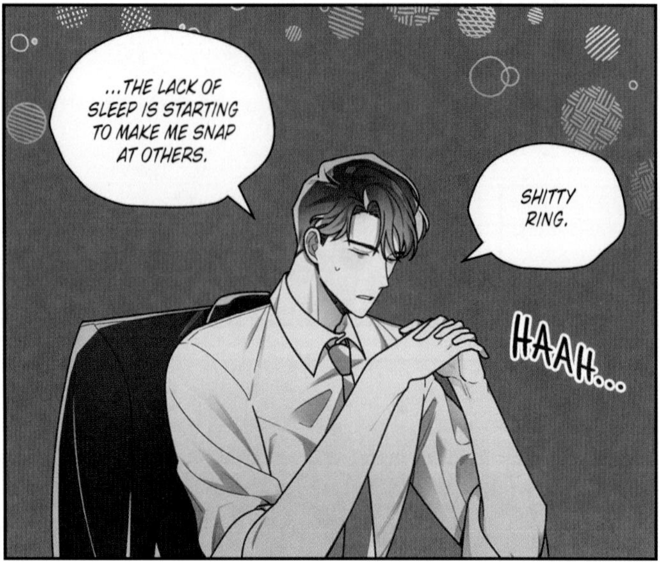
...THE LACK OF SLEEP IS STARTING TO MAKE ME SNAP AT OTHERS.
SHITTY RING.
HAAH...

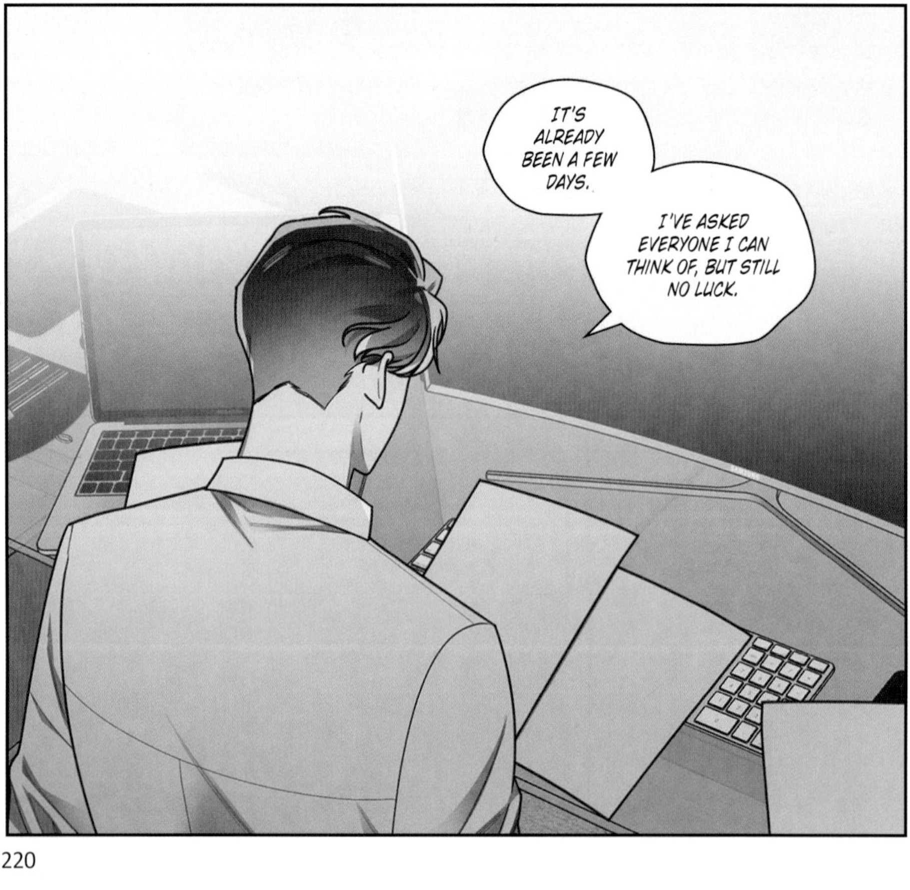
IT'S ALREADY BEEN A FEW DAYS.
I'VE ASKED EVERYONE I CAN THINK OF, BUT STILL NO LUCK.

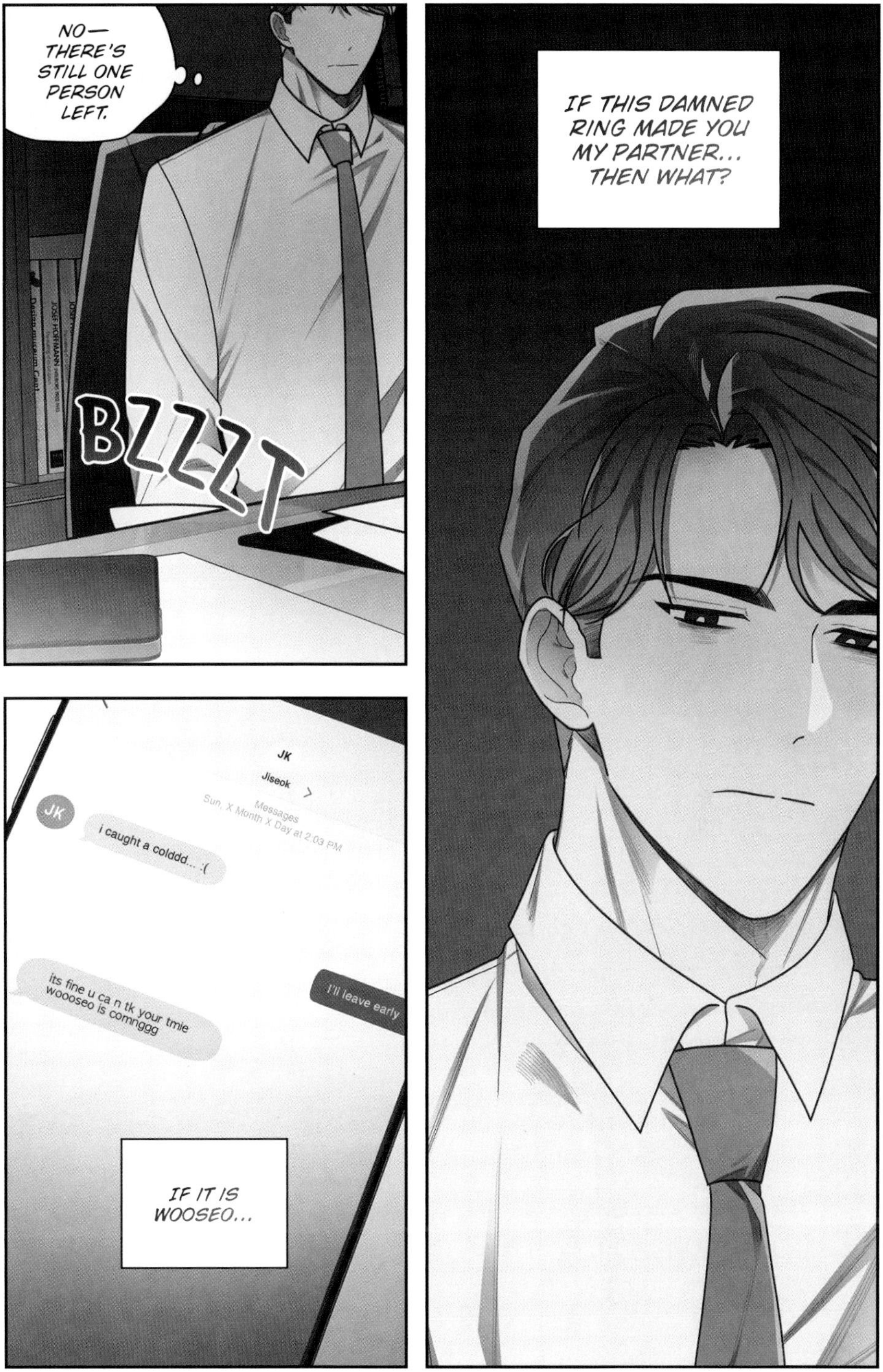
NO— THERE'S STILL ONE PERSON LEFT.
BZZZT
JK
Jiseok
Messages
Sun, X Month X Day at 2:03 PM
i caught a colddd... :(
I'll leave early
its fine u ca n tk your tmie wooseo is comnggg
IF IT IS WOOSEO...
IF THIS DAMNED RING MADE YOU MY PARTNER... THEN WHAT?

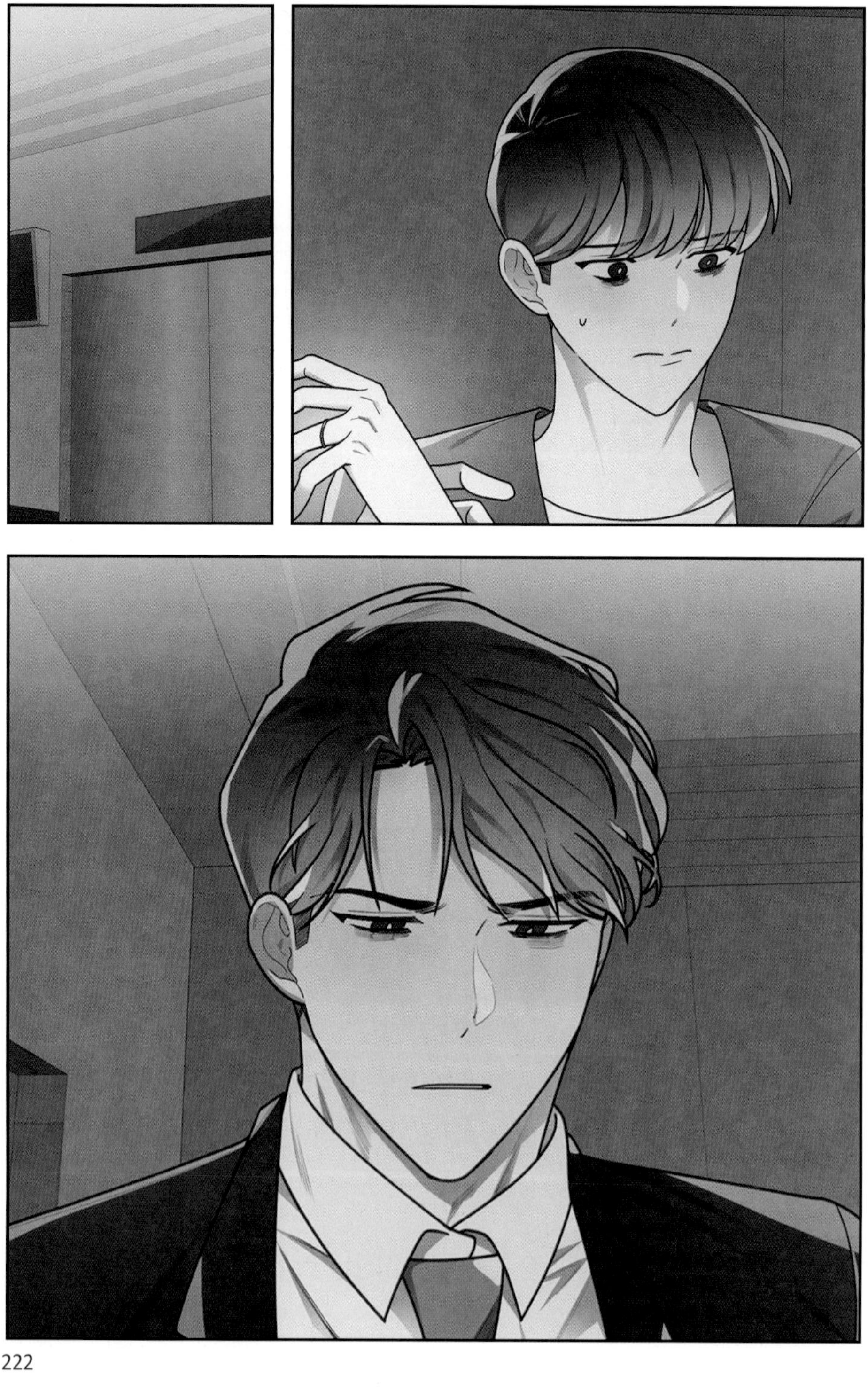

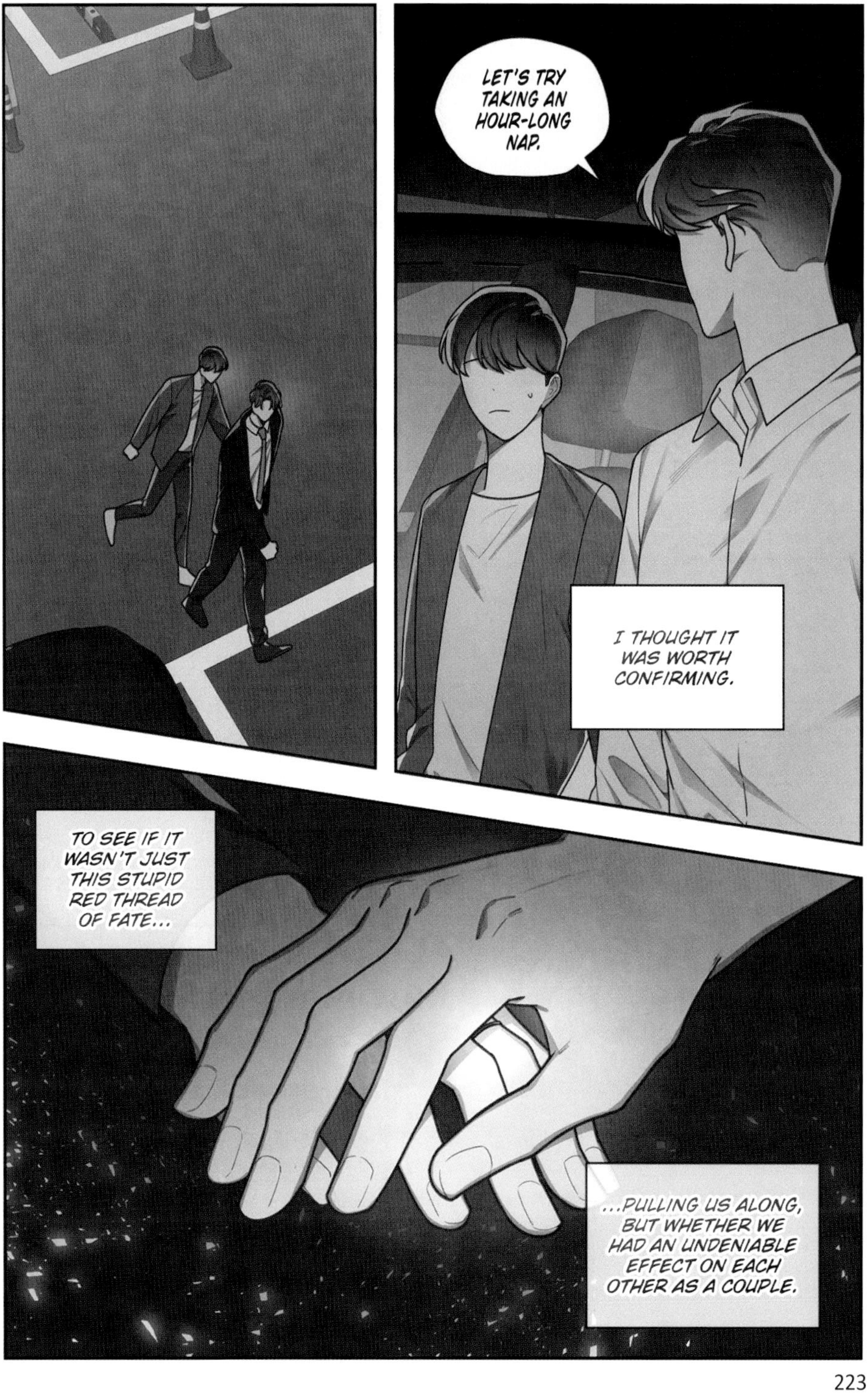
LET'S TRY TAKING AN HOUR-LONG NAP.
I THOUGHT IT WAS WORTH CONFIRMING.
TO SEE IF IT WASN'T JUST THIS STUPID RED THREAD OF FATE...
...PULLING US ALONG, BUT WHETHER WE HAD AN UNDENIABLE EFFECT ON EACH OTHER AS A COUPLE.

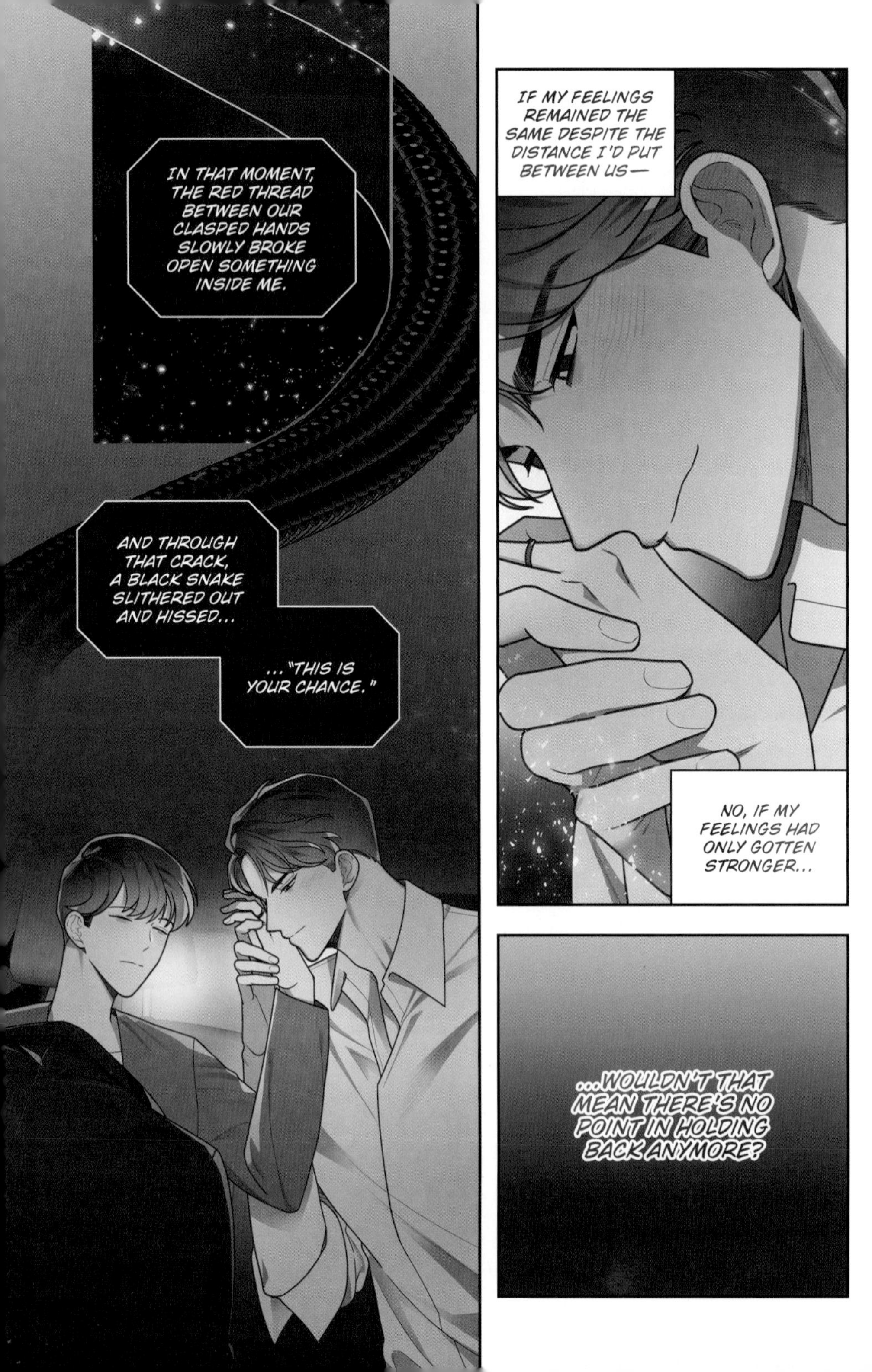
IN THAT MOMENT, THE RED THREAD BETWEEN OUR CLASPED HANDS SLOWLY BROKE OPEN SOMETHING INSIDE ME.
AND THROUGH THAT CRACK, A BLACK SNAKE SLITHERED OUT AND HISSED...
..."THIS IS YOUR CHANCE."
IF MY FEELINGS REMAINED THE SAME DESPITE THE DISTANCE I'D PUT BETWEEN US—
NO, IF MY FEELINGS HAD ONLY GOTTEN STRONGER...
...WOULDN'T THAT MEAN THERE'S NO POINT IN HOLDING BACK ANYMORE?

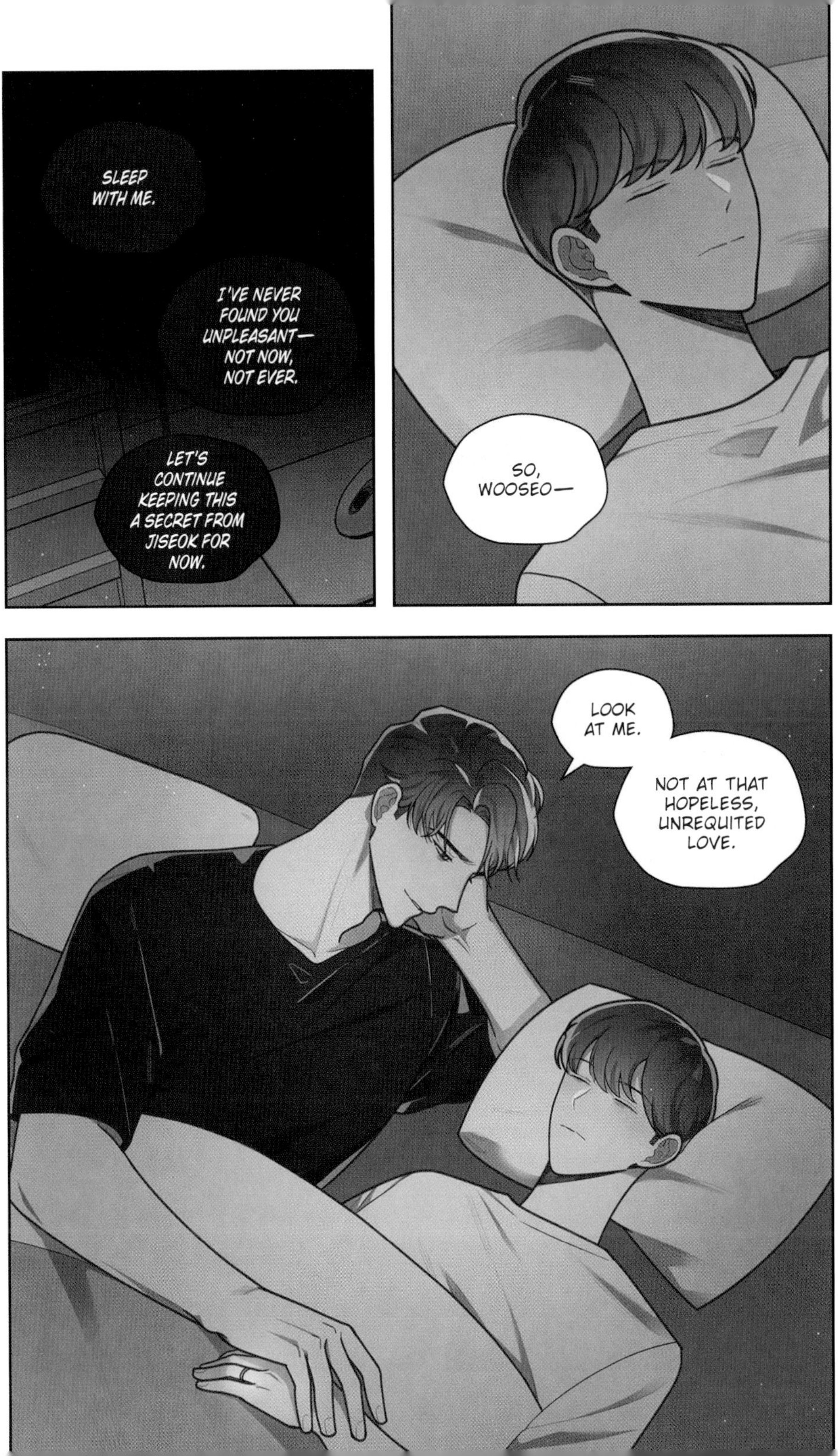
SLEEP WITH ME.
I'VE NEVER FOUND YOU UNPLEASANT—NOT NOW, NOT EVER.
LET'S CONTINUE KEEPING THIS A SECRET FROM JISEOK FOR NOW.
SO, WOOSEO—
LOOK AT ME.
NOT AT THAT HOPELESS, UNREQUITED LOVE.

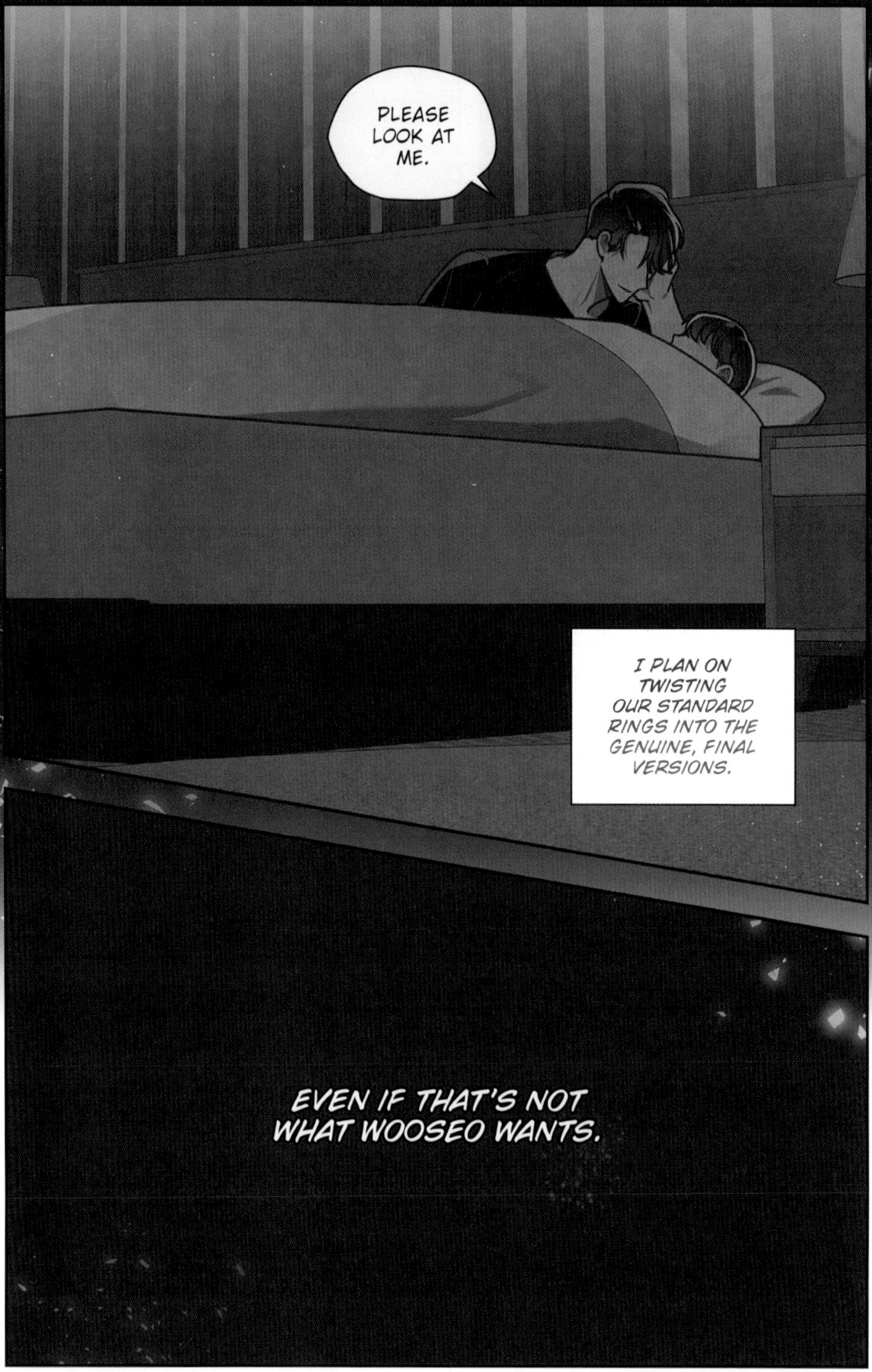
PLEASE LOOK AT ME.
I PLAN ON TWISTING OUR STANDARD RINGS INTO THE GENUINE, FINAL VERSIONS.
EVEN IF THAT'S NOT WHAT WOOSEO WANTS.

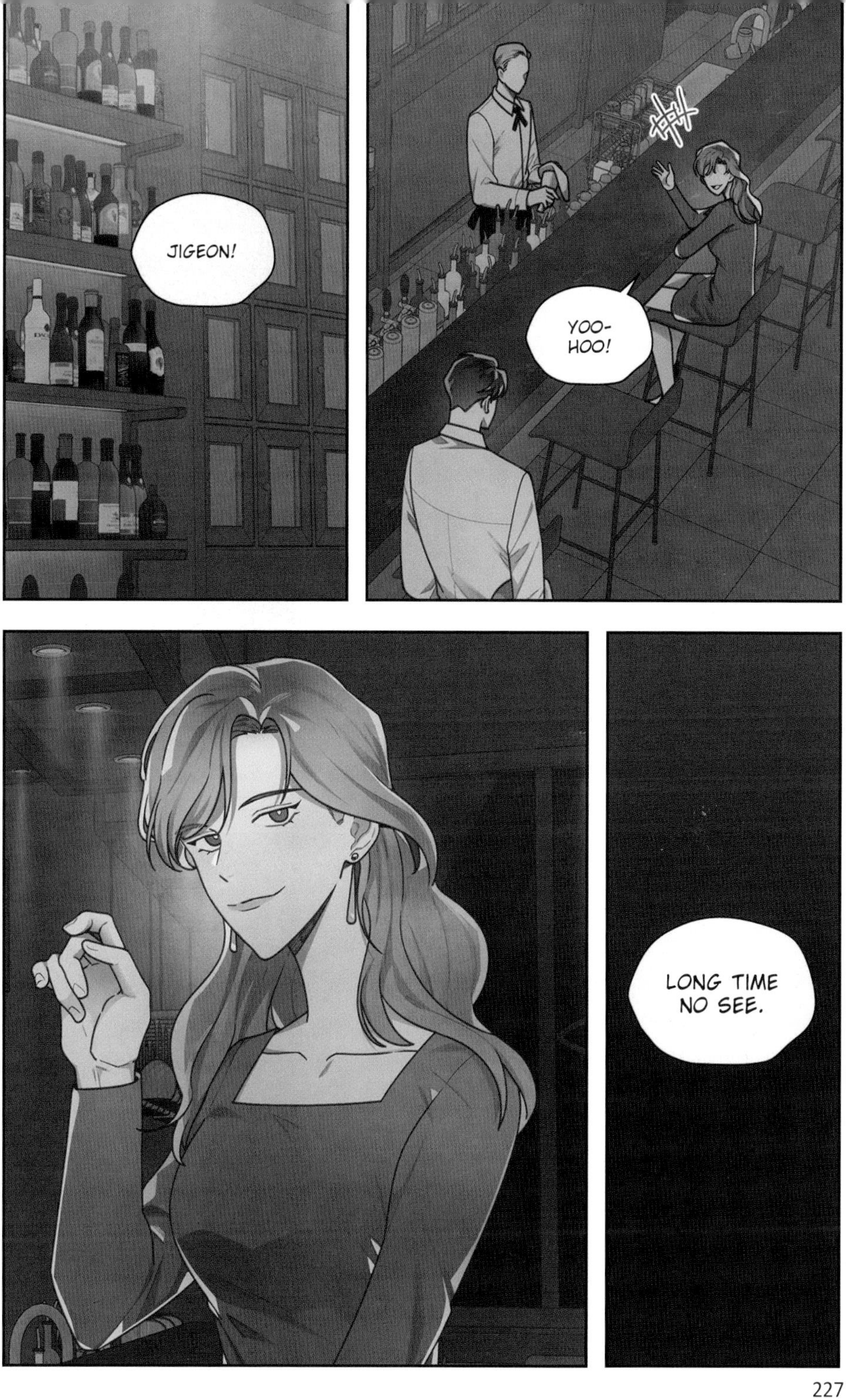
JIGEON!
YOO-HOO!
LONG TIME NO SEE.

Chapter 12

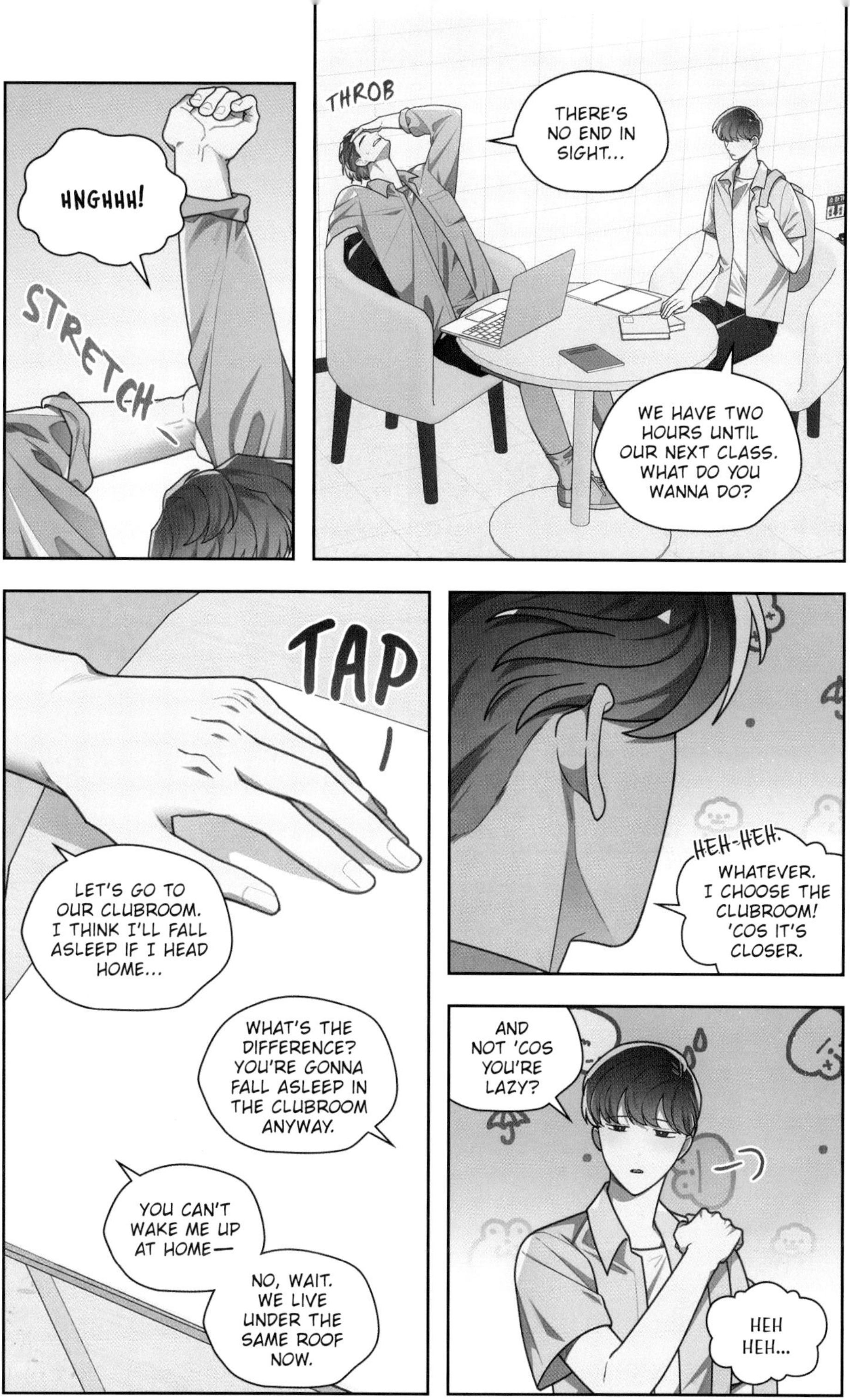
HNGHHH!
STRETCH
THROB
THERE'S NO END IN SIGHT...
WE HAVE TWO HOURS UNTIL OUR NEXT CLASS. WHAT DO YOU WANNA DO?
TAP
LET'S GO TO OUR CLUBROOM. I THINK I'LL FALL ASLEEP IF I HEAD HOME...
WHAT'S THE DIFFERENCE? YOU'RE GONNA FALL ASLEEP IN THE CLUBROOM ANYWAY.
YOU CAN'T WAKE ME UP AT HOME—
NO, WAIT. WE LIVE UNDER THE SAME ROOF NOW.
HEH-HEH.
WHATEVER. I CHOOSE THE CLUBROOM! 'COS IT'S CLOSER.
AND NOT 'COS YOU'RE LAZY?
HEH HEH...

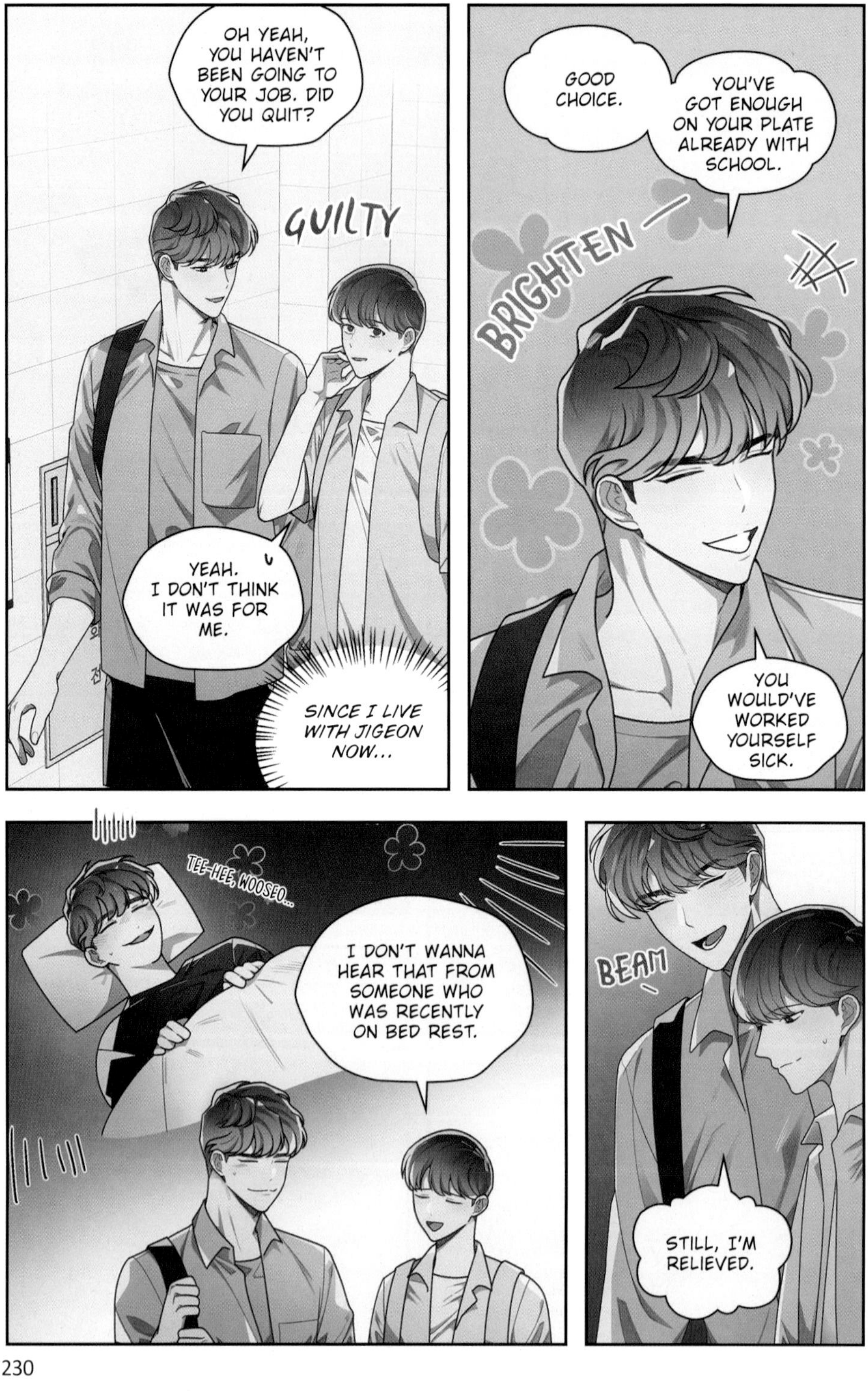
OH YEAH, YOU HAVEN'T BEEN GOING TO YOUR JOB. DID YOU QUIT?
GUILTY
YEAH. I DON'T THINK IT WAS FOR ME.
SINCE I LIVE WITH JIGEON NOW...
GOOD CHOICE.
YOU'VE GOT ENOUGH ON YOUR PLATE ALREADY WITH SCHOOL.
BRIGHTEN
YOU WOULD'VE WORKED YOURSELF SICK.
TEE-HEE, WOOSEO...
I DON'T WANNA HEAR THAT FROM SOMEONE WHO WAS RECENTLY ON BED REST.
BEAM
STILL, I'M RELIEVED.

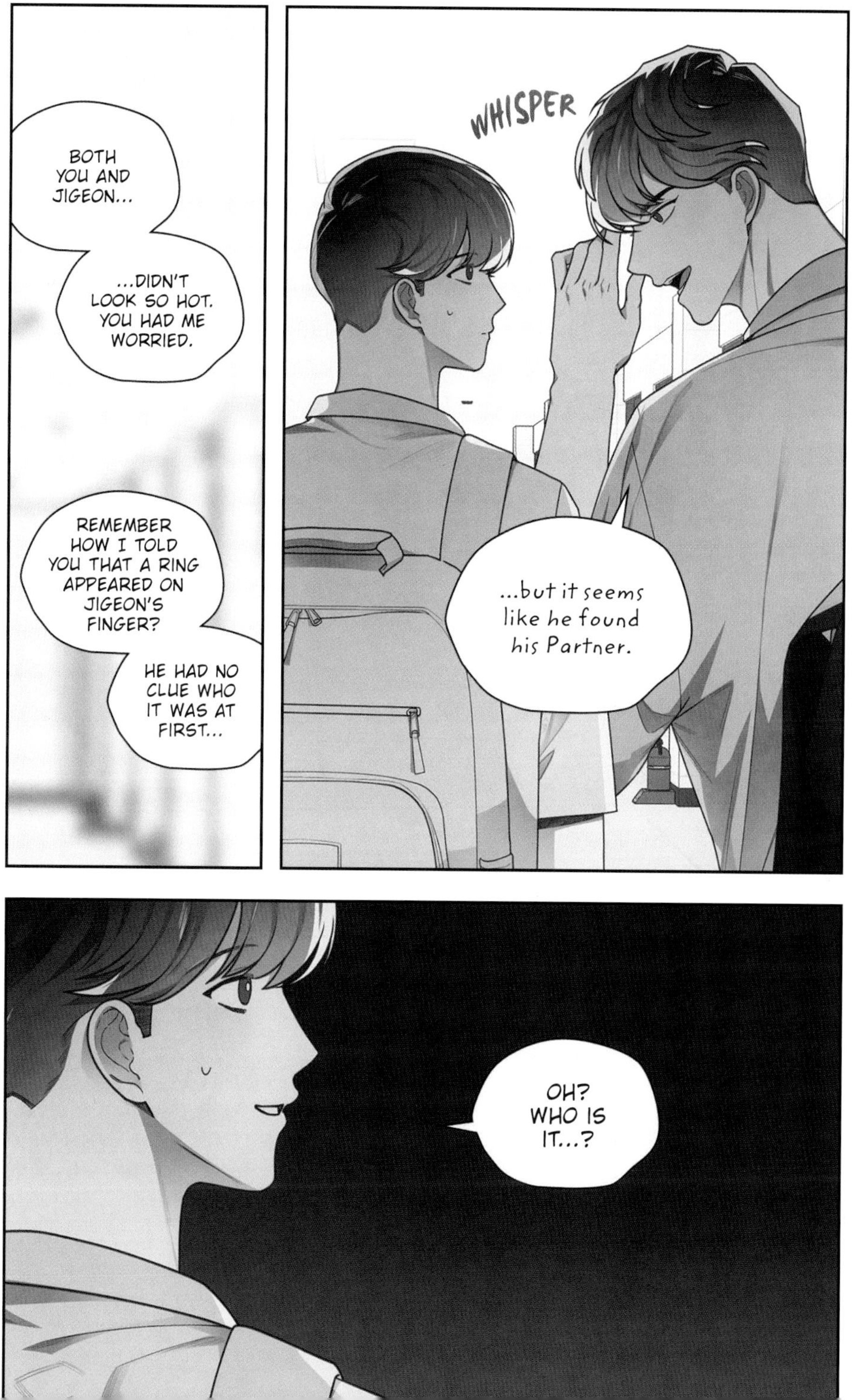
BOTH YOU AND JIGEON...
...DIDN'T LOOK SO HOT. YOU HAD ME WORRIED.
REMEMBER HOW I TOLD YOU THAT A RING APPEARED ON JIGEON'S FINGER?
HE HAD NO CLUE WHO IT WAS AT FIRST...
WHISPER
...but it seems like he found his Partner.
OH? WHO IS IT...?

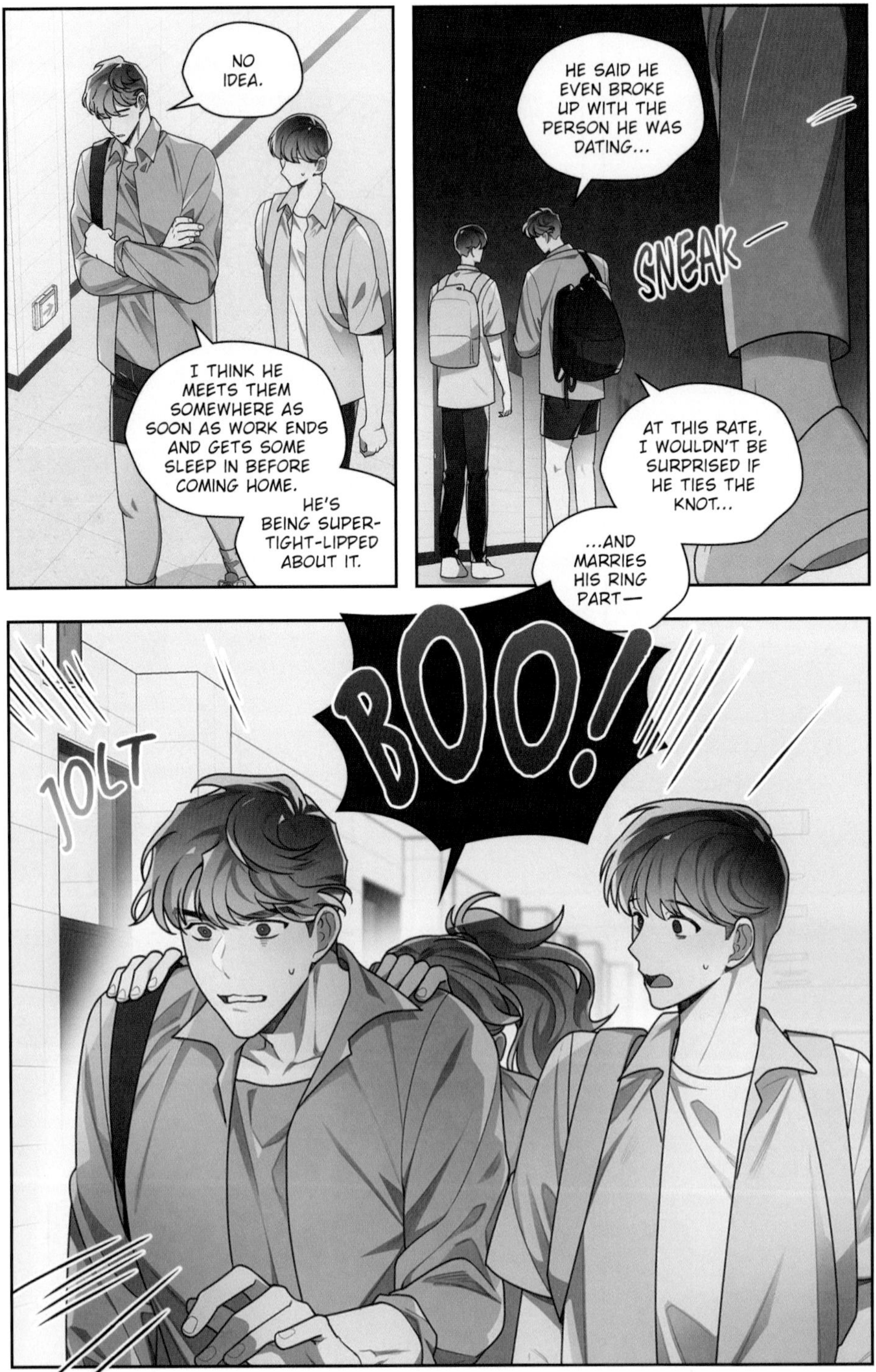
NO IDEA.
I THINK HE MEETS THEM SOMEWHERE AS SOON AS WORK ENDS AND GETS SOME SLEEP IN BEFORE COMING HOME.
HE'S BEING SUPER-TIGHT-LIPPED ABOUT IT.
HE SAID HE EVEN BROKE UP WITH THE PERSON HE WAS DATING...
SNEAK
AT THIS RATE, I WOULDN'T BE SURPRISED IF HE TIES THE KNOT...
...AND MARRIES HIS RING PART—
BOO!
JOLT

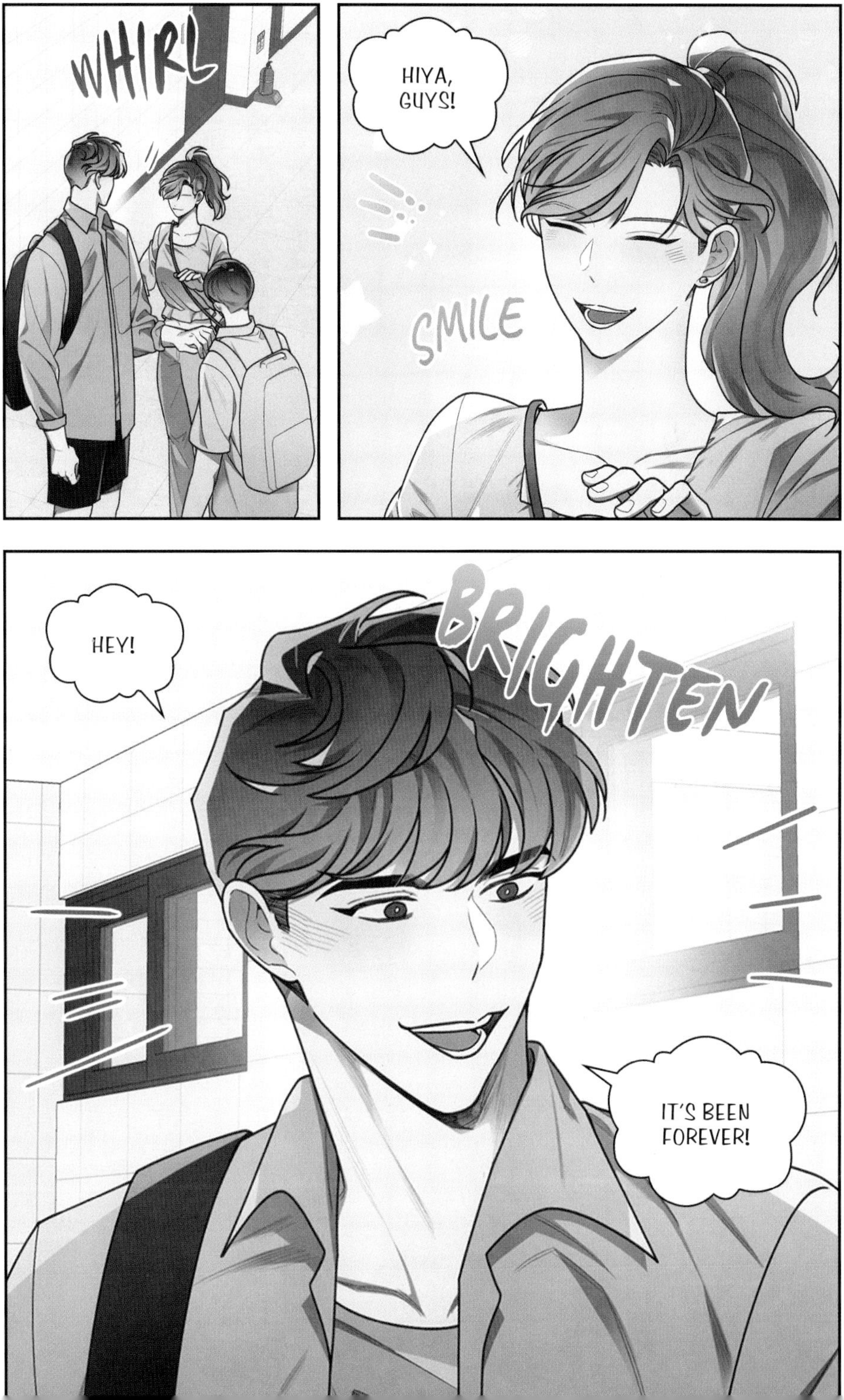
WHIRL
HIYA, GUYS!
SMILE
HEY!
BRIGHTEN
IT'S BEEN FOREVER!

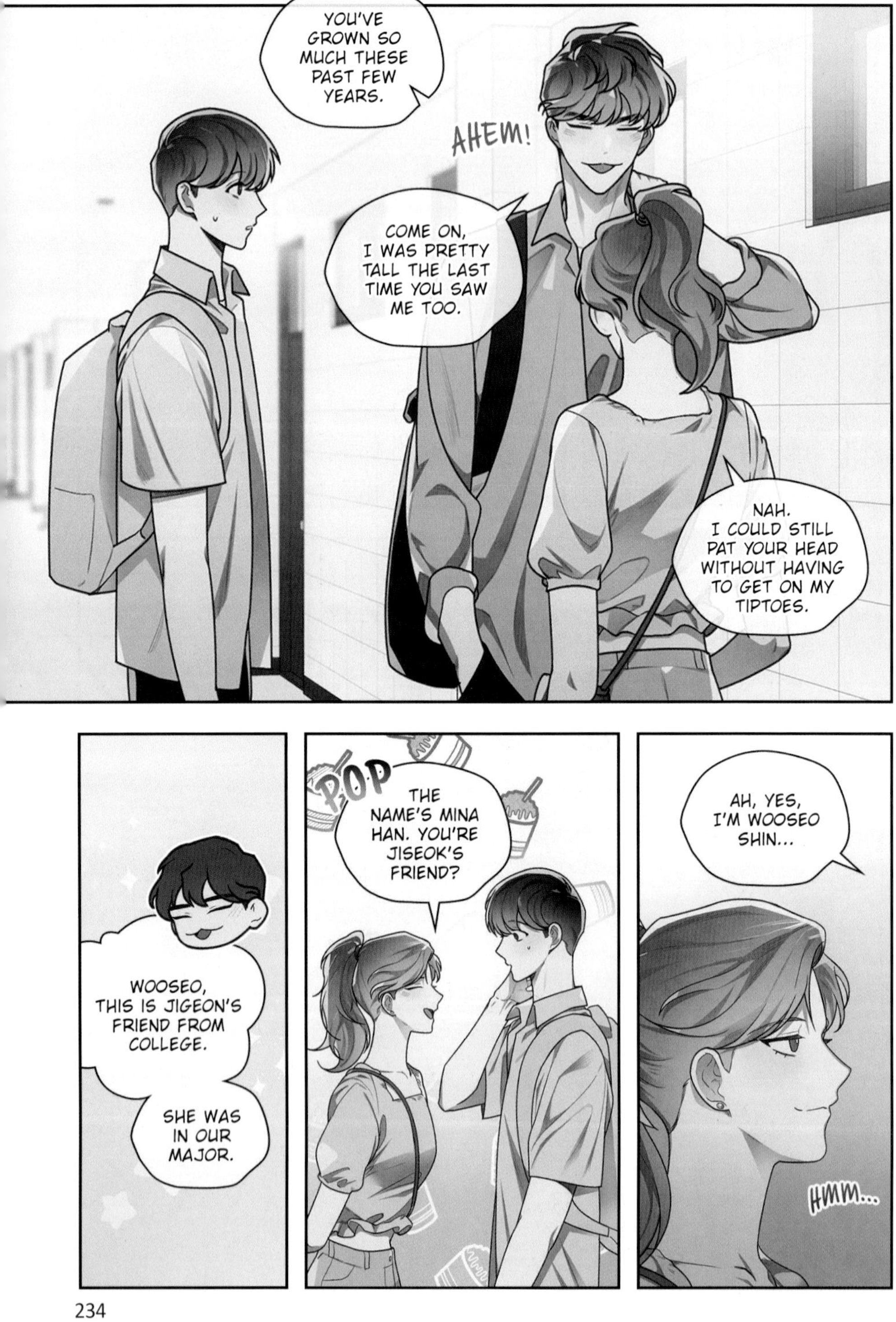
YOU'VE GROWN SO MUCH THESE PAST FEW YEARS.
AHEM!
COME ON, I WAS PRETTY TALL THE LAST TIME YOU SAW ME TOO.
NAH. I COULD STILL PAT YOUR HEAD WITHOUT HAVING TO GET ON MY TIPTOES.
WOOSEO, THIS IS JIGEON'S FRIEND FROM COLLEGE.
SHE WAS IN OUR MAJOR.
POP
THE NAME'S MINA HAN. YOU'RE JISEOK'S FRIEND?
AH, YES, I'M WOOSEO SHIN...
HMM...

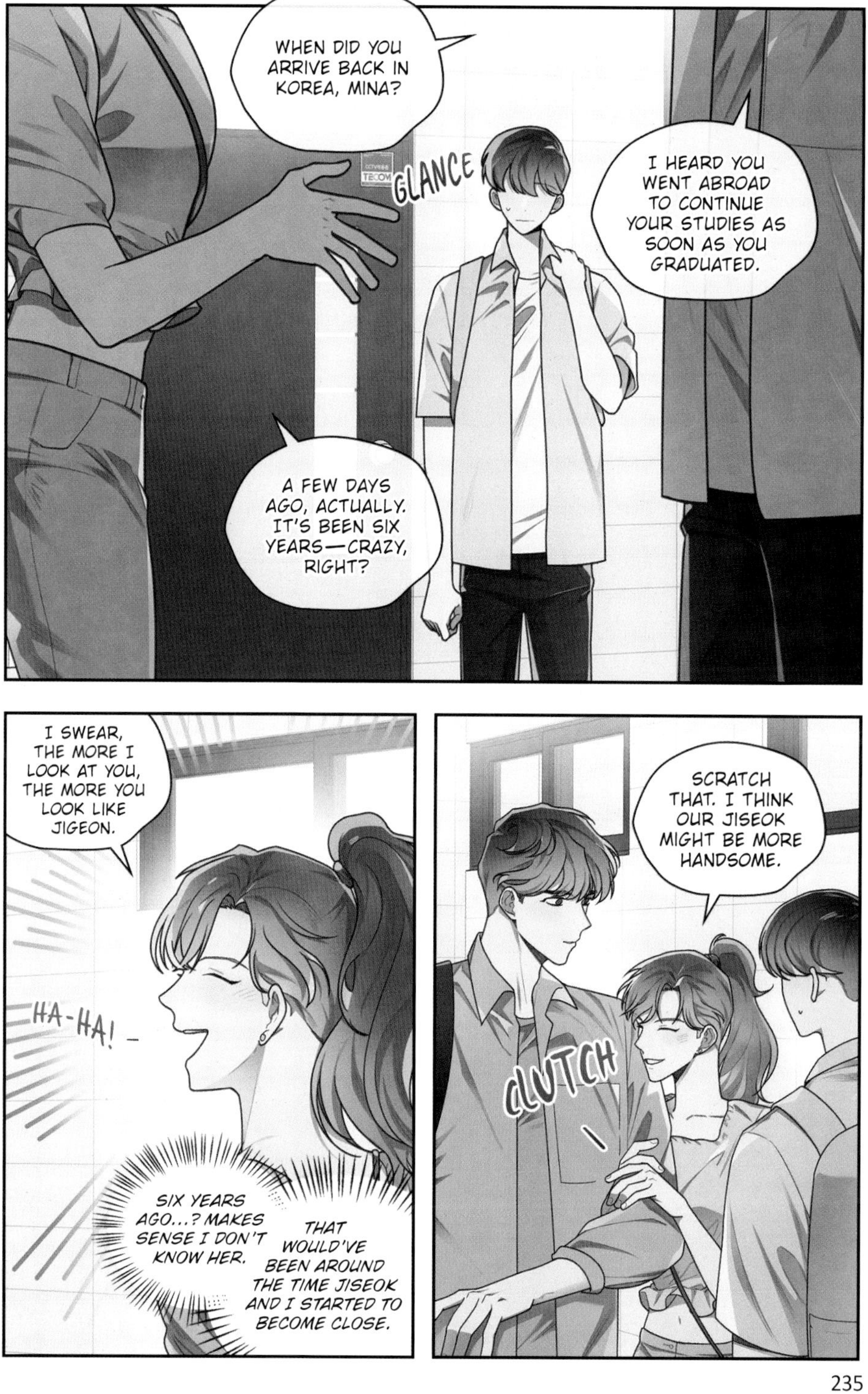
WHEN DID YOU ARRIVE BACK IN KOREA, MINA?
GLANCE
I HEARD YOU WENT ABROAD TO CONTINUE YOUR STUDIES AS SOON AS YOU GRADUATED.
A FEW DAYS AGO, ACTUALLY. IT'S BEEN SIX YEARS—CRAZY, RIGHT?
I SWEAR, THE MORE I LOOK AT YOU, THE MORE YOU LOOK LIKE JIGEON.
HA-HA!
SIX YEARS AGO...? MAKES SENSE I DON'T KNOW HER.
THAT WOULD'VE BEEN AROUND THE TIME JISEOK AND I STARTED TO BECOME CLOSE.
SCRATCH THAT. I THINK OUR JISEOK MIGHT BE MORE HANDSOME.
CLUTCH

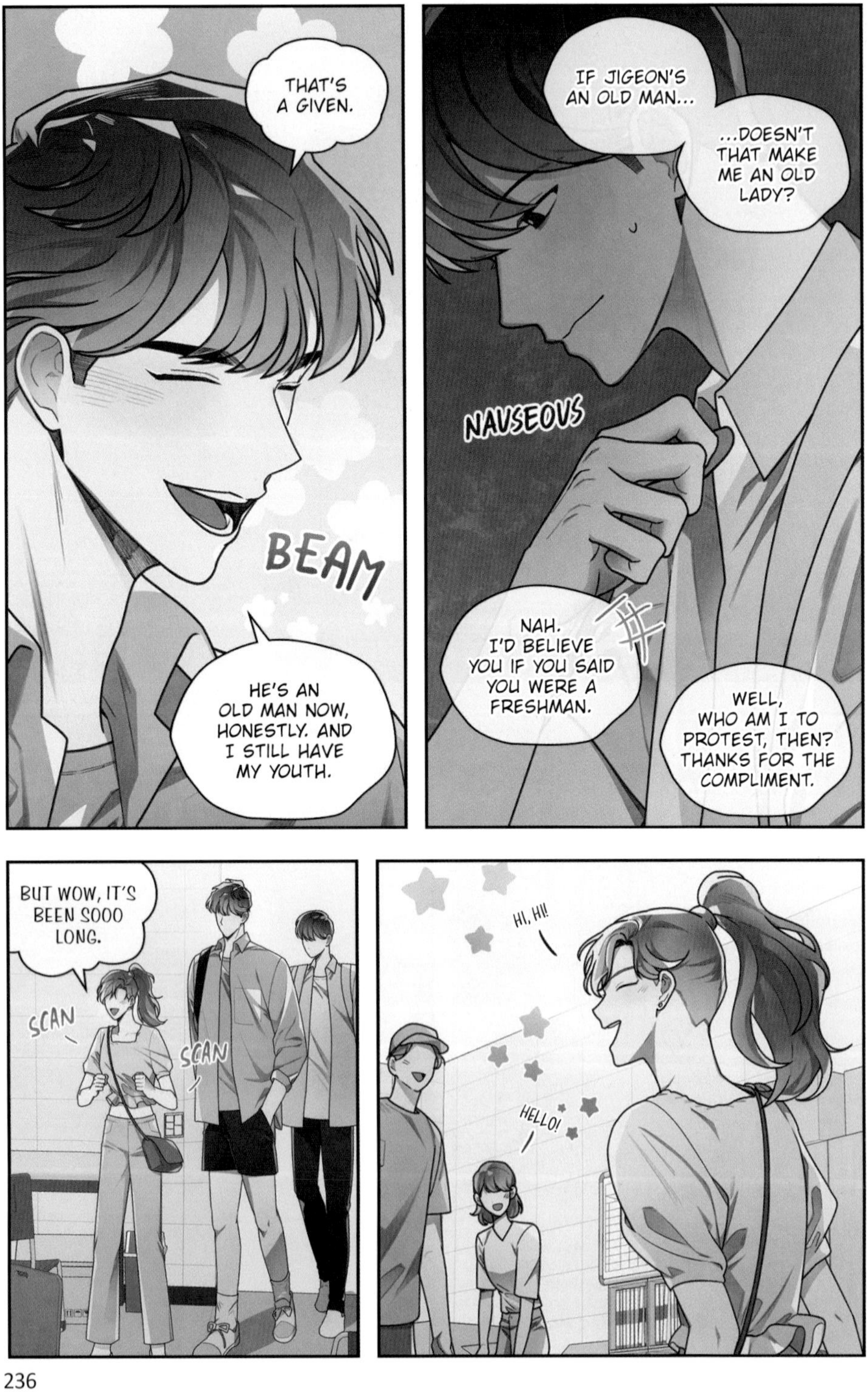
THAT'S A GIVEN.
BEAM
HE'S AN OLD MAN NOW, HONESTLY. AND I STILL HAVE MY YOUTH.
IF JIGEON'S AN OLD MAN...
...DOESN'T THAT MAKE ME AN OLD LADY?
NAUSEOUS
NAH. I'D BELIEVE YOU IF YOU SAID YOU WERE A FRESHMAN.
WELL, WHO AM I TO PROTEST, THEN? THANKS FOR THE COMPLIMENT.
BUT WOW, IT'S BEEN SOOO LONG.
SCAN
SCAN
HI, HI!
HELLO!

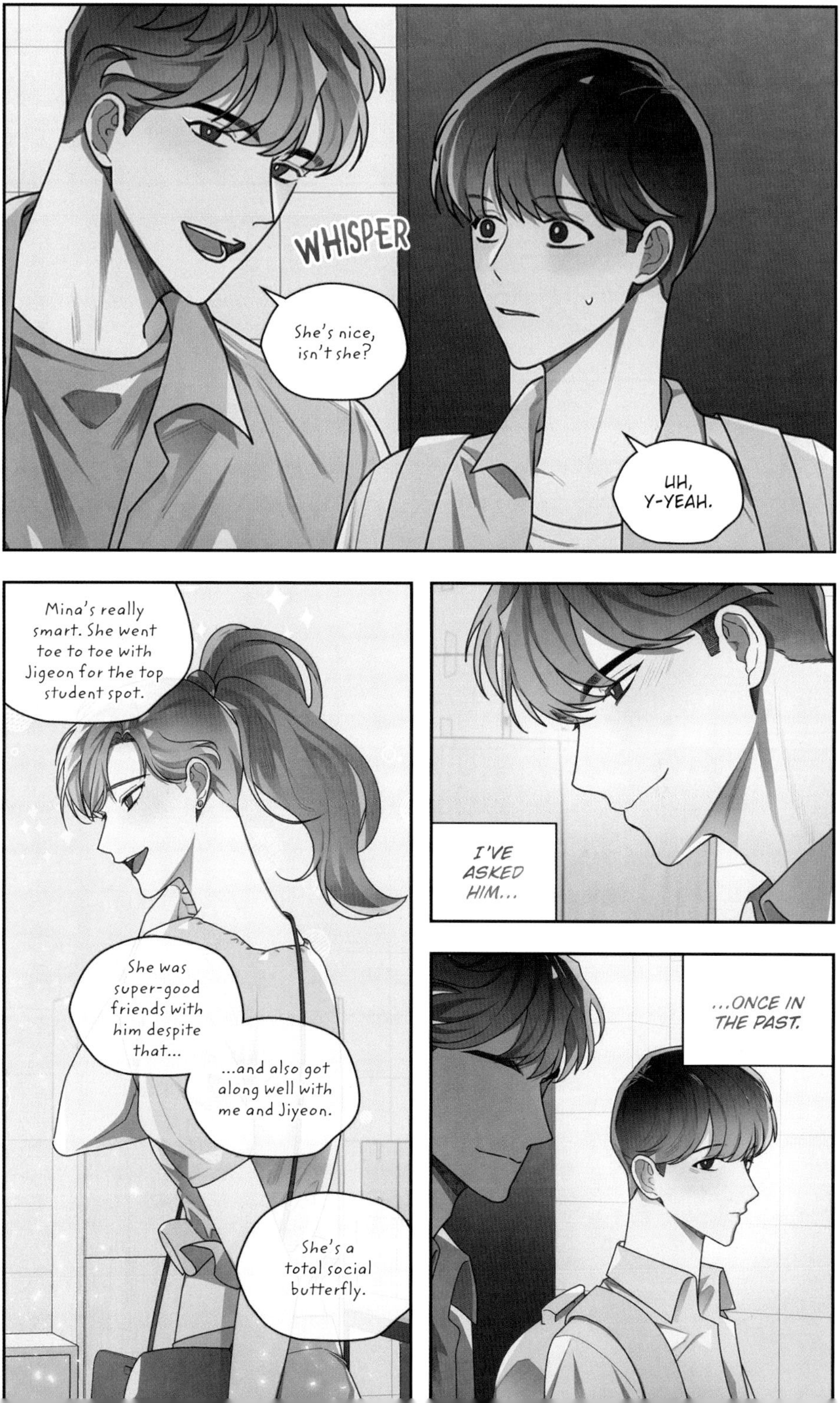
WHISPER
She's nice, isn't she?
UH, Y-YEAH.
Mina's really smart. She went toe to toe with Jigeon for the top student spot.
She was super-good friends with him despite that...
...and also got along well with me and Jiyeon.
She's a total social butterfly.
I'VE ASKED HIM...
...ONCE IN THE PAST.

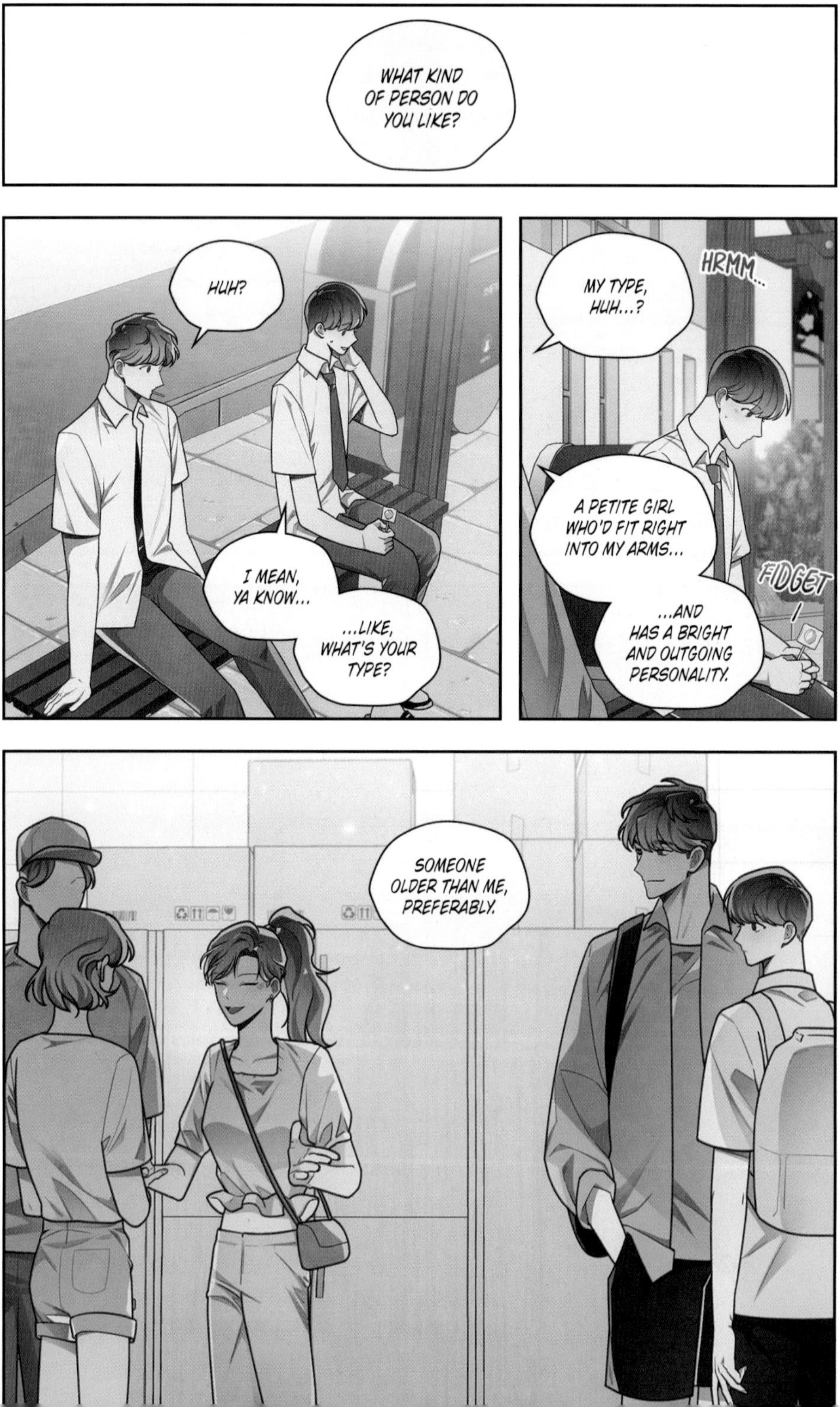
WHAT KIND OF PERSON DO YOU LIKE?
HUH?
I MEAN, YA KNOW...
...LIKE, WHAT'S YOUR TYPE?
MY TYPE, HUH...?
HRMM...
A PETITE GIRL WHO'D FIT RIGHT INTO MY ARMS...
FIDGET
...AND HAS A BRIGHT AND OUTGOING PERSONALITY.
SOMEONE OLDER THAN ME, PREFERABLY.

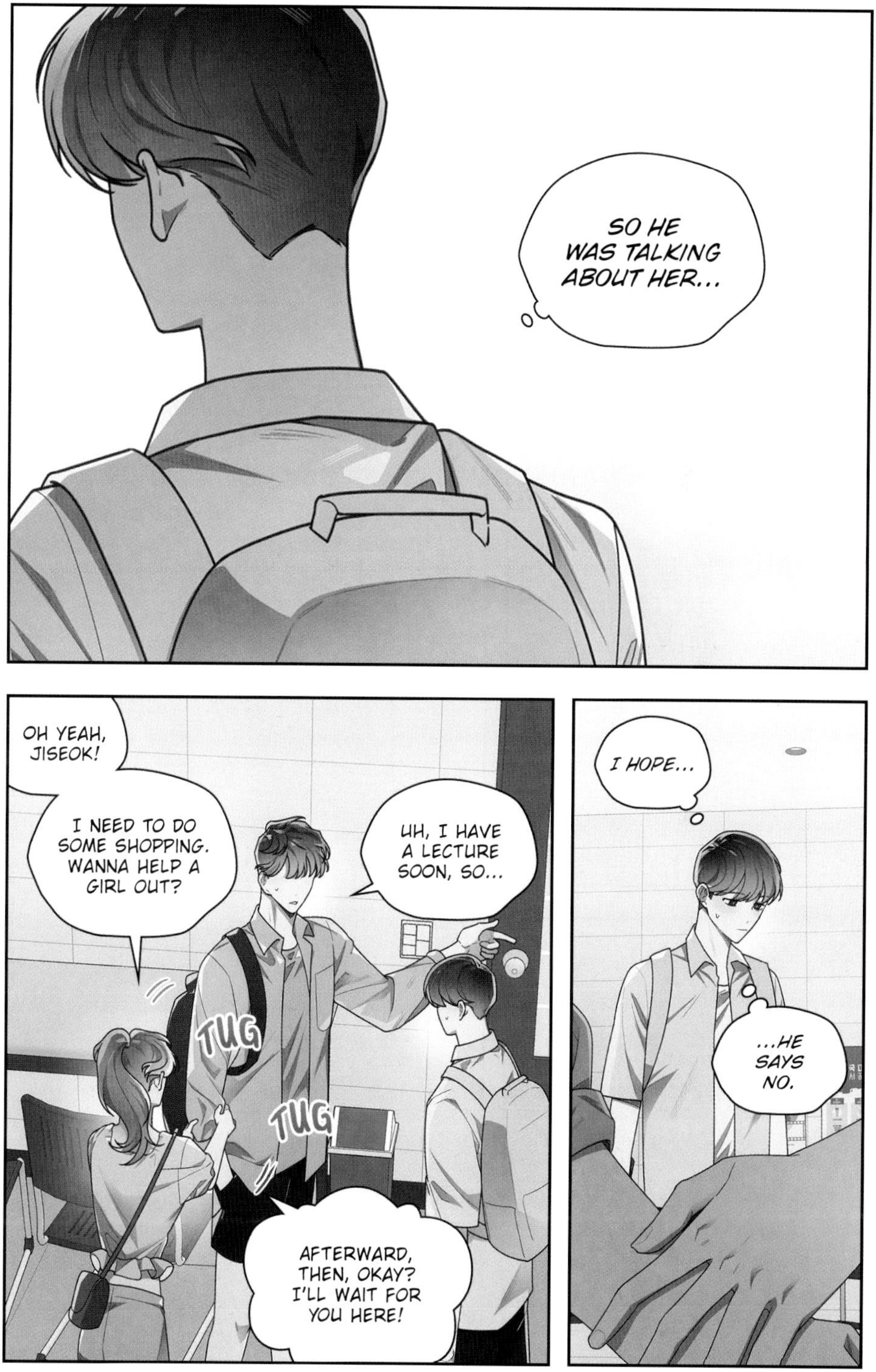

SO HE WAS TALKING ABOUT HER...
OH YEAH, JISEOK!
I NEED TO DO SOME SHOPPING. WANNA HELP A GIRL OUT?
UH, I HAVE A LECTURE SOON, SO...
TUG
TUG
AFTERWARD, THEN, OKAY? I'LL WAIT FOR YOU HERE!
I HOPE...
...HE SAYS NO.

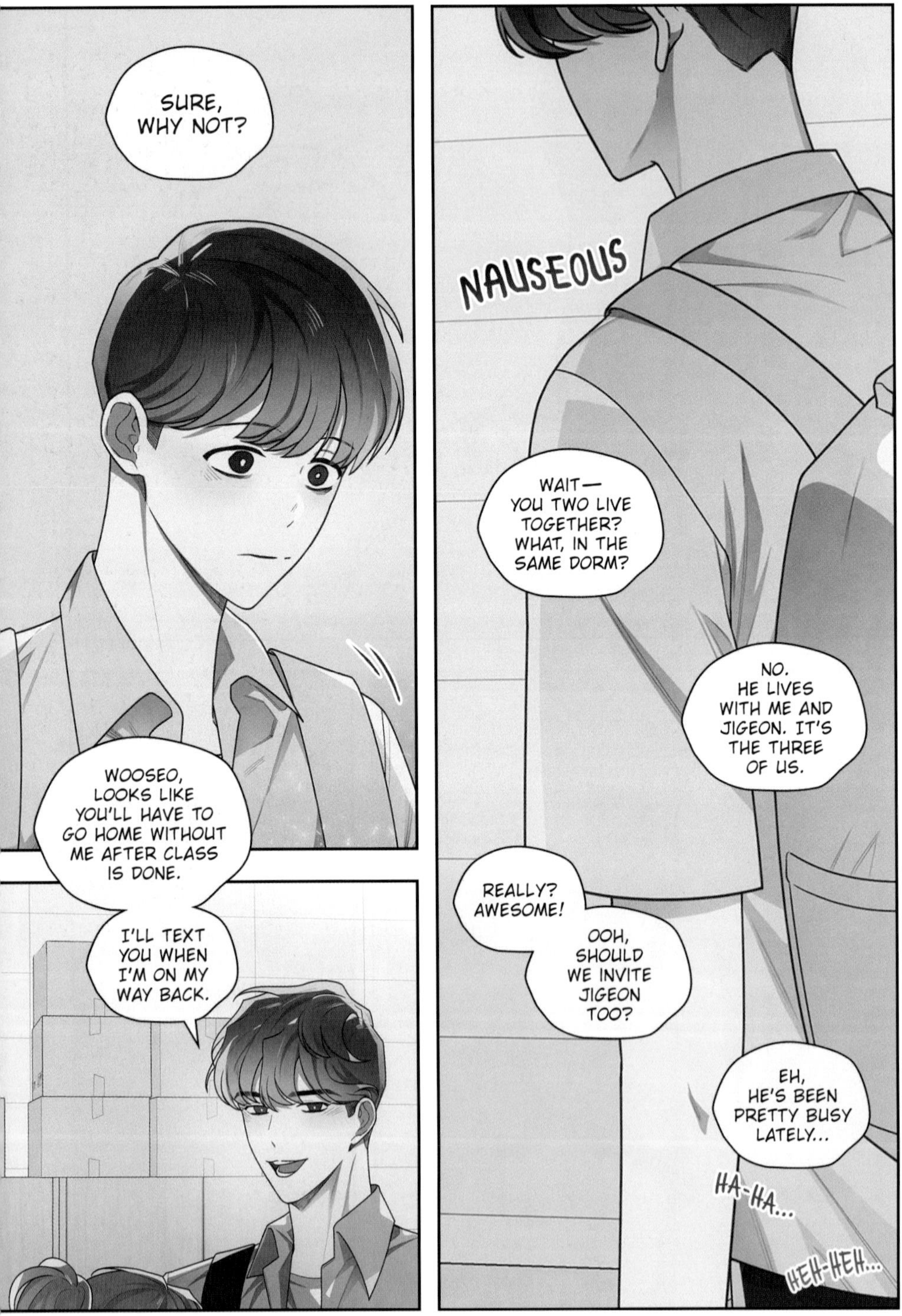
SURE, WHY NOT?
WOOSEO, LOOKS LIKE YOU'LL HAVE TO GO HOME WITHOUT ME AFTER CLASS IS DONE.
I'LL TEXT YOU WHEN I'M ON MY WAY BACK.
NAUSEOUS
WAIT— YOU TWO LIVE TOGETHER? WHAT, IN THE SAME DORM?
NO. HE LIVES WITH ME AND JIGEON. IT'S THE THREE OF US.
REALLY? AWESOME!
OOH, SHOULD WE INVITE JIGEON TOO?
EH, HE'S BEEN PRETTY BUSY LATELY...
HA-HA...
HEH-HEH...

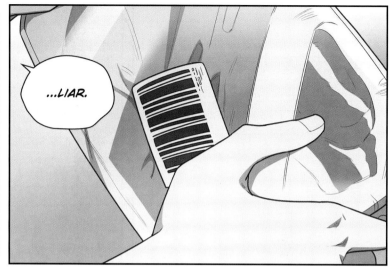

...LIAR.

YOU SAID WE'D GO GROCERY SHOPPING TOGETHER WHEN SCHOOL WAS OVER, BUT YOU JUST LEFT ME.

BITTER

CURRENTLY: GROCERY SHOPPING...

SO? WHAT CAN YOU DO ABOUT IT, WOOSEO?

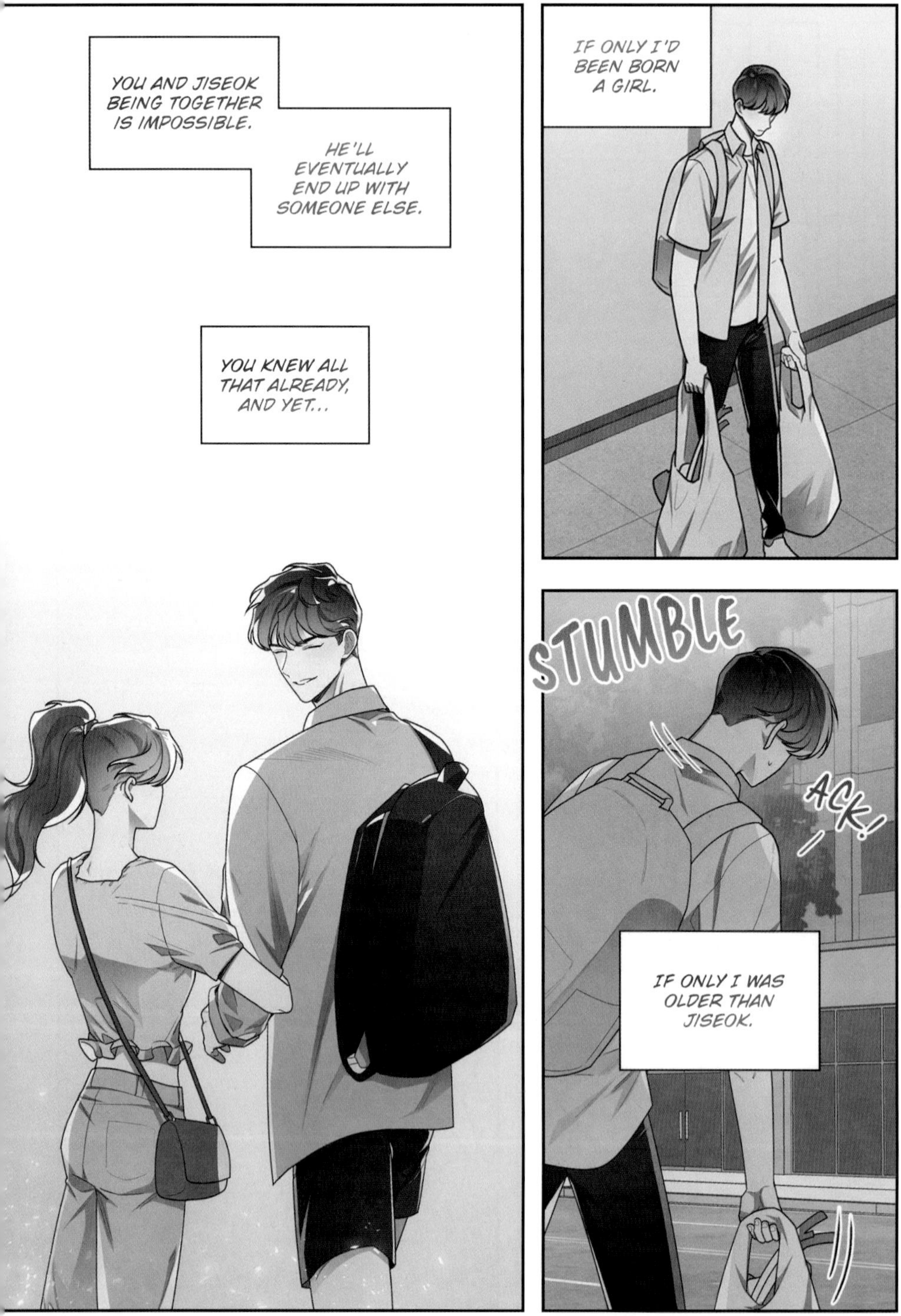
YOU AND JISEOK BEING TOGETHER IS IMPOSSIBLE.
HE'LL EVENTUALLY END UP WITH SOMEONE ELSE.
YOU KNEW ALL THAT ALREADY, AND YET...
IF ONLY I'D BEEN BORN A GIRL.
STUMBLE
ACK!
IF ONLY I WAS OLDER THAN JISEOK.

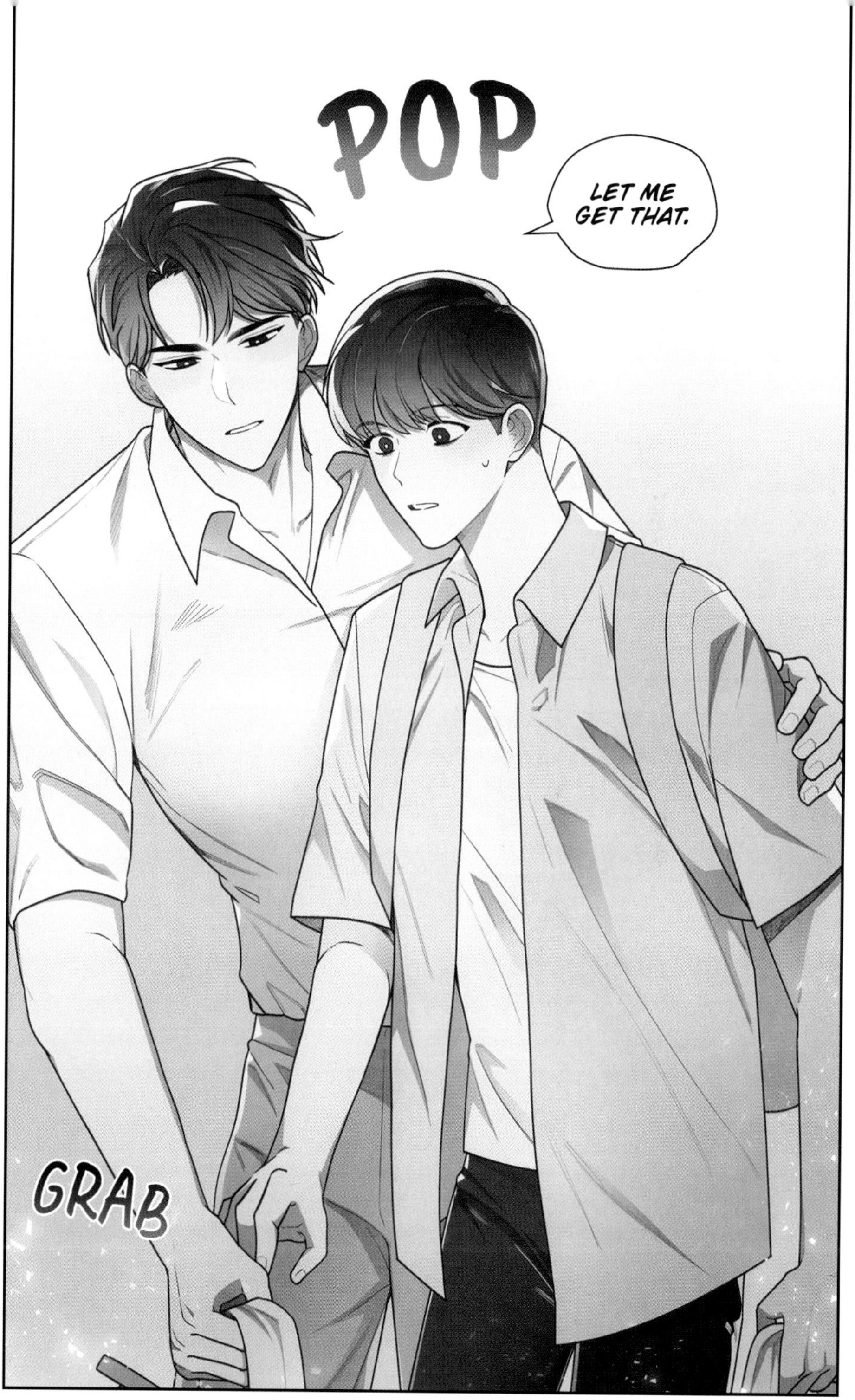
POP
LET ME GET THAT.
GRAB

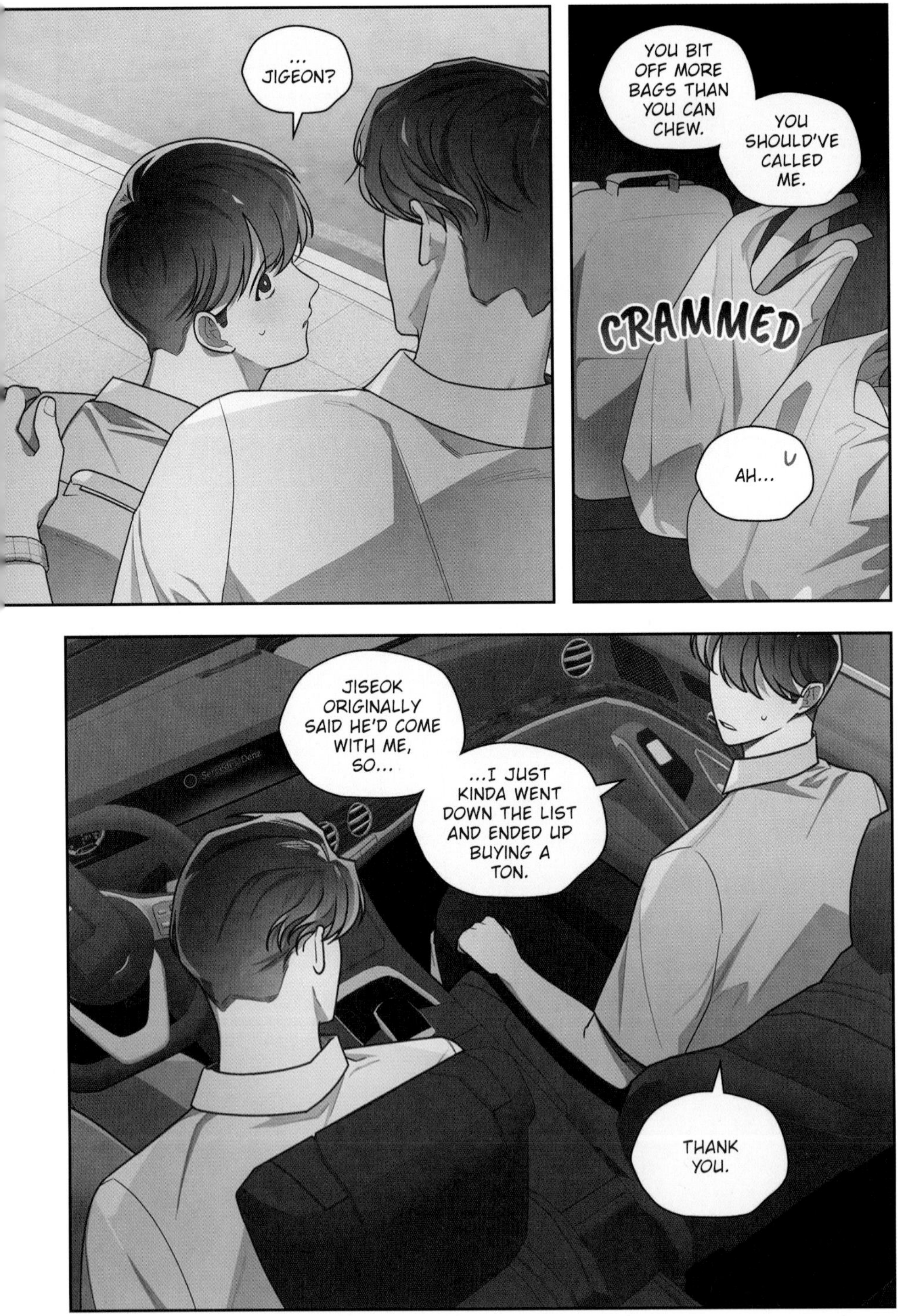
... JIGEON?
YOU BIT OFF MORE BAGS THAN YOU CAN CHEW.
YOU SHOULD'VE CALLED ME.
CRAMMED
AH...
JISEOK ORIGINALLY SAID HE'D COME WITH ME, SO...
...I JUST KINDA WENT DOWN THE LIST AND ENDED UP BUYING A TON.
THANK YOU.

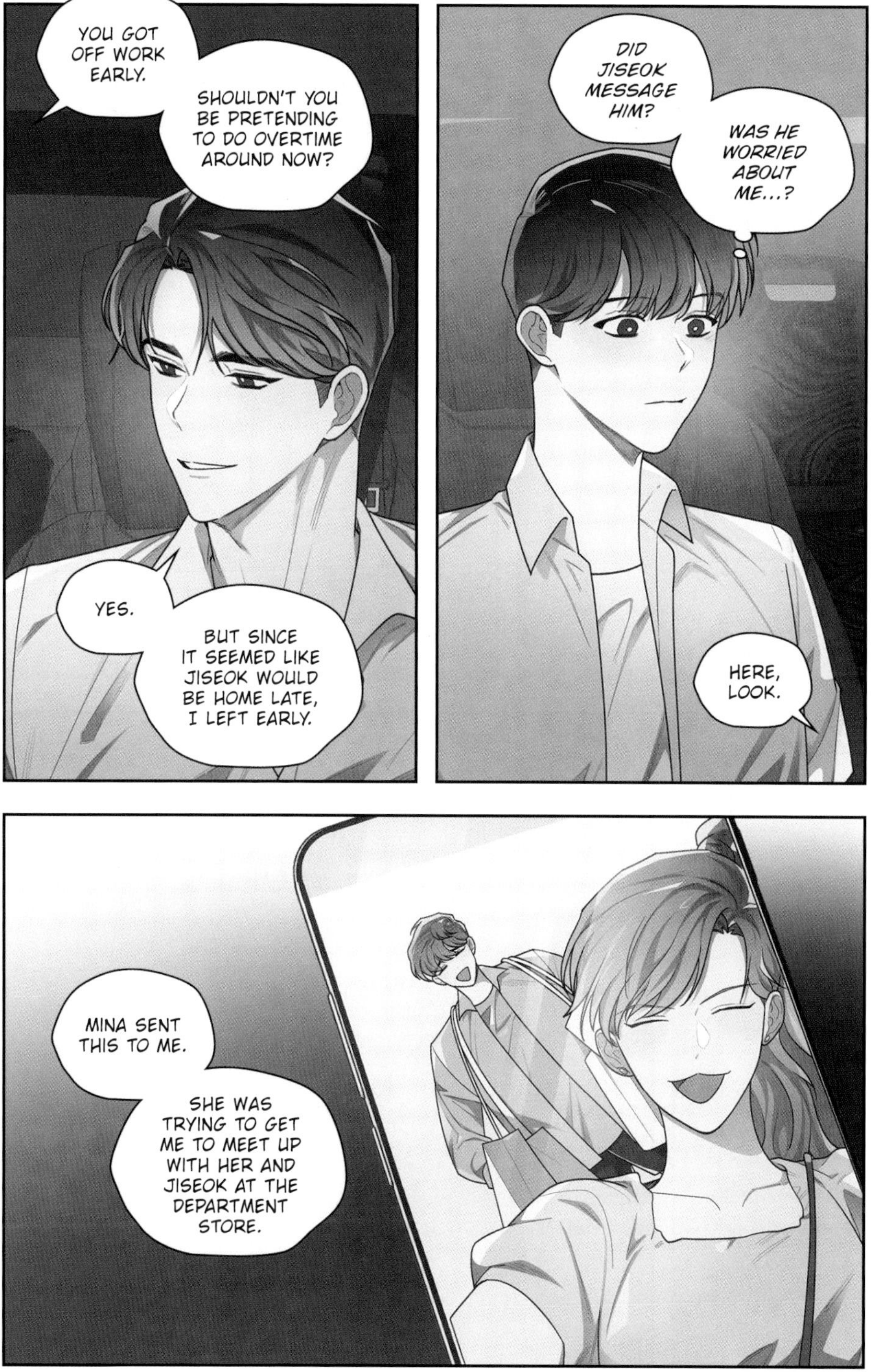
YOU GOT OFF WORK EARLY.
SHOULDN'T YOU BE PRETENDING TO DO OVERTIME AROUND NOW?
YES.
BUT SINCE IT SEEMED LIKE JISEOK WOULD BE HOME LATE, I LEFT EARLY.
DID JISEOK MESSAGE HIM?
WAS HE WORRIED ABOUT ME...?
HERE, LOOK.
MINA SENT THIS TO ME.
SHE WAS TRYING TO GET ME TO MEET UP WITH HER AND JISEOK AT THE DEPARTMENT STORE.

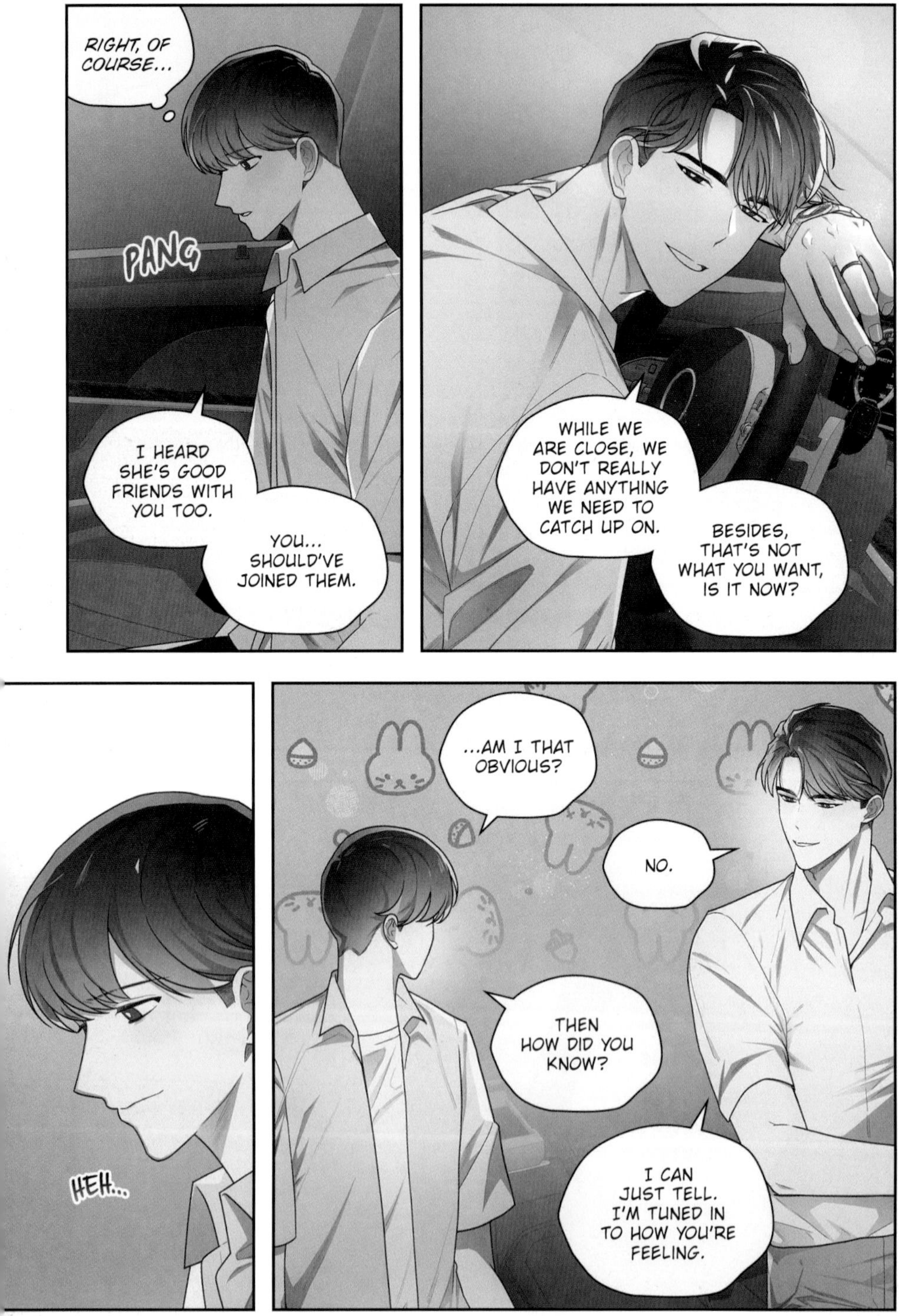
RIGHT, OF COURSE...
PANG
I HEARD SHE'S GOOD FRIENDS WITH YOU TOO.
YOU... SHOULD'VE JOINED THEM.
WHILE WE ARE CLOSE, WE DON'T REALLY HAVE ANYTHING WE NEED TO CATCH UP ON.
BESIDES, THAT'S NOT WHAT YOU WANT, IS IT NOW?
HEH...
...AM I THAT OBVIOUS?
NO.
THEN HOW DID YOU KNOW?
I CAN JUST TELL. I'M TUNED IN TO HOW YOU'RE FEELING.

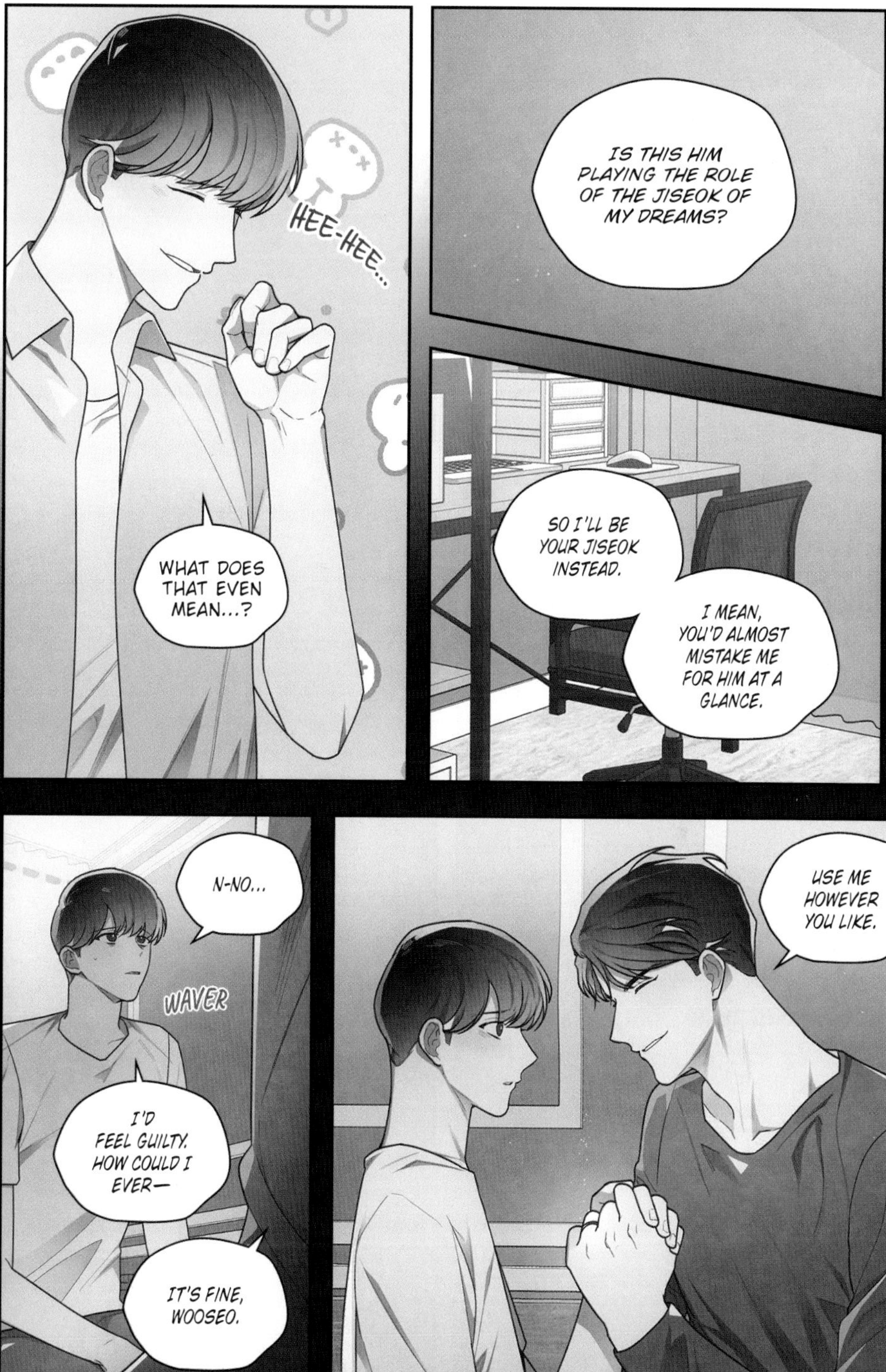
HEE-HEE...
WHAT DOES THAT EVEN MEAN...?
IS THIS HIM PLAYING THE ROLE OF THE JISEOK OF MY DREAMS?
SO I'LL BE YOUR JISEOK INSTEAD.
I MEAN, YOU'D ALMOST MISTAKE ME FOR HIM AT A GLANCE.
N-NO...
WAVER
I'D FEEL GUILTY. HOW COULD I EVER—
IT'S FINE, WOOSEO.
USE ME HOWEVER YOU LIKE.

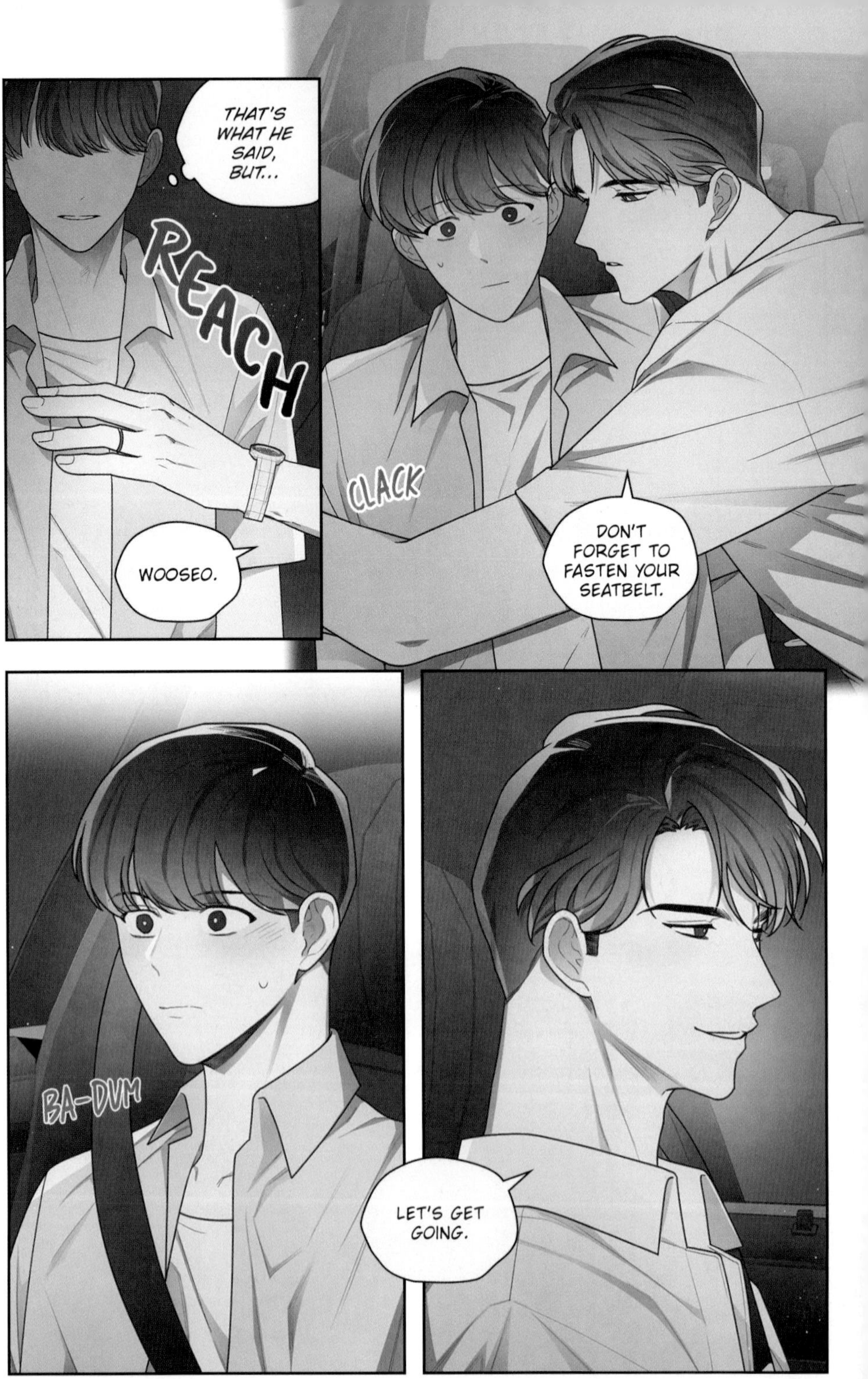
THAT'S WHAT HE SAID, BUT...
REACH
WOOSEO.
CLACK
DON'T FORGET TO FASTEN YOUR SEATBELT.
BA-DUM
LET'S GET GOING.

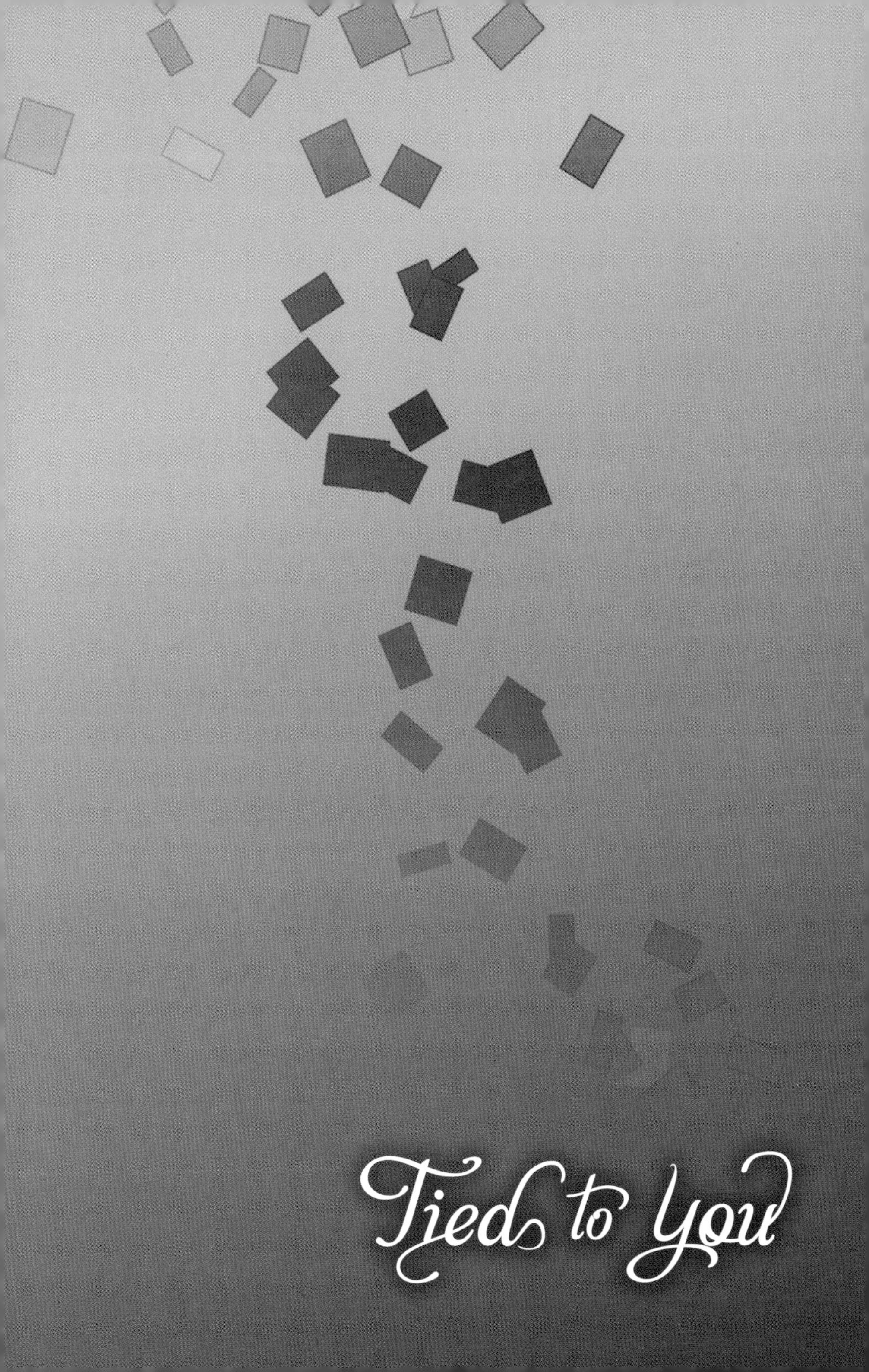

Tied to You

Chapter 13

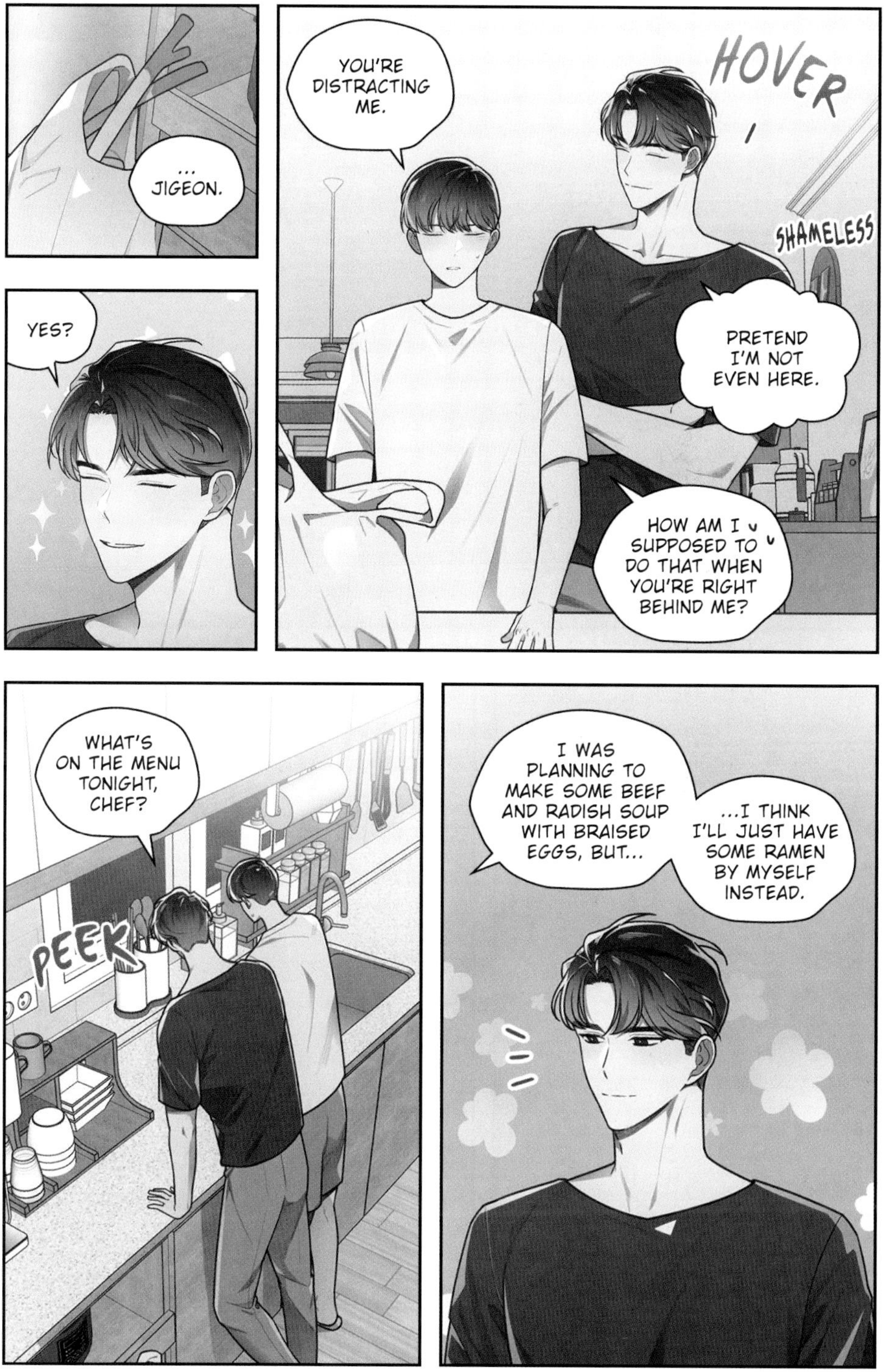
...
JIGEON.
YES?
YOU'RE DISTRACTING ME.
HOVER
SHAMELESS
PRETEND I'M NOT EVEN HERE.
HOW AM I SUPPOSED TO DO THAT WHEN YOU'RE RIGHT BEHIND ME?
WHAT'S ON THE MENU TONIGHT, CHEF?
PEEK
I WAS PLANNING TO MAKE SOME BEEF AND RADISH SOUP WITH BRAISED EGGS, BUT...
...I THINK I'LL JUST HAVE SOME RAMEN BY MYSELF INSTEAD.

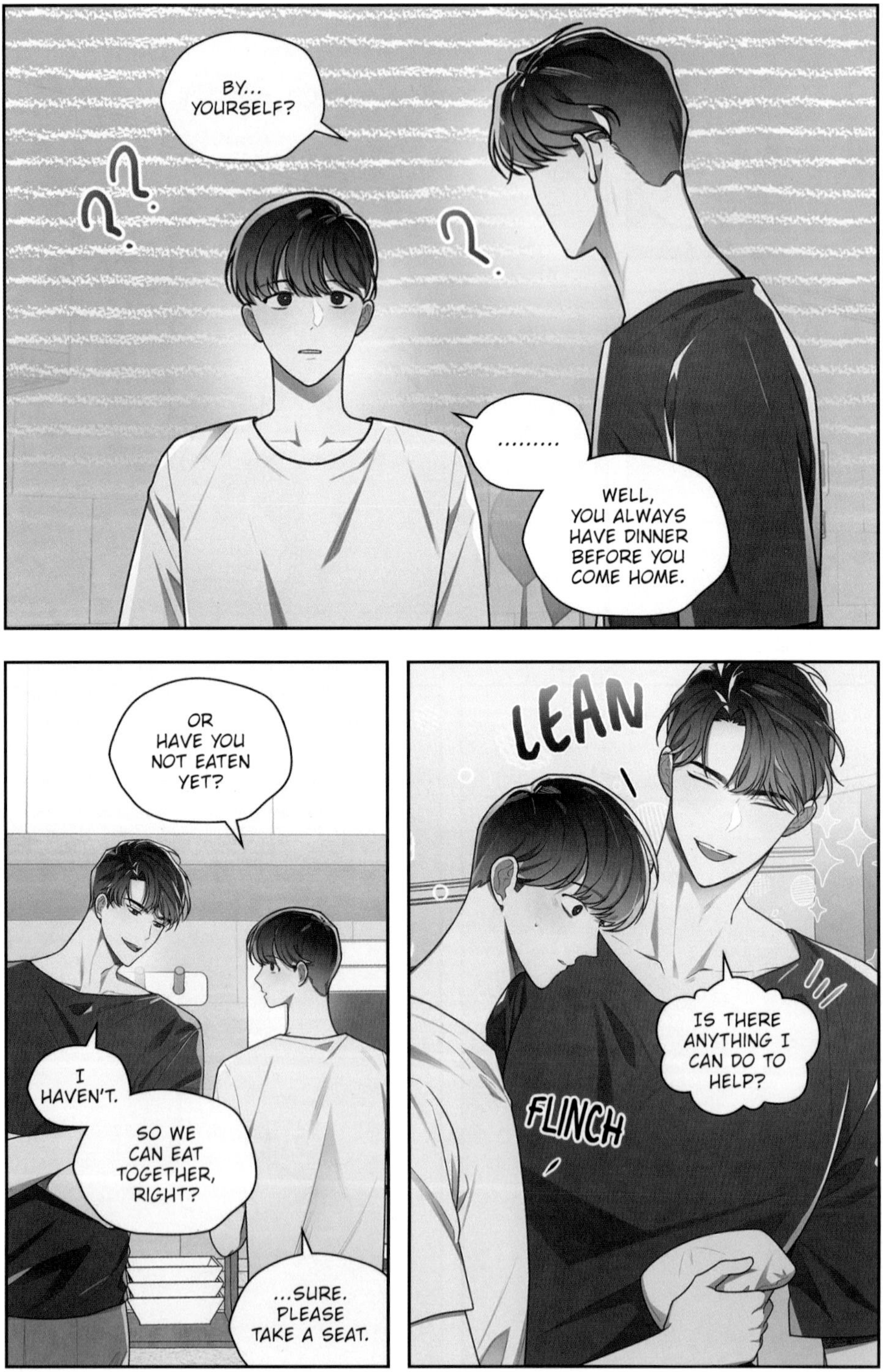
BY... YOURSELF?
....
WELL, YOU ALWAYS HAVE DINNER BEFORE YOU COME HOME.
OR HAVE YOU NOT EATEN YET?
I HAVEN'T.
SO WE CAN EAT TOGETHER, RIGHT?
...SURE. PLEASE TAKE A SEAT.
LEAN
IS THERE ANYTHING I CAN DO TO HELP?
FLINCH

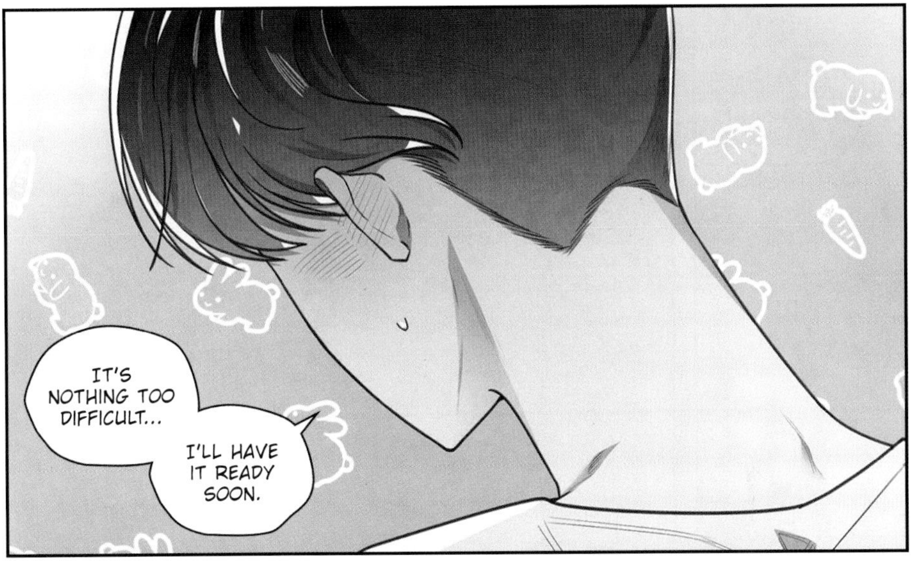
IT'S NOTHING TOO DIFFICULT...
I'LL HAVE IT READY SOON.

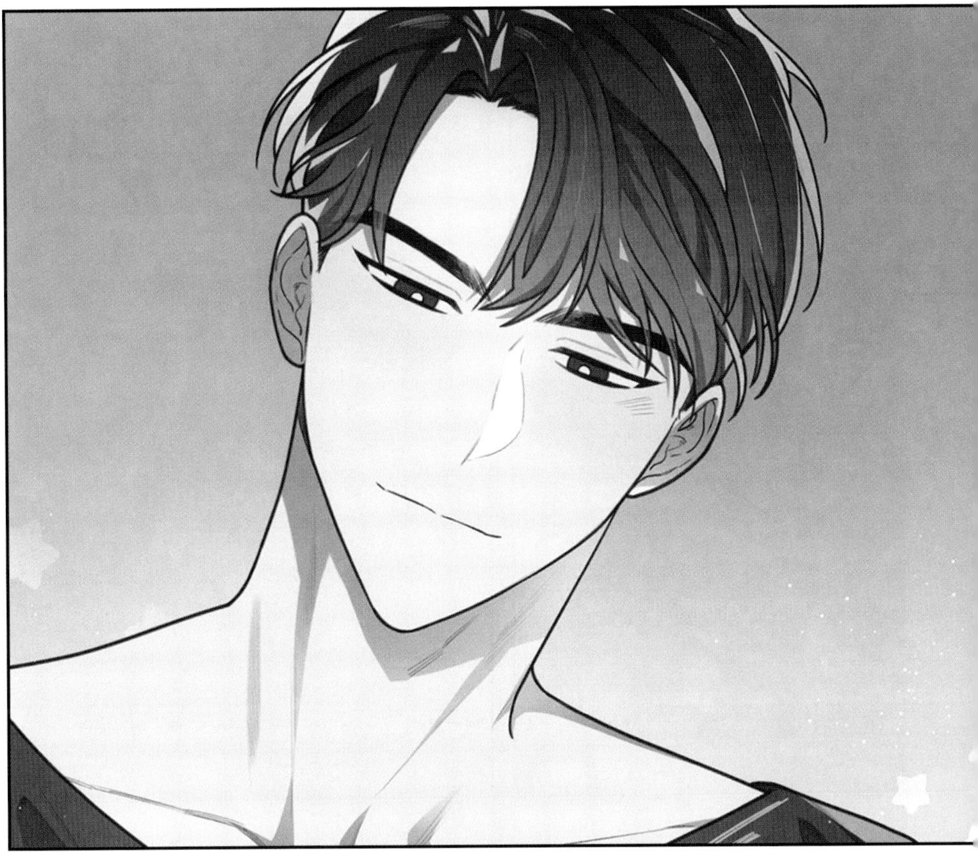

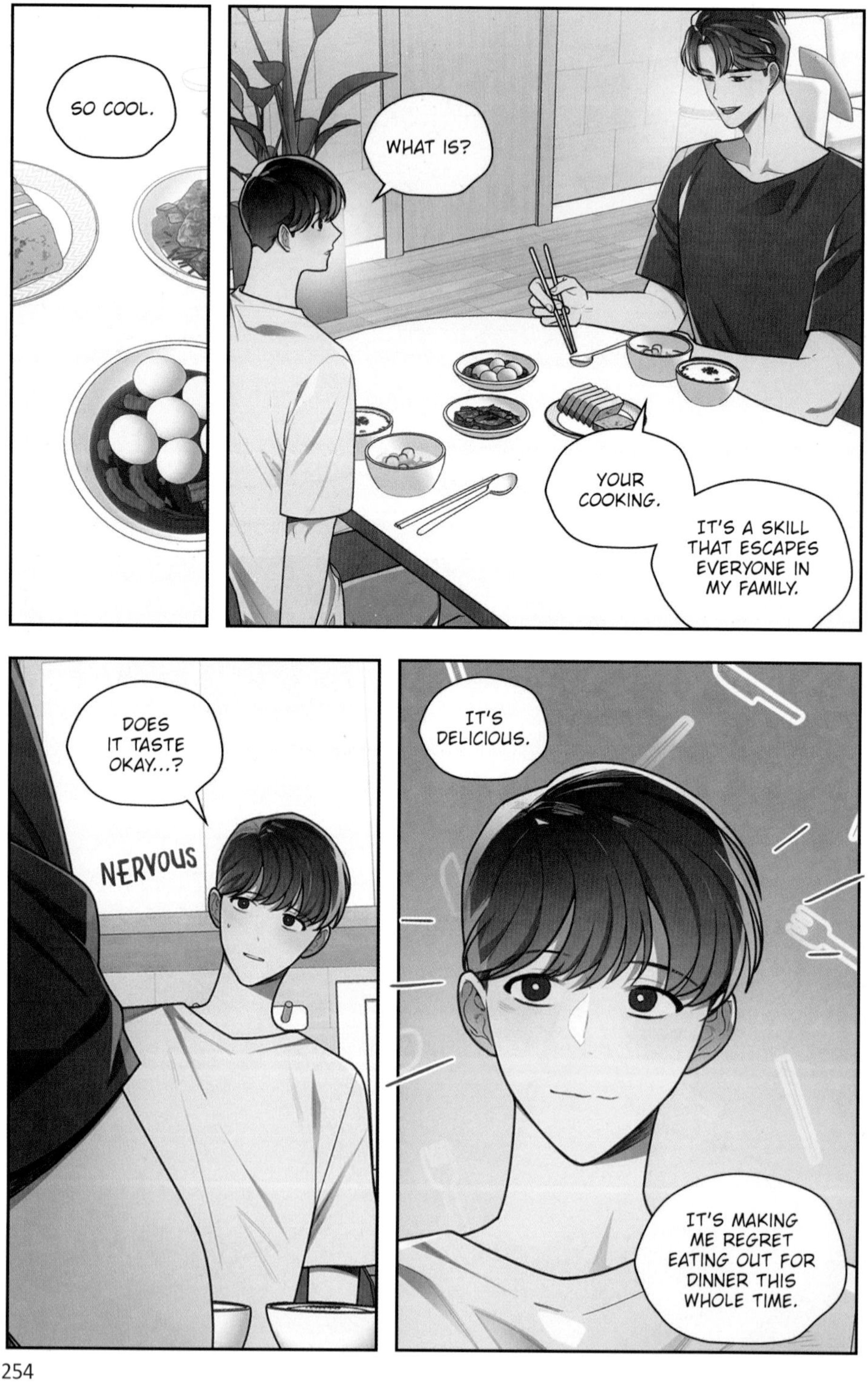
SO COOL.
WHAT IS?
YOUR COOKING.
IT'S A SKILL THAT ESCAPES EVERYONE IN MY FAMILY.
DOES IT TASTE OKAY...?
NERVOUS
IT'S DELICIOUS.
IT'S MAKING ME REGRET EATING OUT FOR DINNER THIS WHOLE TIME.

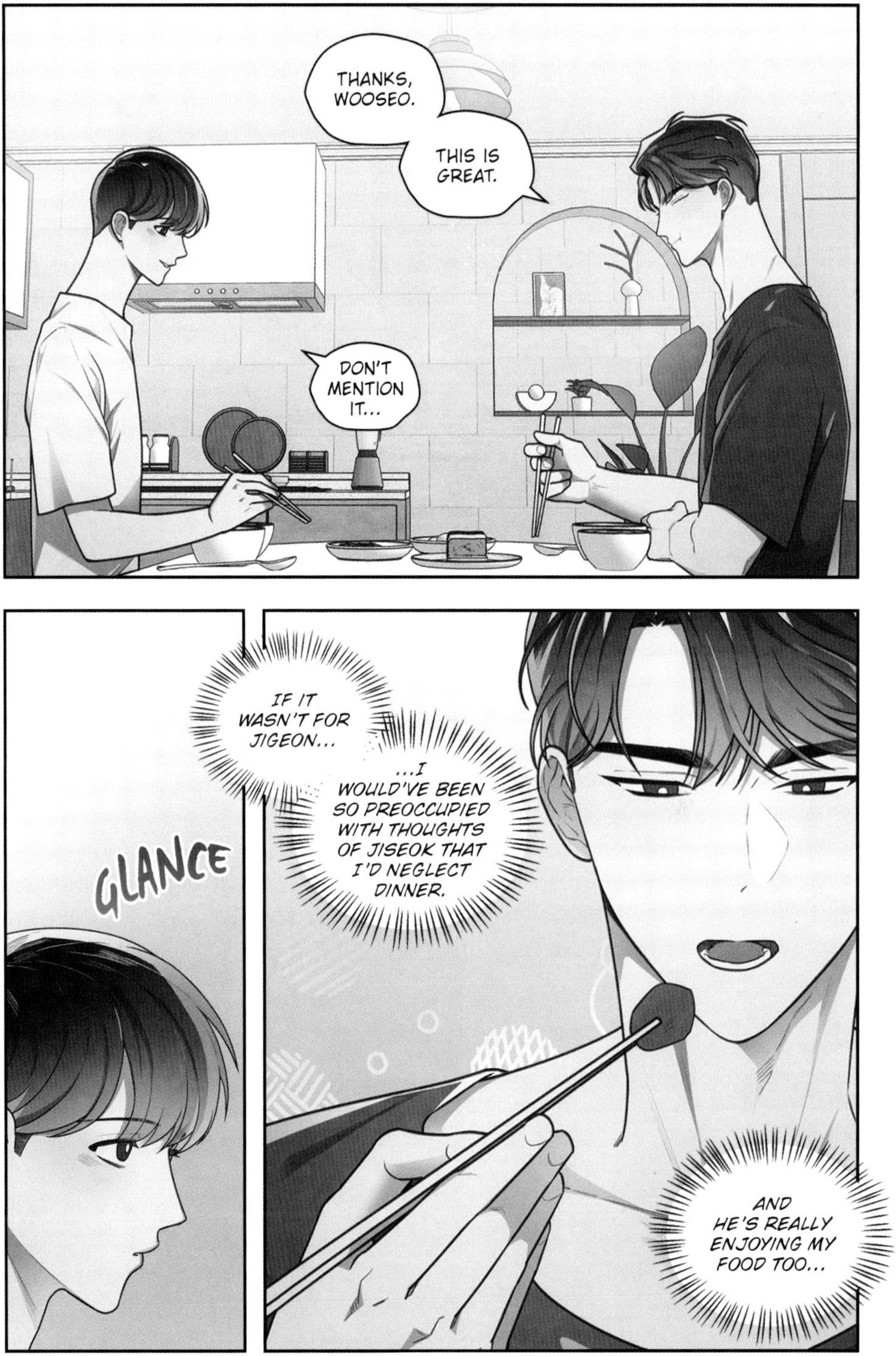
THANKS, WOOSEO.
THIS IS GREAT.
DON'T MENTION IT...
IF IT WASN'T FOR JIGEON...
...I WOULD'VE BEEN SO PREOCCUPIED WITH THOUGHTS OF JISEOK THAT I'D NEGLECT DINNER.
GLANCE
AND HE'S REALLY ENJOYING MY FOOD TOO...

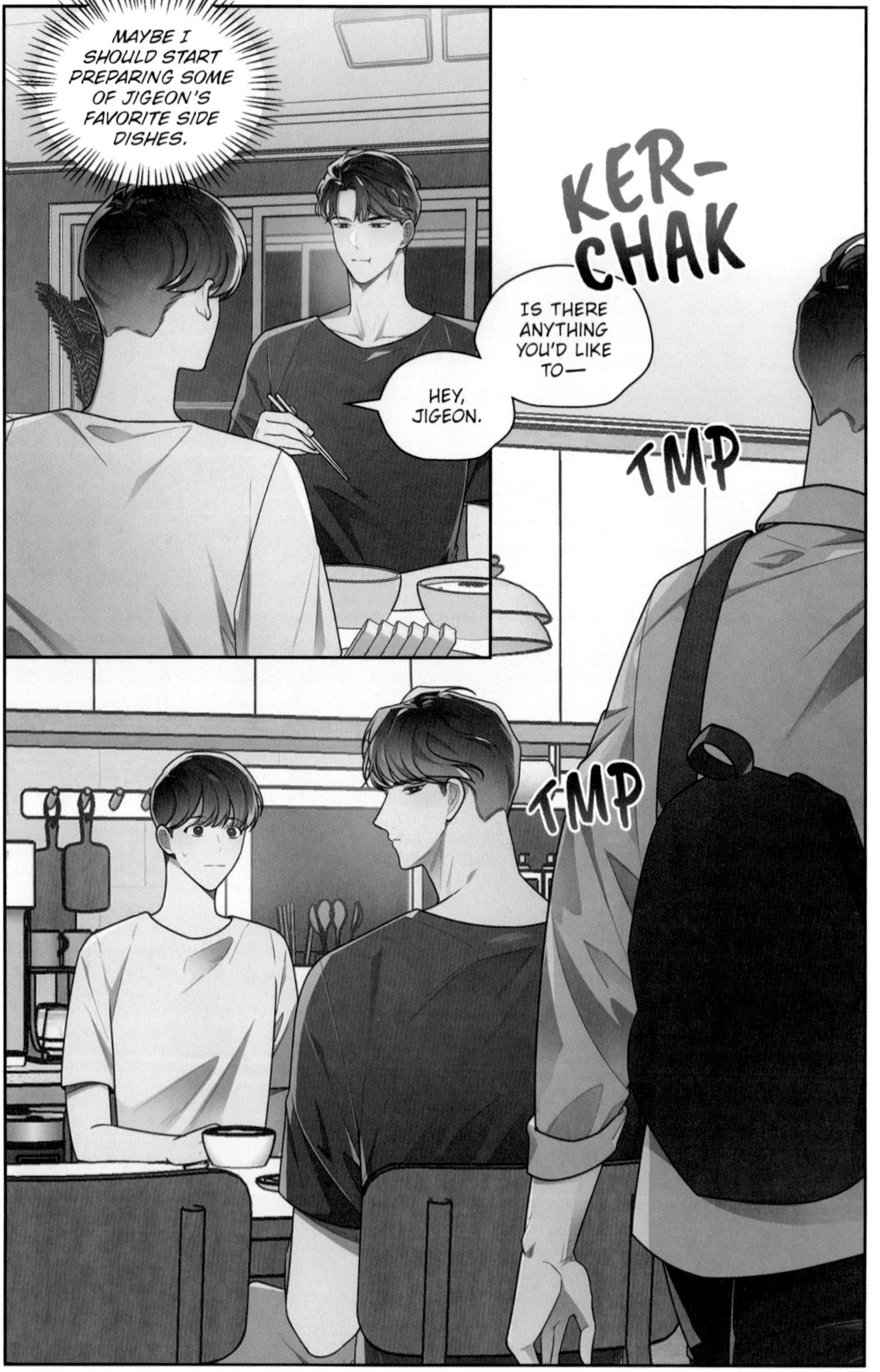
MAYBE I SHOULD START PREPARING SOME OF JIGEON'S FAVORITE SIDE DISHES.
HEY, JIGEON.
IS THERE ANYTHING YOU'D LIKE TO—
KER-CHAK
TMP
TMP

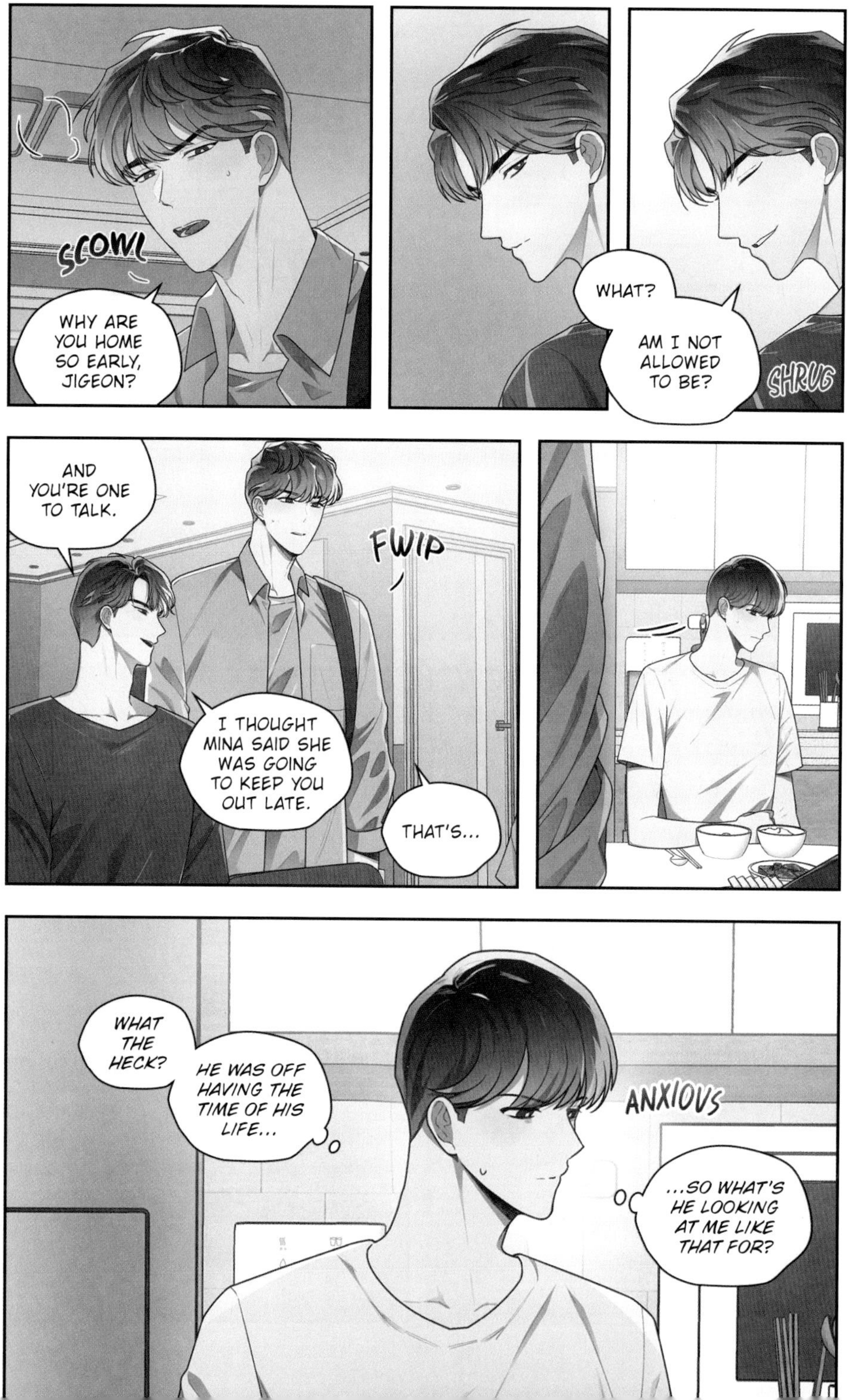
SCOWL
WHY ARE YOU HOME SO EARLY, JIGEON?
WHAT?
AM I NOT ALLOWED TO BE?
SHRUG
AND YOU'RE ONE TO TALK.
FWIP
I THOUGHT MINA SAID SHE WAS GOING TO KEEP YOU OUT LATE.
THAT'S...
WHAT THE HECK?
HE WAS OFF HAVING THE TIME OF HIS LIFE...
ANXIOUS
...SO WHAT'S HE LOOKING AT ME LIKE THAT FOR?

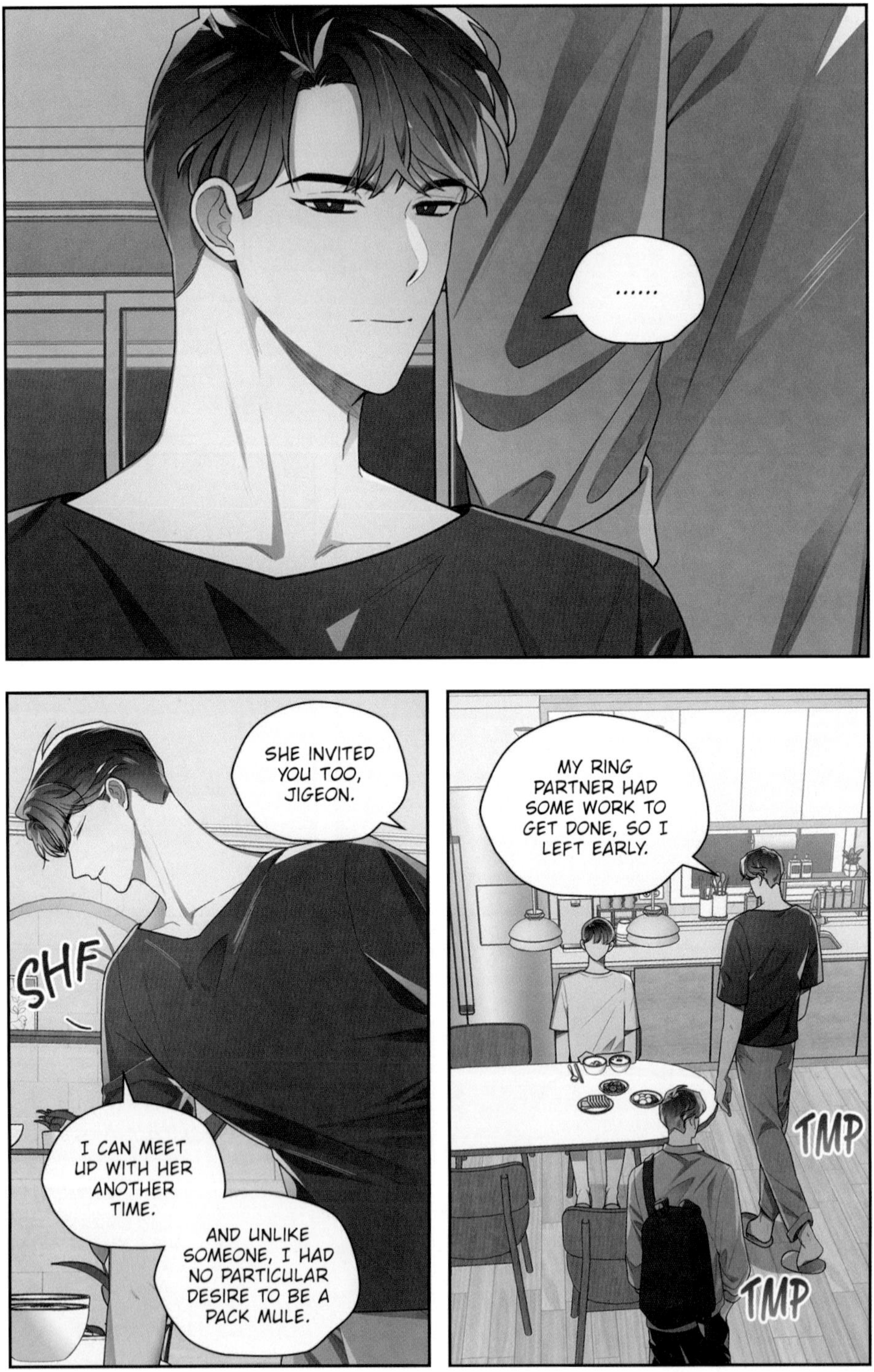
......
SHE INVITED YOU TOO, JIGEON.
SHF
I CAN MEET UP WITH HER ANOTHER TIME.
AND UNLIKE SOMEONE, I HAD NO PARTICULAR DESIRE TO BE A PACK MULE.
MY RING PARTNER HAD SOME WORK TO GET DONE, SO I LEFT EARLY.
TMP
TMP

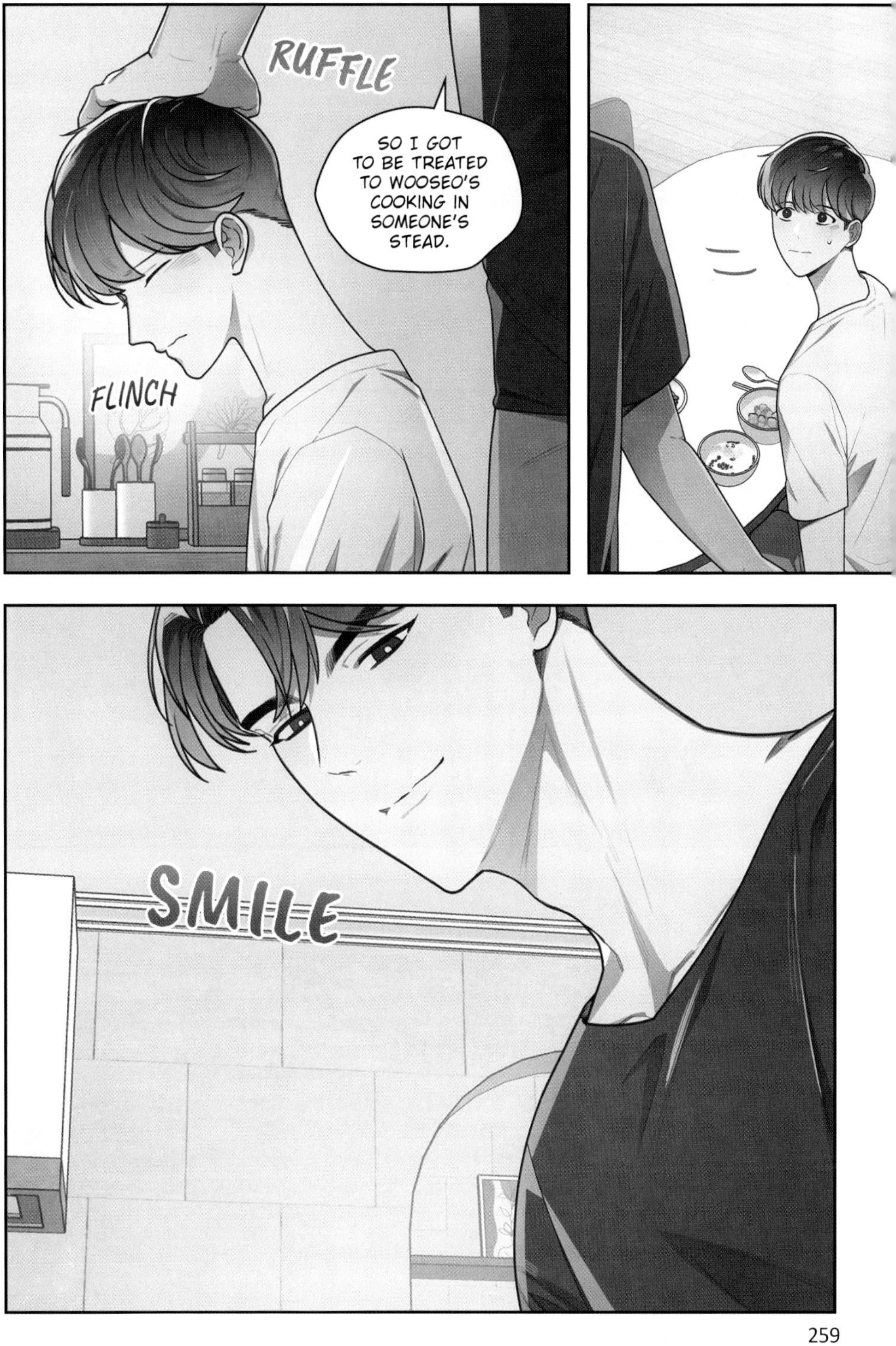
RUFFLE
SO I GOT TO BE TREATED TO WOOSEO'S COOKING IN SOMEONE'S STEAD.
FLINCH
SMILE

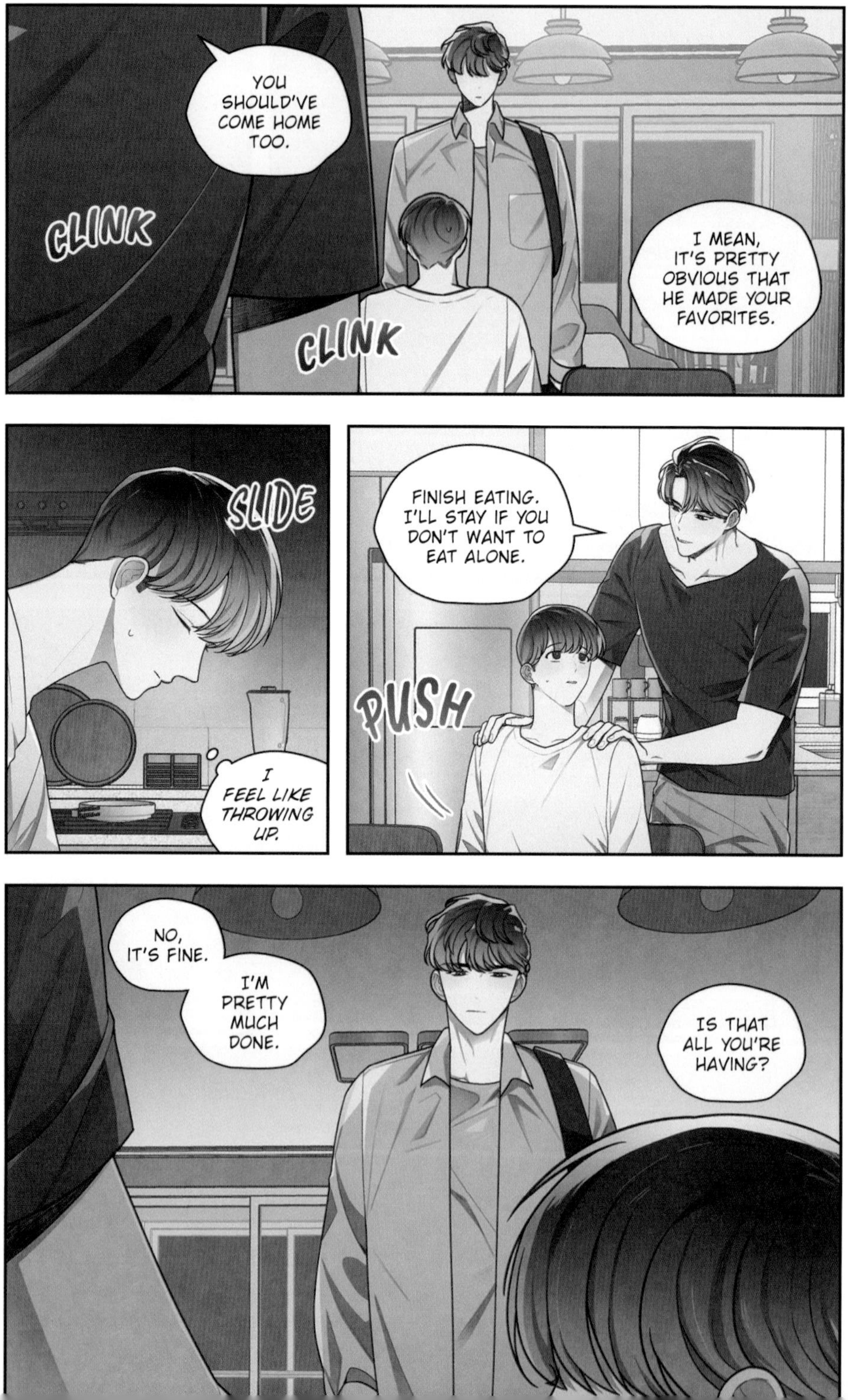
YOU SHOULD'VE COME HOME TOO.
CLINK
CLINK
I MEAN, IT'S PRETTY OBVIOUS THAT HE MADE YOUR FAVORITES.
SLIDE
I FEEL LIKE THROWING UP.
FINISH EATING. I'LL STAY IF YOU DON'T WANT TO EAT ALONE.
PUSH
NO, IT'S FINE.
I'M PRETTY MUCH DONE.
IS THAT ALL YOU'RE HAVING?

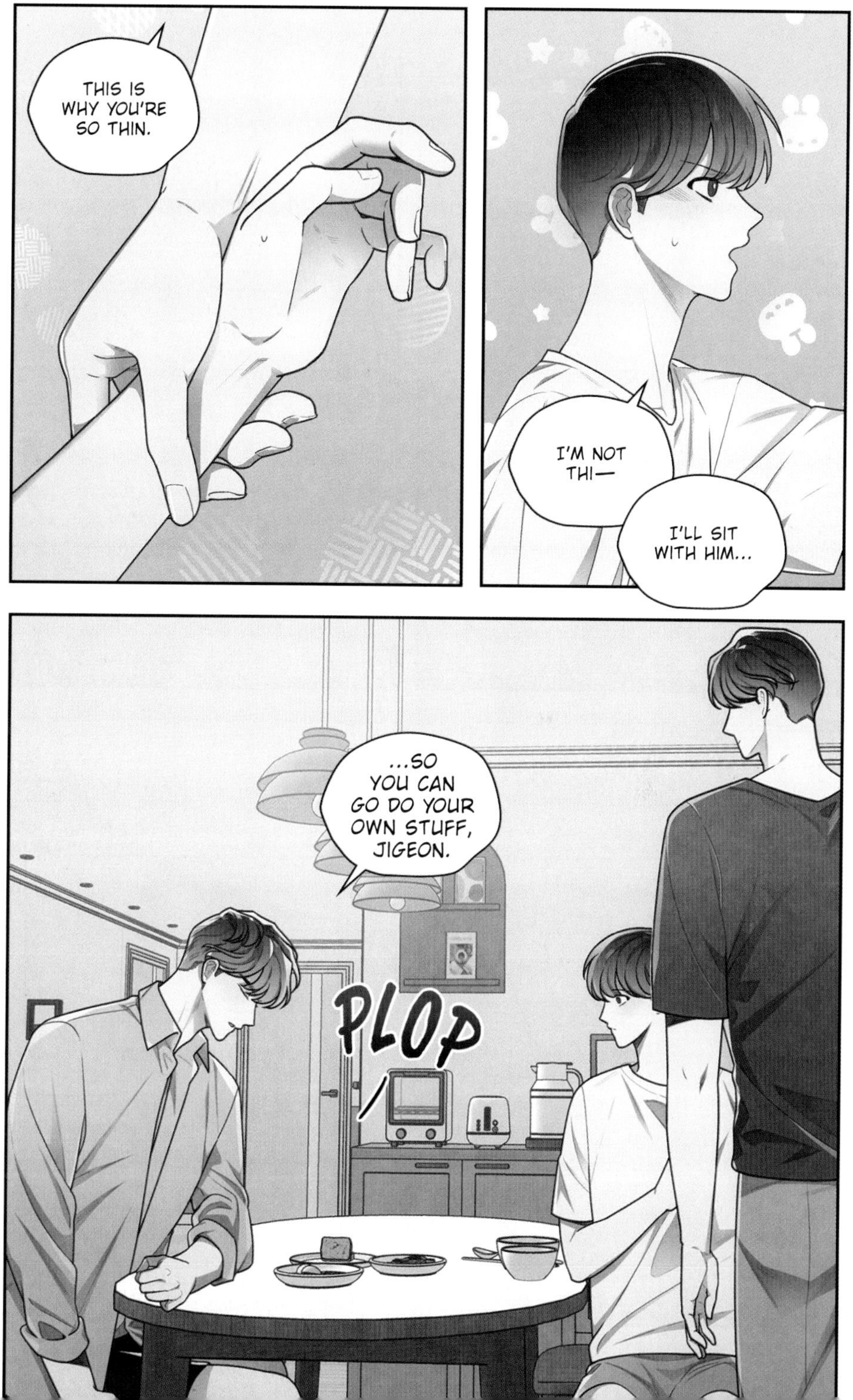
THIS IS WHY YOU'RE SO THIN.
I'M NOT THI—
I'LL SIT WITH HIM...
...SO YOU CAN GO DO YOUR OWN STUFF, JIGEON.
PLOP

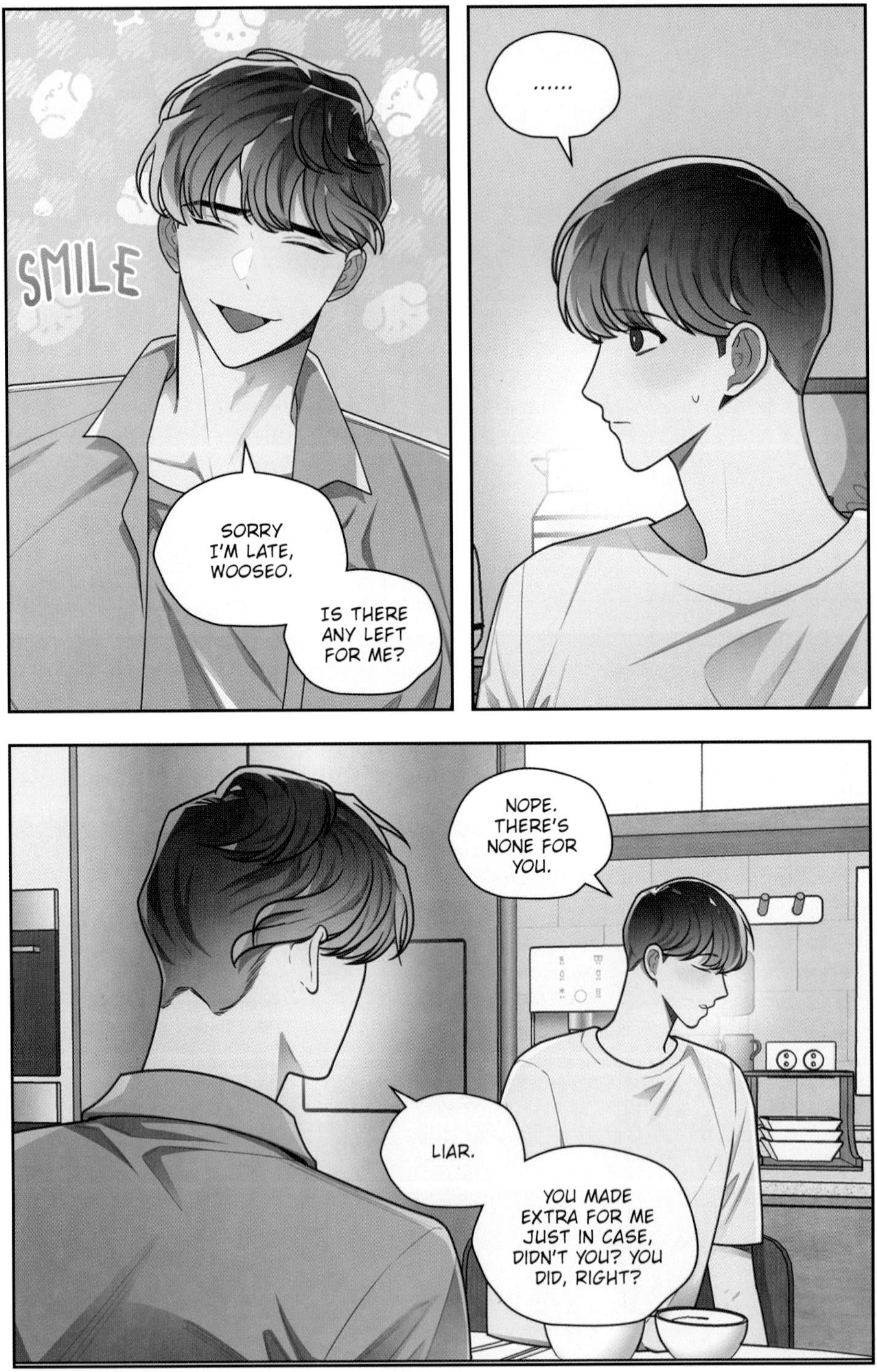
SMILE
SORRY I'M LATE, WOOSEO.
IS THERE ANY LEFT FOR ME?
......
NOPE. THERE'S NONE FOR YOU.
LIAR.
YOU MADE EXTRA FOR ME JUST IN CASE, DIDN'T YOU? YOU DID, RIGHT?

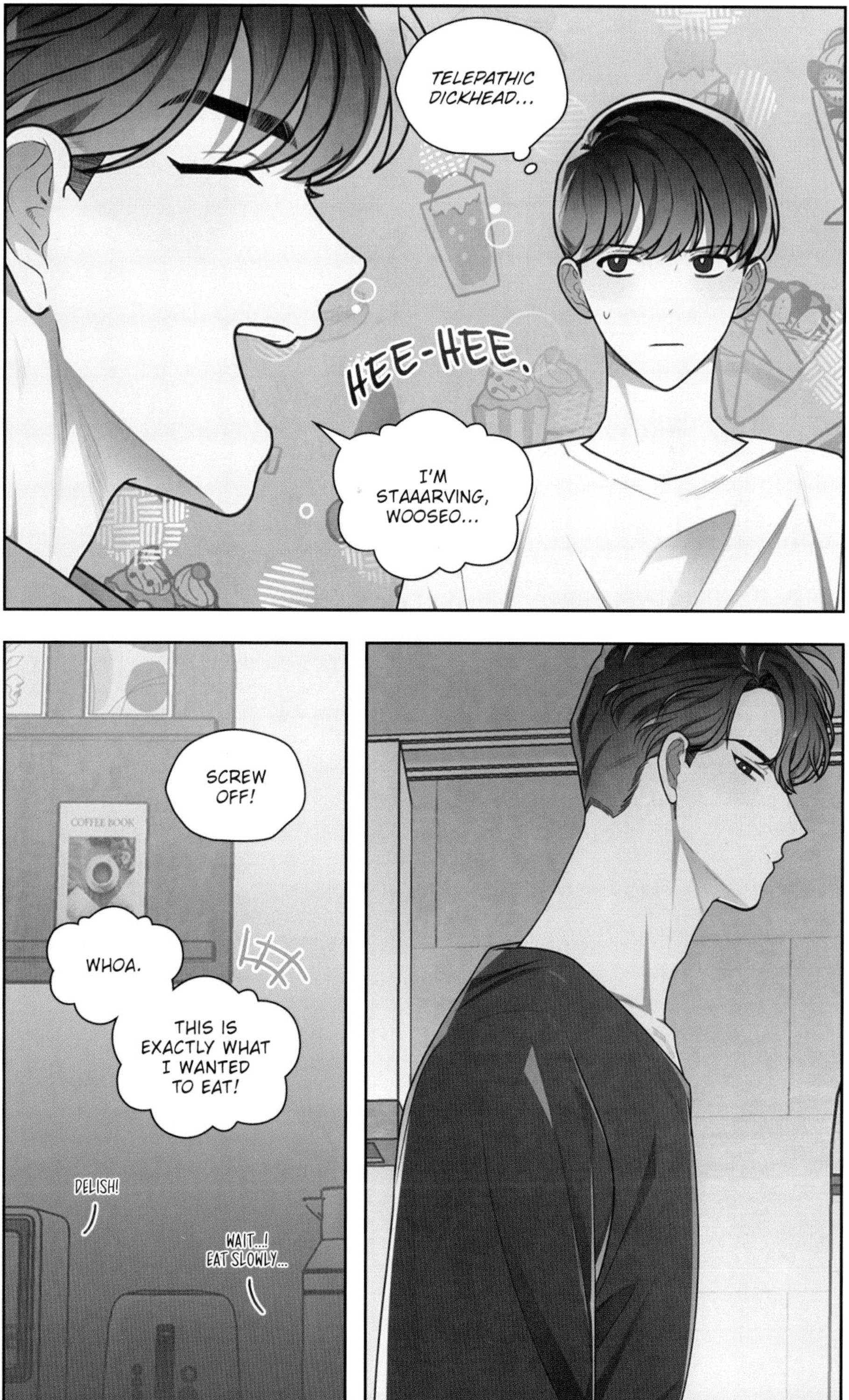
TELEPATHIC DICKHEAD...
HEE-HEE.
I'M STAAARVING, WOOSEO...
SCREW OFF!
COFFEE BOOK
WHOA.
THIS IS EXACTLY WHAT I WANTED TO EAT!
DELISH!
WAIT...! EAT SLOWLY...

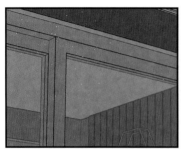

CLACK

CLACK

IT'S ALREADY MIDNIGHT, BUT I HAVEN'T HEARD FROM HIM...

SILENT ～—

I'VE GOT CLASS IN THE MORNING... MAYBE I SHOULD GO TO HIS ROOM...

DOESN'T HE HAVE WORK TOMORROW? WILL HE BE OKAY STAYING UP SO LATE?

A. WAIT LIKE USUAL

B. SNEAK OVER QUIETLY!

TIPTOE

TIPTOE

IS JISEOK ASLEEP ALREADY?

I'LL BE CAREFUL JUST TO BE SAFE...

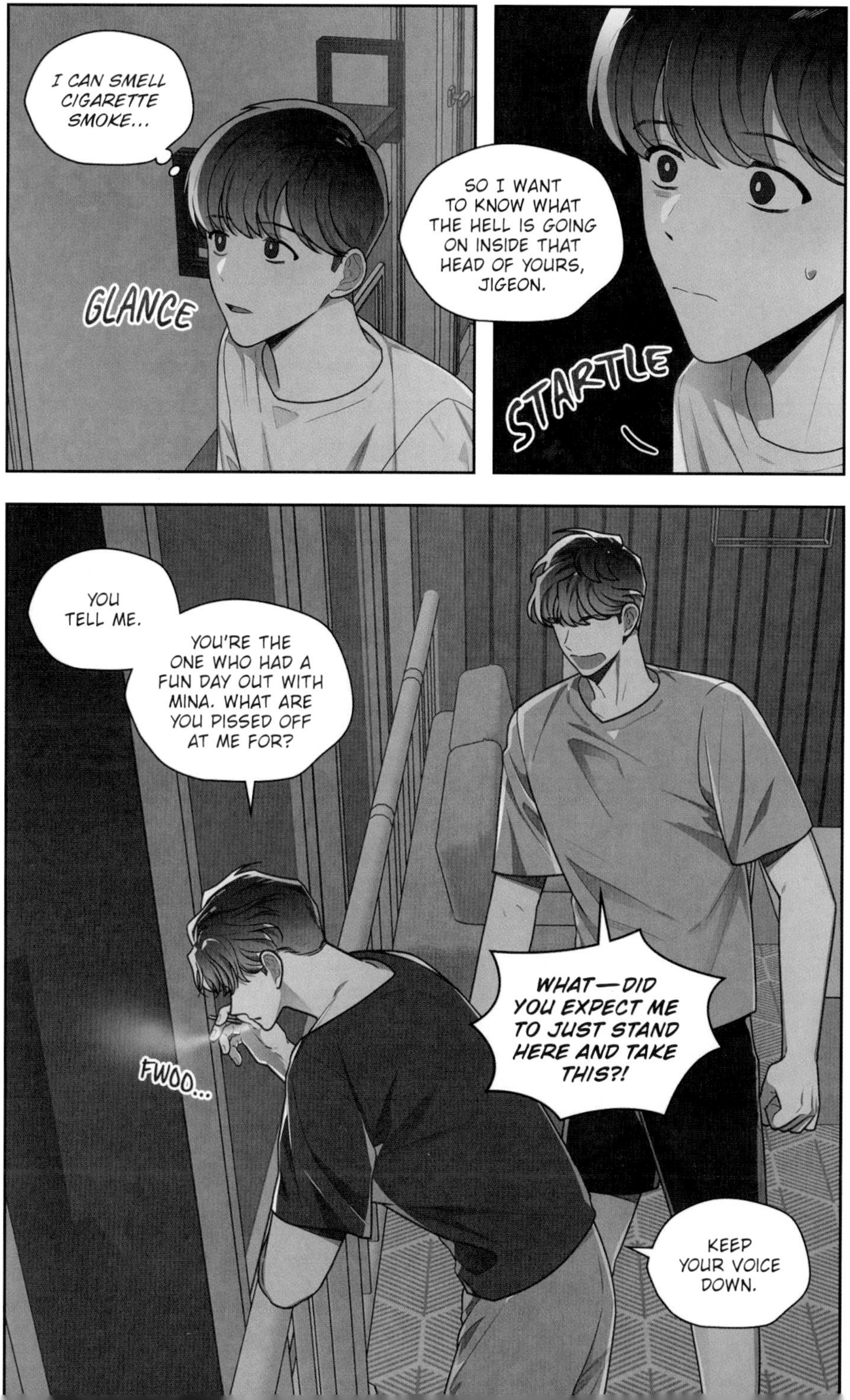
I CAN SMELL CIGARETTE SMOKE...
GLANCE
SO I WANT TO KNOW WHAT THE HELL IS GOING ON INSIDE THAT HEAD OF YOURS, JIGEON.
STARTLE
YOU TELL ME.
YOU'RE THE ONE WHO HAD A FUN DAY OUT WITH MINA. WHAT ARE YOU PISSED OFF AT ME FOR?
WHAT—DID YOU EXPECT ME TO JUST STAND HERE AND TAKE THIS?!
FWOO...
KEEP YOUR VOICE DOWN.

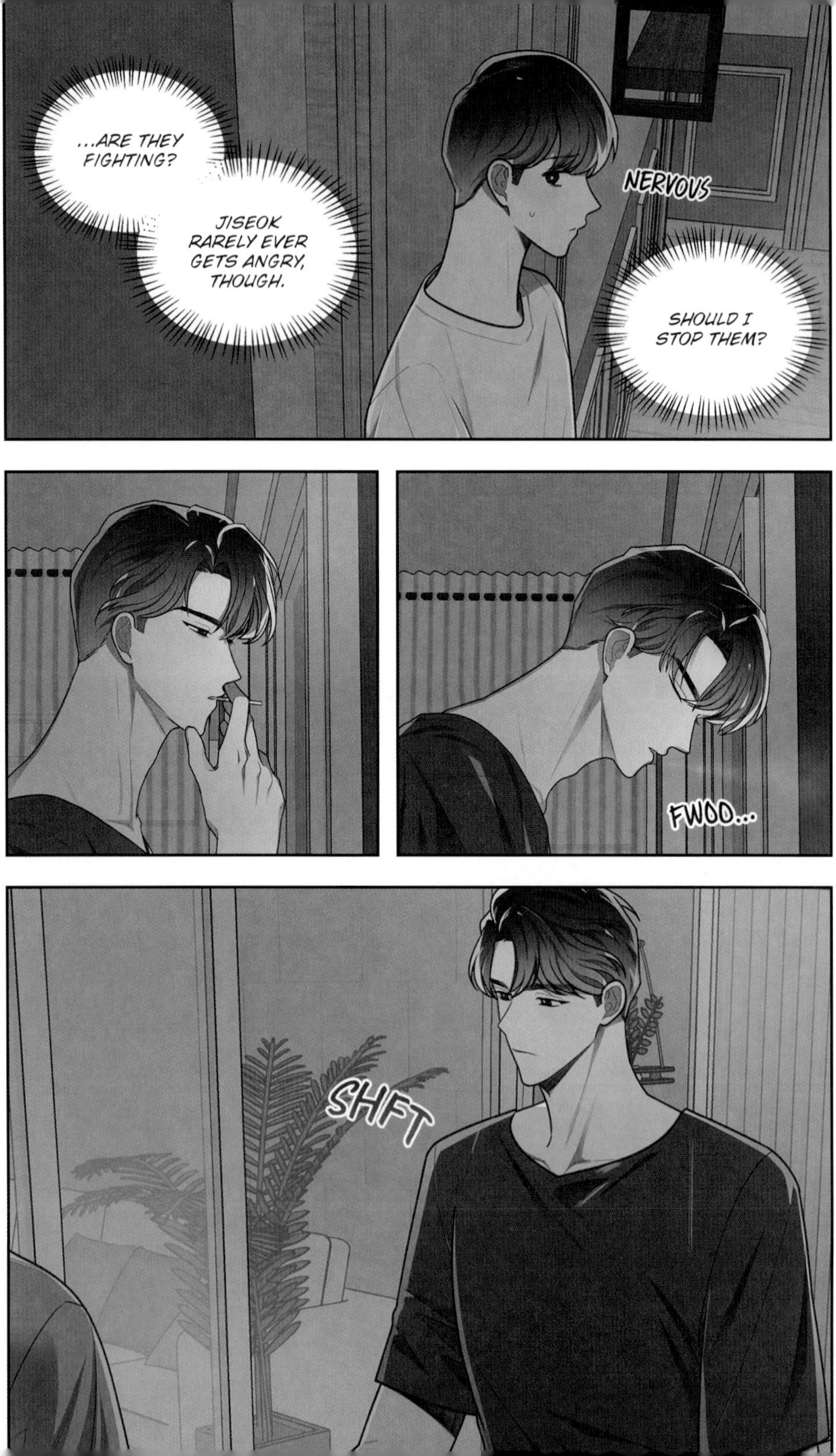
...ARE THEY FIGHTING?
JISEOK RARELY EVER GETS ANGRY, THOUGH.
NERVOUS
SHOULD I STOP THEM?
FWOO...
SHFT

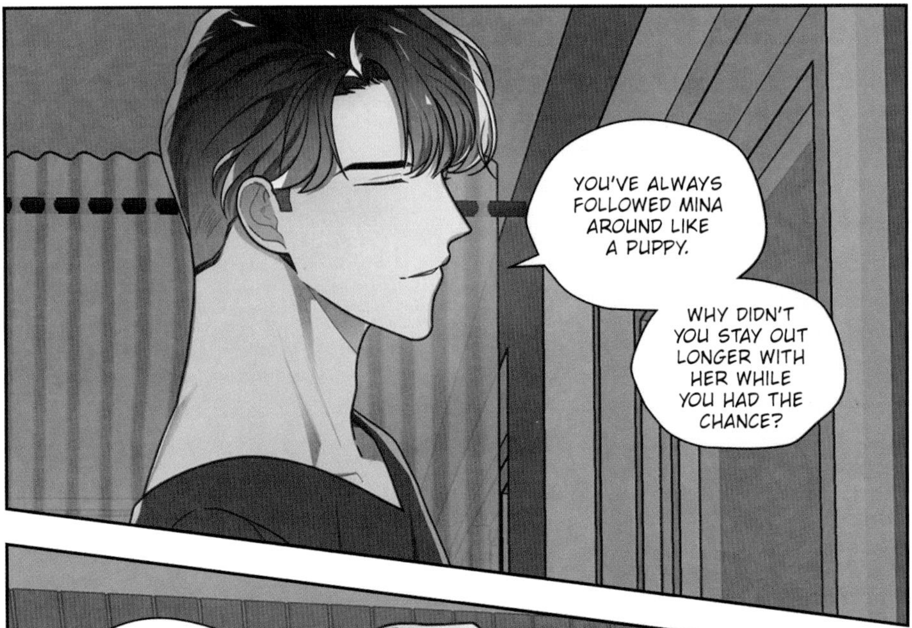
YOU'VE ALWAYS FOLLOWED MINA AROUND LIKE A PUPPY.
WHY DIDN'T YOU STAY OUT LONGER WITH HER WHILE YOU HAD THE CHANCE?

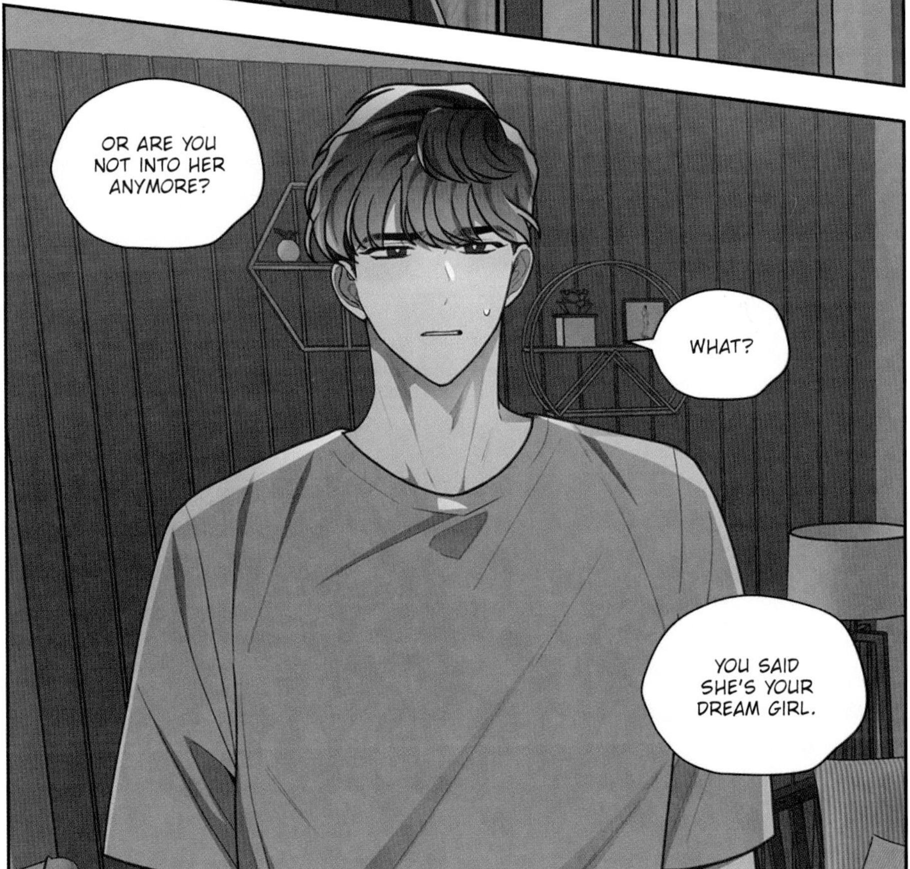
OR ARE YOU NOT INTO HER ANYMORE?
WHAT?
YOU SAID SHE'S YOUR DREAM GIRL.

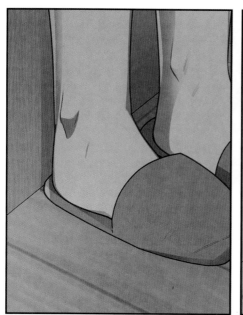

I DO LIKE HER.

FREEZE

I'M STILL INTO MINA— I AM!

BUT...!

TSSS

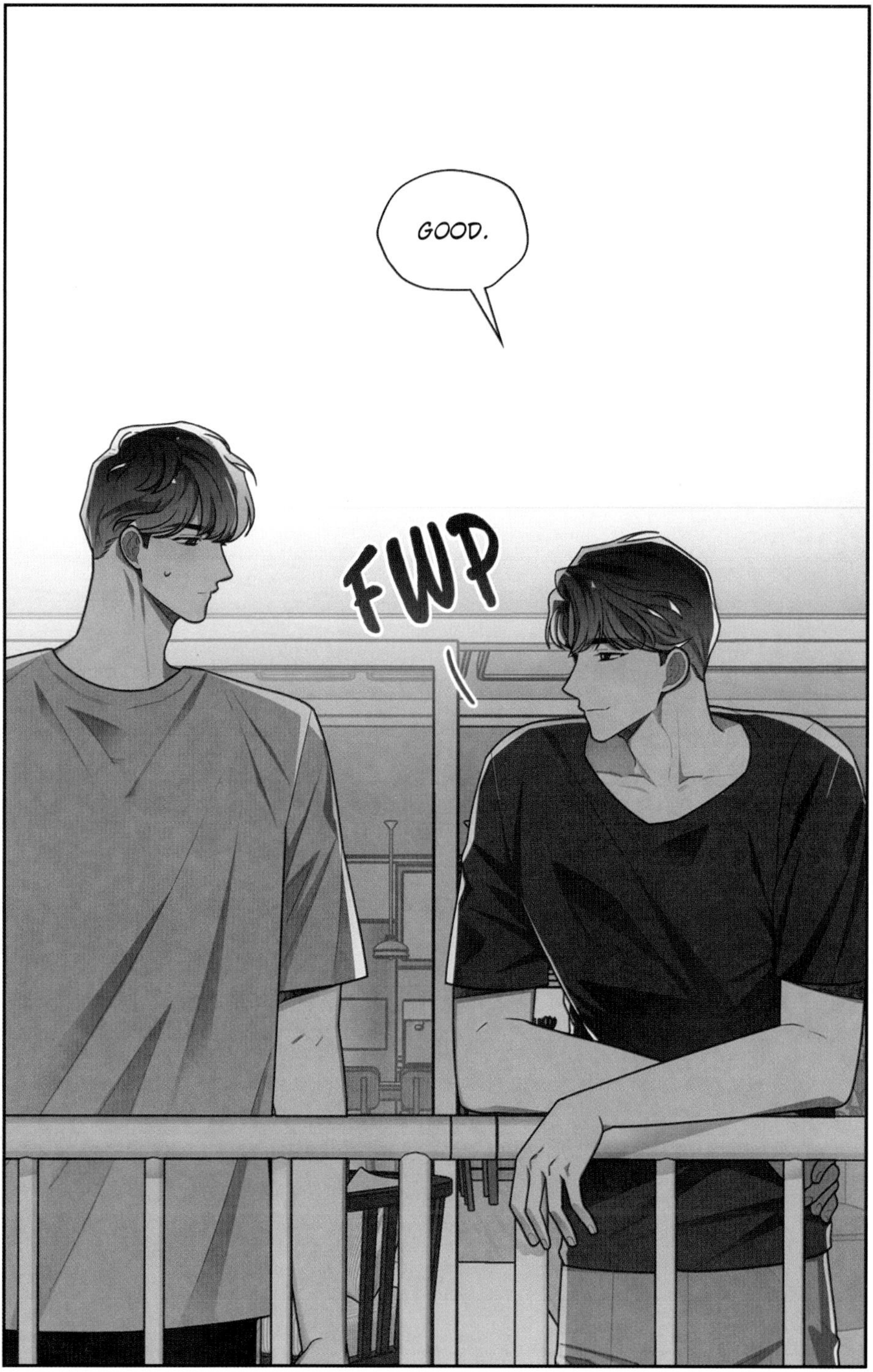
GOOD.
FWP

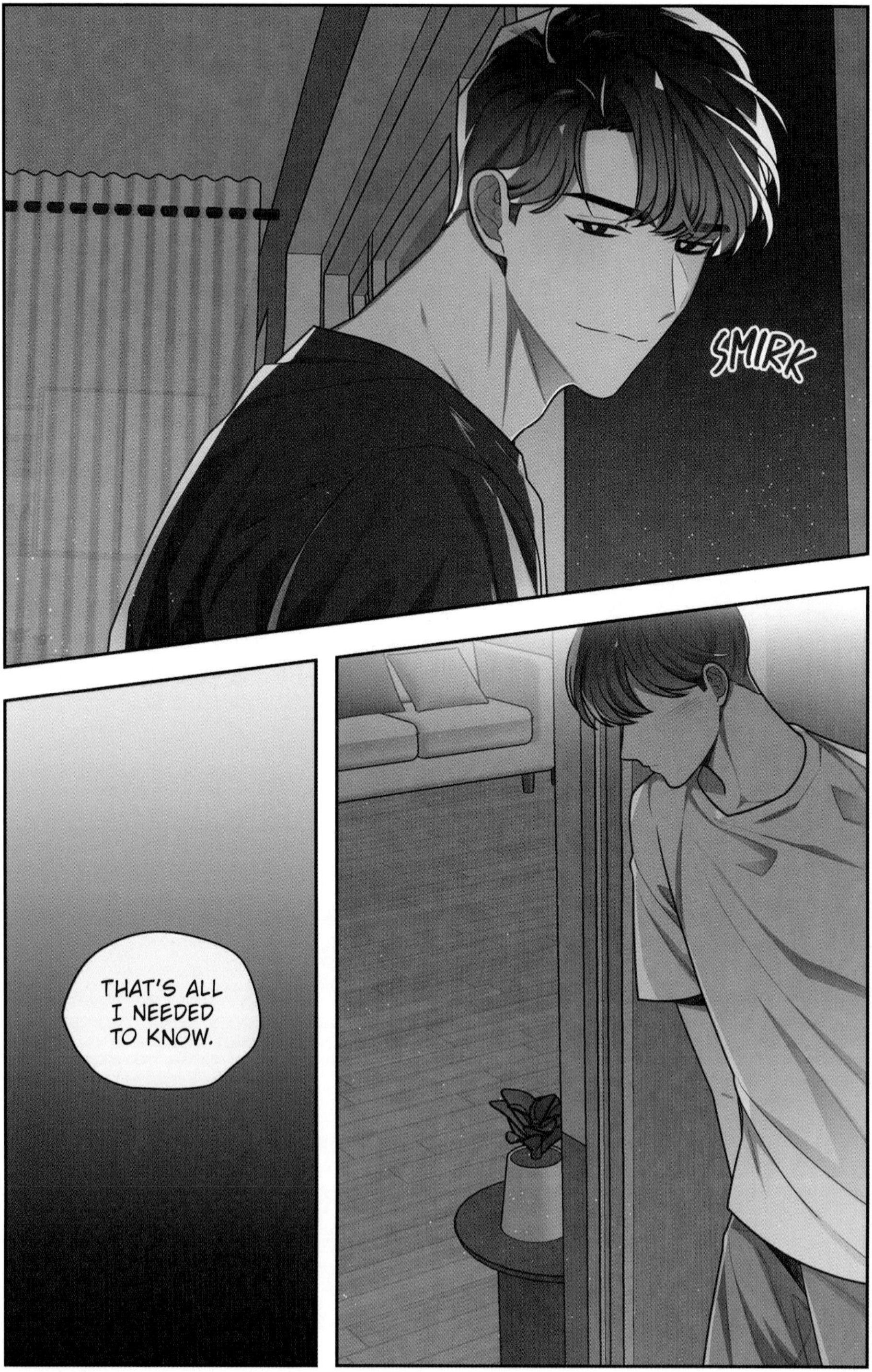
SMIRK
THAT'S ALL I NEEDED TO KNOW.

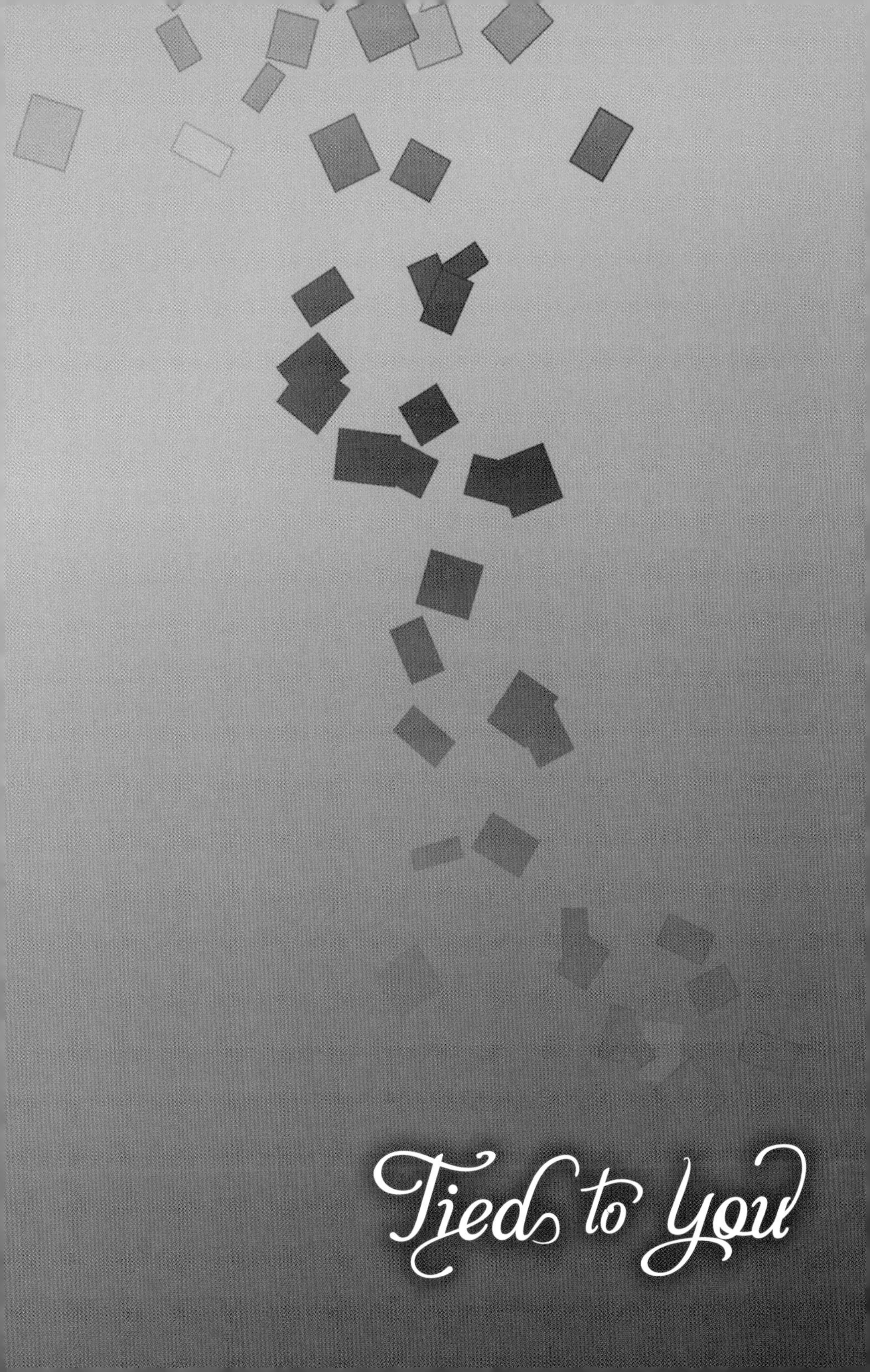

Tied to You

Chapter 14

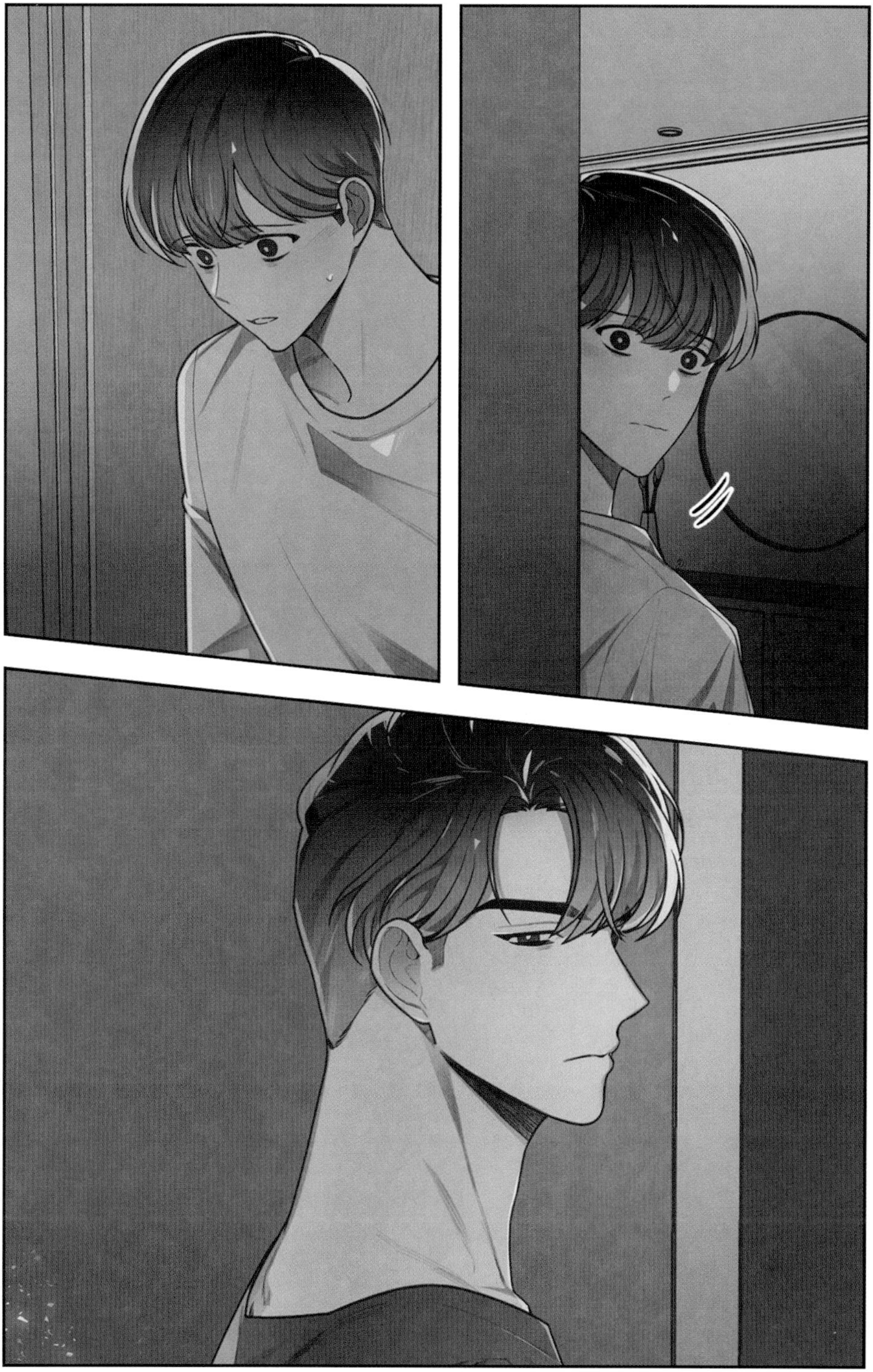

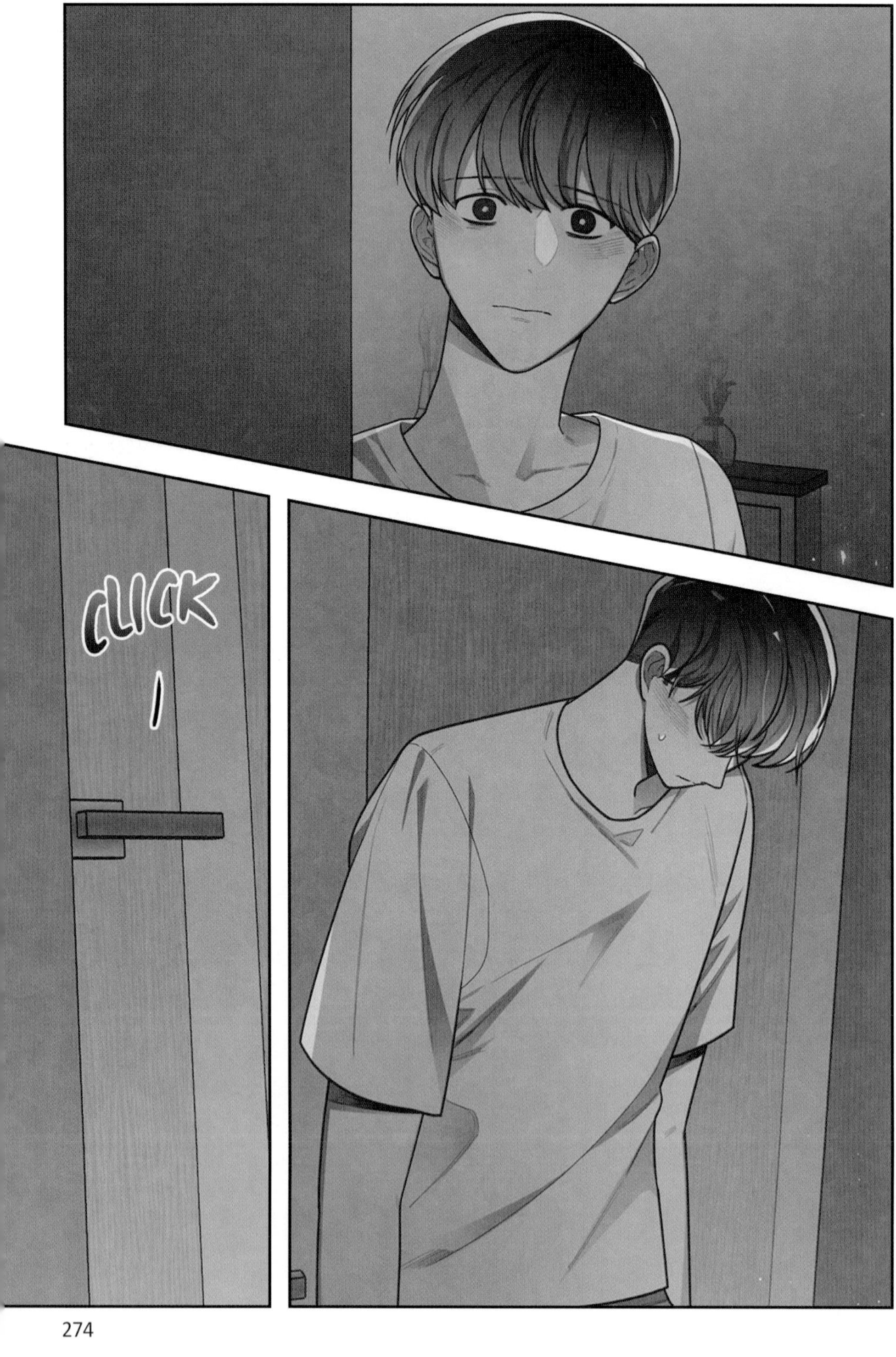
CLICK

Come to my room. I'll comfort you.

JG

Message

WHAT COULD HE POSSIBLY SAY...

...THAT WOULD MAKE ME FEEL BETTER?

DO I EVEN HAVE THE RIGHT TO BE COMFORTED IN THE FIRST PLACE?

FIDGET

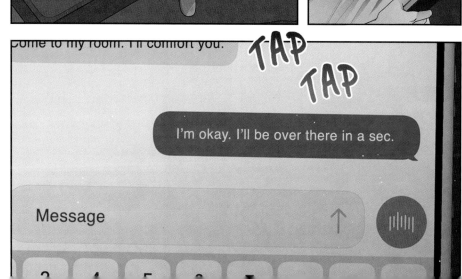

Come to my room. I'll comfort you.

TAP

TAP

I'm okay. I'll be over there in a sec.

Message

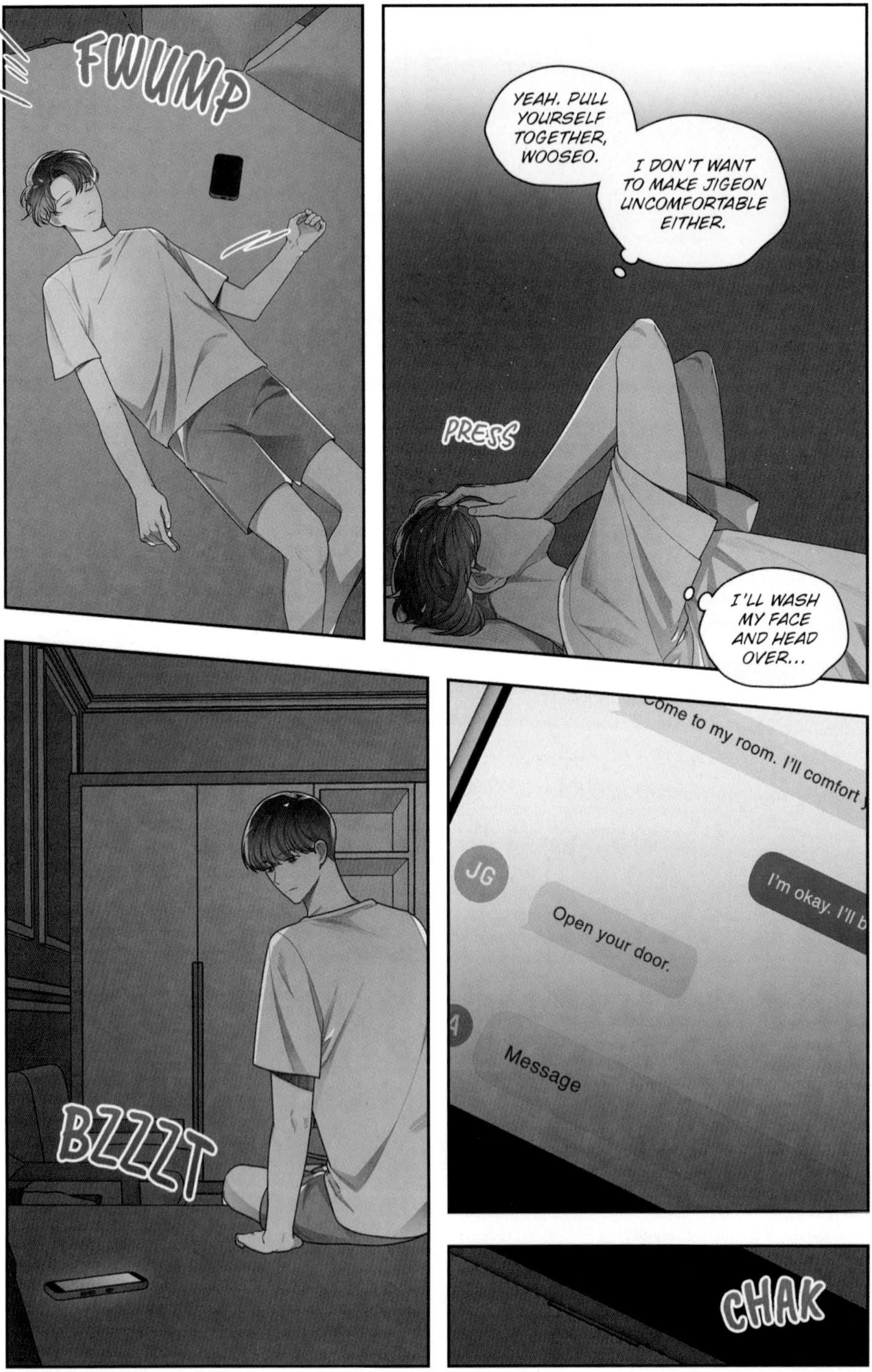
FWUMP
YEAH. PULL YOURSELF TOGETHER, WOOSEO.
I DON'T WANT TO MAKE JIGEON UNCOMFORTABLE EITHER.
PRESS
I'LL WASH MY FACE AND HEAD OVER...
BZZZT
Come to my room. I'll comfort
JG
I'm okay. I'll b
Open your door.
Message
CHAK

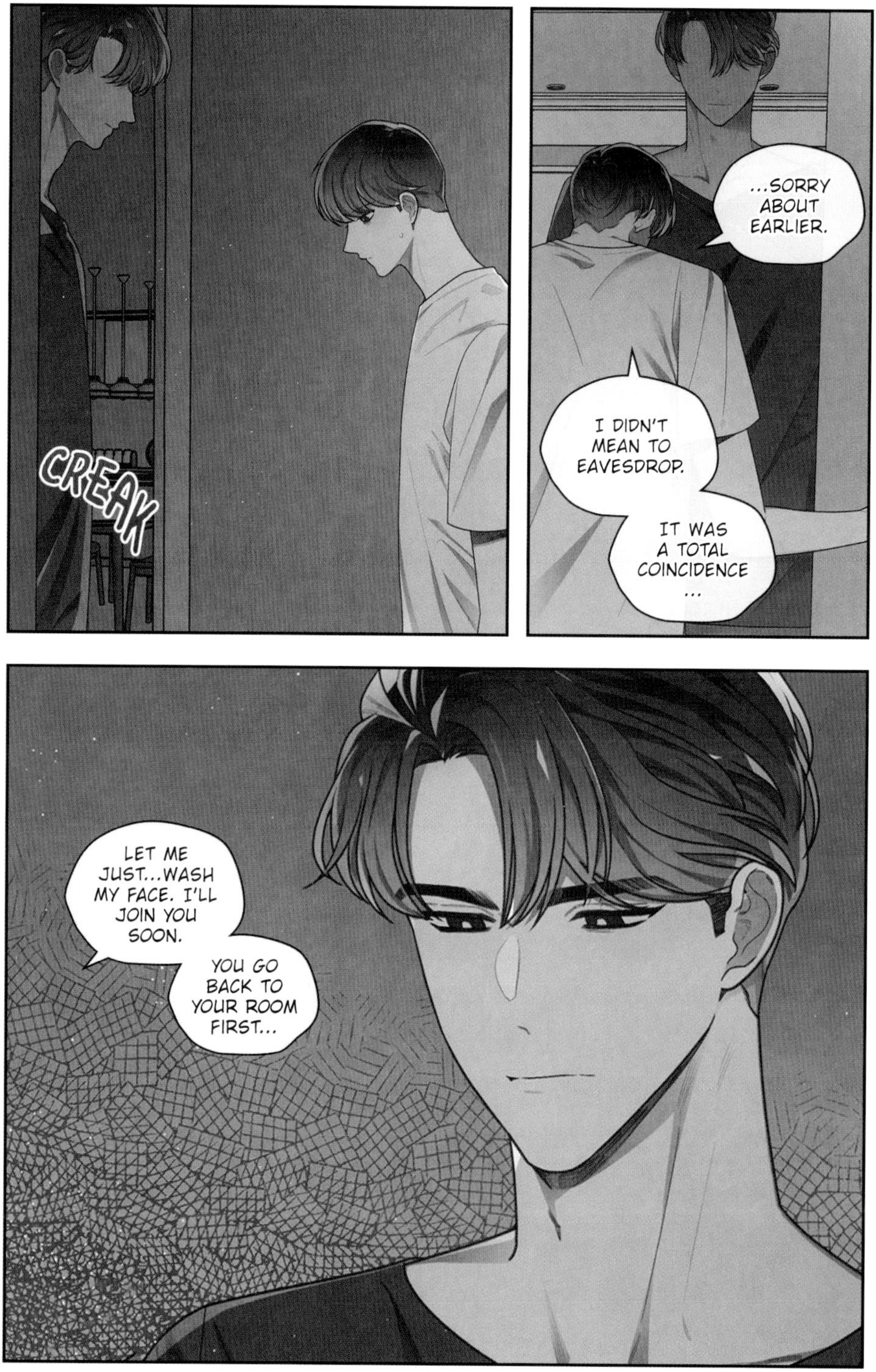
CREAK
...SORRY ABOUT EARLIER.
I DIDN'T MEAN TO EAVESDROP.
IT WAS A TOTAL COINCIDENCE ...
LET ME JUST...WASH MY FACE. I'LL JOIN YOU SOON.
YOU GO BACK TO YOUR ROOM FIRST...

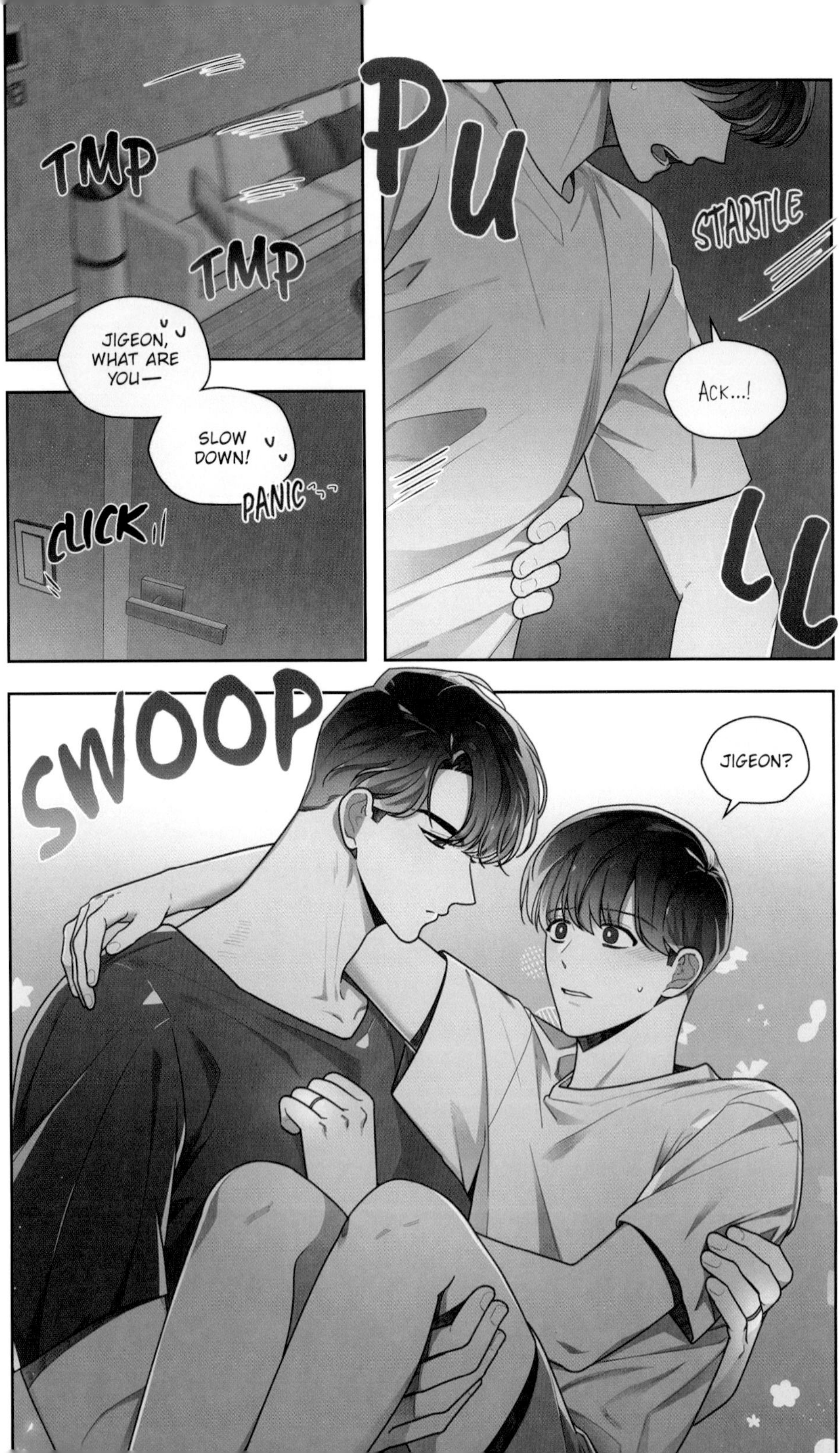
TMP
TMP
JIGEON, WHAT ARE YOU—
SLOW DOWN!
PANIC
CLICK
PU
STARTLE
ACK...!
LL
SWOOP
JIGEON?

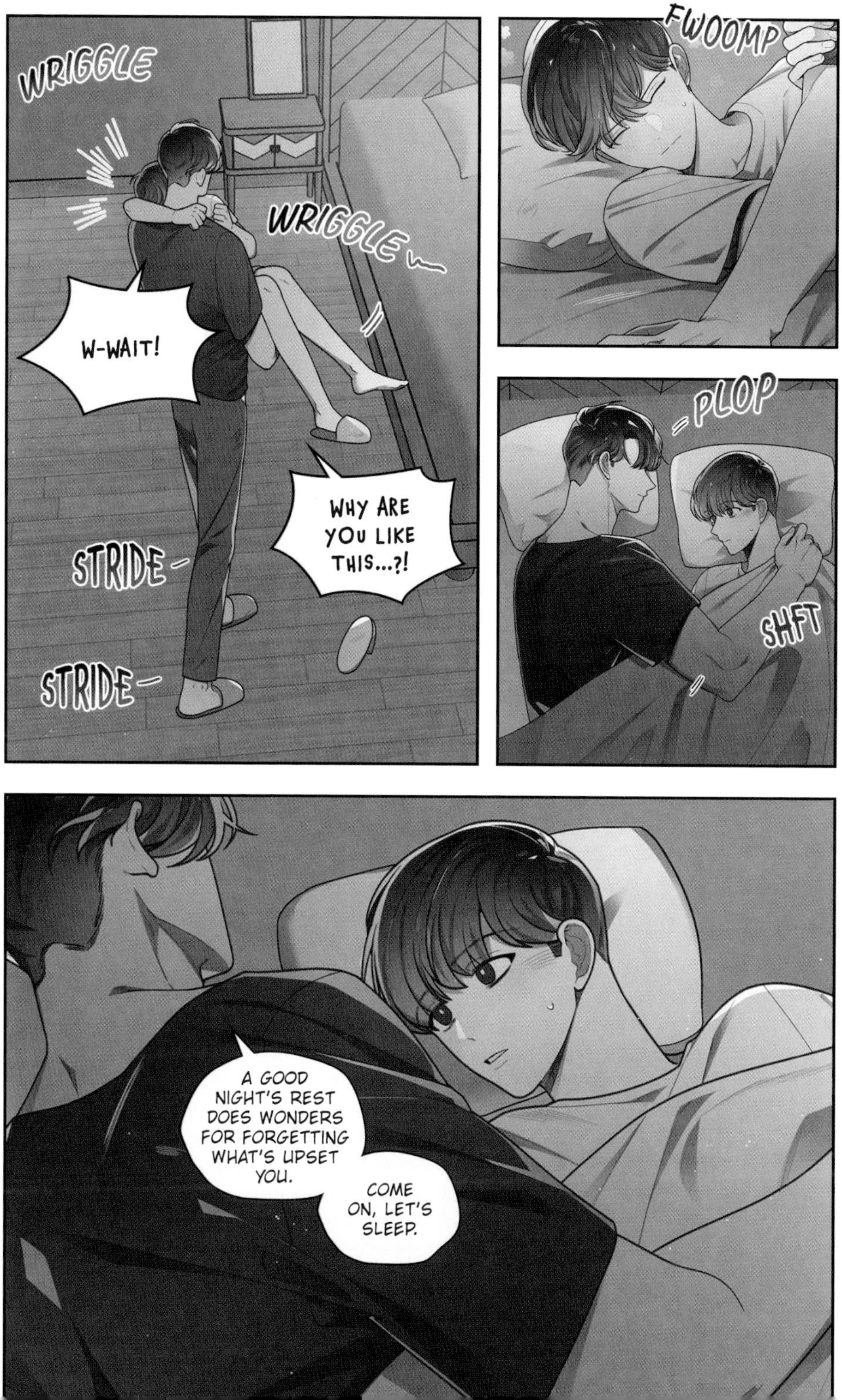
WRIGGLE
WRIGGLE
W-WAIT!
WHY ARE YOU LIKE THIS...?!
STRIDE
STRIDE
FWOOMP
PLOP
SHFT
A GOOD NIGHT'S REST DOES WONDERS FOR FORGETTING WHAT'S UPSET YOU.
COME ON, LET'S SLEEP.

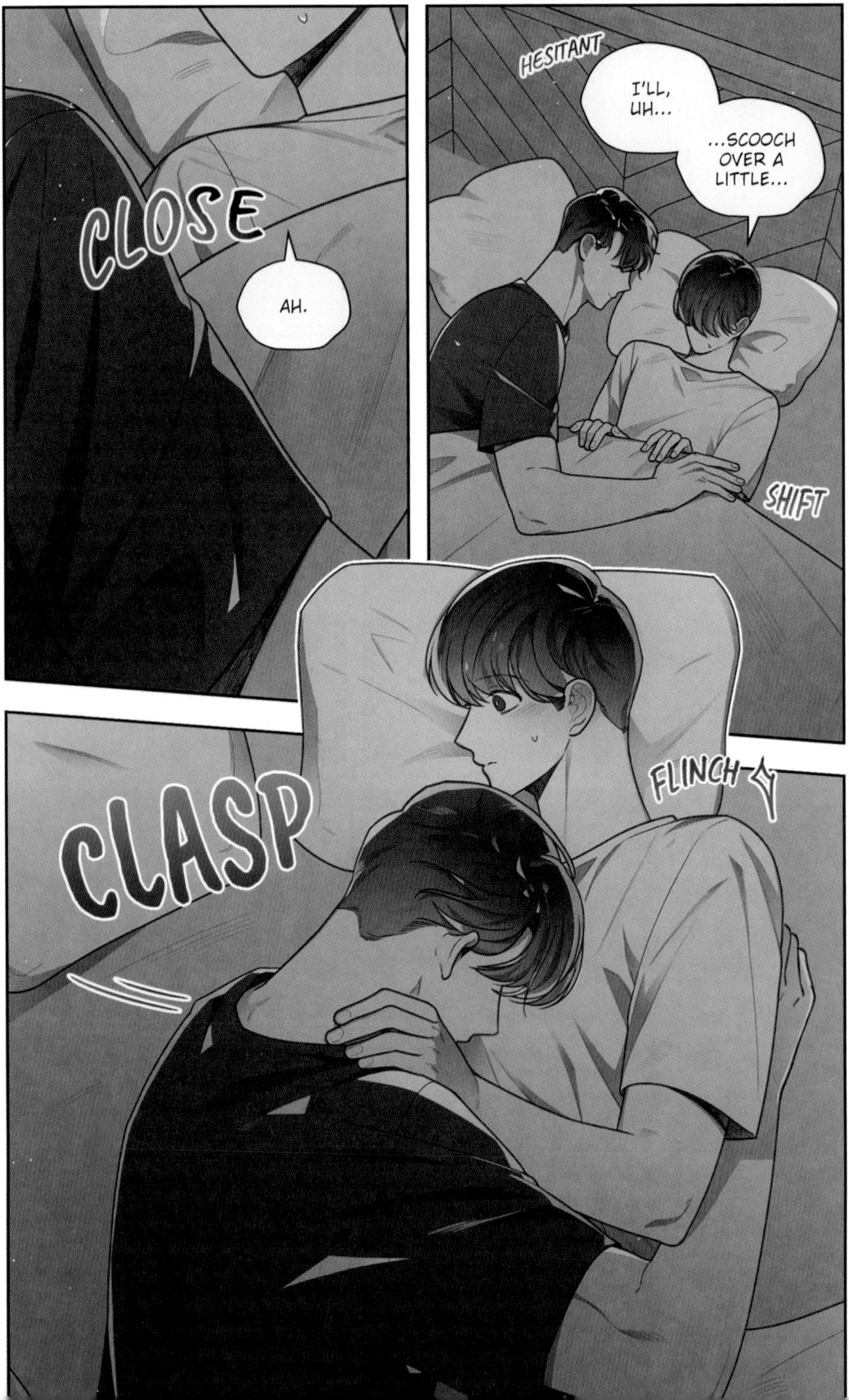
CLOSE
AH.
HESITANT
I'LL, UH...
...SCOOCH OVER A LITTLE...
SHIFT
FLINCH
CLASP

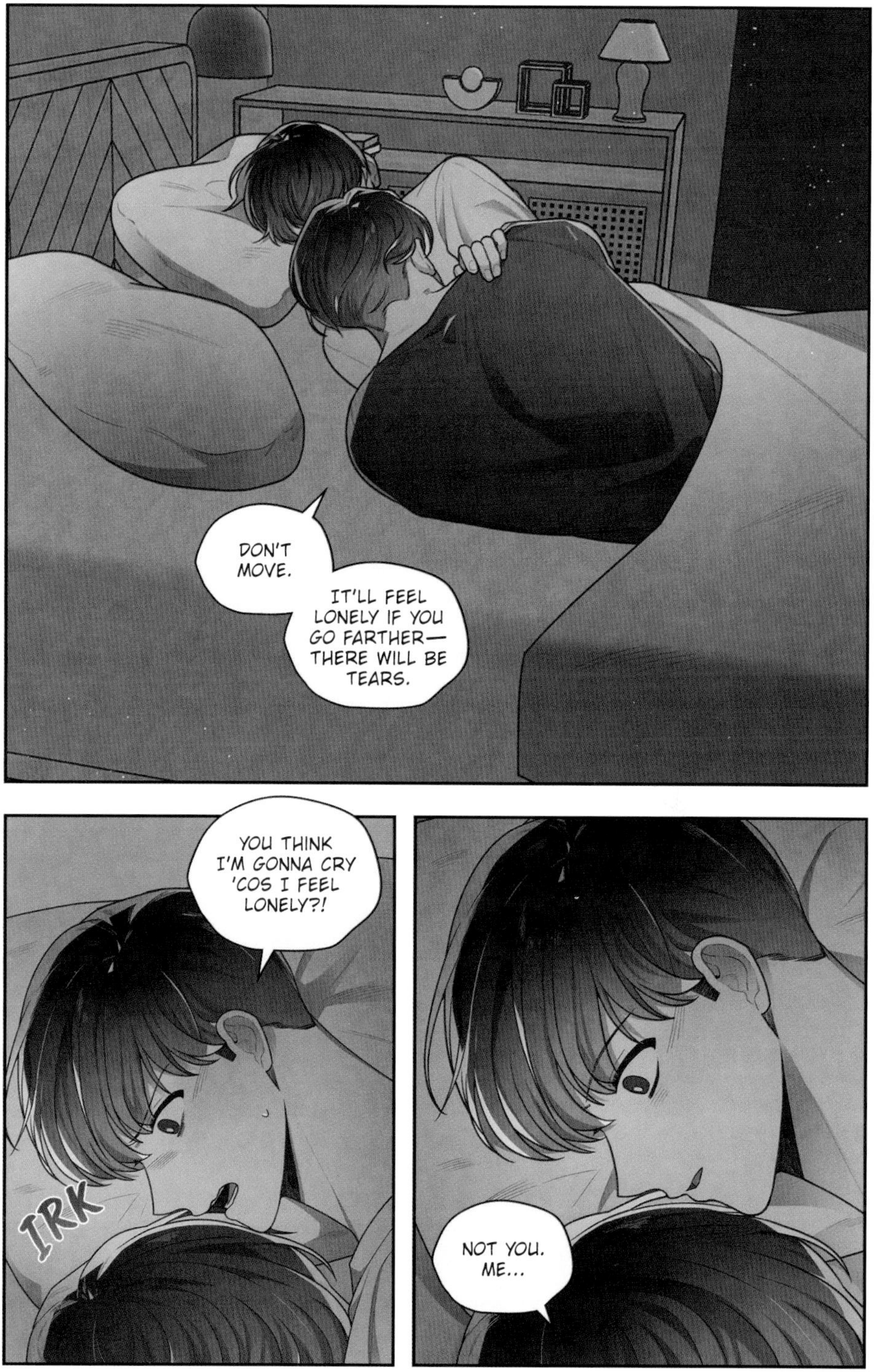
DON'T MOVE.
IT'LL FEEL LONELY IF YOU GO FARTHER— THERE WILL BE TEARS.
YOU THINK I'M GONNA CRY 'COS I FEEL LONELY?!
IRK
NOT YOU. ME...

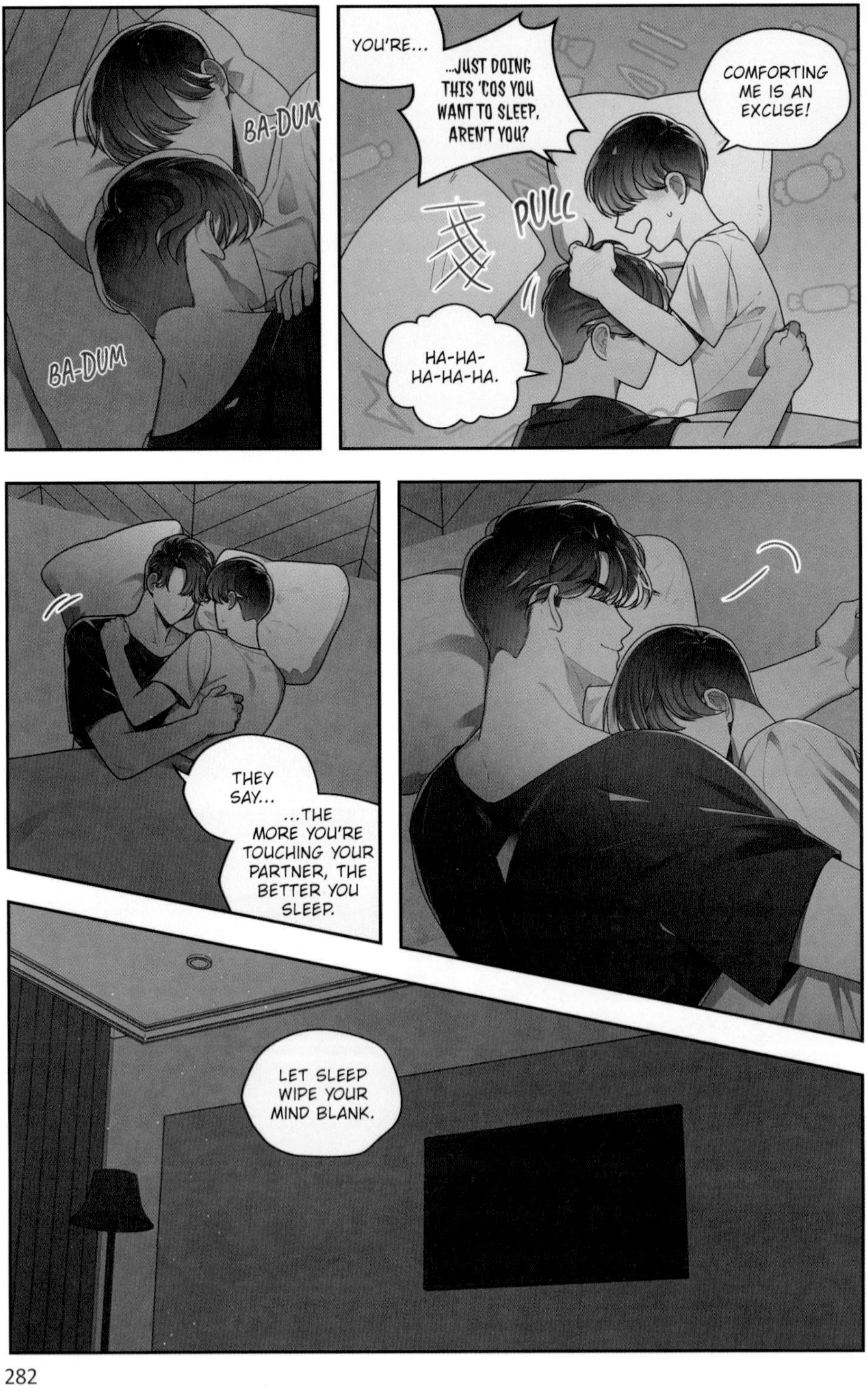
BA-DUM
BA-DUM
YOU'RE...
...JUST DOING THIS 'COS YOU WANT TO SLEEP, AREN'T YOU?
COMFORTING ME IS AN EXCUSE!
PULL
HA-HA-HA-HA-HA.
THEY SAY...
...THE MORE YOU'RE TOUCHING YOUR PARTNER, THE BETTER YOU SLEEP.
LET SLEEP WIPE YOUR MIND BLANK.

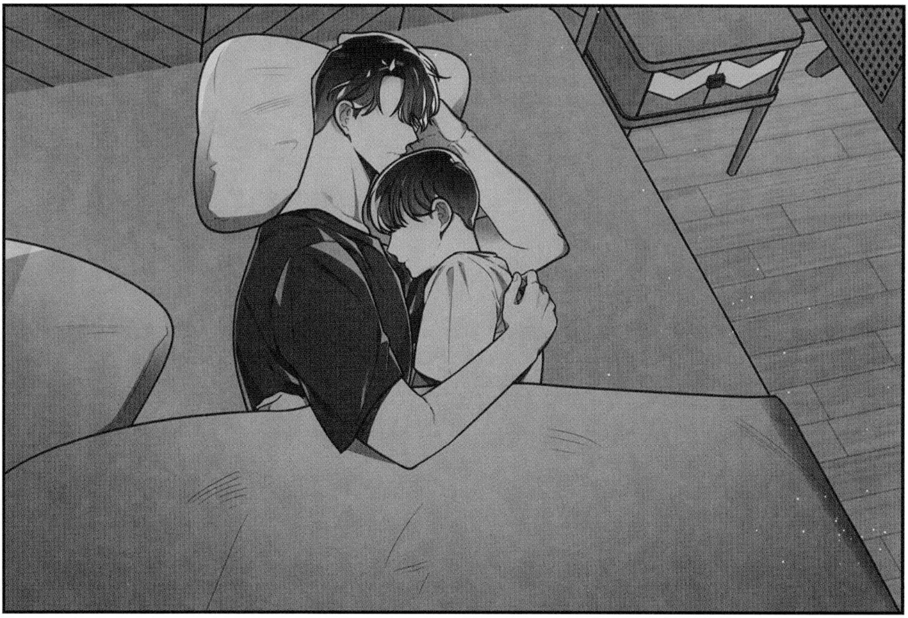

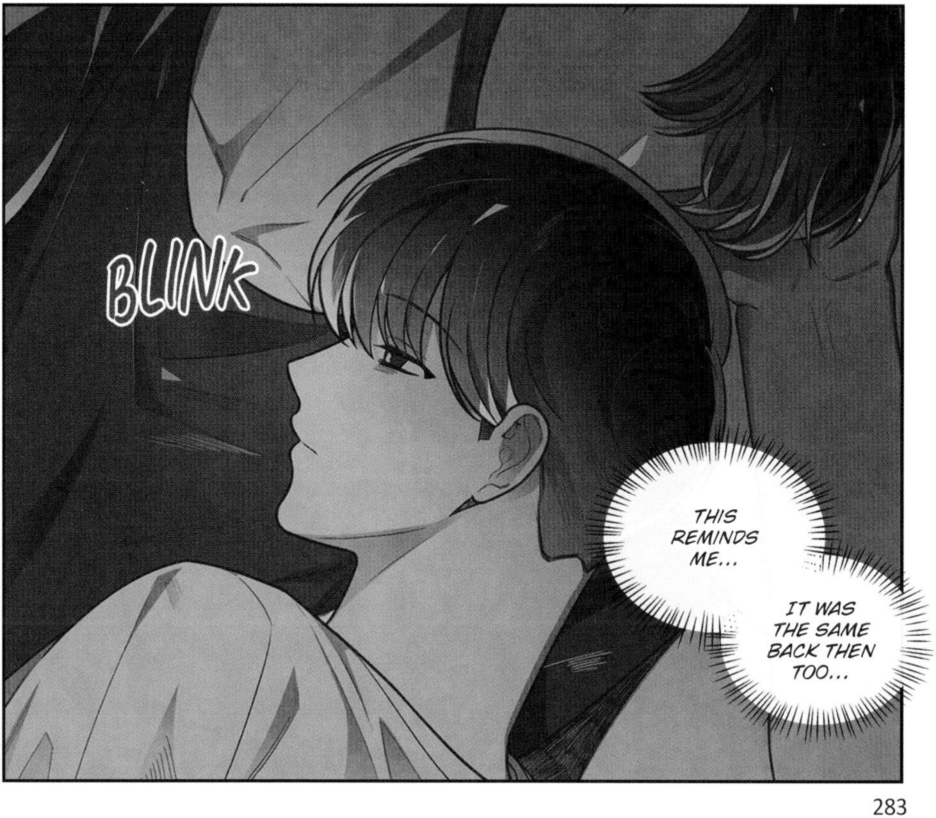
BLINK
THIS REMINDS ME...
IT WAS THE SAME BACK THEN TOO...

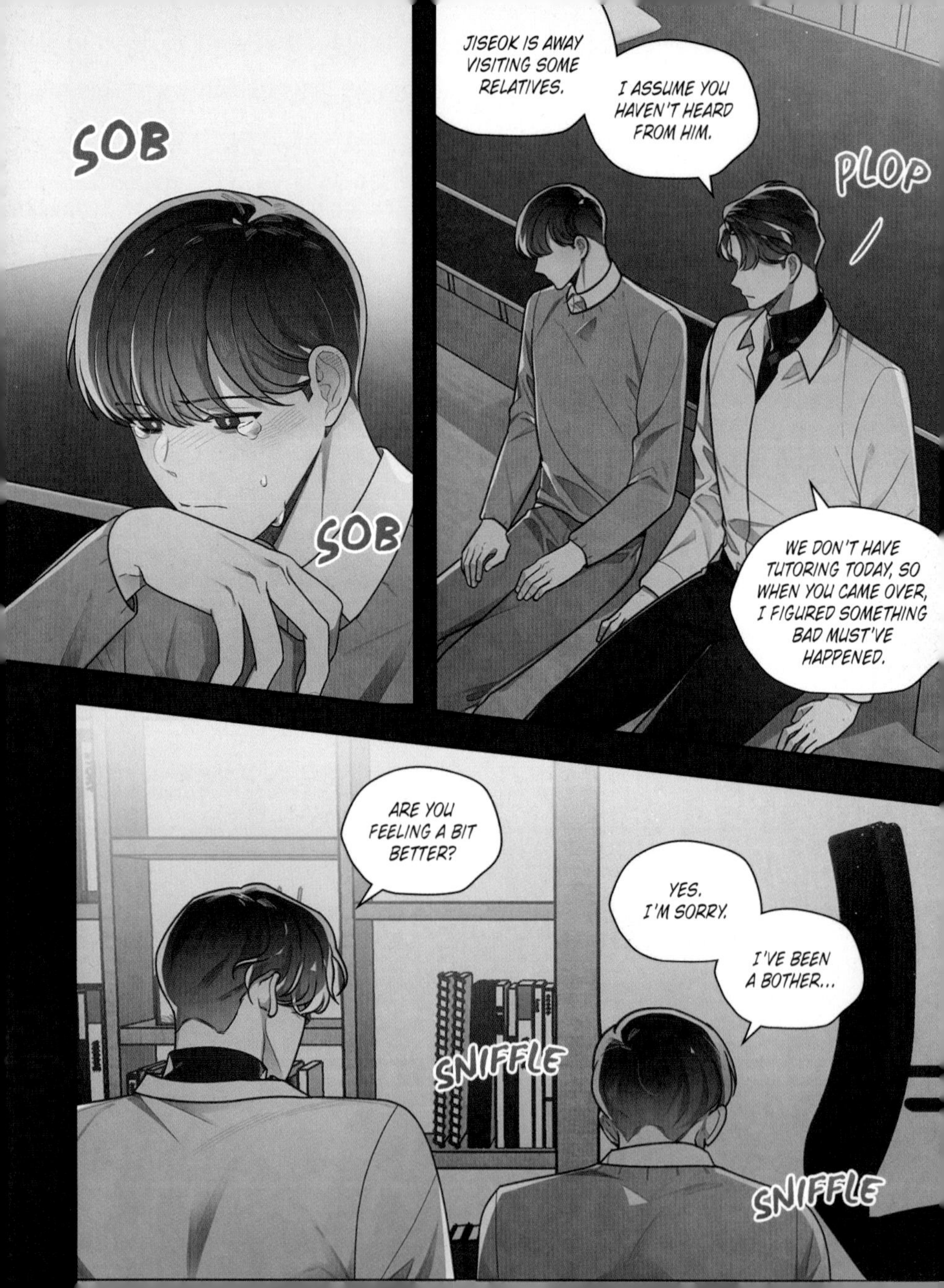
SOB
SOB
JISEOK IS AWAY VISITING SOME RELATIVES.
I ASSUME YOU HAVEN'T HEARD FROM HIM.
PLOP
WE DON'T HAVE TUTORING TODAY, SO WHEN YOU CAME OVER, I FIGURED SOMETHING BAD MUST'VE HAPPENED.
ARE YOU FEELING A BIT BETTER?
YES. I'M SORRY.
I'VE BEEN A BOTHER...
SNIFFLE
SNIFFLE

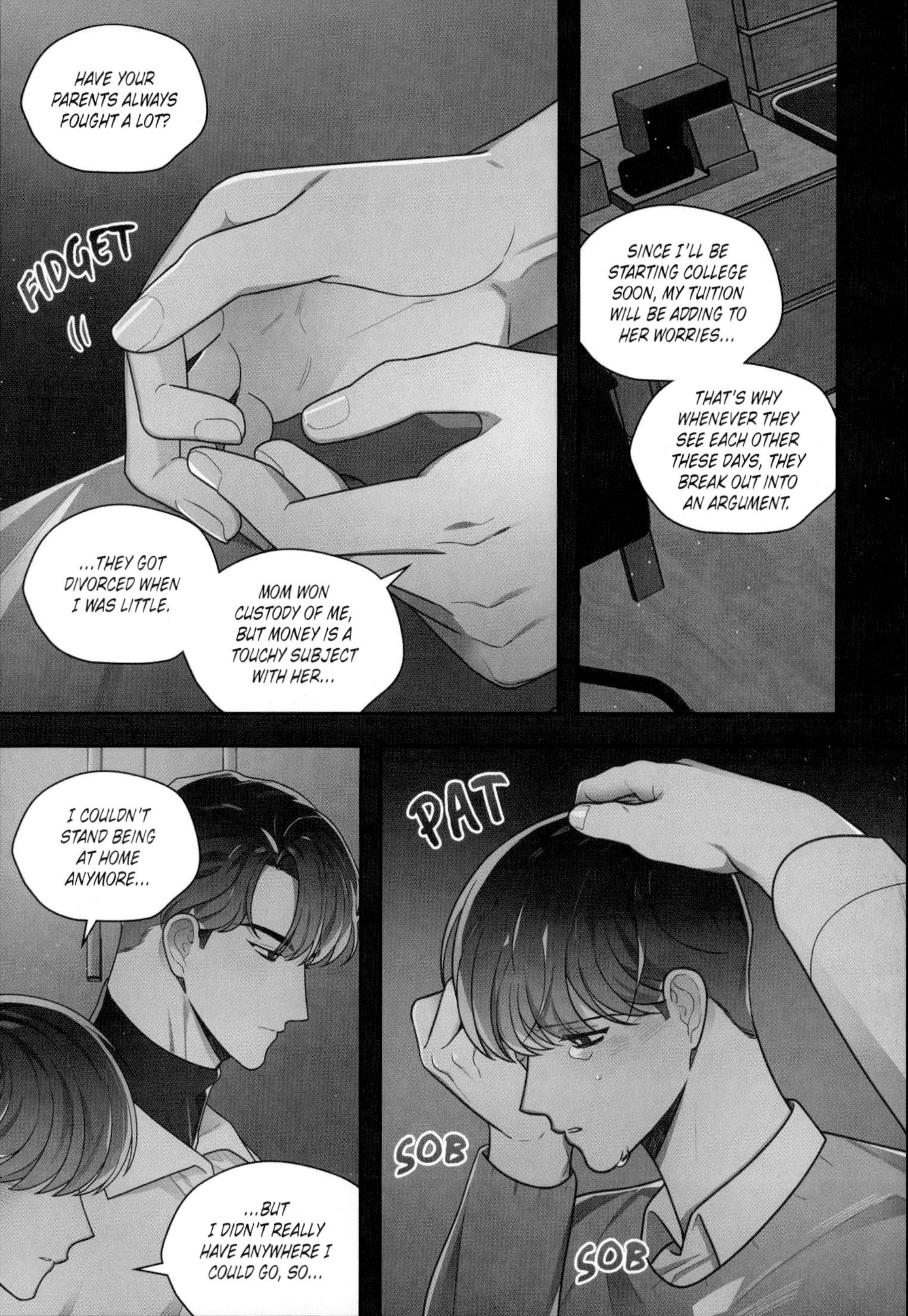
HAVE YOUR PARENTS ALWAYS FOUGHT A LOT?
FIDGET
...THEY GOT DIVORCED WHEN I WAS LITTLE.
MOM WON CUSTODY OF ME, BUT MONEY IS A TOUCHY SUBJECT WITH HER...
SINCE I'LL BE STARTING COLLEGE SOON, MY TUITION WILL BE ADDING TO HER WORRIES...
THAT'S WHY WHENEVER THEY SEE EACH OTHER THESE DAYS, THEY BREAK OUT INTO AN ARGUMENT.
I COULDN'T STAND BEING AT HOME ANYMORE...
...BUT I DIDN'T REALLY HAVE ANYWHERE I COULD GO, SO...
PAT
SOB
SOB

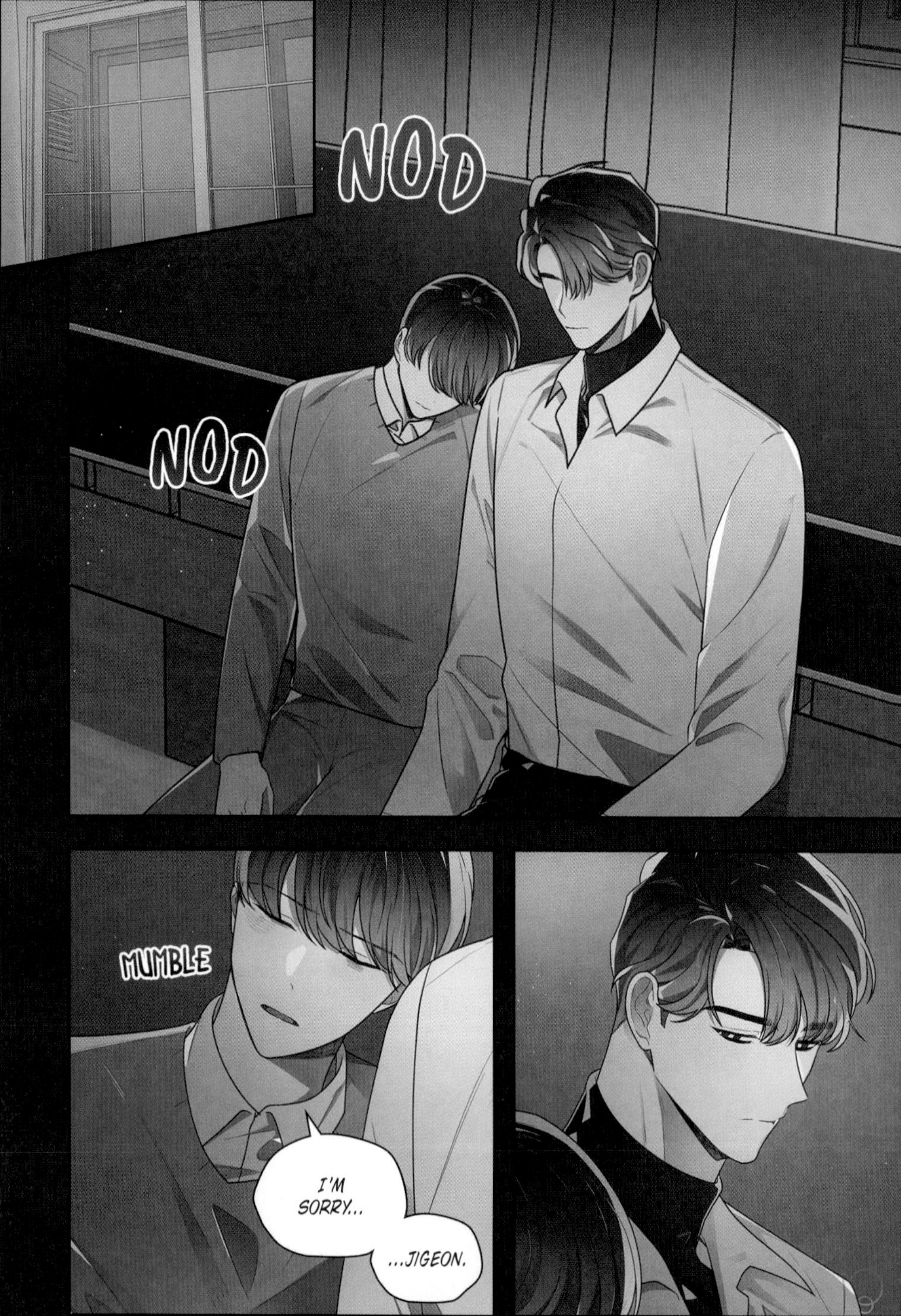
NOD
NOD
MUMBLE
I'M SORRY...
...JIGEON.

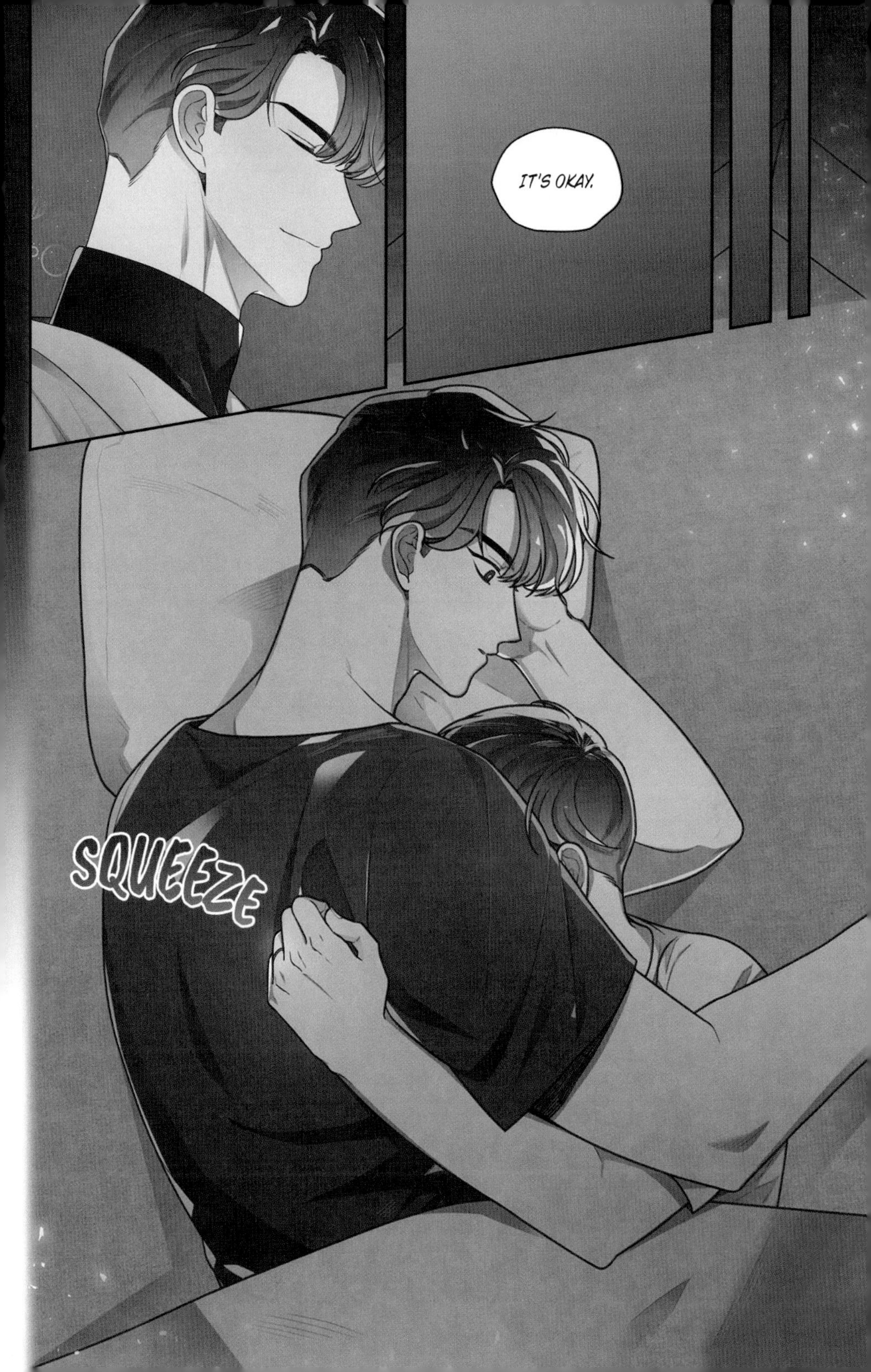
IT'S OKAY.
SQUEEZE

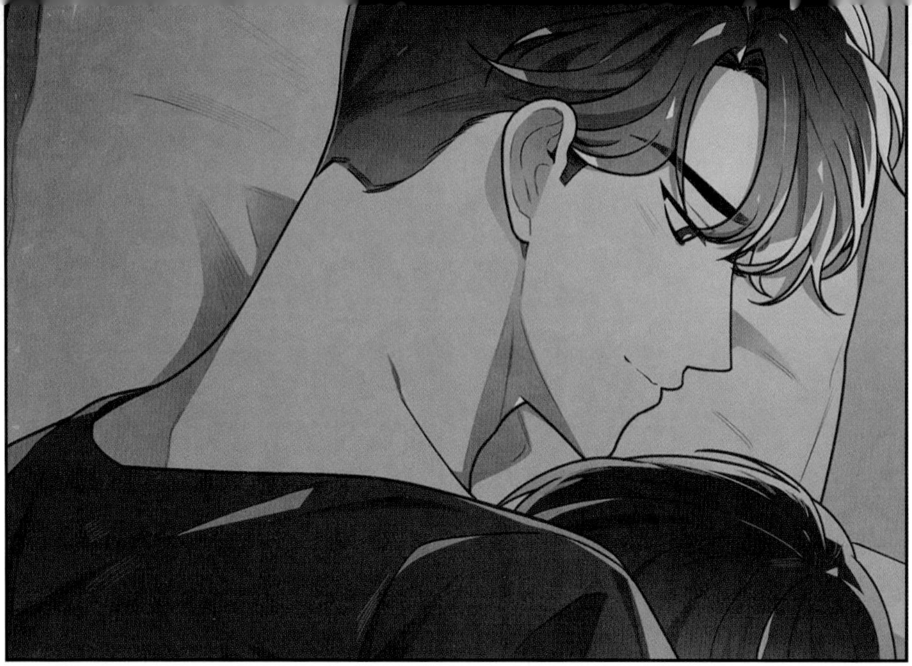

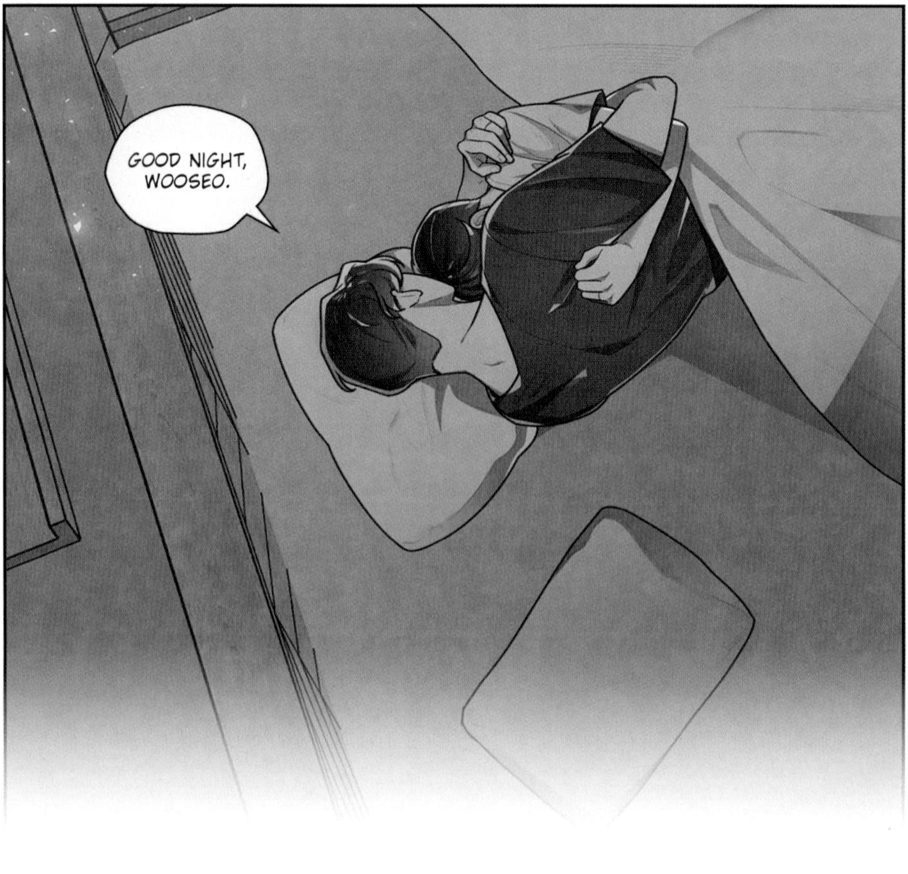
GOOD NIGHT, WOOSEO.

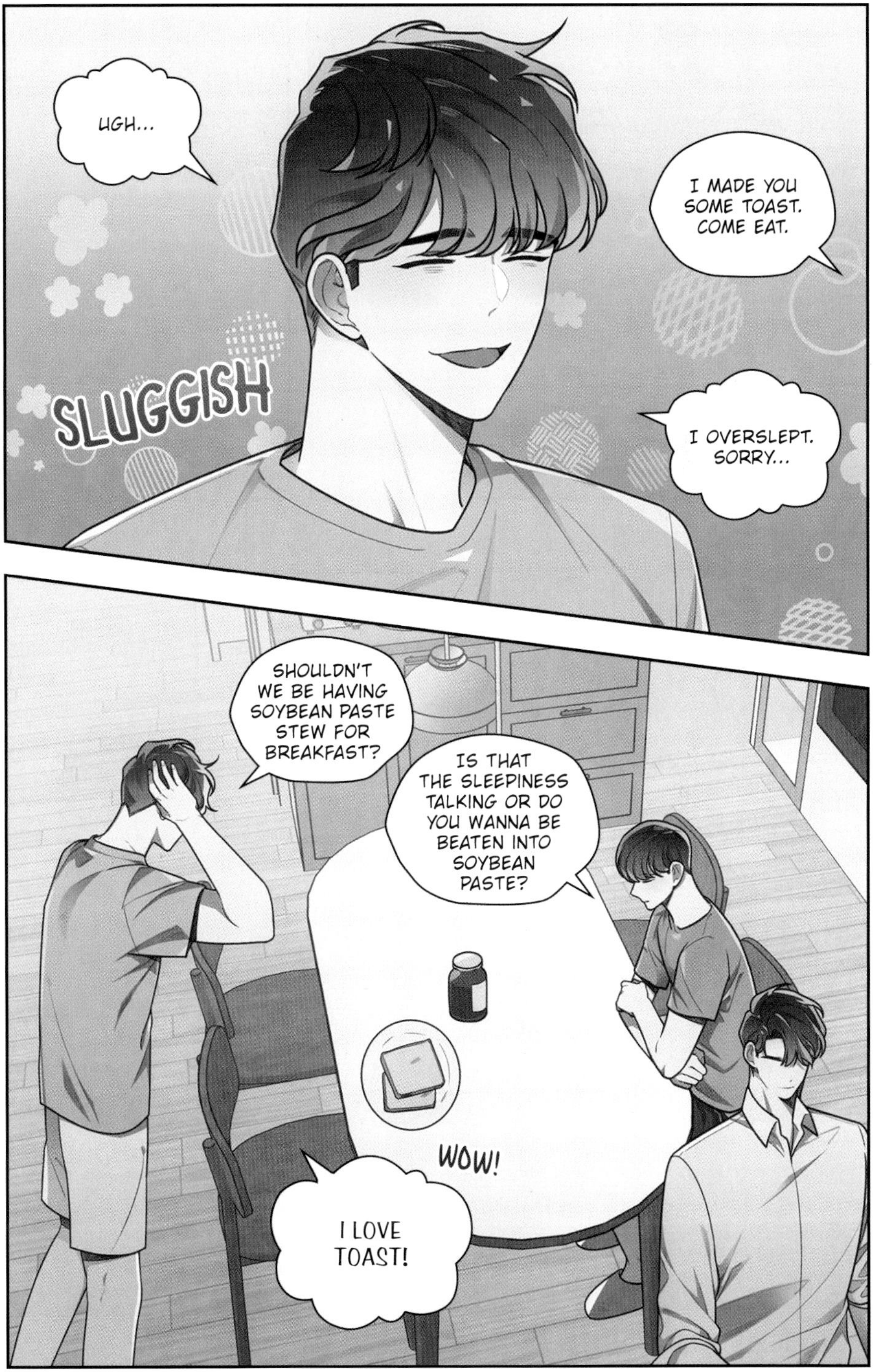
UGH...
I MADE YOU SOME TOAST. COME EAT.
SLUGGISH
I OVERSLEPT. SORRY...
SHOULDN'T WE BE HAVING SOYBEAN PASTE STEW FOR BREAKFAST?
IS THAT THE SLEEPINESS TALKING OR DO YOU WANNA BE BEATEN INTO SOYBEAN PASTE?
WOW!
I LOVE TOAST!

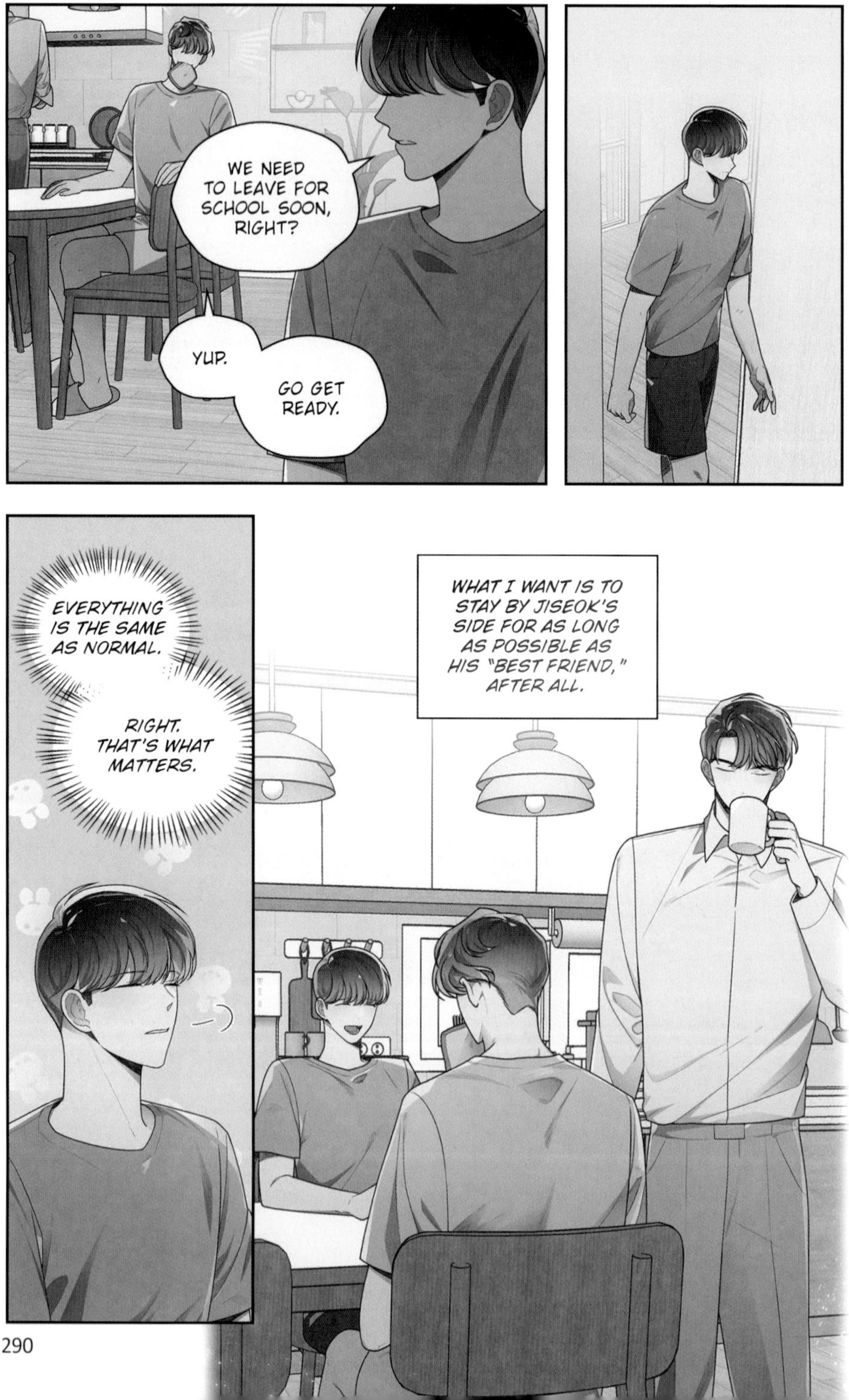
WE NEED TO LEAVE FOR SCHOOL SOON, RIGHT?
YUP.
GO GET READY.
EVERYTHING IS THE SAME AS NORMAL.
RIGHT. THAT'S WHAT MATTERS.
WHAT I WANT IS TO STAY BY JISEOK'S SIDE FOR AS LONG AS POSSIBLE AS HIS "BEST FRIEND," AFTER ALL.

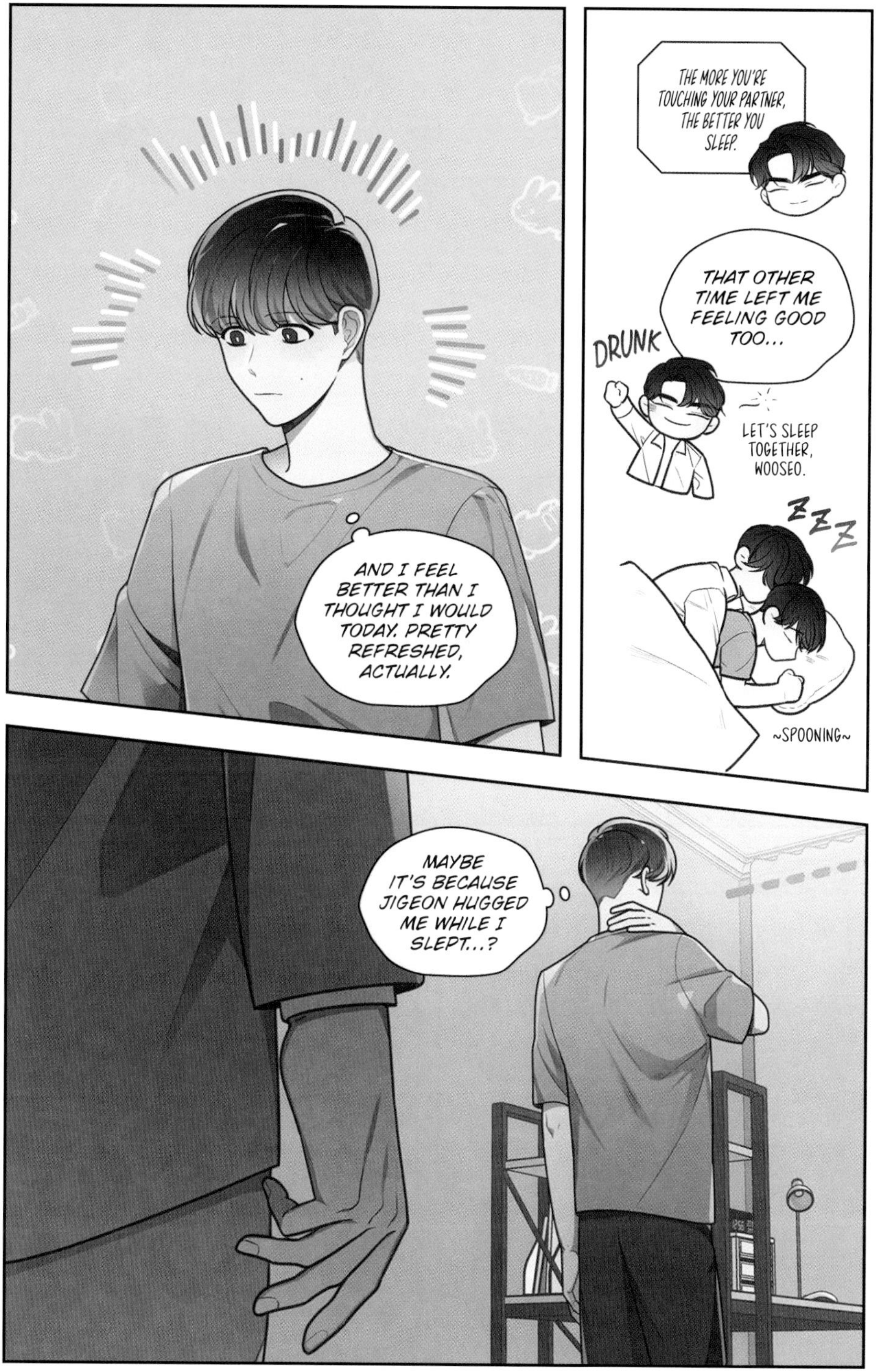
AND I FEEL BETTER THAN I THOUGHT I WOULD TODAY. PRETTY REFRESHED, ACTUALLY.
THE MORE YOU'RE TOUCHING YOUR PARTNER, THE BETTER YOU SLEEP.
THAT OTHER TIME LEFT ME FEELING GOOD TOO...
DRUNK
LET'S SLEEP TOGETHER, WOOSEO.
ZZZ
~SPOONING~
MAYBE IT'S BECAUSE JIGEON HUGGED ME WHILE I SLEPT...?

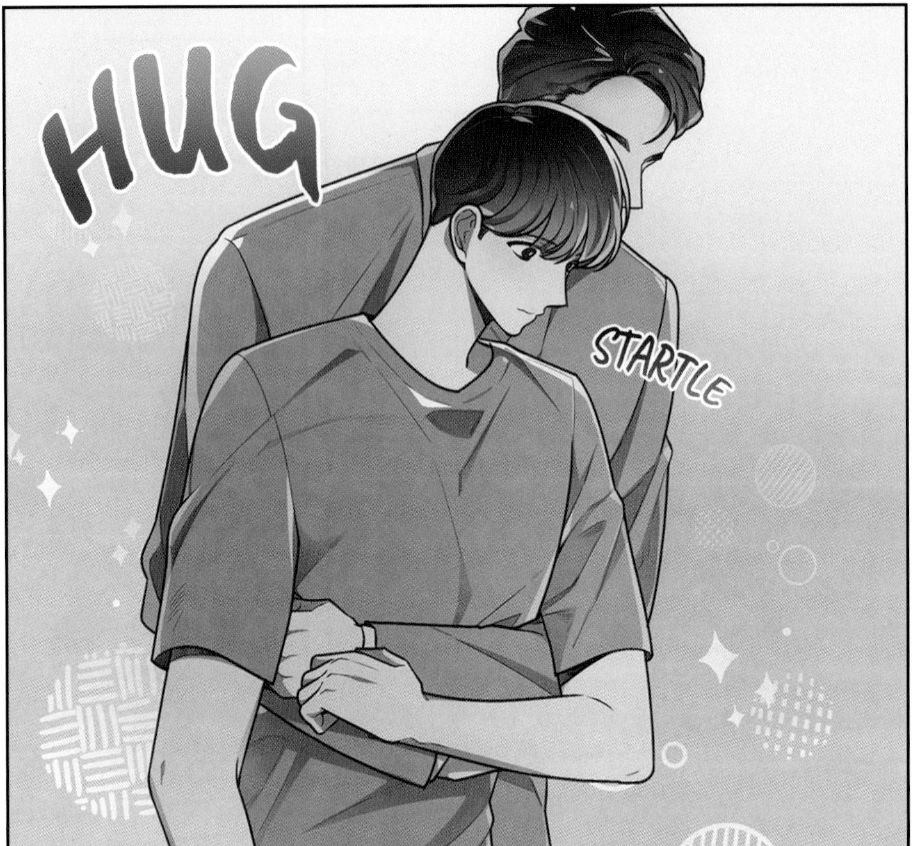
HUG
STARTLE

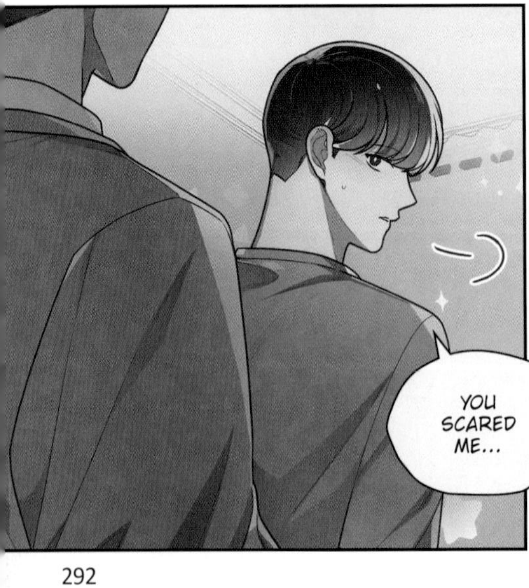
YOU SCARED ME...

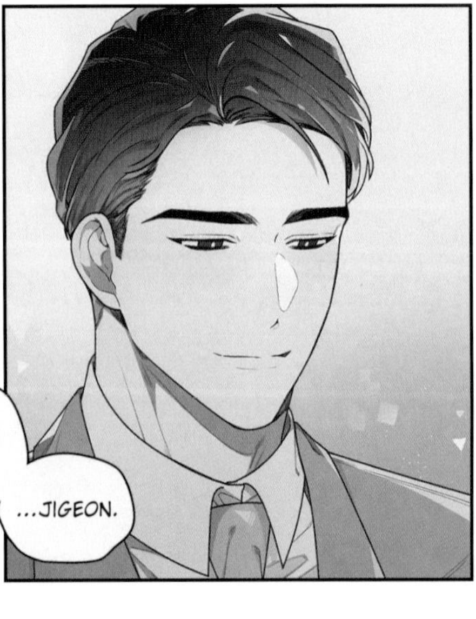
...JIGEON.

Tied to you

Chapter 15

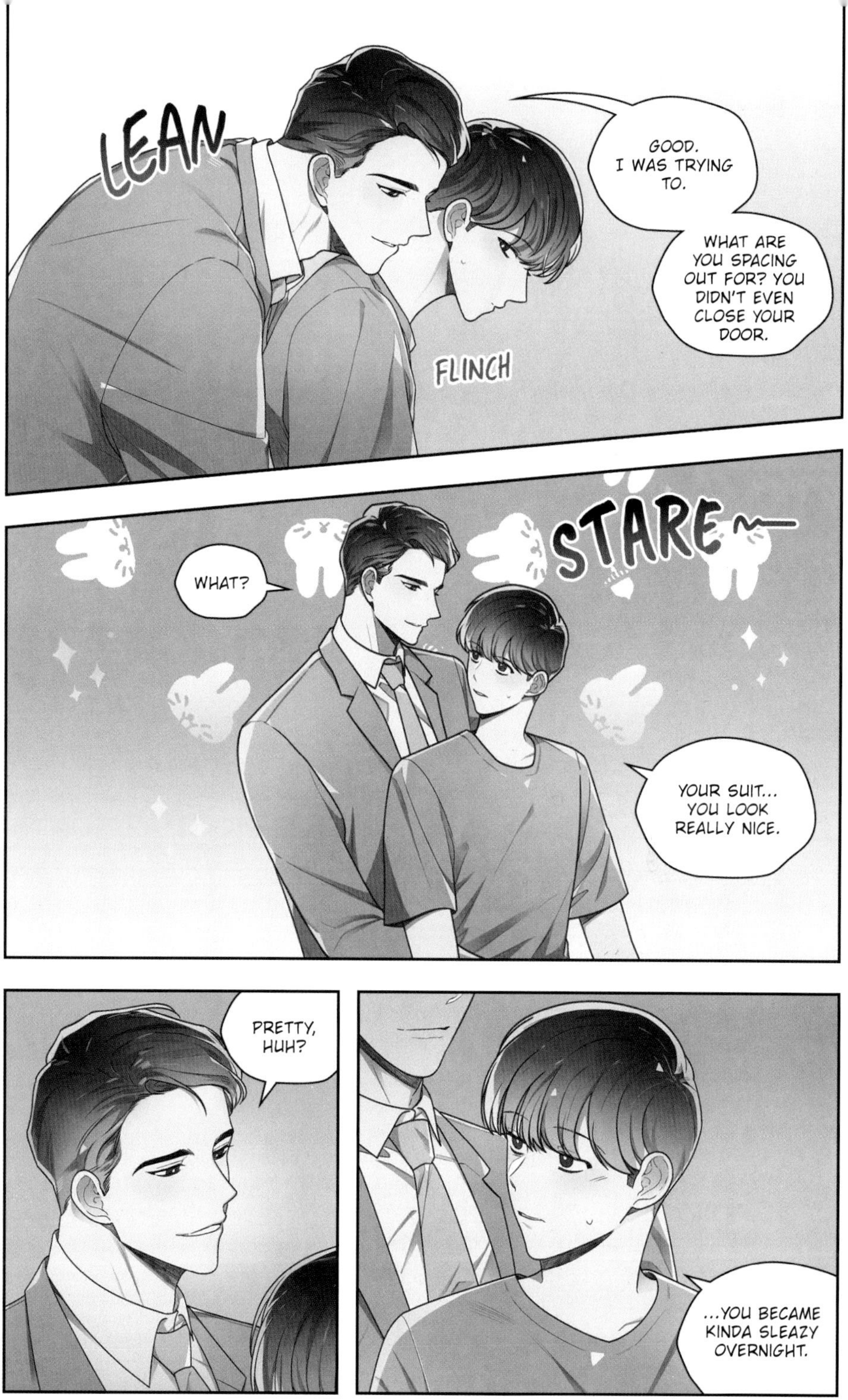
LEAN
GOOD. I WAS TRYING TO.
WHAT ARE YOU SPACING OUT FOR? YOU DIDN'T EVEN CLOSE YOUR DOOR.
FLINCH
STARE~
WHAT?
YOUR SUIT... YOU LOOK REALLY NICE.
PRETTY, HUH?
...YOU BECAME KINDA SLEAZY OVERNIGHT.

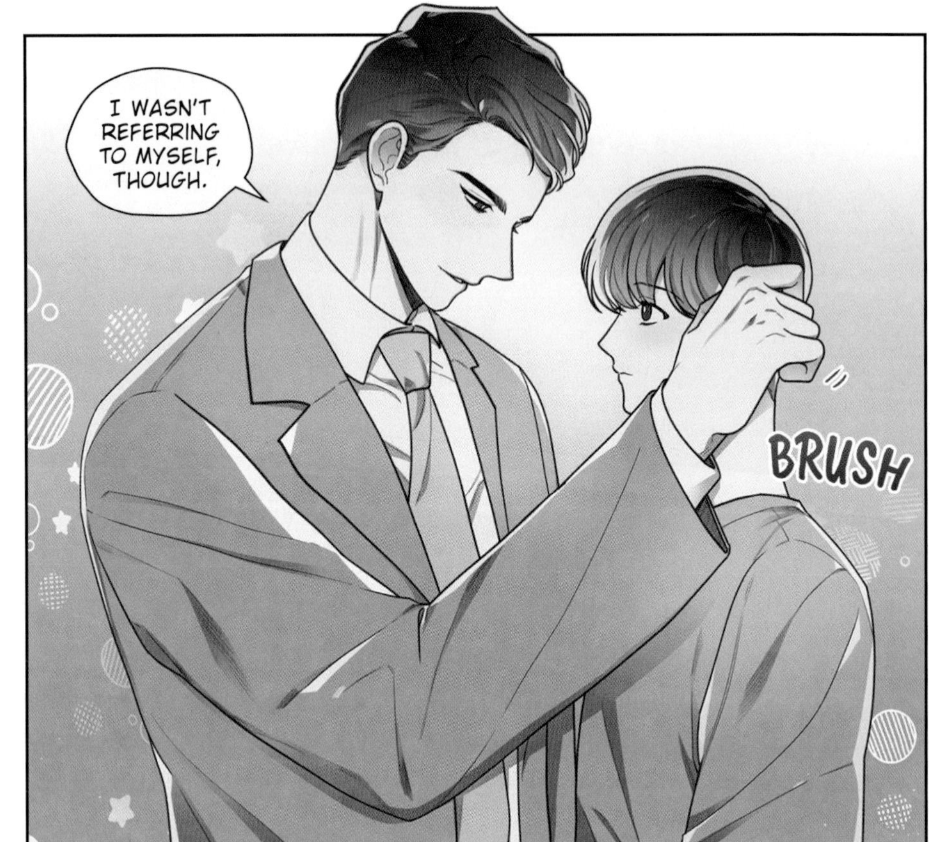
I WASN'T REFERRING TO MYSELF, THOUGH.
BRUSH

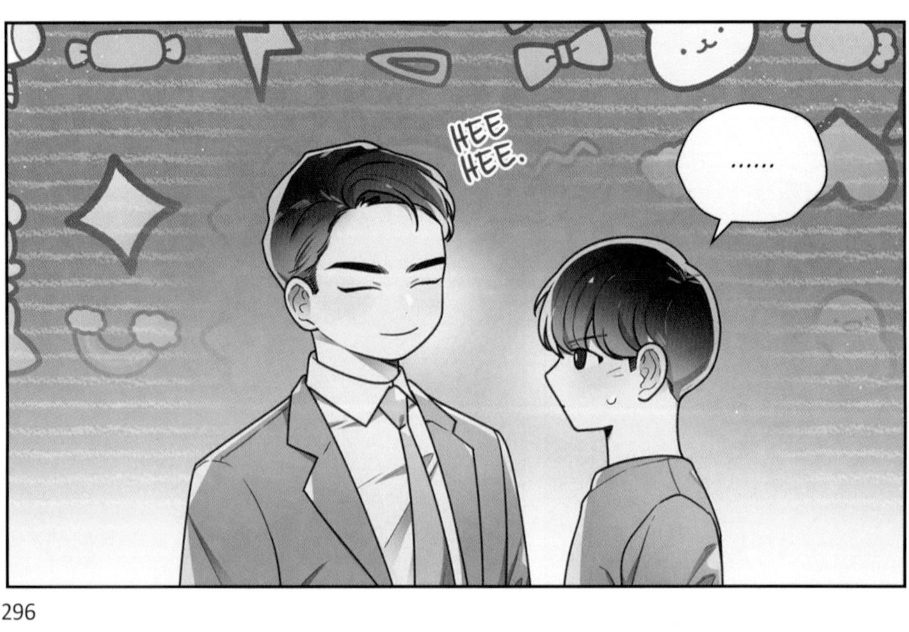
HEE HEE.
......

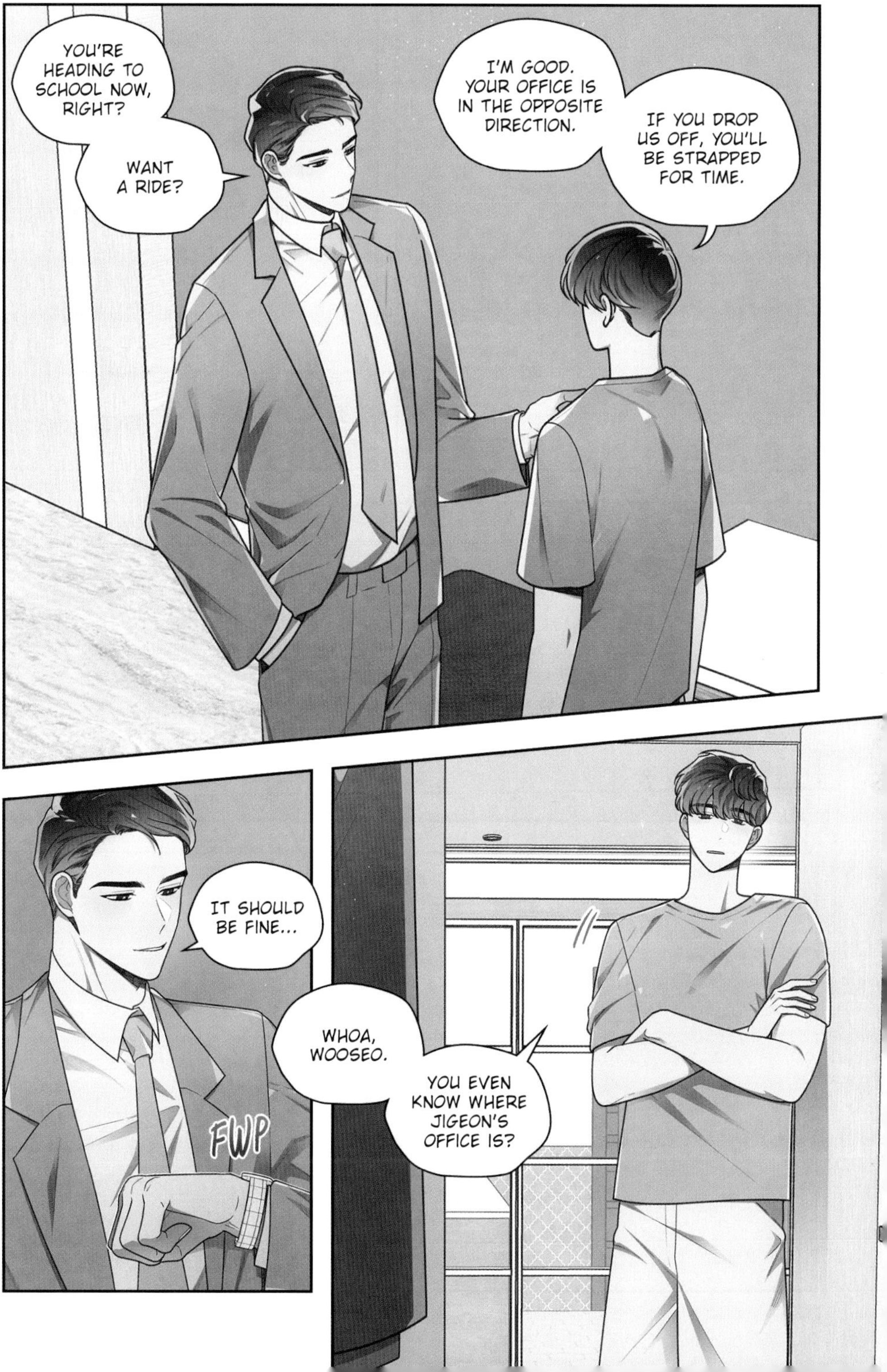
YOU'RE HEADING TO SCHOOL NOW, RIGHT?
WANT A RIDE?
I'M GOOD. YOUR OFFICE IS IN THE OPPOSITE DIRECTION.
IF YOU DROP US OFF, YOU'LL BE STRAPPED FOR TIME.
IT SHOULD BE FINE...
FWP
WHOA, WOOSEO.
YOU EVEN KNOW WHERE JIGEON'S OFFICE IS?

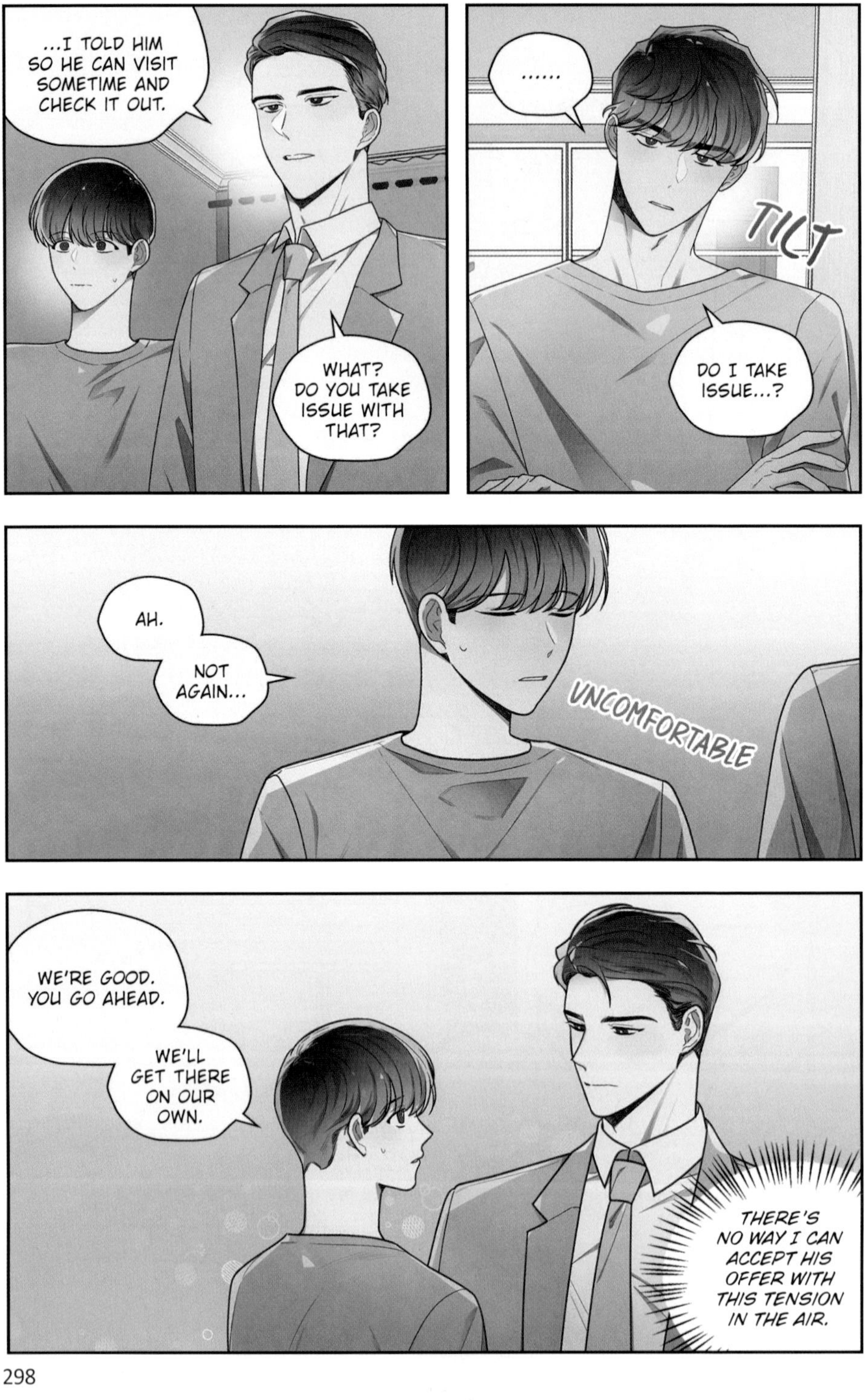
...I TOLD HIM SO HE CAN VISIT SOMETIME AND CHECK IT OUT.
WHAT? DO YOU TAKE ISSUE WITH THAT?
......
TILT
DO I TAKE ISSUE...?
AH.
NOT AGAIN...
UNCOMFORTABLE
WE'RE GOOD. YOU GO AHEAD.
WE'LL GET THERE ON OUR OWN.
THERE'S NO WAY I CAN ACCEPT HIS OFFER WITH THIS TENSION IN THE AIR.

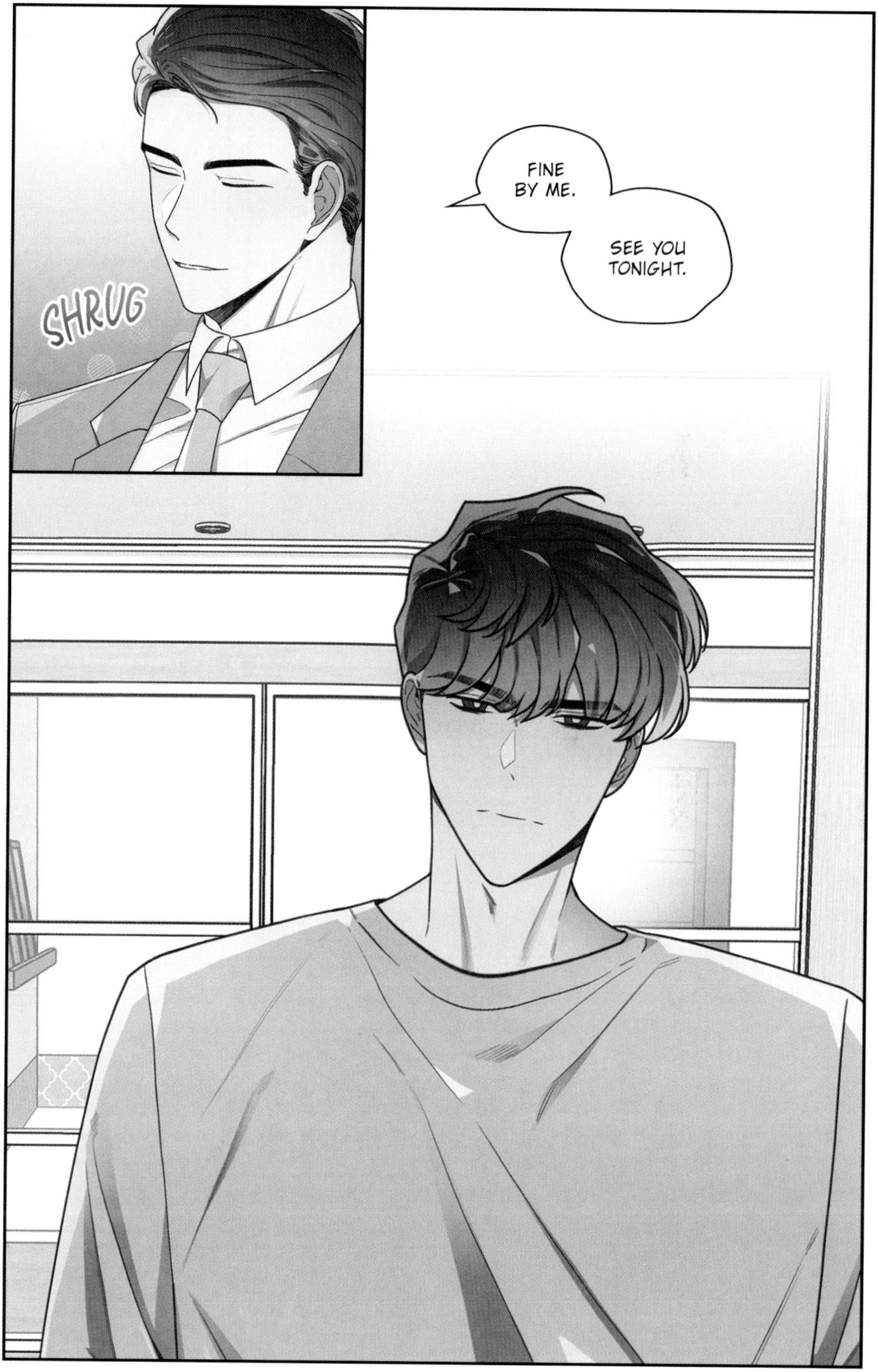
SHRUG
FINE BY ME.
SEE YOU TONIGHT.

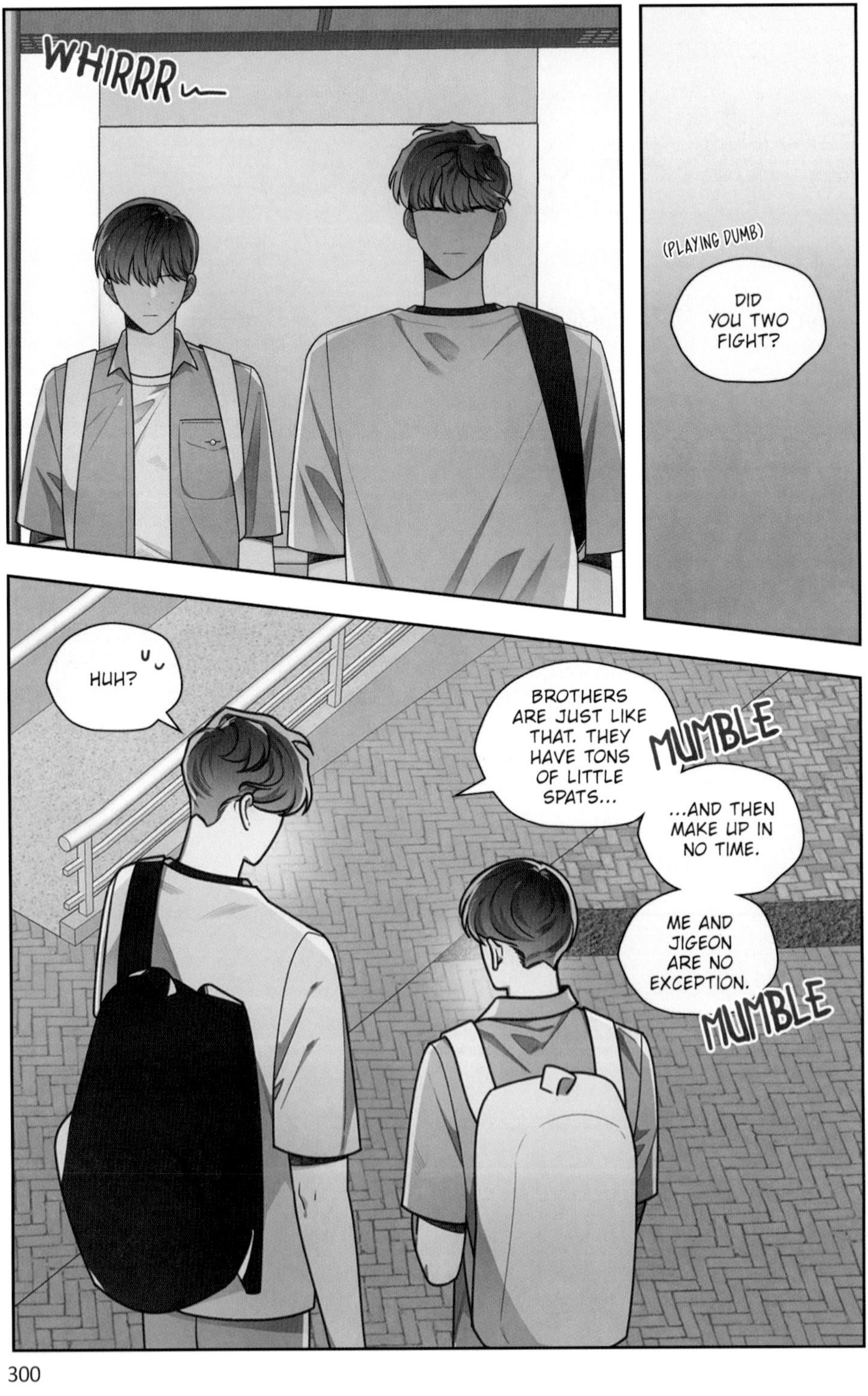
WHIRRR
(PLAYING DUMB)
DID YOU TWO FIGHT?
HUH?
BROTHERS ARE JUST LIKE THAT. THEY HAVE TONS OF LITTLE SPATS...
MUMBLE
...AND THEN MAKE UP IN NO TIME.
ME AND JIGEON ARE NO EXCEPTION.
MUMBLE

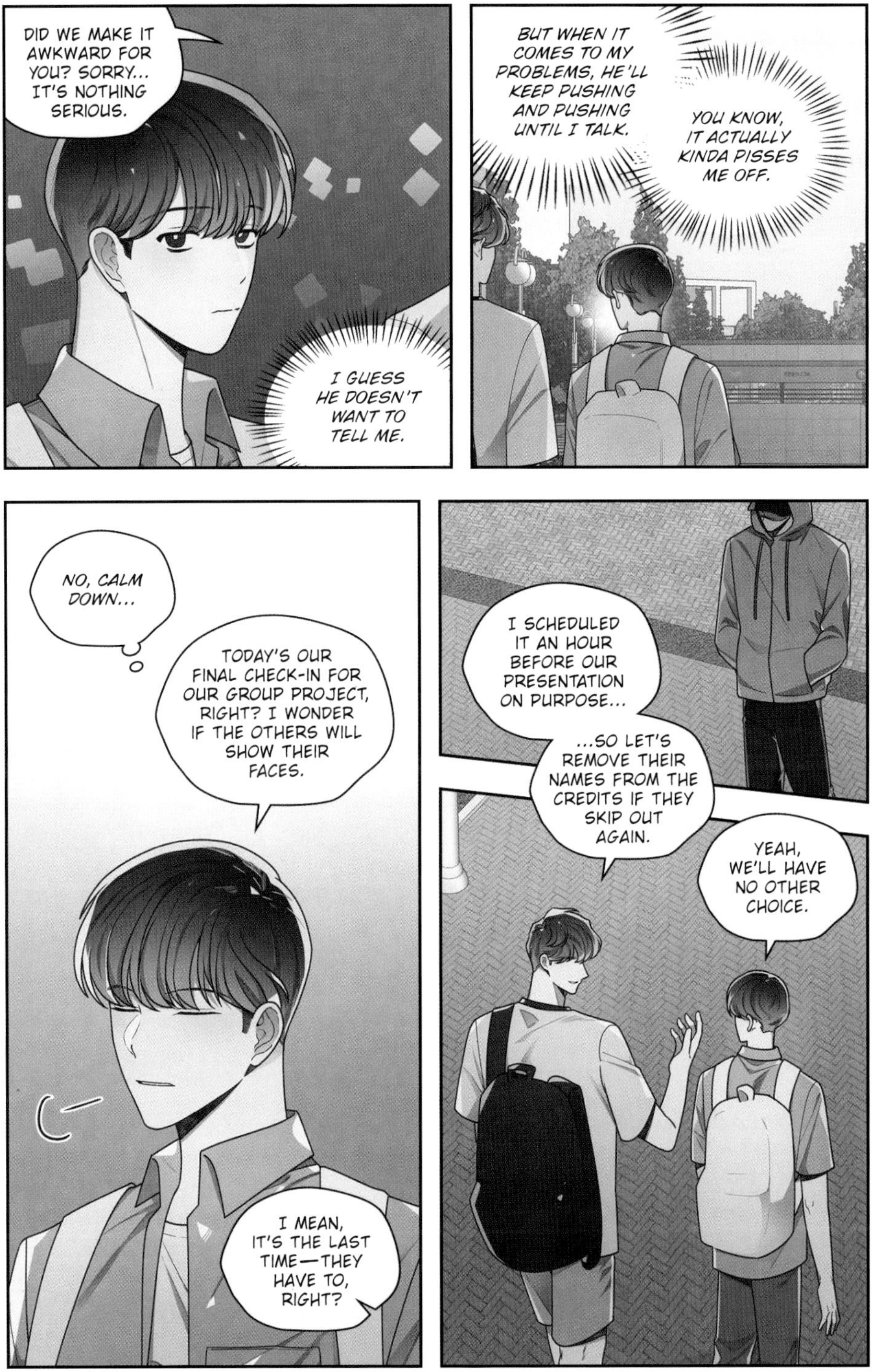
DID WE MAKE IT AWKWARD FOR YOU? SORRY... IT'S NOTHING SERIOUS.
I GUESS HE DOESN'T WANT TO TELL ME.
BUT WHEN IT COMES TO MY PROBLEMS, HE'LL KEEP PUSHING AND PUSHING UNTIL I TALK.
YOU KNOW, IT ACTUALLY KINDA PISSES ME OFF.
NO, CALM DOWN...
TODAY'S OUR FINAL CHECK-IN FOR OUR GROUP PROJECT, RIGHT? I WONDER IF THE OTHERS WILL SHOW THEIR FACES.
I MEAN, IT'S THE LAST TIME—THEY HAVE TO, RIGHT?
I SCHEDULED IT AN HOUR BEFORE OUR PRESENTATION ON PURPOSE...
...SO LET'S REMOVE THEIR NAMES FROM THE CREDITS IF THEY SKIP OUT AGAIN.
YEAH, WE'LL HAVE NO OTHER CHOICE.

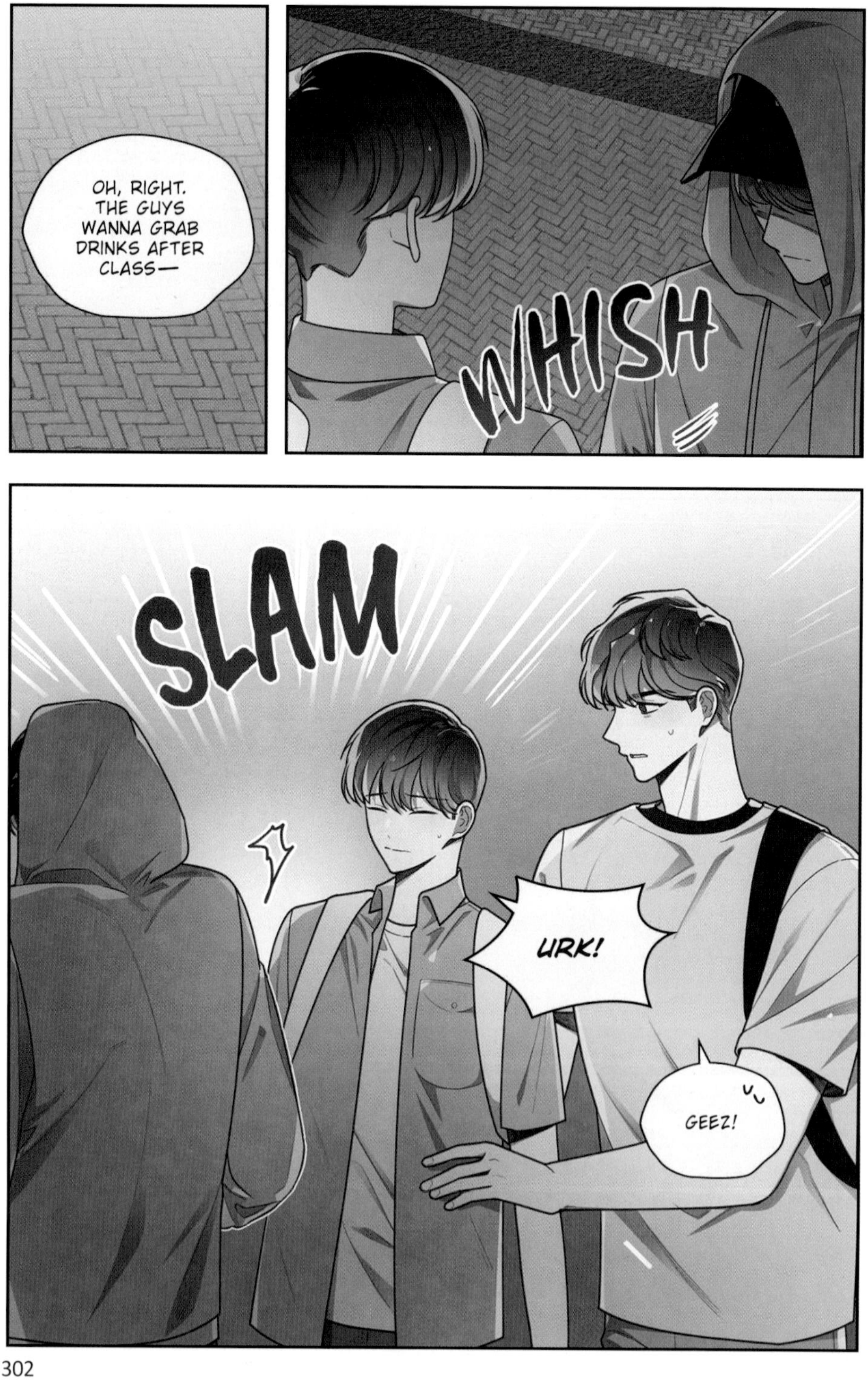
OH, RIGHT. THE GUYS WANNA GRAB DRINKS AFTER CLASS—
WHISH
SLAM
URK!
GEEZ!

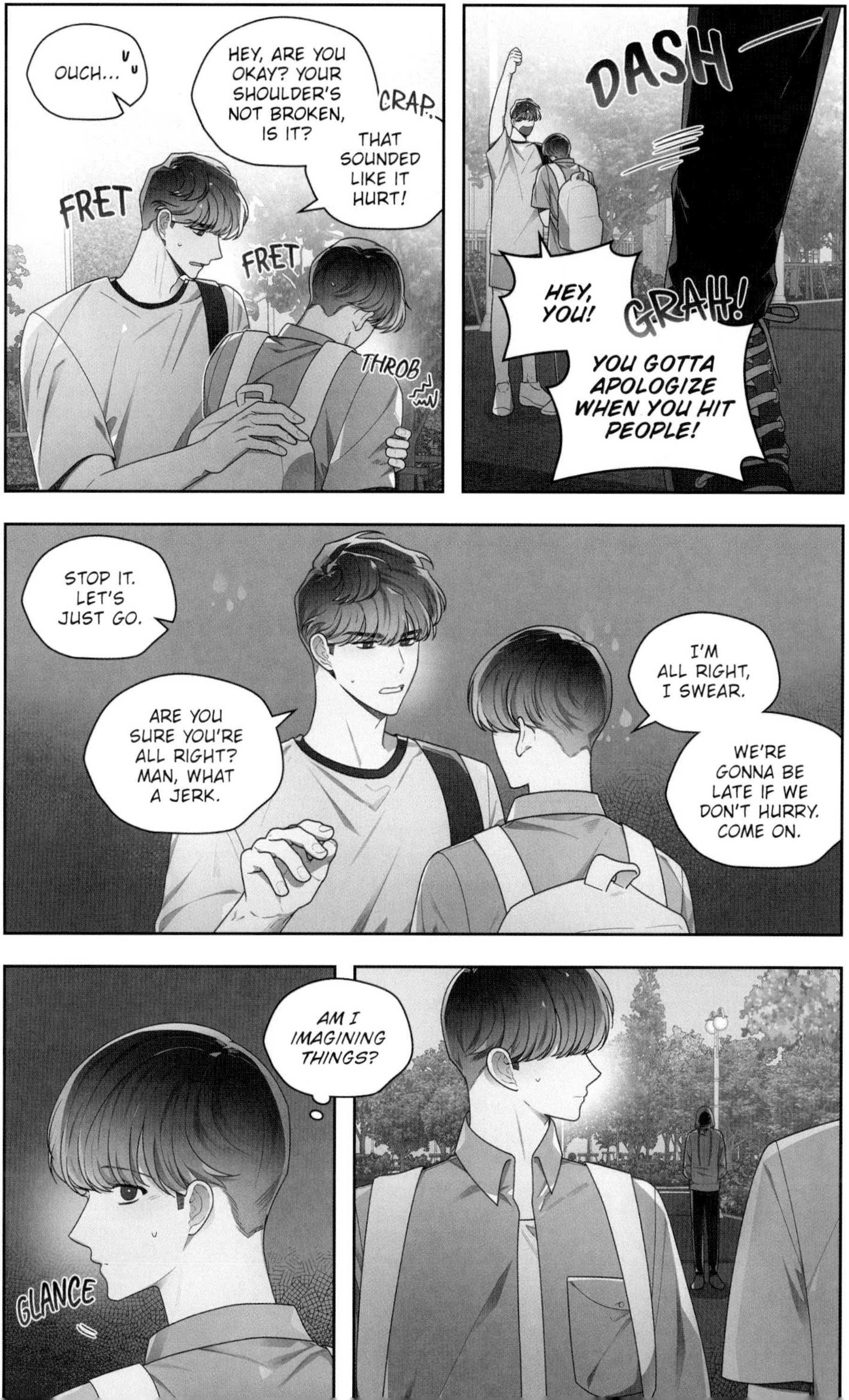
OUCH...
HEY, ARE YOU OKAY? YOUR SHOULDER'S NOT BROKEN, IS IT?
CRAP...
THAT SOUNDED LIKE IT HURT!
FRET
FRET
THROB
DASH
HEY, YOU!
GRAH!
YOU GOTTA APOLOGIZE WHEN YOU HIT PEOPLE!
STOP IT. LET'S JUST GO.
ARE YOU SURE YOU'RE ALL RIGHT? MAN, WHAT A JERK.
I'M ALL RIGHT, I SWEAR.
WE'RE GONNA BE LATE IF WE DON'T HURRY. COME ON.
AM I IMAGINING THINGS?
GLANCE

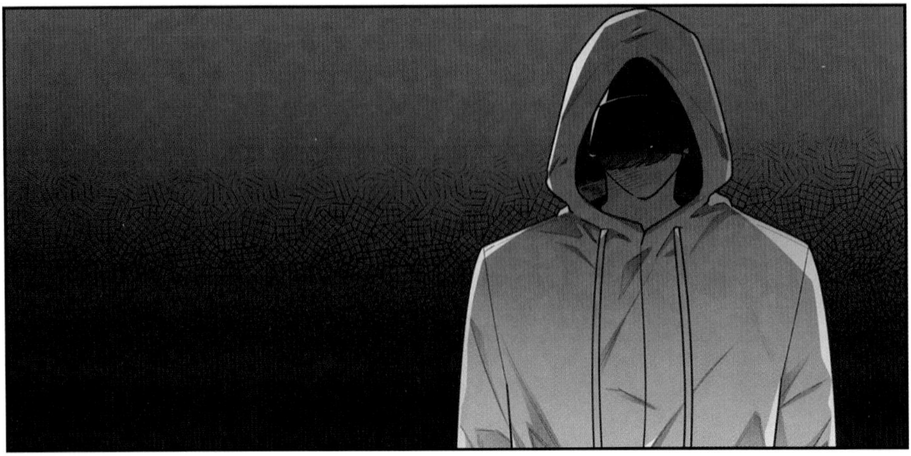

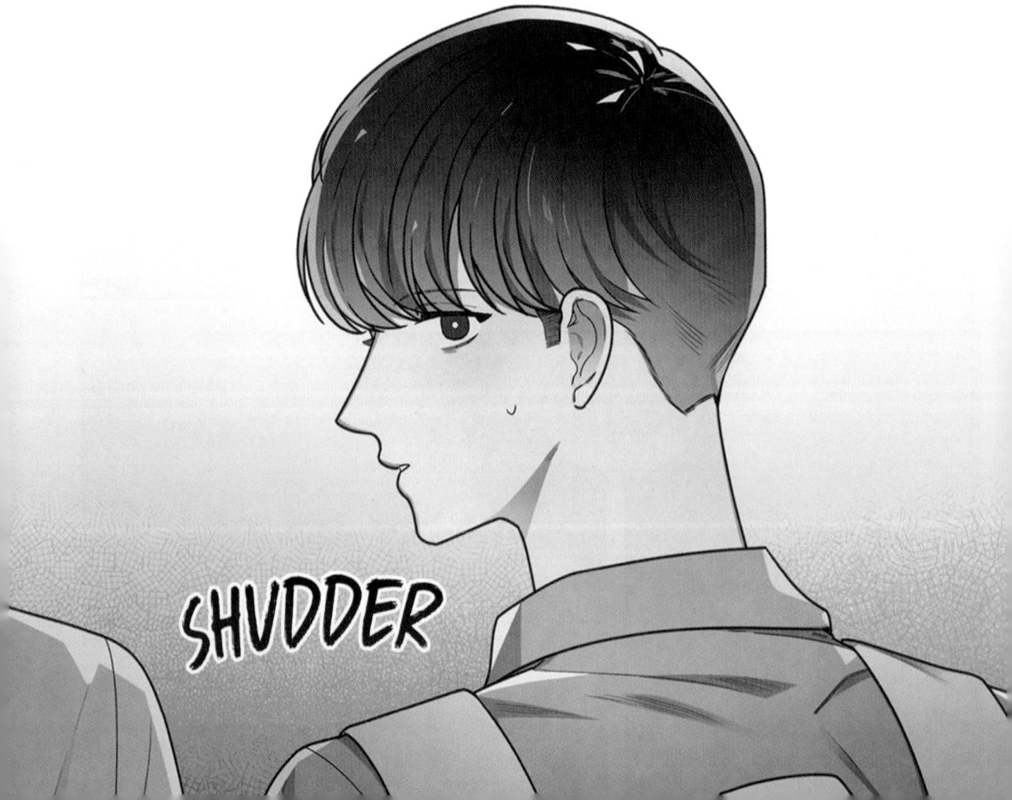
SHUDDER

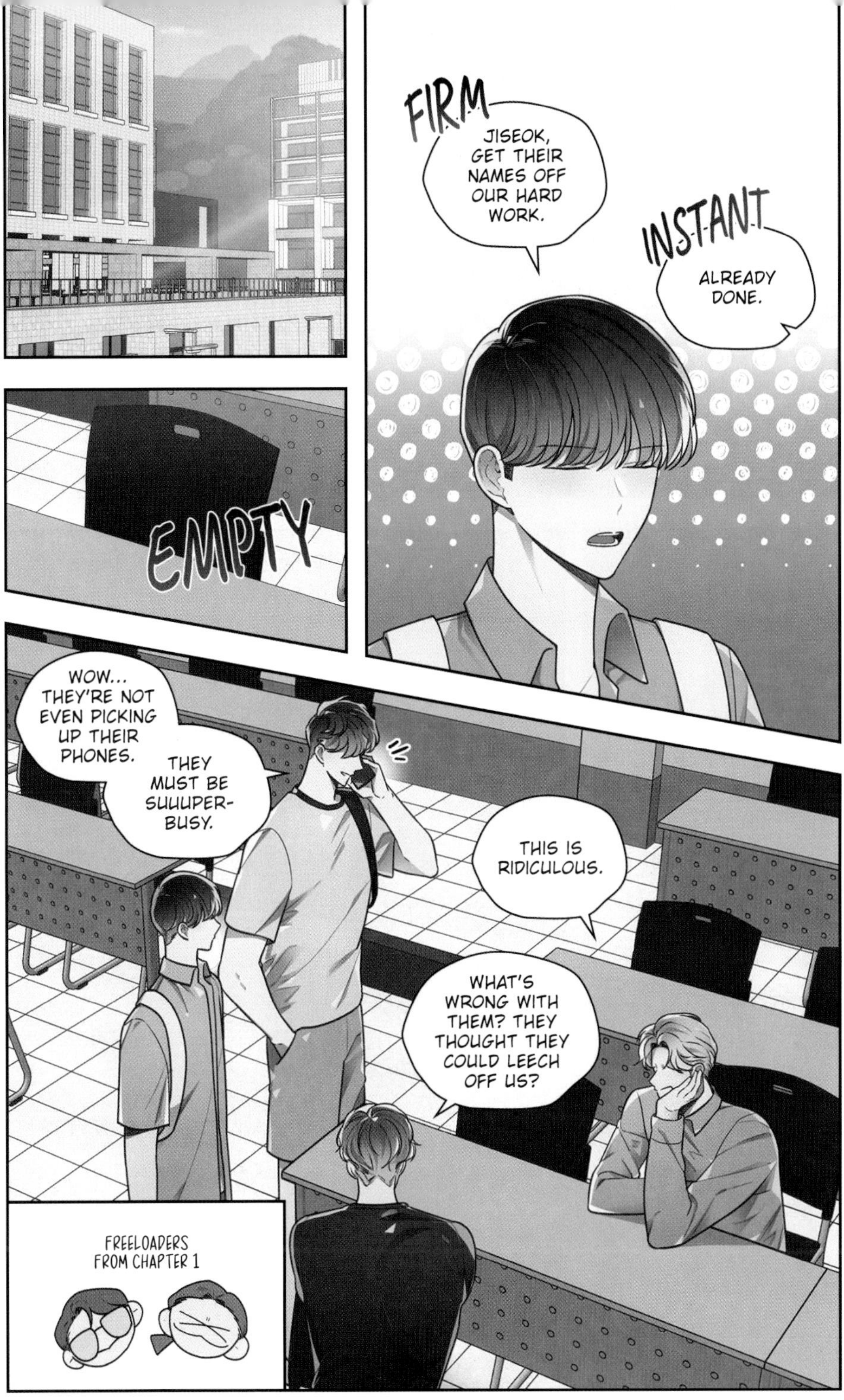
FIRM
JISEOK, GET THEIR NAMES OFF OUR HARD WORK.
INSTANT
ALREADY DONE.
EMPTY
WOW... THEY'RE NOT EVEN PICKING UP THEIR PHONES.
THEY MUST BE SUUUPER-BUSY.
THIS IS RIDICULOUS.
WHAT'S WRONG WITH THEM? THEY THOUGHT THEY COULD LEECH OFF US?
FREELOADERS FROM CHAPTER 1

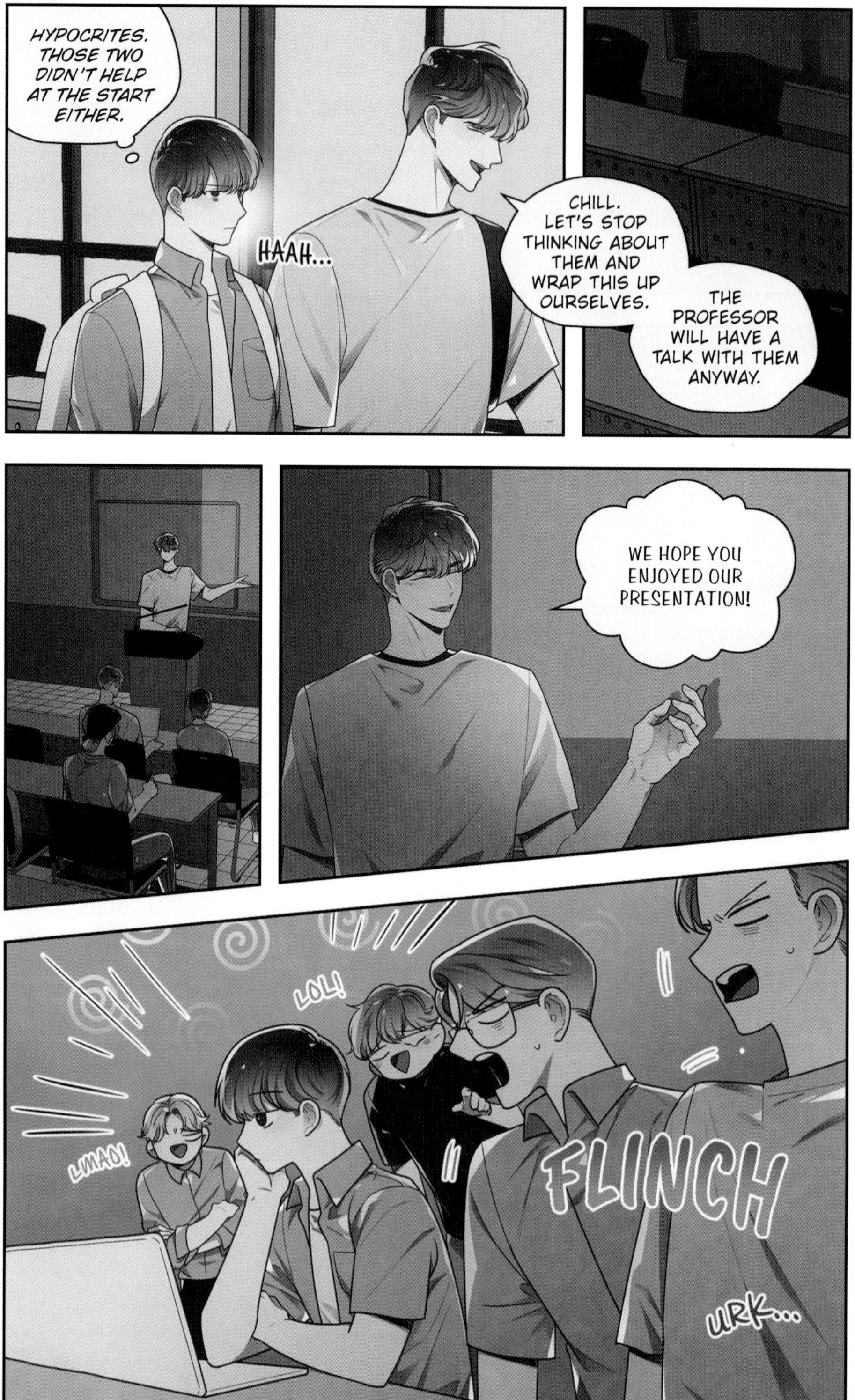
HYPOCRITES. THOSE TWO DIDN'T HELP AT THE START EITHER.
HAAH...
CHILL. LET'S STOP THINKING ABOUT THEM AND WRAP THIS UP OURSELVES.
THE PROFESSOR WILL HAVE A TALK WITH THEM ANYWAY.
WE HOPE YOU ENJOYED OUR PRESENTATION!
LOL!
LMAO!
FLINCH
URK...

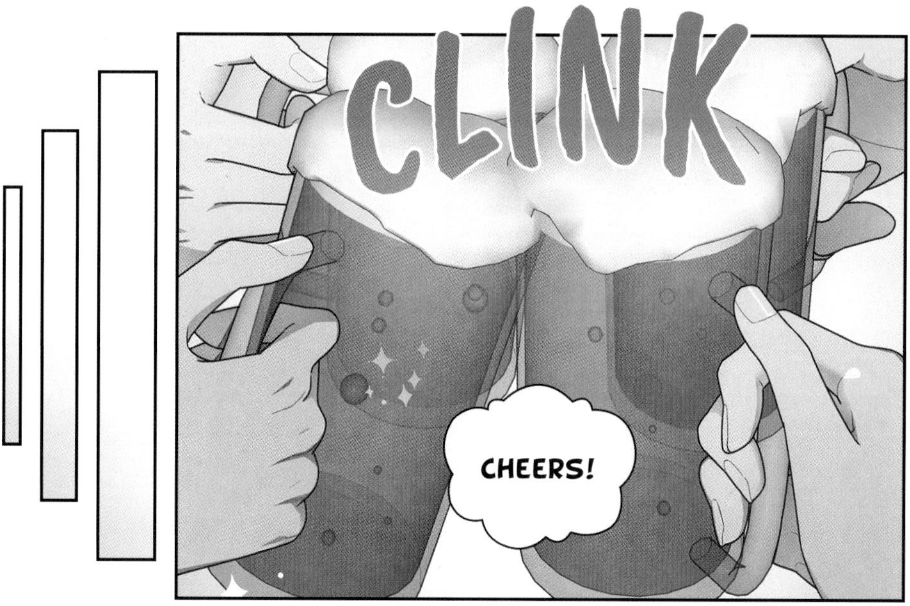
CLINK
CHEERS!

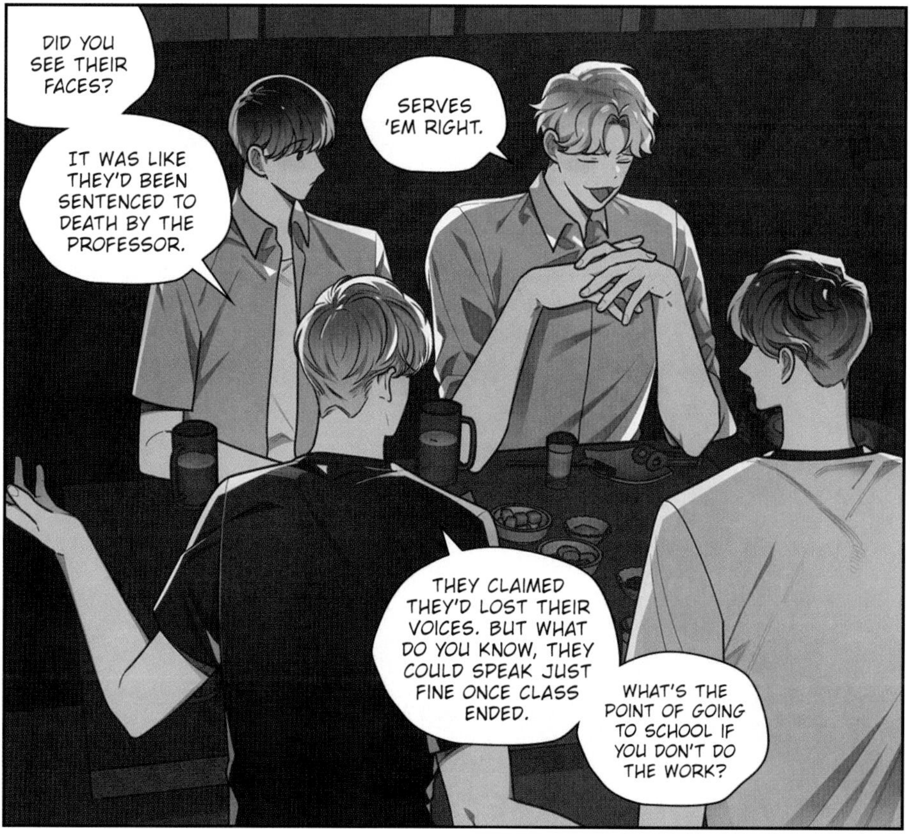
DID YOU SEE THEIR FACES?
IT WAS LIKE THEY'D BEEN SENTENCED TO DEATH BY THE PROFESSOR.
SERVES 'EM RIGHT.
THEY CLAIMED THEY'D LOST THEIR VOICES. BUT WHAT DO YOU KNOW, THEY COULD SPEAK JUST FINE ONCE CLASS ENDED.
WHAT'S THE POINT OF GOING TO SCHOOL IF YOU DON'T DO THE WORK?

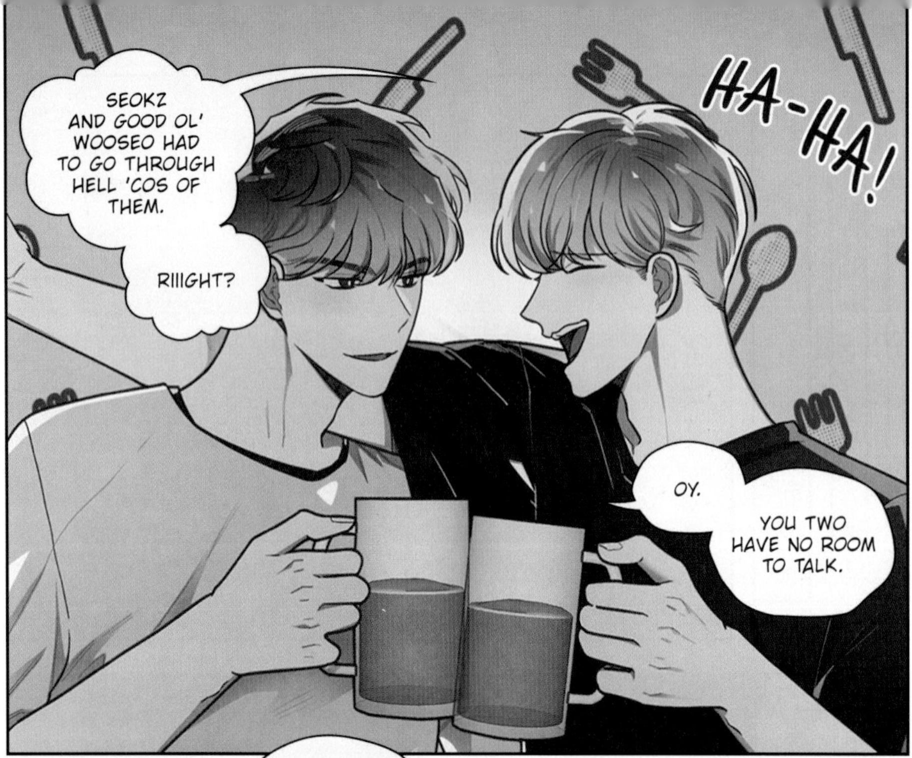
SEOKZ AND GOOD OL' WOOSEO HAD TO GO THROUGH HELL 'COS OF THEM.
RIIIGHT?
HA-HA!
OY.
YOU TWO HAVE NO ROOM TO TALK.

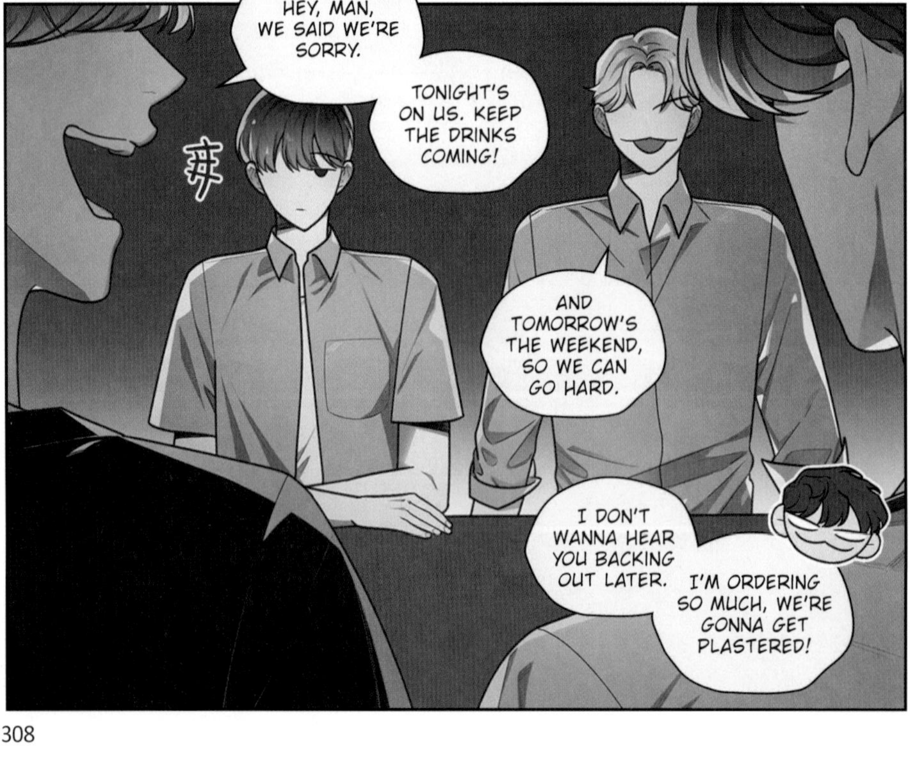
HEY, MAN, WE SAID WE'RE SORRY.
TONIGHT'S ON US. KEEP THE DRINKS COMING!
AND TOMORROW'S THE WEEKEND, SO WE CAN GO HARD.
I DON'T WANNA HEAR YOU BACKING OUT LATER.
I'M ORDERING SO MUCH, WE'RE GONNA GET PLASTERED!

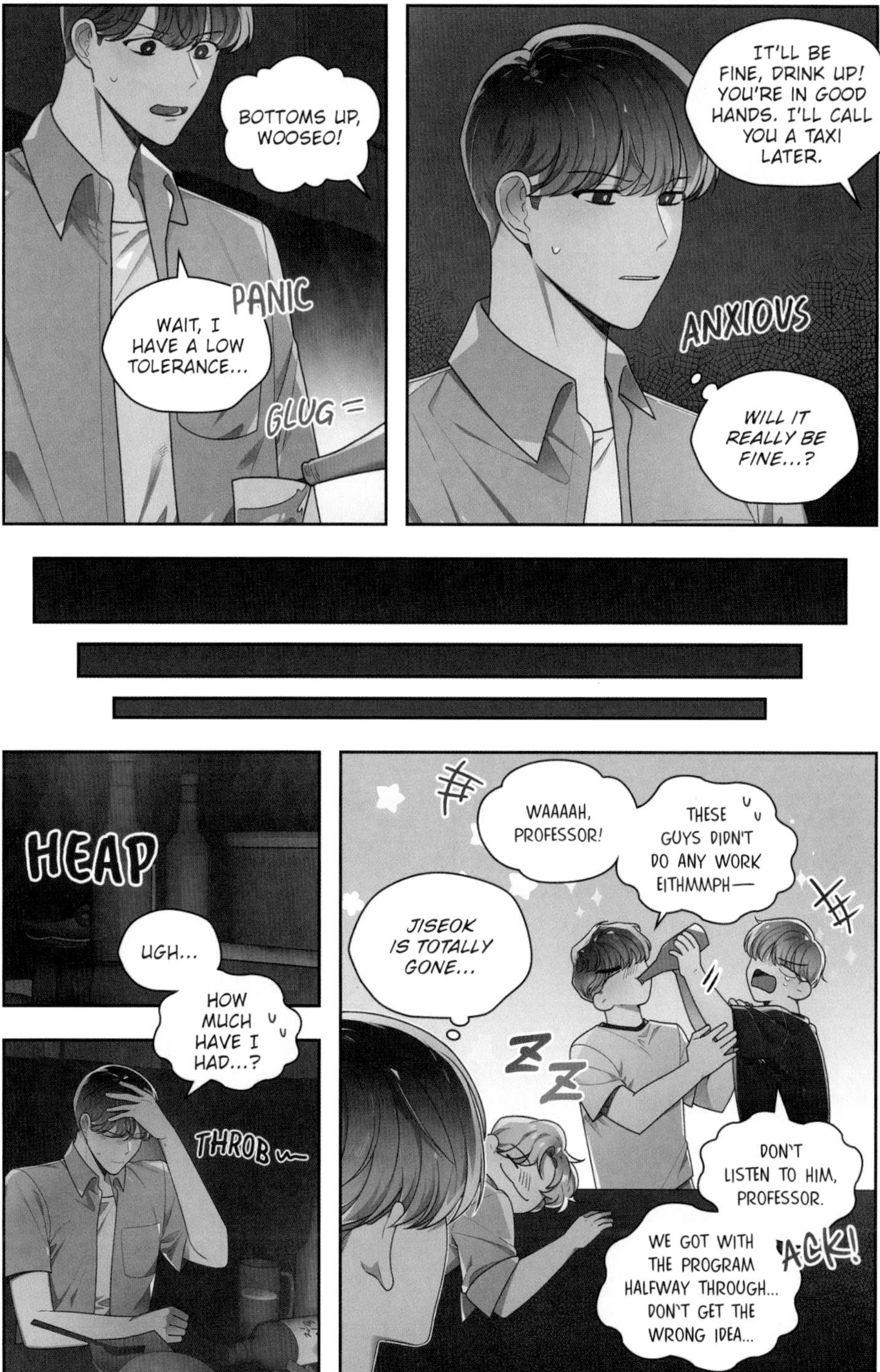
BOTTOMS UP, WOOSEO!
PANIC
WAIT, I HAVE A LOW TOLERANCE...
GLUG
IT'LL BE FINE, DRINK UP! YOU'RE IN GOOD HANDS. I'LL CALL YOU A TAXI LATER.
ANXIOUS
WILL IT REALLY BE FINE...?
HEAP
UGH...
HOW MUCH HAVE I HAD...?
THROB
WAAAAH, PROFESSOR!
THESE GUYS DIDN'T DO ANY WORK EITHMMPH—
JISEOK IS TOTALLY GONE...
ZZ
DON'T LISTEN TO HIM, PROFESSOR.
'ACK!
WE GOT WITH THE PROGRAM HALFWAY THROUGH... DON'T GET THE WRONG IDEA...

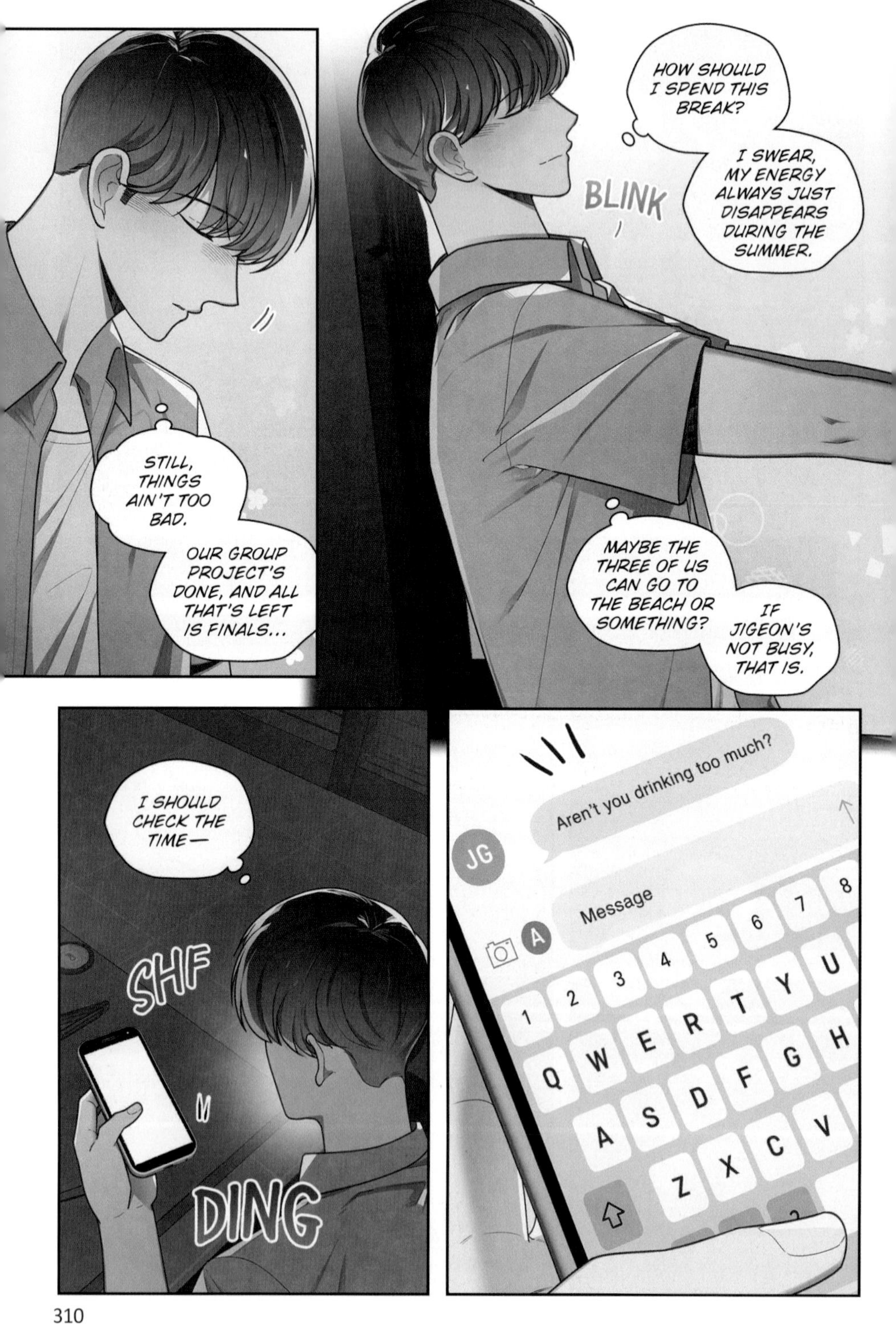
HOW SHOULD I SPEND THIS BREAK?
I SWEAR, MY ENERGY ALWAYS JUST DISAPPEARS DURING THE SUMMER.
BLINK
STILL, THINGS AIN'T TOO BAD.
OUR GROUP PROJECT'S DONE, AND ALL THAT'S LEFT IS FINALS...
MAYBE THE THREE OF US CAN GO TO THE BEACH OR SOMETHING?
IF JIGEON'S NOT BUSY, THAT IS.
I SHOULD CHECK THE TIME—
SHF
DING
Aren't you drinking too much?
JG
Message

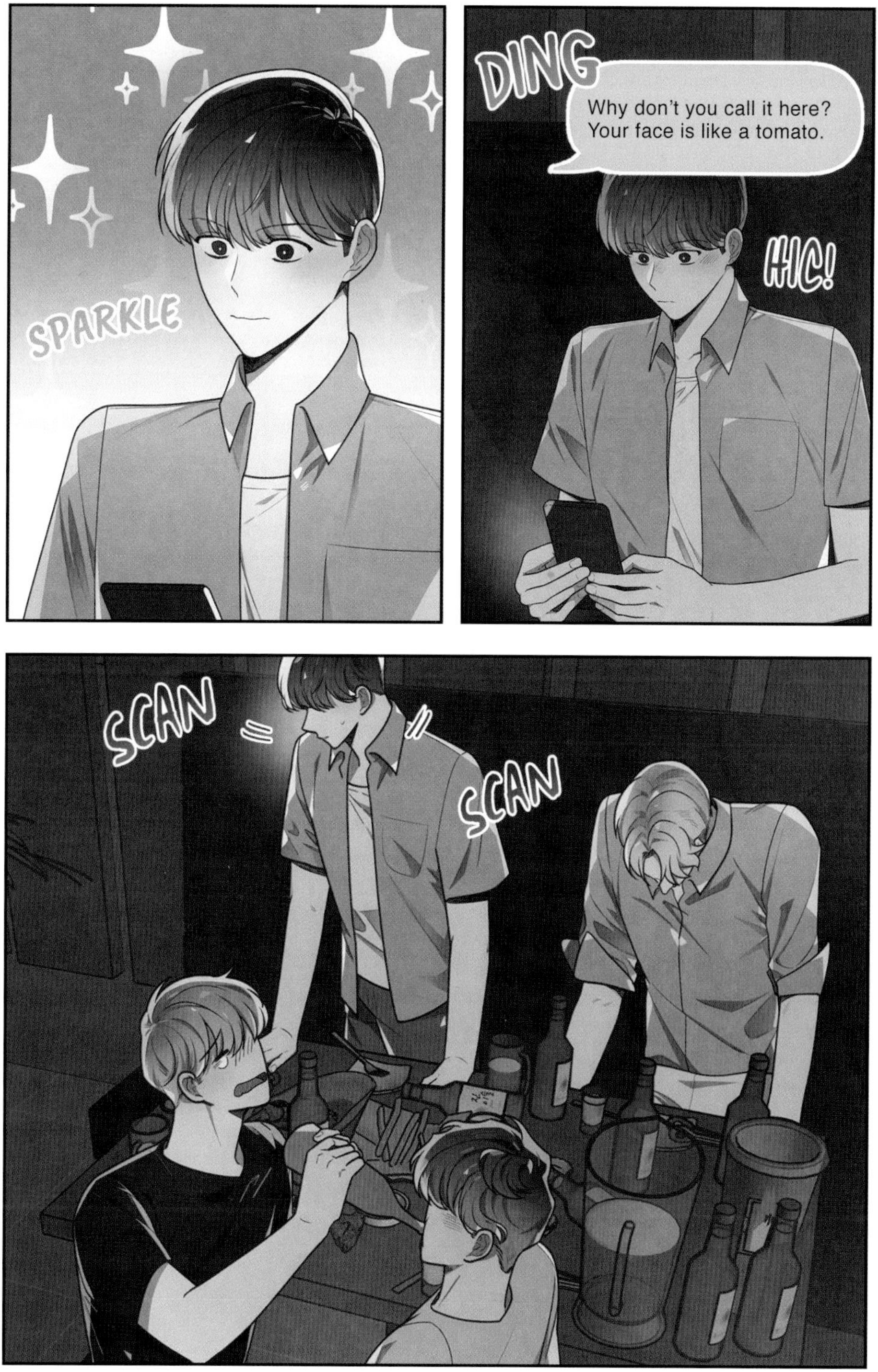
SPARKLE
DING
Why don't you call it here? Your face is like a tomato.
HIC!
SCAN
SCAN

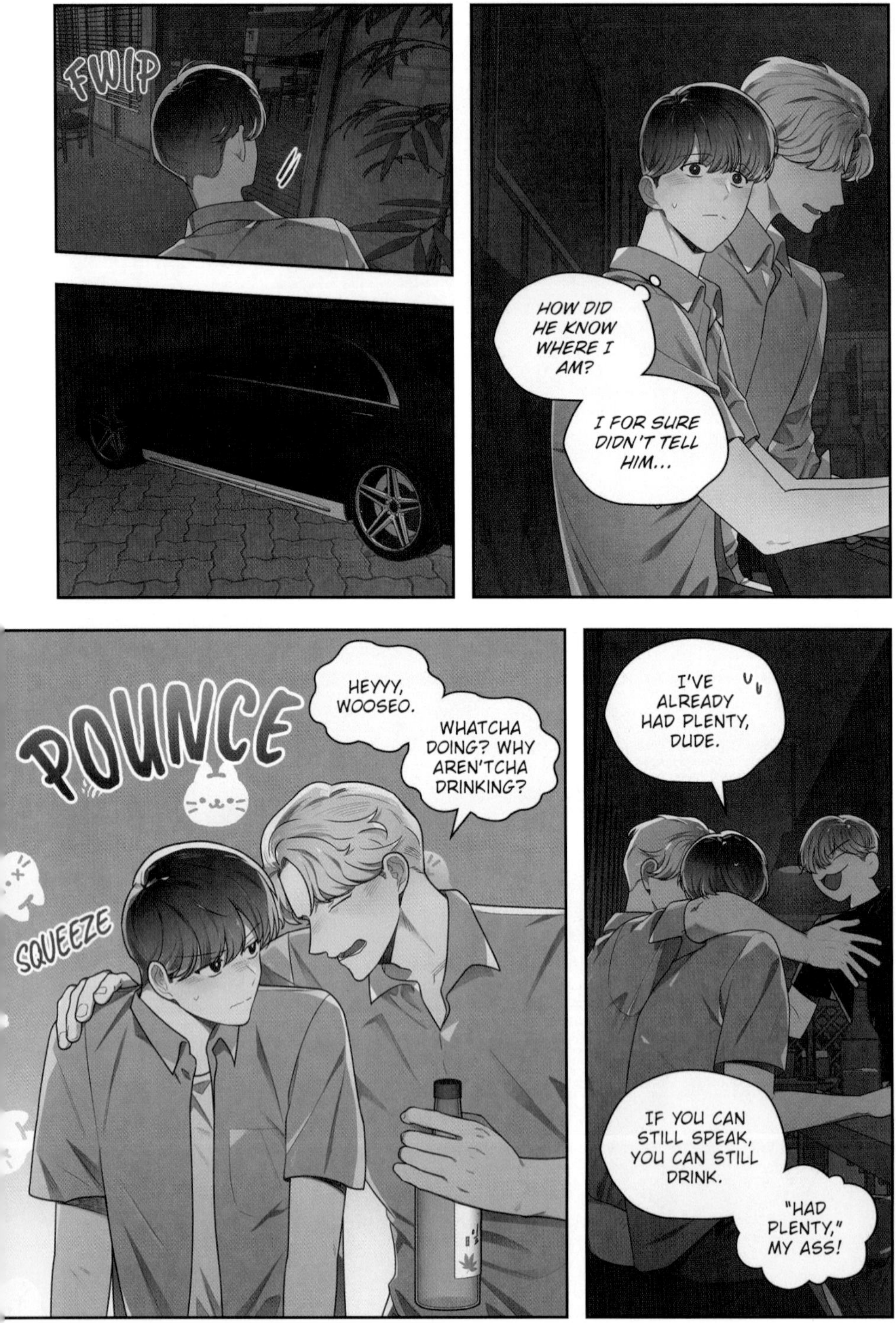
FWIP
HOW DID HE KNOW WHERE I AM?
I FOR SURE DIDN'T TELL HIM...
POUNCE
SQUEEZE
HEYYY, WOOSEO.
WHATCHA DOING? WHY AREN'TCHA DRINKING?
I'VE ALREADY HAD PLENTY, DUDE.
IF YOU CAN STILL SPEAK, YOU CAN STILL DRINK.
"HAD PLENTY," MY ASS!

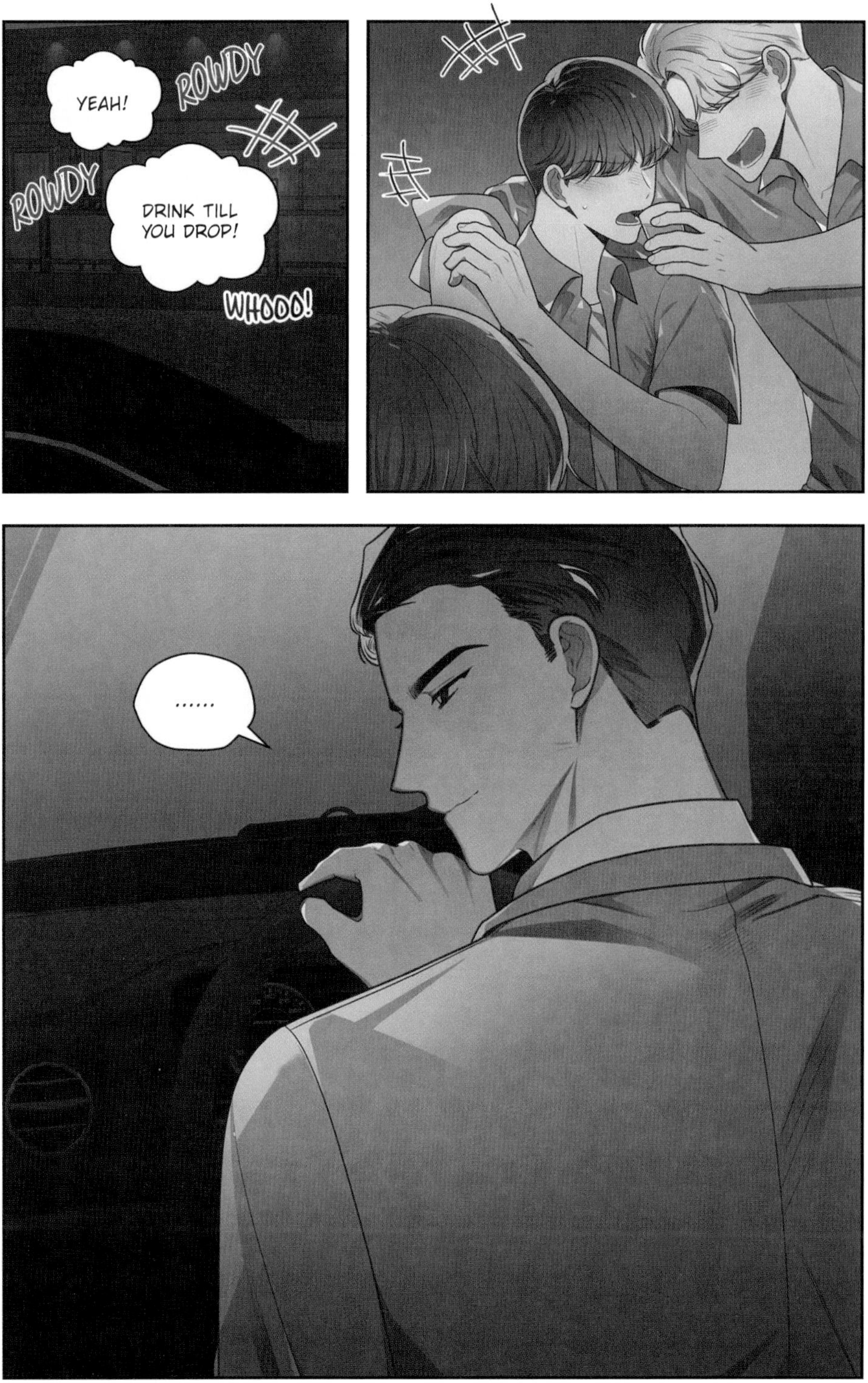
YEAH!
ROWDY
ROWDY
DRINK TILL YOU DROP!
WHOOO!
......

Chapter 16

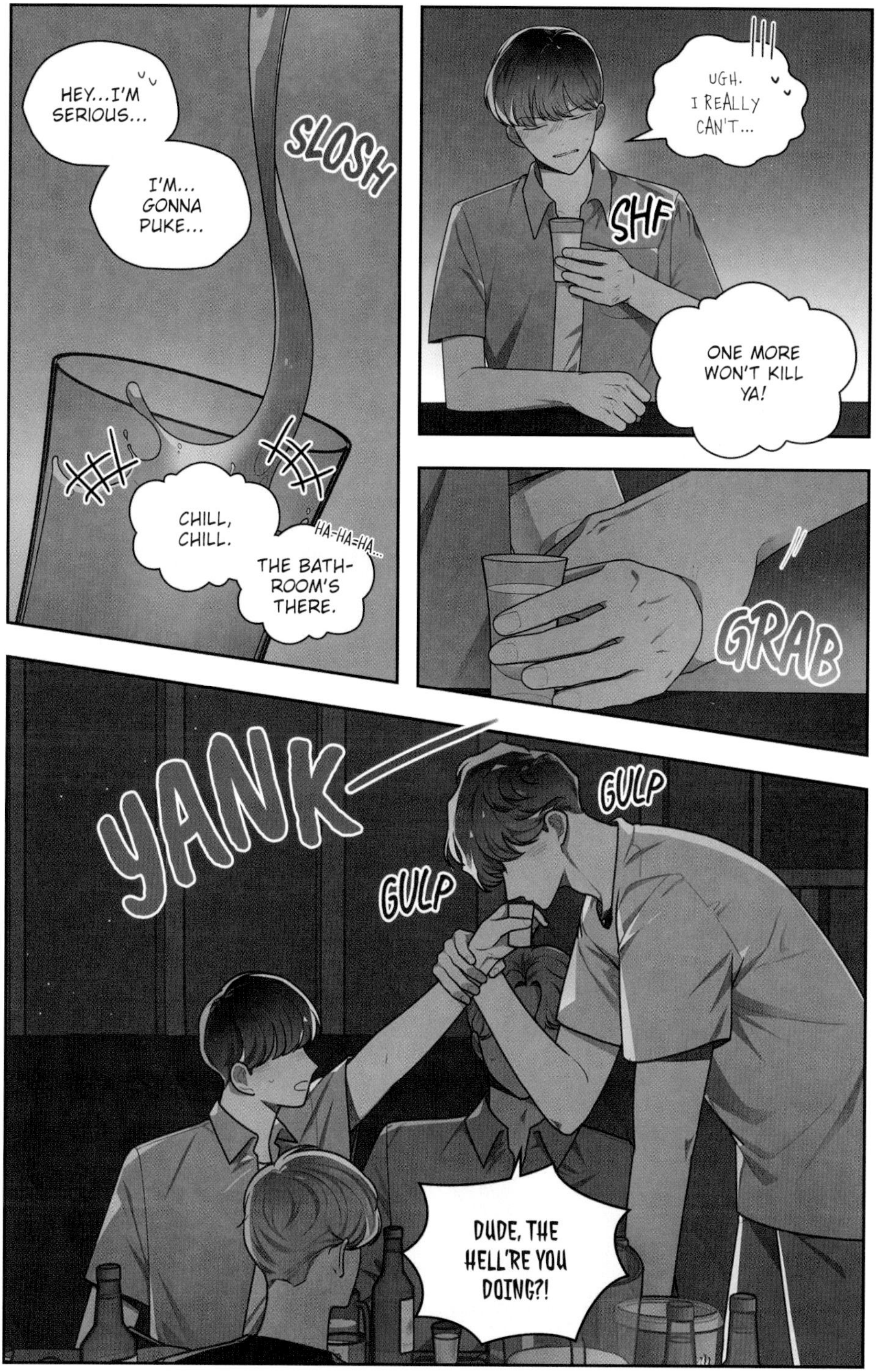

HEY...I'M SERIOUS...
I'M... GONNA PUKE...
SLOSH
CHILL, CHILL.
HA-HA-HA...
THE BATH-ROOM'S THERE.
UGH. I REALLY CAN'T...
SHF
ONE MORE WON'T KILL YA!
GRAB
YANK
GULP
GULP
DUDE, THE HELL'RE YOU DOING?!

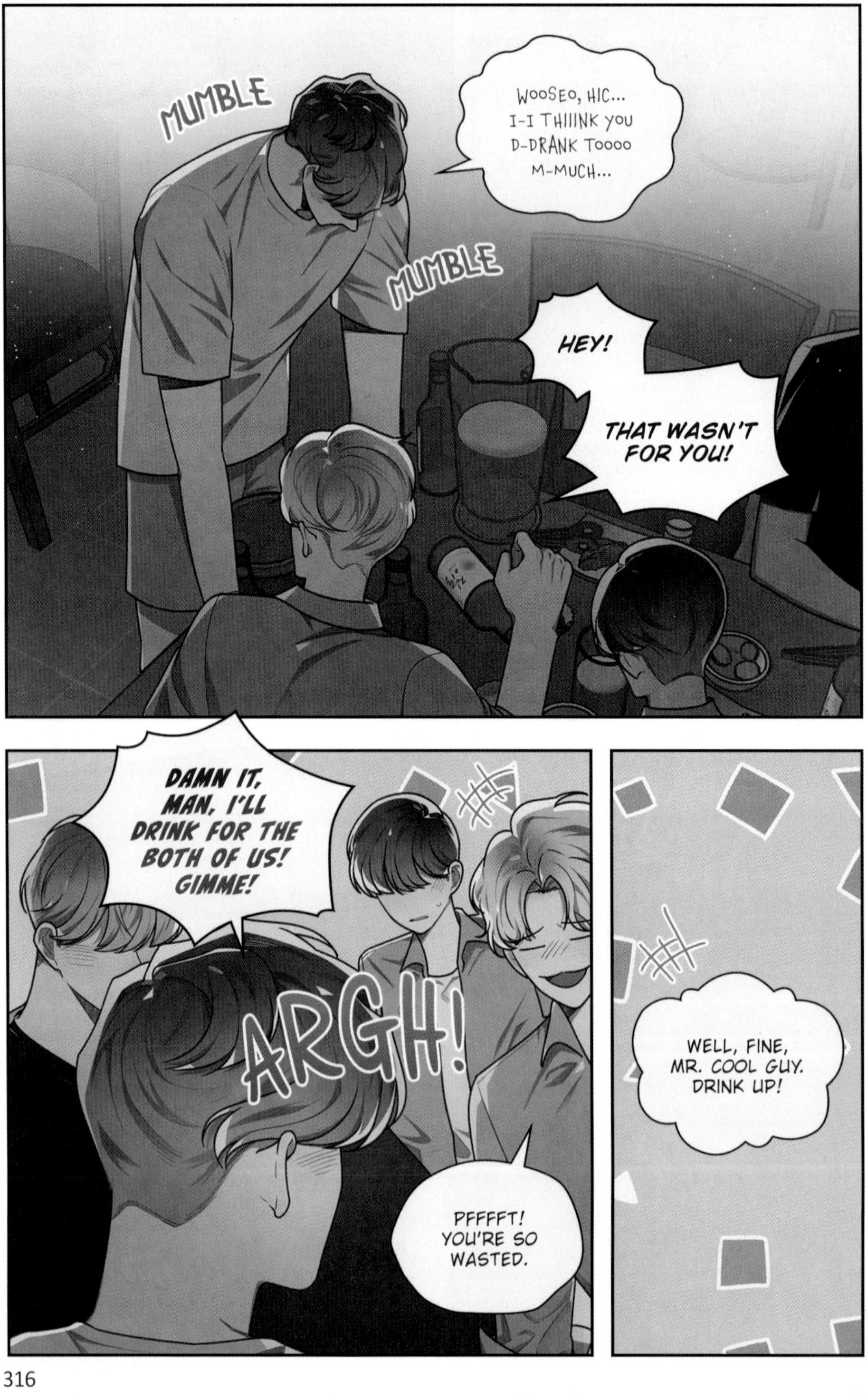
MUMBLE
WOOSEO, HIC... I-I THIIINK YOU D-DRANK TOOOO M-MUCH...
MUMBLE
HEY!
THAT WASN'T FOR YOU!
DAMN IT, MAN, I'LL DRINK FOR THE BOTH OF US! GIMME!
ARGH!
PFFFFT! YOU'RE SO WASTED.
WELL, FINE, MR. COOL GUY. DRINK UP!

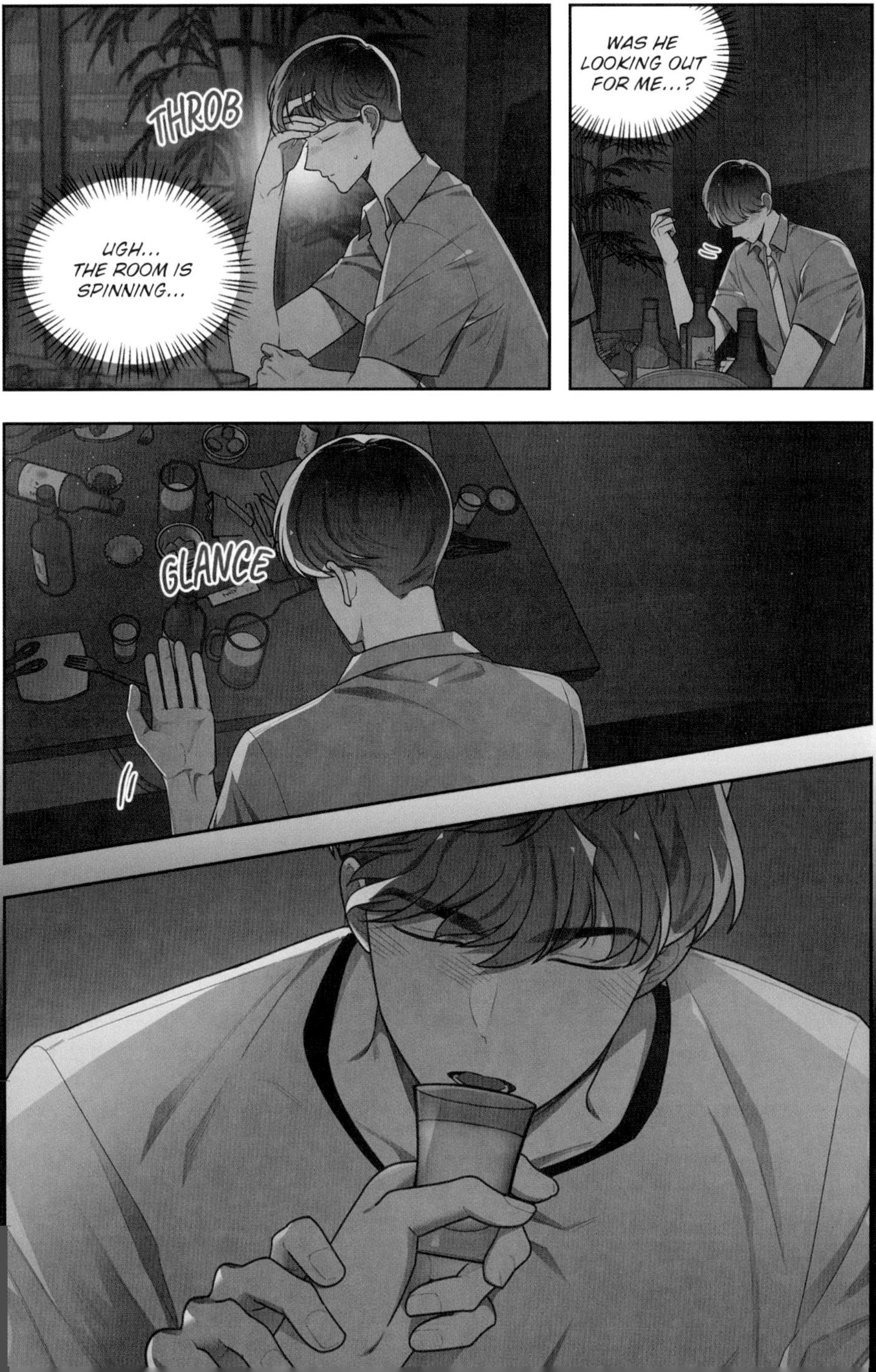
THROB
UGH... THE ROOM IS SPINNING...
WAS HE LOOKING OUT FOR ME...?
GLANCE

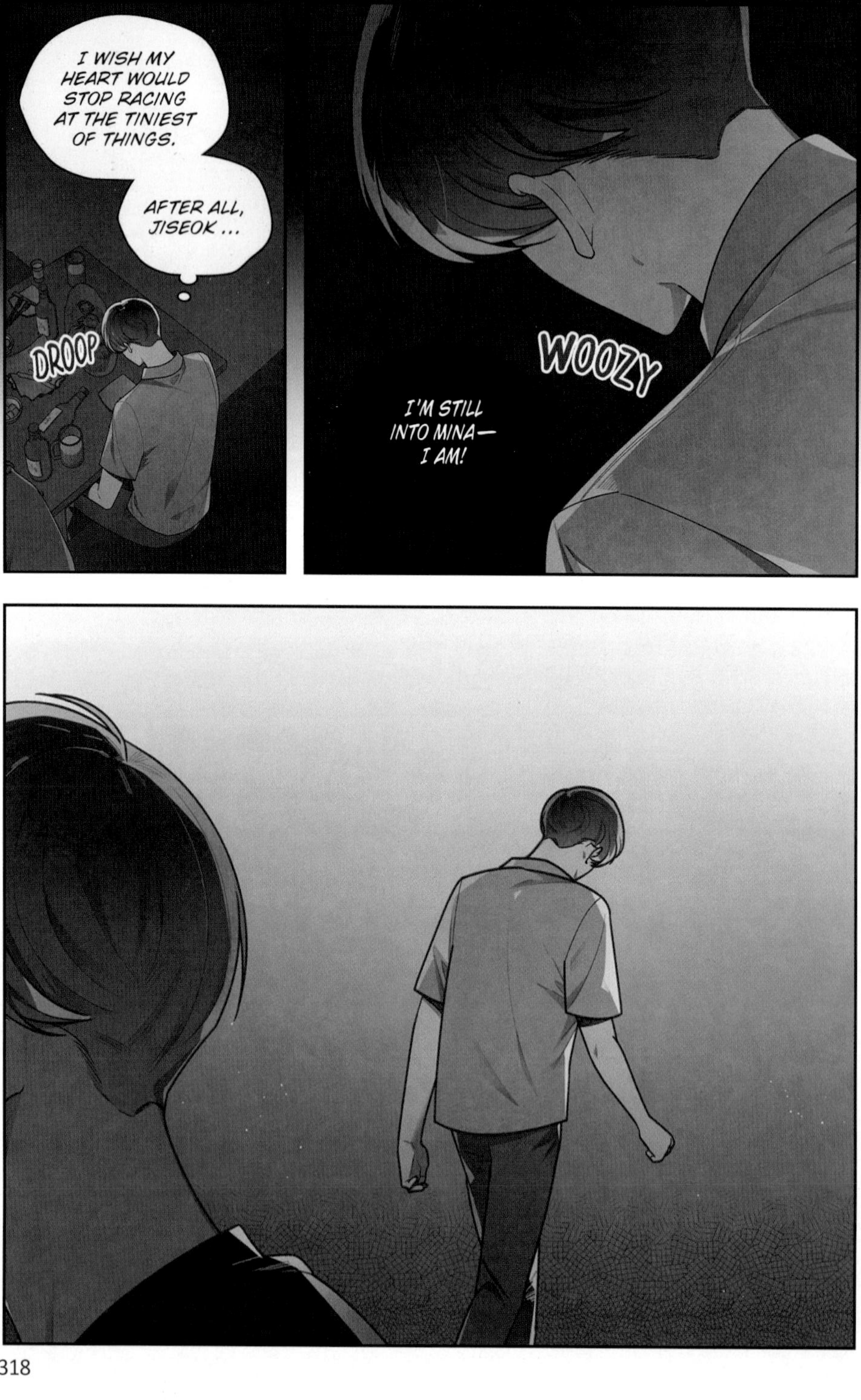

I WISH MY HEART WOULD STOP RACING AT THE TINIEST OF THINGS.
AFTER ALL, JISEOK ...
DROOP
WOOZY
I'M STILL INTO MINA— I AM!

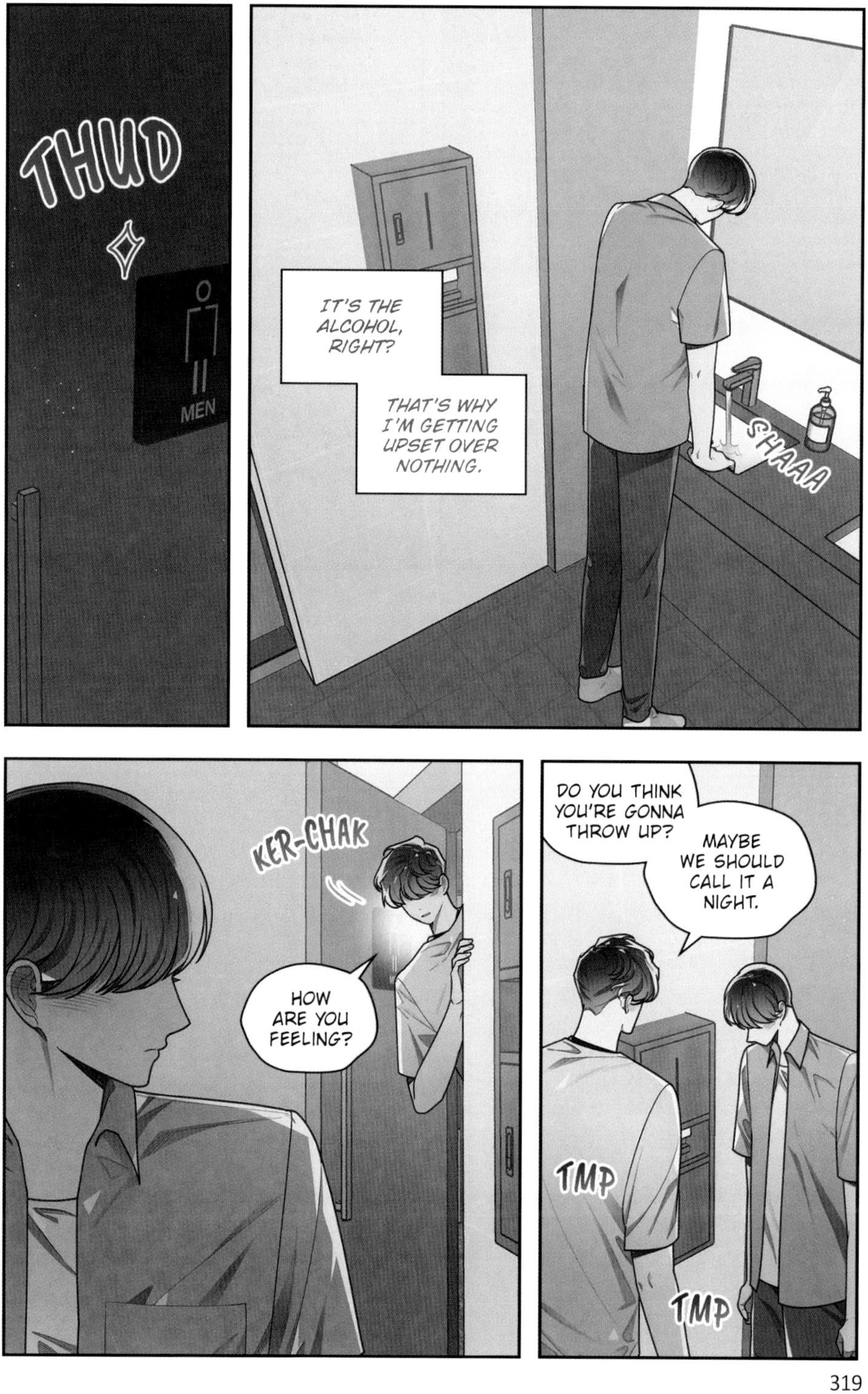
THUD
MEN
IT'S THE ALCOHOL, RIGHT?
THAT'S WHY I'M GETTING UPSET OVER NOTHING.
SHAAA
KER-CHAK
HOW ARE YOU FEELING?
DO YOU THINK YOU'RE GONNA THROW UP?
MAYBE WE SHOULD CALL IT A NIGHT.
TMP
TMP

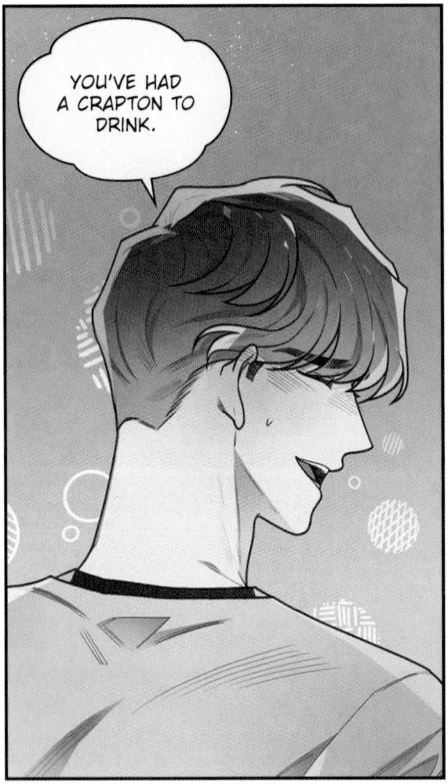
YOU'VE HAD A CRAPTON TO DRINK.

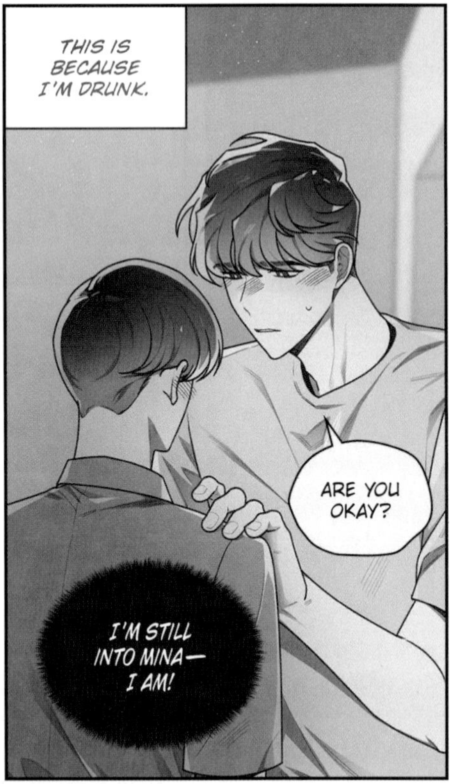
THIS IS BECAUSE I'M DRUNK.
ARE YOU OKAY?
I'M STILL INTO MINA— I AM!

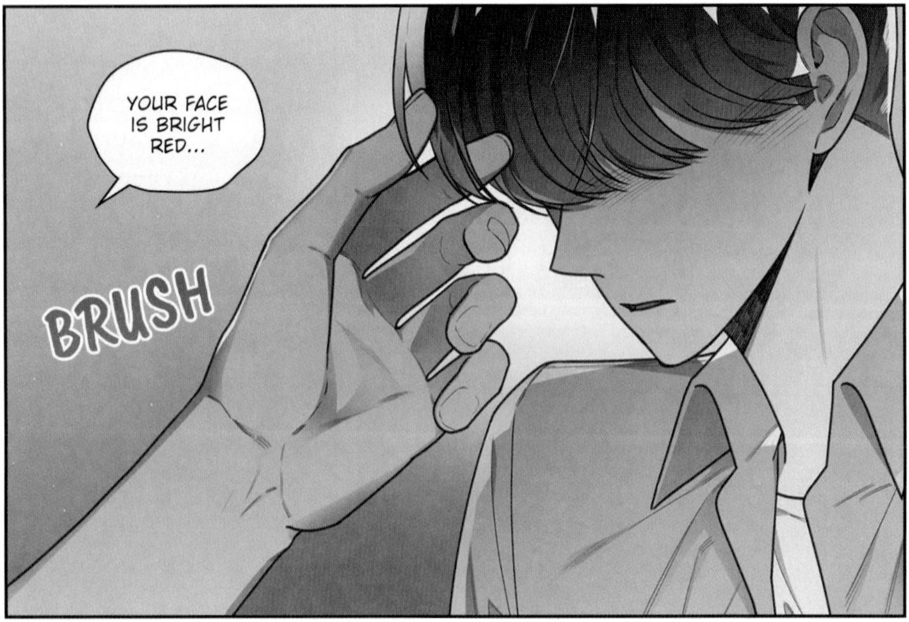
YOUR FACE IS BRIGHT RED...
BRUSH

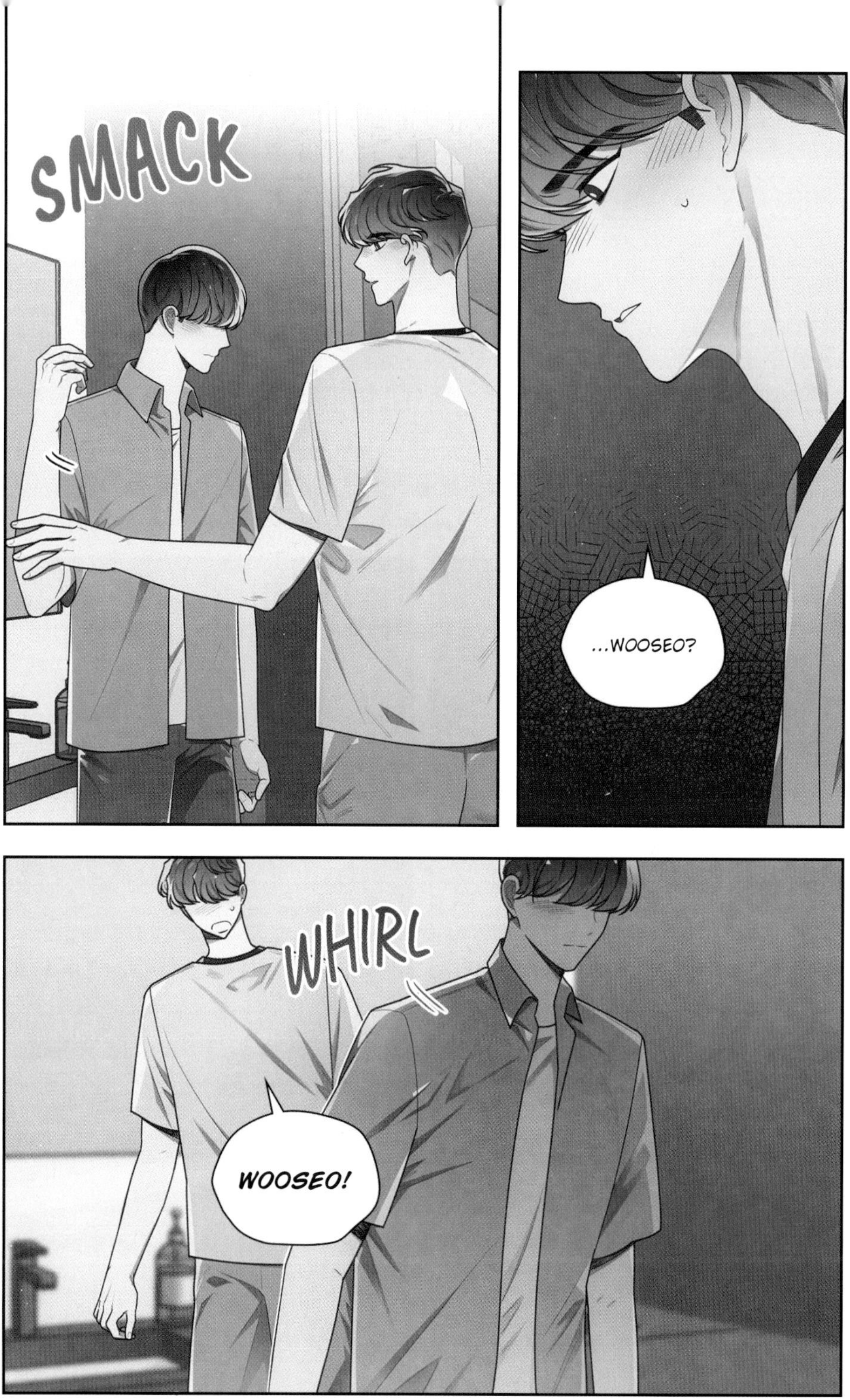
SMACK
...WOOSEO?
WHIRL
WOOSEO!

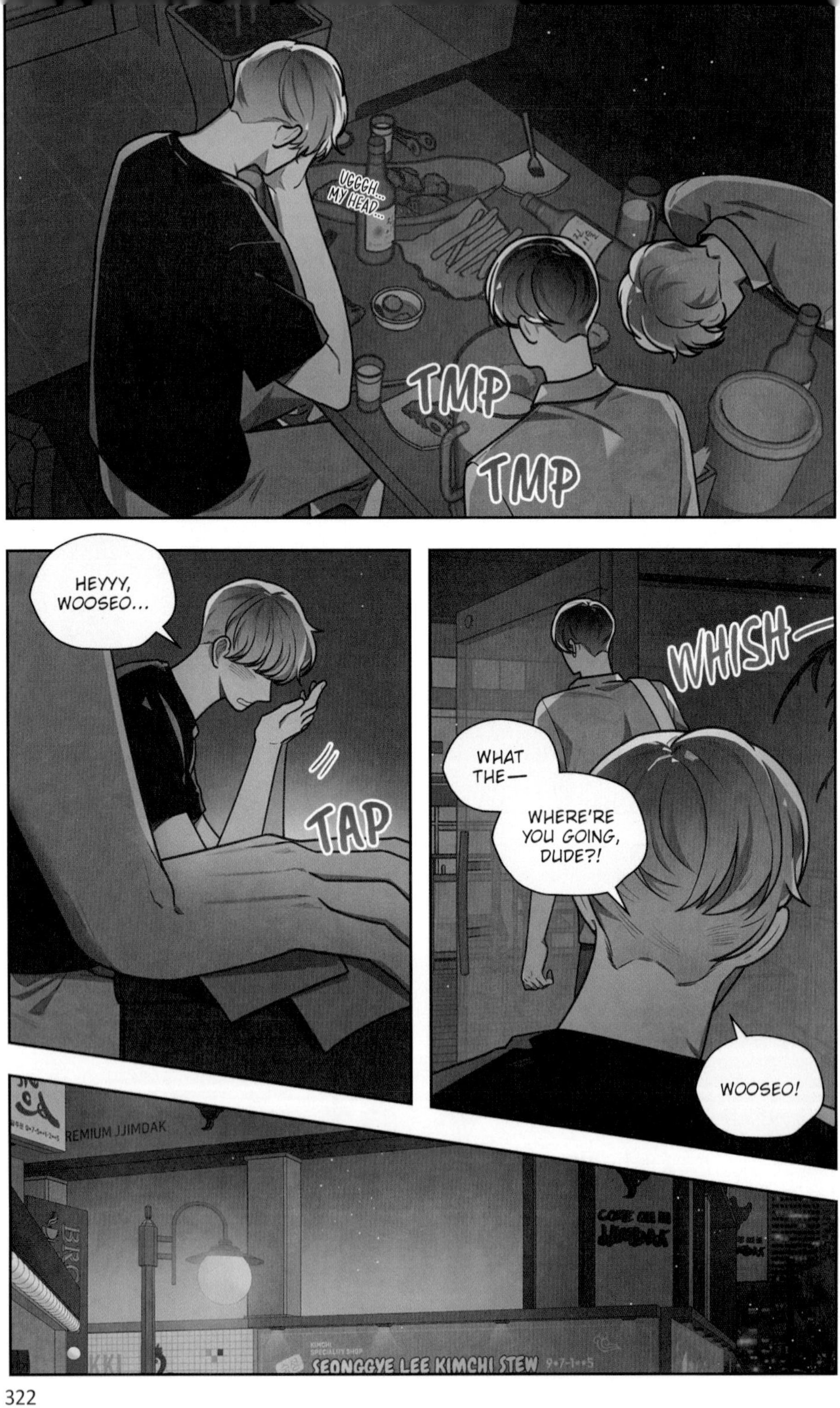
UGGGH... MY HEAD...
TMP
TMP
HEYYY, WOOSEO...
TAP
WHISH—
WHAT THE—
WHERE'RE YOU GOING, DUDE?!
WOOSEO!
PREMIUM JJIMDAK
KIMCHI SPECIALTY SHOP
SEONGGYE LEE KIMCHI STEW

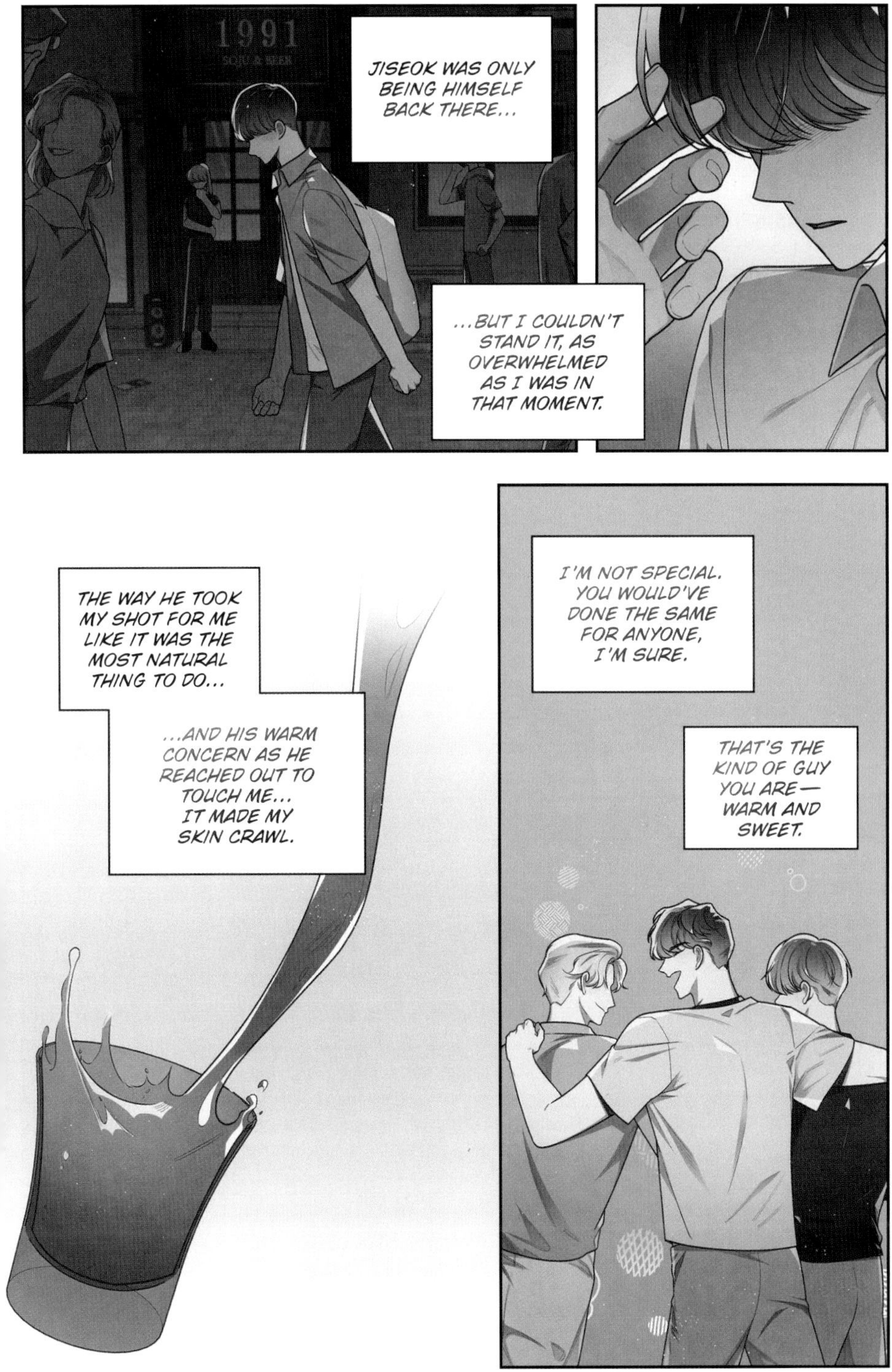
1991
JISEOK WAS ONLY BEING HIMSELF BACK THERE...
...BUT I COULDN'T STAND IT, AS OVERWHELMED AS I WAS IN THAT MOMENT.
THE WAY HE TOOK MY SHOT FOR ME LIKE IT WAS THE MOST NATURAL THING TO DO...
...AND HIS WARM CONCERN AS HE REACHED OUT TO TOUCH ME... IT MADE MY SKIN CRAWL.
I'M NOT SPECIAL. YOU WOULD'VE DONE THE SAME FOR ANYONE, I'M SURE.
THAT'S THE KIND OF GUY YOU ARE— WARM AND SWEET.

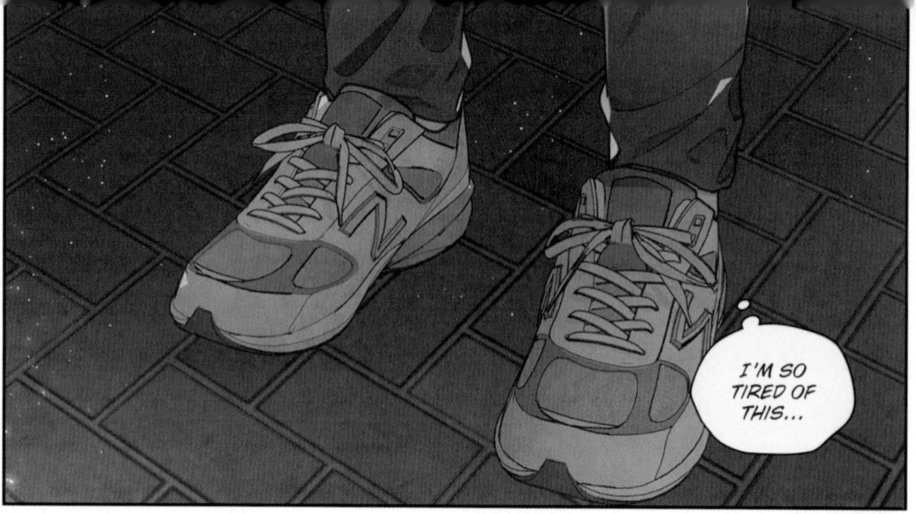
I'M SO TIRED OF THIS...

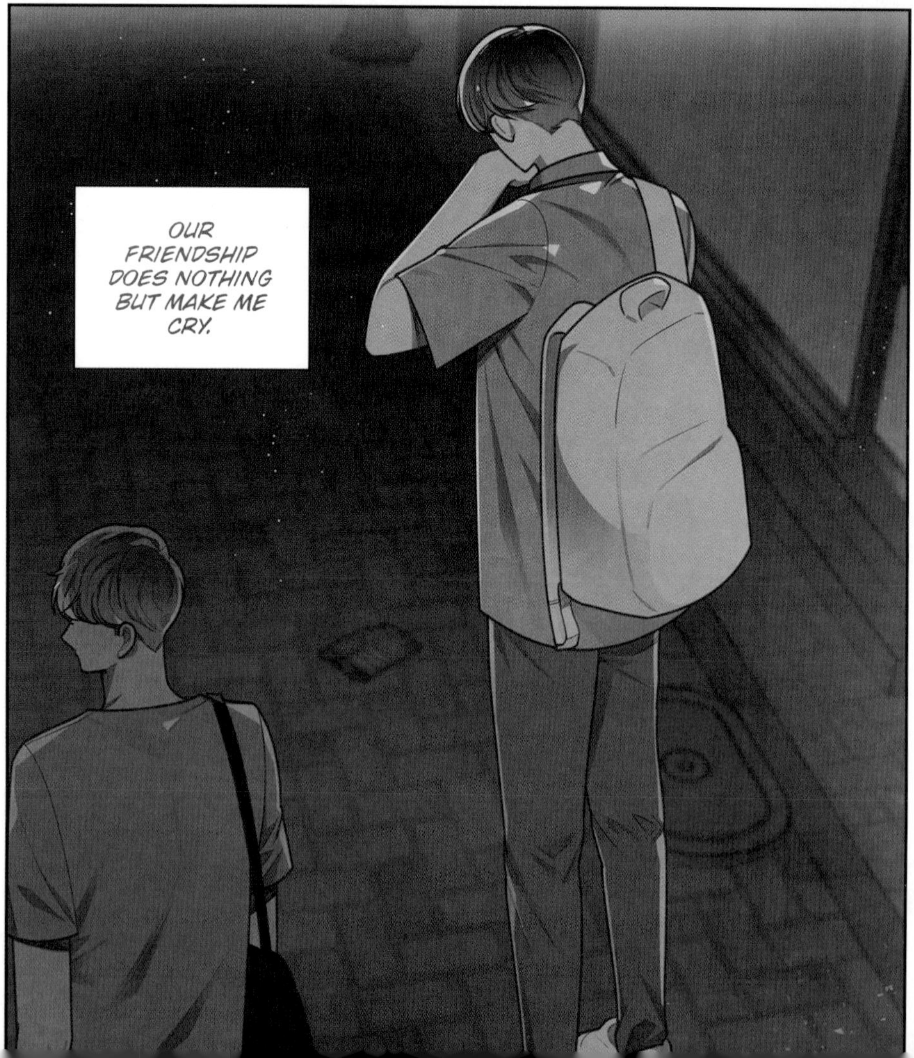
OUR FRIENDSHIP DOES NOTHING BUT MAKE ME CRY.

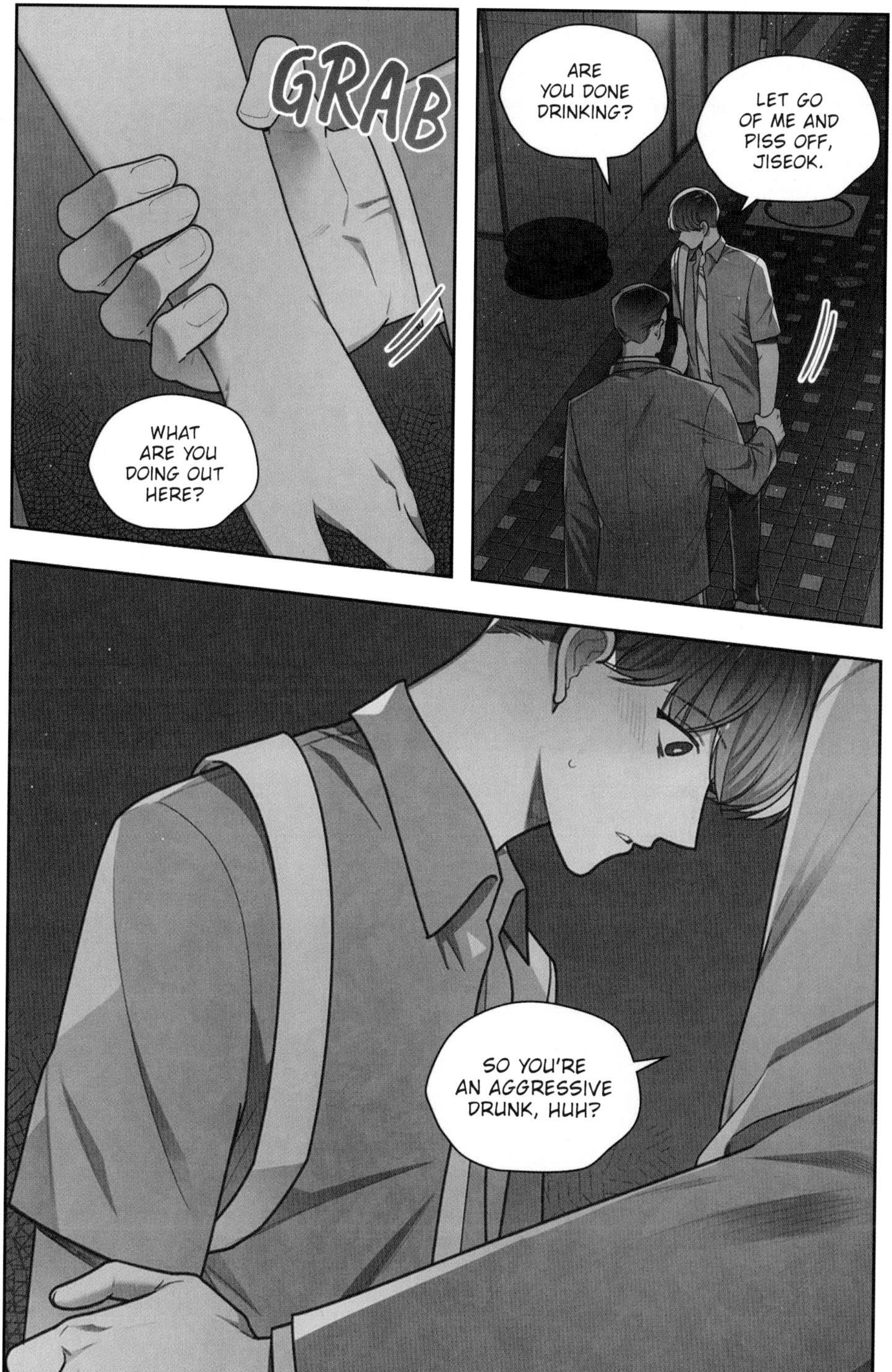
GRAB
WHAT ARE YOU DOING OUT HERE?
ARE YOU DONE DRINKING?
LET GO OF ME AND PISS OFF, JISEOK.
SO YOU'RE AN AGGRESSIVE DRUNK, HUH?

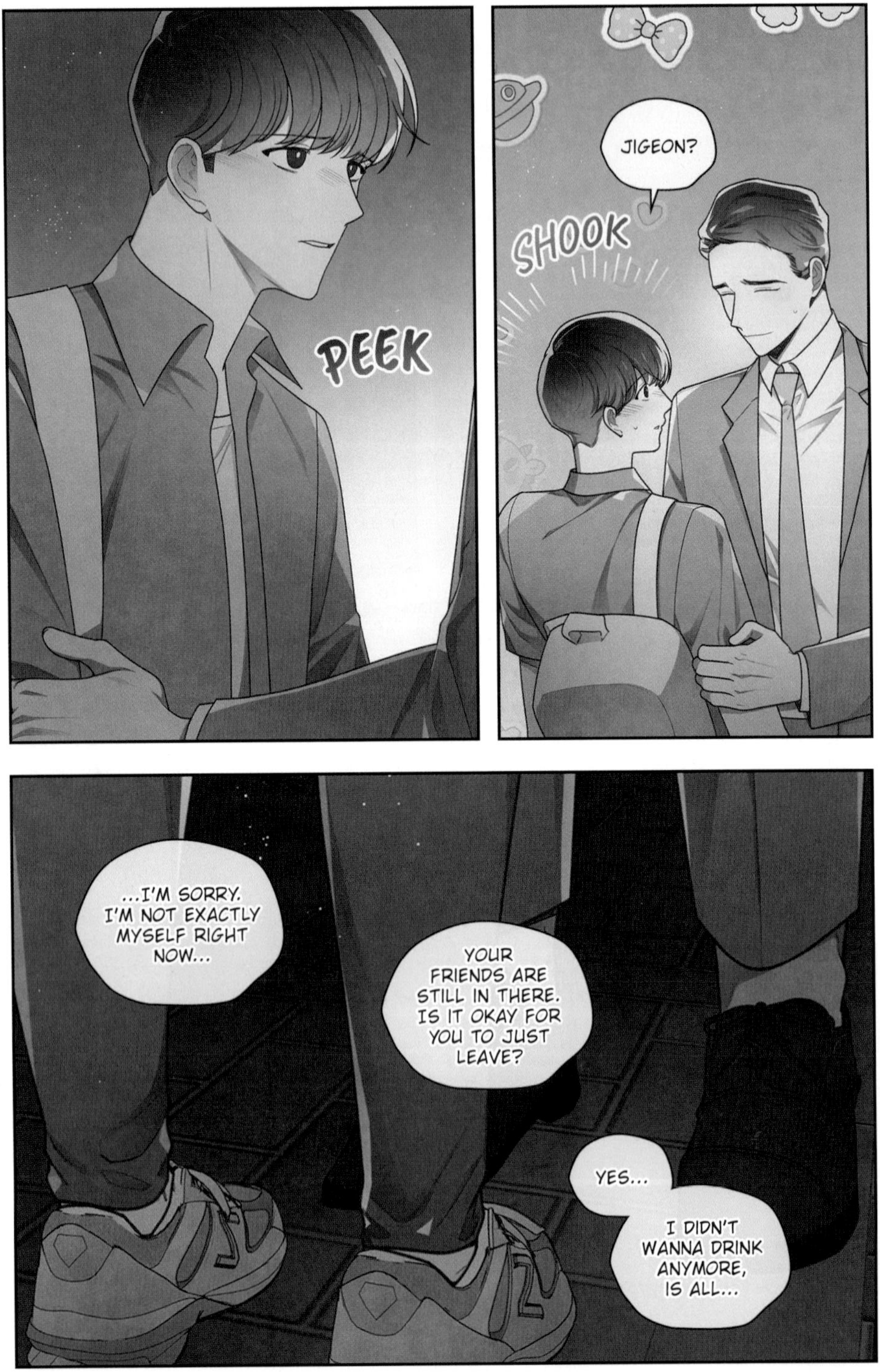
PEEK
JIGEON?
SHOOK
...I'M SORRY. I'M NOT EXACTLY MYSELF RIGHT NOW...
YOUR FRIENDS ARE STILL IN THERE. IS IT OKAY FOR YOU TO JUST LEAVE?
YES...
I DIDN'T WANNA DRINK ANYMORE, IS ALL...

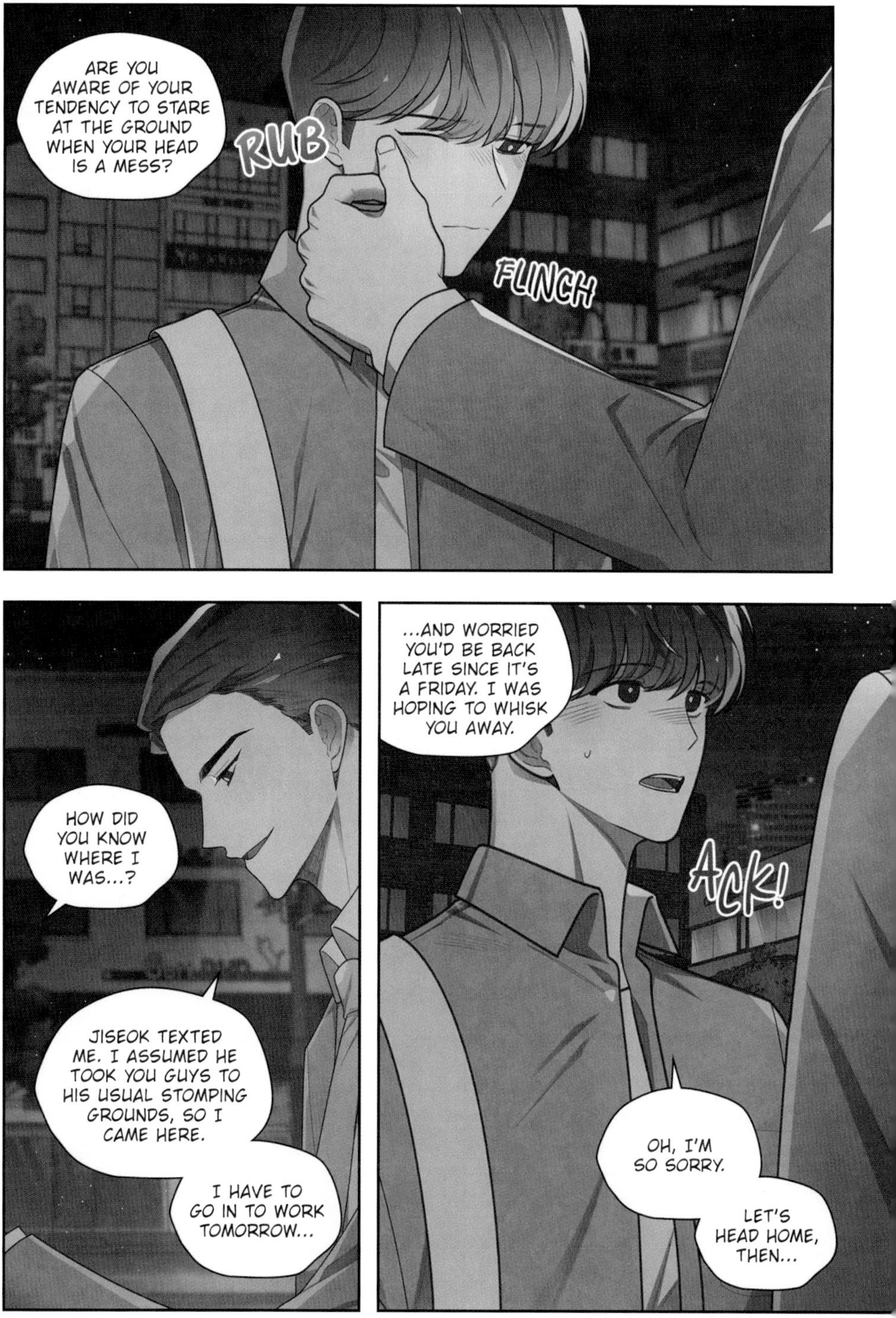
ARE YOU AWARE OF YOUR TENDENCY TO STARE AT THE GROUND WHEN YOUR HEAD IS A MESS?
RUB
FLINCH
HOW DID YOU KNOW WHERE I WAS...?
JISEOK TEXTED ME. I ASSUMED HE TOOK YOU GUYS TO HIS USUAL STOMPING GROUNDS, SO I CAME HERE.
I HAVE TO GO IN TO WORK TOMORROW...
...AND WORRIED YOU'D BE BACK LATE SINCE IT'S A FRIDAY. I WAS HOPING TO WHISK YOU AWAY.
ACK!
OH, I'M SO SORRY.
LET'S HEAD HOME, THEN...

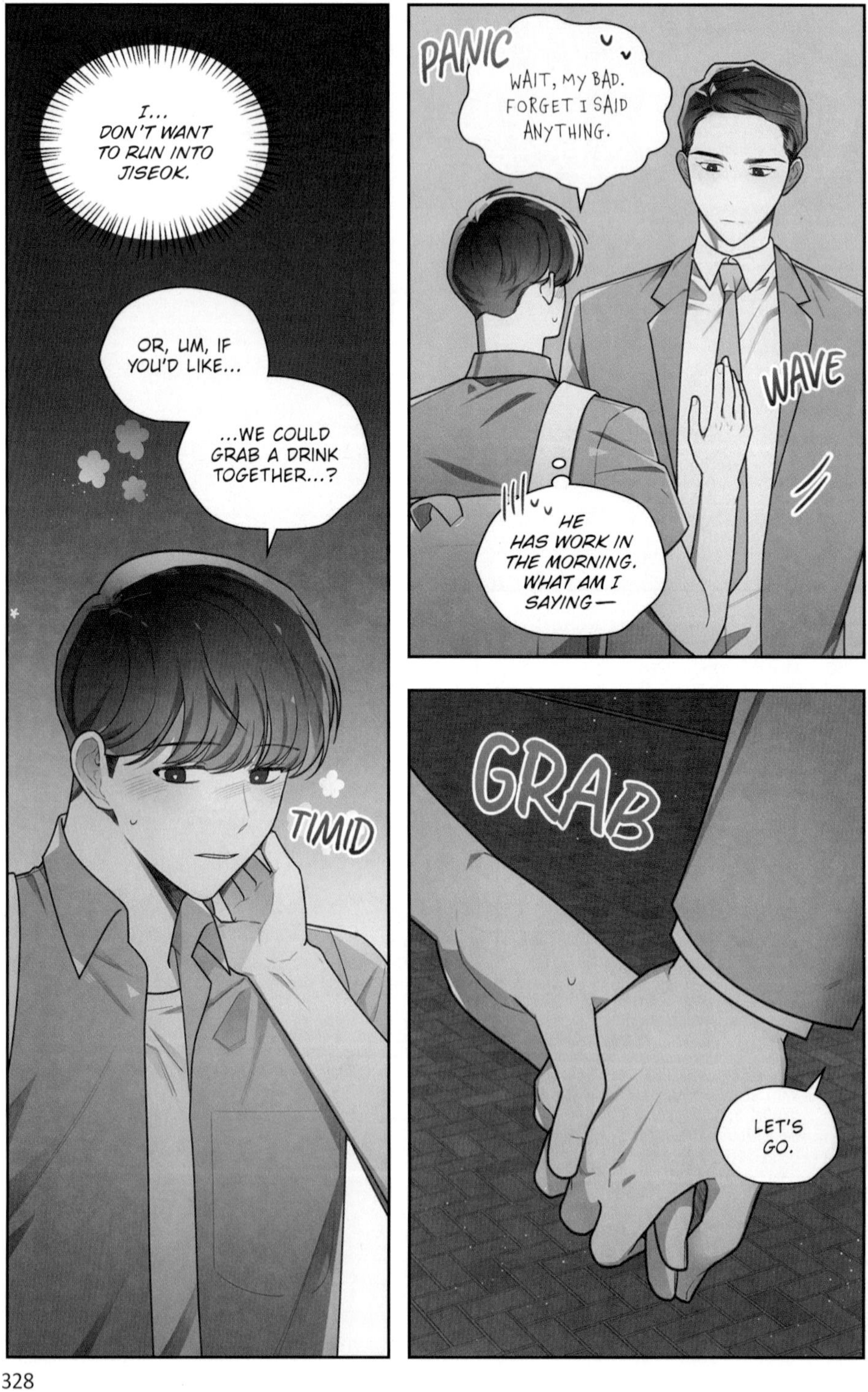
I...
DON'T WANT
TO RUN INTO
JISEOK.
OR, UM, IF
YOU'D LIKE...
...WE COULD
GRAB A DRINK
TOGETHER...?
TIMID
PANIC
WAIT, MY BAD.
FORGET I SAID
ANYTHING.
WAVE
HE
HAS WORK IN
THE MORNING.
WHAT AM I
SAYING—
GRAB
LET'S
GO.

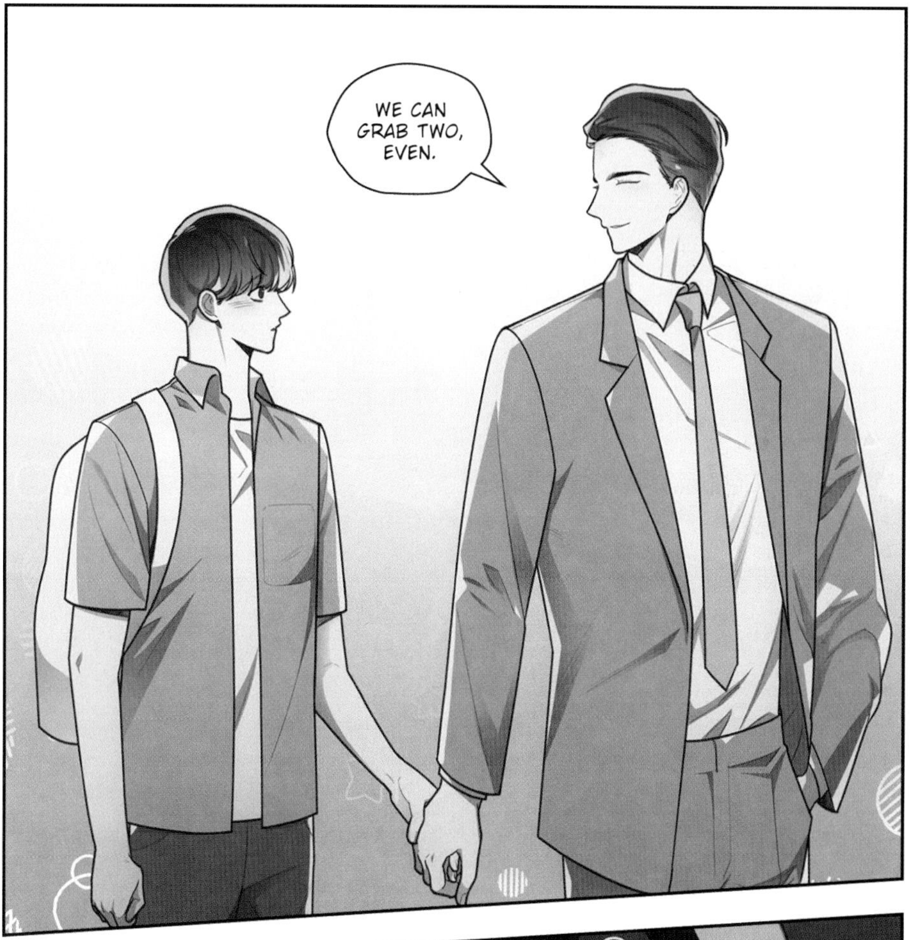
WE CAN GRAB TWO, EVEN.

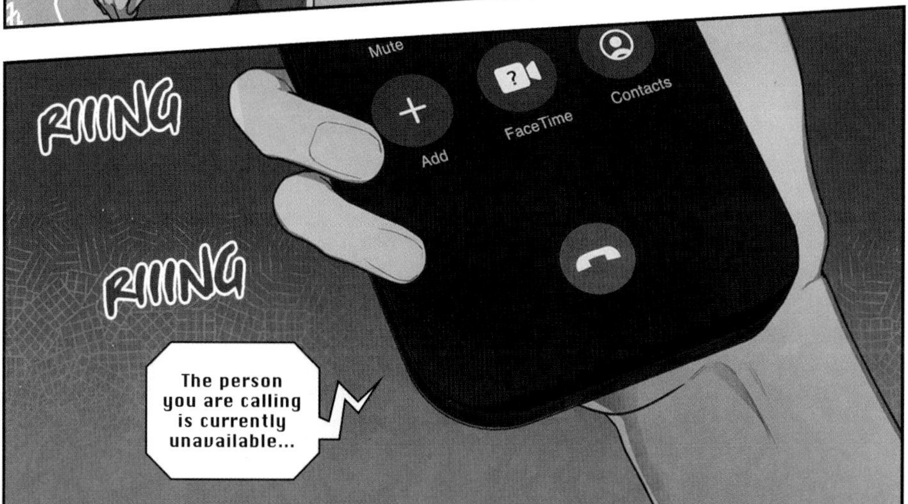
Mute
Add
FaceTime
Contacts
RIIING
RIIING
The person you are calling is currently unavailable...

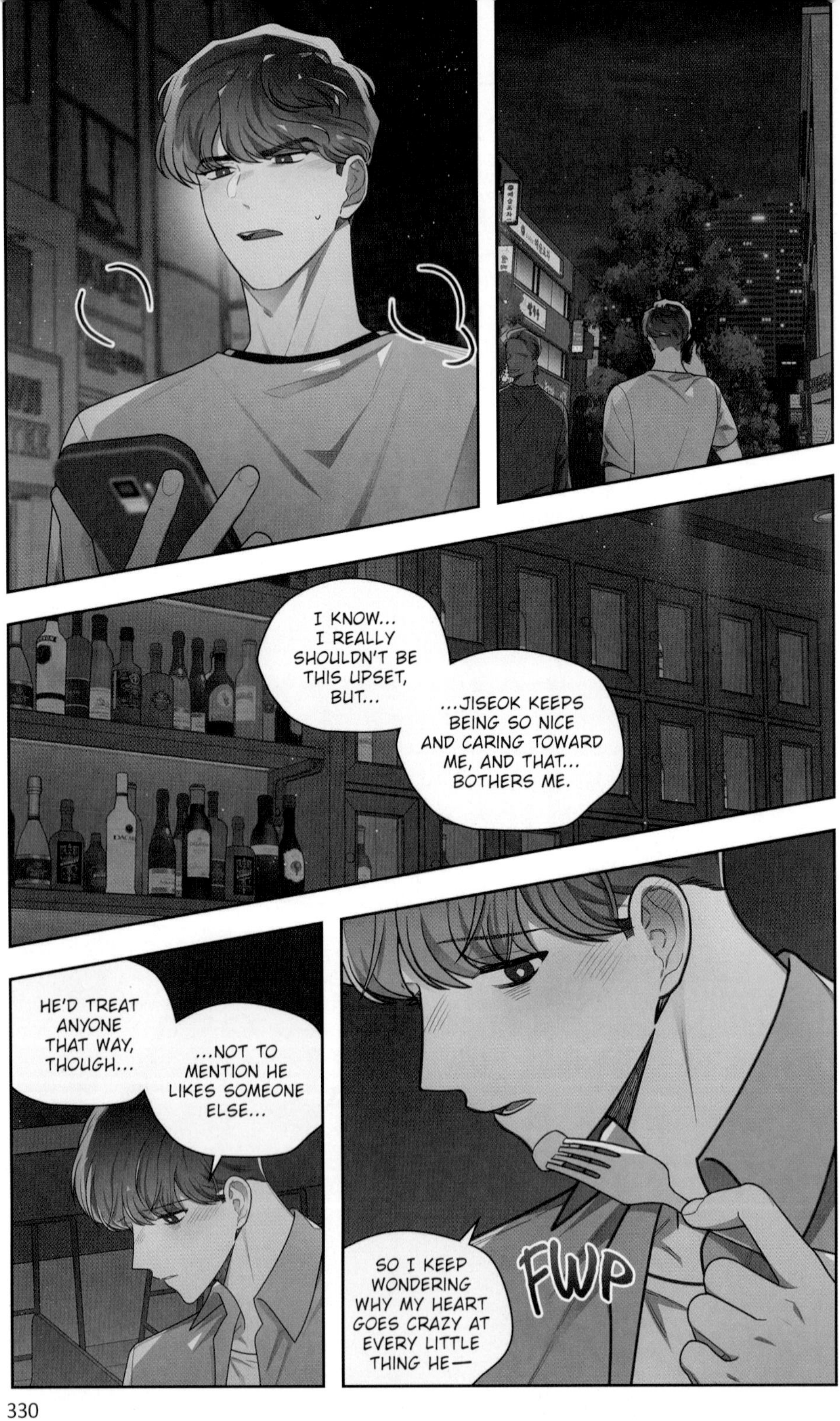
I KNOW... I REALLY SHOULDN'T BE THIS UPSET, BUT...
...JISEOK KEEPS BEING SO NICE AND CARING TOWARD ME, AND THAT... BOTHERS ME.
HE'D TREAT ANYONE THAT WAY, THOUGH...
...NOT TO MENTION HE LIKES SOMEONE ELSE...
SO I KEEP WONDERING WHY MY HEART GOES CRAZY AT EVERY LITTLE THING HE—
FWP

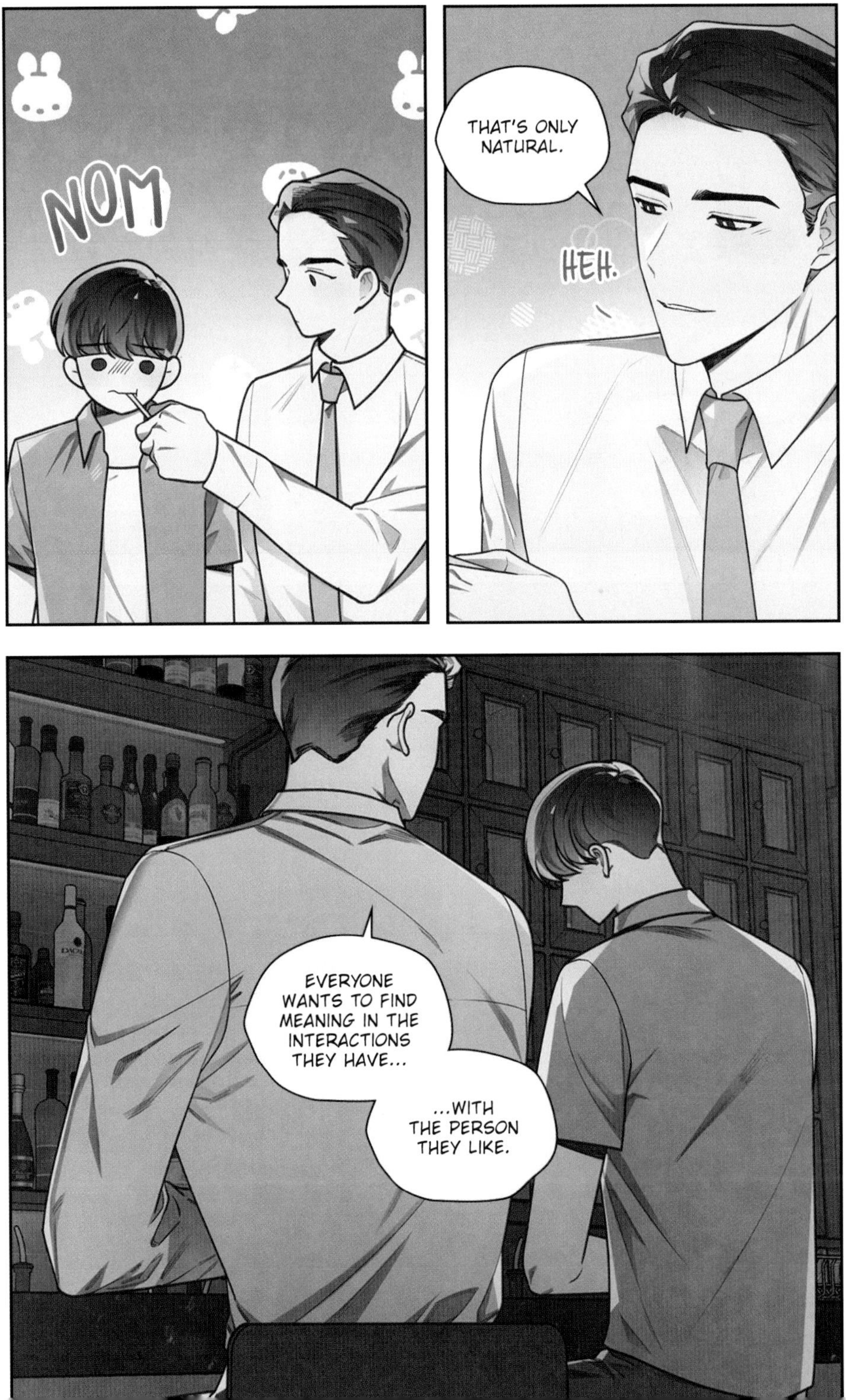
NOM
THAT'S ONLY NATURAL.
HEH.
EVERYONE WANTS TO FIND MEANING IN THE INTERACTIONS THEY HAVE...
...WITH THE PERSON THEY LIKE.

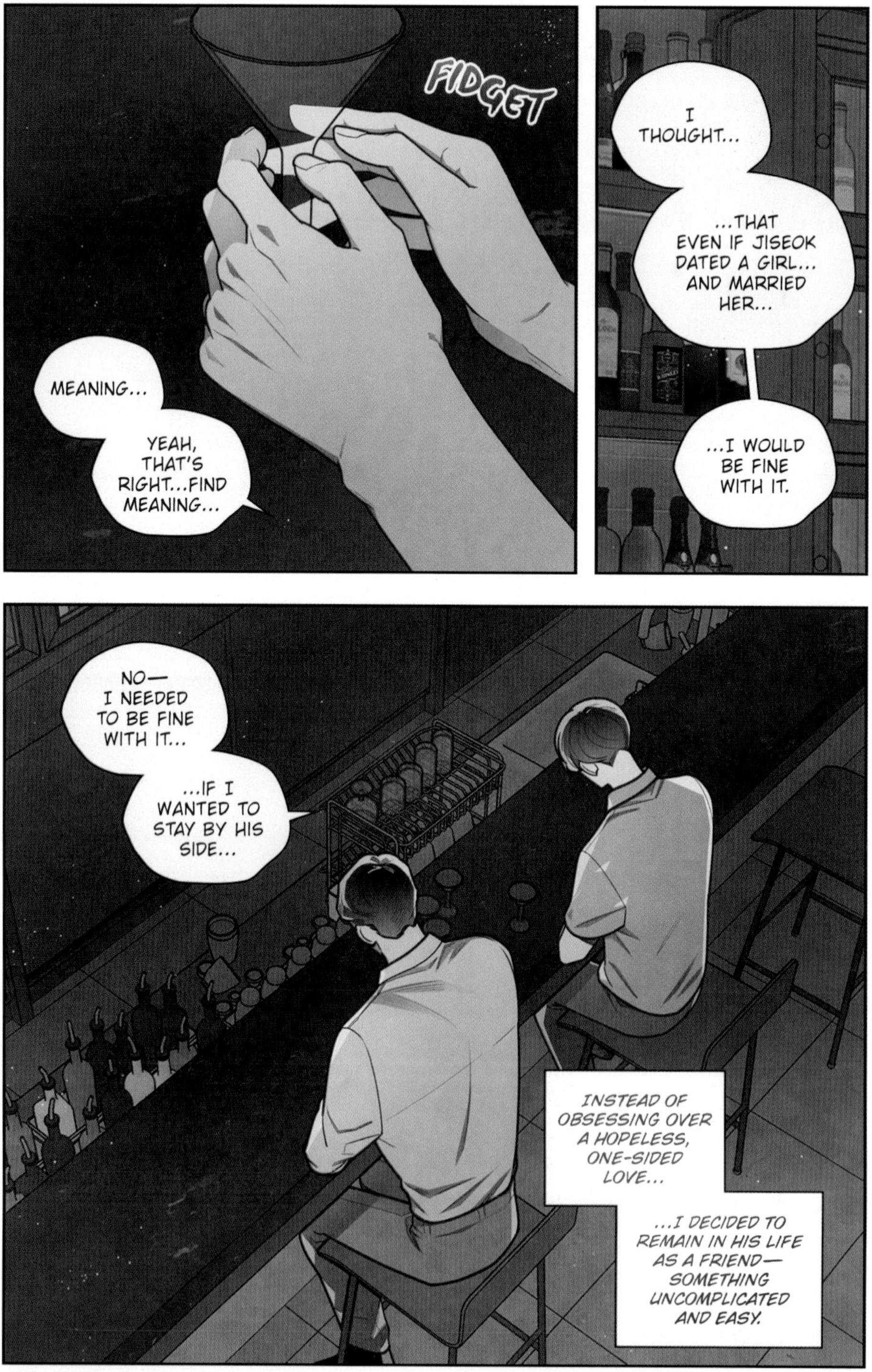
FIDGET
MEANING...
YEAH, THAT'S RIGHT...FIND MEANING...
I THOUGHT...
...THAT EVEN IF JISEOK DATED A GIRL... AND MARRIED HER...
...I WOULD BE FINE WITH IT.
NO— I NEEDED TO BE FINE WITH IT...
...IF I WANTED TO STAY BY HIS SIDE...
INSTEAD OF OBSESSING OVER A HOPELESS, ONE-SIDED LOVE...
...I DECIDED TO REMAIN IN HIS LIFE AS A FRIEND— SOMETHING UNCOMPLICATED AND EASY.

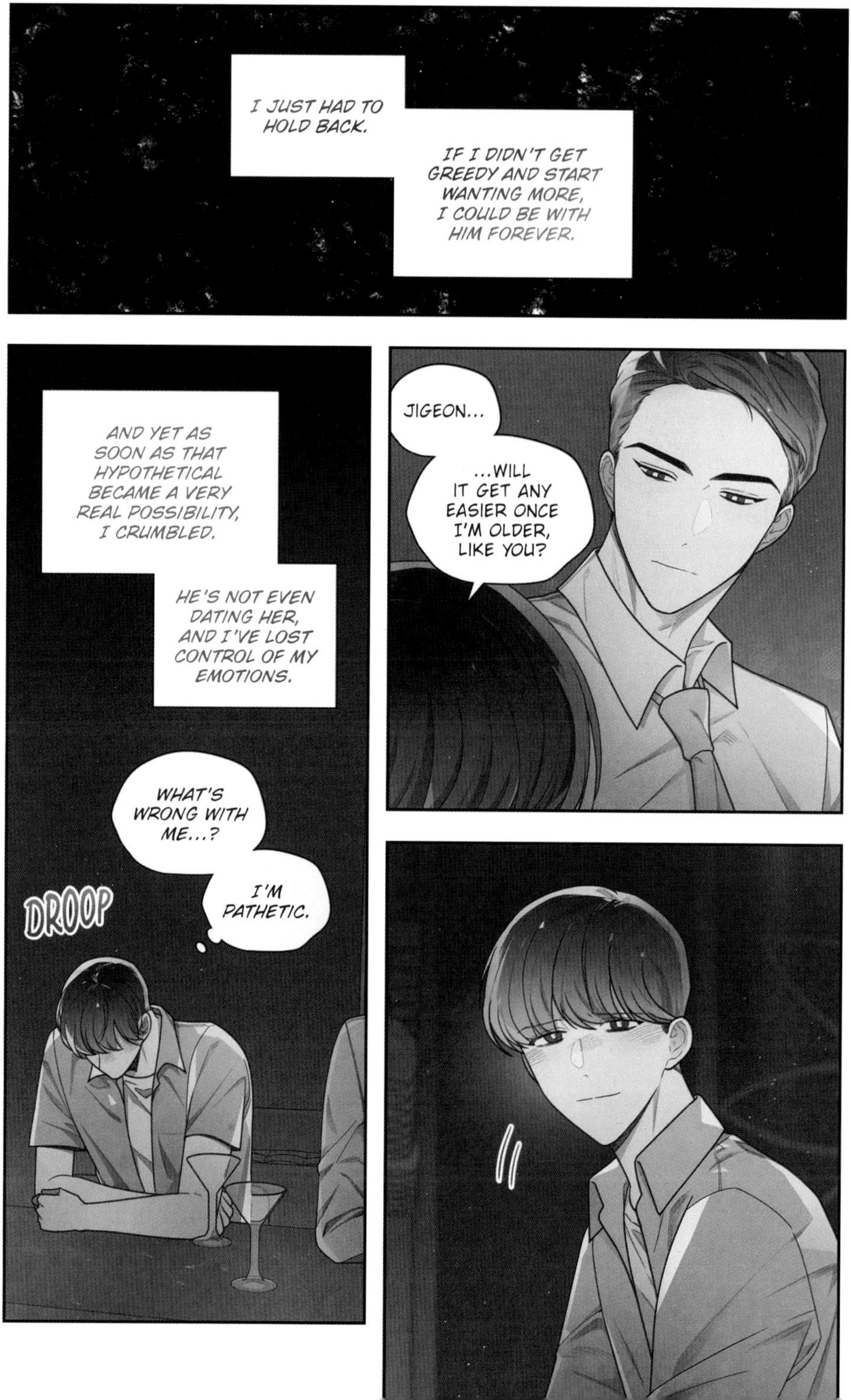

I JUST HAD TO HOLD BACK.
IF I DIDN'T GET GREEDY AND START WANTING MORE, I COULD BE WITH HIM FOREVER.
AND YET AS SOON AS THAT HYPOTHETICAL BECAME A VERY REAL POSSIBILITY, I CRUMBLED.
HE'S NOT EVEN DATING HER, AND I'VE LOST CONTROL OF MY EMOTIONS.
WHAT'S WRONG WITH ME...?
I'M PATHETIC.
DROOP
JIGEON...
...WILL IT GET ANY EASIER ONCE I'M OLDER, LIKE YOU?

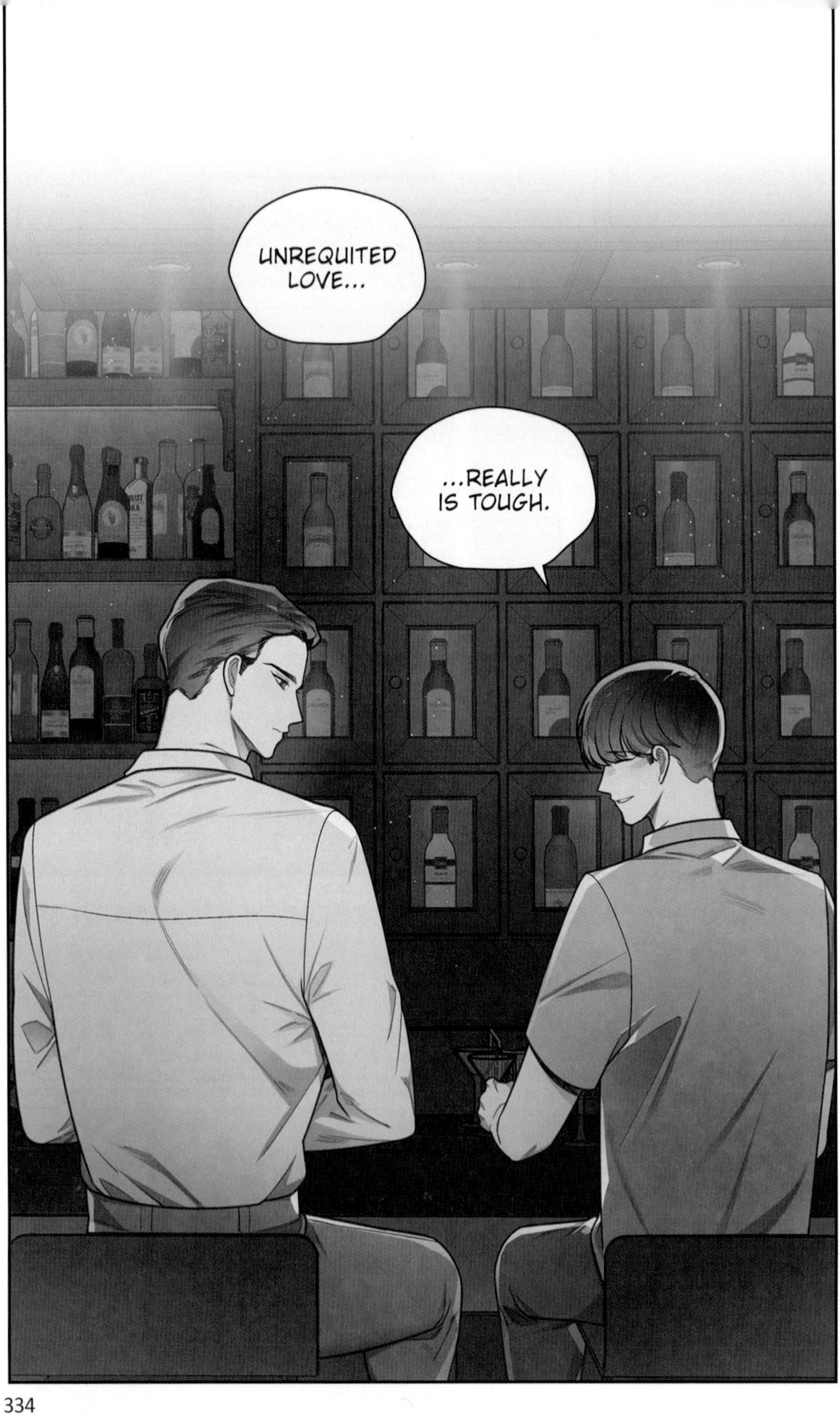
UNREQUITED LOVE...
...REALLY IS TOUGH.

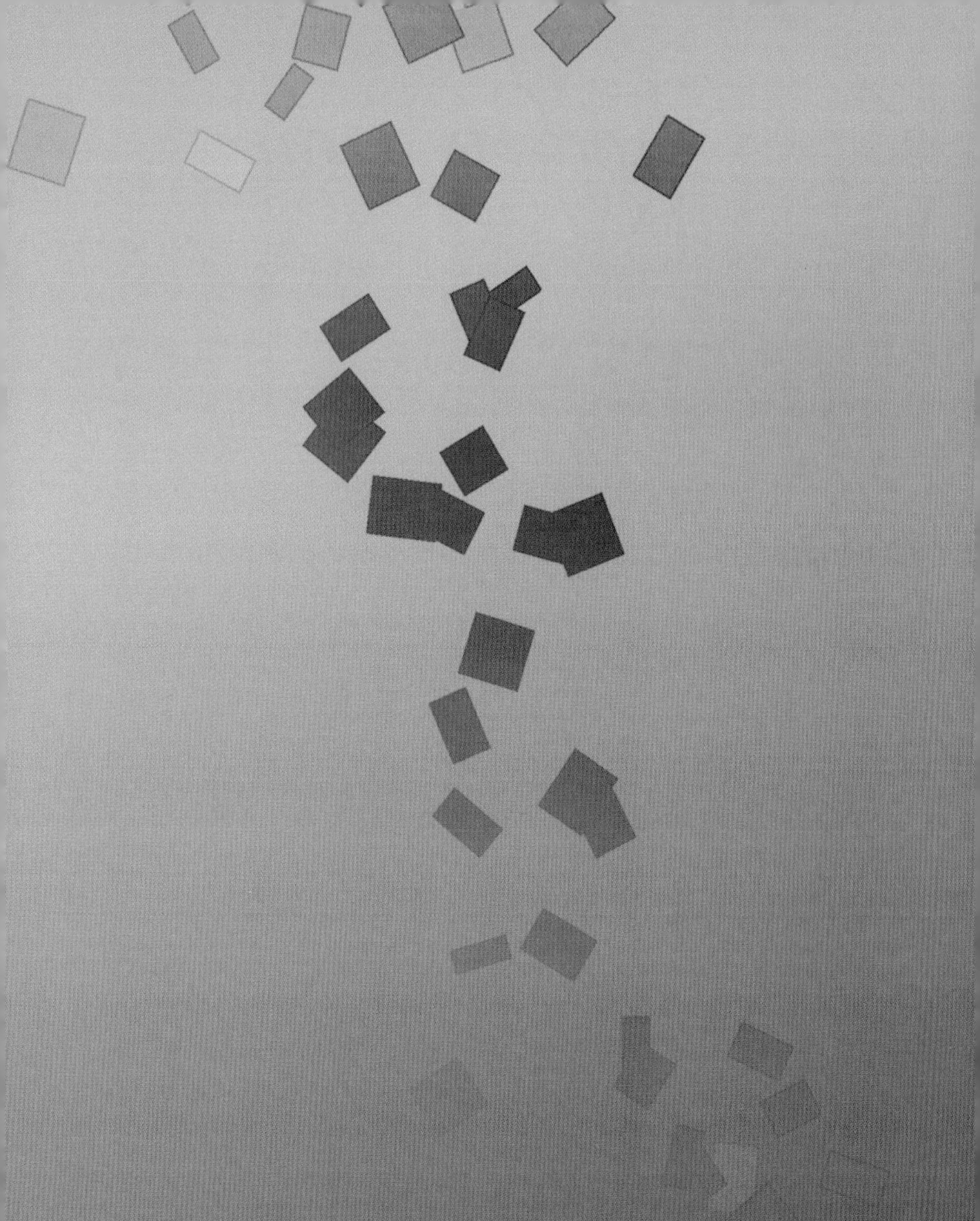

Tied to You

To be continued in Volume 2

Tied to you 1

Art by **WHAT** Original story by **Chelliace**

Translation: **Micah Kim** Lettering: **Chi Bui**

Tied to You, Volume 1
© WHAT, Chelliace 2021 / JS Contents
All rights reserved.
English edition published by arrangement
with JS Contents through RIVERSE Inc.

English translation © 2024 Ize Press

Ize Press
150 West 30th Street, 19th Floor
New York, NY 10001

Visit us at izepress.com ∞ facebook.com/izepress
twitter.com/izepress ∞ instagram.com/izepress

First Ize Press Edition: May 2024
Edited by Ize Press Editorial: Liz Marbach, Won Young Seo
Designed by Ize Press Design: Lilliana Checo

Library of Congress Control Number: 2023951864

ISBN: 979-8-4009-0159-1

1 3 5 7 9 10 8 6 4 2

TPA

Printed in South Korea